Belgium
& Luxembourg

Mark Elliott

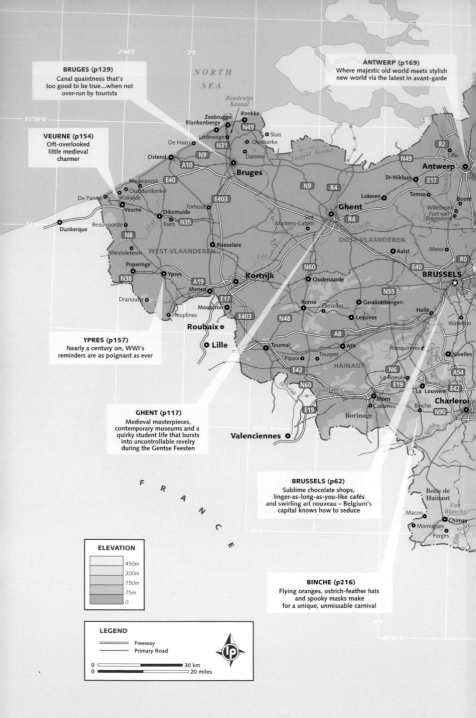

BRUGES (p129)
Canal quaintness that's too good to be true...when not over-run by tourists

ANTWERP (p169)
Where majestic old world meets stylish new world via the latest in avant-garde

VEURNE (p154)
Oft-overlooked little medieval charmer

YPRES (p157)
Nearly a century on, WWI's reminders are as poignant as ever

GHENT (p117)
Medieval masterpieces, contemporary museums and a quirky student life that bursts into uncontrollable revelry during the Gentse Feesten

BRUSSELS (p62)
Sublime chocolate shops, linger-as-long-as-you-like *cafés* and swirling art nouveau – Belgium's capital knows how to seduce

BINCHE (p216)
Flying oranges, ostrich-feather hats and spooky masks make for a unique, unmissable carnival

NORTH SEA

Boudewijn Kanaal

Zeebrugge
Blankenberge
Knokke
Lissewege
Sluis
De Haan
Oostkerke
Ostend
Damme
Leopold Kanaal
Bruges

Nieuwpoort
Oostduinkerke
Koksijde
De Panne
Veurne
Torhout
Diksmuide
Esen
Beauvoorde
Ghent
Sint-Martens-Latem
Dunkerque

Roeselare

Leie

WEST-VLAANDEREN

Westvleteren
Poperinge
Ypres
Menen
Dranouter
Mouscron
Houplines
Kortrijk

Oudenaarde

OOST-VLAANDEREN

Aalst
Meise

BRUSSELS

Roubaix

Ronse
Ellezelles
Geraardsbergen
Lessines
Halle
Waterloo

Lille

Tournai
Pipaix
Tourpes
Ath
Ronquières
Nivelles

HAINAUT

Scheldt

Valenciennes

Le Roeulx
Mons
Cuesmes
La Louvière
Binche
Charleroi

Borinage

St-Niklaas
Lokeren
Temse
Willebroek
Fort van Breendonk
Boom

Antwerp

Lillo

F R A N C E

Botte de Hainaut
Eau Blanche
Macon
Chimay
Momignies
Forges

ELEVATION

450m
300m
150m
75m
0

LEGEND

Freeway
Primary Road

0 ——— 30 km
0 ——— 20 miles

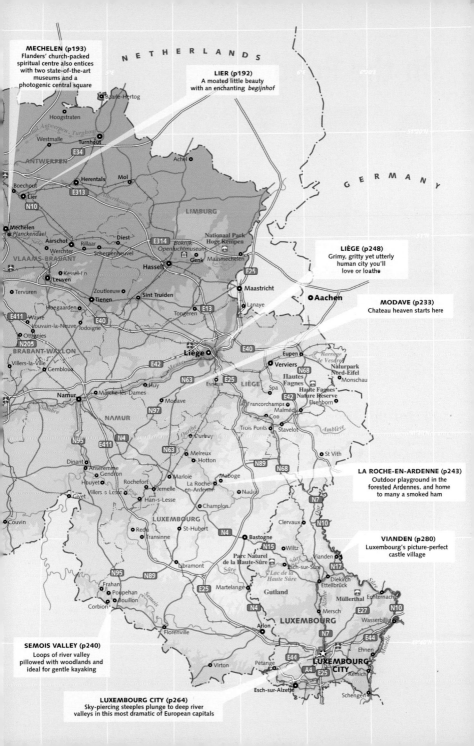

MECHELEN (p193)
Flanders' church-packed spiritual centre also entices with two state-of-the-art museums and a photogenic central square

LIER (p192)
A moated little beauty with an enchanting *begijnhof*

LIÈGE (p248)
Grimy, gritty yet utterly human city you'll love or loathe

MODAVE (p233)
Chateau heaven starts here

LA ROCHE-EN-ARDENNE (p243)
Outdoor playground in the forested Ardennes, and home to many a smoked ham

VIANDEN (p280)
Luxembourg's picture-perfect castle village

SEMOIS VALLEY (p240)
Loops of river valley pillowed with woodlands and ideal for gentle kayaking

LUXEMBOURG CITY (p264)
Sky-piercing steeples plunge to deep river valleys in this most dramatic of European capitals

NETHERLANDS

GERMANY

Baarle-Hertog
Hoogstraten
Westmalle
Turnhout
Achel
ANTWERPEN
Boechout
Herentals
Mol
Lier
Mechelen
Planckendael
Aarschot
Rillaar
Diest
Werchter
Schermenheuvel
VLAAMS-BRABANT
Kessel-Lo
Leuven
Tervuren
Hoegaarden
Wavre
Louvain-la-Neuve
Jodoigne
Ottignies
BRABANT-WALLON
Villers-la-Ville
Gembloux
Namur
Marche-les-Dames
NAMUR
Dinant
Anseremme
Gendron
Hpuyet
Rochefort
Jemelle
Givet
Villers s Lesse
Han-s-Lesse
Couvin
Redu
Transinne
LUXEMBOURG
St-Hubert
Libramont
Frahan
Poupehan
Bouillon
Corbion
Florenville
Virton

LIMBURG
Bokrijk
Openluchtmuseum
Nationaal Park
Hoge Kempen
Hasselt
Genk
Maasmechelen
Zoutleeuw
Tienen
Sint Truiden
Maastricht
Tongeren
Lanaye
Aachen
Liège
Eupen
Verviers
Huy
Esneux
LIÈGE
Spa
Hautes Fagnes
Naturpark Nord-Eifel
Monschau
Modave
Francorchamps
Haute Fagnes Nature Reserve
Elsenborn
Malmédy
Coo
Trois Ponts
Stavelot
Durbuy
St Vith
Melreux
Hotton
Marloie
Maboge
La Roche-en-Ardenne
Champlon
Nadrin
Clervaux
Bastogne
Wiltz
Vianden
Parc Naturel de la Haute-Sûre
Esch-sur-Sûre
Diekirch
Ettelbrück
Müllerthal
Echternach
Martelange
Lac de la Haute Sûre
Gutland
Mersch
Wasserbillig
Arlon
LUXEMBOURG
LUXEMBOURG CITY
Ehnen
Pétange
Remich
Esch-sur-Alzette
Schengen

On the Road

MARK ELLIOTT Coordinating Author

Charleroi (p222) was proving fascinating beyond all expectations. A caretaker revealed his museum's 'secret' vaults containing an astounding collection of late-19th-century art. Another let me climb the city's belfry ('it's not really open but…'). Then came a tip-off from my Belgian wife: 'Have you seen the plane? No, not at the airport. Beside the motorway! Sit on the wing and order yourself a margarita!'

MY FAVOURITE TRIP

Of course I adore Ghent (p117) – show me someone who doesn't! Bruges (p129) is impossibly beautiful and Brussels (p62) is somewhere one never stops discovering. But Belgium's charms are also found in many less-spectacular corners. At the risk of sounding eccentric I have a great soft spot for Verviers (p259), Grimbergen (p113), Enghien (p213) and Aarschot (p202). I am moved by the love that's constantly poured into the little-visited Musée de la Rubanerie (Ribbon Museum; p163) in Comines, find Hoogstraten's belfry (p191) a wonder of the world and am utterly intrigued by the cartographic eccentricity that is Baarle-Hertog (see the boxed text, p192). And as for all those castles…

ABOUT THE AUTHOR

As a small child, Mark was dragged up a bizarre conical hill to meet a giant lion (Waterloo), then let loose inside a giant chemistry set (the Atomium). To a baby Brit, Belgium already looked pretty weird. But that was just the start. Years later a chance encounter in Turkmenistan (a camel market, a blues jam, too much Turkish wine…) saw him tumble into the arms of the lovely Danielle, a Belgian belle with whom he's lived ever since. In between writing guidebooks to far-flung destinations (Iran, Greenland, Azerbaijan, Siberia) he's revelled ever since in the crazy carnivals, beer-lubricated festivals and endlessly appealing cafes that all help make the Benelux one of the world's most underestimated destinations.

Traveller Highlights

Belgium and Luxembourg are complex countries with distinct cultures, and long and fascinating histories. Travellers and Lonely Planet staff and authors share their top travel experiences in these two destinations.

MARTIN MOOS

① GRAND PLACE, BRUSSELS

Whichever way you look at it, meeting for drinks at 'The King of Spain' (Le Roy d'Espagne; p102) in Brussels' Grand Place (p76) just has to be a rendezvous with history.

Neil Manders, Lonely Planet Staff

BRUCE ESBI

2 BRUGES

We saw the best of Belgium by hiring bicycles from the hostel in Bruges (p129) and cycling our way along a beautiful path that runs along a canal. Passing windmills, the path took us all the way to Damme, a quaint little town where we sat outside at one of the many cafes, quenched our thirst with a Leffe beer, and ordered mussels that came by the kilo, steaming in delicious broth.

Diana Steicke, Traveller, Australia

LEANNE LOGAN

3 YPRES

At the fascinating In Flanders Fields museum in beautiful Ypres (Ieper; p157) I was deeply moved by the personal stories of those who lived, fought and died throughout 'The Great War'. The drive around the surrounding WWI battlefields, cemeteries and trenches brought the horror and inhumanity of war even further alive. By 8pm I was back in town for the haunting Last Post ceremony. Finally, we kicked back in town with some fabulous food and beer, because, after all, that's also what life is very much about in Flanders.

Annelies Mertens, Lonely Planet Staff

ROCHEHAUT

The Belgian Ardennes appeals to the Dutch who don't have contours of their own. For the rest of us the scenery often seems a little underwhelming but a truly impressive exception is the wonderful valley view from Rochehaut (p240).

Mark Elliott, Lonely Planet Author

4

JOHNNY70 / ISTOCK

BEER

The highlight of my trip to Belgium was the beer (p48) and food, and attempting to sample as many different types as possible. While we drank *kriek* and *witbier*, ate *stoemp* and waffles, we came away with a great appreciation of the benefits of living in Belgium (though how they got anything done is beyond me).

Ryan Miller, Lonely Planet Staff

5

MARTIN MOOS

6

GHENT

If no one has suggested taking mosquito repellent to Ghent (p117) then they should! One of the few downsides to this really beautiful city. It's a city of walking, low-key eating, drinking and really relaxing. Slightly eerie Gothic architecture looks stunning in the low sun of autumn. I would highly recommend a long weekend there.

Vicki Huggett, Traveller, UK

JONATHAN SMITH

LEANNE LOG

7 LUXEMBOURG

Luxembourg (p263) is Europe's richest country and on my first visit I was naive enough to really imagine it packed almost border to border with banks. Of course not. Nonetheless all the rural castles and forested hills were quite a surprise. And Luxembourg City's dramatic river-canyon setting never ceases to blow me away...especially when it's reverberating to the joyous twangs of the fabulous Blues & Jazz Rallye (p18).

Mark Elliott, Lonely Planet Author

KEVIN GEORGE / AL

8 LIER, DIEST OR TURNHOUT

For Cole Porter a *beguine* meant a slow rumba. But in medieval Belgium *béguines* were single women who wanted the safety of a convent without the restriction of a nun's vows. They've effectively died out nowadays but their homes (*béguinages/begijnhoven;* see the boxed text, p137) remain – adorable enclosed communities of whitewashed houses set around pretty lawns. Over a dozen are now listed by Unesco, including my favourites at Turnhout, Diest and lovely Lier (pictured; p192).

Mark Elliott, Lonely Planet Author

Contents

Regional Map Contents

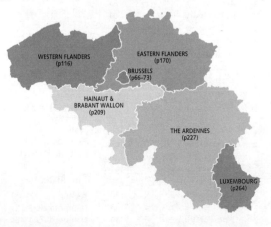

Destination Belgium & Luxembourg

Self-deluding foreigners who've never been here often quip that nobody can name five famous Belgians. Or that Belgium is 'boring'. 'So there's beer and mussels, but what else?' Belgians' downbeat, self-deprecating sense of humour means that locals are more than happy to let such folks fool themselves. If foreigners want to ignore the country's astonishing art history, its 60-plus Unesco sites, and bizarre carnivals that make Rio's look unimaginative, so be it. As one Antwerp resident half-mockingly suggested, 'Don't waste your time here, Amsterdam is so much prettier!' Meanwhile tiny Luxembourg sits even further off most tourist radars, except perhaps for those savvy enough to fill up their petrol tanks as they drive through. Not that Luxembourgers mind. They're already Europe's richest people (per capita). Feel free to not realise that their forested hills are pimpled with medieval castles or that their capital is so photogenically perched on a spectacular river canyon. *Bonne route!*

Belgium is a country of two distinct halves. Dutch-speaking Flanders (northern Belgium) has a flat, often monotonous landscape, but it is interspersed with fabulous historic cities. These lie close together and are conveniently interconnected by regular trains, making travel by public transport seamless. In French-speaking Wallonia (southern Belgium), however, most attractions are contrastingly rural: caves, castles, bucolic valleys and outdoor activities. Staying in village inns and stringing together several minor countryside attractions can make for a truly delightful experience if you're driving or have strong cycling legs. However, if you're limited to public transport you'll quickly get fed up with rural Wallonia's infrequent buses and you'll struggle to make any real sense of the area's charms. Logistically speaking, Luxembourg falls somewhere between the two.

Belgium's division is very much political too. Wallonia's rust belt is littered with the scars of its once-vibrant heavy industries and the Walloon economy noticeably lags behind that of go-ahead Flanders. Fed up with 'subsidising' their French-speaking neighbours, more than a few Flemish nationalists call for the country to split. The majority wouldn't go that far. But as years go by so Belgium's two halves drift further and further apart, if only by default and for the lack of any common language/media. Only Brussels makes even any pretence at seeking bilingualism, and in the modern age kids in both halves often prefer to learn English than a second 'Belgian' language. This is especially true of the Francophone Belgians whose unpreparedness to learn Dutch is a constant gripe. But does this mean that Belgium is bound to split? Most people doubt that, if only because it would be too expensive…and who would get Brussels? Nonetheless, in 2006 when a spoof 'breaking news' documentary on Francophone TV announced that Flanders had declared independence, a remarkable proportion of the viewers actually believed it.

Despite all this, beneath the surface both communities actually share many similar attitudes. Both display a vague disdain for authority, a quiet self-confidence and a gentle streak of surrealism – rather fitting for such a joyously 'illogical' country whose independence was set in motion not by a freedom-fighting terror campaign but with an 1830 opera. Another common attitude is the unguarded disdain each community feels for its co-linguistic neighbour across the border (ie the Flemish for the Dutch, the Francophone Belgians for the French). And both share common worries over law and order and a deep ambivalence over immigration – whether newcomers enrich the cultural mix or drain the national purse; that didn't stop politicians wasting most of 2007 discussing a boundary-line question (see p35) that even many (mainly Francophone) Belgians didn't understand. This left Belgium without a national government for almost a year. The economic crisis of 2008 suddenly knocked heads together. While many Brits and Americans panicked over how to refinance their mortgages and credit-card debts, Belgians tore their hair out over where to shift their savings. So when two major Belgian banks seemed to be teetering towards bankruptcy more than a few households raced to pull out what they could, exacerbating the situation for the enfeebled banks. Finally spurred into action, politicians stopped bickering and put together a bank rescue package that was initially lauded for its boldness. But feelings rapidly soured; prompt action came to be seen as a rash response. Reports emerged of unethical political pressure having been placed on the judiciary to force the measures through, and in December 2008 Prime Minister Yves Leterme's government fell. Into the prime ministerial job came Leterme's replacement, Herman Van Rompuy – somewhat against his own will. Nicknamed 'the Sphinx' for his poker-faced inscrutability, Van Rompuy's low-key approach rapidly proved inclusive and effective. But just as the press were hailing him 'Super Rompuy' the prime minister was headhunted as President of Europe (November 2009). A second chance then for Yves Leterme whose reputation among many voters has never recovered from a TV interview where, when asked to sing the Belgian national anthem, he mistakenly sang the French one instead. A sceptical press welcomed his re-appointment with headlines like 'Est-il fait pour le job?' ('Is he up to the job?').

A major continuing challenge for any prime minister is facing up to the country's massive budget deficit. The Belgian bureaucracy is an expensive animal to feed. Indeed it's the most expensive per capita in all of Europe, according to October 2009 press reports. That's not so surprising when you realise that each language community (Dutch-, French- and German-speaking) and region (Flanders, Wallonia, Brussels) has its own parliament and civil service, who together employ a remarkable 18.5% of the country's workforce – the highest percentage of any OECD nation. That costs around €7.5 billion a year, yet curiously few locals complain. In contrast the royal family costs a paltry €13.8 million per year (under €1.50 per Belgian), yet a July 2009 poll suggested that 70% of Belgians thought that too much, while 32% wanted to stop financial support to the royals altogether.

Whatever the state of the economy, both Belgium and Luxembourg remain countries where people live well. There are strong social support systems, liberal attitudes, imaginative museums, a vibrant theatrical and artistic life and fabulous food. Belgian beers are divine and endlessly varied. And Luxembourg's sparkling wines are merrily quaffed on many a summer street terrace. Crisis or no crisis, big new attractions for visitors continue to blossom. Recent additions to Belgium's portfolio include state-of-the-art galleries in Mons and Leuven, the superb new Hergé museum at Louvain-la-Neuve, and the Magritte Museum and subterranean Coudenberg experience in Brussels. Then there's the incredibly ambitious Grand Curtius in Liège, which is also where one of Europe's most extraordinary 21st-century architectural talking points, Liège-Guillemins station, opened in 2009.

Belgium is much more than chips and chocolate, Luxembourg far more than boring banks. Come prepared for plenty of positive surprises as you discover the good life in this fascinatingly undersold duo.

FAST FACTS BELGIUM/ LUXEMBOURG

Population: 10.6 million/480,000

Area: 30,528/2586 sq km

Unemployment: Flanders 10%; Wallonia 18%; Brussels 21%; Luxembourg 3.5%

Inflation: 4.5%/1.5%

GDP: US$390 billion/ US$31 billion

Minimum gross monthly salary: €1210/€1467

Annual beer consumption per head (Belgium): 100L

Annual chocolate consumption per head (Belgium): 16kg

Smoking: banned in restaurants, but not (yet) in cafés (pubs/bars)

Sex: 58% of Belgians are satisfied with their sex life (worldwide average 44%)

Getting Started

WHEN TO GO

Come to Brussels in the last week of August and you'll wonder where everyone is. The reality is that much of urban Belgium simply packs up and goes away on holiday from 1 July to 31 August. But come 1 September, the capital's ring road is suddenly back to its gridlocked normality. The situation is somewhat similar in Antwerp and Luxembourg City, but reversed in the rural Ardennes and along Belgium's 66km coastal strip of sandy beach, where you'll find things jam-packed throughout the summer. But by October these areas are heading into a long annual slumber.

This whole scenario also plays out in miniature through any given week: savvy travellers can save a packet by sleeping at weekends in business cities (Brussels, Luxembourg City, Kortrijk) and heading for tourist honeypots (Bruges, Durbuy, La Roche-en-Ardenne) midweek in low season. And given Belgium's modest size and Luxembourg's remarkable compactness, it's not hard to shuttle about to fit these patterns.

See our Climate Charts (p289) for at-a-glance temperature information.

The one predictable thing about Belgian weather is its unpredictability. Winters of 2007–8 and 2009–10 saw abundant snows, while in 2008–9 the Ardennes slopes barely got a single skiable week. Winters are traditionally fairly mild, but both 2008 and 2009 saw the mercury dip to around -20°C in places – unprecedented. Local summers are often grey and drizzly, yet in 2009 sunshine reigned for months on end. The fact is that you'll need to be prepared for a range of conditions. And an umbrella is always worth having tucked away.

You might want to time your trip for a local celebration. Both countries are so big on festivals that even the highlights run to several pages (see p16).

COSTS & MONEY

Belgium is, on average, slightly cheaper than Luxembourg, except for fuel. In both countries, accommodation and dining can quickly melt holes in an over-used credit card, but budget options are available. You'll save a packet by eating weekday set-lunches rather than dinners at the same restaurants. And clever timing (staying weekends in business cities and weekdays in tourist areas) can result in significant accommodation savings. Meanwhile, comparatively cheap public transport, coupled with the diminutive size of both countries, makes getting around a relatively minor expense.

LONELY PLANET INDEX

Belgium/ Luxembourg

Litre of petrol €1.40/1.15

Litre of bottled water €0.80/0.75

250mL of draught beer from €1.80/2.20

Souvenir T-shirt €13/15

Street snack – frites €2.10/croissant €1.50

DON'T LEAVE HOME WITHOUT...

- A sense of humour – being pelted by oranges or flapped in the face with a dried herring just might be meant as an honorific blessing (see Laetare, p16).
- An umbrella and extra jumper – optimism isn't always quite enough.
- A water bottle – neither cafés (pubs/bars) nor restaurants, not even fast-food places, will give away tap water, so if you'd rather not pay for it, fill up a flask in your hotel/hostel each morning.
- Soap and a towel – budget hostels provide sheets, but not the washing wherewithal.
- Nerves of steel – essential for drivers, especially before you've internalised the arcane meaning of priorité à droite (see Look Right!, p304).
- Your favourite hangover cure.

By staying in hostels, visiting relatively few museums, filling up on sandwiches or fast fodder and downing just an occasional beer or two, it's possible to get by on €40 per day. Those opting for hotels with full amenities and midrange restaurants should figure around €120.

Families can minimise expenses by staying at self-catering guesthouses (p285). Restaurants often have discounted children's meals; children under 12 years of age travel free on Belgian trains and often get free entrance to museums.

TOP 10

FOLKLORIC FESTIVALS

There are numerous excellent summer music festivals, film festivals and town fairs. However, Belgium also has some unique cultural offerings the like of which you'll see nowhere else. For more details and other festivals, see p16.

1 Cwarmé (p16), Malmédy
2 Rosenmontag, Eupen
3 Carnival (p16), Binche
4 Burning of Winter (p16), Bouge
5 Penitents' Procession (p16), Lessines
6 Laetare (p16), Stavelot
7 Le Doudou (p17), Mons
8 Heilig-Bloedprocessie (p17), Bruges
9 Festival Outremeuse (p18), Liège
10 Giants' Procession (p18), Ath

INDUSTRIAL MUSEUMS

There are plenty of excellent history-based museums, Mechelen's science and toy museums are unbeatable in their fields and Louvain-La-Neuve's Hergé Museum is a masterpiece. However, one great strength is the selection of imaginative museum experiences that provide a fascinating insight into industrial processes and jobs:

1 Making sugar in Tienen (p205)
2 Blowing glass in Seraing (p254)
3 Fishing in Oostduinkerke (p153)
4 Processing flax in Kortrijk (p164)
5 Baking in Veurne (p154)
6 Distilling gin in Hasselt (p204)
7 Wool-crafting in Verviers (p259)
8 Making cheese in Passendale (p161)
9 Weaving in Ghent (p121)
10 Mining in Rumelange (p274)

ART GALLERIES

From primitive passions to Rubens' nudes, surrealism to contemporary installations, porcelain to photography, the artistic heritage is superb:

1 MSK, Ghent ((p121)
2 MNHA, Luxembourg City (p266)
3 Groeningemuseum, Bruges (p133)
4 KMSKA, Antwerp (p179)
5 Verbeke Foundation, Stekene (p190)
6 Magritte Museum & Musées Royaux des Beaux-Arts, Brussels (p82)
7 Photography Museum, Charleroi (p222)
8 M van Museum, Leuven (p200)
9 Musée de l'Art Wallon, Liège (p250)
10 Grand Curtius, Liège (p251)

WEEKLY PLANNER

Some interesting visits or activities are only possible on specific days, so it pays to plan ahead:

- **Monday** – beware, most museums are closed
- **Tuesday** – see bakery demonstrations in Veurne (p154)
- **Wednesday** – climb the Antwerp cathedral tower (p171); free entry evenings to see contemporary art at Wiels (p85), Brussels
- **Thursday** – see weaving demonstrations at MIAT (p121) and enjoy free jazz at Hotsy Totsy (p127), both in Ghent
- **Friday** – join the Roller Parade in Brussels (p112; summer evenings only)
- **Saturday** – take the De Wit tapestry-makers' tour (p196) and visit De Mijpaal railway museum (p196; May, June & September), both in Mechelen; join a perfumery tour (p228) in Namur; at night visit Bruges' ultraweird Retsin's Lucifernum (p144)
- **Sunday** – spend an afternoon at Lillo's Poldermuseum (p190) or at Aubechies' Archeosite (p212), where craftsmen bring prehistory alive

TRAVEL LITERATURE

A Tall Man in a Low Land (Harry Pearson) A hilarious tale of holidaying in Belgium packed with anecdotes spotlighting the peculiarities and idiosyncrasies of everyday life. Think Bill Bryson with a Geordie accent. Occasionally rambles a little too far into the world of cycle-racing, but magnificent nonetheless.

Luxembourg & the Jenisch Connection (David Robinson) Fictional tale of an Englishman's holiday in Luxembourg that turns into a murder mystery. It's set during the record-breaking hot summer of 2003.

The Factory of Facts (Luc Sante) Belgian-born but US-raised, Luc Sante returns at the age of 35 to explore the country he left behind. An interesting account of his thoughts and opinions on all things Belgian.

INTERNET RESOURCES

Most towns have an extensive civic website at www.<townname>.be.

Association of Historic Buildings & Gardens of Belgium (www.demeures-historiques.be)

Belgian Tourist Office (www.visitbelgium.com)

Belgium online in English (www.xpats.com) Belgium's international community provides lots of information, including local news in English and an entertainment agenda.

Belgiumview (www.belgiumview.com) Internauts vote on their hit parade of most beautiful Belgian sites, giving a delightfully random set of highlights. Many good photos.

Horest (www.horest.be) Town-by-town hotel and restaurant listings that are especially helpful for rural backwaters.

Lonely Planet (www.lonelyplanet.com) Postcards from other travellers, the best beds to book and the Thorn Tree travel forum, where you can ask questions before you go or dispense advice when you get back.

Luxembourg Internet Directory (www.luxweb.lu) Links to cinema, cultural, weather and football sites for Luxembourg.

Luxembourg National Tourist Office (www.ont.lu)

LuxAlbum (www.luxalbum.com) Photos of every village in Luxembourg.

HOW MUCH?

Belgium

Midrange hotel double
€60-160

Baguette sandwich €3

Kilogram of pralines
€20-70

Cinema ticket €6

Bike hire per day
free-€14

Luxembourg

Midrange hotel double
€70-200

Baguette sandwich €3.50

Bottle of sparkling wine
€7-15

Cinema ticket €7

Bike hire per day €15-20

Events Calendar

The truly extraordinary wealth of festivals in Belgium and Luxembourg takes many visitors quite by surprise, especially the bizarre Lenten/Carnival pageants. Francophone website www.quefaire.be offers a great range of regularly updated what's-on information from sport to concerts to folklore. Summer spells music festivals and town fairs in the region. Some major ones include Festival van Vlaanderen (Flanders and Brussels, www.festival.be), Festival de Wallonie (Wallonia, www.festivaldewallonie.be) and Summer in the City (Luxembourg, www.summerinthecity.lu).

characters oversee proceedings while on seven distant surrounding hilltops other coordinated conflagrations are lit.

LAETARE   4th Sat of Lent 2 Apr 2011, 13 Feb 2012, 4 Feb 2013, 24 Mar 2014
Stavelot's sinister Pinocchio-like *Blanc Moussis* stuff confetti down women's clothes, dangle smelly dried herrings in people's hair and beat bystanders with dried pigs' bladders. It's all part of the unique Laetare carnival (www.laetare-stavelot.be; p256).

FEBRUARY–MARCH

CWARMÉ   weekend before Lent
In Malmédy (p260) a bizarre multi-day carnival climaxes with a Sunday afternoon parade dominated by masked *Haguète*. These odd characters wearing blood-red capes and pirate hats stuffed with ostrich feathers use *hapes-tchâr* (great extendible wooden pincers) to force bystanders to kneel and repent their sins.

ROSENMONTAG   Mon before Lent 7 Mar 2011, 20 Feb 2012, 11 Feb 2013, 3 Mar 2014
Superbly joyful and colourful carnival fills the streets of Eupen (p262)

CARNIVAL   Shrove Tue 8 Mar 2011, 21 Feb 2012, 12 Feb 2013, 4 Mar 2014
One of the world's oddest carnivals unfolds in Binche (p216) where the orange-throwing, mask-wearing Gilles don their giant ostrich-feather hats in the afternoon if the winds stay calm. In Aalst (map p116) there's the hilarious if raucous Voil Jeanetten (cross-dressed 'dirty prostitutes') carnival. And dozens of other towns have their own smaller-scale carnivals.

BURNING OF WINTER   1st Sun of Lent 13 Mar 2011, 26 Feb 2012, 17 Feb 2013, 9 Mar 2014
The spirit of winter is ceremonially cremated in Belgian village fields and with cruciform fires on hillsides across Luxembourg (where the day's called 'Buergsonndeg'). The biggest and most dramatic bonfire is at Bouge on Namur's eastern outskirts. An odd cast of costumed folkloric

MARCH–APRIL

PENITENTS' PROCESSION   Good Fri 22 Apr 2011, 6 Apr 2012, 29 Mar 2013, 18 Apr 2014
After dusk in Lessines (p213) the lights go out as eerie figures in monks habits and KKK-styled conical hoods parade moodily around town carrying flaming torches in a procession that dates back to 1475.

ARS MUSICA   mid-Mar–early-Apr
Respected festival of contemporary classical music (www.arsmusica.be) at various Brussels venues.

SERRES ROYALES   late Apr
The royal greenhouses (above) open to the public for 10 days.

MAY–JUNE

HANSWIJK PROCESSION   Sun before Ascension
Part religious tableau, part medieval pageant, thousands dress up and parade through Mechelen (p193), starting from Keizerstraat at 3pm. It's to thank the Virgin Mary for sparing the town from plague back in 1272. See www.hanswijkprocessie.org for more info. In 2013 there'll be the added bonus of a four-times-a-century Ommegang featuring folkloric giants.

ZINNEKE PARADE   late May, even years
Thoroughly contemporary one-day multicultural parade designed to bridge social divides and expose Brussels' zanier side (www.zinneke.org).

HEILIG-BLOEDPROCESSIE   Ascension Day
2 Jun 2011, 17 May 2012, 9 May 2013,
29 May 2014 (always a Thursday)
Pageantry and big crowds watch Bruges' biggest folklore event (www.holyblood.com), the parading around town of an enormously revered reliquary supposedly containing a few drops of Christ's blood. Book early for a grandstand seat on the Markt.

KATTENFESTIVAL   2nd Sun in Jun
12th-century Ypres' citizens believed that cats personified evil spirits. As a result poor pussies suffered a bizarre ritual in which they were hurled off the Lakenhalle's belfry. Animal lovers will be glad to hear that these days the falling felines are only toys. Every third year (next in 2012) the festival adds a parade of giant cats (Kattenstoet).

BRUSSELS JAZZ MARATHON
last weekend of May
Three fabulous evenings of free, non-stop jazz, blues and zydeco concerts on stages and in pubs all over Brussels (www.brusselsjazzmara thon.be).

SPRINPROZESSION
(ST WILLIBRORD PAGEANT)   Whit Tue
14 Jun 2011, 3 Jun 2012,
15 May 2013, 10 Jun 2014
A three-day Whitsun pilgrimage celebrating Echternach's (p277) Anglo-Saxon founding father culminates after dawn on Tuesday. From around 9am the cobbled streets fill with rows of dancers linked by white handkerchiefs in a time-honoured religious procession (www.willi brord.lu).

LE DOUDOU   Trinity Sun 19 Jun 2011,
29 May 2012, 20 May 2013, 15 Jun 2014
After a golden 'coach' of relics has been paraded through town, Mons (p214) goes completely crazy as St George fights the dragon on the Grand Place to the insistent drum beats of soldiers in 18th-century costumes. Unesco listed, very physical.

WATERLOO BATTLE RE-ENACTMENTS
mid-Jun
On the weekend nearest 18 June over a thousand costumed 'soldiers' recreate scenes from the classic 1815 battle near Waterloo (www.water loo1815.be), see p219.

VITRINE   late Jun
For 10 days top fashion designers display their creations all around Ghent (odd years) or Antwerp (even years). See www.ffi.be/en/vitrine.

LUXEMBOURG NATIONAL DAY   22-23 Jun
The Grand Duchy's biggest event starts with fireworks from Pont Adolphe in Luxembourg City on the evening of 22 June. Later there's dancing on Place d'Armes followed by an all-night party, with *cafés* (pubs/bars) around town open 'til dawn. On 23 June a military parade winds through the capital's streets and festivities are held nationwide.

COULEUR CAFÉ   last weekend in Jun
Excellent, three-day festival of world-music concerts, workshops and ethnic-dining opportunities attracts over 75,000 people to Brussels' Tour & Taxis complex (www.couleurcafe.be; p91).

JULY

WILTZ FESTIVAL   Jul
Impressive month-long theatre-, jazz- and music-festival in the château grounds at Wiltz (www .festivalwiltz.online.lu; above).

OMMEGANG   1st Thu
Brussels' biggest medieval-style procession (www.ommegang.be) originally celebrated the audacious kidnap from Antwerp of the Sablon's miracle-working Virgin Mary statue (see p83). Totally transformed over the centuries, Ommegang is now effectively a costumed re-construction of Charles V's magnificent *Joyous Entree* parade of 1549. Watching the cavalcade wind around town from the Sablon costs nothing, but to see the lavish finale and dance in the illuminated Grand Place you'll need tickets (book well ahead).

ROCK WERCHTER   1st week
Held in fields at Werchter north of Leuven, this is one of Europe's biggest rock festivals (www. rockwerchter.be), the four-day Belgian equivalent of Glastonbury or Roskilde.

LES FRANCOFOLIES DE SPA   1st week
Spa (p257) hosts one of Belgium's biggest French-language cultural festivals (www.francofolies.be), notable for attracting some of the biggest names in chanson.

DE GENTSE FEESTEN mid-Jul
This fabulously raucous 10-day festival (www
.gentsefeesten.be, in Dutch) transforms the heart
of Ghent into a youthful party of music and street
theatre characterised by packed streets and merry
drinking. You'll pay for the Blue Note jazz festival
(www.bluenotefestival.be) and '10 Days Off...'
(www.10daysoff.be; one of Europe's biggest
techno parties) but most other events are free.

MACRÂLES 20 Jul
At dusk Vielsalm (p255) briefly hands over the
keys of the city to a band of witches who perform
a mesmerising half-comic, half-spooky 'coven' in
full Walloon dialect in a dark corner of the town's
woodland park.

BELGIUM NATIONAL DAY 21 Jul
A military parade passes in front of Brussels' Royal
Palace (p81) by day. At night expect fireworks
in many towns, most spectacularly in Brussels
around Mont des Arts (map p70).

LUXEMBOURG JAZZ & BLUES RALLYE
mid-Jul
The Grund and Clausen areas of Luxembourg City
party all night to a fine array of free concerts
(www.bluesjazzrallye.lu).

PENITENTS' PROCESSION last Sun
Held since 1644, the *Boetprocessie* in Veurne (p154)
is a solemn street parade by hundreds of Biblically-
costumed players. Human tableaux illustrate 40
scenes from Jesus' life, death and resurrection
interspersed by masked 'penitents' in brown
monks'-style robes. By far the most famous image
(scene 36) sees dozens of such cowled figures lum-
ber past carrying heavy wooden crosses.

AUGUST

FESTIVAL MUSICA ANTIQUA 1st week
Weeklong festival of medieval music in Bruges
(www.mafestival.be).

LA NUIT DU LIVRE 1st Sat
All night book-fest in Redu (p237) accompanied
by music and midnight fireworks.

FOLK DRANOUTER 1st weekend
One of Europe's most important folk-music
festivals held in Dranouter, a small town 12km
southwest of Ypres (Map p116; www.folkdra
nouter.be).

MEYBOOM 9 Aug
With many bar-stops en route, this merrily low-key
Brussels' folkloric procession winds down from
the Sablon around 2pm, parades through the
Grand Place then returns to plant a quite misnamed 'May-tree' at the corner of Rue des Sables
and Rue du Marais just before 5pm.

SINT-ROCHUSVERLICHTING 15 Aug
In Aarschot (p202), electric lamps are extinguished
from dusk to midnight, replaced by flickering lines
of candles along windowsills and footpaths. The
magical family-friendly scene is accompanied
by folk dances and brass bands. Don't miss the
chance of perambulating within the magnificent
half-lit central church.

FESTIVAL OUTREMEUSE 15th Aug
A week of raucously drunken celebrations in old
Liège's 'Republic of Outremeuse' (www.fgfw.be/
rlom) culminates on 15 August when sermons
are read in full Walloon dialect, then everyone
gets tipsy on *pékèt* (Wallon for gin). Expect fire
crackers, puppet shows, traditional dances, a
folkloric procession of giants and vast, possibly
unruly crowds. Next day from 5pm, the surreal
Enterrement de Mâti l'Ohé is the cremation
and burial of a bone symbolically marking the
end of festivities. A 'mourning' parade shuffles
around the Outremeuse district, its brass band
interspersing up-tempo carnivalesque music with
sombre dirges accompanied by hammy weeping.
Hilarious. Dress in black and bring celery!

TAPIS DE FLEURS mid-Aug, even years
Alternate years an incredible 'carpet' of intricately
placed flower petals transforms Brussels' Grand
Place into a giant magic carpet (www.flowercar
pet.be). It's free to walk past, €3 to view it from
the town hall balcony or well worth paying a beer
to see it from an upper *café* window.

GOLDEN TREE PAGEANT end Aug
(every 5th year)
Roughly every five years in Bruges this grandiose
procession celebrates the 1468 marriage of Charles
the Bold to Margaret of York. Next in 2012.

GIANTS' PROCESSION 4th weekend
Ath (p213) holds a series of parades featuring enormous World Heritage-listed models
with Biblical and folkloric connections. One
such giant, Goliath (Gouyasse), has his trousers
'burnt' on Friday night, gets married on Saturday
(3pm at St-Julien's Church) then fights David

(5pm at the town hall). The biggest parades are on the Sunday. See http://laducassedath01 .skyrock.com.

SEPTEMBER

BELGIAN GRAND PRIX early Sep
Formula 1 comes to Spa-Francorchamps (p259), resulting in full occupancy at virtually every hotel in eastern Wallonia.

HERITAGE DAYS 2nd weekend
Open Monumentendag (http://openmonu menten.zita.be) in Flanders, Journées du Patrimoine (www.journeesdupatrimoine.be) in Wallonia both see the opening of an annually varying selection of monuments to the public, many of which are not otherwise accessible.

MECHELS GILDEJUWEEL 2nd Sun
Mechelen's Grote Markt is invaded by troops of guildsmen in medieval-style costumes. Various folk dances and musical performances are interspersed with beer quaffing and the 4pm 'Bell-Throwing', when twenty bells are sent flying down a lengthy wire strung between the cathedral tower and the city hall. Each releases a flutter of smaller plastic bells of which one is a lottery-style 'winning' bell.

HERITAGE DAYS, BRUSSELS 3rd weekend
Heritage days (see above) come a week later in the capital.

COMBAT DE L'ÉCHASSE D'OR 3rd Sun
In Namur, a week of festivities (the Fêtes de Wallonie, www.fetesdewallonie.be) culminate in this jousting competition between two teams of stilt-walkers dressed in medieval garb. Starts 4pm on Place St-Aubain.

OCTOBER

NOCTURNE DES COTEAUX 1st Sat
Liège comes alive at dusk with 20,000 candles forming beautiful patterns on the city's vertiginous stairway, Montagne de Bueren (p250). Some 60 historic buildings (many usually closed) open their doors, there are numerous free concerts and at 11.30pm fireworks cap things off. See www .lanocturnedescoteaux.be.

HASSELTSE JENEVERFEESTEN 3rd Sat
The most celebrated moment in Hasselt's famous gin festival (p204) comes at 4.30pm when the town's iconic little Borrelmanneke Fountain (St-Jozefsstraat) briefly pours forth jenever (gin) instead of water.

KLAPSTUKFESTIVAL from mid-Oct
Leuven's month-long international contemporary dance festival (www.stuk.be).

DECEMBER

Christmas markets are common, with a fine example in Brussels' Grand Place (p76).

Itineraries
CLASSIC ROUTES

GEM CITIES OF THE LOWLANDS
10 days / Brussels to Antwerp

Four of northern Europe's most memorable historic cities are so hand-ily close together that an hour's train ride is enough to get between any of them. So you *could* just about glimpse them all in a long weekend. However, even 10 days wouldn't really do them full justice.

Start with Europe's capital, **Brussels** (p62), whose **Grand Place** (p76) is one of the world's most beautiful squares. Explore seductive chocolate shops, wonderful cafes, great galleries, fine museums and art nouveau buildings. And don't miss the unique 1958 **Atomium** (p90).

Medieval architecture and endless canalside charm make beautiful **Bruges** (p129) one of Europe's most romantic getaways. Less tourist-oriented, grittier yet somehow more satisfying is magical **Ghent** (p117), whose inti-mate medieval core is complemented by a vibrant student vibe and some wonderful museums. Larger **Antwerp** (p169) is an eclectic port city whose historical credentials are balanced by its vibrant nightlife, *café*-culture and cutting-edge designer fashions.

The specific order in which you visit these fabulous cities is relatively unimportant transport wise. Be cash-savvy by spending your weekend nights in Brussels or Antwerp, with week nights in Bruges. If you've got a little longer add in Mechelen and Lier too.

THE ESSENTIALS
One Month / Ghent to Vianden

This tour takes you the length of Belgium and Luxembourg along a route easily achievable by public transport (mostly by train, but with a few bus hops thrown in too). Start with glorious **Ghent** (p117) and incomparable **Bruges** (p129). Allow three days apiece, though each could keep you busy for weeks. Once you can tear yourself away nip swiftly along the coast, seeing the remarkable **Atlantikwall WWII fortifications** (p149) near **Ostend** (p147) en route to historic **Veurne** (p154). A couple of days is probably enough to ponder the remarkably reconstructed cloth towns **Diksmuide** (p156) and **Ypres** (p157), though you'll need more if you want to thoroughly investigate the numerous poignant WWI sites nearby. Admire the five-towered, part-Romanesque **cathedral** (p210) at **Tournai** p209 then zip across country to **Brussels** and, a few days later, on to the underrated historic cities of **Leuven** (p199) and **Mechelen** (p193) – easily worth two days apiece. Party your way round **Antwerp** (p169) for two or three days then calm down in the beautiful *begijnhoven* of **Lier** (p192) and **Diest** (p203). To learn about Belgium's industrial heritage try the inspired sugar museum at **Tienen** (p204) or the Val St-Lambert glassworks in ugly **Seraing** (p254) outside **Liège** (p248), itself a big, perversely fascinating city where gaping at the astonishing new Guillemins station is reason enough to stop. A railway line winds through the hilly Ardennes to **Luxembourg City** (p264), a wealthy little capital whose dramatic river-canyon setting is much more spectacular than most visitors anticipate. If you're spending a few days in the Grand Duchy don't miss visiting **Vianden** (p280), the most memorable of its many castle towns.

Straightforward by public transport, this 750km route samples the best-known art cities but also introduces lesser-known sights tha first-time visitors often speed past. If you're doing the trip by car, there'll be lots of extra stops en route as you head south.

ROADS LESS TRAVELLED

CASTLES, CAVES & CANALS   Two Weeks / Wallonia & Luxembourg

Regal **Belœil** (p212) is nicknamed 'Belgium's Versailles'. If driving there on a Sunday don't miss the Archeosite, a reconstructed Iron Age settlement at **Aubechies** (p212). Heading east via **Mons** (p214) peruse the remarkable canal workings (p216) at **Ronquières**, **Strépy Thieu** and **La Louvière**. There are some forgotten castles around **Gembloux** (p221) while for sheer scale it's hard to beat the grey, imposing citadel-fortresses of **Namur** (p228) and **Dinant** (p235), both dominating historic, if slightly tired, cities along the River Meuse. In the area, spot Dave from **Wépion** (p230), visit **Annevoie** (p234) or **Freÿr** (p235) for their formal gardens and cut across country to see the cute mansion-tower at **Crupet** (p234).

Castle village **Lavaux-Ste-Anne** (p237) makes a peaceful accommodation alternative to **Han-sur-Lesse** (p236) once you've visited Han's world-famous cave system, though you might prefer the less commercial caves at **Rochefort** (p236) or **Hotton** (p245). Nearby **La Roche-en-Ardenne** (p243) offers various outdoor pursuits and is crowned by an archetypal castle crag ruin that's only challenged for Crusader-era atmosphere by **Bouillon** (p238) in the lovely Semois Valley.

Returning north via **Durbuy** (p246), **Modave** (p233) has one of the finest interiors of any Belgian chateau, **Huy** (p233) has another Dinant-style citadel and **Jehay** (p234) is the most photogenic moated beauty imaginable.

Alternatively head south for Luxembourg where **Luxembourg City** (p264) is one vast canyon-citadel and virtually every town sports a castle. The most memorable are in **Vianden** (p280), **Bourscheid** (p279), **Bourglinster** (p276), **Beaufort** (p278) and **Larochette** (p276).

Belgium and Luxembourg have numerous under-appreciated rural gems, but realistically you're going to need a car to enjoy them. Consider breaking the itinerary into a series of shorter trips. Remember that on summer weekends rural accommodation gets overbooked, but in Luxembourg City hotel prices plummet.

TAILORED TRIPS

BELGIUM'S BEER TRAIL

None of the Trappist monastery-breweries offer individual visits and only **Orval** (p241) even allows visitors into the abbey grounds. However, **Westvleteren** (p155), **Westmalle** (p190), **Chimay** (p225) and Orval all have 'official' *cafés* near their respective abbeys. All serve their Trappist classics, with the latter two also offering unique (if simple) draught beers available nowhere else.

West Flanders' famous hop-crop is celebrated with a hop museum in **Poperinge** (p156) while Bruges' Den Dijver (p143) is among the most famous restaurant exponents of beer cuisine. Fabulous **Bruges** (p129) is also home to **De Halve Maan** (p136), one of very few Belgian breweries to allow drop-in visits. Once a month you can see the unique Dubuisson steam brewery go into action at **Pipaix** (p212). One place to witness the production of Brussels' unique self-fermenting lambics is **Cantillon Brewery** (p91).

Small breweries at **Achouffe** (La Chouffe, p246), **Aulne** (Blonde des Pères, *p223*), **Ellezelles** (Quintine, *p213*), **Mariembourg** (Super des Fagnes, p224) and **Esen** (Oerbier, p156) all have interesting brewery-*cafés,* most overlooking the brew-stills, while **Hoegaarden** (p205) offers an imaginative museum-like 'white-beer experience'. Historic **Leuven** is home to international mega-lager Stella Artois (visits possible by arrangement; p201) and also brews luscious Leffe, though the original Leffe Abbey still stands in **Dinant** (p235).

24

History

Belgium, Luxembourg and the Netherlands share a fascinatingly tangled history. The current borders of these three 'Low Countries' only appeared in the 19th century but what went before was far from uneventful.

EARLY SETTLEMENTS

For a resource index of articles, books and subjects on Belgian history, see http://vlib.iue.it/hist-belgium.

Belgian talent for industry and trade was already apparent 6000 years ago when Neolithic miners dug extensively to create high-quality flint tools at Spiennes (p215) and traded them throughout the region.

The term Belgium takes its historical roots from a Germano-Celtic group of tribes called the Belgae. As Belgian school kids will proudly tell you, Belgae warriors were the 'bravest' opponents of Julius Caesar during the Roman conquests of Gaul (57 to 50 BC). Since Belgium's 1830 creation, Belgae resistance leader Ambiorix has been resurrected as a national icon, albeit with a slightly self-mocking Asterix-style comic-book persona.

The Romans held Gallia Belgica for 500 years. They founded settlements at Tournai (p209) and Tongeren (which still retains part of its original Roman rampart, p206) and built many a castrum and villa, notably at Arlon (p241) and Echternach (p277). Many other settlements formed along the major Cologne–Bavai–Amiens Roman road, a long straight line that's still called Romeinseweg in places and still forms a major highway in sections around Tongeren. By the Middle Ages the route had become mystically renamed the Chaussée Brunehaut (Route of Brunhilda) in honour of a Visigoth queen who was reputed to have built the road in a single day with help from the devil.

In the 5th century, with the Roman Empire collapsing, Germanic Franks took control of Flanders. Meanwhile in the south, Merovingian kings set up a kingdom in Tournai that eventually controlled much of northern France. The south thus moved into a Latin linguistic orbit, creating a linguistic division with the Germanic north that remains to this day. However, politically the lines were to be frequently redrawn.

COUNTIES & DUCHIES

Parties of raiding Vikings caused havoc in the 9th and early 10th centuries, looting churches and pillaging villages even deep into the Ardennes. In reaction, feudal domains developed with locals offered the protectorship of increasingly powerful counts and dukes but in turn having to fund them. By the 10th century the region was divided into a jigsaw of seven major feudal territories, nominally subservient to either the Ottonian German Empire (the counties/duchies of Brabant, Namur, Luxembourg and Limburg) or to the French kings (counties of Hainaut, Artois and Flanders). The dividing line fol-

TIMELINE

57–51 BC	AD 466	AD 980
Julius Caesar's invading Roman legions find unexpectedly stiff resistant from brave Belgae warriors around Tongeren.	Birth near Tournai of Clovis, uniting king of the Frankish clans whose conversion to Catholicism has lasting effects throughout the region.	Liège becomes an independent prince-bishopric, a status it will keep for over 800 years.

lowed the Scheldt River, with Ottonian border fortresses at Antwerp, Ename (p167) and Valenciennes (now in France). Each area was mostly left alone to manage its own affairs so long as it behaved. In the midst of all this was a curious patchwork of church territories ruled autonomously by the prince-abbots of Stavelot-Malmédy (p260) and the prince bishops of Liège (p248), in which some of proto-Belgium's finest medieval metallurgy developed.

THE RISE OF FLANDERS

Unlike Liège, Flanders lacked much in the way of natural resources but once Viking threats had receded its citizens found an ingenious way to riches – by turning imported raw materials into top-quality textiles. As the reputation of Flemish cloth grew, so Ypres, Bruges and Ghent became extremely wealthy, blooming over the 12th and 13th centuries into international trading towns. Merchant ships from all over Europe docked in Bruges to trade Flemish cloth for English wool, coal, lead and tin. Wine arrived from Spain, silks and spices from Venice and Genoa and furs from as far away as Russia and Bulgaria. Cosmopolitan ideas flooded in too, resulting in many innovations including those in art and architecture.

This flurry of activity bred a class of rich merchants who wanted increased political power. Craftsmen and traders joined forces to form groups known as guilds, setting standards for their craft and establishing local trade monopolies. But it wasn't long before the aspirations of the burghers clashed with those of the local counts. Rights, privileges and taxes were the source of frequent heated disputes. Then there were also conflicts between the lords and their kings. Flanders was in a particularly tricky situation. The Count of Flanders was vassal to the French king. However Flanders' weaving economy relied on a steady supply of high-quality wool from England. So when Flanders sided with their English trade partners during Anglo-French conflicts, the French army showed up to teach them a lesson. In 1302, bloody confrontations known as the Bruges Matins (see p132) kicked off a famous anti-French revolt that had its high point (from the Flemish point of view) at Kortrijk's Battle of the Golden Spurs (see p166) – where the French knights were dramatically (if temporarily) defeated. Since 1830 the battle has become romanticised as a symbol of Belgian (and more recently Flemish) pride. However the revolt actually culminated in a humiliating 1305 treaty that forced Flanders to pay huge indemnities and give France a large tract of its territory including Lille (Rijsel in Dutch).

In the 1340s when England and France went to war yet again England's king Edward III cut off wool exports and numerous Flemish weavers were effectively forced to move across the channel (more than a few British families are still called Fleming, though many of their ancestors emigrated during later religious disputes). This was also the time of the Black Death. Plague killed a remarkably high percentage of Europe's population between 1339 and 1341 and those that

11 July, the anniversary of the 1302 Battle of the Golden Spurs, is still celebrated as Flanders' 'national' holiday.

1302	Early 14th century	1339–1341
At Kortrijk the Flemish win a landmark victory over French knights at the Battle of the Golden Spurs.	Ghent becomes the biggest city in Europe after Paris and Constantinople.	The Black Death ravages northern Europe.

survived often turned to superstitious religion in thanks for being spared – the distant basis behind many of Belgium's odd religious parades.

THE BURGUNDIAN EMPIRE

The later 14th century saw renewed prosperity. Ghent had become the largest city in northern Europe after Paris and many Flemish cities built magnificently ornate belfries, market houses and town halls as symbols of wealth and hard-won civic liberties. The region's political landscape had changed significantly under Philip the Bold (r 1363–1404) who had been 'given' Burgundy by his father the French king and went on to acquire Flanders by tactical marriage. His grandson, extraordinary Philip the Good (Phillipe-le-Bon, Philip III) of Burgundy (r 1419–67) continued playing off France and England while collecting counties much as a philatelist collects stamps. He inherited Hainaut and Limburg then simply purchased Namur, Luxembourg and Antwerp. Thus by the end of his reign most of proto-Belgium (except Liège) joined northeastern France and the Netherlands in what would be remembered as the Valois Burgundian Empire.

Although the Burgundian court had a palace in Dijon (France), Philip had been born in Bruges and ruled his empire from Brussels, earning him the title Conditor Belgii (Belgium's founder). Philip was the richest man in Europe and his court the height of culture and fashion. In Brussels the magnificent city hall was built (p76) flanked by elaborately decorated guildhalls. The arts flourished, particularly tapestry making and painting, with the emergence of the so-called Flemish Primitives (p39).

When Philip's successor died in battle in 1477, his only offspring was the as yet unmarried 19-year-old Mary of Burgundy. Many a European king salivated at the idea of marrying a son to so eligible a teenager. Had she married the French dauphin as she'd been pressured to do, Belgian history would have turned out quite differently. However, guided by her wily British-born stepmother, Margaret of York, she finally married Maximilian of Austria. This yanked the Burgundian empire into the rapidly expanding Hapsburg empire. Her son would become Philip I, the first Hapsburg king of Spain, her daughter (Margaret of Austria) the de-facto ruler of the Low Countries. Based in Mechelen where her rule ushered in a massive cultural blooming, Margaret also acted as guardian to her nephew, Philip I's son, the future Charles Quint.

HAPSBURG RULE

Hapsburg/Holy Roman Emperor Charles Quint (see right) ruled an empire on which the sun never set three centuries before Queen Victoria could claim the same. Born in Ghent, Charles grew up in Mechelen and ruled initially from the splendid Coudenberg Palace (p82) in Brussels, where he was advised by the great humanist Desiderius Erasmus (p91). Later he ruled from Spain leaving his sister, Mary of Hungary, responsible for the Low Countries.

1429–1467	15th century	1425
The formerly antagonistic duchies and counties of proto-Benelux are brought together within the Burgundian empire.	Duke Philip the Good sponsors classic Flemish Primitive artists including Jan Van Eyck and Hans Memling.	Belgium's first university is established at Leuven.

CHARLES QUINT OR KEIZER KAREL?

What do Charles Quint, Keizer Karel, Charles V, Carlos I and Kaiser Karl all have in common? Answer: They were all the same person. Born in Ghent in 1500, Charles was arguably the most powerful teenager in human history. You'll notice his name turning up in all sorts of Belgian contexts from beer labels to historical tours to the Brussels Ommegang once you've learnt the various possible alternative renderings.

By the ripe old age of 15 Charles already ruled the Low Countries (as Charles II of Burgundy). The next year he also became king of Spain (as Carlos I), a position of extraordinary wealth in the 16th century given Spain's brutal seizure of the New World (ie Mexico, Peru and the Caribbean) and its hoards of Inca and Aztec gold. Then in 1519 he was crowned king of Hapsburg Austria and the Germanic 'Holy Roman Empire' as Emperor Charles/Karel/Karl V. He wasn't yet 20.

Suffering increasing competition from manufacturers in England, the great Flemish cloth towns were feeling an economic pinch. So when Charles imposed a series of taxes to finance his foreign wars, the burghers of Ghent planned an uprising. Charles returned to suppress the revolt in 1540, making the defeated ringleaders walk around town wearing nooses, source of a nickname for Ghent folk that's used even today (p117). Thereafter Charles made conscious efforts to encourage Antwerp's growth rather than rely on the troublesome West Flemish towns. In 1555 Charles abdicated leaving his Germanic territories to one son (Ferdinand) and his western empire, including the Low Countries, to another son (Philip II), whose conservatively Catholic Spanish education would prove very significant.

RELIGIOUS REVOLT

From the mid-15th century, the development of semi-mechanised printing sowed the seeds of a social revolution. At first the result was a blooming of education, and humanist thinkers including Erasmus and Thomas More were attracted to the vibrant intellectual centres of Mechelen and Brussels. However, printing also made it progressively easier for literate 'ordinary' people to read the Bible. Suddenly priests who had grown wealthy by 'selling' indulgences (the right to sin) could no longer claim such practices were God's will. The result was a wave of revolutionary Protestantism, the 'Reformation'. Rulers felt threatened and attacked this Protestantism by declaring it 'heresy'.

On paper the death penalty had already existed for heretics in Charles Quint's Low Countries. However, Philip II took a much more zealous approach to sniffing them out and was already well-versed in the techniques of the Spanish Inquisition. Yet Philip's anti-Protestant edicts did little to stifle dissent and rising taxes enforced by the Spanish mercenaries he sent in stirred up passions all the more. In 1566 many Protestants ran riot ransacking churches in what's become known as the Iconoclastic Fury since they intentionally destroyed the religious

The 'Mercator Projection' world map that misleadingly makes Greenland look as big as Africa was familiar in classrooms right up until the 1970s. Yet it was designed by Gerardus Mercator (aka Gheert Cremer), a Flemish cartographer born back in 1512 in Rupelmonde (p190).

1500	1562	1566
The birth in Ghent of future Holy Roman Emperor Charles V, who will later become one of the most powerful rulers in European history.	Although faithful servants of the Spanish crown, Counts Egmont and Hoorn vocally oppose the introduction of the Inquisition in the Low Countries.	Iconoclastic riots and Protestant idealism set off decades of fighting. In these 'Dutch Revolts' the Spanish Netherlands attempts with varying degrees of success to break free of Catholic Spain.

icons they considered idolatrous. Philip retaliated with a force of over 10,000 troops led by the Duke of Alba (Alva). Alba's tenure as governor of the Low Countries was infamous for its cruelty, starting in 1568 with the 'Council of Blood' and the execution of leading dissenting nobles including Brussels heroes Egmont and Hoorn (whose statues grace the Petit Sablon, p83). This kicked off 80 years of turbulence known variously as the Dutch Revolt, the Wars of Religion or the 80 Years War. British involvement was blatant with England's Protestant Queen Elizabeth actively supporting the revoltees against Philip, her stepbrother-in-law. It was to punish English meddling in Flanders that Spain sent the ill-fated Armada in 1588. And among Catholic Brits who joined anti-Protestant Spanish forces in the Low Countries was one Guy Fawkes, later infamous for his botched British gunpowder plot (1605).

Brussels-born Andreas Vesalius (1514–1564), son of Charles Quint's valet-pharmacist, wrote the first modern textbook on human anatomy, effectively launching the subject as a new science.

THE SPANISH NETHERLANDS

After decades of destruction, the Netherlands expelled the Spaniards and emerged as an independent Protestant entity. However, Spain steadily recaptured Belgium and Luxembourg (the 'Spanish Netherlands'). In the territories recaptured by Spain the populous was fed a heavy dose of Catholicism. In this counter-Reformation, Protestants, religious minorities and anti-Spanish freethinkers (including much of the merchant class) moved north to the Netherlands or across the channel to England. The economy thus stagnated though an exception was in Liège: as a large independent prince-bishopric Liège had been spared the worst historical convulsions and its businessmen prospered around this time.

In 1598 Philip II had handed the Spanish Netherlands to his daughter Infanta Isabella and her husband (and nephew), Archduke Albert of Austria. While wars rumbled on sporadically, their flamboyant court sponsored new industries like lace making and diamond processing. Bombastic baroque churches were built to underline the Catholic Church's power and were filled with magnificent statues, huge wooden pulpits and vast artworks stressing a religion where the faithful were offered the hope of magical redemption. Artists like Pieter Paul Rubens (p179) and Anthoon (Anthony) Van Dyck saw their order books fill up.

In 1648 the Peace of Westphalia treaties finally recognised the independence of the Netherlands (along with Switzerland, Sardinia etc) from Spain and the Holy Roman Empire. However, this newly confirmed 'peace' caused further economic disaster for the Spanish Netherlands. A clause of the treaty demanded that part of the Scheldt River be closed to all non-Dutch ships. As a result Antwerp's trade collapsed while a golden age dawned for Amsterdam, the region's new premier port. Much of the Spanish Netherlands sunk further into poverty while the 'peace' proved very short-lived. France had already helped itself to parts of Flanders and southern Wallonia in the 1650s. Then in 1667, with Spain fighting Portugal and Holland battling England, the way lay open for Louis XIV to grab much more. The Dutch and British patched

1604	1609	1659
After a devastating four-year seige, Ostend becomes the last major Benelux town to be recaptured by the Spaniards. Fishing communities like Raversijde are depopulated.	Rubens' arrival in Antwerp coincides with a 12-year ceasefire in the 80 Years War between Spain and the proto-Netherlands.	The Treaty of the Pyrenees makes Philippeville a French fort within the Spanish lowlands, and also formalises Flanders' loss of Artois.

things up to prevent further French advances. Indeed the countries became strong allies after England's 'Glorious Revolution' returned that country to Protestantism, with Dutchman William of Orange becoming England's King William III (as co-monarch with Mary II). Nonetheless, Franco-Dutch wars continued to sweep proto-Belgium for much of the following decades, reaching a climax in 1695 when Louis XIV bombarded Brussels to splinters. Once again France occupied much of the area, sending in military engineer Vauban to fortify military strongholds such as Namur (p228), Ypres (p158), Philippeville (p224) and Luxembourg.

The Dutch Revolt by Geoffrey Parker is a superb resource for getting to grips with the 16th-century religious and political changes that proved so pivotal an era in both Belgian and Dutch history.

AUSTRIAN RULE & FRENCH OCCUPATION

When Charles II of Spain died childless in 1700 his will passed the Spanish Netherlands to a French prince. This implied that the French and Spanish empires would eventually be joined into one superpower. The prospect horrified Britain and Holland and resulted in the War of Spanish Succession (1701–13). French and English forces skirmished for a decade until the Treaty of Utrecht forced a curious compromise in which Spain handed over proto-Belgium (as well as much of Italy) to the Hapsburg Austrians, who ruled from 1713 to 1794 and, influenced by the Enlightenment, relaxed censorship and encouraged development.

In 1789 the French Revolution threw European politics into a new maelstrom. The Paris revolutionaries were anti-religious, anti-monarchic 'troublemakers' who threatened the European status quo. Britain, Austria and Prussia's attempts to quash France backfired with French armies rapidly growing in stature. In 1794 the Austrian Netherlands fell to French forces. French revolutionary laws were ushered in including the repression of the Catholic Church. The long independence of Liège's prince-bishopric ended, many churches were ransacked and Belgium's once-magnificent monasteries were looted, their lands nationalised and many abbey churches demolished as an easy source of building stone.

Napoleon Bonaparte's briefly created new French Empire came crashing down with his ill-advised 1812 attempts to conquer Russia. But 'Boney' made a remarkable last-gasp return in 1815 where the whole future of Europe was decided by mud, rain and a few hours of fighting near Brussels at the pivotal Battle of Waterloo (see boxed text, p218). After Napoleon's defeat, the Congress of Vienna created the United Kingdom of the Netherlands. This incorporated what are today the Netherlands and Belgium. Meanwhile the newly restored Grand Duchy of Luxembourg (then twice its current size) was declared the personal property of the Dutch King who concurrently became Grand Duke.

THE UNITED KINGDOM OF THE NETHERLANDS

The United Kingdom of the Netherlands was created largely to preserve the balance of power in Europe and to create a buffer state should France have any

1695	1713–14	1789–1796
Louis XIV's French troops bombard and largely destroy Brussels. Miraculously the magnificent city hall survives.	After decades of war with France, a Europe-wide peace deal is agreed that includes the break-up of the Spanish Empire. The Spanish Southern Netherlands are given to the Austrian Hapsburgs.	Proto-Belgium is swallowed by the ideas then the troops of revolutionary France, resulting in the looting, destruction and privatisation of its once-magnificent abbeys. After over a millennium, Liège loses its status as an independent prince-bishopric.

northward ambitions. The fact that people of different religions and customs were being forced together was of little consequence. William of Orange-Nassau, crowned King William I in Brussels, was given the throne and he divided his time equally between Brussels and the new kingdom's twin capital, The Hague. But William made enemies quickly after refusing to give southern Belgium fair political representation and trying to impose Dutch as the national language. The latter angered not only Francophones but also Flemish speakers who regarded their language as distinct from Dutch. Few would have imagined a Brussels opera performance to be the spark to set off a revolution, yet that's what happened on 25 August 1830 (see boxed text, p107).

BELGIAN INDEPENDENCE

The January 1831 Conference of London recognised Belgian independence (initially incorporating Luxembourg) and the country was officially declared a neutral state. Unemployed royal wannabe Léopold of Saxe-Coburg Gotha was bundled out of the British court where he'd been moping since his wife's untimely death, and sent ashore at what's now De Panne (p153) to be crowned King of the Belgians. However, Belgium's independence was only finally recognised by the Netherlands in 1839 once Belgium agreed to 'give back' the eastern half of Luxembourg (the section that's now independent Luxembourg) over which the Dutch king was recognised as Grand Duke.

The industrial revolution got off to a roaring start with coal mines developed in the Borinage (around Mons and Charleroi) and iron-making in Liège and later in Luxembourg. The strategically located Grand Duchy, while still a possession of the Dutch crown, had meanwhile joined the German Zollverein customs union. This made it a source of tensions between France and Prussia. Eventually to stop a war breaking out, the 1867 Second Treaty of London agreed to recognise once and for all Luxembourg's neutrality and underlined the point by tearing down Luxembourg City's main fortifications. The Grand Duchy nonetheless remained under the Dutch crown until 1890 when a quirk in its rules of succession (see p264) meant that its previously notional independence suddenly became a reality.

LÉOPOLD II

It will never be known for sure how many Congolese people died in Léopold II's 'private garden': the Congo archives were destroyed after he forfeited the territory. According to Adam Hochschild's fascinating book *King Leopold's Ghost*, the furnaces in the Congo offices in Brussels burnt for over a week.

Coming to the throne in 1865, Léopold II was committed to transforming his father's little kingdom into a world-class nation. He put great effort into bolstering Brussels, commissioning the construction of monumental buildings such as the Musées Royaux des Beaux-Arts (p82), home today to Belgium's finest art collection, and the daunting Palais de Justice (p83).

Then in 1885, mainly through a series of dubious treaties and contracts, Léopold personally acquired a huge slice of central Africa that was 70 times larger than Belgium. This he disingenuously named the 'Congo Free State'. However, while appearing to set up Christian help schemes and philanthropic

1815	1830	1885
Napoleon's surprise comeback is quashed at Waterloo, just south of Brussels. Luxembourg is designated as a Grand Duchy under the Dutch crown.	An opera in Brussels sparks revolution and Belgium is born, much to its own surprise.	Belgium's King Léopold II personally acquires the Congo, ultimately leading to the fabulous regeneration of Brussels and the gruesome fate of 10 million Africans.

THIRD TIME LUCKY

Incredibly for Léopold I, Belgium's throne was a third choice. He'd narrowly missed out on ruling England after his wife Princess Charlotte (the British heir apparent and cousin of future Queen Victoria) died in childbirth. He was then offered the throne of newly reborn Greece but thought that Greek independence had little future. Few really imagined that newly created Belgium would fare any better. Nonetheless Leo decided to make a go of it and was crowned the first king of the Belgians on 21 July 1831, a date that's now the country's national day.

fronts to 'protest' the slave trade, in fact 'his' Congolese people were anything but free. The rubber plantations proved extremely lucrative for Léopold (tyres were developed in the mid-1890s) but Congo army manuals from that time describe women and children kept hostage to force men to fulfil rubber quotas. To keep account of ammunition, troops had to bring back the severed right hand of those killed. Over the next 25 years, reports suggest that up to half of the Congolese population perished directly or indirectly due to Léopold's rule. Writers including Mark Twain and Sir Arthur Conan Doyle were vocal campaigners for Congolese reforms and Joseph Conrad's novel *Heart of Darkness* (the inspiration for the movie *Apocalypse Now*) was set in Léopold's Congo. Finally in 1908 the king was stripped of his possession by the Belgian state, embarrassed by the terrible reputation it had brought the nation. Congo nonetheless remained an important Belgian colony until 1960.

WWI

When Léopold II died in 1909 he was succeeded by his 21-year-old nephew Albert I (r 1909–34). Five years later the whole world changed as WWI broke out and Germany occupied neutral Belgium. However, fast as it was, the German advance was crucially slowed by the plucky defence of Liège. And in the far north at Nieuwpoort, it was halted altogether by the old defensive trick of flooding low-lying fields. This required the opening of the canal sluice gates, a dicey operation undertaken under daily fire by brave volunteers. Thus protected, a tiny triangle of Belgian land around Veurne remained unoccupied and King Albert took up residence here to personally lead the Belgian army. Further German advances towards the strategic French coastal towns were prevented. But Allied counterattacks proved futile. The armies dug trenches and became bogged down for four years of futile sorties which killed hundreds of thousands and reduced to rubble the formerly glorious cloth cities of Ypres (Ieper in Dutch), Nieuwpoort and Diksmuide (p156). They've since been carefully rebuilt and the surrounding area (p160) holds many wartime reminders.

After WWI the Treaty of Versailles abolished Belgium's neutral status and the country was given reparations from Germany which included a chunk of land known today as the Eastern Cantons (p260) along with Germany's

In northwestern Belgium over 200 tonnes of WWI munitions (10% containing chemical weapons) are still being unearthed every year as the result of farming or building operations. That's almost two bombs a day!

Early 20th century	1905–1914	1914–1918
Wallonia's steel and glass manufacturers put the country at the forefront of modern technology.	Booming Brussels embraces the sinuous aesthetics of art nouveau.	Belgium and Luxembourg are invaded by Germany. At the heart of the fighting, Ypres, Nieuwpoort and Diksmuide are wiped off the map. Long after the war they are meticulously rebuilt.

BELGIUM'S RULERS AT A GLANCE

- **Léopold I** (1790–1867) – became Belgium's first king in 1831 almost by accident (p31)
- **Léopold II** (1835–1909) – bearded 'brute' with controversies in Congo (p31)
- **Albert I** (1875–1934) – brave tin-hatted 'soldier king' of WWI (p31)
- **Léopold III** (1901–1983) – questions over his dealings with Hitler caused the 'Royal Question' (opposite) – abdicated 1951
- **Charles** (1903–1983) – acted as regent (not officially king) during Léopold III's Swiss exile (1944–1950) then retired to Ostend (p149) where he became an artist
- **Baudouin** (1930–1993) – popular bespectacled 'priestly' king (p34)
- **Albert II** (born 1934) – present monarch

former colonies of Burundi and Rwanda in central Africa. In 1934 much-loved Albert I died in a mysterious rock-climbing accident and was succeeded by his son, Léopold III (r 1934–51).

WWII

On 10 May 1940 the Germans launched a surprise attack and rapidly occupied the Netherlands, Belgium and Luxembourg. Unlike his father, Belgian King Léopold III put up little resistance and quickly surrendered to the Germans, leaving the Allies in a precarious state. The Belgian government opposed the king's decision and fled to London where it operated in exile throughout WWII. A strong resistance movement developed during Nazi occupation, but there was also collaboration from fascist elements of Belgian society, notably Léon Degrelle's Francophone Rexists and parts of the Flemish nationalist movement. Belgium's Jewish population fared terribly during the war and the country's small Roma (gypsy) minority was all but wiped out. Belgium and Luxembourg were liberated in September 1944, though many were still to lose their lives during the Battle of the Ardennes (see boxed text, p243), Hitler's last-gasp attempt at a counter attack. Both countries were left battered by aerial bombing from both sides. Some monuments that had survived the air raids were spitefully dynamited (like Hoogstraten's belfry) or set on fire (Brussels' Palais de Justice) by the retreating Germans as they fled in 1944.

AFTER WWII

After WWII the 'Royal Question' (opposite) over Léopold III's questionable wartime actions caused a constitutional crisis in Belgium, leading eventually to Léopold's 1951 abdication. Economically, while they had taken a serious wartime beating, both Luxembourg and Belgium rebounded rapidly, their coal and iron reserves being much in demand for the post-war recon-

1939–1944	Christmas 1944	1951
Germany again invades both Belgium and Luxembourg and they remain occupied for most of WWII.	In a last-gasp German counter-offensive, the 'Battle of the Bulge' devastates many towns and villages across Luxembourg and the Belgian Ardennes.	King Léopold III abdicates following the complex 'Royal Question' over his supposed wartime collaboration.

THE ROYAL QUESTION

Things had started badly for Léopold III. In 1935 when newly crowned, he was driving along the shores of Lake Lucerne when he crashed, killing his Swedish-born wife, the overwhelmingly popular Queen Astrid (mother of the present king). In 1940, Léopold III's WWII surrender to the Germans was a stark contrast to Albert I's WWI heroism. His decision to stay on in occupied Belgium was highly controversial and far from appreciated by the Belgium government in exile in London. Nonetheless, at first Léopold retained the people's affections. However, his image as a lonely imprisoned victim was severely undermined once news emerged that (during German occupation in 1941) he had secretly remarried. Léopold's somewhat startling views in his *Political Testament* and his seemingly cosy relationship with Hitler added to the shock waves. Over several years the 'Royal Question' developed as to whether his actions had forfeited his moral rights to stay on as king. In 1944 Léopold had been deported to Germany but although liberated in 1945 he was discouraged from returning for fear of public reaction. Instead he lived in exile in Geneva while his brother Charles took his place as regent. Finally in 1950 his status was made the subject of a national referendum. A marginal majority supported his return. However, when he got back he was greeted by riots and strikes in Wallonia. Fearing that this could lead to civil war, Léopold abdicated in favour of his eldest son, 20 year old Baudouin, whose pious modesty proved popular and rapidly revived the fortunes of the monarchy.

struction effort. Local workforces proved insufficient to staff all the mines and large numbers of immigrants (especially Italians) were enticed to settle in the industrial areas, often under extremely difficult conditions. Around Charleroi some workers lived for years in crude metal huts that had originally been built as camps by the wartime German occupation forces. Only after 264 workers died (136 of them Italian) in a catastrophic 1956 fire at the Bois du Cazier mine (p223) did political attention finally switch from maximising production to looking at safety and workers' rights.

In 1958 a great World Fair gave Belgium the chance to show the world how its industries were advancing, a message driven home by the unique architecture of the Atomium (p90). The same year Brussels became the provisional seat of the European Commission and the Council of Ministers, the executive and decision-making bodies of what has since become the EU (see boxed text, p85). Both Belgium and Luxembourg (which had dumped its neutral status after WWII) were founder members and both joined NATO (North Atlantic Treaty Organisation). In 1967 NATO moved its HQ to Brussels from France, a year after the French had withdrawn from NATO's military wing.

60s & 70s

Differences between Belgium's linguistic groups had been growing since the 19th century. Feelings hardened in WWI (when orders given in French to Dutch-speakers caused some entirely avoidable tragedies) and differences were deliberately played up for divide-and-rule purposes by the German

1958	1960	1969
The Atomium is built as the centrepiece for the last Brussels World Fair.	Belgian Congo (later Zaire) gains independence.	Growing intercommunal tensions reach a violent peak in Leuven.

occupation regime during WWII. To defuse mounting tensions, a language frontier was officially delineated in 1963 creating four language areas (Dutch-, French- and German-speaking plus bilingual Brussels), the first stage in an ongoing process of growing cultural autonomy. As in most Western nations the peace-and-love attitude of the Flower Power era was shaken in 1968 with violent student-led demonstrations. In Belgium these riots took a particular intercommunal turn at Leuven where the Francophone part of the city's world-famous university (p200) was effectively forced to leave the stridently Flemish city, decamping eventually to Louvain-La-Neuve (p220).

During the 1970s the global economy was hard hit by an overnight quadrupling of oil prices (sparked by OPEC production cuts in reaction to the 1973 Yom Kippur/Arab-Israeli war). At the same time the 'old' heavy industries (mining, glass, iron) were slumping, causing a major problem in Wallonia and Luxembourg, whose economies were based around steel and iron-ore. Luxembourg found a cunning way out of their economic problems by wooing foreigners with favourable banking and taxation laws. Newspapers advertisements for 'Luxembourg, where the banks are open on Saturdays' was interpreted by many tax-dodging Belgians as an invitation to drive south with stacks of dubious cash which they didn't need to convert (well before the euro and the Belgian and Luxembourg francs had been freely interchangeable).

In contrast the Belgian reaction to the crisis was quite different. Well-intentioned attempts to shore up its moribund factories with subsidies and socialist rhetoric proved futile and the Walloon economy stagnated. Flanders, whose industry was more diversified and smaller scale, was less harshly hit and in later years its economy surged ahead as investment in newer technologies bore fruit. Increasingly an economic angle was added to the intercommunal disputes.

80s & 90s

Following state reforms in 1980 and 1988 three linguistic communities emerged, themselves overlaid by three regions (Flanders, Wallonia and Brussels-Capital) which took a step closer to being fully fledged states when Belgium was declared a federal state in 1993. Numerous powers were devolved to regional level.

In 1990 a bill legalising abortion passed through parliament, putting King Baudouin in an awkward position. It was his constitutional duty to sign it into law, but doing so was entirely against his piously Catholic conscience. In an extraordinary piece of Belgian compromise, his solution was to have himself declared 'unable to govern' for two days until the bill had been signed. Many admired Baudouin's principled stance on this and many other matters. Indeed he was seen as a major uniting force during an era in which the country was otherwise pulling apart. His sudden death in 1993 led to an outpouring of common grief that transcended linguistic boundaries. Childless Baudouin was succeeded by his younger brother, the jovially approachable present king, Albert II.

For those born into a world of on-demand downloads it's hard to conceive just how 1960s teenagers relied on Radio Luxembourg as the only non-pirate radio station broadcasting new 'pop' music into the UK, years before Radio 1 and way before MTV.

The Belgian royals have their own website www .monarchie.be, while news feeds on their wide-ranging activities appear on www.royalty.nu/ Europe/Belgium.html.

1974	1970s	1992
Belgian cycling champion Eddie Merckx wins a fifth Tour de France.	Economic stagnation sets in as heavy industry becomes uncompetitive in Wallonia and Luxembourg.	Poperinge-born Dirk Frimout becomes Belgium's first astronaut, while back on earth the country's last coal mine closes.

INTO THE 21ST CENTURY

Towards the end of the 20th century Belgium was rocked by infamous paedophile scandals and rising racism. The 1999 elections booted out the Christian Democrat party after 40 years in power. Partly to block the progress of the ultra-right-wing Vlaams Blok, a government was cobbled together from Liberals, Socialists and Greens under Liberal Prime Minister Guy Verhofstadt, which pushed through new moral freedoms and a program to phase out nuclear power in favour of cleaner energy sources. In 2003 Belgium vocally sided with France and Germany against the US-led war in Iraq despite veiled threats that this could result in NATO moving its HQ to somewhere more compliant. After two terms and major progress in reducing Belgium's budget deficit, Verhofstadt's party lost ground at the 2007 elections. The resounding overall victor in 2007 seemed to be Yves Leterme, nicknamed 'Mr 800,000 Votes' after what was a remarkable tally by the standards of Belgium's heavily compartmentalised voting system. However, his party's ambitious election promises to Flemish voters precluded many potential partners from joining a necessary government-forming coalition. A major stumbling block was 'BHV' (see below), an arcane question of administrative borders that to any non-Belgian would have seemed trivial. Yet for almost a year there was deadlock with no national government in power.

Once a government finally emerged, it lasted less than a year before being brought down by a controversial bank-rescue package in the wake of the 2008 credit crunch. In notable contrast to the political turmoil in Belgium, Luxembourg has had the same prime minister (Jean-Claude Juncker) since 1995. He's now the EU's longest serving. However, in 2008's heated debates over legalising euthanasia, the country faced a constitutional crisis when the respected Grand Duke Henri (equivalent of king) said he'd be unable to sign a legalisation bill. As a result a constitutional amendment was rushed through, stripping him of legal powers so that his conscience wouldn't be sullied. Luxembourg's banks have had to deal with greater transparency (Belgians with accounts here can now be shopped to the tax man) and the global economic dislocation of 2008, but the Grand Duchy's economy remains the strongest per capita in Europe.

In May 2005 the *Times* (London) called Belgium 'the last surviving artificially created state in Europe after the collapse of the Soviet Union, Czechoslovakia and Yugoslavia'.

Find out what the Belgian prime minister is up to at www.premier.fgov.be.

BHV (BRUSSELS-HALLE-VILVOORDE)

A peculiarity of Belgium's linguistic division is that if you happen to live in Wallonia you can't vote for a Dutch-speaking party. And if you live in Flanders you can't vote for a French-speaking one. One illogical exception to this illogically disenfranchising rule is Halle-Vilvoorde, within Flanders on the Brussels periphery. Here the electoral district is fused with bilingual Brussels, much to the chagrin of many Flemish politicians, but to the relief of its Francophone voters. Sounds trivial? Not to Belgian politicians who spent most of 2007–2008 unable to form a government thanks to the issue. And it still hasn't been solved.

1993	1996	2009
Belgium becomes a three-part federal state comprising Flanders, Wallonia and Brussels-Capital.	After a spate of paedophile kidnappings and murders, a massive street protest (the White March) is held to complain about police incompetence in tracking the perpetrators.	Belgium's mild-mannered prime minister, Herman Van Rompuy, is headhunted to become the new EU 'President'.

The Culture

THE NATIONAL PSYCHE

Their country is an illogical and wantonly artificial 1830 creation so it's hardly surprising that many Belgians wallow in delicious deadpan surrealism. Where else can you find a pissing boy and a bowler hat as national icons? Even serious news programs on Belgian TV are laced with unvoiced visual gags. And with linguistic divisions virtually ruling out patriotism (Flemish nationalism's a different issue), Belgians instead use semidefeatist humour when discussing anything from the weather to ubiquitous dog poo to the nation's poor showings in international sport. But behind such defeatism lies the self-satisfied knowledge that Belgium has one of the world's best standards of living. Fab food, sublime chocolates and world-beating beers are accepted as part of daily life. Almost everyone moans about the sky-high taxes yet simultaneously takes pride in the excellent health-care system and generous social safety-net that means there's very little obvious street-poverty. Meanwhile, beneath the surface of one of Europe's most modern and determinedly liberal societies, lie hidden roots of pious Roman Catholicism along with an amazing array of weird and wonderful folkloric festivals.

Luxembourgers' national motto, *Mir wëlle bleiwe wat mir sin* (We want to remain what we are), sums up their independent spirit. Like Belgians, Luxembourgers are unrelentingly polite and helpful without being pushy or overly hospitable. Both peoples pride themselves on their openness, honesty and tolerance, at least on the surface. While Belgian fashion designers are world news, local dress codes are low-key. Showy wealth is gently frowned upon and while snobbism is alive and well, it's expressed with measured subtlety.

Belgium was the second European country after the Netherlands to legally recognise both same-sex unions (2003) and euthanasia (2002).

The Linguistic Divide

French-speaking locals describe themselves without complex as Belgians (not as 'Walloons', which would imply speaking one of the almost-folkloric Walloon languages). However, most people in Flanders consider themselves as primarily Flemish. With everything from the media to political parties divided on language lines, there is a remarkable lack of mutual communication between Wallonia and Flanders. Francophones tend to stereotype the Flemish as arrogant and humourless. Meanwhile the Flemish see Francophone Belgians as corrupt, lazy or feckless, an exaggerated image jocularly accepted by some southerners without rancour. With Flanders' economy roaring along, many in Flanders resent financially propping up the poorer south. That has led to a strong rise in Flemish nationalism with increasing calls for greater autonomy or even Flemish independence. Contrastingly, Walloon nationalism is virtually unknown and, while TV immerses most Francophone Belgians in French popular culture, very few would actually consider joining France in the case of a national split. Indeed Francophone Belgians consider the French far more disparagingly than they do their brother Flemish. Flemish nationalism is often associated

FLANDERS

⊗ **Brussels**

FLANDERS

COMMINES

WALLONIA

● Dutch-speaking
● French-speaking
▨ German-speaking
○ Bilingual

with the worrying tide of casual racism, though in reality immigration is a major political issue for both communities.

CELEBRATIONS

Life's cycles (birthdays, weddings, funerals) are celebrated much as in any other Western nation. So too are the year's major Christian-based festivals. However, some notably Belgian traditions include the following:

- **Birth of a child**: proud new parents give fancily wrapped sugared almonds (*suikerbonen/dragées*) to relatives and friends.
- **Lent**: the six weeks leading up to Easter are time for Belgium's craziest and most fabulous festivals.
- **1 May**: men present their female friends or colleagues with a sprig of lily of the valley (*lelietje-van-dalen/muguet*), especially in Wallonia.
- **Easter Sunday**: kids eagerly await not only the Easter Bunny but also the 'Bells of Rome', which fly all the way from the Vatican to drop small chocolate eggs from the sky over Belgium.
- **1 November (All-Saints' Day)**: traditionally the day to visit cemeteries and remember the dead.
- **6 December (St Nicholas Day)**: in addition to Christmas (when Belgians also get presents), 'good children' receive gifts from red-coated, bushy-bearded Sinterklaas/St-Nicholas, who supposedly arrives by boat from Spain, riding a white horse. However, he's accompanied by club wielding Zwarte Piet (Black Peter – now sometimes simply called 'Peter' for political correctness) from whom 'bad children' get nothing but a token thwack. A speciality for the day is fancily shaped *speculaas* (cinnamon-flavoured biscuits).

For national holidays, see p291.

'Lenten and Easter carnivals are a fabulous way to experience Belgium's love of folklore and pageantry'

Lenten & Easter

Lenten and Easter carnivals are a fabulous way to experience Belgium's love of folklore and pageantry. Steeped in oddly twisted religious traditions, festivities trace back to the Middle Ages and include goings-on that defy modern imagination. Almost every town has its own carnival celebration, the focus of which is typically a noisy parade through the streets watched by crowds of families and merrily inebriated *café*-goers throwing sweets and paper confetti. However, the most famous, lavish or downright odd carnivals tend to star a cast of particular characters. See the Events Calendar, p16, for details on specific celebrations.

POPULATION

Belgium's population is basically split in two. Speaking Dutch, the Flemish make up 60% of the population, mostly in Flanders (Vlaanderen). This heavily urbanised northern half of Belgium is one of the most densely populated corners of Europe, with 400 people per square kilometre, compared with 240 in Britain and just 100 in France. In somewhat more rural southern half of Belgium, Wallonia (La Wallonie), the population mostly speaks French. In Wallonia's Eastern Cantons (Ost Kantonen), including Eupen and St-Vith, live around 70,000 German speakers.

And then there's Brussels. Officially bilingual but predominantly French-speaking, it lies physically surrounded by Flanders but is governed separately. Brussels' population includes about 100 different nationalities among the foreign-born residents, and while many Belgian cities have large immigrant communities none are as multicultural as the capital.

MONTHLY PLANNER

A few interesting sights only open once or twice a month. Also, certain cities have one day a month on which entry to the civic museums is free, so careful planning pays dividends.

- First Wednesday (afternoon only) – Brussels' city-owned museums are free
- First weekend – visit Brussels Maison Cauchie (p87)
- First Saturday (from 9am) – visit Pipaix brewery (p212)
- First Sunday – visit Spiennes flint mine (p215). Numerous museums in Tournai, Liège, Mons and other Walloon cities have free entry (see www.consoloisirs.be/dimanches/guide.html for the growing list)
- Second Saturday – climb the towers of Brussels' cathedral (p80)
- Second and fourth Sunday – visit Laermolen in Hoogstraten (p191)
- Last Wednesday – Antwerp city-run museums are free to enter

MULTICULTURALISM

Luxembourg is on paper the most multicultural country in Europe. But only if you base that on the percentage of foreigners (30%, the EU's highest). However, as most such foreigners are Italian, Portuguese and other Western Europeans, you shouldn't expect a radical ethnic melting pot. Belgium's main immigrant communities are French and Italian. Smaller but still sizable and much more visible groups are Moroccans, Turks, Kurds and those from Belgium's former colonies of Congo, Rwanda and Burundi. Many immigrants arrived in the 1960s to work in the mines. Today sections of La Louvière and Charleroi are predominantly Italian (albeit reasonably well-integrated) while Brussels communes of Schaerbeek and St-Josse/St-Joost plus the Antwerp suburb of Borgerhout are predominantly Turkish/Kurdish and/or North African in character.

According to official statistics (http://statbel.fgov.be) around 1800 Congolese, 2000 Italians, 3000 Turks and 8000 Moroccans become naturalised Belgian citizens every year.

While relationships vary, according to some, these latter communities have failed to integrate into Belgian society even after two generations, contributing to a high level of casual racism among Belgians towards them (and among them towards Belgo-Belgians living in 'their' areas). This was most worryingly apparent in the 2000 local elections when an ultra right-wing Flemish nationalist party, the Vlaams Blok, gained 30% of votes in Antwerp. In 2004 a court banned that party on the grounds of its 'permanent incitement to segregation and racism'. It swiftly rebranded itself as Vlaams Belang though its popularity has waned since, replaced in some measure by the new List Dedecker (founded by a Belgian judo champion), whose nationalist and straight-talking right-wing message speaks to a similar audience without recourse to unguarded racism.

MEDIA

Predictably, Belgium's media divides along linguistic lines. The print media ranges from serious to superficial but has little of the sensationalist tabloid journalism common elsewhere, such as in the UK. Daily newspapers *De Standaard* (www.standaard.be, in Dutch), *Le Soir* (Francophone) and *Grenz-Echo* (www.grenzecho.be, Germanophone) are the pick of the crop.

The world's first newspaper, *Nieuwe Tydinghen*, was invented in Antwerp by Abraham Verhoeven in 1606.

Until very recently, Belgium was far ahead of everyone in the TV stakes, thanks to the introduction of cheap access to analogue cable in the 1960s. About 95% of homes are hooked to this system, and can access 40-plus TV channels. This satisfaction with the status quo explains why relatively few Belgians feel the need to embrace digital or satellite TV. The unquestioned bilingualism of Luxembourgers is quite apparent on TV, with programs in *Letzeburgesch* making no attempt to translate interviews done in French.

RELIGION

Christianity was established early in the Low Countries and, after the 16th-century Dutch Revolt, proto-Belgium was force-fed a heavy dose of Roman Catholicism. Church attendance has plummeted since the 1970s, with only 3% of the Flemish population now going to church weekly. Nonetheless roughly 75% of Belgians (and 87% of Luxembourgers) still considers themselves Catholic, at least as a badge of social status and political enlightened-conservatism. While religion continues to influence many aspects of daily life, including education and many major festivals, church mass tends to attract mainly elderly folk along with younger Polish immigrants. Belgium's most important place of Catholic pilgrimage at Scherpenheuvel (p203) still sees a steady stream of candle-lighting faithful. And in October 2009 Belgium celebrated its latest saint with the canonisation of Father Damien (famous for his work with lepers on Molokai). In true secular-sceptic fashion, the Belgian press concentrated mostly on how much Damien's canonisation had cost, who'd verified his supposed 'miracles' and the expense accounts for flying Belgium's royalty out to Rome to attend the ceremony.

At Petit Somme, near Durbuy (p246), a fine castle is home to a thriving community of Hare Krishnas. Visits are possible.

Antwerp is home to Belgium's largest Jewish community, who mostly arrived from Eastern Europe in the late 19th-century.

Over 400 mosques dot the country, with Brussels and Antwerp having the most sizeable Muslim populations – mostly immigrants from Morocco, Turkey, Algeria and Pakistan.

ARTS

World-famous artworks, architectural grandeur, dynamic dance, crazy comics… Belgium's art world is remarkably developed for such a small country.

Visual Arts

From Rubens, Breugel and Van Eyck, to surrealists Magritte and Delvaux, museums around the country can fill their walls with top rate 'Belgian' canvases without needing to look further afield.

FLEMISH PRIMITIVES

Belgium's celebrated art heritage first blossomed in 15th-century Bruges with painters now known as the 'Flemish Primitives'. It's an odd choice of term given that not all were Flemish and that their remarkable sophistication was anything but primitive. Their use of radiant colours and incorporation of intricately detailed depictions of secular subjects greatly influenced the course of European art. Especially notable was Jan Van Eyck (c 1390–1441), who became remarkably wealthy combining painting with a lucrative sinecure as royal valet to the powerful Dukes of Burgundy. Van Eyck lived in Bruges, whose Groeningemuseum (p133) has some particularly superb Flemish Primitive canvases, though his most celebrated artwork, *The Adoration of the Mystic Lamb* (1426–32), is in Ghent's St-Baafskathedraal (p119). Other major names of the era include Rogier Van der Weyden (c 1400–64), Frankfurt-born Hans Memling (c 1440–94) and Dutchman Gerard David (c 1460–1523), all predominantly Bruges-based.

Their contemporary Hieronymus Bosch (c 1450–1516) worked mainly in the Netherlands, though the distinction between Dutch and Flemish painting is rather an artificial one since before the late 16th century, Belgium and the Netherlands were simply known as the Low Countries and artists moved from one royal court or town to another. Bosch's most fascinating paintings are nightmarish scenes, visual parables filled with gruesome beasts and devilish creatures often devouring or torturing agonised humans. Bosch's work had obvious influences on the great 16th-century Flemish painter, Pieter Breugel the Elder (for details on Breugel and his painter sons, see the boxed text, p84).

Get an idea of Jan Van Eyck's intricate masterpieces from the comfort of home on www jan-van-eyck.org.

BAROQUE COUNTER-REFORMATION
Styles changed dramatically following the Counter-Reformation of the 17th century. Suddenly big, powerful canvases full of chubby cherubs and angelic awe were just the thing to remind upstart citizens of the Catholic God's mystical power. And few artists proved so good at delivering such dazzling works than Antwerp-based Pieter Paul Rubens (p179). His most celebrated altarpieces were painted for Onze Lieve Vrouwekathedraal (p171), Antwerp's delightful cathedral, and can still be seen there. However Rubens was so prolific that after you've spent some time in Antwerp it's almost a relief to find a museum that doesn't feature his works.

Rubens' studio nurtured artists such as Antoon (Anthony) Van Dyck (1599–1641), who focused on religious and mythical subjects, as well as portraits of European aristocrats. In 1632 he was appointed court painter by Charles I of England and knighted. His contemporary Jacob Jordaens (1593–1678) specialised in depicting everyday Flemish life and merrymaking. Both artists are widely represented in Belgian collections, notably at Antwerp's KMSKA (p179).

MODERN ART
Three big Belgian names dominate in the latter 19th century, each taking art in notably different directions. In mid-career Constantin Meunier (1831–1905; p89), Belgium's most famous sculptor, took the morally brave step of giving up lucrative bourgeois commissions to concentrate on painting social-realist scenes depicting the lives and difficulties of workers in industrial Belgium. Meanwhile James Ensor (p149) pioneered expressionism way ahead of his time and Fernand Khnopff (1858–1921) developed a beguiling 'symbolist' style reminiscent of contemporary pre-Raphaelites Rosetti and Byrne Jones. Khnopff's work decorates part of St-Gilles town hall (p88) and his (largely rebuilt) childhood home is now the Hotel Ter Reien (p140) in Bruges.

Like Argenteuil to French Impressionism, rural St-Martens-Latem (p129) was the creative crucible of Belgian expressionism after 1904 with two formative groups of painters setting up home in the village. The best known artist of the set was Constant Permeke (1886–1952), whose bold portraits of rural Flemish life blended cubism, expressionism and social realism. Meanwhile Mechelen-born Rik Wouters (1882–1916), a prime figure of Brabant fauvism, sought the vibration of light in sun-drenched landscapes, bright interiors and still-life canvases. Under-rated Jean Brusselmans (1884–1953) also had his fauvist period, experimented with Braque-style cubism and developed a wide palate of bold imagery that's sometimes evocative of Gauguin.

SURREALISM & BEYOND
Developed in Paris in the 1920s, surrealism used images from the subconscious to define a new way of perceiving reality. It found fertile ground in Belgium, where artists had grown up with the likes of Bosch and Breugel. Belgium's best-known surrealists were René Magritte (p82) and Paul Delvaux (p153).

In 1948 an international group called CoBrA (short for Copenhagen, Brussels, Amsterdam) developed an interest in the iconography of children's painting and the primitive world of the mentally ill. Promoting free artistic expression of the unconscious, they used intense, expressive colours to create avant-garde canvases. Belgian founder-member Christian Dotremont went on to create 'logogram' painted poems. The most famous Belgian CoBrA, Pierre Alechinsky (1927–), has gained international prominence for his works, notably in inks.

One of Belgium's best-known contemporary artists is Antwerp-born Henri Van Herwegen (1940–), better known as Panamarenko (www.panamarenko .org). Obsessed with space and flight, he creates bizarre sculptures and installations fusing authentic and imaginary flying contraptions. Even his pseudonym, a bastardised abbreviation of 'Pan American Airlines Company', harks to this theme. His works are often displayed at Ghent's SMAK (p121) and Ostend's Mu.Zee (p149).

Jan Fabre (1958–), stage designer and playwright as well as contemporary artist, has enjoyed the rare accolade of a solo exhibition at Paris' Louvre. His most remarkable work to date is a ceiling of Brussels' Royal Palace (p81), which he turned iridescent using thousands of beetle wing-cases.

Luc Tuymans (1958–), considered Belgium's most prominent living artist, covers subjects from major historical events (the Holocaust, Belgian Congo controversies), to the inconsequential and banal. His works were amongst the first to be exhibited in Brussels' brand new contemporary gallery, Wiels (p85).

Architecture
Belgium is endowed with a fine legacy of architectural delights, though naturally, given the succession of wars that have swept through, almost all have been repeatedly restored over the centuries. Unesco's World Heritage list includes a large selection of Belgian buildings plus the whole old-town centres of Luxembourg City (p264) and Bruges (p129).

Some of Belgium's finest cathedrals and most of its great abbey churches were ripped down during the anti-religious turmoil of the 1790s: the once grandiose abbeys at Aulne (p223) and Villers-la-Ville (p220) still lie in atmospheric ruins from that time. However, a great many splendid religious structures did survive, including the sturdy Romanesque Collégiale Ste-Gertrude in Nivelles (p219). Romanesque architecture, characterised by very hefty columns and semicircular arches, disappeared gradually over the 12th and 13th centuries once new understandings of building technology allowed the introduction of light, pointed arches and the development of soaring Gothic vaulting. Tournai's cathedral (p210), built in three clearly differentiable sections, offers a vivid example of that architectural progression.

In the cloth trading towns of the medieval Low Countries, wealth and education led to precocious ideas about rights and personal freedoms. Architecturally these notions were embodied in the grand guild-houses on market squares and, particularly, in the construction of secular belfries (Bruges' is particularly incredible) and ornate city halls, most memorably in Brussels (p62) and Leuven (p199).

Once the Catholic rulers had definitively suppressed iconoclasm and Protestantism in proto-Belgium (after the Dutch Revolt, p27), art and architecture followed a whole new baroque trend. This Counter-Reformation underlined ideas about God's mystical nature along with the limitless powers of kings by use of dazzlingly ornate and exuberant decoration. Although starting from Italian artistic roots, this heavy Flemish baroque developed as its own distinct style that reaches a stylistic peak in Antwerp's St-Carolus-Borromeuskerk (p177).

Belgium has 286 castles, according to www .demeures-historiques .be. That's more castles per square kilometre than anywhere in Europe, says www.chateauxde belgique.be, which shows you many that can be visited, slept in or even purchased if you've got a little spare cash.

For most of the 18th century, while Belgium was under Austrian rule, architecture took on a cold, rational, neoclassical style as typified by Brussels' Place Royale (p81). After independence, but especially under its second king, Léopold II (r 1865–1909), Belgium focused on urban redevelopment. Leopold realised that making Brussels more aesthetically appealing would boost its economic potential. Partly using vast personal riches he'd gained through exploitation of the Congo, he funded gigantic public buildings like the Palais de Justice (p83), created the monumental Cinquantenaire (p87) and laid out vast suburban parks linked to the city by splendidly wide thoroughfares like Ave Louise and Ave Tervuren. Much of this expansion coincided with a late 19th-century industrial boom that saw Belgian architects experimenting with new materials including glass and iron. From the early 1890s, Brussels was at the forefront of art nouveau design, using sinuous lines, organic tendrils and floral motifs to create a genuinely new architectural aesthetic. One of the best examples, the Old England Building (p82), combines wrought ironwork frames, round windows, frescoes and sgraffito, a distinctive art nouveau technique of incised mural that's most stunning example graces the facade of Maison Cauchie (p87). Antwerp also has some excellent art nouveau facades, found especially in the Zurenborg suburb (p180). But art nouveau wasn't only about facades – several buildings from this era only reveal their secrets once inside (see p92).

After WWI the feminine curves of art nouveau were progressively replaced by the harder, rectilinear lines of art deco, presaged very early by buildings like Ghent's 1912 Vooruit (p128) and Brussels' 1911 Palais Stoclet (p92), and later by the cruel 1950s brutalism that marks Brussels' Bibliothèque Royale. One high point from that era is the futuristic 1958 Atomium (p90).

Tragically, earlier 20th-century styles were largely unvalued during the 1960s and '70s and some of Belgium's finest art nouveau buildings were torn down. Worldwide protests over the 1965 destruction of Horta's Maison du Peuple (see p184) helped bring about laws protecting Brussels' heritage and ARAU (p92) was formed to save and renovate city treasures. The former Belgian radio and TV building, Flagey (p89), was one art deco landmark to be rescued but other swathes of cityscape have gone under the demolition ball, notably in Brussels to make way for the bland glass buildings that typify the EU quarter. Luxembourg's EU zone is almost as uninspired.

Despite some public acclaim, Belgium's 21st-century architecture has mostly proved less than majestic. Antwerp's sail-topped Justitiepaleis (p180) is certainly memorable but fails to offer the wow factor of the Bilbao Guggenheim, whose spirit it seems to envy. Bruges' red-elephant Concertgebouw (p137) feels like a modernist token and even the fine new galleries in Mons (p214) and Leuven (p199) aren't genuinely beautiful. There is, however, one major exception: Santiago Calatrava's truly astonishing Guillemins station (p252) in Liège. This is contemporary architecture that'll really blow your hat off.

Fashion & Decorative Arts

Given its historical associations with weaving, it's hardly surprising that Belgium has been innovating with textile design for centuries. Some of the world's greatest tapestries were created in Brussels and Oudenaarde (p166). Major innovations in lace production were made in medieval Bruges (see p129), Binche, Geraardsbergen (p167) and 19th-century Brussels while Comines (p163) was a world leader in ribbon making.

'From the early 1890s, Brussels was at the forefront of art nouveau design, using sinuous lines, organic tendrils and floral motifs to create a genuinely new architectural aesthetic'

THE NINTH ART

In Belgium comic strips (*stripverhalen* in Dutch, *bandes dessinées* [BD] in French) certainly aren't only for kids – indeed they're considered the 'Ninth Art'. Best known is boy-reporter Tintin (see p221), who set off on his first mission (*Tintin in the Land of the Soviets*) back in 1929. The series is still Belgium's top international seller, with over 200 million sold in various languages. In June 2009, one of the nation's most awesome new museums opened to honour Tintin's creator, Hergé, in Louvain-la-Neuve. Less imaginative but housed in a classic art nouveau building, Brussels' Centre Belge de la Bande Dessinée (p80) showcases the nation's best, and the capital's streets have many comic murals which you can follow on the Comic Strip Route (p81).

One of the most admired contemporary comic-strip characters is Philippe Geluck's *Le Chat* (The Cat), a curiously static figure often appearing in single-frame scenes making simple yet cleverly thought-provoking observations. Domestically, the best selling comic-book series is Willy Vandersteen's delightful *Suske and Wiske* (*Bob and Bobette* in French), which started in 1945 but reappeared in major movie form during 2009. Other enduring postwar classics include *Lucky Luke*, a classic Western parody by Morris (Maurice De Bevère); *Blake and Mortimer*, a sci-fi strip by Edgar P Jacobs; Marc Sleen's *Nero;* and the little blue *Smurfs* (*Les Schtroumpf*) by Peyo (Pierre Culliford). OK, so some comics *are* for kids.

Meuse valley dependencies of the Liège Prince Bishops, early-medieval Huy (p233) and Dinant (p235) were at the forefront of new techniques in metallurgy that led to beautiful Mosan metalwork (p230). Both Belgium and Luxembourg were major iron makers in the 19th century, providing the raw materials and technical know-how for the early 20th-century experimentation in art nouveau architectural forms. Around the same time, glassware had grown to be one of Belgium's major exports, with glassmakers developing fanciful forms for chandeliers and two-coloured cut-glass tableware, which remains highly prized by collectors and is still made at Seraing (p254).

Antwerp's recent reputation as a major player in designer fashion started in the 1980s with the Antwerp Six (see p177), of whom the best known are probably Dries Van Noten and Anne Demeulemeester. The reputation has snowballed ever since with the city's fashion academy (p173) turning out ever more promising designers. More recent 'Antwerp' names to look out for include Véronique Branquinho, Raf Simons and Columbian-born Haider Ackermann. Brussels has its own fashion school, La Cambre, and its own stars including Xavier Delcour. Other names to watch are Nicholas Woit, Kaat Tilley (www.kaattilley.com) and self-taught Ypres-born back-to-the-fifties designer Annemie Verbeke.

If there's one advantage in having a monarchy it's that queens need hats – reason enough for Belgium to have nurtured two world-class hatters, Christophe Coppens and Olivier Strelli. The latter has branched out into a whole range of chain-boutique clothing.

The sudden growth of Brussels, Enghien (p213) and Oudenaarde (p166) as major tapestry making centres was partly caused by the siege and destruction of Arras by French King Louis XI, 1477-82. That caused many of Arras' world-famous tapestry artisans to flee to lands still in friendly Burgundian hands.

Literature

Celebrated Flemish writers include Guido Gezelle (1830–99) and Hendrik Conscience (1812–83), whose historical-fiction *Lion of Flanders* has led to many romanticised misconceptions about the 1302 Battle of the Golden Spurs (p166). Easier to find in English translation is Hugo Claus' 1983 masterpiece *Het Verdriet van België* (The Sorrow of Belgium), a beautifully nuanced novel using a well-paced historical narrative to reflect upon Nazi collaboration during WWII.

Belgium's most prolific novelist was Liège-born Georges Simenon (1903–89; p251), creator of the detective character Inspector Maigret. Contemporary Francophone writers include Amélie Nothomb, whose novel *The Stranger*

Next Door relates strange events in the Belgian countryside. Her break-through 1999 work, *Stupeur et Tremblements* (Fear and Trembling), featured a Belgian office girl working in 20th-century Japan and was a particular triumph both as a short novel and as a 2003 movie.

> Belgian poet and author Marguerite Yourcenar was the first woman elected (in 1980) to the male-dominated Académie Française.

Francois Weyergans' work often explores psychological problems and in 2005 he won France's prestigious Prix Goncourt with *Trois Jours Chez Ma Mère* (Three Days at My Mother's), musing imaginatively on writer's block.

The poem *Rénert* (Fox) by Michel Rodange (1827–76), the first literary work published in *Letzeburgesch* (the Luxembourg language), takes a teasing look at Luxembourg's 19th-century society and has been translated into English.

Cinema

Belgium's best known filmmakers are brothers Luc and Jean-Pierre Dardenne, rare double-winners of the Palme d'Or at Cannes. Their hard-hitting classics include *L'Enfant,* about a petty crook coming to grips with fatherhood, and *Rosetta,* about a girl searching for work and meaning to her life. Both are gritty affairs filmed in miserable suburbs of Liège. Neither do much for that city's tourist image.

The country's biggest export to Hollywood is the 'Muscles from Brussels', actor Jean-Claude Van Damme. Van Damme's career took off in the late 1980s after he put on an impromptu martial arts display outside a posh restaurant for the head of a Hollywood studio.

> In 1929, *My Fair Lady* screen superstar Audrey Hepburn was born to a Dutch mother in Brussels. Their home at Rue Key-enveld 46 (Map pp72–3) has a commemorative plaque.

Luxembourg is little known for film though the 2003 Vermeer-inspired movie *Girl with a Pearl Earring* was partly filmed there. Low-budget 2008 hip-hop comedy *Reste Bien Mec!* shows an alternative side of Luxembourg but it's only available in French.

Ghent and Bruges both have film festivals while Brussels has two, the International Festival of Fantastic Film plus Anima, focusing on cartoons.

Music

CLASSICAL

Opera has been important since 1830, when a production sparked Belgium's revolution (see the boxed text, p107). There are opera houses in Brussels (p107), Ghent (www.vlaamseopera.be) and Liège (www.operaliege.be), where romantic composer César Franck was born. Top orchestras include the Flanders Symphony (www.symfonieorkest.be) and the Liège Philharmonic (www.op l.be).

JAZZ & BLUES

Jazz has a special place in Belgium. Dinant-born Adolphe Sax (1814–94) invented the saxophone, gypsy guitar-maestro Django Reinhardt (1910–53) hailed from Hainaut, and octogenarian Toots Thielemans (1922–) still enthrals audiences with his legendary harmonica playing. Brussels' Jazz Marathon (p17) and Luxembourg's marvellous Jazz and Blues Rallye (p18) both fill their respective cities with fabulous free music. Fans of upbeat blues have a unique ally in Walter de Padua, DJ of the incomparable Sunday night radio show *Dr Boogie* (radio Classic 21). Belgium's Seatsniffers (www.seatsniffers.be) play romping rockabilly and psychobilly aficionados shouldn't miss Turnhout's raucous Grasshopper Festival (www.rockinaroundturnhout.be).

POP, ROCK & CHANSON

Long after his death, Jacques Brel (1929–78) remains Belgium's most iconic singer. His bitter-sweet evocations of Belgium's 'flat country' were mixed with upbeat humorous vaudeville take-offs of local characteristics. Fans can visit a

Brussels museum in his honour (see p78). Other classic Belgian pop-chanson stars include Maurane, Adamo and (more recently) Axelle Red, who plies her trade in French despite Flemish roots. Dapper crooner Helmut Lotti still pumps out reworked classics beloved by his (typically aging) fans.

Belgian novelty acts to briefly hit international consciousness included 'le punk' Plastic Bertrand, and singing nun, Soeur Sourire (*Dominique-a-nique-a-nique*), whose unlikely life story was made into a 2009 movie.

Widely popular across Europe are Dani Klein's Latin-influenced group Vaya Con Dios while 1970s rock band Machiavel has made a comeback, playing when drummer/co-singer Marc Ysaye gets time off from his day job managing a national radio station. Ostend-born Arno (Arno Hintjens) is the 'Belgian Tom Waits'.

Popular contemporary Belgian artists include K's Choice, dEUS, Ozark Henry and Ghinzu. Hooverphonic make mellifluous lounge-trip-hop, and Praga Khan offers heavy techno. Brothers David and Stephen Dewaele are known internationally for their mixing skills under various monikers including 2ManyDJs, Soulwax and Kawasaki.

Belgian summers are packed full of music festivals in all genres, notably Werchter and Dour for mainstream rock. Antwerp is known for a cutting-edge club scene and its trance and house parties.

Brush up on Belgium's 'forgotten' pop, blues and rock bands (Burning Plague, Dr Downtrip, the Pebbles…) using the remarkably comprehensive website http://houbi.com/belpop.

Theatre & Dance

Belgium's history of contemporary dance starts in 1959 with Maurice Béjart's ground-breaking *Rite of Spring* production in Brussels, but Béjart's Ballet du XXe siècle moved to Lausanne in 1987. Today the Belgian scene centres on two companies, Anne Teresa De Keersmaeker's group Rosas (www.rosas.be; p109) in Brussels and Charleroi/Danses (p222) in Charleroi. The country's drama scene is also inspiring. To combine the two, investigate Brussels' KunstenFESTIVALdesArts (www.kfda.be). Antwerp is the realm of classical ballet – see the Koninklijk Ballet van Vlaanderen (www.koninklijkballetvanvlaanderen.be). Most theatre and dance companies take a break during July and August.

SPORT

Although Justine Henin and Kim Clijsters have given Belgian tennis a few unexpected years in the world spotlight, the nation's greater sporting passions are cycling, football, motorsports and…um…birds.

Cycling

Take a Sunday drive down almost any Flemish country lane and you'll probably come across groups of cyclists in full logo-daubed lycra. Some are highly fit semiprofessionals following in the pedal-straps of Belgium's great sports icon Eddy Merckx. But many others are paunchy pleasure-bikers who'll spend almost as much time in the roadside *cafés* lingering over beery refreshment.

Despite a series of damaging doping scandals and organisational disagreements, professional cycling remains one of Belgium's most popular spectator sports. Belgium's top cycling events include the following:

Ronde van Vlaanderen (Tour of Flanders; www.rvv.be; 🕑 early Apr) Incorporating an infamously steep, cobbled ascent in Geraardsbergen (p167). The race is celebrated by a major cycling museum in Oudenaarde (p166).

La Flèche Wallonne (www.letour.fr/indexFWH_us.html; 🕑 late Apr) Usually between Charleroi and Huy.

Liège-Bastogne-Liège (www.letour.fr/indexLBL_us.html) Nicknamed La Doyenne, a day after the Flèche Wallonne.

Football

Belgium's monarchy and the national football team (nicknamed the Red Devils) have long been joked to be the only things keeping the country together. So in the early 21st century, the team's humiliatingly dismal form has been particularly worrisome. Things will hopefully pick up in time for the 2018 or 2022 World Cups, which Belgium hopes to co-host with the Netherlands (see www.thebid.org). This should finally put to rest memories of the 1985 Heysel tragedy, in which 39 people died as Liverpool and Juventus fans clashed during the European Cup final held at Brussels' foremost stadium (p108). Meanwhile Belgium has a vibrant club-football scene with tickets relatively easy to procure even for major-league teams like Anderlecht (www.rsca.be), Bruges (www.clubbrugge.be) or Standard Liege (www.standardliege.be).

Nicknamed the mauves, RSC Anderlecht (www.rsca.be) is Belgium's best-known and most historically successful football team. It's unusual for having a wide supporter base in both Dutch and Francophone linguistic communities and beyond.

Motorsport

Though long retired, Belgian Formula One stars Jacky Ickx (www.jacky-ickx-fan.net) and Thierry Boutsen remain local heroes and the **Belgian Grand-Prix** (www.f1belgium.com) is widely cited as one of the world's most exciting, thanks to the testing course at Spa-Francorchamps (p259).

Other Sports

BIRD-SPORT

Thousands of enthusiasts in Flanders are passionately keen on pigeon races (see www.duivenbode-bds.be), a sport that gained greatly in popularity after the birds proved important messengers during WWI. There's even a Brussels statue to the Great War's 'Soldier Pigeons' (Map p70). Meanwhile an estimated 13,000 *vinkeniers* (finch fanciers) regularly enjoy the particularly eccentric pastime of vinkenzettingen (finch-sitting; see www.avibo.be). Dating from the late 16th century, the idea is for a caged chaffinch, shielded within a wooden box, to chirrup more times in a timed hour than those of competitor finches. Only a specific 'susk-WEET' sound is acceptable, with some potty *vinkeniers* claiming that birds from Wallonia can't chirrup in correct Flemish! The televised national championship (last Sunday of June) sees about 2000 birds compete for a prize of around €3000. Contests are usually held in rural villages but some Sunday mornings in summer you might spy *vinkeniers* in a quiet lane in Bruges (p145).

BALLE-PELOTTE (KAATSEN)

This archetypal Belgian ball-game (also called Jeu-de-Balle and Jeu-de-Paume) is generally played on specially marked village squares. Two five-member teams bat a small hard-rubber ball between them using gloved hands, sometimes accompanied by the boozy oompah of local trumpeters. For the full, somewhat complex rules see http://users.swing.be/sw123868/god.htm or visit the specialist museum in Ath (p213). For league fixtures consult www.frnp-knk.be (in French) or http://users.telenet.be/kaatsen (in Dutch).

Food & Drink

From chic restaurants to casual brasseries, chip shops to *chocolatiers*, quality is the yardstick and word-of-mouth recommendations spread rapidly in Belgium and Luxembourg. So it's generally a reassuring sign if an eatery has been open for years. Nonetheless, if you're looking for something stylishly modernist, the region has that well covered too. And when it comes to drinking, the range of characterful *café* (pub/bar) options is trumped only by the incredible variety of world-beating beers to drink inside them.

LOCAL FOOD

At an upmarket restaurant in Belgium or Luxembourg, locals will typically expect to find French-influenced cuisine. These places tend to offer straight-forwardly cooked quality meats (perhaps with foie gras to add flavour and price); fresh, relatively unfussy fish dishes (monkfish, sole or perhaps cod); and starters including pâtés, garlic snails and scallops. However, there's also an altogether more hearty style of 'real' Belgian food: *ballekes* (meatballs), stews and *stoemp,* a mashed together veg-and-potato dish originally made to use up leftovers. These foods were, till quite recently, seen as lower class or relegated to home cooking, but they're increasingly being reincarnated both as *café* snack-meals and with gourmet twists in restaurants.

In between lie classic local dishes like *waterzooi* (a cream-based chicken or fish stew), eel in sorrel, and seasonal specialities like asparagus, game and mussels (p52).

Luxembourg's cuisine adds a Germanic element. The national dish is *judd mat gaardebounen* – slabs of smoked pork served in a thick, cream-based sauce with chunks of potato and broad beans. Other specialities include *liewekniddelen mat sauerkraut* (liver meatballs with sauerkraut) and *kachkeis* (a cooked cheese).

Locals show no qualms whatsoever about eating frogs' legs, veal, rabbit, foie gras, tripe or horse meat, which might seem inhumane or distasteful to some foreign visitors. Also, note that steaks are generally served rather more bloody than many visitors may anticipate: *à point* translates in phrase books as 'medium' but tends to approach what many Anglophones consider as rare. 'Blue' steaks will barely have bounced off the grill.

'FOREIGN' FOOD

There's no lack of international flavours in this region. While spaghetti and lasagne feature cheaply on virtually any cafe menu, you'll also find many decent Italian restaurants along with plentiful tapas (not always fully Spanish) and numerous good-value Greek, Turkish, Vietnamese and Chinese restaurants. Thai food is available in a wide variety of price-brackets, but Indian food tends to be comparatively upmarket. Note that in Belgium steamed rice almost always comes free with any Asian main course.

Most towns will have one or two Moroccan or North African restaurants, typically twinkling with colourful lamps. If you've never tried a *tajine* (slow-cooked stew), couscous or *mechoui* (North African spit-roast lamb) this could be your chance. In Brussels there are numerous sub-Saharan African choices too, see the boxed text, p101.

If you're invited to eat at someone's home it would be rude to arrive without a gift – typically flowers, chocolates (a decent brand) and/or a (well-chosen) bottle of wine.

Written back in 1997 by the creators of a London-based Belgian restaurant, *The Belgo Cookbook* is a zany, in-your-face cookbook with advice on good tunes to play while cooking guinea fowl in raspberry beer, among other things.

DRINKS
Non-alcoholic Drinks

Belgian tap water (*kraantjeswater/eau du robinet*) is perfectly drinkable. However, dare to ask for some in a restaurant and you can expect at least a very contemptuous look, more likely a flat refusal. Locals fall into line and buy costly bottles of mineral water: choose *plat/plate* (flat) or *bruisend/pétillante* (sparkling).

Order a coffee in any normal cafe and you'll generally get something approximating to an Americano in strength and style (even though it's frequently called an espresso). Such coffee usually comes accompanied by a biscuit or chocolate and, unlike in France, you don't normally pay extra for milk (real or evaporated). Beware that in Belgium a 'cappuccino' is usually a regular coffee topped with sweetened whipped cream. If that's not how you like it you can find 'real' cappuccinos in a new breed of coffee-shops, many calling themselves *caffè* rather than cafe (in Brussels, several are in Ixelles, p105). Unlike in Amsterdam, Belgian coffee-shops really do serve coffee rather than marijuana. For barista reviews read http://caffenation.blogspot.com. Belgium's only Starbucks (so far) is at Brussels Airport.

To the general annoyance of British visitors, tea is usually served as a steaming glass of water with separate dunk-it-yourself tea-bag, albeit often in a wide variety of flavours. If you want top-quality tea by the pot, squeeze into Brussels' Comptoir Florian (p105).

Alcoholic Drinks
BEER

In the margin: A beer's colour is mainly influenced by the malt, well-roasted malts resulting in darker brews, though sweeteners like caramel and candy sugar can also affect appearance.

In Belgium, beer rules. No other country boasts a brewing tradition more richly diverse. Standard Belgian lagers, notably Jupiler, Maes and Stella Artois are world class. That's what you'll get if you just ask at any *café* (pub/bar) for a *pintje/bière* (typically €1.80 for 250mL). But what really gets connoisseurs in a tizzy are the angels and demons – big bold brews that often derive from old monastery recipes or compete for the most diabolical names (Duvel = devil, Forbidden Fruit, Judas). The most famous of all, the six Trappist beers, are still brewed in active abbeys.

The religious link is historical. When plague broke out in the Middle Ages, St Arnold convinced locals to drink beer rather than water. As beer was boiled, this preventative trick proved rather effective. St Arnold became the patron saint of brewers and beer became an everyday drink. To enhance the flavour they added honey and spices, including coriander, believed to protect against hangovers. A wise move with beers, which – ranging as high as 13% alcohol by volume – are designed to be very slowly sipped and savoured, certainly not chugged by the pint.

Today, although there are hundreds of varieties, every beer is served in its own glass, uniquely embossed and specially shaped to enhance the taste and aroma. The most outlandish include a thistle-shaped creation for the very un-Belgium sounding Gordons' Scotch and Kwak's glass-on-a-stand, which looks like a science-lab escapee.

In the margin: Tim Webb's excellent Good Beer Guide Belgium (http://booksaboutbeer.com) gives a bar-by-bar account of what to taste, where to taste it and which breweries welcome devotees.

Trappist & Abbey Beers

In medieval times, beer was healthier than water and approximated to barley soup – a meal in itself. In the early 19th century monastic beer production developed into a source of revenue for rebuilding monasteries that had been ravaged in the anti-religious convulsions following the French Revolution. Today many fine, flavourful Belgian brews remain 'abbey beers' in name only since the monks have sold their labels and recipes to big brewery chains as with Grimbergen, Maredsous and ubiquitous Leffe. However, six

---

'MUST-TRY' BELGIAN BEERS

- **The Trappists** – mythic **Westvleteren 12** consistently tops the list, but good luck getting any except at In de Vrede (p155). **Orval**, **Rochefort 10** and **Westmalle Triple** come in just behind.
- **Pannepot** (p156) – like liquid, alcoholised black chocolate, this unique and powerfully delicious brew takes some effort to find.
- If **Leffe** (p235) and archetypal white-beer **Hoegaarden** (p205) seem a bit corny, try the lesser known, higher-strength **Leffe 9°** or sturdy **Hoegaarden Grand Cru**.
- **Duvel, Grimbergen Triple, Double Enghien, St-Bernardus, Ename Triple, Brugse Zot** and **La Chouffe** are all readily available golden brews that are well structured and deceptively strong.
- **De Koninck** – a characteristic brown ale of mild strength. In Antwerp, where it's ubiquitous, just ask for a *bolleke* (a 'little bowl' as the glass is nicknamed).
- **Silly Pils** (p213) – fun to find if only for the name.
- **Kriek Boon** – if you hate fruit beers and can't understand lambics (p91), this remarkable cherry beer just might change your mind.
- **Kwak** – a characterful red beer served in a hilarious glass that shouts 'I'm a tourist!'
- **Oerbier** – a complex, Marmitey dark brew that's best on draught as served at De Dolle Brouwers (p156).
- **Garre** – this 11% draught marvel with an incredibly floral head is only available in one pub, see p144. Handle with extreme care!

---

abbeys of the strict Cistercian order still make their own 'Trappist Beers'. Widely considered the epitome of the Belgian beer experience, these brews come in varying colours and strengths, but all are rich, smooth and intriguingly complex. Relatively easy to find are Chimay (p225), Orval (only one style, p241) and Westmalle (p190). It takes just a little more persistence to seek out excellent Rochefort (p236) or 'newcomer' Achel (www.achelsekluis.org), which was only revived in 1999, the abbey having closed in WWI. But the Holy Grail for Belgian beer-fans is Westvleteren, whose beers aren't even labelled and can only be identified by the colour of their caps. The yellow cap 12 (10.8% alcohol) is a dark, unfiltered, malty beer whose intense complexity sees it regularly voted among the world's very best beers (see www.ratebeer.com). The trouble is finding any to taste, as supply is deliberately kept very limited. The best hope is generally to go in person to the abbey *café* In de Vrede (p155). Even there, if you want to buy more than a six-pack, you'll need an appointment. It all adds to the thrill and mystique.

White Beers
Known as *witbier/bière blanche* in Dutch/French, white beers are thirst-quenching wheat beers, typically cloudy, flavoured with hints of orange peel and cardamon and drunk ice-cold with a twist of lemon on summer afternoons. Best known is Hoegaarden (see p205), though Brugs Tarwebier (from Bruges) is also a good choice.

Lambics & Fruit Beers
In the Senne Valley southwest of Brussels mysterious airborne microorganisms allow the spontaneous fermentation of archetypal lambic beers (*lambiek* in Dutch). The idea is magical. However the taste of pure lambic is uncomfortably sharp and acidic. It's rendered less unpalatable by barrel-maturing for up to three years, then blending (to make *gueuze*), sweetening with sugar/caramel (for *faro*) or by adding fresh soft fruit, notably cherries

If you can't find a bar serving Westvleteren, consider sipping St Bernardus (www.sintbernardus.be) from nearby Watou. Although not a Trappist brewery itself, after WWII the brewers here were assisted by a St-Sixtus Abbey master-brewer, so some beer fans consider this an 'alternative Westvleteren'.

(for *kriek*) and raspberries (for *framboise*). Visiting the fascinating little Cantillon Brewery (p91) helps you understand lambic production. If you find Cantillon's fruit beers too harsh (or Belle-Vue's too sickly sweet), don't be put off – Mort Subite and Lindemans brands have a fuller fruit flavour and gentler tartness, while the excellent Boon (www.boon.be) brand from Lembeek is most beautifully balanced.

Other Brews

Not all beers fit into neat categories, and not all abbey-style brews are abbey beers. A plethora of small-production artisan breweries produce special beers, sometimes experimenting with curious vegetable additions (see Pipaix, p212), historic recipes or coming up with 'seasonal' beers. One of Belgium's most-beloved brews, Duvel (www.duvel.be) is a golden ale with a dense, creamy head and strong, distinct flavour. If you wonder why it's called 'devil' try drinking a few too fast.

The Belgian Brewers website (www.beerpara dise.be) catalogues beers and brewery contacts.

WINE

Wine (*wijn/vin*) is the standard accompaniment to fine dining. Almost all is imported, though Luxembourg's Moselle Valley (p274) produces some decent Rieslings and excellent sparkling Méthode Traditionelle. Belgium's tiny home-grown wine industry, re-started in the 1970s, has three appella-tions: Hageland, based around the villages of Rillaar and Zoutleeuw east of Leuven; Haspengouw, in the eastern part of Limburg province; and Côtes de Sambre et Meuse in Wallonia.

JENEVER (PÉKÈT)

Jenever (*genièvre* in French, *pékèt* in Walloon) is an archetypal Dutch-Flemish spirit, originally distilled as a medieval medicament and flavoured with juniper berries. The historical precursor of modern gin, it's sipped straight, never diluted with tonic. At outdoor festivals *pékèt* comes in tiny plastic shot-glasses. In bars you'll pay rather more but receive a bigger, sherry-style glassful. For beginners the most palatable choices are the sweetened fruit ver-sions. However, ask for a *witteke* (literally a 'little white one') to get a classic *jenever*, which is almost colourless when *jonge* (young) or yellow-tinged (*oude*) after it's been matured in wooden barrels for at least eight years. Hasselt boasts a *jenever* museum (p204) and an annual *jenever* festival (p19), while seemingly endless mini-shots of *pékèt* are de rigueur during Liège's chaotic 15 August celebrations (p18).

WHERE TO EAT & DRINK

Outside hotels, the best place to find a sit-down (usually light) breakfast (*ontbijt/petit déjeuner* in Dutch/French) is in a bakery-cafe. Typical break-fasts consist of fresh breads and croissants with butter and jam, served with coffee or tea. Fuller versions add cold sliced meats, cheese and possibly eggs. Restaurants generally open from around noon to 2.30pm for lunch (*middagmaal/déjeuner* in Dutch/French, though often called 'lunch' in either language), often offering great-value set lunch menus (weekdays only) and a *dagschotel/plat du jour* (dish of the day). Most then re-open for dinner (*avondmaal/dîner* in Dutch/French; around 6.30pm to 10pm). A restaurant menu (*de kaart/la carte*) will be divided into starters (*voorgerechten/entrées*) and main courses (*hoofdgerechten/plats*). Most restaurants (apart from tapas bars) will be annoyed if you order a starter without a subsequent main course and may charge a supplement or refuse outright. Typical desserts include ice cream (*roomijs/glace*), various cakes and tarts or perhaps crème brûlée (cus-tard topped with caramelized sugar). For better-known restaurants you'll be

---

HANDY CHAINS

Lonely Planet rarely suggests chain restaurants. Nonetheless three Belgian chains warrant a mention:

- **Le Pain Quotidien/Het Dagelijks Brood** (www.painquotidien.com; sandwiches €6-8, salads €10-13) Rapidly going global, this Belgian bakery-cafe chain's defining feature is the big farmhouse-style wooden table creating a curious social experiment by gently offering the possibility for customer interaction. Newspapers available.

- **Lunch Garden** (www.lunchgarden.com; 1-/3-course meals from €5.95/10) While far from exotic, these bargain-value, cafeteria-style eateries (65 branches in Belgium) offer a sit-down hot meal or salad bar for barely the price of a *croque monsieur*. Typically hidden away in shopping arcades or city-fringe hypermarkets.

- **Exki** (www.exki.be; ✸ breakfast & lunch) A gently hip, ground-breaking chain specialising in bio- and eco-friendly 'fast' food, salads, health juices, sandwiches and good coffee that costs only €1 before 11am.

---

wise to book at least the morning before…though you might wait months for a table reservation at certain Michelin-starred places. Note that restaurants that stay open mid-afternoon usually serve only cakes and pancakes *(crêpes)* at that time, rather like the (often florally twee) tea rooms they temporarily emulate. However, many *cafés* and brasseries will serve at least rudimentary meals all day, notably simple pastas and *croques* (toasted sandwiches). The best known, a *croque monsieur* (with ham and cheese), typically costs around €8 with a generous salad garnish, roughly half that without. Remember that while all *cafés* will serve you a coffee, a Belgian *café* is more the equivalent of a pub-bar elsewhere, concentrating mostly on serving beers and alcoholic drinks. Smoking is banned in restaurants across Belgium and Luxembourg. In 2010 the ban was extended to Belgian *cafés* that serve food.

Soup *(soep/potage)* offers another inexpensive, relatively hearty option. A recent revival means there are now modern soup kitchens in major cities, some of which offer all-you-can-eat fresh soup and bread for around €5.

Quick Eats

The Belgians swear they invented *frieten/frites,* so don't think of calling them French fries here. At a proper *frituur/friture* (chip stand), *frieten/frites* are given a to-order second crisping before being served in a paper cone, smothered with large blobs of thick mayonnaise or flavoured sauces. There are dozens of sauces – if stumped for choice, try Andalouse, like very mildly spiced 1000-island dressing.

Belgium's home-grown hamburger chain, Quick (www.quick.be), competes with McDonalds (www.mcdonalds.be), whose Belgian restaurants usefully offer free wi-fi.

A popular and economic quick lunch for office folk is a *belegd broodje/ sandwich,* half a baguette filled with one of an array of prepared fillings (around €3). *Crudités* (a sprinkling of added salad) might be included but can add around €0.50 extra to the price. Buy early as many *cafés* and takeaway sandwich shops run out of bread by 2pm. Some cafes serve *botterham/tartine* (open) sandwiches or simple slices of bread with DIY topping rather than a French bread sandwich.

Pitas (stuffed pita bread) make common late-night street snacks. When meat-filled they're known as *gyros* or doner kebabs, depending on the server's original nationality. A *dürüm* is a similar kebab rolled into flat *lavash* bread.

Websites www.resto.be, www.la-carte.be, www. deltaweb.be and www. resto.lu list thousands of restaurants in Belgium and Luxembourg, many with customer reviews. In Dutch, www.pocket resto.be reprints useful restaurant press-reviews.

MUSSELLING IN

Belgium's signature Zeeland mussels are succulent and conspicuously larger than French equivalents, though most aren't actually Belgian at all and instead hail from just across the Dutch frontier. Fresh mussels open spontaneously during cooking, so if you find one hasn't opened don't force it: it might be off. Forget forks – eat them local-style using an empty mussel shell as a pair of tweezers. Chez Léon (p97) is Brussels' classic place for mussels, but not necessarily its cheapest. In season (traditionally September to April, exact dates vary each year), endless restaurants, supermarket cafeterias and even motorway service stations will serve them, sometimes *à volonté* (all you can eat). Invariably accompanying *frites* are included. When comparing prices remember to look at the portion sizes, which can vary from 650g (pretty small considering most of that's shells) to 1.2kg (very hefty). The basic cooking method is to steam them in a salty onion-and-celery broth, but a wide variety of alternatives add garlic, wine, *pastis* or various other flavourings, usually adding only a euro or two to the cost.

On the coast and at winter markets, steaming bowls of whelks (sea-snails, *wulloks/caricolles*) are dished up from sidewalk stalls.

Belgium's classic waffles (*wafel/gaufre*) should be cooked as you wait and served piping hot. Don't worry if you're asked if you'd like a little *slagroom* on top. That's the Dutch word for whipped cream, not an indecent proposal. Still, if you want to act local you'll decline: the 'real' way to eat Brussels' light, rectangular waffles is with just a light sprinkling of icing sugar. Heavier, rounded Liège waffles are already sweetened and need no adulteration whatsoever. But if you fancy smothering either type in fruit, syrup or chocolate, there's many a tourist-savvy stall that can oblige. It's your holiday after all.

VEGETARIANS & VEGANS

Though it focuses more on the Netherlands, www.etenvooreentientje.nl also links to numerous Belgian restaurants where you can eat a full meal for under €10.

Salads appear on most standard menus, however, the majority contain some form of cheese or meat product. And although mainstream bistros and restaurants generally offer at least one vegetarian option, it's typically a non-meat pasta, a cheese omelette or maybe a plate of the boiled mixed veg that would otherwise be used as garnish. Bigger cities (especially student towns like Ghent and Leuven) do have specialised vegetarian restaurants, most catering to vegans and using organic ('bio') ingredients, but often open only for lunch. For dinner you'll usually find a range of sensibly priced vegetarian fare at one of the ubiquitous Chinese, Vietnamese or Thai restaurants. Extensive listings of vegetarian options in Flanders and Brussels are available in Dutch on www.vegetarisme.be.

CHOCOLATE

Recognising that livestock production contributes up to 20% of the planet's 'greenhouse gasses', Ghent announced that as of 2009, Thursdays would be Veggie Days for the city's councillors, civil servants and school kids.

Chocolate is fundamentally a mix of cocoa paste, sugar and cocoa butter in varying proportions. Dark chocolate uses the most cocoa paste, milk chocolate mixes in milk powder, and white chocolate uses cocoa butter but no cocoa paste at all. Mouth-watering Belgian chocolate is arguably the world's best because it sticks religiously to these pure ingredients, while other countries allow cheaper vegetable fats to replace some of the cocoa butter (EU regulations allow up to 5%). Another prime factor in chocolate quality is the 'conching' (stirring) process – grainy chocolate just hasn't been conched enough. If you never thought your average block of chocolate was grainy before, you'll think differently after trying silky-smooth Belgian pralines. You'll find bars of elephant-emblazoned Côte d'Or (now owned by Kraft) along with the seashell-shaped Guylian chockies in many supermarkets. But what's really special are the 'pralines', filled chocolates sold from a wide range of *chocolaterie* shops. Domestically, the most ubiq-

---

THE BIRTH OF BELGIAN CHOCOLATE

In 1857 Swiss confectioner Jean Neuhaus (www.neuhaus-chocolates.com) opened a 'medicinal sweet shop' in Brussels' glorious Galeries St Hubert (it's still there, p110). In 1912 Neuhaus' grandson is credited with inventing the praline (pronounced 'prah-*leen*') by filling an empty chocolate shell with sweet, flavoured fillings. Three years later Neuhaus' wife invented the *ballotin*, a colourful cardboard presentation box. Pralines, still mostly sold in *ballotins*, are now a Belgian institution and make the ideal gift to take when visiting friends.

---

uitous chain is Leonidas, original 1930s pioneers of the cream-filled *manon*. Comparatively inexpensive Leonidas pralines (€19.80 per kg) are quite superb by non-Belgian standards, yet many locals regard the brand with a somewhat snobby condescension, preferring pricier Neuhaus, Corné or Galler (around €48 per kg). Galler's Kaori chocolate sticks, to be dipped in various provided flavour pots, are portrayed as a confectioner's metaphor for Japanese calligraphic art. Respected independent *chocolateries* include Burie and Del Rey in Antwerp (see p183) and Mary's in Brussels. Stylish black-box presentation, specialist bean sources and innovative flavours (including tea) make Pierre Marcolini chocolates a top choice for the wealthy and fashion conscious (€70 per kg).

Whichever brand you choose, entering a Belgian chocolate shop involves a shift of consciousness. The atmosphere is calm and seductive. Row upon row of assorted pralines await in air-conditioned comfort, attended by glove-clad assistants who'll patiently wrap whatever you select should you decide against one of the pre-packaged selections (125g to 1kg). Either way the price per kilogram stays the same. It's even fine to buy just a single chocolate.

Some useful choco-terms:

- *Manon* – luscious pralines filled with soft, creamy *crème fraîche*. Limited shelf life.
- *Ganache* – blend of chocolate, fresh cream and extra cocoa butter flavoured with coffee, cinnamon or liqueurs.
- *Gianduja* – smooth blend of milk chocolate and hazelnut paste.
- *Praliné* – mix of chocolate and finely ground toffee or nuts.
- *Praliné nougatine* – ditto but uses larger pieces of nuts or toffee to provide the crunch.

EAT YOUR WORDS

To recognise horse from herring, get behind the cuisine scene by memorising some key foodie terms in both Dutch and French. For pronunciation guidelines see p309 and p313.

Food Glossary

DUTCH
Meat

bloedworst	*bloot*·worst	black pudding
eend	eynt	duck
everzwijn	*ey*·vuhr·zweyn	boar
hersenen	*her*·suh·nuhn	brains
hert	hert	venison
hesp	hesp	ham
kalfsvlees	*kalfs*·vleys	veal
kalkoen	kal·*koon*	turkey
kip	kip	chicken

TRAVEL YOUR TASTEBUDS

- *anguille* – eel (don't confuse with *andouille,* a strong flavoured sausage made with intestines and stomach parts).
- *asperges* – spring asparagus, most famous from Mechelen.
- *ballekes/boulettes* – meatballs typically served in *tomatensaus/sauce tomate.* A speciality in Liège, the dish has long been seen as decidedly lower class elsewhere but has recently returned to fashion. Try them acting trendy with cherries.
- *boudin* – various forms of sausage incorporating milk and breadcrumbs, many edible raw. Boudin is also a mild Francophone insult meaning fatso (for women).
- *canibale* – basic *filet américain* used as a sandwich filling.
- *Vlaamse stoofkarbonade/carbonade flamande* – Flemish beer-based hot-pot using chunks of tasty but usually low-quality stewing steak (usually beef, sometimes horse).
- *chèvre chaud* – literally means 'hot goat', but in reality refers to warm goats' cheese, generally as salad with honey dressing.
- *gegratineerde witloof/chicons au gratin* – endives wrapped in ham and smothered in cheesy white-sauce.
- couscous – various North African dishes based on 'grains' that are actually tiny balls of formed semolina.
- *croque monsieur* – grilled ham-and-cheese sandwich. Other *croques* add egg, pineapple etc.
- *filet américain* – a misleading name for Belgium's equivalent of steak tartare, ie a blob of high-grade, raw minced beef, prepared with small quantities of onion, seasoning and egg.
- *fondue* – while cheese versions do exist, a 'fondue' in Belgium most commonly means a *fondue bourguignonne,* with chunks of meat that you skewer and cook on the table in a pan of sizzling hot oil. However, as 'fondue' means 'melted' the word can appear in various other contexts on a menu.
- *gaufres* – waffles.
- *gibier* – general term for seasonal game meat (pheasant, wild boar etc).
- *kalfszwezerik/ris de veau* – veal sweetbreads.
- *konijn met pruimen/lapin aux pruneaux* – rabbit cooked until tender in a sauce with prunes.
- *mosselen/moules* – mussels (see the boxed text, p52).
- *paardefilet/steak de cheval* – horse steak.
- *paling in 't groen/anguilles-au-vert* – eel in spinach sauce. Not the most visually appetising of dishes, nor is it moreish after the fourth chunk; try it as an entree.
- *rognon* – kidney, a highly regarded delicacy.
- *speculaas/speculoos* – cinnamon flavoured gingerbread most typically formed as biscuits (served with coffee) or shaped as St Nicholas for 6 December festivities.
- *St-Jacobsschelpen/coquilles St Jacques* – scallops.
- *stoemp* – potatoes mashed with a vegetable-of-the-day then tarted up with toppings such as ham, sausage, bacon or (less often) fried egg.
- *stoverij/stoofvlees* – stew, often synonymous with *carbonade flamande.*
- *tajine* – Moroccan slow-cooked stew usually served in a dish with a distinctive conical 'hat'.
- *truite à l'Ardennaise* – trout poached in a wine sauce and served sprinkled with almonds.
- *waterzooi* – cream-based soupy-stew traditionally made with chicken though regional variations such as *Oostendse waterzooi* substitute fish.

konijn	ko-*neyn*	rabbit
lam	lam	lamb
lever	*ley*-vuhr	liver
paard	paart	horse
parelhoen	*paa*-ruhl-hoon	guinea fowl
rund	ruhnt	beef
slak	slak	snail
spek	spek	bacon
varkensvlees	*var*-kuhns-vleys	pork
worst	worst	sausage

Fish & Seafood

baars	baars	bream
forel	foh-*rel*	trout
garnaal	khar-*naal*	shrimp
haring	*haa*-ring	herring
inktvis	*ingt*-vis	squid
kabeljauw	ka-buhl-*yaw*	cod
oester	*oos*-tuhr	oyster
paling	*paa*-ling	eel
St-Jacobsschelpen	sint-*yaa*-kop-skhelp	scallops
steurgarnaal	*steur*-khar-naal	prawn
tong	tong	sole
tonijn	to-*neyn*	tuna
zalm	zalm	salmon
zeebaars	*zey*-baars	sea bream

Vegetables

aardappel	*aart*-a-puhl	potato
ajuin	a-*yöyn*	onion
artisjok	ar-tee-*shok*	artichoke
asperge	as-*per*-zhuh	asparagus
aubergine	oa-buhr-*zhee*-nuh	eggplant
boon	boan	bean
champignon	sham-pee-*nyon*	mushroom
courgette	koor-*zhet*	zucchini
erwtjes	*erw*-tyuhs	peas
groene/rode paprika	*khroo*-nuh *pap*-ree-ka	green/red pepper (capsicum)
komkommer	kom-*kom*-uhr	cucumber
kool	koal	cabbage
look	loak	garlic
olijf	o-*layf*	olive
peterselie	pay-tuhr-*say*-lee	parsley
pompoen	pom-*poon*	pumpkin
prei	pray	leek
selder	*sel*-duhr	celery
spinazie	spee-*naa*-zee	spinach
spruitjes	*spröy*-tyes	Brussels sprouts
witloof	*wit*-loaf	chicory
wortel	*wor*-tuhl	carrot

Miscellaneous

azijn	a-*zayn*	vinegar
boter	*boa*-tuhr	butter
brood	broht	bread

ei	ey	egg
geitenkaas	*khey*·tuhn·kaas	goat's cheese
kaas	kaas	cheese
konfituur	kon·fee·*tewr*	jam
melk	melk	milk
peper	*pey*·puhr	pepper
rijst	reyst	rice
suiker	*söy*·kuhr	sugar
water	*waa*·tuhr	water
zout	zawt	salt

Cooking Methods

gebakken	khuh·*ba*·kuhn	baked
gegratineerd	khuh·khra·tee·*neyrt*	browned on top with cheese
gegrild	khuh·*khrilt*	grilled
gegrild aan 't spit	khuh·*khrilt* aant spit	spit-roasted
gepaneerd	khuh·*pa*·neyrt	coated in breadcrumbs
gerookt	khuh·*rohkt*	smoked
geroosterd	khuh·*rohs*·tuhrt	roasted
gesauteerd	khuh·soh·*teyrt*	sautéed
gestoomd	khuh·*stohmt*	steamed
gevuld	khuh·*vuhlt*	stuffed

FRENCH
Meat

agneau	a·nyo	lamb
bœuf	berf	beef
boudin noir	boo·dun nwar	black pudding
brochette	bro·shet	kebab
canard	ka·nar	duck
cervelle	sair·vel	brains
charcuterie	shar·kew·tree	cooked/prepared meats
cheval	sher·val	horse
chevreuil	che·vrer·yer	venison
dinde	dund	turkey
entrecôte	on·trer·koat	rib steak
escargot	es·kar·go	snail
foie	fwa	liver
jambon	zhom·bon	ham
lapin	la·pun	rabbit
marcassin	mar·ka·sun	boar
pintade	pun·tad	guinea fowl
porc	por	pork
poulet	poo·lay	chicken
saucisson	so·see·son	sausage
veau	vo	veal

Fish & Seafood

anguille	ong·gee·yer	eel
brème	brem	bream
cabillaud	ka·bee·yo	cod
calmar	kal·mar	squid
coquilles St Jacques	ko·kee·yer sun zhak	scallops
crevette	krer·vet	shrimp
dorade	do·rad	sea bream

CASSO-CONFUSTION

On French menus don't confuse a *cassolette* with a *cassoulet* (silent 't'). The former refers to a little cooking pot (often copper, sometimes ceramic), which could hold virtually anything the chef's created, often imaginative. However a *cassoulet* is a rich bean-and-meat casserole originally from southern France.

---

hareng	a·rong	herring
huître	wee·trer	oyster
langouste	long·goost	crayfish
raie	ray	ray
saumon	so·mon	salmon
scampi	skom·pee	prawn
thon	ton	tuna
truite	trweet	trout

Vegetables

ail	ai	garlic
artichaut	ar·tee·sho	artichoke
asperge	a·spairzh	asparagus
aubergine	o·bair·zheen	eggplant
champignon	shom·pee·nyon	mushroom
chicon	shee·kon	chicory
chou	shoo	cabbage
choux de Bruxelles	shoo der brew·sel	Brussels sprouts
citrouille	see·troo·yer	pumpkin
concombre	kong·kombr	cucumber
courgette	koor·zhet	zucchini
échalote	ay·sha·lot	shallot
épinards	ay·pee·nar	spinach
haricot	a·ree·ko	bean
oignon	on·yon	onion
persil	pair·sil	parsley
petit pois	pay·tee pwa	peas
poireau	pwa·ro	leek
poivron rouge/vert	pwav·ron roozh/vair	red/green pepper (capsicum)
pomme de terre	pom der tair	potato
truffe	trewf	truffle

Miscellaneous

beurre	bur	butter
confiture	kon·fee·tewr	jam
eau	o	water
fromage	fro·mazh	cheese
(fromage de) chèvre	(fro·mazh der) she·vrer	goat's cheese
lait	lay	milk
œuf	erf	egg
pain	pun	bread
poivre	pwa·vrer	pepper
riz	ree	rice
sel	sel	salt
sucre	sew·krer	sugar
vinaigre	vee·nay·grer	vinegar

Cooking Methods

à la broche	a la brosh	spit-roasted
à la vapeur	a la va·per	steamed
au four	o foor	baked
farci	far·see	stuffed
fumé	foo·may	smoked
gratiné	gra·tee·nay	browned on top with cheese
grillé	gree·yay	grilled
pané	pa·nay	coated in breadcrumbs
rôti	ro·tee	roasted
sauté	so·tay	sautéed

Environment

As a small, densely populated country that's been at the heart of European development (and wars) for centuries, it's hardly a surprise that Belgium's environment is now highly degraded. The country is already chock-full of cities and needs further space to develop internationally competitive new-generation businesses, leaving little space for 'low-carbon' energy solutions. Nonetheless, Belgium and Luxembourg signed up to the Kyoto Protocol and Rio Convention on Biodiversity (www.cbd.int). There's an active green movement, and various fiscal approaches to petrol pricing, rubbish collection and energy efficiency have helped gently push a somewhat ambivalent public towards more ecologically considerate behaviour.

THE LAND

Belgium is small. Doze off for a couple of hours on the Paris–Amsterdam Thalys and you've missed it. But it's still almost 12 times the size of tiny Luxembourg. The pair are nestled between France, the Netherlands and Germany.

Belgium also sports 66km of North Sea coast that's unexpectedly sandy, albeit backed by an almost unbroken parade of uninspired apartment-block resort towns. Flanders, Belgium's northern half, does have some vaguely pretty undulations around Borgloon and Oudenaarde (p166). However the vast majority of its landscapes are either sprawling, suburbanised villages or flat monotonous fields punctuated only by belfries, steeples and grazing cattle. As you head into northern Wallonia, rolling contours become the norm – attractive patchworks of fields and woodlands occasionally interspersed by abrupt river gorges. The hills get somewhat higher and more heavily wooded in the Ardennes of southeast Belgium and Luxembourg, but don't think 'mountains' – Belgium's highest point, the Signal de Botrange (694m; see p261), is a gently domed plateau, not a peak. Nonetheless the surrounding moorland bogs and swamps of the Hautes Fagnes (p261) have a certain wild fascination.

Belgium's two great rivers, the Scheldt (Schelde/Escaut in Dutch/French) and Meuse (Maas in Dutch), are fed by major tributaries including the industrialised Sambre, prettier Ourthe and attractive Lesse. Canals linking to the sea or between river arteries continue to be of considerable significance and Belgium sports some particularly original boat lifts and lock systems (p216). Transportation of heavy goods by barge is partly regaining ground in recent years as ecological sensitivity grows over truck exhaust emissions. Liège, on the Meuse, is Europe's third-largest inland port.

WILDLIFE
Animals

Before the last Ice Age, Belgium was home to mammoth and later to bears and bison; however, centuries of hunting and urbanisation has meant that the biggest wild critters left today are deer, wild boars, foxes, badgers, red squirrels and rabbits. Hunting is still a beloved pastime in the Ardennes, notably around the town of St-Hubert (p238). The season runs from 15 October to 15 January.

For twitchers, Belgium isn't a prime location, but the coastal reserves have a reasonable diversity of regional and migratory species (see National Parks, p60). Storks are being successfully bred in Het Zwin and the critically endangered black grouse *(Tetrao tetrix)* has found its last refuge in the

If there's no room on land, there's always the sea. Check out www.C-power.be to read about Belgium's new offshore wind power scheme.

Nearly a fifth of Belgium's total land area is covered with buildings, in Flanders it's 26.2%. For more official statistics see http://stat bel.fgov.be.

The very extensive 2003 study *Biodiversity in Belgium* can be downloaded free as a series of pdf files on www.biodiv.be/bio diversity/bib/implemen tation/docs/books/bib

Hautes Fagnes Nature Reserve, which has adopted it as the park's emblem. Protected in Belgium, these birds live in moorland habitats and, if you're lucky, can be spotted in bare branches of trees. The males are black with a noticeable red bonnet.

On the outskirts of Brussels, the Forêt de Soignes (p113), a majestic (if 'artificial') beech forest is home to one of Europe's largest populations of sparrow-hawks. However, cuckoos, turtle doves and golden orioles have largely disappeared and researchers are worried by a general diminution in birdlife that has seen lark and partridge populations collapsing by as much as 90% since the 1970s.

Plants

The native forests that once covered much of Belgium have been destroyed by centuries of clearing for agriculture and pasturage. Today's forests – concentrated in the Ardennes – are largely coniferous monocultures used for logging and are unable to sustain the diversity of plant and animal species that once lived in this region. Other isolated patches of forest, mainly beech, birch and oak, are dotted around the countryside. These, too, are generally planted rather than purely 'natural' as with Brussels' majestic Forêt de Soignes (p113). Belgium's National Botanic Garden (see Nationale Plantentuin Van België, p113) boasts one of the largest collections of plants in Europe, including many indigenous plants.

While an overall net deforestation persisted until 2000, the Flemish government has a set goal of adding 10,000 hectares of forested land by 2010 (based on a 1994 baseline).

NATIONAL PARKS

Best known of Belgium's protected natural areas is the Hautes Fagnes Nature Reserve (see p261), a mesmerising if bleak fen-land area that was once a commercial source of peat. The 5700-hectare Nationaal Park Hoge Kempen (www.nationaalpark.be) between Genk and Maasmechelen comprises a swath of heather fields, pine forest, lakes and hills partly accessible from a recreation area known as Kattevennen near Genk.

Straddling the Dutch border, Kalmthoutse Heide Nature Reserve (www.grensparkzk.nl), north of Antwerp, features important wet and dry heath as well as active and inactive sand dunes. Over 90% of Belgium's dragonfly species live here.

The coastal nature reserves of Het Zwin (p152) and nearby Zwin-Polder protect a wetland ecosystem that's maintained by North Sea flooding. The reserves include salt marshes, coastal dunes and freshwater wetlands, and provide sanctuary for numbers of bird and rare flora species, such as glasswort and seablite, which thrive on salty soil. De Westhoek Vlaams Natuurreservaat, a 340-hectare coastal reserve abutting the French border near De Panne (p154), shelters about a third of the wildflower species found in Flanders. A popular winter haven for migratory birds, it's also home to warblers, nightingales, the endangered crested lark, the little ringed plover and several rare species of spiders, insects, toads and newts.

ENVIRONMENTAL ISSUES

From 1999 the two main green political parties, Agalev (Flemish, now renamed Groen!) and Ecolo (Francophone), fared well in elections and became part of the ruling coalition until 2003. During this time their most important success was an agreement in which Belgium agreed to phase out its nuclear power stations between 2015 and 2025. With nuclear power then providing two-thirds of the country's energy, this was a daring and

Website http://waarnemingen.be is a fabulous interactive resource for naturalists, including sightings lists for birds, mammals, butterflies, plants and much more. More visual http://natuurpunt.be (in Dutch) is also a great resource.

Kris Decleer's 2008 book *Ecological Restoration In Flanders* outlines northern Belgium's recent nature-regrowth strategy. It's available via www.inbo.be (€13, 160pp).

The International Union for Conservation of Nature (www.iucn.org) is a big global network of environmentally active groups and individuals helping in the search for pragmatic solutions to ecological problems.

much-lauded decision. However, it relied on a rapid effort to develop renewable energy sources from an almost standing start. Although vast wind turbines have been sprouting across the country ever since, Belgium's seven nuclear stations still produced over half the nation's electricity in 2008. In October 2009 the government controversially postponed the nuclear shutdown by at least 10 years. Belgium was already struggling to meet Kyoto emissions promises, but the justifications given also included the global economic crisis leaving a big budget hole. Agreed revenues of around €245 million a year from the power company Electrabel should help.

The nuclear back-track underlined that Belgium needs better vision and action to increase its proportion of sustainable energy sources. Mixed messages over solar energy haven't helped. Citizens were initially offered major tax credits to install photovoltaic roof panels. But a recent shift in policy has preferentially stressed domestic energy saving through better insulation and efficiency. On the other hand, wind power is steadily gaining ground – the first six gigantic wind turbines of the C-Power wind farm (www.C-power. be) are already installed some 20km offshore in the North Sea. One of the small advances at the Copenhagen climate conference was an agreement between several European governments (including Belgium) to form a grid for wind-power sharing.

Another concern is water quality. While Belgian tap water is treated and drinkable, Belgium's largest rivers are heavily polluted and as recently as 2006, Brussels put untreated sewage straight into the Senne River, as it had done for centuries. An OECD report released the same year said that Belgium had the worst water in the industrialised world, with the highest concentrations of nitrates and pesticides. And according to a 2008 report Belgian coastal waters are the EU's most polluted (apart from Romania's), with only six out of 40 beaches satisfying new hygiene norms.

Belgium's urban air pollution becomes most noticeable on certain summer days – when smog alerts are announced the speed limits on key motorways drop to 90km/h. Preferential taxes on fuel efficient and low emissions vehicles are also designed to reduce the problem in the longer term, though Belgium's high proportion of company cars reduces the efficacy of such pricing structures. Meanwhile Flanders' Pendelplan sets out to reduce car-commuting by encouraging cycle-to-work schemes and making bicycles increasingly available at train stations.

Progress has been made with recycling. While systems vary between communes, variable pricing systems on domestic-refuse removal have encouraged a large proportion of Belgian households to separate rubbish, with paper, metal-plastic waste and compostable matter each collected individually. Communal glass-disposal banks are also common. The Bebat program (www .bebat.be), funded by battery eco-taxes, recycles nearly 60% of all batteries sold in Belgium, the best record in Europe. For more complex household waste (electronics, washing machines etc), a similar scheme (www.recupel. be) obliges the manufacturer or seller to take responsibility for recycling the components, a service for which an eco-tax is levied on each piece of equipment according to the estimated difficulty of recycling.

IBGE-BIM (www.brux ellesenvironnement.be) is the capital's environmental monitoring unit. They publish numerous online files on locally relevant initiatives and, among many other things, award businesses that fulfil eco-initiative goals.

Brussels

The fascinating capital of Belgium and Europe sums up all the contradictions of both. It's simultaneously historic yet hip, bureaucratic yet bizarre, self confident yet un-showy and multicultural to its roots. The city's contrasts and tensions are multilayered yet somehow consistent in their very incoherence – Francophone versus Flemish, Bruxellois versus Belgian versus Eurocrat versus immigrant. And all this plays out on a cityscape that swings block by block from majestic to quirky to grimily rundown and back again. It's a complex patchwork of overlapping yet distinctive neighbourhoods that takes time to understand. Organic art nouveau facades face off against 1960s concrete disgraces. Regal 19th-century mansions contrast with the brutal glass of the EU's real-life Gotham City. World-class museums lie hidden in suburban parks and a glorious beech forest extends extraordinarily deep into the city's southern flank. This whole maelstrom swirls forth from Brussels' medieval core, where the truly grand Grand Place is surely one of the world's most beautiful squares.

Constant among all these disparate images is the enviable quality of everyday life – great shopping, consistently excellent dining at all price ranges, sublime chocolate shops and a *café* scene that could keep you drunk for years. But Brussels doesn't go out of its way to impress. Its citizens have a low-key approach to everything. And their quietly humorous, deadpan outlook on life is often just as surreal as the classic Brussels-painted canvases of Magritte.

HIGHLIGHTS

- **Europe's most beautiful square?** Ponder the question over a few beers on the gorgeous Grand Place (p76)
- **Big balls** Nine of them arranged like a school chemistry set form the amazing Atomium (p90)
- **Drinkers' delight** *Cafés* ancient and modern, including an inspiring selection of classics scattered around the Bourse (p103)
- **Art history** Old masters and surrealists at the Musées Royaux des Beaux-Arts (p82), with its shiny new Magritte Museum annex
- **Art nouveau** The wonderful Old England Building (p82) – one of many art nouveau masterpieces (p82)
- **Dino discovery** Palaeontology comes to life at the magnificent Musée des Sciences Naturelles (p85)
- **Forgotten treasure** Extraordinary riches lurk in the vast Musées Royaux d'Art et d'Histoire (p87)

★ Atomium

Classic Cafés — Old England Building
Grand Place ★★
★★ Musées Royaux
d'Art et d'Histoire
★ Musée des
Musées Sciences Naturelles
Royaux
des Beaux-Arts Tervuren ★

- POPULATION: 1,081,000
- LANGUAGES: FRENCH & DUTCH

BRUSSELS IN...

One Day

Gape in wonder at the **Grand Place** (p76), Brussels' gorgeous central square. Discover that the **Manneken Pis** (p77) is much smaller than you'd imagined then stroll through the **Galeries St-Hubert** en route to finding his 'squatting sister', the **Jeanneke Pis**. Admire the colourful scene that is the **Rue des Bouchers** (p78), then move on for a seafood lunch in the convivial **Ste-Catherine** area (p104). Window shop up Rue Antoine Dansaert, exploring the compact, quirky **Fashion District** (p79) then grab a drink in the **Cirio** (p103) or one of the other fabulous classic *cafés* around the **Bourse** (p78). Admire the cityscape as well as the musical instruments at the majestic **Old England Building** (p82), nip across the road to the new **Magritte Museum**, then have a drink in the eccentric **La Fleur en Papier Doré**, where Magritte himself used to booze. Admire the bulky **Palais de Justice** and preen a little as you stroll past the antique shops and pretty people on the Sablon. Have an exotic pita snack in the art nouveau *café* **Perroquet** (p100) or head straight to lively **Délirium Café** (p104) to sample a range of fine Belgian beers. Quickly realise that you should have stayed a week.

One Week

Buy a 72-hour **Brusselscard** (p76) for three intense pre-paid days of brilliant museums, but remember to start it on a Tuesday, Wednesday, Thursday or Friday – otherwise you'll 'waste' a day. With the card in hand don't miss the **Musée des Sciences Naturelles** (p85), **Cinquantenaire museums** (p87), **Africa Museum** (p92), **Chinese Pagoda** (p90) or your free beer at **L'Arbre d'Or** (p77) on the Grand Place. Once the card has expired discover lambic beers at the **Musée Bruxellois de la Gueuze** (p91), visit the unique **Atomium** (p90), peruse the comic-strip murals (p81), discover the restaurants, cultural complexities and **art nouveau houses** of Ixelles (p88), bus out to the **Waterloo Battlefield** (p217), and meet up with a **Tof person** (see the boxed text, p87). And all the while, never stop drinking your way through our list of inspirational *cafés* (p102). Santé!

HISTORY

According to legend, St-Géry built a chapel on a swampy Senne (Zenne) River island back in AD 695. A settlement that grew around it had become known as Bruocsella (from *bruoc*, marsh, and *sella*, dwelling) by 979 when Charles, Duke of Lorraine moved here from Cambrai. He built a fort on St-Géry island amid flowering irises, which have since become the city's symbol. By 1100 Bruocsella was a walled settlement and capital of the Duchy of Brabant. In 1229 Brabant's Duke Henri I published the first Brussels charter guaranteeing protection for (and expectations of) the town's citizens. In 1355 the Count of Flanders, then Brabant's neighbourhood enemy, invaded and seized Brussels. However, a year later, Brussels citizens, led by Everard 't Serclaes, ejected the Flemish to considerable jubilation. 't Serclaes went on to become a prominent local leader fighting for ever more civic privileges, a stance which finally saw him assassinated in 1388. This caused a furore in Brussels, whose towns-folk blamed the lord of Gaasbeek and took revenge by burning down his castle (p113). Today, an anachronistic statue of 't Serclaes' corpse (Grand Place 8, p77) is still considered a potent source of luck.

Meanwhile, the cloth trade was booming. By the 15th century, prosperous markets filled the streets around the Grand Place selling products for which some are still named: Rue au Beurre (Butter St), Rue des Bouchers (Butchers' St) etc. The city's increasingly wealthy merchant guilds established their headquarters on the Grand Place, where medieval tournaments and public executions took place in the shadow of a towering Hôtel de Ville.

From 1519 Brussels came to international prominence as capital of Charles Quint's vast Hapsburg Empire (see p27). In 1549 Charles' future-successor, Philip II of Spain, was welcomed to the city in an incredibly lavish pageant that today forms the basis of the Ommegang (p17). But fanatically Catholic Philip was unimpressed with the lowlanders' brewing Protestantism. His

Spanish Inquisition resulted in thousands of executions including those of anti-Spanish Counts Egmont and Hoorn in front of the Maison du Roi.

In 1695, Louis XIV's French army under Marshal De Villeroy bombarded Brussels for 36 hours, hoping to divert Dutch attention from its attempts to regain Namur (Namur being temporarily occupied by France at this stage). The damage was truly catastrophic. Around 4000 houses were destroyed, around a third of the city was reduced to rubble and contemporary estimates calculated damages at 50 million florins (equivalent to some €5 billion in today's terms). The Grand Place was virtually obliterated though miraculously the Hôtel de Ville survived relatively intact. And within five years most of the square's guildhalls were rebuilt, making them even more impressive than they'd been before.

Austrian rule in the 18th century fostered urban development, with the construction of grand squares such as Place Royale and completion of the royal palace at Laeken (1784). Many of the Upper Town's architectural gems were built during this time and in the brief eras of French and Dutch rule that followed. In 1830 Brussels proved the unlikely starting point of the curious 1830 'operatic' revolt (see boxed text, p107) that led Belgium to entirely unexpected independence.

At this stage Brussels was home to around 100,000 people. However, the city grew enormously in both population and stature during the next century, greatly funded by Wallonia's industrial revolution along with King Léopold II's plunder of the Congo. While millions of Congolese died, Brussels lavished itself with some of Europe's finest belle époque and art nouveau buildings.

Unlike much of the country, Brussels survived both world wars comparatively unscathed. The city underlined a new era of postwar optimism by hosting the 1958 World's Fair in the shadow of one of the era's most extraordinary constructions, the Atomium (p90. Brussels' growth was further boosted when it became the headquarters of NATO and EEC (later EU). However, in the city's drive for progress and modernism, much of the capital's once-fine architecture is torn down to make way for mediocre concrete office buildings, a form of architectural vandalism that's now widely known as *Brusselization*. A stint as Cultural Capital of Europe in 2000 finally gave the city the push it needed to start properly protecting heritage buildings and sprucing up neglected neighbourhoods. Nonetheless, brutal steel-and-glass redevelopment has continued apace in the EU and Bruxelles-Midi areas while plenty of grimy urban areas still await attention.

ORIENTATION

Most of Brussels is surrounded by 'the Ring' ('R0'), a far-from-ring-shaped motorway that gets blocked almost solid with rush-hour traffic from September to June. Lengthy connectors involving long tunnel sections (and thus invisible on many maps) link to a much smaller 'inner ring' that traces a rough pentagon along lines that were once the city walls. The central Senne River is effectively invisible, having been covered over in the late 19th-century for health reasons (cholera outbreaks and the like).

Best explored on foot, Central Brussels' historic core includes the **Lower Town** (Map p70) around the imposing Grand Place, the partly gentrified working-class **Marolles** (Map pp72–3) and the much grander **Upper Town** (Map pp68–9) with its royal buildings, museums and snooty Sablon.

Southeast of the inner ring, the vibrantly multicultural area of **Matonge** (p89) is home to the capital's African community while further east, between **Etterbeek** and the monumental arch of the **Cinquantenaire**, lies the **EU quarter** (p85).

Built by Léopold II to access his new forest park at La Cambre, the patchily grand, upmarket Ave Louise runs south through vibrant **Ixelles** (Elsene in Dutch; Map pp72–3), which is liberally dotted with art nouveau architecture, as is somewhat down-at-heel **St-Gilles** (Map pp72–3) to its direct west.

Just north of the inner ring lie the rundown, if once grand, immigrant neighbourhoods of **Schaerbeek** (Map pp66–7) and **St-Josse** (Map pp68–9) and the Gare du Nord. Directly southeast of the station is a pink-windowed red-light district, yet to its north lies a shiny new tower-block business district resembling a miniature Manhattan. Post-industrial **Molenbeek** (Map pp66–7) is the city's modern-day port on the Charleroi–Antwerp canal. Further north, **Laeken** is where the Belgium's royal family lives and in **Heysel** you'll find that intriguing space-age leftover from the 1958 World's Fair, the Atomium.

BILINGUAL BRUSSELS

The 19 *communes* of the Brussels Capital Region (Brussels Hoofdstedelijk Gewest in Dutch, Région de Bruxelles-Capitale in French) comprise the only area in Belgium that's officially bilingual. For simplicity in this book we have only used one version of each name (the French) but in fact on buildings, train stations, road signs, you name it, there are two versions. That explains why certain Brussels street names look so flabbergastingly long. In fact they're saying the same thing twice. For example, in 'Rue de l'Ecuyer Schildknaapstraat', both Rue de l'Ecuyer (French) and Schildknaapstraat (Dutch) mean Squire Street. Handily, the grammatical form of the two languages means that the French terms *rue/avenue* (street/avenue) always come first while in Dutch *straat/laan* are tacked on to the end. This allows for a space-saving trick when the core name doesn't need translating, ie a sign might end up reading something like 'Ave Maxlaan' (ie literally Ave Max Avenue). In the Marolles, street names even add a third version in Bruxellois (the city's traditional dialect).

Brussels is surrounded by Flanders, where all signs are in Dutch. So for places like Tervuren, Zaventem (the airport) and Grimbergen covered in this chapter but beyond Brussels' official regional boundary, the street names are given in Dutch. If you want to see normally placid Belgians get inexplicably heated, ask them what they think about the six Faciliteitengemeente/ Communes à Facilité on the edge of Brussels (where people 'should' speak Dutch but in reality the majority speak French).

Brussels has numerous train stations. Major international services invariably arrive at Bruxelles-Midi, whose down-at-heel surroundings are gradually being punctuated by stark contemporary tower buildings. Generally you're advised to hop straight on any connecting train (four minutes) to subterranean Bruxelles-Central, which is handiest for the historic centre. Use Bruxelles-Luxembourg or Bruxelles-Schuman for the EU Area.

INFORMATION
Bookshops
Anticyclone des Açores (Map p70; ☎ 02-217 5246; Rue du Fossé aux Loups 34) Travel specialist.
FNAC (Map pp68-9; ☎ 02-209 2211; www.fnac.be; City 2 shopping centre, Rue Neuve; ◷ 10am-7pm Mon-Sat, to 8pm Fri) Book department-store with events ticketing agency.
Sterling Books (Map p70; ☎ 02-223 6223; www.sterlingbooks.be; Rue du Fossé aux Loups 38; ◷ 10am-7pm Mon-Sat, noon-6.30pm Sun) English-language bookshop with comfy sofas and a kids' play area.
Waterstones (Map p70; ☎ 02-219 2708; Blvd Adolphe Max 71-75; ◷ 9am-7pm Mon-Sat, 10.30am-6pm Sun) Large English-language bookshop with numerous international magazines.

Internet Access
There's free wi-fi at Flanders Info (p76), the Cercle des Voyageurs (p104), Zabar (p105) and many other *cafés*. Matonge has numerous phone-internet shops.

Other central options:
Belgium Internet (Map p70; Rue du Marché au Charbon; per hr €2; ◷ 24hr) Three terminals oddly plonked in a central all-night grocery store.
Touistrading (Map p70; ☎ 02-219 5493; Rue de Flandre 118; per hr €1; ◷ 11am-11.30pm) Typical phone shop.

Laundry
Aquatic Wash Laundry (Map pp72-3; Rue Montserrat 9; per load €3.20; ◷ 5.30am-11pm) Self-service laundrette.
Salon Lavoir de la Chapelle (Map p70; Rue Haute 7; per 5kg load €6.50; ◷ 8am-6pm Mon-Fri) Old-fashioned, full-service laundrette.

Left Luggage
Bruxelles-Midi Station Luggage office (per article per day €2.50; ◷ 6am-9pm); Luggage lockers (per 24hr small/large €3/4) Maximum 72 hours for lockers.

Medical Services
Community Help Service (☎ 02-648 4014; www.chsbelgium.org; ◷ 24hr) English-speaking crisis helpline. Can also help find English-speaking doctors, dentists and other health professionals.
Dr Van Breusegem Clinic (Map p70; ☎ 02-502 1407; Rue L Lepage 12; ◷ 9am-10am & 5pm-6pm Mon-Fri) Central location. Consultations without appointment €23.
Hôpital St-Pierre (Map pp72-3; ☎ 02-535 3111; www.stpierre-bru.be; Rue Haute 290-322; ◷ emergency 24hr, consultation 8am-5pm) Central hospital offering emergency assistance.

(Continued on page 76)

GREATER BRUSSELS

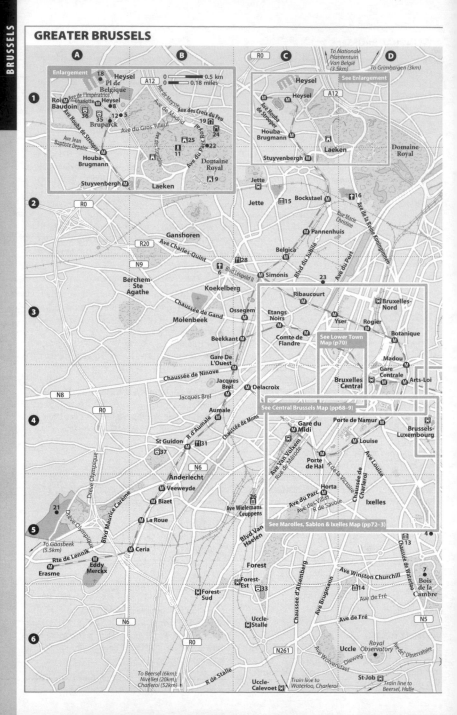

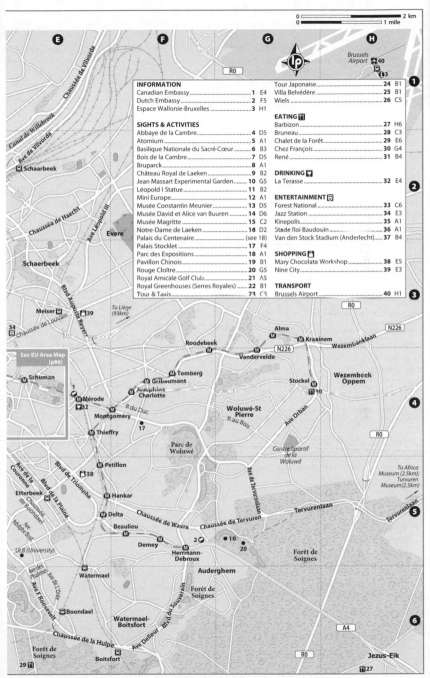

0 — 2 km
0 — 1 mile

INFORMATION
Canadian Embassy.................................. **1** E4
Dutch Embassy.. **2** F5
Espace Wallonie-Bruxelles...................... **3** H1

SIGHTS & ACTIVITIES
Abbaye de la Cambre............................... **4** D5
Atomium... **5** A1
Basilique Nationale du Sacré-Cœur......... **6** B3
Bois de la Cambre.................................... **7** D5
Bruparck... **8** A1
Château Royal de Laeken......................... **9** B2
Jean Massart Experimental Garden........ **10** G5
Léopold I Statue.................................... **11** B2
Mini Europe.. **12** A1
Musée Constantin Meunier.................... **13** D5
Musée David et Alice van Buuren........... **14** D6
Musée Magritte..................................... **15** C2
Notre-Dame de Laeken........................... **16** D2
Palais du Centenaire.......................... (see 18)
Palais Stocklet...................................... **17** F4
Parc des Expositions............................. **18** A1
Pavillon Chinois.................................... **19** B1
Rouge Cloître.. **20** G5
Royal Amicale Golf Club........................ **21** A5
Royal Greenhouses (Serres Royales)....... **22** B1
Tour & Taxis.. **23** C3

Tour Japonaise...................................... **24** B1
Villa Belvédère...................................... **25** B1
Wiels... **26** C5

EATING 🍴
Barbizon.. **27** H6
Bruneau... **28** C3
Chalet de la Forêt.................................. **29** E6
Chez François.. **30** G4
René.. **31** B4

DRINKING 🍷
La Terasse... **32** E4

ENTERTAINMENT 🎭
Forest National..................................... **33** C6
Jazz Station... **34** E3
Kinepolis... **35** A1
Stade Roi Baudouin............................... **36** A1
Van den Stock Stadium (Anderlecht)...... **37** B4

SHOPPING 🛍
Mary Chocolate Workshop..................... **38** E5
Nine City... **39** E3

TRANSPORT
Brussels Airport.................................... **40** H1

CENTRAL BRUSSELS

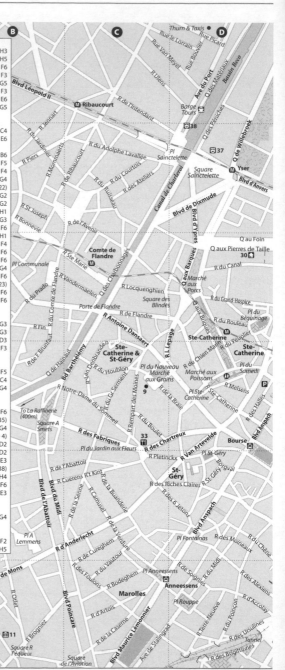

INFORMATION
Amazone	**1**	H3
Australian Embassy	**2**	H5
BIP (Tourist Info)	**3**	F6
FNAC	**4**	F3
French Embassy	**5**	G5
Post Office	**6**	F3
Salon Lavoir de la Chapelle	**7**	E6
USA Embassy	**8**	G5

SIGHTS & ACTIVITIES
Atelier Christophe Coppens	**9**	C4
Bibliothèque Royale	**10**	E6
Cantillon Brewery (Musée Bruxellois de la Gueuze)	**11**	B6
Cathédrale des Sts Michel & Gudule	**12**	F5
Centre Belge de la Bande Dessinée	**13**	F4
Colonne du Congrès	**14**	G4
Coudenburg	(see 22)	
De Ultieme Hallucinatie	**15**	G2
Église Ste-Marie	**16**	G2
Halles de Schaerbeek	**17**	H1
Le Botanique	**18**	G3
Magritte Gallery	**19**	F6
Maison Autrique	**20**	H1
Money Museum	**21**	F4
Musée BELvue	**22**	F6
Musée des Instruments de Musique	**23**	F6
Musée du Jouet	**24**	G4
Musées Royaux des Beaux-Arts	**25**	F6
Old England Building	(see 23)	
Palais Royal	**26**	F6
Statue of Godefroid de Bouillon	**27**	F6

SLEEPING
Centre Vincent van Gogh	**28**	G3
HI Hostel Jacques Brel	**29**	G3
Hooy Kaye Lodge	**30**	D3
Sleep Well	**31**	F3

EATING
Galerie Ravenstein	**32**	F5
In 't Spinnekopke	**33**	C4
Le Bier Circus	**34**	G4

ENTERTAINMENT
BoZar	**35**	F6
Cinematek	(see 35)	
Cirque Royal	**36**	G4
FNAC	(see 4)	
Kaaitheater	**37**	D2
K-Nal	**38**	D2
Koninklijke Vlaamse Schouwburg	**39**	E3
LibertineSupersport	(see 38)	
Mirano Continental	**40**	H4
Musée du Cinéma	**41**	F6
Théâtre National	**42**	E3

SHOPPING
Mary	**43**	G4

TRANSPORT
Eurolines	**44**	F2
Touring Club de Belgique	**45**	H5

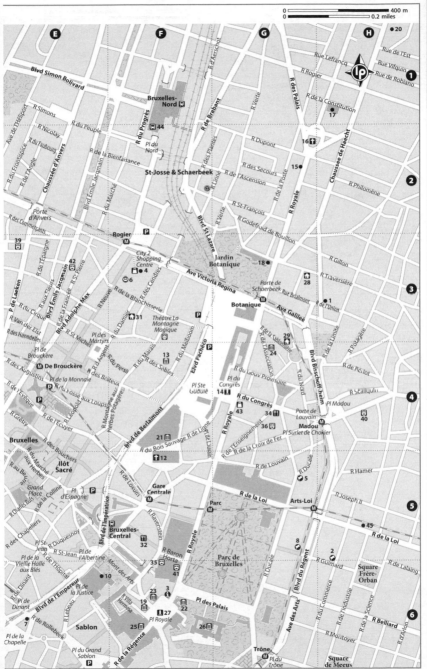

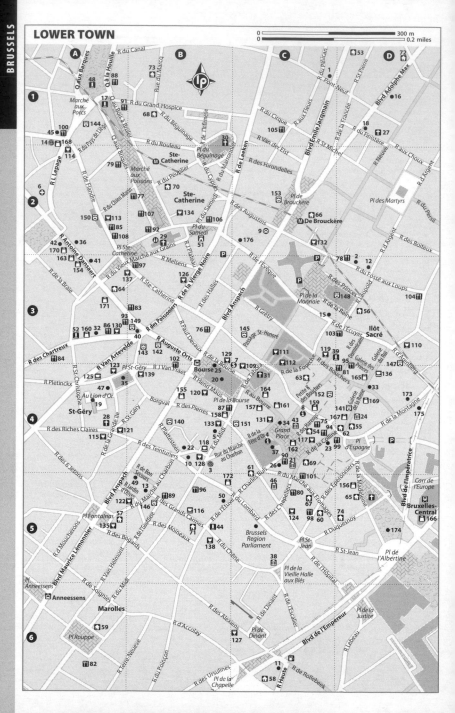

LOWER TOWN

MAROLLES, SABLON & IXELLES

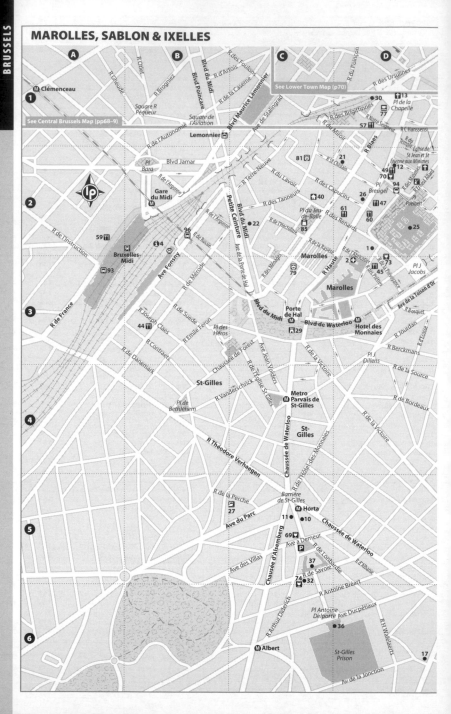

See Lower Town Map (p70)

See Central Brussels Map (pp68–9)

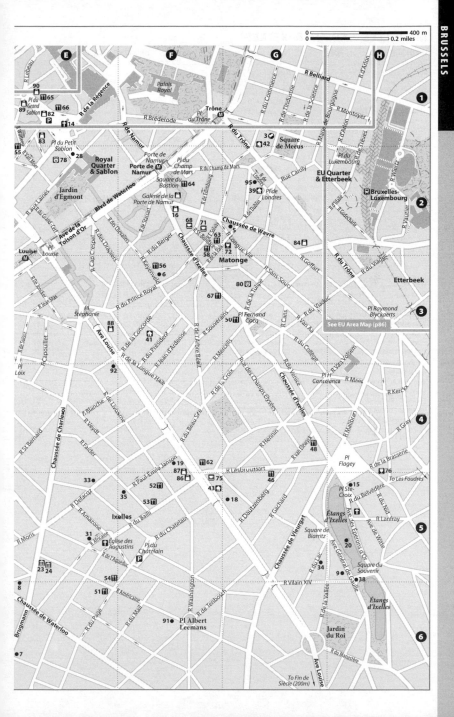

To Fin de
Siècle (200m)

BRUSSELS

MAROLLES, SABLON & IXELLES

BRUSSELS TRANSPORT MAP

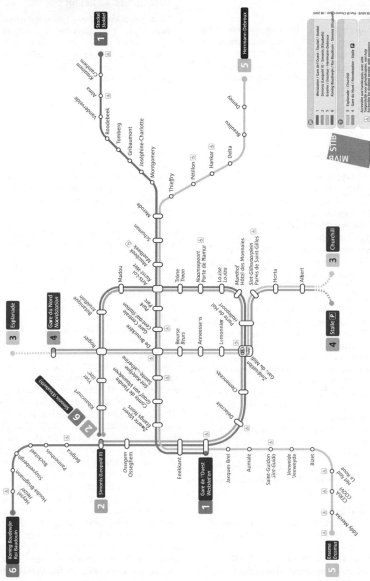

(Continued from page 65)

Money

ATMs and exchange facilities are found near the Bourse, at Bruxelles-Midi station and Brussels Airport. **Eurogold** (Map p70; Rue de la Bourse 32; ☉ 9am-5.30pm Mon-Thu, 9am-6pm Fri) offers comparatively good exchange rates without commission.

Post

Post office Main (Map p70; Blvd Anspach 1; ☉ 8am-6pm Mon-Fri, 10.30am-4.30pm Sat); Gare du Midi (Map pp72-3; Ave Fonsny 1e; ☉ 7am-7pm Mon-Fri, 10am-3pm Sat); City 2 shopping centre (Map pp68-9; Rue Neuve; ☉ 9.30am-6.30pm Mon-Fri, 10am-1pm Sat)

Tourist Information

BIP (Map pp68-9; ☎ 02-548 0458; www.biponline.be; Rue Royale 2-4; ☉ 10am-6pm) Official Brussels region tourist office. More spacious and much less crowded than Brussels International (see above). Hotel bookings and information are available but no financial transactions.

Brussels International (Map p70; ☎ 02-513 8940; www.brusselsinternational.be; Grand Place; ☉ 9am-6pm Mon-Sat, Mon-Sun in summer) The main city tourist office, located inside the town hall. Often crammed full, it sells discount booklets and the Brusselscard (see boxed text, right). Booth at Bruxelles-Midi train station.

Espace Wallonie-Bruxelles (Map pp66-7; ☎ 02-504 0200, 02-725 5275; www.belgique-tourisme.net; arrivals hall, Brussels Airport; ☉ 8am-9pm) Information on Brussels and Wallonia, not Flanders.

Flanders Info (Map p70; ☎ 02-504 0390; www.visit flanders.com; Rue du Marché aux Herbes 63; ☉ 9am-6pm Apr-June & Sep, 9am-7pm Jul-Aug, 9am-5pm Oct-Mar, to 4pm Sun Oct-Mar, closed 1-2pm weekends) For Flanders information, obviously. Free wi-fi.

Use-It (Map p70; ☎ 02-725 5275; www.use-it.be; Rue de l'Écuyer; ☉ 9am-12.30pm & 1-6pm Tue-Fri & 1pm-5pm Sat). Their superb free guide-maps are full of spot-on local tips and irreverent humour. Copies are available from a door dispenser even when the office is closed, and also from hostels or by download.

Travel Agencies

Airstop (Map p70; ☎ high toll 070-233 188; www .airstop.be; Blvd Emile Jacqmain 76; ☉ 10am-6pm Mon-Fri, 10am-5pm Sat)

Connections (Map p70; ☎ high toll 070-233 313, 02-550 0130; www.connections.be; Rue du Midi 19; ☉ 9.30am-6.30pm Mon-Fri, 10am-5pm Sat)

SIGHTS

The medieval grandeur of the Grand Place has an immediate wow factor that rarely fails to impress. And further afield are numer-

---

DISCOUNTS & FREEBIES

On the first Wednesday afternoon of each month, most of Brussels' major museums are free to enter. At other times the cheapest way to see a bunch of top sites is with the **Brusselscard** (www.brusselscard.be; 24/48/72 hours €20/28/33). The card gets you into 30 major museums and provides free city transport plus discounts for other attractions, some shops and restaurants. It's available through Brussels International (left), six STIB agencies and four of the bigger museums. Pre-paying online saves €1. When picking your dates don't forget that most museums close Mondays. And when collecting the pass, ensure that its magnetic stripe has been properly validated.

---

ous excellent museums. But much of the fun in Brussels is found simply wandering the streets, enjoying the bizarre mismatch of architectural styles, spotting the quirky little details and dropping regularly into the fabulous *cafés* en route.

Grand Place

Brussels' magnificent Grand Place (Map p70) is one of the world's most unforgettable urban ensembles. Oddly hidden, the enclosed cobblestone square is only revealed as you enter on foot from one of six narrow side alleys: Rue des Harengs is the best first approach.

The focal point is the magnificently spired 15th-century city hall but each of the fabulous antique guildhalls (mostly 1697–1705) has a charm of its own. Most are unashamed exhibitionists adorned with fine baroque gables, gilded statues and elaborate guild symbols.

Alive with classic *cafés*, the square takes on different auras at different times. Try to visit more than once and don't miss looking again at night when the scene is magically (and tastefully) illuminated. On Monday, Wednesday and Friday mornings there's a flower market and at various other times the square might host anything from Christmas fairs to rock concerts to the extraordinary biennial 'flower carpet' (see p18).

HÔTEL DE VILLE (CITY HALL)

Laboriously built between 1444 and 1480, the splendid, slightly asymmetric **Hôtel de Ville** (City Hall; Map p70; ☎ visitors office 02-279 4347) was almost the only building on the Grand Place to escape the 1695 French bombardment – ironic considering it was their primary target. The creamy stone facade is lavished with Gothic gargoyles and reliefs of nobility. Its intricate tower soars 96m, topped by a gilded statue of St-Michel, Brussels' patron saint. For 45-minute **guided tours** (€3; ☼ 3.15pm Tue & Wed year-round, 12.15pm Sun from Apr-Sep), turn up at Brussels International (opposite) 40 minutes before scheduled departure times to buy tickets.

MAISON DU ROI

This fanciful feast of neogothic arches, verdigris statues and mini-spires is bigger, darker and nearly 200 years younger than the surrounding guildhouses. Once a medieval bread-market, the current masterpiece dates from an 1873 rebuild and nowadays houses the **Brussels City Museum** (☎ 02-279 4350; www.bru city.be; adult/concession/Brusselscard €3/2.50/free; ☼ 10am-5pm Tue-Sun) whose old maps, architectural relics and paintings give a historical overview of the city. Don't miss Pieter Breugel the Elder's 1567 *Cortège de Noces* (Wedding Procession).

HOUSES & GUILDHALLS

The Grand Place's gorgeous buildings and guildhouses are listed here according to their street number and traditional name, along with their original guild where appropriate:

1: Maison des Boulangers – Bakers Now the café Le Roy d'Espagne. The gilded bronze bust above the door is Bakers' patron, St-Aubert.

2: La Brouette (The Wheelbarrow) – Grease-makers Notice the faint gold wheelbarrows above the door. The statue of St-Gilles was added in 1912.

4: Le Sac (The Bag) – Cabinet-makers Incredibly ornate.

5: La Louve (The She-Wolf) – Archers The golden phoenix rising from the ashes signifies the rebirth of the Grand Place after the 1695 bombardment.

6: Le Cornet (The Horn) – Boatmen Stern-shaped gable.

7: Le Renard (The Fox) – Haberdashers

8: L'Étoile (The Star) The square's smallest building, where city hero Everard 't Serclaes (p63) died in 1388. A fairly contemporary 'tradition' claims you'll garner good luck by rubbing a 1902 brass statue of Everard's reclining corpse. Holes have been worn into Everard's forearm from all the rubbing. The statue adorns the house's arcaded north wall in Rue Charles Buls, the road separating the house from the Hôtel de Ville. Also notice the lovely 1899 gilded art nouveau plaque dedicated to the city by its appreciative artists.

9: Le Cygne (The Swan) – Butchers In 1847 this lovely house hosted Karl Marx. Ironically it's now home to the square's finest upmarket restaurant.

10: L'Arbre d'Or (The Golden Tree) – Brewers Notice the hop plants climbing columns here. Still the Belgian brewers' headquarters, two atmospheric but small basement rooms now house a cursory **Brewery Museum** (☎ 02-511 4987; www.beerparadise.be; adult/Brusselscard €6/free, ☼ 10am-5pm daily Easter-Nov, noon-5pm Sat & Sun Dec-Easter). Entry includes a beer supped amid barrels and delightfully antiquated wooden brewers' tools. Tickets seem overpriced if you're paying but with the Brusselscard it's a great opportunity for a free drink.

13-19: Dukes' of Brabant Mansion Six 1698 houses behind a single palatial facade reworked in 1882. Had the imperial governor had his way after 1695, the whole square would have looked rather like this.

24-25: La Chaloupe d'Or (The Golden Boat) – Dressmakers Now a particularly splendid *grand café* whose upper storey rooms (when open) offer fine views across the square.

26-27: Le Pigeon – Artists Victor Hugo lived here during his exile from France in 1852.

South of Grand Place
MANNEKEN PIS

Don't be surprised to 'meet' Van Gogh posing on Rue Charles Buls, Brussels' most unashamedly tourist-oriented shopping street, whose chocolate and trinket shops lead the camera-toting hoards three blocks to the **Manneken Pis** (Map p70; cnr Rue de l'Étuve & Rue du Chêne). This fountain-statue of a little boy cheerfully taking a leak is comically tiny and a perversely perfect national symbol for surreal Belgium. More often than not the tiny statue's nakedness is largely hidden beneath a costume relevant to an anniversary, national day or local event. The costume diary is posted on http://ordre -manneken-pis.blogspot.com (in French). His ever-growing wardrobe is partly displayed at the Maison du Roi (opposite).

The present-day bronze Manneken Pis design was sculpted by Jerôme Duquesnoy in 1619, but it's not the original. A stone version named Little Julian stood here from the mid-14th century.

CHANSON & LACE

The excellent **Musée du Costume et de la Dentelle** (Map p70; Costume & Lace Museum; ☎ 02-213 4450; Rue de la Violette 12; adult/Brusselscard €3/free; ☼ 10am-12.30pm & 1.30-5pm Mon, Tue, Thu & Fri, 2-5pm Sat & Sun) has a fine collection. At the time of research, however,

> **OTHER PISSERS**
>
> The Manneken Pis (p77) has a much younger little squatting 'sister', the 20th-century **Jeanneke Pis** (see below; Map p70) and there's also **Zinneke** (see opposite; Map p70), a mongrel dog standing with cocked (if dry) leg as though to show his contempt for the surrounding Fashion District.
>
> Meanwhile, if you go to **Geraardsbergen** (p167) you'll find many locals who insists that *their* Manneken Pis is actually the original.

the museum building was almost entirely commandeered for a major exhibition on 1950s fashions. The **Jacques Brel Foundation** (Map p70; ☎ 02-511 1020; www.jacquesbrel.be; Place de la Vieille Halle aux Blés 11; adult/concession €8/5; ⏲ 10.30am-6.30pm Tue-Sat, last entry 5pm) is an archive centre and museum dedicated to Belgium's raspy-voiced chanson superstar (see the boxed text, p77).

Ilôt Sacré

GALERIES ST-HUBERT

When opened in 1847 by King Léopold I, the glorious **Galeries St-Hubert** (Map p70; Galerie du Roi, Galerie de la Reine, Galerie des Princes) formed Europe's very first shopping arcade. Many enticing shops lie behind its neoclassical glassed-in arches flanked by marble pilasters. Several eclectic *cafés* spill tables onto the gallery terrace, safe from rain beneath the glass roof. For a surreal introduction to Brussels' charms walk through Belgique Gourmande confectionery shop (Galerie de la Reine 17) and descend into some brick-vaulted subterranean tunnels. Here a soundtrack of jazz and dripping water announces **Brussels on Stage** (Map p70; ☎ 02-502 0973; www.bruxelles-enscene.be; adult/child/Brusselscard €6/5/4.50; ⏲ 10am-5pm). Imaginative ideas, from iris pools to sliced-open trams, illustrate the city's history and culture but when we last visited some scenes were broken and 'Manneken Pis alley' had run dry.

RUE DES BOUCHERS

Northwest of the *galeries* are uniquely colourful Rue and Petite Rue des Bouchers, a pair of narrow alleys jam-packed with pavement tables, pyramids of lemons and iced displays of fish and crustacea. It's gloriously photogenic and space heaters keep things working year-round but before being enticed in by the waiter-touts, read the boxed text, p98.

Up a dead-end alley here you'll find the Manneken Pis's recently re-plumbed 'sister' **Jeanneke Pis** (Map p70; Impasse de la Fidélité) squatting behind locked railings (see the boxed text, left).

Returning towards the Grand Place, don't miss peeping inside Toone (p108) and into the wonderful, age-old biscuit shop **Dandoy** (Map p70; ☎ 02-511 0326; Rue au Beurre 31), full of splendid old moulds for *speculaas*/*speculoos* (traditional spiced biscuit) figures.

Bourse

The **Bourse** (Map p70; Place de la Bourse) is Belgium's 1873 stock exchange building. You can't enter but its grandiose neoclassical facade is brilliantly festooned with friezes and sculptures, reclining nudes, lunging horses and a multitude of allegorical figures. Some of the work is by Rodin, then a young apprentice sculptor. Directly outside, an archaeological site called **Bruxella1238** (⏲ from 10.15am 1st Wed of each month) has uncovered the scanty remains of a former Franciscan convent that was bombarded into ruins in 1695. Most of the site is visible by peeping through the glass windows set into the pavement roughly outside the Cirio *café* (p103).

Five of Brussels' most archetypal and historic *cafés* are within stumbling distance of the Bourse, three of them hidden away down minuscule medieval passageways (p103).

The nearby **Église St-Nicolas** (Church of St-Nicolas; Map p70; Rue au Beurre 1; ⏲ 8am-6.30pm Mon-Fri, 9am-6pm Sat, 9am-7.30pm Sun) is a pint-sized edifice as old as Brussels itself. What really makes it notable is its virtual invisibility – the exterior is almost totally encrusted with shops. Appropriately enough, it's dedicated to the patron saint of merchants.

St-Géry

Surrounding Place St-Géry you'll find a lively, compact area of popular *cafés* and good-value Asian restaurants. Until 1799 the square had been dominated by a medieval Gothic church. But it was demolished under the antireligious French regime and replaced by a market square featuring a curious pyramidal monolith-fountain. In 1881 a superb neo-Renaissance brick-and-wrought-iron meat market, the **Halles St-Géry** (Map p70; www.hallessaintgery.be), was built right around this monument. The market lay derelict for much of the 1980s but has since been beautifully renovated and is now a combined bar-*café*, night club and exhibition space.

JACQUES BREL

Born in Schaerbeek in 1929, Belgium's greatest 20th-century singer started his career in 1952 in the Brussels cabaret La Rose Noire. The following year he headed to Paris, where he mixed with songwriters and fellow artists including Édith Piaf. His first record was released in 1954 and he rapidly became an idol. His passionate, transcendent songs were performed with astounding intensity. As one fan described it 'he sang like a boxer and usually lost a kilo during each performance'. The wide-ranging themes of his songs include love, spirituality, nostalgia, the hypocrisy of the bourgeoisie and beautiful evocations of Belgium's contradictions. Despite the latter, he was often thought of as French, and became a 'French' film star in the late 1960s. In 1973 he quit performing to sail around the world. He spent the last two years of his life in the remote Marquesas Islands of French Polynesia, where he's now buried near French painter Paul Gauguin, having died of lung cancer in 1978.

Top five Brel songs:

- *Bruxelles* – upbeat nostalgic favourite in which he somehow gets away with turning the capital into a verb (approximately translated as *'That was the time when Brussels Brusseled'*)
- *Ne me Quitte Pas* – the classic tear-jerker
- *Madeleine* – don't be fooled by the jolly banjo sound…waiting for a Brussels tram has never sounded so poignant
- *Le Plat Pays* – rain, fog and dismal Belgian landscapes are somehow rendered as poetic idylls
- *Les Flamands* – light-heartedly mocks the po-faced lifestyle of the Flemish even though his family was originally of Flemish descent

Black steel gates beside the bistro Le Lion St-Géry lead into a private (but often open) courtyard in which one branch of the mostly covered Senne River has been uncovered along with a reconstructed historical mooring point. The stream is bridged by the vaulted 1811 brick, neogothic **Au Lion d'Or** building. The courtyard also offers interesting views of the bulb-spired church, **Église Notre-Dame des Riches Claires**.

Fashion District

You don't have to be a fashion hound to enjoy the quirky facades, shops and idiosyncrasies of this compact area that neatly divides St-Géry and Ste-Catherine. Heading northwest from the Bourse, you'll pass the magnificent wrought-iron frontage of the Beursschouwburg (see p106), a cultural centre originally built in 1885 as a grand brasserie. A block north, ponder who would actually want to sit on the translucent plastic chairs displayed on the white-lit disco flooring at **Kartell** (Map p70; Rue Antoine Dansaert 2) furniture shop. Veer west here on Rue des Chartreux to admire the flamboyant art nouveau ironwork over the entrance to Brussels' classic chess-*café*, Le Greenwich (see p104). Nearby is the surreal lighting specialist **Espace Bizarre** (Map p70; www.espacebizarre.com; Rue des

Chartreux 19), the first place to look should you need a lamp in the form of a life-sized horse. On the next corner is a typically Brussels-style piece of street humour, the statue of a cock-legged dog Zinneke (ie 'Mongrel', see the boxed text opposite).

The main area of fashion boutiques lies two short blocks north on Rue Antoine Dansaert. Stijl (p110) and secondhand specialist Idiz Bogam (p110) are much less daunting to enter than the hallowed boutiques of **Annemie Verbeke** (Map p70; Rue Antoine Dansaert 64) or ring-the-bell **Martin Margiela** (Map p70; Rue de Flandre 114). Window shoppers might find **Linders** (Map p70; Rue Antoine Dansaert 84) more intriguing: it specialises in the archaic-looking white-ruffed black 'togas' still worn by top Belgian lawyers. Across the road, designer eyewear specialist **Hoet** (Map p70; Antoine Dansaert 97) has an extraordinary line in silver filigree eyeshades. Do look up to admire the Parisian-style gables above. And look back to the upper facade of the outwardly uninspired KBC bank building to notice an unexpected frieze of bananas. A block west, **Atelier Christophe Coppens** (Map pp68-9; ☎ 02-538 0813; www.christophecoppens.com; Nouveau Marché aux Grains 23) is perhaps the most visually remarkable of all the boutiques, a stage-like affair on which the 'performer' is a circular

BRUSSELS

white-curtained changing space, the 'audience' neat rows of hats and scarves.

Ste-Catherine

It's hard to imagine today, but fishing boats once sailed up the now-invisible River Senne, mooring in the heart of Ste-Catherine, which was for centuries a major fish market. Although the river has been covered over since 1870, the area's reputation for fish persists and the main reason you're likely to visit is to choose from the numerous well-regarded seafood restaurants around Pl Ste-Catherine. There's also a curious mixture of cheaper bars and eateries sprinkled along Rue de Flandre.

The area sports two notable if smog-blackened churches. **Église Ste-Catherine** (Place Ste-Catherine; ⊗ rarely open) must be one of the only religious buildings that positively encourages folks to urinate on its walls (there's a 'pissoir' on its northwest flank). Inside is a black statue of the Virgin and Child that Protestants once hurled into the Senne (1744) but was found again 'miraculously' floating on a chunk of turf. The 1657 **Église St-Jean-Baptiste au Béguinage** (Map p70; Place du Béguinage) is a Flemish baroque masterpiece designed by Luc Fayd'Herbe, a student of Rubens. It's often cited as Belgium's most beautiful church but is rarely open.

Boxed in on three sides and incongruously dwarfed by the back of a Novotel Hotel is the ivy draped **Tour Noire** (Place du Samedi), a remnant of Brussels' original city wall.

Other minor curiosities include the **Pigeon Soldat memorial** commemorating the brave carrier pigeons of WWI. Beside the monolithic **Anspach Fountain**, notice the bronze crocodiles and lizards set to leap out of the water…at least when the pool has any water.

Rue Neuve Area

Pedestrianised **Rue Neuve** (Map p70) is central Brussels' busiest shopping street but certainly not its loveliest. To escape the lacklustre '70s architecture, meditate awhile in the 18th-century **Église Notre-Dame du Finistère** (Map p70; ⊗ 9am-6.30pm), whose great baroque interior features a remarkable 1758 altarpiece, its giant wooden canopy held aloft by flying cherubs. The neoclassical **Place des Martyrs** should eventually look pretty grand once the glacially slow renovations are finally complete. Already one terraced café has started 'reclaiming' parts of this square that had, till recently, been eerily forgotten. At its centre is a monument to 467 people who died in the 1830 revolution. The haphazard spark to the revolution (see the boxed text, p107) had been lit by excitable opera-goers leaving the La Monnaie/De Munt, still Brussels' most prestigious cultural venue (see p107).

Cathedral Area

CATHÉDRALE DES STS-MICHEL & GUDULE

Host to coronations and royal weddings, Brussels' grand, twin-towered **cathedral** (Map pp68-9; www.cathedralestmichel.be; Place Sainte-Gudule; admission/treasury free/€2.50; ⊗ cathedral 8am-6pm, treasury 10am-12.30pm & 2-5pm Mon-Fri, till 3.45pm Sat, closed Sun morning) bears at least a passing resemblance to Paris' much better known Notre Dame. Begun in 1226, the construction took some 300 years. Stained-glass windows flood the soaring nave with light while column-saints brandish gilded tools. An enormous wooden pulpit, sculpted by Antwerp artist Hendrik Verbruggen, sees Adam and Eve driven out of Eden by fearsome skeletons. To climb the cathedral towers (10am on the second Saturday of each month, €5), sign up a day or two ahead.

MONEY MUSEUM

Unexpectedly absorbing, the 15-room **National Bank Museum** (Map pp68-9; ☎ 02-221 2206; www.nbbmuseum.be; Rue du Bois Sauvage 10; adult/student/child/Brusselscard €5/4/free/free; ⊗ 10am-6pm Tue-Sun) is far more than just a coin collection. Well-presented exhibits trace the very concept of money all the way from cowrie shells to credit cards. Entrance is free at weekends, on Wednesday afternoon and throughout summer.

COLONNE DU CONGRÈS

Brussels' 25m-tall version of Nelson's Column is an 1850s monolith (Map pp68-9) topped by a gilded statue of King Léopold I. It commemorates the Belgian constitution of 1831. The four female figures around its base represent the four constitutionally upheld freedoms of religion, association, education and the press. The last of these encouraged Victor Hugo, Karl Marx and others to visit Belgium back when such freedoms were much more restricted in other parts of Europe. Between two bronze lions, an eternal flame honours Belgian victims of the two world wars.

CENTRE BELGE DE LA BANDE DESSINÉE

Though the Hergé Museum (p220) is much more memorable, the **Belgian Comic Strip Centre**

(Map pp68-9; ☎ 02-219 1980; www.comicscenter.net; Rue des Sables 20; adult/concession/Brusselscard €7.50/5/free; ☺ 10am-6pm Tue-Sun) offers a definitive overview of the country's vibrant comic-strip culture (see p43). Even if you're not excited by the 'Ninth Art', do peep inside the impressive 1906 art nouveau building, a Victor Horta (see the boxed text, p89) classic with wrought-iron superstructure and a glass roof. You don't have to pay an entrance fee to enjoy the central hallway or to drink a coffee (€2.20) at the attached *café*.

Place Royale Area

A short stroll up the Mont des Arts steps from the Grand Place area, Place Royale forms the heart of Brussels' regal Upper Town area. The neoclassical square features a bold equestrian **statue of Godefroid de Bouillon**, the crusader knight who very briefly became the first European 'king' of Jerusalem in 1099 (see the boxed text, p239). It's flanked with fascinating museums and has a curious secret lurking beneath (see Coudenberg, p82). North of the Royal Palace is a spacious formal **park** dotted with classical statues.

ROYAL PALACE

When the king takes his summer holidays you can visit his official workplace, the 19th-century **Palais Royal** (Map pp68-9; ☎ 02-551 2020; www.monarchy.be; Place des Palais; admission free; ☺ 10.30am-4pm Tue-Sun late Jul-early Sep). It's an expansive pile that looks something like a less-inspired cousin to Buckingham Palace. Although officially residence to the Belgian monarchs, a king hasn't actually lived here since Léopold III decamped to Laeken (p90) after 1935. The first few rooms might feel a little soulless but the throne room is impressively overloaded with chandeliers and gilt. And for a breathtaking climax you end up in the former 'Congo Room'. Here artist Jan Fabre has created an extraordinary iridescent wonder by covering the ceiling with the wing-cases of 1.4 million Thai jewel beetles.

BELVUE

Attached to the Royal Palace's western end, **Musée BELvue** (Map pp68-9; ☎ 02-545 0800; www.belvue.be; Place des Palais 7; adult/senior/youth/child/Brusselscard €5/4/3/free/free; ☺ 10am-5pm) introduces Belgian history through a series of documents, images and videos. There are masses to take in and the computerised map of Europe's changing borderlines (morphing year by year 1000AD to 1830) is especially engrossing. However, unless you're already fairly familiar with the events covered you might be left with as many questions as answers.

COMIC-STRIP MURALS

Over 40 comic-strip murals currently enliven alleys and thoroughfares throughout the old city centre, with more added year after year. Most are mapped on www.brusselscomics.com/en/route_bd.cfm and a more detailed free brochure is available from Brussels International (p76). Moseying past a few of these cheery murals makes a great excuse to explore less-visited neighbourhoods. Some favourites:

■ **Tibet & Duchateau** (Map p70; Rue du Bon Secours 9) – very effectively sees a life-sized figure teetering towards a trompe l'œil window

■ **Tintin** (Map p70; Rue de l'Étuve)

■ **Broussaille** (Map p70; Rue du Marché au Charbon) – depicts a young couple arm-in-arm. The original 1991 version showed a couple of very ambiguous sex that the neighbouring gay establishments used to promote the quarter. However, a 1999 repaint seemed to give the black-haired figure a more feminine hairstyle, earrings and (slightly) bigger breasts. Creeping homophobia or honest mistake? Nobody knows.

■ **Peeping Policeman** (Map pp72-3; Rue Haute) – Hergé character uses the terrace end brilliantly for a little spying

■ **Manneken Pis Displaced** (Map p70; Rue de Flandre)

■ **Néron** (Map p70; Pl St-Géry) – a human stack reaching for the birds

■ **Le Chat** (Map pp72-3; Blvd du Midi) – bricklaying himself into place

BRUSSELS' ART NOUVEAU MASTERPIECES

Brussels excels in art nouveau architecture. In the city centre don't miss the Old England Building (below) or the magnificent *café* Falstaff (p103). Many other top examples are scattered fairly widely but there are decent concentrations of fine facades in St-Gilles (p88) and Ixelles (p88), where a classic art nouveau house hosts a museum dedicated to maestro architect Victor Horta (p89). Near the Cinquantenaire monument, the loveliest of all art nouveau townhouses is the Maison Cauchie (p87). In Schaerbeek Maison Autrique (p88) appeals to some Horta aficionados, while drinking at De Ultieme Hallucinatie (p88) offers tantalising glimpses of some marvellous art nouveau interiors. The famous Palais Stoclet (p92), now Unesco-listed, is undergoing extensive restoration.

ARAU tours (p92) can get you into some normally closed gems including the **Hôtel Solvay** (Map pp72-3; Ave Louise 224) and Hôtel Van Eetvelde (p87), whose facades barely hint at the wonders within. Brussels International tourist office and Horta Museum sell the map-guide *Brussels: Living Art Nouveau* (€3). An extensive if slightly dated art nouveau brochure and map can be downloaded from www.brusselsartnouveau.be.

COUDENBERG

Coudenberg Hill (now Place Royale) was the site of Brussels' original 12th-century castle. Over several centuries this was transformed into one of Europe's most elegant and powerful palaces, most notably as the 16th-century residence of Holy Roman Emperor Charles V (Charles Quint; p27). Around the palace, courtiers and nobles in turn built fine mansions. However, the vast complex was destroyed in a catastrophic 1731 fire. Its ruins were eventually levelled to create newly laid out Place Royale but beneath street level the basic structure of the palace's long-hidden lower storeys remains. Whole stretches of medieval street layout are now discernable thanks to considerable archaeological work. The **Coudenberg** (adult/senior/youth/child/Brusselscard €5/4/3/free/free, combined with BELvue €8/5/4/free/free) subterranean site is entered from BELvue. You'll emerge near the Old England Building.

OLD ENGLAND BUILDING

This 1899 former department store is an art nouveau showpiece with a superlative black facade all aswirl in wrought iron and arched windows. It contains Brussels' **Musical Instrument Museum** (Musée des Instruments de Musique; Map pp68-9; ☎ 02-545 0130; www.mim.fgov.be; Rue Montagne de la Cour 2; adult/concession/Brusselscard €5/3.50/free; ⏱ 9.30am-4.45pm Tue-Fri, 10am-4.45pm Sat & Sun, last entry 4pm), one of the world's biggest collections of historic, modern and world instruments. Stand near each exhibit to automatically hear the instrument's sound played on your audioguide. And don't miss the rooftop *café* for a superb city panorama.

MUSÉES ROYAUX DES BEAUX-ARTS

Brussels' foremost **art gallery** (Map pp68-9; ☎ 02-508 3211; www.fine-arts-museum.be; Rue de la Régence 3; permanent collection adult/senior/student/Brusselscard €8/5/2/free, Magritte Museum €8/5/2/free, audio-guide €4, combination ticket €13/9/3/free, temporary exhibitions €9/6.50/2.50/9; ⏱ 9.30am-5pm Tue-Fri, 10am-5pm Sat & Sun) has a truly stupendous collection. Sadly, by no means is all of it currently on display.

Permanent Collection

With some 30 rooms closed indefinitely for asbestos removal, you can currently see only the highlights of the superb pre-18th-century collection. It's particularly strong on surreal and macabre 16th-century masterpieces (Bosch, Dirk Bouts etc) and includes a room full of Breugel. You're then swept into the pot-bellied pomposity of Counter-Reformation art with numerous gigantic Rubens and Jordaens canvases and plenty more 17th- and 18th-century fare.

Way down in the bowels of the gallery, the 'modern' art section starts with 19th-century work but is notable for its wealth of fine early 20th-century pieces by Belgian artists plus the odd Seurat, Dali and Miro.

Magritte Museum

A separate ticket is required for the gallery's beautifully presented **Magritte Museum** (www .musee-magritte-museum.be). Opened in June 2009, it has the world's largest collection of the surrealist pioneer's paintings and drawings. Watch his style develop from colourful Braque-style cubism in 1920 through a Dali-esque phase and a late-1940s period of Kandinsky-like brushwork to his trademark bowler hats of the 1960s. Regular screenings of a very professional 52-minute documentary give interesting insights into the artist's unconventionally conventional life (see the boxed text, below).

Sablon

The Sablon is a cobbled square whose *cafés*, antique shops and *chocolatiers* are typically frequented by the see-and-be-seen Brussels upper crust. Surrounding lanes sport plenty more intriguing antique shops and the square itself hosts a Sunday antique market. The Sablon's large, flamboyantly Gothic church, the **Église Notre-Dame du Sablon** (Map pp72-3; Rue de la Régence; ⓨ 9am-7pm), started life as the 1304 archers' guild chapel. However, a century later it had to be massively enlarged to cope with droves of pilgrims attracted by the supposed healing powers of its Madonna statue. The statue was procured in 1348 by way of an audacious theft from a church in Antwerp – apparently by a vision-motivated husband-and-wife team in a rowing boat! It has long since gone but a boat behind the pulpit commemorates the curious affair that went on to inspire Brussels' original Ommegang (p17).

ÉGLISE NOTRE-DAME DE LA CHAPELLE

Brussels' oldest surviving **church** (Map pp72-3; Place de la Chapelle; admission/guide-pamphlet free/€3; ⓨ 9am 7pm Jun Sep, 9am 6pm Oct-May) now curi-

ously incorporates the decapitated tower of the 1134 original as the central section of a bigger Gothic edifice. Behind the palm-tree pulpit, look on the wall above a carved confessional to find a small memorial to 'Petro Brevgello', ie Pieter Breugel the Elder (see the boxed text, p84), who once lived in the nearby Marolles.

Nearby, the barely used Bruxelles-Chapelle commuter train station is topped by a skate area and hosts **Recyclart** (Map pp72-3; ☎ 02-502 5734; www.recyclart.be; Rue des Ursulines 25), an urban regeneration project hosting anything from debates to art to cutting-edge DJ parties.

PLACE DU PETIT SABLON

About 200m uphill from Place du Grand Sablon, this charming little garden (Map pp72–3) is ringed by 48 bronze statuettes representing the medieval guilds. Standing huddled on a fountain plinth like two actors from a Shakespearean drama are Counts Egmont and Hoorn, popular city leaders who were beheaded on the Grand Place in 1568 for defying Spanish rule. The site of Egmont's grand former residence lies behind.

Palais de Justice

Larger than St Peter's in Rome, this colossal 2.6 hectare complex of **law courts** (Map pp72-3; ☎ 02-508 6410; Place Poelaert; admission free; ⓨ 8am-5pm

---

MR MAGRITTE

Celebrated by a fine new museum (opposite), René Magritte (1898–1967) was Belgium's most prominent surrealist artist. He's best known for a simple painting consisting of a pipe and the words 'this is not a pipe' (in French). The joke is recycled endlessly by Belgian newspapers, advertisers and even on the door of one of Magritte's favourite drinking holes, La Fleur en Papier Doré (p105), whose *café* walls still preserve some of his scribbles.

But many of his works go much deeper, blending images of the ordinary with those of the subconscious. One fascinating element in Magritte's personality was his apparent conventionality. Unlike many fellow artists he was sociable, happily married and unimpressed by the bohemian lifestyles of the Paris surrealist set. From 1930 the Magrittes moved into the very ordinary suburban house that's now Brussels' 'other' **Musée Magritte** (Map pp66-7; ☎ 02-428 2626; www.magrittemuseum. be; Rue Esseghem 135; adult/concession €6/5; ⓨ 10am-6pm Wed-Sun), exhibiting his passport, photos, furniture and, predictably enough, a pipe. Here Magritte painted most of his famous works – setting up his easel in the kitchen and painting while wearing a three-piece business suit. The kitchen window offered a view of a postage-stamp garden and a brick wall that was Magritte's 'looking glass into another world'.

Die-hard Magritte fans can also visit Magritte's bourgeois 1911 **childhood home** (☎ 071-244 926; chatelet-tourisme@skynet.be; Rue des Gravelles 95, Châtelet; ⓨ sporadic) in the sorry ex-mining town of Châtelet (Map p209) outside Charleroi, now a venue for very occasional art exhibits. Or admire (from outside) the house in Lessines (p213), where Magritte was born.

THE BREUGEL FAMILY

Spell it Breugel or Breughel, this family dominated Flemish art in the late 16th and early 17th centuries. Pieter Breugel the Elder (c 1525–69) was undeniably the family's master. His work ranged from powerful landscapes to satirical allegories likened to those of Hieronymus Bosch. But he's best remembered for his quirky scenes of contemporary peasant life woven around portentous religious events and myths. Many of his works were painted in the step-gabled brick house now nicknamed **Breugel House** (Map pp72-3; Rue Haute 132), which can be visited, but only by arranging a private guided tour through Brussels International (p76). Book way ahead.

Breugel's first son, Pieter Breughel the Younger (1564–1638) might have added an h but he largely copied his father's style, earning the nickname 'Hell Breughel' for his preoccupation with scenes of damnation. Contrastingly, second son Jan Breughel (1568–1625) spent most of his artistic life in Antwerp painting sensitive landscapes and flower arrangements, leading to his sobriquet, 'Velvet'.

Mon-Fri) was the world's biggest building when constructed (1866–83). Designed to evoke the temples of the Egyptian pharaohs, it was sited on the hill dominating the working-class Marolles as an intimidating symbol of law and order. When its architect Joseph Poelaert went insane and died during its construction, legends promptly suggested he'd been struck down by the witchcraft of the numerous Marolles residents evicted to make way for the building. The term *skieven* (twisted) *architekt* remains a characteristic insult in the old Bruxellois dialect (right). However, some claim that the term dates back much earlier to when the City Hall's tower was built off-centre in the 15th century (p76).

While the labyrinthine Palais de Justice is undoubtedly grand, it is not easy to secure. Indeed in several high-profile cases criminals have managed to abscond from its precincts.

Behind the building a pavement **terrace** offers wide panoramas over the Brussels rooftops, with the Atomium and Koekelberg Basilica as stars of the skyline show. A glass **elevator** (Pl Breugel, Rue de l'Epée; free; 7.30am-11.45pm) leads down into the Marolles.

Marolles

Brussels' once resolutely working-class quarter, the Marolles has partly shed its proletarian image with a rash of intimate restaurants and funky interior-design shops setting up along the main streets, Rue Haute and Rue Blaes. Nonetheless, pockets of original Bruxellois character can still be found, notably around the **Place du Jeu-de-Balle**, home to a classic early morning flea market (see p109). At a few of the down-market *cafés* here you might overhear people speaking in the earthy Bruxellois dialect

(see boxed text, below). Note that despite the name, Jeu-de-Balle (aka *balle-pelotte*; p46) is no longer played here. Further west, Sunday's **Marché du Midi** (6am-1pm Sun) is Brussels' biggest market with a colourful, predominantly North African and Mediterranean feel.

PORTE DE HAL

For centuries Brussels was surrounded by a grand 8km fortress wall. It was partially demolished in the 1790s then removed altogether on Napoleon's orders in 1810. Well, almost. In fact a few isolated remnants survived, including one of the seven very imposing 14th-century gatehouse towers that the

BRUXELLOIS

The old Marolles-Brussels dialect, Bruxellois, is a curious mixture of French, Dutch and Walloon with elements of Spanish and Yiddish thrown in. These days very few people beyond Place du Jeu-de-Balle actually speak the full dialect. Nonetheless, certain Bruxellois words are used, consciously or otherwise, to punctuate local French whether for comic effect or because no better word exists. Classic examples that hint at the playful Bruxellois character:

- *blèter* – to snivel, complain
- *in stoemelings* – sneakily, on the quiet
- *papzak* – fatso
- *zatlap* – habitual drunkard
- *zieverair* – time-waster, idiot
- *zieverer* – to mess around

French preserved for use as a military prison. This **Porte de Hal** (Blvd du Midi; adult/concession/child/Brusselscard €5/4/free/free; ☺ 9.30am-5pm Tue-Fri, 10am-5pm Sat & Sun, last entry 4.15pm) was converted into a museum in 1847 and romantically embellished with statuary, windows and neogothic turrets thereafter. Today an audio-guide leads you round its decent little city-history museum and exhibition of armour. Then there's the opportunity to climb for views to the 6th-storey battlements. Despite recent landscaping of surrounding gardens, the tower's fairy-tale appearance jars with its location on a traffic island within the inner-city ring road.

Forest (Vorst)

Forest is a completely misleading name for this run-down, inner-city *commune* dominated by a vast car factory. It's well off the usual tourist track, but in a converted former brewery building towards Bruxelles-Midi (tram 82), you'll find **Wiels** (Map pp66-7; ☎ 02-340 0050; www.wiels.org; Ave Van Volxemlaan 354; adult/concession/Brusselscard €6/4/free; ☺ noon-7pm Wed-Sat, 11am-6pm Sun), the capital's new centre for contemporary art exhibitions. Entry is free on Wednesday evenings.

EU Area

Along the thundering thoroughfares Rue de la Loi and Rue Belliard, tragically bland office blocks are packed so close together they form dark concrete canyons. To the east, EU office buildings cut a brutally modern gash through a once attractive neighbourhood behind Bruxelles-Luxembourg station. But it's not all horror. The EU Area (Map p86) also has lovely gardens, fountains and some fine early 20th-century houses notably around Sq Marie-Louise.

EU PARLIAMENT

The European Parliament looks like a gigantic greenhouse for triffids. It's nicknamed 'Caprice des Dieux' (Whim of the Gods), not because it's divinely inspired, but because its facade resembles a so-named French cheese – or at least the cheese's blue-oval box. Visitors can sit in on parliamentary sessions in the huge debating chamber (the 'hemicycle'), or take free multilingual audio-guided **tours** (☺ 10am & 3pm Mon-Thu, 10am Fri) when parliament's not meeting. Start at the **visitor's centre** (Map p86; ☎ 02-284 3457; Rue Wiertz 43).

From central Brussels, access is easiest by suburban train to **Bruxelles-Luxembourg** (15 minutes, four times an hour on weekdays). It's Belgium's oldest train station, though only a token section of stone facade remains of the 19th-century original – a startling contrast to the new modernist station (with Hergé mural) and to the ghetto of businesslike EU offices that back it. These line a central concourse that's as impersonal and charmless as a Le Corbusier sketch.

PARC LÉOPOLD

Steep-sloping Parc Léopold was Brussels Zoo till 1880 and now forms an unexpectedly pleasant oasis hidden away just behind the EU Parliament. Fine century-old buildings like the attractive **Solvay Library** and **Jacqmain School** are closed to the public and the **Musée Antoine Wiertz**, displaying Wiertz's frenzied 19th-century hell scenes is under long-term reconstruction. But the Musée des Sciences Naturelles (below) alone justifies the trip. Afterwards you can retire to *cafés* on Place Luxembourg or take the chip-challenge at Maison Antoine (Pl Jourdan) – do you think they're really Brussels' best?

Musée des Sciences Naturelles

This inspirational **Museum of Natural Sciences** (Map p86; ☎ 02-627 4238; www.naturalsciences.be; Rue Vautier 29; adult/concession/child/Brusselscard €7/6/4.50/free; ☺ 9.30am-4.45pm Tue-Fri, 10am-6pm Sat & Sun) may well be the best of its type anywhere.

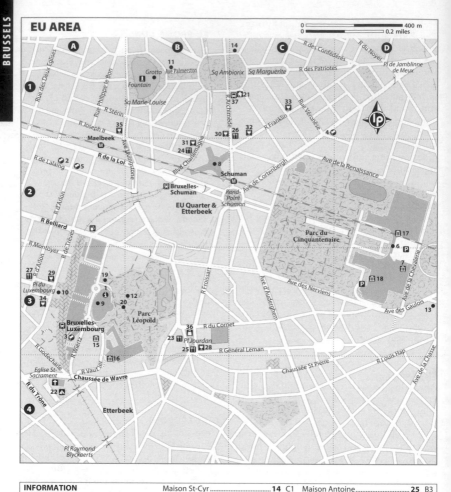

EU AREA

Thought-provoking and highly interactive, the museum has far more than the usual selection of stuffed animals. The undoubted highlight is a unique 'family' of iguanodons – 10m-high dinosaurs found in a Hainaut coal mine back in 1878. A computer simulation shows the mudslide that might have covered them, sandboxes allow you to play dino hunter and multilingual videos give a wonderfully nuanced debate on recent palaeontology. Was T-Rex a giant chicken? You decide! Other delights include a cutaway living beehive, a whale hall and a walk-through Antarctic 'tunnel'.

THE EU COMMISSION
The European Commission, the EU's sprawling bureaucracy, is centred on the vast, four-winged **Berlaymont building** (Map p86; Rue de la Loi 200). Built in 1967, it's striking but by no means beautiful, despite a billion-euro rebuild between 1991 and 2004 that removed asbestos-tainted building materials. Information panels dotted around the building give insight into the history of this neighbourhood and Brussels' international role. From Bruxelles-Central take Metro 1A to Schuman or a handy suburban train to Brussels-Schuman (12 minutes).

Cinquantenaire & Around
The **Cinquantenaire** (Map p86) is a triumphal arch reminiscent of Paris' *Arc de Triomphe*. It was designed to celebrate Belgium's 50th anniversary ('cinquantenaire') in 1880 but took so long to build that by that date only a temporary plaster version was standing. The full beast wasn't completed till 1905. In summer, the arcade forms the curious backdrop to a drive-in cinema screen, while around it are several grand-scale museums. Access is easiest by Metro 1A to Schuman or Mérode.

MUSÉE ROYAL DE L'ARMÉE ET D'HISTOIRE MILITAIRE
Getting onto the top of the Cinquantenaire Arcade is possible if you visit this free **museum** (Map p86; ☎ 02-737 7811; www.klm-mra.be; Parc du Cinquantenaire 3; admission/audio-guide free/€3; ☒ 9-11.45am & 1-4.30pm Tue-Sun). It boasts a truly staggering collection of all things military dating back to Belgian independence.

AUTOWORLD
Across the big, cobbled square (free parking), **Autoworld** (Map p86; ☎ 02-736 4165; www.autoworld

<table>
<tr><td>

INSIDE INFORMATION

Brussels' EU world is often viewed by outsiders as a faceless bureaucracy. Well, perhaps it is. But it is also a community of real people from 27 real countries, a remarkable opportunity to share culture and understanding that is all too often missed. The interesting scheme, **Tof People** (www.brusselstofpeople .eu), aims to overcome the inertia by putting you in touch with a whole range of Brussels-based folks from all over the union.

</td></tr>
</table>

.be; adult/concession/Brusselscard €6/4.70/free, camera €2.50; ☒ 10am-6pm Apr-Sep, 10am-5pm Oct-Mar) displays one of Europe's biggest ensembles of vintage and 20th-century cars. Among all the four-wheelers, notice the Harley Davidson the present king gave to Belgium's police force when he decided his biker days were over.

MUSÉES ROYAUX D'ART ET D'HISTOIRE
Few Belgians realise there's a treasure trove lurking within this cavernous **Antiquities Museum** (Map p86; ☎ 02-741 7211; www.kmkg-mrah.be; Parc du Cinquantenaire 10; adult/concession/child/Brusselscard €5/4/free/free; ☒ 9.30am-5pm Tue-Fri, 10am-5pm Sat & Sun). The astonishingly rich, global collection ranges from Ancient Egyptian sarcophagi to Meso-American masks, to icons to wooden bicycles. It's worth having a clear idea what you want to see before coming or the sheer scope can prove overwhelming. Visually attractive spaces include the medieval stone carvings set around a neogothic cloister and the soaring Corinthian columns (convincing fibreglass props) that bring atmosphere to an original 420 AD mosaic from Roman Syria. Labelling is in French and Dutch so the English-language audio-guide (€3 extra) is worth considering.

ART NOUVEAU HOUSES
Brussels' greatest art nouveau gem is the **Maison Cauchie** (Map p86; ☎ 02-733 8684; www.cauchie. be; Rue des Francs 5; adult/child €5/free; ☒ 10am-1pm & 2-5.30pm 1st Sat & Sun of each month, plus 6pm-8.30pm most evenings May-Aug), whose stunning 1905 facade is lavishly adorned with stylised female figures. It looks like a Klimt painting transformed into architecture. When it's open, wait in a gallery of Cauchie's expressionist paintings and read about the building's miraculous 1980s salvation until the next tour (around 30 minutes)

is ready to take you into the fabulous sgraffito-adorned rooms upstairs.

Currently hidden by renovation scaffolding, the narrow **Maison St-Cyr** (Map p86; Sq Ambiorix 11; ☙ closed) has a classic 1903 facade that's remarkable for its naturalistic copper-framed window, filigree balconies and a circular upper portal. It's crowned by a devil-may-care topknot of extravagantly twisted ironwork.

A great highlight of an ARAU tour (p92) is getting into the otherwise closed **Hôtel Van Eetvelde** (Map p86; Ave Palmerston 2-4). While the outside of this building is not Brussels' most gripping, its interior is a Horta masterpiece studded with exotic timbers and sporting a central glass dome infused with African-inspired plant motifs. Its owner, Baron Van Eetvelde, was at that time Minister for the Congo and, not coincidentally, the country's highest-paid civil servant.

Schaerbeek

The rather seedy area around the **Gare du Nord** (Bruxelles-Nord) is a weird human jumble. Motorists cruise lasciviously past prostitutes in their 'pink windows' while local Muslim ladies pass by obliviously, dressed in fully scarfed modesty.

Looking east along Rue Royale your gaze is unavoidably drawn to the very distinctive **Église Ste-Marie** (Map pp8-9; Pl de la Reine), an octagonal 19th-century church in neo-Byzantine style, replete with buttresses and a star-studded central cupola. Nearby *café* **De Ultieme Hallucinatie** (Map pp68-9; www.ultiemehallucinatie.be; Rue Royale 316; beer from €2.20; ☙ 10.30am-2am Mon-Sat) is a classic townhouse refitted with art nouveau interiors in 1904. The front salon is truly marvellous, with original lamps, brass radiator-covers and stained glass. The brasserie area (behind) that's publicly accessible is much less interesting but buying a drink earns you a walk-through glimpse of the highlights.

The 1901 former food market **Halles de Schaerbeek** (☎ 02-218 2107; www.halles.be; Rue Royale Ste-Marie 22) is a great example of glass and wrought-iron industrial architecture that's been restored as an arts venue.

Horta fans may enjoy his 1893 **Maison Autrique** (☎ 02-215 6600; www.autrique.be; Chaussée de Haecht 266; adult/senior/concession €6/4.30/3; ☙ noon-5.30pm Wed-Sun). It shows little luxury or extravagance but many design elements hint at the art nouveau wave that was just about to sweep Brussels to architectural glory. It hosts regularly changing exhibitions and the website offers an interesting downloadable walking guide to the neighbourhood (www.autrique.be/docs/promenade/plan.en.pdf).

Trams 92 or 93 pass near all of the above.

St-Gilles (Sint-Gillis)

One of Brussels' overlooked architectural wonders is **Saint-Gilles town hall** (Maison Communale de Saint-Gilles; Map pp72-3; ☎ 02-536 0211; www.stgilles.iris net.be; Pl Maurice van Meenen), a splendid Napoleon III style palace sporting a soaring brick belfry dotted with gilt statuary. Occasional exhibitions and a major **Comics Festival** (www.comics festivalbelgium.com; ☙ early Oct) are held here but otherwise visits are only by arrangement, so you can't be sure of seeing the wedding hall ceiling, painted by Belgian symbolist artist, Fernand Khnopff.

The surrounding area has a couple of great *cafés* and plenty of century-old houses. Although many are grimy and neglected and virtually none are open for visits, walking past a selection of fine facades whets one's appetite for the Horta Museum (opposite) and makes a pleasant way to discover this very eclectic area. Examples:

- **Ave Paul Dejaer 9** Colourfully refurbished art nouveau house
- **Ave Paul Dejaer 16** Sadly abandoned former charcuterie store, inside which 'lives' a giant rooster fashioned out of spoons
- **Rue de Savoie 66** Art nouveau house
- **St-Gilles Prison** (Ave Ducpétiaux) Crenellated white-stone facade that imitates a veritable Crusader-era fortress
- **Ave Ducpétiaux 18-24** Fine archetypal townhouses
- **Hôtel Hannon** (Ave de la Jonction 1; ☙ 11am-6pm) Superb art nouveau stained-glass windows
- **Ave Brugmann 55** Archetypal art nouveau circular window-tops and little owls over the door
- **Ave Brugmann 30** Round-ended art deco tower apartment

Ixelles (Elsene)

Trams 91 or 92 get you close to the following sights.

In what seems an outwardly typical Ixelles townhouse, the **Musée d'Art Fantastique** (Map pp72-3; ☎ 0475-412 918; www.maisonbizarre.be; Rue Américaine 7; admission €7; ☙ 2-5pm Sat & Sun) hits you with jumbled rooms full of cyborg body parts,

Terminator heads and vampire cocoons, then lets you electrocute a troll.

A few doors away a much more sedate attraction is the art nouveau **Musée Horta** (Map pp72-3; ☎ 02-543 0490; www.hortamuseum.be; Rue Américaine 25; admission €5; ☺ 2-5.30pm Tue-Sun). It occupies two adjoining houses designed and built between 1898 and 1901 by Brussels' most renowned architect, Victor Horta (see below), who lived here himself until 1919. The exterior has distinctive dome ironwork but it's the interior that impresses. Radiating from an iron-laced staircase, airy rooms sport mirrored walls, glorious timber panelling, intimate stained-glass inlays and curly door handles.

Other nearby art nouveau houses (closed to the public):

■ **Rue Africaine 92** Creamy tones, harmonious lines and a big circular window
■ **Rue Defacqz 71** 1893 house designed by prominent art nouveau architect Paul Hankar (1859–1901) as his own studio
■ **Rue Faider 83** Beautiful, gilded sgraffito design at the top

FLAGEY AREA

Centre of an up-and-coming nightlife area is the 1938 'liner' building, **Flagey** (Map pp72-3; www .flagey.be; Place Flagey), originally conceived as the national radio building. With its distinctive round 'periscope' tower, it's an art deco classic that now hosts a hip cafe and various entertainment venues.

Leading north are the pretty **Ixelles Ponds** (Étangs d'Ixelles) flanked by an artistic though modest **WWI Memorial** and many grand mansions. Private art nouveau house-facades to admire include the crazy wrought-iron railings on the otherwise stern **Ave Général de Gaulle**

38-39 and the slightly grubby 1904 **Rue du Lac 6**, with circular windows, super stained glass and a lovely 2nd-floor balcony.

Access is by trams 81 or 82 from Bruxelles-Midi.

MATONGE

Taking its name from a square in Kinshasa, Congo, **Matonge** is home to Brussels' African community though the compact area also encompasses a much wider ethnic mix. Like parts of Kinshasa, the architecture has its fair share of tired old 1960s concrete but even the dreary **Galerie d'Ixelles** comes to life with a dozen African hair-stylist shops, down-market bars and an outlet for Congolese CD/DVDs. On Chaussée de Wavre travel agencies offer cheap flights to Bujumbura and Kigali. Snack bars serve cheap, tasty portions of African delicacies such as Yassa, Mafe or Moambe (see the boxed text, p101). Grocery shops at numbers 17, 27, 36 and 130 are the place to look for plantains, yams, leaf-wrapped cassava or even dried caterpillars. But don't come expecting endless quaint boutiques selling folkloric African village-art. The only such place here is **Africamäli** (☎ 02-503 0074; Chaussée de Wavre 83).

MUSÉE CONSTANTIN MEUNIER

This intimate **museum** (Map pp66-7; ☎ 02-648 4449; Rue de l'Abbaye 59; admission free; ☺ 10am-noon & 1-5pm Tue-Fri) occupies an Ixelles townhouse that was the last home and studio of Brussels-born artist Constantin Meunier (1831–1905). He's best known for his emotive sculptures and social realist paintings, including larger-than-life bronzes depicting muscular miners from Hainaut, dockworkers from Antwerp and men reaping fields. Take tram 93 or 94.

HORTA'S CREATIONS

Victor Horta (1861–1947) was an architectural chameleon mostly remembered for his daring, light-suffused art nouveau buildings using trademark elements of wrought iron and glass. His once-celebrated Maison du Peuple (see p184) was torn down in 1965 but surviving masterpieces include Rue Américaine 25 (now the Musée Horta, opposite) and Grand Magasin Waucquez (now the Centre Belge de la Bande Dessinée, p80), along with Horta's first truly art nouveau house, the 1893 **Hôtel Tassel** (Map pp72-3; Rue Paul-Émile Janson 6) and his first civic commission, the **Jardin d'Enfants** (Map pp72-3; Rue St-Ghislain 40) schoolhouse.

Horta's WWI 'exile' in England and the USA marked a transition in styles – gone was the sensuous art nouveau and in its place stood the clean-cut functionalism of art deco. From 1922 to 1928 Horta designed the bold but severe Palais des Beaux-Arts (see BoZar, p107), while his disappointing last major work was the drably functional, post–art deco train station, Bruxelles-Central.

Uccle (Ukkel)

Uccle is an affluent, middle-class *commune*, though you'd hardly think so from a first glance at the graffiti-tagged station Uccle-Stalle.

In a 1928 art deco showpiece house you'll find the exquisite **Musée David et Alice van Buuren** (Map pp66–7; ☎ 02-343 4851; www.museumvan buuren.com; Ave Léo Errera 41; adult/senior/student/child €10/8/5/free, garden only €5/4/2.50/free; ☀ 2-5.30pm Wed-Mon), where five rooms are crammed with sublime furnishings, stained glass and top-quality paintings covering five centuries of art. Also notable are more than 30 works by van Buuren's talented symbolist protégé, van de Woestyne and a Vincent van Gogh sketch for the latter's classic *Peeling Potatoes*. Take tram 23 or 90.

BOIS DE LA CAMBRE

This remarkably extensive forest park (Map pp66–7) forms Brussels' great green lungs. It stretches from regal Ave Louise to the Forêt de Soignes, whose soaring beech trees then extend all the way to Waterloo (p217). Established in 1862 the park has lawns, playgrounds, a 'pocket' theatre, roller-skating rink and an island on an artificial lake, where the historic Chalet Robinson *café*-restaurant was recently rebuilt after a tragic fire.

Laeken

The **Domaine Royal** (Royal Estate) contains a trio of palace-villas that are home to Belgium's ruling family. All are out of bounds to tourists but two or three weeks a year (exact dates announced each January) you can join the enthusiastic queues to visit the magnificent **Royal Greenhouses** (Serres Royales; Map pp66–7; ☎ 02-551 2020; www.monarchy.be; Ave du Parc Royal 61; admission €2; ☀ late Apr-early May), designed in 1873 by Alphonse Balat (Horta's teacher). The construction was an engineering marvel of its day and the contents include many fabulous and rare tropical species. Take bus 53 from Metro Bockstael.

Deceased Belgian royals are laid to rest in the **crypt** (☀ 2pm-5pm Sun & special holidays) of the splendid, triple-spired stone church of **Notre-Dame de Laeken** (Map pp66–7; ☎ 02-479 2362; www.ndlaeken-olvlaken.be; Parvis Notre-Dame; ☀ 2-5pm Tue-Sun, Jan-Nov).

A pair of realistic East Asian pagodas form the key attractions in the **Musées d'Extrême-Orient** (☎ 02-268 1608; http://orient.kmkg-mrah.be/japan/index_fr.html; Ave Jules Van Praet 44; adult/concession/child/

Brusselscard €4/3/1.50/free, 1-4.45pm 1st Wed of month free; ☀ 9.30am-4.30pm Tue-Fri, 10am-4.30pm Sat & Sun). Both are Léopold II leftovers, built in 1905 after the king had seen similar towers at the 1890 Paris World's Fair. An underpass leads from the ticket desk to the vermillion **Tour Japonaise** (Japanese Tower; Map pp66–7) fronted by a fabulous Japanese pavilion with occasional art nouveau flourishes, such as in the stained-glass windows. Inside the gloriously glittering **Pavillon Chinois** (Chinese Pavilion; Map pp66–7), the decor swings from gilded belle époque to Khajuraho-Indian. Both pagodas display priceless Asian decorative arts while an easily overlooked Japanese Arts museum shows off swords, samurai armour and ukiyo-e painting. Get off tram 4 or 23 at 'Araucaria'.

Stretching west to the Atomium, the expansive **Parc de Laeken** is dotted with magnolia and mature chestnut trees. Its focal point is an 1880 **Léopold I statue**.

Heysel

The astounding Atomium (see below) dominates a sprawling complex of trade-fair exhibition halls including the distinctive 1930 art deco **Palais du Centenaire** (Map pp66–7) featuring terraced tiers capped by statues. Nearby you'll also find the national football stadium, Belgium's original multiplex/IMAX cinema and a subtropical water fun-park. Metro station Heysel is handy, tram 81 is more scenic and car access is easy from the Brussels ring. If you're driving or cycling note that less than 6km north, historic Grimbergen village (p113) is an entirely different world.

ATOMIUM

The space-age **Atomium** (Map pp66–7; ☎ 02-475 4777; www.atomium.be; adult/concession/Brusselscard/child €9/6/6/free; ☀ 10am-5.30pm) looms 102m over north Brussels' suburbia like a gleaming steel alien from a '60s Hollywood movie. It consists of nine house-sized metallic balls linked by steel tube-columns containing escalators and lifts. The balls are arranged like a school chemistry set to represent iron atoms in their crystal lattice…except these are 165 billion times bigger. It was built as a symbol of postwar progress for the 1958 World's Fair and was originally destined for demolition thereafter. However, it rapidly became an architectural icon and received a shiny makeover in 2006.

Visits take you by lift to the top panorama sphere where, disappointingly, the views aren't labelled and queues are possible. Back at the bottom, escalators and stairs show you four other spheres. Displays focus on the building's construction and the 1958 fair but you'll need to have paid the extra €2 for an audio-guide to learn much from them.

At night the spheres sparkle magically and, except during midsummer, the panorama-level **restaurant** (☎ 02-479 5850; www.belgiumtaste. com; mains €12-20) reopens at 7.30pm, putting starched cloths on its functional tables and serving decent dinners with a view. Dinner guests don't pay the tower entrance fee but reservations are 100% essential.

MINI EUROPE
Want to fool your friends that you saw all of Europe? Easy. Just photograph the dozens of 1/25th scale models of the continent's top monuments at **Mini Europe** (Map pp66-7; ☎ 02-478 1313; www.minieurope.com; adult/child €11.80/8.80; 10am-5pm Apr-Dec, 9.30am-8pm Jul-Aug). On certain midsummer Saturday nights it stays open till midnight, with firework displays at 10.30pm.

Koekelberg
NATIONAL BASILICA
Ghastly but gigantic, **Basilique Nationale du Sacré-Cœur** (Map pp66-7; ☎ 02-421 1669; www.basilique .be; Parvis de la Basilique 1; 9am-5pm May-Sep, 10am-4pm Oct-Apr) is the world's fifth-largest church and, by some measures, the world's largest art deco building. When construction started in 1905 (to celebrate Belgium's 75th anniversary), a truly magnificent feast of neogothic spires was planned. However, WWI left state finances impoverished so a 1925 re-design shaved off most of the intricate details. The lumpy result, finally completed in 1969, has some attractive stained glass but is predominantly a white elephant of dull, brown brick and green copperwork. The central dome is visible for miles, commanding the northwest end of ruler-straight Blvd Léopold II. Take the lift (adult/Brusselscard €4/2.40) to a 53m-high panorama balcony for wide views including an interesting perspective on the Atomium. Enter from door 6 (southwest side).

Molenbeek
TOUR & TAXIS
A postal sorting shed doesn't sound like an immediate tourist draw but the **Tour & Taxis complex** (Map pp66-7; ☎ 02-420 6069; www.tourtaxis

.be; Rue Picard 3) is in fact an architectural masterpiece – its 21st-century revamp creating a fine exhibition and commercial space in these Victorian warehouses and customs depots. It's all part of an ongoing gentrification of Brussels' run-down **canal district**, from where you can now take a variety of summer **barge cruises** (www.brussels bywater.be).

Anderlecht
Internationally best known for its **football team** (Map pp66-7; ☎ 02-522 1539; www.rsca.be; Van den Stock Stadium, Ave Théo Verbeeck 2), this sprawling western suburb now has a rather grimy, run-down reputation. However, back in 1521 it was still a country village when the world-famous humanist Erasmus came to 'play at farming'. The lovely brick home where he stayed for five months is now the **Erasmus House Museum** (☎ 02-521 1383; www.erasmushouse.museum; Rue du Chapitre 31; admission €1.25; 10am-5pm Tue-Sun). It's an unexpected little gem furnished with fine artworks including several Flemish Primitive paintings and some priceless manuscripts. There's an attractive 'philosophy garden' behind and the already modest entry fee also allows access to Belgium's smallest **begijnhof** (closed noon-2pm). It's now an appealing two-house something-of-everything museum tucked behind the nearby 16th-century Gothic **Church of St-Pierre & St-Guidon** (9am-noon daily & 2pm 5.30pm Thu-Tue). The church has some original murals and was once a major pilgrimage site: right up until WWI, cart-drivers and those suffering fits would arrive here to pray before the reliquary of 10th-century St-Guy (Guidon), the multitasked patron saint of cattle, workhorses, sheds and epileptics. The church's fine, carved white-stone spire looks especially photogenic viewed up narrow Rue Poselein, and it dominates the patchily attractive, café-ringed square **Place de la Vaillance**, where several 1920s buildings have pseudo-medieval facades. Metro Saint-Guidon lies directly behind.

CANTILLON BREWERY
Beer lovers shouldn't miss this unique living brewery-museum, the **Musée Bruxellois de la Gueuze** (Map pp68-9; ☎ 02-521 4928; www.cantillon .be; Rue Gheude 56; admission €5; 8.30am-5pm Mon-Fri, 10am-5pm Sat). Atmospheric and family run, it's Brussels' last operating lambic (p49) brewery and still uses much of the original 19th-century equipment. After a brief explanation, visitors take a self-guided tour including the barrel

rooms where the beers mature for up to three years in chestnut wine-casks. Expect plenty of cobwebs as spiders are considered friends of lambic's spontaneous fermentation process, which occurs (winter only) in a vast, shallow copper tub in the attic room. The entry fee includes two taster-glasses of Cantillon's startlingly acidic brews. Virtually unrecognisable as a brewery, it's located on a faceless backstreet near Metro Clemenceau.

Woluwé & Tervuren
AVENUE DE TERVUREN (TERVURENLAAN)
A 20-minute ride on tram 44 from Metro Montgoméry follows beautiful tree-lined Ave de Tervuren east past opulent embassy villas, the lovely parkland ponds of Woluwé and through the northern reaches of the leafy Forêt des Soignes. Sit on the right (south) side to spot the 1911 **Palais Stoclet** (Map pp66-7; Ave de Tervuren 281; ☽ closed), whose stark, radically geometric exterior is an early premonition of art deco. A Unesco site since June 2009, at the time of research the building was under renovation but hopefully it will one day be possible to visit and admire the interiors, which feature original work by Klimt and Khnopff.

TERVUREN
Tram 44 terminates in verdant Tervuren, just beyond Brussels' eastern city limit. Here the unique **Africa Museum** (off Map pp66-7; Koninklijk Museum voor Midden-Afrika; ☎ 02-769 5211; www .africamuseum.be; Leuvensesteenweg 13, Tervuren; adult/ concession/child/Brusselscard €5/4/free/free, audio-guide €2; ☽ 10am-5pm Tue-Fri, 10am-6pm Sat & Sun) is a veritable palace of a building, purpose-built by King Léopold II to show off Europe's most impressive array of African artefacts. Of course, much of the collection was plundered from Léopold's then-private 'garden' (Congo), where his rule saw a staggering percentage of the Congolese population die (see p30).

The superb collection includes masks, tools, woven baskets and an enormous 22m-long, 3.5-tonne Lengola canoe. And what's displayed is only a fraction of what's still locked in the museum's vaults. Numerous stuffed animals and pinned insects are displayed in a section of the museum that has changed little since it opened in 1910 and whose walls are still adorned with landscapes by symbolist artist Emile Fabry. Most controversial is the section dealing with the history of Congo, where a few statistics do little more than hint at the level of suffering endured by Africans under Léopold's infamously exploitative rule.

The museum's magnificent setting is a vast formal park of lakes and manicured lawns dotted with statuary. Here, in 1897, Leopold's ethnographic exhibition went as far as building whole Congolese villages... and populating them with living Congolese villagers. A shocking idea – even for that era. Yet it was repeated during 1958's World Fair to considerable global consternation.

The museum's gently colonial-themed **cafeteria** (sandwiches €3-7.50, mains €7.80-16.20; ☽ 11.30-3pm) serves a selection of African meals and various beers flavoured with exotic fruits.

ACTIVITIES
Golf
See http://brussels.angloinfo.com/countries/ belgium/golf.asp for general golfing information and www.golfbelgium.be/clubs.html for club listings. Those with EGA recognised handicaps usually qualify for Belgian Golf Federation reciprocal membership and can then play at Anderlecht's 18-hole **Royal Amicale Golf Club** (Map pp66-7; ☎ 02-521 1687; www.golf -anderlecht.com; Rue de la Scholle; green fees week/weekend €38/55) near Metro Eddy Merckx.

Swimming
Piscine Victor Boin (Map pp72-3; ☎ 02-539 0615; Rue de la Perche 38; adult/child €2/1.50; ☽ noon-7pm Mon-Sat, from 2pm Wed) Covered art deco swimming pool in St-Gilles.

TOURS
Brussels City Tours (Map p70; ☎ 02-513 7744; www .brussels-city-tours.com; Rue de la Colline 8; adult/concession/ child €16/14.50/8; ☽ every half hr 10am-4pm Apr-Oct, 10am-3pm Nov-Mar) Hop-on, hop-off double-decker buses with eight-language commentary stopping at 13 places including Bruxelles-Central, Atomium, Place Royale and the EU's Rond Point Schuman. Buy tickets (valid 24 hours) when boarding. Also offered are 2½-hour city tours (10am and 2pm) starting on foot then continuing by bus, one-day bus tours to Ghent and Bruges and other weekly tours visiting places such as Antwerp or Luxembourg.

Heritage conservation group **ARAU** (Map p70; ☎ 02-219 3345; www.arau.org; Blvd Adolphe Max 55) can get you into many of Brussels' architectural gems that are otherwise closed to the public. Their popular three-hour art nouveau bus tours (adult/concession €17/13) usually start 10am Saturdays (English or French/English) April to mid-December. For their other much more sporadic themed tours, see the website.

For cycle tours, see p111.

FESTIVALS & EVENTS

See p16 for Brussels events.

SLEEPING

Brussels has a vast range of accommodation. Unless you're on specific business, try to find accommodation within the central 'pentagon', ideally around the Grand Place or perhaps in nearby Ste-Catherine. Brussels has a reasonable network of B&Bs, many listed and bookable through **Bed & Brussels** (☎ 02-646 0737; www.bnb-br ussels.be).

Camping

Camping Bruxelles-Europe à Ciel Ouvert (Map p86; ☎ 02-640 7967; Chaussée de Wavre 203; tent/person €6/6; ⊙ reception 8am-11pm Jul-Aug) The only campsite in central Brussels is a simple summer-only place hidden away in the garden of a spindle-spired church, Église du St-Sacrement. Rather ropy showers are available and campervans may park outside (€10 without hook-up). The nearest full camping grounds are much further afield in Wezembeek-Oppem, Grimbergen and Beersel (p113).

Budget

Most hostel fees include breakfast and are slightly discounted if you're under 26.

HI Hostel Jacques Brel (Map pp68-9; ☎ 02-218 0187; brussels.brel@laj.be; Rue de la Sablonnière 30; dm/s/d €17.40/34/48; ⊙ 8am-midnight; ☒ ☎ ▯) Neat, presentable and reasonably spacious hostel in a pleasant, nearly central area. The bar has occasional live music (sometimes guests play for their bed!), there's a 2nd-floor terrace, free wi-fi, laundry for €4, no lockout and a partly 'bio' (organic) breakfast is included.

Centre Vincent van Gogh (Map pp68-9; ☎ 02-217 0158; www.chab.be; Rue Traversière 8; dm/s/d €18/33/52; ☒ ▯ ☎) The lobby bar and pool-table veranda are unusually hip for a hostel, but rooms are less glamorous and, from some, reaching the toilets means crossing the garden courtyard. No membership required. Wi-fi €2 per hour.

Sleep Well (Map pp68-9; ☎ 02-218 5050; www.sleepwell .be; Rue du Damier 23; hostel dm/s/d/tr €19.70/30.50/55.40/74.10, hotel s/d/tr €43/62/88; ☒ ▯) Bright cartoon colours and a tinkling Manneken over the door are an inviting contrast to the soulless (if central) surroundings dominated by a multistorey car park. There's plenty of meet-each-other space, a bar, free breakfast, games room, terrace and internet (€1.50 per half hour). Functional, somewhat worn rooms look like student residences. The hostel section has shared facilities (though some rooms have taps and toilets) and can't be accessed between 11am and 3pm.

HI Hostel JOHN Breugel (Map p70; ☎ 02-511 0436; www.jeugdherbergen.be/brussel.htm; Rue du Saint Esprit 2; HI members dm/s/d €19.80/34/48.40; ⊙ lockout 10am-2pm, curfew 1am-7am; ☒ ▯) Superbly central but somewhat institutional with limited communal space. Internet €2 per hour, wi-fi free, lockers €1.50.

2Go4 (Map p70; ☎ 02-219 3019; www.2GO4.be; Blvd Émile Jacqmain 99; dm €22-29, s/d/tr/q €55/69/96/116; ⊙ reception 7am-1pm & 4-11pm) The well-equipped hostel features zany ground-floor furnishings including a chunk of old Atomium sheeting hanging above reception. It's toward the slightly sleazier end of town but on a bright, major street. No lockout, no curfew. Come here to check in even if you've booked their unpretentious 'Grand Place Rooms' (Map p70; Rue des Harengs 6; doubles €59 to €70), which have low ceilings, hefty beams and a fabulously central location. Rates include coffee but not breakfast.

Midrange & Top End

Breakfast is generally included in rack rate prices, but not necessarily when you've scored an internet bargain. Check carefully.

WEEKEND & SUMMER DEALS

With most of Brussels' accommodation scene aimed squarely at Eurocrats and business travellers, many mid- and upper-range hotels drop their rates dramatically at weekends and in summer. Double rooms with September midweek rates of €240 might cost as little as €69 in August – so why use a hostel? Shop around and check carefully for internet deals, especially on chain hotels.

BRUSSELS

GRAND PLACE AREA

Downtown-BXL (Map p70; ☎ 0475-290 721; www.down townbxl.com, www.lacasabxl.com; Rue du Marché au Charbon 118-120; d €76) Near the capital's gay district, this B&B is superbly located for those wanting to dance the night away. From the communal breakfast table and help-yourself coffee bar, a classic staircase winds up to good-value rooms featuring zebra striped cushions and Warhol Marilyn prints. One room features a round bed. Adjacent Casa-BXL offers three rooms in a more Moroccan-Asian style.

La Vieille Lanterne (Map p70; ☎ 02-512 7494; www .lavieillelanterne.be; Rue des Grands Carmes 29; s/d from €76/86, summer €65/75; ☎) Watch the Manneken Pis from the window of room 5 in this neat, unsophisticated six-room B&B-style 'hotel', accessed by steep spiral stairs from an archetypal giftshop. Check in before 10pm. Free wi-fi.

Hotel Alma (Map p70; ☎ 02-219 3119; www.alma hotel.be; Rue des Éperonniers 42; d €80-200) Neat, high-ceilinged rooms with colourfully stripy carpets. The decor is minimalist but somewhat lacking in style. Rear rooms are peacefully quiet and great value if you're offered last-minute walk-in rates of €65 as we were.

Hotel Mozart (Map p70; ☎ 02-502 6661; www .hotel-mozart.be; Rue Marché aux Fromages 23; s/d/tr/q €80/100/130/150;) Mozart? Think Sultanahmet rather than Saltzburg when imagining the sensory overload of this place – lashings of Turkish mosaic-work plus wall fountains, gilt rococo-styled chairs and an incredible crush of imitation 'antiques', paintings and 'art nouveau' lamps. Garish, fun and very central but mattresses are saggy, bathrooms have their defects and you'll need good earplugs in the front rooms, which overlook never-sleeping 'Pita' street.

Hôtel Saint-Michel (Map p70; ☎ 02-511 0956; www .atgp.be; Grand Place 15; without view s/d/tr €65/105/128, with view €120/140/163) Its unique location right on the fabulous Grand Place means you just might forgive the dowdy decor, soft mattresses and a lift like a goods elevator. The views from the front rooms are truly breathtaking but bear in mind you'll also share the sounds of a square that remains alive with activity (and occasional full-scale rock concerts) till the wee hours. Service is very friendly.

Hôtel Arlequin (Map p70; ☎ 02-514 1615; www .florishotels.com; Rue de la Fourche 17; r €85-299; ☎) This well-hidden hotel's outstanding feature is its 7th-floor breakfast room with superb views

across to the City Hall. Recently upgraded room decor has a retro-'60s appeal that's more tasteful than the lobby might suggest. Nonetheless we found loose wires and scuffed corridor walls and at the weekend music from nearby venues can be disturbing. Rates vary radically according to demand. Wi-fi €5/10 per hour/day.

Chambres d'hôtes du Vaudeville (Map p70; ☎ 0471-473 837; www.chambresdhotesduvaudeville.be; Galerie de la Reine 11; d rear/front €115/155; ☎ ✗) This classy new B&B has an incredible location right within the gorgeous (if reverberant) Galeries St-Hubert. Delectable decor styles include African, modernist and 'Loulou' (with 1920s nude sketches). Larger front rooms have claw-foot bathtubs and *galerie* views, but can be noisy with clatter that continues all night. Get keys via the art deco influenced, recently revamped Café du Vaudeville, where breakfast is included. Vaudeville's unique house beer is provided free in the minibar.

Royal Windsor Hôtel (Map p70; ☎ 02-505 5555; www .royalwindsorbrussels.com; Rue Duquesnoy 5; r weekend/inter-net/rack rates from €139/180/350, 'fashion rooms' €199-900; ✗ ✗ 💻 P) This super-central 266-room business hotel has liveried doormen, a brass 'n' glass entranceway and somewhat oppressively low ceilings. Standard rooms offer '30s-style corner cabinets and stylish over-bed draperies. But the unique feature is the hotel's handful of 'fashion rooms' created by cutting-edge Belgian fashion designers including Nicolas Woit, Marina Yee and Kaat Tilley.

Hôtel Amigo (Map p70; ☎ 02-547 4747; www.hotel amigo.com; Rue de l'Amigo 1-3; d from €179/199/319 week-end/summer/weekday, ste from €1299; ✗ ✗ 💻 ♿) Let faultlessly polite besuited staff usher you into Central Brussels' top address. Behind a classical Flemish facade lies a stone-flagged reception area worn smooth by centuries of footsteps. Stylishly redesigned rooms have an airy and imaginative vibe with neo–art deco touches, surreal carved 'fruit' elements and art ranging from signed Goosens caricatures to Magritte prints and framed Tintin figurines.

Hôtel Le Dixseptième (Map p70; ☎ 02-502 5744; www.ledixseptieme.be; Rue de la Madeleine 25; s/d/ste from €180/200/270, weekend €100/100/200; ✗ 💻) A hushed magnificence greets you in this alluring boutique hotel, partly occupying the former 17th-century residence of the Spanish ambassador. The coffee-cream breakfast room retains original cherub reliefs while the bar-lounge has been done out to re-create a similar ambience. The 24 guestrooms are all individually decorated in a wide variety of styles. Spacious executive suites come with four-poster beds. Across a tiny enclosed courtyard-garden in the cheaper rear section, some rooms are less than memorable, though the Creuz Suite has its bathroom tucked curiously into a 14th-century vaulted basement. Lifts stop between floors so you'll need to deal with some stairs.

Hotel Aris (Map p70; ☎ 02-502 6006; www.arishotel .be; Rue du Marché aux Herbes 78; s/d/tr/f €220/240/310/360; 🛜 🏠) Very central. The blandly neutral rooms are overpriced at rack rates but well worth considering when discounted to €69 in summer.

Dominican (Map p70; ☎ 02-203 0808; www.the dominican.be; Rue Léopold 9; r €315-1150; 🗙 🏠 🖳) Combining classic elegance with understated modern chic this excellent top-range palace occupies the site of a former abbey right behind La Monnaie. It's hard to beat for style and the location is wonderfully central albeit in an area suffering from rather patchy architecture and atmosphere.

Le Plaza (Map p70; ☎ 02-278 0100; www.leplaza-brus sels.be; Blvd Adolphe Max 118-126; r €100-400) From outside the architecture looks unsophisticatedly art deco but inside the foyer oozes classical charm. Rooms are refined and unusually spacious and the hotel has a conscious eco-sensitive policy. However, staff seem somewhat overworked and the location, while reasonably central, is marred by the block of sex shops that leads north from here towards the seedier Gare du Nord area. Breakfast €29.

Hôtel Métropole (Map p70; ☎ 02-217 2300, reservations, 02-214 2424; www.metropolehotel.com; Place de Brouckère 31; s/d/ste €330/360/500, weekend rates from €115; 🗙 🏠) This 1895 showpiece has a jaw-droppingly sumptuous French Renaissance-style foyer with marble walls, coffered ceiling and beautifully etched stained-glass back windows. The café is indulgent and the bar (frequent live music) features recently 'rediscovered' murals by a student of Horta. One of the lifts is an 1895 original. Rooms have been recently redecorated in styles varying from art deco to what they describe as 'Venetian Baroque', slightly overcolourful for some tastes. Much of the furniture is restored, from 1930s originals, and some of the chandeliers no doubt are hellishly difficult to dust.

ST-CATHERINE & AROUND

Hôtel Noga (Map p70; ☎ 02-218 6763; www.nogahotel .com; Rue du Béguinage 38; s/d/tr/q from €95/110/135/160, weekends from €70/85/110/135; 🏠 🖳 🛜) This very welcoming family hotel uses model yachts to give the lobby and piano room a certain nautical feel. Sepia photos of Belgian royalty, along with historic bellows, top hats and assorted random kitsch, lead up to variously decorated rooms that are neat and clean without particular luxury. Wi-fi is free for the first hour.

Hooy Kaye Lodge (Map pp68-9; ☎ 02-218 4440; www .hooykayelodge.com; Quai aux Pierres de Taille 22; d €95-125) Calm, elegantly sparse B&B, with Burmese chests and framed antique garments in a 17th-century house, which retains its unpolished 1795 stairway. The Burmese connection continues with the three-tiered 'office' in the garden, shaped like an out-building of Shwedagon.

Hôtel Welcome (Map p70; ☎ 02-219 9546; www.brussels hotel.travel; Rue du Peuplier 1; r €96-210; 🗙 🏠) The wooden-panelled reception area does nothing to prepare guests for the full-colour decor in each uniquely designed room transporting you to, say, Tahiti, Congo, Cuba or Zanzibar.

our pick Maison Noble (Map p70; ☎ 02-219 2339; www.maison-noble.eu; Rue du Marcq 10; s €119-139, d €€129-149; 🏠 🖳 🛜) A stay at this splendidly refined four-room guesthouse starts with a welcome drink in the Flemish neogothic lounge. It's backed by a gorgeous 1920s stained-glass panel and joined to a neo-Renaissance piano room. Guests are free to tickle the ivories and once in a while recitals are held here featuring up-and-coming concert pianists. Fully hotel-standard rooms have rainforest showers, fine linens, and framed Breughel prints over the beds. While the target market is 'married' gay couples, the charming owners are hetero-friendly.

Hotel Café Pacific (Map p70; ☎ 02-213-0080; www .hotelcafepacific.com; Rue Antoine Dansaert 57; s €119-159, d €129-169; 🛜) The hip design look is all you'd expect from this fashion-district address, though the reception is just a desk attached to a revamped café. Most rooms come with high-powered showers and large but subtle black-and-white nudes above the bed. Fabrics by Mia Zia, toiletries by Bvlgari.

TRÔNE

A sedate, oft-overlooked little area that's within easy walking distance of the EU Parliament, yet also handy for the Royal area and lively Matonge.

Chambres en Ville (Map pp72-3; ☎ 02-512 9290; www.chambresenville.be; Rue de Londres 19; s/d €80/100, 2 nights s/d €140/180; 🖳) Impressive B&B in an unmarked 19th-century townhouse featuring part-stripped wooden floors, high ceilings and large, tastefully appointed guestrooms. Furniture new and old combined with striking artwork and curiosities from all over the world (notably antique African statuettes) gives the place a unique character. Duplex top-floor studio available (€1000 per month)

Hôtel Stanhope (Map pp72-3; ☎ 02-506 9111; www.stanhope.be; Rue du Commerce 9; d weekday/weekend from €220/84; ⊠ 🖳 🖳 ⅋) This serene oasis of genteel 'English-style' class has a mock-classical lounge-lobby styled like a club library and guestrooms where timeless fabrics vary from Sanderson-floral to Delftware-effect without feeling chintzy. Breakfast costs €25. Online weekend bargains can be found.

MAROLLES

Hôtel Galia (Map pp72-3; ☎ 02-502 4243; www.hotelgalia.com; Place du Jeu-de-Balle 15; s/d/tr/q from €65/75/90/120; ⊠) Simple rooms with tiny plastic shower-toilet cubicles overlook Brussels' well-known bric-a-brac market square. Prices are constant year-round so it's worth considering booking here during high seasons.

BRUXELLES-MIDI AREA

There are numerous hotels around Brussels' main international station, and prices are often very competitive. But you should be aware that this is not one of Brussels' more salubrious neighbourhoods. Locals probably exaggerate the area's reputation for petty criminality as part of a certain prejudice against largely immigrant districts. Still, there's little real charm here and it's a bit too far from the centre to be truly convenient for visiting Brussels' major sights. Hotels around Place Roupe (three blocks north) don't cost much more but the area's somewhat less daunting and slightly nearer the centre, though still far from a prime location.

Hôtel à la Grande Cloche (Map p70; ☎ 02-512 6140; www.hotelgrandecloche.com; Pl Roupe 10; s/d/tr €68/79/90) Unremarkable, somewhat disjointed and with slightly soft mattresses, this place is nonetheless professionally run and its fixed prices make it a reasonable fall back when everything in the centre is full or overpriced.

IXELLES & AVE LOUISE

Like everywhere in Brussels this area's character can vary substantially block by block, but overall it's one of the capital's most chic and lively inner suburbs.

Hôtel Rembrandt (Map pp72-3; ☎ 02-512 7139; www.hotel-rembrandt.be; Rue de la Concorde 42; s/d without bathroom €50/75, with bathroom €70/95; 🖳) A homely and good-value guest house just a block off Ave Louise. It's a jumble of old ornaments, paintings and polished wooden furnishings. Rooms are well cared for if a tad small, all with showers or baths but the cheaper ones sharing toilets. Reception closes at 9pm.

Thewhitehotel (Map pp72-3; ☎ 02-644 2929; www.thewhitehotel.be; Ave Louise 212; r weekend/weekday from €90/115; 🖳 🖳) The fiendishly hip ultra-minimalist rooms are bright white with designer touches. They're above a similarly stylish bar-lounge offering free internet (wi-fi in contrast costs €5 for two days). It's well placed for the trendy Flagey-Ixelles scene, a tram ride from the city centre and has bikes/scooters available to rent.

EATING

The essential Brussels experience involves old-world restaurants where aproned waiters bustle across tiled floors and diners tuck into hearty Belgian cuisine in wood-panelled surroundings. But trendy minimalism has also swept the scene, and there's no shortage of international cuisine. As ever, *cafés* (p102) are generally cheaper and open longer than restaurants if atmosphere and price is more important than refinement and cuisine.

The cobbled streets around the Grand Place are the natural starting point, though be careful on the quaint Rue and Petite Rue des Bouchers (see p98). For fish and seafood the Ste-Catherine's fish-market area is highly regarded. The streets around Place St-Géry offer a small line-up of great-value Asian eateries. The Marolles shelters several intimate and trendy options while Matonge counterpoints cheap African and world cuisine with hip local fare on Rue St-Boniface. There's a lot more choice around Ixelles. Affluent locals tend to dine considerably further afield in middle-class areas beyond the scope of this book, such as Woluwé, Kraainem and Uccle or semi-rural escapes like Lasne and Linkebeek. Useful sources of restaurant suggestions (some with customer reviews) are www.resto.be and www.deltaweb.be.

Lower Town
FRENCH & BELGIAN

Domaine de Lintillac (Map p70; ☎ 02-511 5123; Rue de Flandre 25; mains €9.50-28; ☺ noon-2.30pm & 6.30-10.30pm Tue-Sat) This warm, colourful French-rustic-style restaurant features a toaster on each checkerboard table. Virtually every dish is duck-related including various duck sausages, pâtés and *cassoulet*, a thick bean-based stew. Prices are very reasonable, especially if you avoid their speciality foie-gras starters.

Fin de Siècle (Map p70; Rue des Chartreux 9; mains €10.23-15.81, beer from €1.91; ☺ bar 4.30pm-1am, kitchen 6pm-12.30am) From *carbonade* (beer-based hotpot) and *kriek* (cherry beer)-chicken to mezzes and tandoori chicken, the food selection is as eclectic as the decor in this low-lit cult place. Tables are rough, music constant, ceilings purple and prices still converted to the centime from Belgian Francs. To quote the barman 'there's no phone, no bookings, no sign on the door…we do everything to put people off but they still keep coming'.

Viva M'Boma (Map p70; ☎ 02-512 1593; Rue de Flandre 17; mains €11-18; ☺ noon-2.30pm & 7-10pm Thu-Sat, plus noon-2pm Mon-Tue) Hefty Belgian classics served in a long, narrow bistro entirely walled in gleaming white tiles like the butchers' shop it once was. A stuffed sheep and pig's head meet and greet.

Brasserie Royal (Map p70; ☎ 02-217 8500; www.royalbrasseriebrussels.be; Rue de Flandre 103; mains €12.50-19, beer €2.20; ☺ noon-10.30pm) Black and dark chocolate walls with white UFOs of light and rows of Bombay Sapphire for decor create a jazzy setting for steaks, fish or traditional Belgian fare. Don't let the abysmal website put you off.

La Villette (Map p70; ☎ 02-512 7550; www.la-villette.be; Rue du Vieux Marché aux Grains 3; mains €16-20.50, mussels €21-23, lunch €14; ☺ noon-2.30pm & 6.30-10.30pm Mon-Fri, 6.30pm-11.30pm Sat) Beams, dark wood and gingham tablecloths create a wonderfully typical atmosphere for traditional Brussels food, along with steaks and various changing beer recipes such as salmon in Hoegaarden or guinea fowl in *kriek*.

In 't Spinnekopke (Map pp68-9; ☎ 02-511 8695; www.spinnekopke.be; Place du Jardin aux Fleurs 1; mains €15-25; ☺ lunch & dinner Mon-Fri, dinner Sat) This age-old classic occupies a 17th-century whitewashed cottage with a summer terrace spilling onto on a newly revamped square. Bruxellois specialities and meats cooked in beer-based sauces are authentic but hardly a bargain and some of the tables feel a tad cramped.

Chez Léon (Map p70; ☎ 02-513 0426; www.chezleon.be; Rue des Bouchers 18; mains €15-27; ☺ noon-11pm) This long-time tourist favourite serves the original 'Mussels from Brussels', and makes a good place to try them if you don't mind that portions (mostly 850g) are somewhat small by Belgian standards. Rooms are spread over several gabled house and decor varies from attractively classic to somewhat tacky depending on where you sit.

Brasserie de la Roue d'Or (Map p70; ☎ 02-514 2554; Rue des Chapeliers 26; mains €15-28; ☺ noon-12.30am, closed Jul) Cosy in a cramped Parisian bistro sort of way, this place serves excellent if somewhat pricey Belgian food. Wall murals and ceiling clouds pay homage to the city's surrealist artists.

Belga Queen Brussels (Map p70; ☎ 02-217 2187; www.belgaqueen.be; Rue Fossé aux Loups 32; mains/weekday lunch/beers from €20/16/2.50; ☺ noon-2.30pm & 7pm-midnight) Belgian cuisine is given a chic, modern twist within a magnificent if reverberant 19th century bank building. Classical stained-glass ceilings and marble columns are hidden behind an indecently hip oyster counter and wide-ranging beer and cocktail bar (open noon till late). In the former bank vaults beneath, there's a cigar lounge

---

TOP RESTAURANTS

Our restaurant reviews focus on ambience and value for money. However, if money is no object check out one of Brussels' dozen Michelin-starred restaurants, many run by internationally known chefs. Beware that even with a plutonium credit card you may need reservations weeks in advance for mythic **Comme Chez Soi** (Map p70; www.commechezsoi.be). Other classics require a lengthy taxi ride from the city centre, including Jean-Pierre Bruneau's **Bruneau** (Map pp66-7; www.bruneau.be) near Koekelberg, Alain Deluc's **Barbizon** (Map pp66-7; www.barbizon.be) in Jezus-Eik, and Pascal Devalkeneer's **Chalet de la Forêt** (www.lechaletdelaforet.be), also set amid towering beeches in the Forêt de Soignes. Central **Sea Grill** (Map p70; www.seagrill.be) is truly superb for fish though oddly located in a typical international business-hotel.

TOO GOOD TO BE TRUE?

Locals tend to steer clear of many undeniably attractive fish restaurants that create such a photogenic scene on the Rue and Petite Rue des Bouchers. Of course there are exceptions. Chez Leon (p97) is a veritable institution for mussels and Aux Armes de Bruxelles is a reliable place for high-class Belgian favourites. But at certain other places we've observed some subtle trickery. In one example we agreed to take a bargain value menu listed on the board outside. But when taking our order, the waiter nonchalantly suggested some vastly more expensive alternatives, implying (if never actually saying) that they were included. A second clever 'scam' was that the 'house wine' turned out to be one of the most expensive options on the wine list. So the moral, on this street at least, is always double check.

---

that morphs into a nightclub after 10pm Wednesday to Saturday. The unique toilets have a memorable surprise in store! Service and food standards here are heatedly debated among city residents but we've always had positive experiences.

our pick L'Ogenblik (Map p70; ☎ 02-511 6151; www .ogenblik.be; Galerie des Princes 1; lunch €11, mains €23-28; ☽ noon-2.30pm & 7pm-midnight) This historic bistro-restaurant has sawdust floors, close-packed tables and plenty of bustle. The atmosphere is much livelier than many upmarket fish restaurants but seafood quality challenges the best (the salmon *mille-feuille* is divine). Steaks and duck dishes are also available.

La Maison du Cygne (Map p70; ☎ 02-511 8244; www.lamaisonducygne.be; Grand Place; mains €37-65, menu €65; ☽ lunch Mon-Fri, dinner Sun-Fri) Gastronomic Belgo-French seasonal cuisine is served in this sophisticated restaurant on the 2nd floor of a classic 17th-century guildhall. Book way ahead to score one of the few tables with a Grand Place view. For something slightly less formal try their 1st-floor Ommegang Brasserie (www.brasseriedelommegang.be; mains €15 to €27; open noon to 2.30pm and 6.30pm to 10.30pm Monday to Saturday).

SEAFOOD

Many Belgian restaurants serve mussels (in season), monkfish and seafood plates but there are also seafood specialists. The best selection is in the Ste-Catherine area. Quality

---

WATER INTO WINE?

Or maybe beer? In midrange restaurants a bottle of water will typically cost €5 to €7. No, tap water isn't an option. But for less than half that price you can usually order a standard beer.

---

is generally high here and menu items fairly similar so it's a matter of finding the atmosphere and price range that suits. Note that drink prices can be disproportionately elevated in the pricier restaurants.

Mer du Nord (Map p70; ☎ 02-513 1192; www.vishandel noordzee.be; Rue Ste-Catherine 45; ☽ 11am-5pm Tue-Sat, 11am-8pm Sun) Well-reputed fishmonger's window catering to a queue of stand-and-snack lunch-grabbers around bare metal outdoor tables.

Vistro (Map p70; ☎ 02-512 4181; Quai aux Briques 16; mains €17-38, menus €22-47; ☽ noon-2.30pm Mon-Fri & 6.30-midnight Mon-Sat) Much less formal and noticeably cheaper than many Ste-Catherine options. Vistro has bare brick walls and A-frame beams upstairs and a pleasant buzz.

Vismet (Map p70; ☎ 02-218 8545; Pl Ste-Catherine 23; mains €24-26; ☽ noon-3pm & 7-10pm Tue-Sat) Vismet is popular and stylish in a simple, vaguely minimalist fashion, with rows of ceiling point-lamps and high-up mirrors like rectangular steersman's windows. Tables can feel slightly cramped but quality is high and there's a daily changing shortlist of recommendations.

Bij den Boer (Map p70; ☎ 02-512 6122; www.bijden boer.com; Quai aux Briques 60; mains €15-28; ☽ noon-2.30pm & 6-10.30pm Mon-Sat) Convivial favourite, with mirror panelled walls, model yachts, sensible prices and a jolly ambience. Wine of the month is €20 a bottle.

La Marie-Joseph (Map p70; ☎ 02-218 0596; Quai au bois à Brûler 47-49; mains €22.50-32, beer/coffee €4.25/4; ☽ noon-3pm & 6.30-11pm Tue-Sun) Bright, modern art on whitewashed timber walls, simple tables and a hushed air of mild formality. The fish meals get consistently good local reviews from those who can afford them.

OTHER EUROPEAN

Comocomo (Map p70; ☎ 02-503 0330; Rue Antoine Dansaert 19; 3/6/9 pintxos €8.50/14/19; ☽ lunch & dinner;

premetro Bourse) *Pintxos* (the Basque version of tapas) snake past on an 80m-long conveyor belt. Colour codes include blue for fish, green for veggies, red for pork, and so on. It's all as predictably hip as you'd expect for this part of town.

A l'Ombra (Map p70; ☎ 02-511 6710; Rue des Harengs 2; pastas €8.50-13, mains €14-18; ☑ noon-3pm Mon-Fri & 6.30pm-11.30pm Mon-Sat) Take a tiny, tile-walled 1920s shop-house. Keep the classic decor, wooden shelf-holders and cashier booth. Insert stools and a narrow communal table. Serve great fresh pasta and see if the customers finally communicate. Perhaps…at least with the farewell grappa.

Ricotta & Parmesan (Map p70; ☎ 02-502 8082; www.ricottaparmesan.com; Rue de l'Écuyer 31; mains €9-15; ☑ noon-2.30pm & 6.30pm-11pm Mon-Sat) Excellent-value Italian food enjoyed in atmospheric decor – a pair of antique buildings filled with olive-oil bottles and antique cooking implements, some fancifully framed.

ASIAN
Lotus Bleu (Map p70; ☎ 02-502 6299; Rue du Midi 70; mains €8-13; ☑ noon-11pm) Simple, generally reliable central place for inexpensive Vietnamese, Chinese and Thai food.

Rêve d'Asie (Map p70; ☎ 02-502 4828; www.reve dasie.be; Rue Jules Van Praet 19; mains €8-15; ☑ noon-11.30pm) A trishaw plunges from the ceiling, chairs and frames burst out of the half plastered walls but all the Buddhas stay predictably calm. Despite the whacky decor, the Thai and Vietnamese food is very well priced and tasty (though hardly gourmet) and served with a smile. Plenty of other Asian options, mostly Vietnamese but also an Indian (with the unlikely name 'Shamrock'), are huddled along the same street.

Ajiyoshi (Map p70; ☎ 02-502 0298; Quai aux Briques 32; noodles €9.50-12, katsudon €15.50, sushi sets from €20.50; ☑ noon-2pm&7-10.15pm) This tiny, typical Japanese eatery strikes a fair balance between price and quality. For detailed customer reviews of numerous other Japanese options in Brussels, see www.ponpokopon.net/resto.html.

VEGETARIAN
Den Teepot (Map p70; ☎ 02-511 9402; Rue des Chartreux 66; ☑ noon-2pm Mon-Sat) Macrobiotic, veggie lunch place attached to a mustard-yellow 'bio' shop.

Picnik (Map p70; ☎ 02-217 3484; Rue de Flandre 109; soup €2-3, daily special €8, 3-course menu €9.50;

☑ 11.30am-4pm Mon-Fri) Vegetarian snack bar that's mostly organic.

AFRICAN
Kokob (Map p70; ☎ 02-511 1950; www.kokob.be; Rue des Grands Carmes 10; veg/meat dishes from €7.90/11.50, rice €1; ☑ 6.30pm-11pm daily & noon-4pm Thu-Sun) Warmly lit Ethiopian bar/restaurant/cultural centre where well-explained dishes are best shared then eaten from and with pancake-like *injera* (€0.75 each). There is live acoustic music one Thursday per month.

LATE NIGHT
Mystical (Map p70; ☎ 02-512 1111; www.mysticalresto.be; Rue des Éperonniers 57; mains €11-24, pasta €8-14; ☑ 6pm-5am Tue-Sun) Bare-brick walls and alternating black and cream seats are attractively lit and surveyed by Buddha and Léopold II. The menu includes grills, mussels, and kangaroo in almond-honey sauce.

Si Bemol (Map p70; ☎ 02-219 6378; www.lesibemol.be; Rue aux Fleurs 20; mains €10.50-21.50; ☑ 7pm-5am; ☎) Traditional cuisine from *stoemp* (potato-veg mash) to steaks to *chicons au gratin* (ham wrapped endives in cheese sauce) available almost till dawn. By the time Si Bemol closes, the *café*s around Place de Jeu-de-Balle (Map pp72–3) will be opening so you needn't go hungry.

QUICK EATS
A range of inexpensive lunchtime sandwich shops lies in and around the Galerie Ravenstein arcade (Map pp68–9:) behind Bruxelles-Central station. Elsewhere, the following snack options include:

Panos (Map p70; Rue du Marché aux Herbes 85) Handy chain-bakery and sandwich shop.

Pita Places (Map p70; Rue du Marché aux Fromages) Pick from a swarm of places along Rue du Marché aux Fromages. Most open at lunchtime then work all night till around 6am. Basic pitas cost from €3. Eat in or take away.

Fritland (Map p70; Rue Henri Maus 49; ☑ 11am-1am) Chips.

Comus & Gasterea (Quai aux Briques 86; ☑ 11am-6pm Mon-Fri, 2-6pm Sun) Modern ice-cream parlour where everything's homemade, including the cones.

Leonidas (Map p70; Rue de la Colline 11; ☑ 9.30am-midnight) Snack on skewers of fresh strawberries dipped in a chocolate fountain (€3).

SELF-CATERING
GB Express (Map p70; Rue au Beurre 25; ☑ 8am-10pm) Small central supermarket.

Congrès

Le Bier Circus (Map pp68-9; (☎ 02-218 0034; www.bier-circus.be; Rue de l'Enseignement 57; mains €13-18, pastas €9-12; ⊗ noon-2.30pm Mon-Fri & 6pm-midnight Mon-Sat) The decor is underwhelming but the Belgian 'beer cuisine' is as good as you'll find and the *café* has a very wide range of brews to wash it all down.

Marolles, Sablon & Ixelles

SABLON

On the Sablon itself you'll often be paying a hefty premium for being seen in the 'right' place, though there are exceptions.

our pick Le Perroquet (Map pp72-3; ☎ 02-512 9922; Rue Watteeu 31; light meals €8-10; ⊗ noon-1am) Lovely art nouveau *café* with stained glass, marble-topped tables and dark-wood panelling. It's a really affordable place for salads and gourmet pitas: try the toasted '*croc pruneaux*' stuffed with cheese, bacon, prunes and green-garnish (€5.90). Bar opens 10am.

Tour D'y Voir (Map pp72-3; ☎ 02-511 0078; www.tourdyvoir.be; Place du Grand Sablon 8-9; mains €15-25, lunch/dinner menus €16/40; ⊗ lunch Mon-Sat, dinner daily) High-backed fashion chairs and modern, semi-abstract art contrasts with rough brick floors and ancient beams in the upper part of a converted medieval chapel. Front windows overlook the Sablon and the light-touch French food is presented with aplomb. The entrance is easily missed beside Wittamer (p109), the square's classic tearoom patisserie.

MAROLLES

Walking distance from the centre, Rue Haute, Rue Blaes and some interconnecting lanes host an up-and-coming dining scene. It's worth strolling around as new places open frequently. For really cheap food and drink from 5am till 5pm try any *café* on Place du Jeu-de-Balle. See map pp72-3.

Quim's (Map pp72-3; ☎ 02-502 3008; www.lequims.be; Rue Haute 204; mains €9.50-19, ⊗ noon-2pm & 7-10.30pm Tue-Sun; ⊠) This Belgo-Portuguese offering has adroitly reworked a classic mirror-panelled *café* into a low-lit fashion-conscious restaurant without losing any of the building's character. Mock clock faces and twinkling candles predominate. Classic Belgian lunch-specials cost under €10.

Restobières (Map pp72-3; ☎ 02-502 7251; www.restobieres.eu; Rue des Renards 32; mains €12-22, menus €18-38; ⊗ noon-3pm Tue-Sat, 6.30-11pm Thu-Sat, 4-11pm Sun) Beer-based twists on typical Belgian meals

served in a delightful two-storey restaurant. The walls are plastered with bottles, grinders and countless antique souvenir biscuit tins featuring Belgian royalty.

Au Stekerlapatte (Map pp72-3; ☎ 02-512 8681; Rue des Prêtres 4; mains around €16; ⊗ dinner Tue-Sun, closed Jul-Aug; ⊠) Behind a grungy facade lies a cavernous casual bistro offering an extensive menu of generous Belgo-French food.

Cinabre de Garance (Map pp72-3; ☎ 02-502 1604; www.cinabredegarance.com; Rue Haute 198; mains €17-19, menu €30; ⊗ noon-2pm & 7-10.30pm Tue-Sun; ⊠) Red and grey walls are patterned with light projections and splashed with abstract art. Sit at consciously battered wooden tables for imaginative meals like kangaroo in fig sauce. Or follow flickering candles up steep rear stairs to the 'secret' handkerchief of tree-shaded terrace.

Les Petits Oignons (Map pp72-3; ☎ 02-512 4738; www.petits-oignons.be; Rue Notre Seigneur 13; mains €18-25, 3-course lunch menu €18, 4-course dinner menu €28; ⊗ lunch Mon-Fri & dinner Mon-Sat) This wisteria-draped 17th-century house has globe lanterns and colour-splash art inside, a garden area behind and puts reliable if limited-choice Belgo-French food on your plate, notably ray wings and lamb knuckle.

GARE DU MIDI AREA

Within the Bruxelles-Midi complex are the usual bars, bakeries and snack-shacks but if you have a long wait for your train there are a couple of dining options nearby that might be worth leaving the station for.

Au Bon Coeur (Map pp72-3; ☎ 02-538 9669; Rue Joesph Claes 27; mains €4-10; ⊗ 6.30-10.30pm Tue-Sun) Despite its cheesy decor and unpromising location, this family-style Greek eatery is an age-old classic for inexpensive *petits os* (short, barbequed spare ribs) served with fresh lemon rather than barbeque sauce. Queues are possible mid-evening. The walk from the station's southeast exit is short but gloomy.

Midi Station (Map pp72-3; ☎ 02-526 8800; www.midistation.eu; Pl Victor Horta 26; mains €20-33; ⊗ 7am-midnight) Attempting to reverse the Bruxelles-Midi station area's negative image, this boldly stylish restaurant also offers an oyster bar, hip cocktail lounge, a cigar bar and live music Thursdays and Fridays (10pm). Several cheap, smoky bars lie on either side if all you want's a €1.60 beer.

MATONGE & ST-BONIFACE

Very inexpensive African, Pakistani, South American, Italian and Belgo-Belgian eateries

EATING AFRICAN

Many restaurants in the compact Congolese district of Matonge offer a selection of African dishes. Common choices are *moambe*, Congo's classic palm-nut stew (fish or chicken), *yassa*, a tangy lemon-flavoured chicken dish originally from Senegal and *mafe* (aka *poulet arachide*), an Africa-wide favourite with chicken in a sauce made from palm oil, peanut paste and tomato purée. Add hot-pepper sauce to taste. Other typical options are grilled whole *tilapia* (St-Peters' fish), curried *gésier* (chicken gizzards) and barbequed goat. All tend to come accompanied with rice (sometimes cassava) with optional cassava-leaf 'spinach' and deep-fried plantain chips.

are located side-by-side along Rue Longue Vie and are liberally scattered on Chaussée de Wavre. Meanwhile one block southwest, St-Boniface is an island of decidedly trendier bistros and coffee shops.

Tartine Zaline (Map pp72-3; Galerie de la Porte de Namur; mains €5-7; 🕑 noon-8pm) Generous portions of pre-prepared African meals packed to take away or microwaved to eat at a single row of simple stools.

Imagin'Air (Map pp72-3; ☎ 02-511 3331; Pl Fernand Cocq 6; mains €9-17; 🕑 10am-10pm Mon-Sat, 10am-6pm Sun, closed Wed in winter) Adorable, organic-food 'Art Café' with exposed brick walls and one of Brussels' prettiest patio terraces decked with plants and bonsai-sized trees. Short, handwritten menus change frequently and dishes can be made to order for those on gluten-free, lactose-free and vegetarian/vegan diets.

Les Brassins (Map pp72-3; ☎ 02-512 6999; www.les brassins.be; Rue Keyenveld 36; mains €10-17; 🕑 noon-2.30pm & 6pm-midnight Mon-Fri, noon-1am Sat, noon-midnight Sun) On a quiet, unpromising back-street, this unpretentious brasserie is decorated with old enamel brewery adverts and serves reliable, well-priced Belgian home-cooked classics such as *carbonade*, *filet américain* and *boulettes* (meatballs), accompanied by perfect *frites* (or *stoemp*, you choose) and washed down by an excellent range of Belgian beers.

Le Dakar (Map pp72-3; ☎ 0498-989 500; http://resto ledakar.com; Chaussée de Wavre 134; beer €2, mains €10.50-13; 🕑 noon-1am Mon-Sat, 6pm-1am Sun) Numerous places nearby serve the same Congolese and Senegalese favourites (see above) for less

money. However, unlike most, the Dakar has a gentle semblance of style and even a pair of artistic lounge seats at which to sip your aperitif.

L'Ultime Atome (Map pp72-3; ☎ 02-513 1367; www .ultime-atome.com; Rue St-Boniface 14; mains €11-17; 🕑 8.30am-1am Mon-Fri, 10am-1am Sat & Sun). This cavernous brasserie has curious train-wheel decor enlivening the pale wooden panelling of an otherwise classic *café*. A youthful crowd keeps things buzzing day and night and the non-stop kitchen turns out great-value meals including cheesy endives, tajines and mussels (€17).

Saint-Boniface (Map pp72-3; ☎ 02-511 5366; Rue St-Boniface 9; mains €15-22; 🕑 noon-2.30pm & 7-10pm Mon-Fri). Enchanting old-world restaurant, featuring gingham tablecloths, walls jammed with framed pictures and authentic dishes from France's southwestern and Basque regions, notably *cassoulet*, Périgord duck, foie gras and *andouillette* (strongly flavoured tripe sausage – very much an acquired taste).

IXELLES & AVE LOUISE

Le Framboisier (Map pp72-3; ☎ 02-647 5144; Rue du Bailli 35; 🕑 noon-11pm Tue-Sun) Imaginatively flavoured ice cream to take away or, in summer, eat in the garden. Sorbets, including some made from Cantillon beers, are the house specialities.

Le Hasard des Choses (Map pp72-3; ☎ 02-538 1863; Rue du Page 31; mains €10-15, 🕑 noon-2.30pm Mon-Fri & 7-10.30pm Sun-Fri) Monty Python-esque lamps and tube vents, rough, bare-brick walls and a tree-shaded backyard area make an unusual venue for salads, delicious pastas or shrimps in green coconut curry (€14).

Fin de Siècle (off Map pp72-3; ☎ 02-648 8041; www .lafindesiecle.be; Ave Louise 423; mains €10-20; 🕑 lunch & dinner) Despite the imposing exterior and plush olde-worlde decor this delightful discovery offers well-prepared (predominantly Italian) meals at remarkably sensible prices. A one-plate lunch costs only €7.95. Garden seating in summer.

Dolma (Map pp72-3; ☎ 02-649 8981; www.dolma.be; Chaussée d'Ixelles 329; 🕑 Tue-Sat) Competent if not especially exotic vegetarian buffet served in a Tibetan ambience. The daily changing selection is posted on their website.

La Tsampa (Map pp72-3; ☎ 02-647 0367; www.tsampa .be; Rue de Livourne 109; daily special €12; 🕑 noon-7.30pm Mon-Fri, closed Aug) Vegetarian restaurant and organic delicatessen with choice of meals till

2.30pm, then salads, pies or set-dish plates till close.

Rouge Tomate (Map pp72-3; ☎ 02-647 7044; www.rouge tomate.com; Ave Louise 190; mains €18-29; ✆ noon-2.30pm Mon-Fri & 7-10.30pm Mon-Sat) Modern Mediterranean cuisine served in an expansive, fashionably updated 1883 townhouse whose rear terrace, shaded by old trees, adds further to the attraction in summer. Try the *lomo* (tenderloin) with mint and almond curry or, for vegetarians, pesto-flavoured *légumes en cocotte*.

La Quincaillerie (Map pp72-3; ☎ 02-533 9833; www.quin caillerie.be; Rue du Page 45; mains €19-35; ✆ noon-2.30pm Mon-Sat, 7pm-midnight daily) A central Victorian stairway and station-style clock dominate this unique brasserie-restaurant. Wooden box-draws, gleaming copperware and green wrought-iron interior date from its days as an upmarket ironmonger's shop. Upper-level seating is cramped but offers unusual views down upon other diners. Menus are multilingual and food standards reliable.

Chez Oki (Map pp72-3; ☎ 02-644 4576; www.chez-oki .com; Rue Lesbroussart 62; lunch €9, mains €20-25, 3-/4-/ 5-course menu €30/39.50/49.50; ✆ noon-2pm Tue-Fri & 6.30-10pm Mon-Sat) Modern minimalism wraps around a patch of 'zen garden' while French-Japanese fusion food works wonders on your plate. Hope that your *yeux fermés* (surprise) menu starts as ours did – with utterly divine foie gras sushi drizzled with caramelised soya. Wow. Wines from €26.

Yamayu Santatsu (Map pp72-3; ☎ 02-513 5312; Chaussée d'Ixelles 141; ✆ lunch Tue-Sat, dinner Tue-Sun) Widely reckoned to be Brussels' most authentic Japanese restaurant by those who can cope with the idiosyncrasies of the notoriously temperamental sushi-master.

Anderlecht

Several *cafés* around the main square have cheap snack meals. For something more satisfying, **René** (Map pp66-7; ☎ 02-523 2876; Place de la Résistance 14; mains €14-26; ✆ lunch & dinner Wed-Sun) is

a quintessential old-world family restaurant serving excellent steaks, *filet américain* finished at your table and seasonal mussels in steaming cauldrons. It overlooks a tree-lined square that hosts a vibrant Saturday market.

DRINKING

In most cities, tourists stop in *cafés* in between visiting the sights. Here the *cafés* are the sights. And visiting a museum or two just gives your liver the necessary respite before another drink. Nearly every street in the city centre has at least one marvellously atmospheric *café*. Styles vary from showy art nouveau places and medieval survivors around the Bourse to hip and heaving options in St-Géry and Ixelles. And there's many an Anglo-Irish pub in the EU quarter. Where oh where will it end?

Lower Town
GRAND PLACE & AROUND
Whether you're sitting on one of the incomparable open-air terraces or within a 17th-century guildhouse, drinking on the grandest of Grand Places is a delight. Our favourites are the bustling **Le Roy d'Espagne** (Map p70; Grand Place 1; beer/coffee from €3/3.10; ✆ 10am-1am) – yes, those are inflated dried pigs' bladders above your head – and the even more indulgent **Chaloupe d'Or** (Map p70; Grand Place 24; beer/coffee from €3.40/3.60; ✆ 10am-midnight), whose 'secret' upstairs room is a particularly superb vantage point though not always open. Not surprisingly prices are steep, so if you're not here to soak up the special Grand Place ambience you can save up to 50% on drinks by walking just a block or two further.

Le Cercueil (The Coffin; Map p70; Rue des Harengs 10-12; beer from €2.80; ✆ 4pm-late Mon-Tue, 1pm-late Fri-Sun) Grungy, all-black madness with coffins for tables and lit mainly by UV.

Goupil le Fol (Map p70; ☎ 02-511 1396; Rue de la Violette 22; ✆ 9pm-5am) Overwhelming weirdness hits you as you acid-trip your way through

---

CHIP CHAMPS

Frying since 1948, **Maison Antoine** (Map p86; Place Jourdan; small chips/large chips/sauce €2/2.20/0.50; ✆ 11.30am-1am Sun-Thu, 11.30am-2am Fri & Sat) is a classic little *fritkot* (take-away chip kiosk) whose reputation as 'Brussels best' is self-perpetuating. 'Best' or not, their chips are certainly top notch and such is their popularity that *cafés* on the surrounding square (including beautifully wrought-iron-fronted L'Autobus) allow *frite* eaters to sit and snack so long as they buy a drink. Another fine contender for the chip crown is **Chez François** (Map pp66-7; Pl Dumon) at outlying Metro Stockel. Handily central Fritland (p99) keeps frying till the wee hours.

BRUSSELS' TOP DRINKING SPOTS FOR...

- Breakfast: Mokafé (p104)
- Bottled-beer choice: Délirium Café (p104)
- Chess: Le Greenwich (p104)
- Classic brown-*café* ambience: À la Mort Subite (below)
- Coffee: Blomqvists Espresso Bar (p105)
- Draught-beer choice: Moeder Lambic Fontainas (p104)
- Eccentricity: Goupil le Fol (opposite), Le Cercueil (opposite)
- *Fin-de-siècle* brilliance: Falstaff (below), Le Cirio (below), Métropole Café (p105)
- Hubble-bubble waterpipes: Imanza (p105)
- Hype: Café Belga (p105)
- Medieval atmosphere: A L'Image de Nostre-Dame (below)
- Ornate interior at bargain prices: Brasserie de la Renaissance (p105)
- Reading: Cercle des Voyageurs (p104), Floreo (p104)
- Tea: Comptoir Florian (p105)

---

this sensory overload of rambling passageways, ragged old sofas and inexplicable beverages mostly based on madly fruit-flavoured wines (no beer available). Unmissable.

Poechenellekelder (Map p70; Rue du Chêne 5) Despite facing Brussels' kitsch-central, this is a surprisingly appealing *café* full of genuine old puppets. It offers a decent selection of fairly priced beers including Oerbier and gueuze on tap.

La Fleur en Papier Doré (Map p70; www.goudblommekeinpapier.be; Rue des Alexiens 53; 11am-midnight Tue-Sat, 11am-7pm Sun) The nicotine-stained walls of this tiny *café* are covered with writings, art and scribbles by Magritte and his surrealist pals, some of which were reputedly traded for free drinks. '*Ceci n'est pas un musée*', quips a sign on the door reminding visitors to buy a drink and not just look around.

BOURSE

Ah, the classics. If you do nothing else in Brussels, visit at least a couple of these close-packed yet easily overlooked gems. Each has its own unique character.

A L'Image de Nostre-Dame (Map p70; beers from €1.60; noon-midnight Mon-Fri, 3pm-1am Sat, 4pm-10.30pm Sun, closes 8pm Wed) Down a tiny hidden alley, Nostre-Dame has an almost medieval feel, but retains a genuine local vibe. Magical... except for the toilets.

our pick **Le Cirio** (Map p70; ☎ 02-512 1395; Rue de la Bourse 18; beer/lasagne €2.20/7.80; 10am-midnight) This

sumptuous 1886 *grand café* dazzles with polished brass-work and aproned waiters yet prices aren't exorbitant and coiffured Mesdames with small dogs still dilute the gaggles of tourists. The house speciality is a half-and-half mix of still and sparkling wines (€3.20).

Au Bon Vieux Temps (Map p70; Impasse Saint Michel; beers from €2.50; 11am-midnight) Duck beneath the bishop then tunnel through the centuries to this lushly panelled 1695 gem. You'll find lavish fireplaces, fascinating characters and even mythical Westvleteren 12 (€10!) on the beer menu.

Falstaff (Map p70; Rue Henri Maus 17; beers/mains from €2.80/13.50; 10am-1am) The interior of this *grand café* is an astonishing festival of century-old art nouveau stained glass and fluidity designed by Horta disciple, Houbion. A wide range of meals are available.

À la Bécasse (Map p70; Rue de Tabora 11; beer/spaghetti from €2.80/5; 11am-midnight) Hidden almost invisibly down a body-wide alley-tunnel. Long rows of tables give the Bécasse a certain Breugelesque quality though it's 'only' been operating since 1877. The unusual speciality is *panaché*, a jug of Timmermans lambic mixed with fruit beer or faro to make it more palatable. Not to everyone's taste.

ILOT SACRÉ

À la Mort Subite (Map p70; Rue Montagne aux Herbes Potagères 7; draught Maes/Chimay €2/4.10; 11am-midnight;) An absolute classic unchanged since 1928, with lined-up wooden tables, arched mirror-panels and entertainingly brusque service.

Toone (Map p70; beer from €2.50; ☾ noon-midnight Tue-Sun) Home to Brussels' classic puppet theatre (p108), this is also a unique and atmospheric drinking den…if you ever get served.

Délirium Café (Map p70; ☎ 02-511 3601; www.deliriumcafe.be; Impasse de la Fidélité; ☾ 10am-4am Mon-Sat, 10am-2am Sun) The barrel tables, beer-tray ceilings and over 2000 world beers were already impressive. Now they've added a rum garden, a tap house and the Floris Bar (from 8pm) serving hundreds of *jenevers*, vodkas and absinthes. No wonder it's lively. Live music at 10.15pm

Mokafé (Map p70; Galerie du Roi; coffee/beer/waffles/breakfast from €2/2/2.60/6.50; ☾ 7.30-11.30pm) Ideal for breakfast or gently indulgent cakes at a terrace in the awesome Galeries St-Hubert.

ST-GÉRY & STE-CATHERINE
Our listing barely scratches the surface of all that's available within a few easy blocks.

ourpick Cercle des Voyageurs (Map p70; ☎ 02-514 3949; www.lecercledesvoyageurs.com; ☾ 11am-10pm Wed-Mon; ☜) Invite Phileas Fogg for coffee to this delightfully calm *café* featuring globes, antique-map ceiling and a travel library. If he's late, flick through old *National Geographics* in your colonial leather chair or use the free wi-fi to see what happened.

Moeder Lambic Fontainas (Map p70; www.chezmoederlambic.be; Impasse de la Fidélité; ☾ 10am-4am Mon-Sat, 10am-2am Sun) A beer pub with design-style decor, dangling trumpet lamps, back lit wall panels and an incredible 640 different brews on draught including Witkap Pater (€3.30).

Le Greenwich (Map p70; ☎ 02-511 4167; Rue des Chartreux 7; beer/coffee/wine from €2.10/2.10/3.50, croque/spaghetti €4/9; ☾ 11am-10pm) High-ceilinged pub with belle époque gilt woodwork and pina-fored waitresses supplying beers to a clientele of chess-playing regulars. The hushed concentration means you can hear a pawn drop.

Floreo (Map p70; ☎ 02-514 3905; www.floreo.be; Rue des Riches Claires 19; beer/coffee/shots/cocktails €1.80/1.90/4.50/6.50, wraps/mains €5.50/11.50; ☾ 11am-late) Big windows and a 1920s/30s charm make this intimate *café* a particularly relaxing place to read the newspapers by day (provided in several languages). On weekend evenings things heat up around 10pm with a DJ perched on the wooden spiral stairs. There's also a soul-funk jam session on Thursday nights around 9.30pm.

Booze'n'Blues (Map p70; Rue des Riches Claires 20; beer from €2; ☾ 4pm-late) Cramped and rough featuring a mannequin torso, an old juke box and an extended bar panelled like a choir stall. Unpredictable, entertainingly grouchy staff.

Los Romanticos (Map p70; ☎ 02-217 6707; Quai au Bois à Brûler 5; beer/mescal/cocktails from €2.50/6/7.50; ☾ noon-late, kitchen till 10pm) Upbeat South American restaurant, cocktail bar and dance floor offering regular tango courses.

Other great choices:

Monk (Map p70; Rue Ste-Catherine 42) Contemporary meets old brown-*café* in this 17th-century gabled house with tiled floors, mirrored walls and a hip clientele.

Fontainas Bar (Map p70; Rue du Marché au Charbon 91) Groovy triangle of 70s retro cool and a great patch of street-terrace.

Zebra (Map p70; Place St-Géry 33) Why do the hippest people like the least comfortable chairs?

Gecko (Map p70; Place St-Géry 16) Rough school-desk seating on the street-terrace and just the right level of planned scruffiness inside. Music favours modern reggae and African vibes.

Gay Bars
Le Belgica (Map p70; www.lebelgica.be; Rue du Marché au Charbon 32; ☾ 10pm-3am Thu-Sat, 8pm-3am Sun) DJs transform what looks like a 1920s traditional brown-*café* into one of Brussels' most popular gay music-pubs. Several other gay venues lie along the same street.

L'Homo Erectus (Map p70; ☎ 0475-831 107; www.lhomoerectus.com; Rue des Pierres 57; ☾ 3pm-dawn Mon-Fri, from 4pm Sat & Sun) One of the capital's most popular gay bars, now with two venues, each easily recognisable by the evolution of man from ape graphically depicted on the front windows. Relatively quiet during the day, crammed at night, and swamped during Pride weekends.

Locals' Cafés
Au Laboureur (Map p70; Rue de Flandre 108; beer €1.60; ☾ 9.30am-10pm) Amid surrounding trendiness, this refreshingly unpretentious place still attracts crusty beer-nursing locals with unfeasibly long moustaches. Hurry before it gentrifies.

Some other solidly local, unpretentious brown *cafés* that are central yet off the typical tourist circuit include **Kafka** (Map p70; Rue de la Vierge Noire 6), **Au Daringman** (Map p70; Rue de Flandre 37) and **Les Postiers** (Rue du Fossé aux Loups 14).

Tea & Coffee

Coffee Company (Map p70; Rue du Midi 45; cappuccinos €2.50; 🕙 7.30-11.30pm) Starbucks-style caffeine fixes for those wanting 'real' cappuccinos.

Imanza (Map p70; Rue van Artevelde 52; soft-drinks/tea €2.50/4, waterpipe €9; 🕙 6pm-1.30am Tue-Sun) Of the capital's many 'shisha bars' (places to smoke fragrant waterpipes), few are as exotically inviting as this triangular Ali Baba's cavern of low brass tables and twinkling Moroccan lamps. No alcohol served.

Métropole Café (Map p70; www.metropolehotel.com; Hotel Métropole, Place de Brouckère 31 beer/coffee/waffles from €3.80/3.80/7) The magnificently ornate belle époque interior easily justifies the hefty drink prices, though curiously a large number of punters still decide to sit on its comparatively unappealing street terrace.

Marolles

Brasserie Ploegmans (Map pp72-3; www.ploegmans.be; Rue Haute 148; mains €12-24; 🕙 noon-2.30pm Tue-Fri & 6pm-10pm Tue-Sat, closed Aug) Old-fashioned mirror-panelled seats and 1927 chequerboard flooring make this a classic local hostelry that's also well regarded for its typical Bruxellois meals.

L'Inattendu (Map pp72-3; Rue de Wynants 13; beers €1.70-3, mains €8-15.50; 🕙 9am-11pm Mon-Thu, 9am-5am Fri) As unexpected as the name suggests, this is one classic little wood-panelled *café*-bistro tourists have largely overlooked. Basic, traditional pub-meals are served including *stoemp* (€9.50) and *waterzooi* (cream-based stew; €12).

Zabar (Map pp72-3; Pl de la Chapelle 7; beer/coffee from €2.50/2.50, pastas €8; 🕙 11am-1am Mon-Fri, 10am-3am Sat, 10am-7pm Sun; 🛜) This retro-stylish *café* is more orange than an orange and offers free wi-fi.

EU Area

Each national group has its own Eurocrat hangouts. On Thursday nights the bars of Place du Luxembourg are especially packed with parliamentary aides on the razz before their three-day weekend. Irish pubs around the Commission are typical Eurocrat favourites including **Kitty O'Shea's** (Map p86; Blvd Charlemagne 42), the **James Joyce** (Map p86; Rue Archimède 34) and oversized **Wild Geese** (Map p86; Ave Livingstone 2), though the **Old Oak** (Map p86; 26 rue Franklin 26; beers from €1.50) is more down-to-earth.

Ville de Dinant (Map p86; Rue de Trèves 30; beers €1.80-3; 🕙 11.30am-7pm Mon-Fri) You don't need a guidebook to find the numerous Eurocrat drinking holes around Place du Luxembourg but if you

want a really local experience nearby come to this uncompromisingly Belgian dive for a draught Grimbergen Blond.

Piola Libri (Map p86; ☎ 02-736 9391; www.piolalibri.be; Rue Franklin 66; 🕙 noon-3pm & 6-8pm Mon-Fri, noon-6pm Sat, closed Aug; 🛜) Italian Eurocrats relax after work on sofas, pavement tables or in the tiny triangle of back garden and enjoy free tapas-style snacks with chilled white wines at this convivial bookshop-*café*-bar.

La Terrasse (Map pp66-7; ☎ 02-732 2851; www.brasserielaterrasse.be; Ave des Celtes 1; beers €2.40-4.50, mains €9.90-18; 🕙 8am-midnight Mon-Sat, 10am-midnight Sun) Handy for the Cinquantenaire, this wood-panelled classic *café* has a tree-shaded terrace and makes an ideal refreshment stop after a hard day's museuming. Snacks, pancakes, ice creams, breakfasts (from €3.90) and decent pub-meals are all available at various times.

Ixelles & St-Gilles

FLAGEY

The area is accessible by tram 81.

Café Belga (Map pp72-3; ☎ 02-640 3508; Place Flagey 18; 🕙 8am-2am Sun-Thu, 8am-3am Fri & Sat) This hip brasserie in a corner of the art deco Flagey 'liner' building (p89) is mellow by day but beats grow ever louder towards closing time.

Nexx (Map pp72-3; ☎ 02-644 5434; www.nexxresto club.be; Chaussée de Boondael 8; beer/wine/cocktails from €2.50/3.50/8, mains €12.50-21.50; 🕙 noon-3am Sun-Thu, noon-5am Fri & Sat) By midnight all conversation is drowned by DJ enthusiasm as *Brussels branché* set pack themselves into a heaving mass of hip blue-neon and silver wall-pads. In the quieter hours of early evening there's remarkably decent food on offer albeit rather haphazardly served.

MATONGE & LOUISE

Kuumba (Map pp72-3; ☎ 02-512 8505; Rue de la Paix 35; 🕙 1pm-10pm Wed-Sat) The appealing *café* of a Flemish-African friendship association with small exhibitions of African art.

Coffee & Tea

If you're seeking 'real' cappuccinos (made with frothed milk rather than Belgian style with sweet whipped cream) try these cafes.

Blomqvists Espresso Bar (Map pp72-3; ☎ 0484-350 644; Rue Francart 14) A Swedish barista works his La Marzocco FB70, an espresso machine that's worth as much as a family car.

Comptoir Florian (Map pp72-3; ☎ 02-513 9103; www.comptoirflorian.be; Rue St-Boniface 17; coffee/tea

€2.50/4.50; 11am-8pm Tue-Sat) Two tiny, supercosy tasting rooms behind a tea-trading store offering six different bean types for its coffees and 200 teas served in an eclectic range of pots.

Natural Caffè (Map pp72-3; Ave Louise 196; espresso/cappuccino €2/2.60; 7.30am-7pm Mon-Fri, 9am-7pm Sat, 10am-6pm Sun) Popular and fashionably brash if you like that upmarket chain sandwich-shop feel.

ST-GILLES
Brasserie de la Renaissance (Map pp72-3; 02-534 8260; Ave Paul Dejaer 39; 9am-midnight) This *grand café* has a single, high-ceilinged room whose walls sport a ludicrously ornate load of gilt stucco tracery. Yet despite the grandeur, drinks are cheap and the food (Portuguese, Italian and Belgo-French) an amazing bargain. The street terrace surveys St-Gilles' lovely town hall.

Moeder Lambic (Map pp72-3; 02-544 1699; Rue de Savoie 68; 4pm-2am) Sample an A to Z of Belgian beers in this compact *café* with bare-brick walls, chunky hand-hewn tables and crates full of well-thumbed comic books to read. Quite a contrast to its hip new sister-act (p104)

ENTERTAINMENT
For extensive listings check www.netevents.be, www.agenda.be, www.kiosque.be or, in print, get the English-language magazine *Bulletin*, Wednesday's MAD supplement in *Le Soir* or (more generally for Belgium) the Mosquito pull-out from *Telemoustique* magazine.

Ticket agencies:
Arsene50 (02-512 5745; www.arsene50.be; 12.30-5.30pm Tue-Sat; Galeries St-Hubert Map p70; Cinéma Arenberg, Galerie de la Reine; Flagey Map pp72-3; Pl Ste-Croix) Last-minute discounted and half-price tickets for cinema, theatre and assorted shows.

Caroline Music (Map p70; 02-217 0731; www.carolinemusic.be; Passage St-Honoré 20) Music shop and ticket agent for contemporary live gigs, festivals and club nights.

FNAC (Map pp68-9; 02-275 1115; City 2 shopping centre, Rue Neuve; 10am-7pm Mon-Sat, 10am-8pm Fri) Tickets for mainstream events.

Cinema
Cinenews (www.cinenews.be) tells you what's on at 37 Brussels cinemas and dozens more beyond. On listings, 'VO' means 'original version' (ie with subtitles, not dubbed) while 'V fr' (French version) implies dubbing into French.

Kinepolis (Map pp66-7; 02-474 2600; www.kinepolis.com; Blvd du Centenaire 1;) Belgium's original multiplex complex with 24 screens and an IMAX theatre.

Cinematek (Map pp68-9; 02-551 1919; www.cinematek.be; BoZar Complex, Rue Baron Horta 9; adult/member €3/1, 2-month membership €15) Cinema buffs swoon at the incredible range of classic and cult choices and it's worth arriving early to browse the museum's old projectors and cinema memorabilia. Almost every day at least one silent movie is screened with live piano accompaniment. Other classic talkies are shown in their original language. To be on the safe side, consider booking a day ahead.

Cinema Nova (Map p70; 02-511 2477; www.nova-cinema.org; Rue Arenberg 3) The ultimate in alternative cinema, Nova shows off-beat international movies that are more thought-provoking than entertaining (subtitles will be French/Dutch) and there's a brilliantly rough student-style bar.

Live Music
ROCK
Ancienne Belgique (AB; Map p70; 02-548 2400; www.abconcerts.be; Blvd Anspach 110) The AB's two auditoriums are favourite venues for mid-level international rock bands and plenty of home-grown talent. Ticket office on Rue des Pierres.

Beursschouwburg (Map p70; 02-513 8290; www.beursschouwburg.be; Rue Auguste Orts 22; exhibition area 10am-6pm Mon-Sat, café 7.30pm-late Thu-Sun) Diverse mix of contemporary music including rock, jazz, rap and disco. The *café* approximates to a free nightclub late on weekend nights.

Forest National (Map pp66-7; 02-340 2211; www.forestnational.be; Ave du Globe 36) The city's temple for larger international gigs and local favourites. Take tram 81.

Also see **Halles de Schaerbeek** (p88).

JAZZ & BLUES
L'Archiduc (Map p70; 02-512 0652; www.archiduc.net; Rue Antoine Dansaert 6; beer/wine/cocktails €2.70/3.60/8; 4pm-late) This intimate, split-level art deco bar has been playing jazz since 1937. It's an unusual two-tiered circular space that can get incredibly packed but remains convivial. You might need to ring the doorbell. Saturday concerts are free, Sundays bring in international talent and admission charges vary.

Music Village (Map p70; 02-513 1345; www.themusicvillage.com; Rue des Pierres 50; cover €7-20; from 7.30pm Wed-Sat) Polished 100-seat jazz venue housed in two 17th-century buildings with dinner (not compulsory) available from 7pm and concerts starting 8.30pm, or 9pm weekends. The performers squeeze onto a small podium that's visible from any seat. Bookings advised.

Sounds Jazz Club (Map pp72-3; ☎ 02-512 9250; www .soundsjazzclub.be; Rue la Tulipe 28; ☿ 8pm-4am Mon-Sat) Unassuming but immensely popular little Ixelles venue. It has concerts most nights, styles varying from modern to big band to salsa. The website has click-through links to artists' MySpace pages. Cover charges vary and acts typically start around 10pm.

Jazz Station (Map pp66-7; ☎ 02-733 1378; http://jazz station.be; Chaussée de Louvain 193a; ☿ exhibitions 11am-7pm Wed-Sat, concerts 6pm Sat & 8.30pm some weeknights) An appealing new venue in what was once an 1885 station building. There are also exhibitions, a multimedia jazz-archive and practice rooms, where you can listen in on musicians honing their art.

Bizon (Map p70; ☎ 02-502 4699; www.cafebizon .com; Rue du Pont de la Carpe 7; admission free; ☿ 6pm-late) Happening little grunge bar in St-Géry featuring home-grown live blues, a range of beers and a selection of *jenevers*.

OPERA & CLASSICAL

La Monnaie/De Munt (Théâtre Royal de la Monnaie/ Koninklijke Muntschouwburg; Map p70; ☎ 02-229 1372; www.demunt.be; Place de la Monnaie) It was high-spirited revellers leaving this premier opera and dance venue who kick-started the 1830 revolution that led to Belgium's very formation (see the boxed text, below). The season runs September to June.

BoZar (Map pp68-9; ☎ 02-507 8215, bookings 02-507 8200; www.bozar.be; Rue Ravenstein 23) Celebrated classical-music venue, home to the National Orchestra and Philharmonic Society. From outside the Horta-designed 1928 art deco building lacks much charm but its Henri Le Bœuf Hall is considered to be one of the five best in the world for acoustic quality.

Conservatoire Royal de Musique (Royal Music Conservatory; Map pp72-3; ☎ 02-511 0427; Rue de la Régence 30) Classical-music venue.

Cirque Royal (Map pp68-9; ☎ 02-218 2015; www .cirque-royal.org; Rue de l'Enseignement 81) This converted indoor circus is now a venue for dance, operetta, classical and contemporary music.

Flagey (www.flagey.be) Ixelles' flagship venue has several concert halls. See p89.

Maison de la Bellone (Map p70; ☎ 02-513 3333; www.bellone.be; Rue de Flandre 46) The glass-vaulted courtyard of this 18th-century stunner is used for occasional concerts.

Nightclubs

Consult **TheClubbing** (www.theclubbing.com) or **Noctis** (www.noctis.com) for what's-on listings or ask at music shops like Caroline Music (opposite) or **Dr Vinyl** (Map p70; ☎ 02-512 7344; Rue de la Grande Île 1; ☿ noon-7pm Tue-Sat, open late for DJs Thu). Note that clubbing does not mean holing up in the capital – there's plenty more in and around Antwerp.

K-Nal (Map pp68-9; Ave du Port 1) On Saturday nights from 11pm, the capital's latest 'place to be' is K-Nal's Libertine Supersport (http://libertine supersport.be), which kicked off in October 2009 following an intense Facebook buzz. Libertine level plays house/disco/lounge music while Supersport invites the biggest names in electro. Certain Fridays K-Nal also hosts 'Fight Club' and 'Anarchic', each once a month.

REVOLUTIONARY PERFORMANCE

An enchanting if highly simplified story of Belgium's foundation starts on 25 August 1830 with the Brussels premiere of French composer Daniel Auber's then-new opera, *La Muette de Portici* at La Monnaie (above) in Brussels. The story, sung in French, centres on a 1647 Naples uprising against the Spanish, featuring large crowd scenes and dramatic effects. Fired up by the duet *Amour sacré de la patrie* (Sacred love of homeland), the mainly bourgeois Francophone audience poured into the streets to join workers already demonstrating outside the theatre against their Dutch rulers. Together they stormed the Palais de Justice, chased out the Dutch troops and, in a glorious crowning moment, raised the flag of Brabant over Brussels' City Hall. Belgium was born.

For the 175th anniversary of Belgium, the opera was re-performed in Ghent. But this was Flanders 2005. When *Amour sacré de la patrie* started there were no Francophone 'patriots' to be stirred but plenty of Flemish nationalist hecklers ready to interrupt by singing instead the Flemish anthem. But by a pre-prepared and wonderfully Belgian compromise, the protesters left after a few minutes. This time no revolution. At least, not yet.

BRUSSELS

GAY & LESBIAN BRUSSELS

Brussels' compact but thriving Rainbow Quarter is clustered around Rue du Marché au Charbon. Here you'll find a dozen gay-oriented *cafés* (see www.lepetitmarais.eu and p104), and two LGBT information centres/bars, multilingual **Rainbow House** (Map p70; ☎ 02-503 5990; www.rainbowhouse .be; Rue du Marché au Charbon 42; ⓨ 6.30pm-10.30pm Wed-Sat) and Francophone **Tels Quels** (Map p70; ☎ 02-512 3234; www.telsquels.be; Rue du Marché au Charbon 81; ⓨ from 5pm Sun-Tue, Thu & Fri, from 2pm Wed & Sat) who run the telephone helpline, **Telégal** (ⓨ 02-502 0700; 8pm-midnight).

Belgian Gay & Lesbian Pride (www.blgp.be; ⓨ 1st Sat in May) culminates in this area with a vast-scale all-night party. The **Festival du Film Gay & Lesbien de Bruxelles** (www.fglb.org) runs for 10 days in late January and Cinéma Nova (p106) runs occasional **Pink Screen weeks** (www .gdac.org). **Darakan** (Map p70; ☎ 02-512 2076; Rue du Midi 9) is a tiny gay bookshop.

La Démence (www.lademence.com) held at Fuse (below) is a hugely popular gay rave that attracts men from all over Europe and beyond. It's only on once a month; check the website for dates. **Absolutely M** (www.absolutely-m.net; admission €9; ⓨ 9pm-5am Sun) is a new Sunday gay night at the Mirano Continental (p107) and **Chez Maman** (Map p70; ☎ 02-502 8696; www.chezmaman.be; Rue des Grands Carmes 12; ⓨ from 10pm Thu-Sun) is the capital's most beloved transvestite show.

Handily central gay-friendly accommodation includes Downtown-BXL (p94), well placed for the nightlife area, and refined Maison Noble (p95), which is aimed more at couples and business folk.

Fuse (Map pp72-3; ☎ 02-511 9789; www.fuse.be; Rue Blaes 208; admission €3-12; ⓨ 11pm-7am Sat) The Marolles club that 'invented' European techno still crams up to 2000 movers onto its two dance floors. Once a month it also hosts La Démence (above).

Mirano Continental (Map pp68-9; www.mirano.be; Chaussée de Louvain) If you're still in your business suit after postwork Eurocrat pints on Place Luxembourg, this revamped former cinema could be your next destination. Thursdays' AtSeven (www.atseven.eu; from 7pm to 2am) is an early affair with grazing food, wine bar and '80s/'90s dance music while Friday parties and Saturday nights' Just Mirano (www .justmirano.be; €8 to €10; from 11pm to 6am) are mainstream 'friendly' discos.

Club des Halles (Map p70; ☎ 02-289 2660; www.cafe deshalles.be; Pl St-Géry 1) Popular city-centre club in the vaulted cellars beneath the buzzing Café des Halles.

Sport

In Heysel the national stadium, **Stade Roi Baudouin** (Map pp66-7; ☎ 02-479 3654; Ave du Marathon 135), hosts major cycling races, athletics meetings and international football matches. For club matches Brussels' most famous football team is RSC Anderlecht (see p91).

Theatre

Touring international productions occasionally supplement the local-language scene with English-language performances. The theatre season runs September to June.

Le Botanique (Map pp68-9; ☎ 02-218 7935; Rue Royale 236) Cultural centre, exhibition hall and concert venue incorporating an 1826 glass veranda.

KVS (Koninklijke Vlaamse Schouwburg; Map pp68-9; ☎ 02-210 1112; www.kvs.be; Rue de Laeken 146) The Royal Flemish Theatre performs in a bold new auditorium behind a beautifully restored neo-Renaissance facade with plenty of wrought ironwork. Challenging Dutch-language dramas are typical but there are dance and occasional English-language productions.

Théâtre National (Map pp68-9; ☎ 02-203 4155; www.theatrenational.be; Blvd Émile Jacqmain 111-115) The Francophone community's rectilinear glass theatre.

Kaaitheater (Map pp68-9; ☎ 02-201 5959; www .kaaitheater.be; Square Sainctelette 20) Bastion of Flemish avant-garde theatre.

Théâtre Les Tanneurs (Map pp72-3; ☎ 02-512 1784; www.lestanneurs.be; Rue des Tanneurs 75) Known for dynamic drama and dance.

Bronks Youth Theatre (Map p70; ☎ 02-219 7554; www.bronks.be; Marché aux Porcs 15) Theatre, mime and workshops for toddlers and children, most weekends.

PUPPET THEATRE

Théâtre Royal de Toone (Map p70; ☎ 02-511 7137; www.toone.be; Petite Rue des Bouchers 21; adult/student €10/7; ⓨ typically 8.30pm Thu & 4pm Sat, see website) Worth visiting anytime for its pub-*café*, this is also the last bastion of traditional marionette theatre, performed for adults in French and occasionally in Walloon or Bruxellois.

DANCE

Brussels has no resident classical ballet – that's in Antwerp (p187) – but innovative contemporary dance companies do make occasional performances.

Rosas (☎ 02-344 5598; www.rosas.be) This Brussels-based company built around choreographer Anne Teresa De Keersmaeker strikes a winning balance between traditional and avant-garde dance. When not globetrotting they typically perform at La Monnaie (p107) or Kaaitheater (opposite).

Ultima Vez (☎ 02-719 5528; www.ultimavez.com) Brainchild of controversial director/choreographer Wim Vandekeybus, who's big on stark, confrontational images. In Brussels you might catch them at Théâtre Les Tanneurs (opposite). Check the website.

La Raffinerie (off Map pp68-9; ☎ 02 410 3341; www.charleroi-danses.be; Rue de Manchester 21, Molenbeek) This converted 19th-century sugar refinery is second home to Charleroi/Danses (p222).

SHOPPING

Rue Neuve (p80) lacks charm but is a major mainstream shopping street. Tourist-oriented shops selling chocolate, beer, lace and Atomium baubles stretch between the Grand Place and Manneken Pis. The splendid Galeries St-Hubert feature many more chocolate shops sold in a calmer, grander setting. Rue Antoine Dansaert is the nerve centre of Brussels' design and fashion quarter, the Sablon features antiques, while the Marolles are full of quirky interior design shops. Ave Louise is the setting for many up-market chain boutiques.

Art, Antiques & Interior Design

The Sablon area's many antique shops and private galleries resemble miniature museums. Some sell ancient artefacts from around the world. Others specialise in art deco work, glassware or contemporary art.

There's a weekly **antique market** (Map pp72-3; ☻ 9am-6pm Sat, 9am-2pm Sun) on Place du Grand Sablon, which also sports particularly chic shops. Others are dotted along Rue des Minimes, Rue Charles Hanssens and Rue Watteeu. If you're trying to replace a broken

glass from a set of Belgian crystal try **Au Cherche-Midi** (Map pp72-3; ☎ 02-511 2608; Rue Ernest Allard 16; ☻ 10.30am-6pm Tue-Sat, 10.30am-2pm Sun). For a more funky selection of less exclusive ornaments and retro ware, trawl the appealing shops of Rue Haute and Rue Blaes in the Marolles district or rummage through the bric-a-brac of the Place du Jeu-de-Balle flea market (see p84). Haggling is expected at the latter.

Beer

Standard beers like Leffe, Hoegaarden, Chimay etc are usually cheaply available in supermarkets. But if you want rarer types without going to the brewery, there are beer-specialist shops to help you. They'll also sell matching glasses for some, along with various other beer paraphernalia. Shops with wide selections:

Beermania (Map pp72-3; ☎ 02-512 1788; www.beermania.be; Chaussée de Wavre 174; ☻ 11am-8pm Mon-Sat Jan-Nov, daily Dec) Complete with a tasting *café*, international delivery service and online sales.

De Biertempel (Map p70; ☎ 02-502 1906; www.biertempel.be; Rue du Marché aux Herbes 56b; ☻ 9.30am-7pm)

Chocolate
LOCAL PRODUCERS

Mary (www.marychoc.com; Map pp68-9; ☎ 02-217 4500; Rue Royale 73; per kg €56; ☻ 10am-6pm Mon-Sat) Supplies pralines to Belgium's royals plus the odd US president. Their chocolate-making workshop (Map pp66-7; ☎ 02-737 7244; Chaussée de Wavre 950; open 9am to 3.30pm) offers tours with tastings (€8) behind the crenellated facade of the Arsenal building.

Planète Chocolat (Map p70; ☎ 02-511 0755; www.planetechocolat.be; Rue du Lombard 24; per kg €50; ☻ 10.30am-6.30pm) Both moulds and chocolates are made on site. At 4pm Saturday and Sunday there are praline-making demonstrations explaining chocolate's development, culminating in a chance for visitors to create their own chocolates.

Wittamer (Map pp72-3; ☎ 02-512 3742; Place du Grand Sablon 6) One of Brussels' best-known local establishments also runs a nearby posh patisserie and coffee shop, which is one of the places to see and be seen.

Jean-Philippe Darcis (Map p70; ☎ 02-502 1414; www.darcis.com; Petite Rue au Beurre 14) A Marcolini (p110) fashion sense but with the addition of prize-winning patisserie creations, notably 12 flavours of macaroon.

CHAIN CHOCOLATE SHOPS

Leonidas (Map p70; www.leonidas.com; Rue de la Colline 11; per kg €19.80; ⊙ 9.30am-midnight) Though often unfairly maligned by choco-snobs, Leonidas offers bargain-value 100% cocoa-butter pralines from dozens of handy branches. This one opens especially long hours.

Corné Port Royal (Map p70; ☎ 02-512 4314; Rue de la Madeleine 9; per kg €35; ⊙ 10am-8pm) Excellent price-quality ratio.

Galler (Map p70; ☎ 02-502 0266; Rue au Beurre 44; per kg €48; ⊙ 10am-9.30pm) Has a reputation for innovative flavours, many available in bar form.

Neuhaus (Map p70; ☎ 02-512 6359; www.neuhaus .be; Galerie de la Reine 25) Belgium's original – established in 1857. This stunning flagship shop has stained-glass windows and sumptuous displays.

Pierre Marcolini (Map pp72-3; ☎ 02-513 1783; www .marcolini.be; Place du Grand Sablon 39; per kg €70) Rare chocolate beans, experimental flavours (eg tea) and designer black-box packaging make Marcolini's pralines Belgium's trendiest and most expensive.

Comic Books

Brüsel (Map p70; ☎ 02-502 3552; www.brusel.com; Blvd Anspach 100; ⊙ 10.30am-6.30pm Mon-Sat, noon-6.30pm Sun)

Centre Belge de la Bande Dessinée (see p80)

La Maison de la BD (Map p70; ☎ 02-502 9468; Blvd de l'Impératrice 1; ⊙ 10am-7pm Tue-Sun)

Fashion

Antwerp may be Belgium's centre of the avant-garde (see p177), but Brussels has plenty to offer. For an extensive listing of all that's available and links to designer websites, a great first stop is **Modo Bruxellae** (www.modobruxellae.be), the capital's fashion champion, who organises a biennial Designers' Trail (late October in even years). A plus in Brussels is that many top Belgian designer outlets are grouped conveniently close together on Avenue Dansaert (p79), including the boutiques of Annemie Verbeke, Olivier Strelli and Nicolas Woit. For international big-name boutiques, a better hunting ground is around Metro Louise.

Stijl (Map p70; ☎ 02-512 0313; Rue Antoine Dansaert 74) A top address, Stilj is well stocked with Antwerp Six classic designer-ware (Ann Demeulemeester, Dries Van Noten) but also features up-to-the-minute designers including Haider Ackermann, Gustavo Lins (www .gustavolins.com) and Raf Simons. It's a hip

place but not unduly daunting to enter and, unlike many such boutiques, prices are clearly labelled. Has fashion for men and women.

Idiz Bogam (Map p70; ☎ 02-512 1032; Rue Antoine Dansaert 76) Specialises in retro, vintage and global secondhand gear for men and women. Big on furs, hats, shoes and sequins.

Gabrielle (Map p70; ☎ 02-514 7808; Rue des Chartreux 25; ⊙ 1-6.30pm Tue, 11am-6.30pm Wed-Sat) Vintage clothing and accessories from the '20s to '70s.

Delvaux (Map p70; ☎ 02-512 7198; Galerie de la Reine 31) A household name for Belgian leather handbags and accessories.

Les Enfants d'Édouard (Map pp72-3; ☎ men's 02-640 4245, women's 02-640 2448; men's Ave Louise 177, women's Ave Louise 175) Secondhand and end-of-line (red label) stocks of designer and major-brand clothes.

Lace

Manufacture Belge de Dentelles (Map p70; ☎ 02-511 4477; www.mbd.be; Galerie de la Reine 6-8; ⊙ 9.30am-6pm Mon-Sat, 10am-4pm Sun) Excellent stock of antique lace, and staff who love the stuff. For more on lace, see p139.

GETTING THERE & AWAY
Air

Brussels Airport (Map pp66-7; ☎ 02-753 4221, flight information 0900 70 000; www.brusselsairport.be; Zaventem) is 14km northeast of Brussels. There are ATMs on most levels and for stamps there's a postpoint in the Louis Delhaize grocery. The arrivals hall (Level 2) has a money changer (but watch the rates), car-rental agencies and tourist information. The bus terminus and luggage lockers are on Level 0, the train station on Level 1. For airlines information, see p297. For getting to/from the airport, see opposite.

Bus

Eurolines (Map pp68-9; ☎ 02-274 1350; www.eurolines.be; Rue du Progrès 80) operates to London, Amsterdam, Paris and other international destinations from Bruxelles-Nord. See above for details.

Car

Major car-rental companies have offices at Gare du Midi and Brussels Airport but rentals from their downtown premises usually cost less.

Avis (Map pp72-3; ☎ 02-537 1280; www.avis.be; Rue Américaine 145)

Budget (Map pp72-3; ☎ 02-646 5130; www.budget.be; Hotel Bristol, Ave Louise 91)

Train

Bruxelles-Midi (South Station; Map pp72-3) is the main station for international connections: the Eurostar, TGV and Thalys high-speed trains (with prebooking compulsory) only stop here. Most other mainline trains stop in quick succession at Bruxelles-Midi, **Bruxelles-Central** (Gare Centrale, Central Station; Map p70) and, except for Amsterdam trains, also at **Bruxelles-Nord** (Gare du Nord, North Station; Map pp68-9). Information offices at all three stations open early morning to late evening. For all enquiries consult www.b-rail .be or call ☎ 02-555 2555.

The following fares (one-way second-class) are for standard trains from Bruxelles-Central:

Destination	Fare (€)	Duration (min)	Frequency (per hr)
Amsterdam	36.60	164	1
Antwerp	6.60	35-49	5
Binche	8.60	59	1
Bruges	12.90	62	2
Charleroi	8.60	60	2
Ghent	8.10	36	2
Hasselt	11.70	75	2
Kortrijk	11.70	69	1
Leuven	4.80	24-36	4
Liège	13.60	60-80	2
Luxembourg City	33.20	180	1
Mechelen	4	15-28	2
Mons	8.60	55	2
Namur	8.10	62	2
Nivelles	5.10	30	2
Ostend	15.40	75	1
Schiphol (Amsterdam airport)	34.20	148	1
Tournai	11.70	61-73	2
Ypres	16	105	1

For other international train services see p298.

GETTING AROUND
To/From the Airport

Airport City Express (€3; ⏱ 5.30am-12.20am) trains run four times hourly between Brussels Airport and the city's three main train stations, Bruxelles-Nord (15 minutes), Bruxelles-Central (20 minutes) and Bruxelles-Midi (25 minutes). Express-bus 12 links the airport to Bruxelles-Luxembourg via Nato HQ and Metro Schuman (prepurchased/bought-aboard €3/4). It should take around 30 minutes but allow much more at rush hour. After 8pm at weekends slower route 21 is substi-tuted. See www.stib.be for the rather complex timetables. An airport taxi to central Brussels costs around €30 (some accept credit cards) but once you're stuck in rush-hour traffic you'll probably wish you'd taken the train.

Bicycle

Intolerant drivers, slippery cobblestones and tram tracks combine to make Brussels a cyclist's nightmare. However, in 2009 the **Brussels Charter** (www.velo-city2009.com) gave the city international prominence in pushing for increased bicycle mobility and infrastructure. A network of bike paths (separated from the traffic) and bike lanes (usually painted red and marked with white lines) is being somewhat imperfectly introduced and bicycles may legally take certain (marked) one-way streets in the wrong direction: convenient but hazardous, as few car drivers realise. **Cycling in Brussels** (www.bicycle .irisnet.be) gives maps and more information. Bicycles can be carried on metros and trams except at rush hours (7am to 9am and 4pm to 6.30pm), once you've purchased a one-year €15 bike pass.

RENTAL

Villo! (☎ 078-051 110; http://en.villo.be; ⏱ 24 hrs) is an system of 180 automated stations for short-term bicycle rental (30/60/90/120 minutes free/€0.50/1.50/3.50). First you need a subscription (day/week/year €1.50/7/30), then charges accumulate and are debited from your credit/bank card. When making stops the idea is to return the bike to the nearest station and take a new one when continuing. Failure to return the bicycle or to follow the rules could cost you €150. Read the website carefully for details and a station-finder map (note that only major ones issue subscriptions).

For longer bike hires try **FietsPunt/PointVelo** (Map p70; ☎ 02-513 0409; www.recyclo.org; Pl Madeleine; per day/3 days €7.50/15; ⏱ 7am-7pm Mon-Fri), which is also a cycle repair shop. You'll need ID and credit card or a €150 deposit. The shop is somewhat hidden: look left as you leave Bruxelles-Central station via the daytime-only Madeleine exit.

CYCLE TOURS

Cycle tours are available through Centre Vincent van Gogh (p93), **Maison des Cyclistes** (Map pp72-3; ☎ 02-502 7355; www.provelo.be; Rue de Londres 15; ⏱ noon-6pm Mon-Fri, 10am-6pm Sat & Sun Apr-Oct) and **Brussels Bike Tours** (☎ 0484-898 936; www.brussels

biketours.com; adult/student incl bicycle rental €25/22; (🕙 10am Feb-Nov, 10am & 3pm Apr-Sep). The latter's approximately four-hour tours (maximum group size 12) start from the Hôtel de Ville (Grand Place). Many first-time visitors love both the ride and the beers and *frite*-stops along the way (food and drink costs extra).

ROLLERSKATES

Belgium is perhaps unique in having special road rules for 'rollers' (those on rollerskates or rollerblades). On Friday evenings June to September certain major city streets give temporary right of way to rollers from 7pm (see www.belgiumrollers.com).

Car

The slightest hiccup on either ring road brings traffic to a halt especially on Friday afternoons. **Brussels-Mobilty** (www.bruxellesmobilite.irisnet .be) maps real-time congestion problems. For information on road rules, see p305.

Street parking requires meter-payment when signs say *betalend parkeren/stationnement payant* (usually 9am to 1pm and 2pm to 7pm Monday to Saturday).

Public Transport

Brussels' integrated bus-tram-metro system is operated by **STIB/MIVB** (www.stib.be) Main kiosk (Map p70; ☎ 02-515 2000; Rue de l'Évêque 2; 🕙 10am-6pm Mon-Sat); Branch kiosk (Map pp72-3; Gare du Midi; 🕙 7.30am-5.30pm Mon-Sat, 8.30am-2pm Sun). Public transport runs from about 6am to midnight, after which it's taxi only except on Friday/Saturday and Saturday/Sunday nights, when 17 Noctis night-bus routes (€3 single) operate twice hourly from midnight to 3am, most starting from Place de Brouckère.

TICKETS & PASSES

Tickets are valid for one hour and are sold at metro stations, STIB/MIVB kiosks, newsagents and on buses and trams. Single-/five-/10-journey STIB/MIVB tickets cost €1.60/7.30/11.20 including transfers. Unlimited one-/three-day passes cost €4.20/9.20. Note that airport buses are excluded and slightly higher 'jump' fares apply if you want to connect to city routes operated by De Lijn (Flanders bus), TEC (Wallonia bus) or SNCB/NMBS (rail). Children under six travel free.

Tickets must be validated, before travel, in machines located at the entrance to metro platforms or inside buses and trams. Tickets without validation incur fines of €55. Random checks are made.

Brussels International (p76) sells one-day passes and Brusselscards (p76).

METRO

Metro stations are marked with a white 'M' on a blue background. Lines 1A (northwest–southeast) and 1B (northeast–southwest) share the same central stretch including useful stops at Bruxelles-Central, Ste-Catherine and Schuman (for the EU Area). Line 2 basically follows the Petit Ring. See map p75. Don't expect London-style frequency: trains only run every 10 to 15 minutes. While you wait there's often artwork to peruse. Highlights:

Bourse (Map p70) Paul Delvaux' *Nos vieux trams bruxellois* depicts old trams in the capital.

Horta (Map pp72-3) Relics from Horta's Maison du Peuple integrated into the foyer.

Porte de Hal (Map pp72-3) Old trams and futuristic vehicles merge in scenes mirroring the comic-strips of artist François Schuiten.

Stockel (Map pp66-7) Life-sized murals of Tintin and pals.

TRAM, PREMETRO & BUS

The vast web of bus and tram transport has no central hub so grab a free STIB/MIVB transport map before going too far. Underground *premetro* trams link Brussels-Nord (Gare du Nord) and Brussels-Midi (Gare du Midi) via the Bourse, travelling beneath the boulevard known consecutively as Adolphe Max/Anspach/Maurice Lemonier.

Taxi

Official taxis (typically black or white) charge €2.40 pick-up plus €1.35/2.70 per kilometre within/outside the Brussels region. There's a €2 supplement between 10pm and 6am. Waiting costs €25 per hour. Taxes and tips are officially included in the meter price so you should ignore requests for extra service charges. Taxis wait near the three central train stations, outside Hôtel Amigo (Map p70), near the Grand Place (Map p70) and at Place Stéphanie (Map pp72–3) on Ave Louise. Website www.bruxellesmobilite .irisnet.be/articles/taxi/ou-trouver-un-taxi lists other ranks and taxi operators including **Taxis Bleus** (☎ 02-268 0000) and **Taxis Verts** (☎ 02-349 4949). Cabbies have a reputation for aggressive, overfast driving but if you're seriously dissatisfied you can report them toll-free on ☎ 0800-94001 – the receipt, which they must legally print for you, should have their four-digit taxi ID.

AROUND BRUSSELS

SOUTH OF BRUSSELS

For Waterloo, see p217.

Forêt de Soignes

This vast suburban **forest** (Zoniënwoud in Dutch; www.zonienwoud.be; Map pp66-7) is a botanical cathedral of glorious towering beech trees. Many were planted by proto-Belgium's 18th-century Austrian rulers with oaks added by the French to provide timber for future naval ships. By the time those trees had matured, however, shipbuilders preferred metal, so the trees went uncut. Today the result is a delightful regional park with hundreds of kilometres of cycle, horse and walking paths. Tucked into the forest fringes you'll find the **Jean Massart Experimental Garden** (Map pp66-7; www.ulb.ac.be/musees/jmassart; admission free; 9am-5pm Mon-Fri), arboreta at Tervuren and Groenendaal and an arts centre at **Rouge Cloître** (Map pp66-7; www.rouge-cloitre.be), site of a former 14th-century abbey.

SOUTHWEST OF BRUSSELS

Beersel

The 1310 **Kasteel van Beersel** (02-359 1646; Lotsestraat; adult/concession/child €2.50/1.25/1.25; 10am-noon & 2-6pm Tue-Sun Mar–mid-Nov, Sat & Sun only in winter, closed Jan) is the closest medieval castle to the capital. And from outside it's a beauty. The picture-perfect brick towers, rebuilt in 1498, are topped off with 17th-century roofs and rise proudly above a tree-ringed moat. However, it's an empty shell, the building having been used as a cotton factory in the 19th century. There's an appealing half-timbered restaurant-brasserie outside.

Around 1km west, the cramped, basic but inexpensive **Beersel Camping** (02-331 0561; campingbeersel@pandora.be; Steenweg op Ukkel 75, Beersel; adult/tent/car/caravan/camper-van €3/2/1.50/3/5) is one of the nearest year-round campgrounds to Brussels. Check-in at **Café Camping** (beer/kriek €1.30/1.85; 8am-midnight), a very down-market bar that redeems itself slightly by serving excellent draught Boon Kriek.

GETTING THERE & AWAY

The castle is handily close to the west Brussels 'Ring' motorway (junction 19) and is right outside Beersel train station (west exit). Trains run thrice hourly from **Halle**, whose interesting historic centre is worth a quick look while you're in transit. For the campsite, bus 154 from Halle is more convenient: alight at 'Windmolen'.

Gaasbeek

One of the finest rural castles within striking distance of the capital is the **Kasteel van Gaasbeek** (www.kasteelvangaasbeek.be; adult/senior/youth €6/4/1; 10am-6pm Tue-Sun Apr–mid-Nov, last admission 5pm), set in an extensive 17th-century park 14km southwest of central Brussels. Originally built to guard the medieval Brabant–Flanders border, this was the castle that angry Brussels folk burnt down in response to the 1388 murder of Everard 't Serclaes (see p63). In 1565, Gaasbeek was briefly home to Count Egmond before he was executed by the Spanish (p83). Elements of each era are visible. The castle is furnished inside, romantically crenellated outside and looks quite different when viewed from different angles – though the majority of the structure is the result of an extensive 1897 renovation. By public transport take bus 142 from Metro Erasmus.

NORTH OF BRUSSELS

Nationale Plantentuin Van België

Belgium's **National Botanic Garden** (02-260 0920; www.botanicgarden.be; Domein van Boechout, Meise; adult/concession €4/3; 9.30am-6.30pm Apr-Oct, 9.30am-5pm Nov-Mar, last entry 1 hr before closing) is a 93-hectare park located in the village of Meise, 12km north of downtown Brussels. It's based around two lakes and includes the Kasteel van Boechout, a photogenic moated castle that Léopold II gave to his sister, Princess Charlotte, after her own at Tervuren burnt down in 1879.

Of the 18,000 plant species, the park's most prized orchids, carnivorous plants and famous giant Amazonian water lilies are housed in the 1966 Plantenpaleis (Plant Palace), a series of 13 connecting greenhouses. Other highlights are the outdoor medicinal garden and a small 1864 greenhouse shaped like a king's crown. That was built in by Balat, Horta's teacher and the architect responsible for the Serres Royales (p90). The 18th-century orangery has been converted into a *café* and shop.

De Lijn buses 250/251 run every 15 minutes from Bruxelles-Nord (35 minutes) via Metro Bockstael (20 minutes).

Grimbergen

Briefly its own principality (18th century), **Grimbergen** (www.grimbergen.be/toerisme/index.htm) lies just 2km north of Brussels' ring road, (6km from the Atomium) and is one of Brabant's prettiest towns. The sweet little central square is dominated by **Sint-Servaasbasiliek** (admission free; 9am-6pm), Grimbergen's 1128 abbey-church, which was majestically rebuilt after 1660. Although since truncated it retains one of Belgium's most breathtaking baroque-rococo interiors plus a fine 49-bell **carillon** (bells played 8-9pm Fri, Jul-Aug & 4.30-5.30pm Sun Easter-Sep). Grimbergen is best known today for its abbey **beers** (www.grimbergenbier.be), especially the robust, golden Goud 8°. The beers are actually brewed industrially in Waarloos but there's a little **beer museum** (Abdijstraat 20; by pre-arrangement only) tucked into the former abbey grounds (turn left through the big stone gate and it's opposite a stylish brasserie). Any of the town's tempting pubs and restaurants serve Grimbergen brews but great, atmospheric choices are at two historic watermill-pubs: **Tommenmolen** (02-269 7084; Tommenmolenstraat 18; beer €2.50-3, snacks €4-11, mains €14-18; noon-9.30pm

Fri-Tue) and **Liermolen** (02-269 7690; Vorststraat 8; noon-9pm Wed-Sun). Both are signposted and within 800m of the square. Both offer traditional craft demonstrations on summer weekend afternoons and technically form part of the family-friendly museum **het mot** (02-270 8111; www.mot.be; adult/child €3/1), whose three sites are linked by appealing walking paths. The museum's main building, **Guldenhal** (Guldenhal 20; 9am-5pm daily), is located 1km south of centre in the grand, arcaded former stables of the Merode Castle (Prinsenkasteel), a ruined moated tower of which remains are visible in the grounds. The museum displays '150 years of washing machines', there are lots of child-activity stations and even the toilets are educational.

Half-hourly buses 230/232 link Grimbergen to Brussels' Metro Bockstael (25 minutes). On summer Tuesdays and Thursdays there's a canal boat connection to/from Brussels Quai de Humbeek (€5, one hour) but prebook on 02-218 5410 (see www.bateaubus.be).

Western Flanders

Packed with more than its fair share of historic cities, Western Flanders is unquestionably Belgium's greatest attraction. The fabulous medieval cores of Bruges and Ghent top the bill, but several other belfries and *begijnhoven* are now World Heritage Sites and even lesser-known towns like Oudenaarde and Veurne retain wonderfully picturesque town squares. Ypres and Diksmuide are charming, too, and all the more extraordinary for having been meticulously rebuilt following WWI. Scars and souvenirs of the Great War remain poignant attractions in the surrounding countryside, which also grows hops for some of Belgium's most iconic beers.

Belgian *chansonnier* Jacques Brel poetically described this area's agricultural hinterland as *le plat pays* (the flat country), its cathedrals the only mountains, its mists stretching to infinity. It's not a place of spectacular scenery, but even in the desolate winter one can share Brel's bittersweet adoration for 'a sky so low that canals get lost therein'. Brooding blankets of fog, howling February gales and startlingly bright spring mornings all have their mesmerising charms.

Belgium's coastline is blessed with wide, flat, sandy beaches, however, the visual effect is often marred by unsightly coast-hugging high-rises. Nonetheless there are a few remaining areas of wild dunes. Charming De Haan or bustling Ostend are pleasant exploratory bases, and at Oostduinkerke the tradition of horseback shrimp fishing continues, if only as a folkloric token.

Places here are listed anticlockwise, starting from Ghent. Note that while the term 'Flanders' now refers to all of northern Belgium, historically it was only associated with this western area.

HIGHLIGHTS

- **Canal Contest** Beautiful Bruges (p138) or glorious Ghent (p117) – which is lovelier?
- **Salient Reminder** WWI memories linger around Ypres (p160)
- **Primitive Passions** Medieval masterpieces at Bruges' Groeningemuseum (p133) and Ghent's cathedral (p119)
- **Battle of the beers** Wonderful Westvleteren (p155) or particular Pannepot (De Garre pub, p144)?
- **Bunker Down** WWII sea defences west of Ostend (p149)
- **On your Bike** Bucolic canal-side cycle rides to Damme (p146) and beyond
- **Real or Resurrection?** Magnificent market squares at Ypres (p157), Veurne (p154), Oudenaarde (p166) and Diksmuide (p156). But which are original?

- PROVINCES: OOST-VLAANDEREN (EAST FLANDERS: CAPITAL GHENT), WEST-VLAANDEREN (WEST FLANDERS: CAPITAL BRUGES)
- LANGUAGE: DUTCH

WESTERN FLANDERS

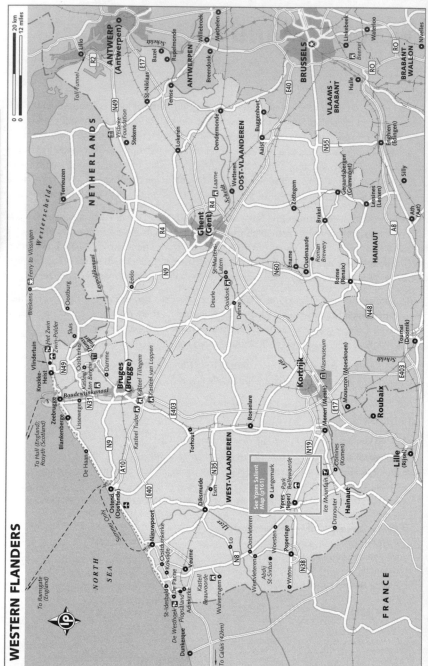

GHENT (GENT)
pop 230,000

Asking citizens of Ghent what they think of their city is a pointless exercise: you'll find only unanimous love. And with good reason. Ghent is one of Europe's greatest discoveries – small enough to feel cosy but big enough to stay vibrant, it has enough medieval frivolity to create a spectacle but retains a gritty industrial edge that keeps things 'real'. Tourists remain remarkably thin on the ground, yet with its fabulous canal-side architecture, wealth of quirky bars and some of Belgium's most fascinating museums, this is a city you really won't want to miss.

History
The seat of the counts of Flanders, medieval Ghent (Gent/Gand in Dutch/French) was a great cloth town that grew to become medieval Europe's largest city after Paris and Constantinople. The hard-working townsfolk were well known for their armed battles, civil liberties, and protests against the heavy taxes imposed on them. In 1540 Ghent-born Holy Roman Emperor Charles V ('Keizer Karel', 'Charles Quint'; p27) was particularly incensed when the townsfolk refused to pay taxes to fund his military forays into France. He came down swiftly and heavily on the city, abolishing the town's privileges and humiliating the guildsmen by making them walk around town wearing nooses round their necks. Ghent-folk are nicknamed 'Stroppendragers' (rope pullers) to this very day. This episode signalled the beginning of a long decline as the Low Countries' centre of gravity moved to Antwerp.

However, in the early 19th-century, Ghent was the first town in Flanders to harness the Industrial Revolution. Many of its historical buildings were converted into flax- and cotton-processing mills and the city became known as the 'Manchester of the Continent'. These days, Ghent is Flanders' biggest university town, more Cambridge than Manchester. But its hotels are still more focused on business than tourism so upper-range places tend to offer weekend and summer discounts. Finding any accommodation at all can prove hard during July's fabulous Gentse Feesten (see p18), when the city's at its liveliest. Then again, at that time you probably won't get any sleep anyway.

Orientation
Ghent's magnificent medieval core comprises three interconnected squares. The easternmost of these, Korenmarkt, is undergoing a massive series of works that means it's likely to feel like a building site until 2012. The main train station, Gent-Sint-Pieters, is about 2km to the south. In between lie the Citadelpark galleries and a big university quarter spread notably along Overpoortstraat. Sleepstraat is the start of a predominantly Turkish quarter.

Information
BOOKSHOPS
Atlas & Zanzibar (Map pp118–19; ☎ 09-220 8799; www.atlaszanzibar.be, www.manymaps.com; Kortrijksesteenweg 19; ⏰ 10am-1pm & 2-6pm Mon-Sat) Ghent's best travel bookshop.
FNAC (Map pp118-19; ☎ 09-223 4080; Veldstraat 88) Books and ticketing.

INTERNET ACCESS
CallShop (off Map p122; ☎ 09 335 5375; Sleepstraat 41; per hr €1; ⏰ 10am-10pm Thu-Tue) Inexpensive internet and phone calls.
Coffeelounge (Map p122; ☎ 09-329 3911; Botermarkt 6; per hr €2; ⏰ 10am-7pm Wed-Mon) Central.
Rail@Net (Map pp118-19; ☎ 09-223 7386; Brabantdam 138, per hr €1.50; ⏰ 9am-8pm Thu-Tue) Spacious Internet room above a grocery.

MONEY
Goffin Change (Map p122; ☎ 09-225 6095; www.goffinchange.be; Henegouwenstraat 25; ⏰ 9.15am-5.45pm Mon-Fri, 10am 4.30pm Sat) Exchanges cash and some travellers cheques.

POST
Main post office (Map p122; Lange Kruisstraat 55; ⏰ 9am-6pm Mon-Fri, 10.30am-4.30pm Sat)

TOURIST INFORMATION
Tourist office (Map p122; ☎ 09-266 5232; www.visitgent.be; Botermarkt 17; ⏰ 9.30am-6.30pm Apr-Oct, to 4.30pm Nov-Mar) In a vaulted cellar entered from the north side of the belfry building.
Use-it (www.use-it.be) Brilliantly opinionated, downloadable guide-maps. Available free in print form from hostels and tourist offices.
Zone09 (www.zone09.be) Dutch-language events-listing magazine available free from street dispenser boxes.

WESTERN FLANDERS

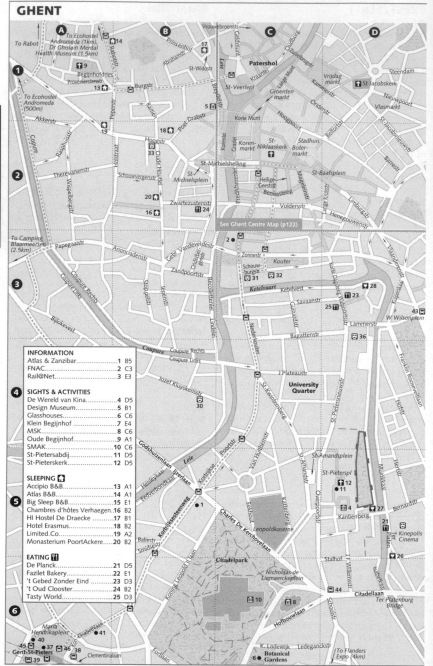

GHENT

See Ghent Centre Map (p122)

INFORMATION
Atlas & Zanzibar...................1 B5
FNAC..2 C3
Rail@Net................................3 E3

SIGHTS & ACTIVITIES
De Wereld van Kina...............4 D5
Design Museum.....................5 B1
Glasshouses...........................6 C6
Klein Begijnhof 7 E4
MSK..8 C6
Oude Begijnhof......................9 A1
SMAK......................................10 C6
St-Pietersabdij.....................11 D5
St-Pieterskerk.....................12 D5

SLEEPING
Accipio B&B.........................13 A1
Atlas B&B..............................14 A1
Big Sleep B&B......................15 E1
Chambres d'hôtes Verhaegen.16 B2
HI Hostel De Draecke 17 B1
Hotel Erasmus.....................18 B2
Limited.Co............................19 A2
Monasterium PoortAckere....20 B2

EATING
De Planck..............................21 D5
Fazilet Bakery.......................22 E1
't Gebed Zonder Eind 23 D3
't Oud Clooster....................24 B2
Tasty World...........................25 D3

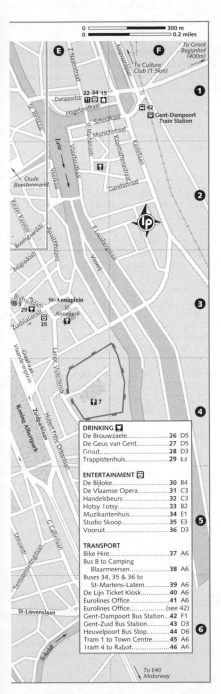

Sights & Activities

BELFORT

Ghent's trio of central squares are dominated by two imposing, if dour, churches, with a third across the St-Michielsbrug bridge. In the middle is a soaring Unesco-listed 14th-century **belfry** (Belfort; Map p122; ☎ 09-233 0772; Botermarkt; adult/concession/child €3/2.50/free; ⏰ 10am-5.30pm mid-Mar–mid-Nov) topped by a big dragon. That's a weathervane not a fire breather and it's become something of a city mascot. Meet previous incarnations of the dragon during an audio-guided climb of the belfry, during which you can also watch an interesting video on bell-making and survey the city from on high. You'll start by climbing stairs through rather claustrophobic wall passages, but from the first landing there's a lift to whisk you further up.

ST-BAAFSKATHEDRAAL

Behind the belfry lies the large stone bulk of **St-Bavo's Cathedral** (Map p122; ☎ 09-269 2045; St-Baafsplein; ⏰ 8.30am-6pm Apr-Oct, to 5pm Nov-Mar). While not especially memorable from outside, its towering interior has some fine stained glass and an unusual combination of brick vaulting with stone tracery. A €0.20 leaflet guides you round the cathedral's numerous art treasures, including a big original Rubens opposite the stairway that leads down into the partly muralled crypts. There's more treasure here. However, most visitors come to see just one magnificent painting – Jan Van Eyck's 1432 'Flemish Primitive' masterpiece, **The Adoration of the Mystic Lamb** (adult/child €3/1.50; ⏰ 9.30am-4.30pm Mon-Sat & 1-4.30pm Sun Apr-Oct, 10.30am-3.30pm Mon-Sat & 1-3.30pm Sun Nov-Mar), see the boxed text, p120. It's kept in a specially temperature-controlled, half-darkened side chapel. An audioguide explains every panel in considerable detail. If you can forgo this and don't want to queue to see the original, a photographic copy is displayed for free in the cathedral's side-chapel 30.

ALONG THE CANALS

To admire Ghent's towers and gables at their most photogenic, stand just west of the little **Grasbrug** bridge at dusk. It's a truly gorgeous scene, though the appealing **Graslei** waterfront facades aren't as old as they look – these 'medieval' warehouses and townhouses were largely rebuilt for Ghent's 1913 World Fair. The antique meat-market building, **Groot Vleeshuis** (Map p122; Groentenmarkt 7; admission free;

WESTERN FLANDERS

ADORING THE MYSTIC LAMB

Van Eyck's 20-panel *Adoration of the Mystic Lamb* (displayed in St-Baafskathedraal) is one of the earliest works of art ever undertaken using oil paints. It's had more than its fair share of adventures: it narrowly survived the Calvinists, was marched off to Paris during the French Revolution and was grabbed by WWII Germans who concealed it in an Austrian salt mine. The nudity of Adam and Eve on its outer panels so horrified Austria's Emperor Joseph II that he had them replaced with clothed versions. Today all but one of the original panels are back in place (while Joseph II's clothed replacements hang for good measure near the cathedral's entrance). The one missing panel, *De Rechtvaardige Rechters* (The Fair Judges), was stolen in 1934 and has never been returned, but a copy that sits in its place is good enough to fool all but the sharpest-eyed critic.

10am-6pm Tue-Sun), is now a promotion and tasting hall for regional agricultural produce, with smoked hams dangling from hefty old wooden beams. **Oude Vismarkt** (Map p122), a large historic fish-market building at the river's Y junction, should look superb once its long-term reconstruction is finally finished. **Boat tours** (adult/senior/child €6/5.50/3.50; 10am-6pm Mar–mid Oct, weekends only in winter) are operated by four companies all based at either the Grasbrug or Vleeshuisbrug bridges. All depart several times hourly according to demand. They all cover essentially the same three-pronged up-and-back route (40 minutes) but **De Gentenaer Rederij** (Map p122; 0473-481 036; www.rederijdegen tenaer.be) adds 10 minutes extra along Ketelvaart then tunnels under Francois Laurentplein to emerge briefly outside the **Duivelsteen** waterfront castle-house.

GRAVENSTEEN

The Counts of Flanders' quintessential 12th-century stone **castle** (Map p122; 09-225 9306; St-Veerleplein; adult/concession & youth/child €8/6/free; 9am-5pm Apr-Sep, to 4pm Oct-Mar) comes complete with moat, turrets and arrow slits. It's a fabulously evocative sight and all the more remarkable considering that during the 19th century the whole site was converted into a cotton mill. Meticulously restored since, the interior now sports the odd suit of armour, a guillotine and a few torture devices. The relative lack of furnishings is compensated by a hand-held 45-minute movie-guide, which sets a historical costumed drama in the various rooms you visit. See who's been thrown in the 5.5m prison pit and join the video characters enjoying great panoramas from the hefty battlements.

If you just want to look *at* the castle, there are beautiful, if slightly obscured, views from Augustijnenstraat and the nearby willow-lined canal outside Hostel De Draecke.

PATERSHOL

Dotted with delightful, half-hidden restaurants, enchanting **Patershol** (Map p122; www.patershol .be) is a web of twisting cobbled lanes whose wonderfully old-world houses were once home to leather tradesmen and to the Carmelite Fathers (*Paters* – hence the name). Don't miss the beautifully restored 1363 children's hospice complex, which now hosts the charming (and cheap) 't Caffetse lawn-*café* (p126), along with the utterly delightful **Huis van Alijn** (Map p122; 09-269 2350; www.huisvanalijn. be; Kraanlei 65; adult/senior/youth €5/3.75/1; 11am-5pm Tue-Sat, from 5pm Sun). The museum's theme is 'life in the 20th century (up to the '70s)' and although little is in English, the exhibits are self-explanatory. The recreated shop interiors are quaint, the '60s/'70s rooms are fun and the engrossing collage of family home videos is unexpectedly moving.

VRIJDAGMARKT & AROUND

Across Zuivelbrug from Patershol notice the 15th-century **Dulle Griet** (Map p122), a 5m-long red super-cannon whose 660mm bore and 250kg cannon balls made it one of the five biggest siege guns of the entire Middle Ages. Just beyond you'll emerge into **Vrijdagmarkt**, a magnificent square that was once the city's forum for public meetings and executions. It's lined with tempting *cafés* and still animated by a large market on Fridays.

DISCOUNT CARD

The three-day **Museumpas** (€20) gives free entrance to all of Ghent's top museums and monuments and allows unlimited travel on trams and city buses. Excellent value. Available at participating museums, major bus offices and the tourist office.

Quirky Onderstraat hides an **art cloister** (Map p122), in the courtyard of no 22, that you can glimpse if you venture up **Werregarensteeg** (Map p122; www.ghentizm.be), a tiny alley where graffiti is positively encouraged as an art form. You'll emerge near the flamboyant Gothic/Renaissance **stadhuis** (Map p122; Hoogpoort). This is a prime spot for weddings, but it's otherwise open only for one-hour **guided visits** (€4; 2.30pm Mon-Thu May-Sep) that start from the tourist office.

DESIGN MUSEUM

A vast toilet-roll 'sculpture' humorously marks the back side of this **museum** (Map pp118-19; ☎ 09-267 9999; http://design.museum.gent.be; Jan Breydelstraat 5; adult/senior & student/child €5/3.75/free; 10am-6pm Tue-Sun), whose collection specialises in furnishings from baroque through art nouveau and '70s psychedelic to '90s furniture-as-art. It's hosted in an architecturally schizophrenic building which catapults you from the 18th century into the 21st, then drags you back again.

MIAT

In a five-floor, 19th-century mill-factory building, the innovative **Museum voor Industriële Archeologie en Textiel** (Industrial Archaeology Museum; Map p122; ☎ 09-269 4220; www.miat.gent.be; Minnemeers 9; adult/senior/youth €5/3.75/1; 10am-6pm Tue-Sun) celebrates Ghent's history of textile production. The thought-provoking (if mostly in Dutch) exhibits consider 250 years of industrialisation and its effects on society. There's a very extensive collection of mechanical weaving equipment all still in working order – prepare for sensory overload on Tuesday or Thursday mornings when they're unleashed.

ST-PIETERSABDIJ

Founded in the 7th century on a barely perceivable rise, 1km south of Korenmarkt, this **former abbey** (Map pp118-19; www.kunstinhuis.be) was the original centre around which Ghent grew. Turned into barracks after the French Revolution, several structures have survived, including the refectory with its remarkable muralled ceilings (under restoration). There are regular art exhibitions in the abbey gallery, but at other times the **main complex** (adult/concession/children €5/3.75/free; 10am-5.45pm Sun Apr-Nov, last 'Alison' tour 4pm) isn't really worth the entry fee unless you fork out €3 extra for the two-hour 'Alison' tour, led by a 'virtual monk' on a video-guide device. For free you

can stroll the vineyards of the **abbey gardens** (10am-5pm Tue-Sun) and look inside the vast 1720 **St-Pieterskerk** (10am-5.30 Tue-Sun).

Across the abbey courtyard, **De Wereld van Kina** (Map pp118-19; ☎ 09-244 7373; www.dewereldvankina.be; St-Pietersplein 14; 9am-4.30pm Mon-Fri, 2pm-5pm Sun) is a mishmash of a natural history museum aimed primarily at school kids. You can meet Pterygotus (a man-sized prehistoric lobster), walk through a human body with pounding heart and get quizzed in the lively sex-education room. Behind an array of old stuffed birds (press play to hear them sing) is a model of Ghent as it looked in the 16th century. Great…but why here?

The stark square surrounding the abbey signals the start of Ghent's vibrant student district.

CITADELPARK GALLERIES

In a park containing rampart remnants and artificial cascades you'll find **SMAK** (Map pp118-19; ☎ 09-221 1703; www.smak.be; Citadelpark; adult/youth/child €6/1/free; 10am-6pm Tue-Sun), Ghent's highly regarded Museum of Contemporary Art. It features regularly changing exhibitions of provocative, cutting-edge installations. Across the road, a building styled like a Greek Temple contains **MSK** (Museum voor Schone Kunsten; Map pp118-19; ☎ 09-240 0700; www.mskgent.be; Citadelpark; adult/senior/youth €5/3.50/1, 10am 6pm), a superb fine-art gallery whose impressive collection includes typically nightmarish works by Hieronymus Bosch, a happy family of coffins by Magritte, luminist canvases by Emile Claus and fine examples of Jean Brusselmans' cubism. Pieter Breughel the Younger's 1621 *Dorpsadvocaat* (room 8) is a brilliant portrait of a village lawyer oozing with arrogance. The museum's a bit of a maze so you'll value the free map handed out at reception.

Nearby the pretty **Botanical Gardens** (Kruidtuin) make for a very pleasant stroll. The gardens' **glasshouses** (Map pp118-19; admission free; 9am-4.20pm Mon-Fri, 9am-11.50am Sat & Sun), containing an impressive tropical plant collection, offer shivering winter travellers what's effectively a free sauna.

MUSEUM DR GUISLAIN

Hidden away in a spooky 1857 neo-Gothic lunatic asylum this enthralling **mental health museum** (off Map pp118-19; ☎ 09-216 3595; www.museumdrguislain.be; Jozef Guislainstraat 43; adult/senior/youth €5/3.50/1; 9am-5pm Tue-Fri, 1pm-5pm Sat & Sun) takes

WESTERN FLANDERS

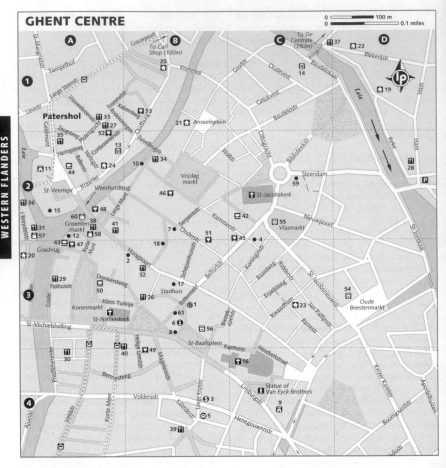

GHENT CENTRE

visitors on a trilingual, multicultural journey through the history of psychiatry, from gruesome Neolithic trepanning to contemporary brain scans via cage beds and phrenology. Dr D'Arsonval's extraordinary 1909 radiographic apparatus looks like a Dr Frankenstein creation, but even more nightmarish are the waxwork models of horrendous genital abnormalities and child-birth complications. North-sector tram 1 from Gravensteen stops outside.

BEGIJNHOVEN

Ghent has three widely separated *begijnhoven* (see the boxed text, p137 ,for more info). Most central, the **Oude Begijnhof** (Map pp118–19) is just a pretty area of lanes of which the most photogenic is Provenierstersstraat.

The enclosed **Klein Begijnhof** (Map pp118-19; www.kleinbegijnhof-gent.be) is an unusually spacious haven, with big lawns, a heavy 1720 baroque church and two 'secret gardens', but the quaint houses are mostly hidden behind whitewashed garden walls. Enter opposite Lange Violettestraat 118.

The well preserved 1874 **Groot Begijnhof** (off Map pp118–19) is a comparatively modern and slightly austere affair in the suburb of Sint-Amandsberg, 600m east of Gent-Dampoort Train Station.

Festivals & Events

During mid-July's raucous **Gentse Feesten** (Ghent Festivities; www.gentsefeesten.be), the city's many squares become venues for a vast variety of street-theatre performances and there are big associated techno and jazz festivals. Those wanting a merrily boozy party atmosphere will love it. But consider avoiding Ghent at this time if you don't.

Sleeping

Ghent offers innovative accommodation in all budget ranges. See **Bed & Breakfast Ghent** (www. bedandbreakfast-gent.be) for information on over 60 B&Bs and approximate availability. Note that our listings include Ghent's new €2.50 per person tourist tax, which is rarely mentioned in accommodations' own quoted prices.

BUDGET

Camping Blaarmeersen (off Map pp118-19; ☎ 09-266 8160; www.gent.be/blaarmeersen; Zuiderlaan 12; campsites per adult/child/car/tent/caravan Mar-May, Sep & Oct €4.50/2/2/4/4, Jun-Aug €5.50/2.50/2.50/5/5; ☻ Mar-Oct) This campsite is part of a recreational park featuring Ghent's only 'beach', 3.5km west of the centre. It's accessible by bus 8 from Gent-Zuid via Gent-St-Pieters.

HI Hostel De Draecke (Map pp118-19; ☎ 09-233 7050; www.vjh.be; St-Widostraat 11; dm/tw €18.80/46; ☒ 🖥 🛜) Behind a pseudo-medieval facade lies a slightly institutional modern hostel facing a picturesque willow-lined central canal. Rates include buffet breakfast. Wi-fi or internet costs €2 per half-hour, lockers €2, towels €1.50. No lockout. Book ahead.

Ecohostel Andromeda (off Map pp118-19; http://eco hostel.be; Bargiekaai 35; dm €24.50-26.50, d/tr €68/102.50; ☻ reception 11am-8pm Jun-Sep, to 5pm Oct-May, closed Feb) Sleep on a 'recycled' barge where 19 ergonomic dorm beds share 14 pillows and some unexpectedly stylish communal bathrooms. The small, peaceful, open-top deck is great for conversations with fellow hostellers. The organic breakfast costs €4 extra. The boat is moored on the canalside around 600m northwest of the Oude Begijnhof. Or take north-sector tram 1 from Gravensteen to Witte Kaproenenplein, then walk two minutes south on Alois Joosstraat through a slightly daunting housing estate.

ourpick Hostel 47 (Map p122; www.hostel47.com; Blekerijstraat 47; dm €26.50-29.50, d/tr €71/97.50; ☻ check-in by 10pm) Virginal white walls, spacious bunkrooms and designer fittings make this an unusually inviting hostel. It's set in a historic high-ceilinged house with small garden. The price includes free lockers and a cursory breakfast with excellent coffee. Central yet wonderfully calm. No bar.

Hotel Flandria (Map p122; ☎ 09-223 0626; www. flandria-centrum.be; Barrestraat 3; s/d with washbasin €43/50, s/d/tr/q with bathroom €58/65/98/125; ☻ reception 7am-10pm Mon-Fri, 8am-7pm Sat, 8am-10pm Sun; 🖥 🛜) Map-plastered walls beckon you into this helpfully central budget hotel, whose friendly new owners are working to iron out some of the place's dowdier features. The six cheapest rooms share two bathrooms.

WESTERN FLANDERS

GAY & LESBIAN GHENT

A great online resource is www.holebi gent.be. While it's all in Dutch, clicking 'Horeca' on the top menu gives an easily understandable listing of gay B&Bs and *cafés*, plus many more that are gay friendly *(Holebivriendelijke Horeca)*. **Hephaestion** (Map p122; ☎ 09-335 3461 www.hephaestion.be; Kammerstraat 29; ☾ 10am-7pm Mon-Thu, 2pm-1am Fri & Sat) is a friendly GLBT bookshop, cafe and information centre. Two skips away, comfy lounge-bar **Foyer Casa Rosa** (Map p122; ☎ 09-269 2816; www.casarosa.be; Belfortstraat 39; ☾ 3pm-3am) is Ghent's foremost gay *café*. If you're looking for a raunchier scene, go to Antwerp.

MIDRANGE

Limited.Co (Map pp118-19; ☎ 09-225 1495; www.limited-co.be; Hoogstraat 58; s/d/t/q €52.50/70/102.50/120; ☎) Located above a *café*-restaurant (open noon to 2pm Monday to Friday and 6pm to 10pm Monday to Saturday, mains €7-10) of modern simplicity are five great-value, stylish rooms with lime-green walls, black floors and smart white bathrooms. Call to make arrangements if arriving outside restaurant hours.

Big Sleep B&B (Map pp118-19; ☎ 09-233 4352; s.deravet@worldonline.be; Hagelandkaai 38; s/d €55/60) Friendly B&B whose three rooms have showers but shared toilets. The lovely high-ceilinged 1890 townhouse is decorated with souvenirs of world travels, while the quietest 'Green Room' has a swirling '70s decor, hand-painted by a renowned local artist. A swimming pool is under construction in the small back garden. It's handy for Gent-Dampoort station.

Atlas B&B (Map pp118-19; ☎ 092334991; www.atlasbenb .be; Rabotstraat 40; s/d from €57/73; 🖳) This fine 1863 townhouse has some gorgeous belle-époque, art deco and art nouveau touches, and features plentiful maps and globes. Room choice is between small exotic 'Africa', roomier 'Asia' or Tuscan 'Europe', the latter with separate bathroom. An orangery and new garden are planned.

Galerie Link (Map p122; ☎ 09-223 5942, 0475-795 178; Blekersdijk 39; s/d/loft from €57.50/90/100) House, gallery and B&B merge into one memorable experience facing a quiet but central canal. The extraordinarily vast loft is an art-packed beamed duplex apartment that could sleep a football team. There's no sign.

our pick Accipio B&B (Map p122; ☎ 0486-559 498; www.accipio.be; St-Elisabethplein 26; s/d/t/q €75/95/130/160; 🖳) There are two super-stylish family-sized suites in this historic house, with 19th-century beams and lots of personality. Especially excellent value for single or double occupancy. Breakfast and a Senseo coffeemaker awaits you in your kitchenette.

Hotel Erasmus (Map pp118-19; ☎ 09-224 2195; www .erasmushotel.be; Poel 25; s/d/tr/q €81.35/104/147.50/170, luxury s/d €101.50/155; ☾ reception 7am-10.30pm; ☎) This renovated 16th-century house has an ivy-draped garden, and a suit of armour guarding your €10 breakfast. Some of the dozen rooms have stained-glass windows and oak-beamed ceilings, but decor is more twee than antique. The location is superb.

Simon Says (Map p122; ☎ 09-233 0343; www.simon -says.be; Sluizeken 8; d €95; ☎) Located above a coffee-shop cafe in a brightly coloured corner house with art-nouveau facade. Guest rooms are fashionably minimalist in style.

TOP END

Hotel Harmony (Map p122; ☎ 09-324 2680; www .hotel-harmony.be; Kraanlei 37; s/d/ste from €130/145/220; ☒ 🖳 ☎ 🖾 ☜) Old-meets-new boutique hotel with luxuriously heaped pillows, fine white linens, Miro-esque art and chocolate-raspberry colour-schemes beneath 18th-century beams. Views from the 3rd-floor common balcony and from 'exceptional' rooms (s/d €155/180) are possibly the best in all of Ghent. The rear deck has an 8m-by-4m outdoor pool. Wi-fi per hour/day costs €2/10.

Ghent Marriott (Map p122; ☎ 09-233 9393; www. marriottghent.be; Korenlei 10; d standard/weekend-special from €159/119; ☎) Enter from behind and this top new 150-room hotel appears to be a four-storey modernist bubble of glass and concrete. But looking from Korenlei all you'll see is a traditional facade incorporating four traditional house-fronts. Canal-view rooms (€50 extra) have superb waterfront panoramas. Wi-fi per day costs €19.95; breakfast €23.

Ghent River Hotel (Map p122; ☎ 09-266 1010; www. ghent-river-hotel.be; Waaistraat 5; s/d/ste from €165/180/300, weekends €140/165/185, internet rates from €99; ☎) This 77-room hotel imaginatively combines an 18th-century mill-warehouse and a 1518 Renaissance house, where a contemporary chandelier dangles through the two-storey atrium-foyer. Room interiors are modern, but many retain quirky historical features. Atmospheric canal-side rooms (some rather small) are light-suffused even though the views aren't especially lovely. Wi-fi per hour/day costs €5/20.

Chambres d'hôtes Verhaegen (Map pp118-19; ☎ 09-265 0765; www.hotelverhaegen.be; Oude Houtlei 110; d €195-265; ☒ reception 2pm-6pm) This grandly classical 1770s home enjoys a sumptuous blend of historical renovation with well-placed modernist and retro touches. There's a dazzling salon, an 18th-century dining room and neatly manicured parterre garden. Superb 'Paola's Room' is named for the then young Italian princess who stayed here long before becoming Belgium's present queen. Breakfast costs €15.

Eating

You'll find cosy, upper-market restaurants, covering most cuisines, in the delightful little alleyways of Patershol. For fast food, there's plenty of choice around Korenmarkt, while for Turkish food and cheap pizzas the prices generally keep falling the further you go up Sleepstraat. Nowhere in Belgium offers more choice of vegetarian and organic foods and the tourist office produces a useful free **Veggieplan Gent** guide map.

De Planck (Map pp118-19; ☎ 0486-743 337; www.deplanck.be; Ter Platen; sandwiches/pastas from €3/8; ☒ noon-2.30pm & 6.30-10pm Wed-Mon) Yes, palm trees grow in Ghent, albeit small ones on the deck of this appealing barge-*café*. In winter the open terrace is space-heated or you can retreat into the very cosy bar below. Try their pleasantly hoppy 6.8% Planckske house beer.

't Gebed Zonder Eind (Map pp118-19; ☎ 09-329 0397; Walpoortstraat 13; mains €7-22, draught Primus/Tongerlo €1.80/2.80; ☒ 4pm-1am Tue-Sat, kitchen 6pm-11pm) Decorated with enamel signs, varnished wooden tables and vintage lamps this classic *café* is great for a drink, pub snack or savoury pancake (€12). It also serves a changing menu of finer food, including seasonal artichokes.

Amadeus (Map p122; ☎ 09-225 1385; www.amadeus spareribsrestaurant.be; ; Plotersgracht 8/10, Patershol; mains €7.50-16.85, 3-course menu €16; ☒ 6.30pm-11pm) Great value all-you-can-eat spare ribs (€13.95) at two addresses (the other is at Goudenleeuwplein 7, Botermarkt), both within ancient buildings that are full of atmosphere, bustle and cheerful conversation.

't Oud Clooster (Map pp118-19; ☎ 09-233 7802; Zwartezusterstraat 5; mains €9-17; ☒ dinner Mon-Sat) Served in an atmospheric room built onto the wall-ruins of a former historic nunnery,

the unpretentious food is such good value that you'll probably need to book.

Eethuis Avalon (Map p122; ☎ 09-224 3724; www.restaurantavalon.be; Geldmunt 32; mains €10.80-12.50; ☒ 11.30am-2.30pm Mon-Sat; **V**) 'Live well and laugh often' is the Avalon's sage suggestion, backed up with copious, reliably delicious vegetarian and vegan lunches. Eat in their intriguing warren of little rooms or on a delightful tree-shaded rear terrace.

Brasserie Pakhuis (Map p122; ☎ 09-223 5555; www.pakhuis.be; Schuurkenstraat 4; mains €13.50-29, lunch €12, menus €25-42; ☒ kitchen noon-11pm Mon-Thu, to midnight Fri & Sat, bar 11.30-1am, closed Sun) This hip, if mildly ostentatious, modern brasserie/bar/restaurant is set in a magnificently restored former textile warehouse. It retains the original century-old wrought ironwork and an incredible roof. It's well worth popping inside even if you only stop for a drink.

Mimosa (Map p122; ☎ 09-233 5520; Kongostraat 2; tajines €14-16; ☒ noon-2.30pm & 6.30-10pm Wed-Mon) Mismatched tiles, plastic foliage and lurid elements of '70s decor can't spoil the taste of the tajines in this reliable little neighbourhood Moroccan restaurant.

Avonden (Map p122; ☎ 09-233 5349; Ham 39; mains €14-21; ☒ dinner Tue-Sun) It's almost like being invited to a casual dinner party in a Belgian home. The food here is thoroughly Flemish, the menu's a blackboard and the cosy townhouse setting fills with jolly conversation from an ever appreciative local crowd. Bookings advised.

De Tempelier (Map p122; ☎ 09-233 0305; www.brasseriedetempelier.be; Meerseniersstraat 9; mains €14-16; ☒ 6pm-10pm Wed-Sun) Formerly a cult cafe known for its weird Gothic church-style interior decor, De Tempelier was re-launched in late 2009 as a cosy brasserie-restaurant serving just a handful of daily changing dishes.

ourpick House of Eliott (Map p122; ☎ 09-225 2128; www.thehouseofeliott.be; Jan Breydelstraat 36; mains €15-24; ☒ noon-2pm & 6-11pm, Thu-Mon Oct-Aug) Oozing a delightful pseudo-1920s charm this gently camp, canal-side gem is full of flapper mannequins and sepia photos. There's nothing old fashioned about the stylishly presented cuisine, which creates some truly marvellous flavour combinations.

Belga Queen (Map p122; ☎ 09-280 0100; www.belgaqueen.be; Graslei 10; mains €19-40; ☒ noon-11pm, tearoom 2.30-7pm, cigar-lounge 7pm-late Mon-Sat) Several eateries jostle to position their tables on the Graslei's gorgeous canal-side terrace, but

Belga Queen's plastic bucket-seats grab the most tourist-prized spot. Inside, the stylish, extensive yet somewhat cramped spaces offer a choice of lounge-style sofa seating or stool perches.

De Blauwe Zalm (Map p122; ☎ 09-224 0852; www .deblauwezalm.be; Vrouwebroersstraat 2; mains €22-40; ☽ noon-1.30pm Tue-Fri & 7-9.30pm Mon-Sat) Considered among Belgium's top seafood restaurants, the Blauwe Zalm's refined decor is given pizzazz by a quite astonishing jellyfish chandelier.

QUICK EATS

Soup'r (Map p122; Sint-Niklaasstraat 7; small/large soup €3/4.50, sandwiches €2.50-4; ☽ 11am-6.30pm Tue-Sat) Attractive, modern soup kitchen that's great for a light, fast meal.

Tasty World (Map p122; ☎ 09 225 7407; www.tasty world.be; Hoogpoort 11; light meals €3-7.50; ☽ 11am-7pm Mon-Sat) Good variety of organic light meals, veggie burgers and delicious fresh juices to eat in or take away. There's another branch near Vooruit (Map pp118-19; ☎ 09-330 7527; Walpoortstraat 38).

Brooderie (Map p122; ☎ 09-225 0623; www.broo derie.be; Jan Breydelstraat 8; breakfast/soup/main/menu from €5/3.50/9.50/19; ☽ 8am-6pm Tue-Sun) Rustic bakery-tearoom serving breakfasts, soups and savoury snacks. They also have simple, colourful B&B rooms with shared bathrooms.

SELF-CATERING

Contact GB (Map p122; Hoogpoort 42; ☽ 9am-6pm Mon-Sat) Central supermarket.

Organic market (Map p122; Groentenmarkt; ☽ 9am-1pm Fri)

Fazilet Bakery (Map pp118-19; Dampoortstraat 36; ☽ 6am-8pm Sat-Thu) Fresh baked bread and delicious Turkish pastries to take away.

Drinking

Ghent's fabulous *café* scene is endlessly inspiring, with more than 280 choices in the centre alone. If you want cheap beer rather than character, forget our selection and head to the endless student hang-outs that line Overpoortstraat. After 3am Charlatan (opposite) and surrounding bars are usually the most central places still open, though Het Spijker (opposite) often continues till 5am.

't Caffetse (Map p122; ☎ 09-269 2350; Kraanlei 65; beer/cava €1.30/3.50; ☽ 11am-5pm Tue-Sat) Charming yet remarkably inexpensive *café* whose lawn seats are set within the cloister of a 14th-century almshouse. Although it's accessed

through the Huis Van Alijn (p120), you don't have to pay the museum's entry fee if you just want a drink.

Het Waterhuis aan de Bierkant (Map p122; ☎ 09-225 0680; www.waterhuisaandebierkant.be; Groentenmarkt 12; ☽ 11am-1am) With an interior draped in dried hops this brilliant though unavoidably touristy beer-pub is a photogenic sight. There are exclusive house beers on draught and it shares an enticing waterfront terrace with atmospherically austere *jenever* (Dutch-style gin) bar 't Dreupelkot (open from 4pm).

Coffee & Curiosa (Map p122; ☎ 09-328 0738 Geldmunt 6; beer/coffee/cava/champagne from €1.80/2/4.50/6.50; ☽ 11am-6pm Tue-Thu & Sun, to 10pm Fri & Sat) Calmly sedate tea house and champagne lounge in a superbly preserved art deco shop-house. It's also good for soup-lunches (€3.50) and cakes.

Herberg De Dulle Griet (Map p122; Vrijdagmarkt 50; ☽ 4.30pm-1am Tue-Sat, noon-7.30pm Mon) Heavy beams, a heraldic ceiling, barrel-tables, lacy lampshades and the odd boar's head all add character to one of Ghent's best-known beer pubs.

Pink Flamingo's (Map p122; ☎ 09-233 4718; www .pinkflamingos.be; Onderstraat 55; ☽ noon-midnight Sun-Thu, 2pm-3am Fri & Sat) Brilliantly kitsch-overloaded *café* with Barbie lamps, 1970s wallpaper and oodles of plastic fruit. It's lively for a drink and decent value for sandwiches (€3.50) or pastas (from €8).

Rococo (Map p122; ☎ 09-224 3035; Corduwanierstraat 5; coffee/beer/wine €2.50/4/4; ☽ from 10pm) Lavish *café*-bar with carved wooden ceilings, where the only lighting is provided by candles. It's an ideal place for late-night conversation and spontaneous music, should someone decide to fire up the piano.

Limonada (Map p122; ☎ 09-233 7885; www.limonada .be; Heilige Geeststraat 7; beers/cocktails from €1.80/5.50; ☽ 10pm-3am Mon-Sat) Seventies-retro lounge with beanbag seats around low luminous tables.

Callisto Tearoom (Map p122; ☎ 09-233 0452; Hooiaard; ☽ very seasonal) Although unashamedly tourist-centred, Callisto's terrace is hard to beat and prices for drinks and light snacks are unexpectedly reasonable. On colder days its interior offers unbeatable waterway views, while balloon-lanterns, funky colours and traditional glass chandeliers make for a warm, cosy atmosphere.

Mocabon (Map p122; ☎ 09-225 7195; Donnersteeg 35; ☽ 8am-7pm Mon-Sat year-round plus 11.30am-6.30pm Sun Oct-Easter) The delightful aroma of freshly roasted beans entices passers-by into this classic, old-world coffeeshop.

Het Spijker (Map p122; ☎ 09-329 4440; Pensmarkt 3; Primus/Tongerlo/cava €2/2.80/4; ☯ 10am-5am) Tongues of flames lick the entrance portal of this medieval, heavy-beamed stone *café*. A lively place that's usually the most central drinking spot to stay open really late.

De Geus van Gent (Map pp118-19; ☎ 09-220 2875; www.geuzenhuis.be; Kantienberg 9; ☯ 7pm-late) Congenial, multifaceted *café* with very eclectic decor, jam nights on term-time Wednesdays and comedy nights in June.

De Brouwzaele (Map pp118-19; ☎ 09-224 3392; Ter Platen 17; ☯ 11am-11pm) Local gents unwind with a beer and a newspaper in this low-key classic *café*. It's set in a triangular former brewery-house whose giant copper brew-still is now the focal point of a very original hop-decked bar.

Gruut (Map pp118-19; ☎ 09-233 6821; www.gruut.be; Grote Huidevettershoek 10; beer €2; ☯ 11am-1am) Ghent's new brewery-pub where you taste the blonde that's maturing beside you.

Trappistenhuis (Map pp118-19; www.trappistenhuis.be; Brabantdam 164; ☯ noon-1am Mon-Fri 6pm-1am Sat) Trappistenhuis is an archetypal beer-pub with 150 (somewhat pricey) brews and a taste for blues music. It makes a decent pitstop when walking to or from the Kleine Begijnhof.

't Velootje (Map p122; Kalversteeg 2; beer €4; ☯ from 9pm, very variable) Unique doesn't begin to describe this extraordinary Patershol pub, which looks like an escaping jumble sale. Flouting every possible fire-safety rule the interior is crammed from floor to ceiling with all manner of junk and riches, notably dusty virgins and antique bikes. Once you've squeezed your way onto one of the hilariously cramped benches there's still the problem of persuading the temperamental owner to actually serve you. Unforgettable, but avoid the toilets.

Entertainment

While most websites are in Dutch, clicking 'agenda' on any site is the best way to see what's planned. Alternatively grab free *Week-Up* pamphlets or the *Zone 09 Magazine* (free from distribution boxes round town), also in Dutch. Also see **Muziekclub Democrazy** (www.democrazy.be) for an imaginative and varied network of clubs and events at various venues.

LIVE MUSIC & NIGHTCLUBS

Most *café*s don't charge entry fees for concerts, but might add a small supplement to listed drink prices.

Hot Club de Gand (Map p122; ☎ 0498-541 117; www.hotclubdegand.be; Schuddevisstraatje; ☯ 3pm-late) Hidden down the tiny alley behind 't Dreupelkot *jenever* bar, this is a great place to seek out live acoustic music. Be it jazz, gypsy, blues or flamenco, there's likely to be a concert most term-time nights at around 9pm.

Hotsy Totsy (Map pp118-19; ☎ 09-224 2012; www.hotsytotsy.be; Hoogstraat 1; beer from €1.70; ☯ 6pm-1am Mon-Fri, 8pm-2am Sat & Sun) A 1930s vamp pouts above the zinc bar of this marvellous 'artist's *café*' with silver-floral wall paper, black-and-white film photos, chess sets for quiet nights and free live jazz at 9pm most Thursdays (October to April). It was founded by the brothers of famous Flemish author Hugo Claus.

Charlatan (Map p122; www.charlatan.be; Vlasmarkt 6; ☯ 7pm-very late) The Charlatan remains a perennial favourite, offering live music in virtually any genre (around 10pm several nights weekly) and opening times that should leave you ready for breakfast.

Cafe Video (Map p122; www.cafevideo.be; Oude Beestenmarkt 7; ☯ 8pm-late, Tue-Sat) This compact DJ *café* spins contemporary beats and hosts an eclectic selection of live bands, from shoegazers to purveyors of indie-electronica.

Muzikantenhuis (Map pp118-19; ☎ 04/6-502 877; http://muzikantenhuis.be; Dampoortstraat 50; ☯ noon-midnight Tue-Sat Sep-Jul, concerts 9pm Thu-Sat) Ropes, horse harnesses and the sayings of Rumi give this very inexpensive *café* a slightly cheesy atmosphere but the free traditional Turkish music concerts are the attraction. You might also find jazz and Latin styles.

Café Trefpunt (Map p122; ☎ 09-233 5848; www.trefpuntvzw.be; Bij St-Jacobs 18; ☯ from 5pm) Most of the week this is a laid-back pub, but on Monday evenings, when most other places close, there are jam sessions or live concerts. Standards tend to be high as performers want to impress the owners, who also organise the Gentse Feesten (p18). DJs on Sundays.

De Centrale (off Map p122; ☎ 09-265 9828; www.decentrale.be; Kraankindersstraat 2; ☯ café 2pm-midnight) Multicultural centre offering an interesting range of 'world' music concerts and dances (flamenco, Turkish, North African, Asian). There's also a restaurant providing jobs for unemployed immigrants and a reading cafe with a wide range of international newspapers.

Culture Club (off Map pp118-19; ☎ 09-267 6441; www.cultureclub.be; Afrikalaan 174; admission €8/10 before/after midnight; ☯ Sat 11pm-dawn Oct-May) One British magazine rated this the 'world's hippest club'. Themes and cover charges vary. It's roughly 1.5km north of Gent-Dampoort station via Koopvaardijlaan.

Flanders Expo (off Map pp118-19; ☎ 09-241 9211; www .flandersexpo.be; Maaltekouter 1) Though primarily for trade fairs, Flanders Expo also hosts occasional big-name rock concerts. It's at tram 1's southern terminus, 4km beyond Gent-St-Pieters.

PERFORMING ARTS

Pre-booking online is wise though most websites are in Dutch.

Vooruit (Map pp118-19; ☎ 09-267 2828; www.vooruit .be; St-Pietersnieuwstraat 23; ☯ cafe 11.30am-2am Mon-Sat, 4pm-1am Sun) A visionary premonition of art deco, the 1912 Vooruit building is a prominent venue for dance, rock concerts, film and visiting theatre companies. Its lively *café* also hosts occasional low-key free concerts and serves draught Moinette 'bio-beer'.

De Bijloke (Map pp118-19; ☎ 09-269 9292; www. debijloke.be; Jozef Kluyskensstraat 2) Good selection of classical music concerts on a site recycled from a historic abbey and hospital.

De Vlaamse Opera (Map pp118-19; ☎ 070-220 202; www.vlaamseopera.be; tickets €9-95; Schouwburgstraat 3) Ghent's 1840 opera hall boasts horseshoe-shaped tiered balconies and elegant salons.

Handelsbeurs (Map pp118-19; ☎ 09-265 9160; www.han delsbeurs.be; Kouter 29) Central concert-hall for anything from classics to Latin to blues.

NT Gent Schouwburg (Map p122; ☎ 09-225 0101; www.ntgent.be; St-Baafsplein 17) Home to Ghent's premier theatre company. It also offers interesting 'open rehearsals' and workshops but naturally almost everything's in Dutch. Its cafe-restaurant, de Foyer, has a great terrace overlooking the square.

Poppentheater (Map p122; ☎ 09-269 2367; www. huisvanalijn.be; Kraanlei 65; adult €3; ☯ 2.30pm Wed & Sat Sep-Jun) Traditional puppet shows in the Huis van Alijn (p120).

Shopping

South of Korenmarkt, pedestrianised Veldstraat sports standard department stores, while two blocks east Mageleinstraat and its offshoots are fashion hunting-grounds.

Home Linen (Map p122; ☎ 09-223 6093; Korenlei 3; ☯ 10am-6pm Tue-Sun) stocks art deco tablewear and a large collection of Belgian linen.

Mustard makers since 1790, **Tierenteijn-Verlent** (Map p122; ☎ 09-225 8336; Groentenmarkt 3) is an atmospheric pharmacy-styled shop that also sells jams and spices.

Getting There & Away

About 2km south of the city centre **Gent-St-Pieters** (Map pp118-19) is Ghent's main train station. It's a fortress-like affair with romantic, heraldic murals and an alluring yet inexpensive mock-medieval station *café* (closes 9pm). Trains run at least twice hourly to Antwerp (€8.60, 50 minutes), Bruges (€5.90, fast/slow 25/40 minutes), Brussels (€8.10, 36 minutes), Kortrijk (€6.30, fast/slow 20/36 minutes), Ostend (€8.60, fast/slow 38/55 minutes) and Oudenaarde (€4, 30 minutes). Ostend–Bruges–Antwerp, Kortrijk–Antwerp and local Eeklo-bound trains also stop at **Gent-Dampoort** (Map pp118-19), which is more conveniently close to the city centre than Gent-St-Pieters.

Though its ticket office is near Gent-St-Pieters, **Eurolines** (Map pp118-19; ☎ 09-220 9024; www.eurolines.be; Koningin Elisabethlaan 73; ☯ 9am-1pm & 2-5.45pm Mon-Fri, 9am-12.15 Sat) international buses depart from Gent-Dampoort station. Many regional **De Lijn** (www.delijn.be) services start from **Gent-Zuid bus station** (Map pp118-19).

Getting Around

Tram and bus tickets for city services are cheaper bought from ticket machines or De Lijn's **information kiosks** Gent-St-Pieters (Map pp118-19; ☯ 7am-7pm Mon-Fri); Botermarkt (Map p122; ☯ 7am-7pm Mon-Fri, 10.30am-5.30pm Sat). These kiosks also give away useful city transport maps but beware that during extensive works on Korenmarkt, the normally handy tram routes 1 and 4 can't pass through the centre so both routes are currently divided into two disconnected sectors.

From Gent-St-Pieters, tram 1 to the centre departs from within the tunnel to the left as you exit the station. Tram 4 starts from the station square, loops past Rabot and eventually doubles back to Patershol. Change at Rabot for tram 1's north-sector route for the HI and Andromeda hostels. Useful bus 5 from Vlasmarkt runs to Vooruit, St-Pietersabdij and Heuvelpoort (handy for the Citadelpark galleries). **Night buses** (www.delijn.be; ☯ 11.30pm-2.30am Fri & Sat only) are free.

Bicycles can be rented from **Biker** (Map p122; ☎ 09 224 29 03; Steendam 16; half-/full day €6.50/9; ☯ 9am-12.30pm & 1.30-6pm Tue-Sat) or from the Gent-St-Pieters **station luggage room** (bagagekantoor; ☎ 09-241 2245; per day €9.50, plus €12.50 deposit) – ID required. Beware that police will confiscate illegally parked bikes.

AROUND GHENT
Deurle & St-Martens-Latem
pop 8300

Greater Ghent peters out into woodlands and meadows in the upmarket suburban villages of Deurle and St-Martens-Latem. A century ago, this attractive area was home to several symbolist and expressionist artists, notably Gustave de Smet and Constant Permeke. De Smet returned in his retirement to what is now the somewhat odd **Museum Gustave de Smet** (☎ 09-282 7742; De Smetlaan 1, Deurle; admission free; 2-6pm Wed-Sun May-Sep, 2-5pm Wed-Sun Oct-Apr, closed Jan), displaying a selection of the artist's work within what's still a lived-in family house.

Hidden away some 400m north up the next lane west is a trio of small side-by-side galleries displaying regularly changing selections of modern and/or contemporary art. The most active is the **Museum Dhondt-Dhaenens** (☎ 09-282 5123; www.museumdd.be; Museumlaan 14, Deurle; admission depending on exhibition €3-5; 10am-5pm Tue-Sun).

Overlooking the meadows and meandering river, **Auberge du Pecheur** (☎ 09-2823144; www.auberge-du-pecheur.be; Pontstraat 41, Deurle; d €95-150) has a brasserie, tea-room and Michelin-starred restaurant plus four architecturally varied hotel buildings, including two fine historic houses, each with stylish modern fittings.

From Ghent buses 34, 35 or 36 (direction De Pinte) depart approximately twice hourly taking around 40 minutes from Gent-Dampoort (bus platform 4) or 25 minutes from the south (back) side of Gent-St-Pieters station. The De Smetdreef stop is 30m from the Museum Gustave de Smet.

Amid pollarded trees across the river (around 3km by road) is the splendidly moated, bulb-spired **Kasteel Ooidonk** (☎ 09-282 2638; www.ooidonk.be; Ooidonkdreef 7, Bachte-Maria-Leerne; adult/child €7/2, gardens only €1/0.30; castle 2pm-5.30pm Sat Jul-Aug & Sun Apr–mid-Sep, grounds 9am-6pm Tue-Sun), a privately owned medieval castle set in attractive grounds beyond a dinky little gateway tower.

Laarne
Just east of Ghent, **Kasteel Laarne** (adult/senior/child €7/6/2; 3pm Sun Easter-Sep & Thu Jul-Aug) is a fine castle that oozes medieval atmosphere, with a moat and stone-cone 14th-century towers. Should you arrive on the right day (see opening times above) you could peruse its tapestries, paintings and celebrated silver collection. Wetteren-bound bus 34 takes 22 minutes from Gent-Dampoort, departing at a quarter-past each hour.

BRUGES (BRUGGE)
pop 117,000

If you set out to design a fairy-tale medieval town it would be hard to improve on central Bruges (Brugge in Dutch). Picturesque cobbled lanes and dreamy canals link exceptionally photogenic market squares lined with soaring towers, historic churches and old whitewashed almshouses. And there's plenty of it. The only downside is that everyone knows. That means that there's an almost constant crush of tourists, especially through the summer months. So to really enjoy Bruges stay overnight (day-trippers miss the fabulous evening floodlighting) and try to visit midweek (avoiding floods of British weekenders). There's a special charm in spring when daffodils carpet the tranquil *begijnhof* or in winter (except Christmas) when you can have the magnificent, if icy, town almost to yourself.

History
The fortress around which Bruges would grow was originally constructed by Baldwin Iron Arm, first count of Flanders, just beyond the head of a long sea channel called the Zwin. As with other Flemish cities, Bruges' medieval prosperity came from trading and manufacturing textiles from high-quality English wool. Trade came via the Zwin and a linking waterway from nearby Damme village (p146). Thirteenth-century traders meeting at the Bruges house of a certain Van de Burse (Vlamingenstraat 35) were the first to formalise stock trading and to this day stock exchanges are still called *bourses* in many languages. By 1301 Bruges' citizens were already so wealthy that French king Philip the Fair's wife, Joanna of Navarre, purportedly claimed: 'I thought I alone was queen, but I see that I have 600 rivals here'.

Despite occasional rebellions (see the boxed text, p132), Bruges' zenith came in the 14th-century. As a key member of the Hanseatic League (a powerful association of northern-European trading cities), international trading houses set up shop here and ships laden with exotic goods from all over Europe and beyond docked at the Minnewater (p136).

Prosperity continued under the dukes of Burgundy, especially Philip the Good (r 1419–67), who arrived in 1430 to marry

WESTERN FLANDERS

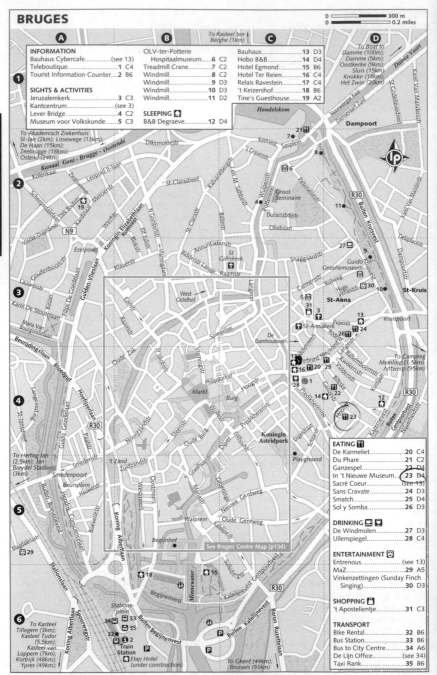

BRUGES

0 — 300 m
0 — 0.2 miles

INFORMATION
Bauhaus Cybercafe..............(see 13)
Teleboutique.........................1 C4
Tourist Information Counter....2 B6

SIGHTS & ACTIVITIES
Jeruzalemkerk.......................3 C3
Kantcentrum......................(see 3)
Lever Bridge..........................4 C2
Museum voor Volkskunde......5 C3

OLV-ter-Potterie
Hospitaalmuseum.......6 C2
Treadmill Crane.................7 C2
Windmill.........................8 C2
Windmill.........................9 D3
Windmill........................10 D3
Windmill........................11 D2

SLEEPING
B&B Degraeve.............12 D4

Bauhaus....................13 D3
Hobo B&B.................14 D4
Hotel Egmond.............15 B6
Hotel Ter Reien...........16 C4
Relais Ravestein..........17 C4
't Keizershof..............18 B6
Tine's Guesthouse.......19 A2

EATING
De Karmeliet..............20 C4
Du Phare...................21 C2
Ganzespel.................22 D4
In 't Nieuwe Museum...23 D4
Sacré Coeur.............(see 13)
Sans Cravate.............24 D4
Smatch....................25 D4
Sol y Somba..............26 D3

DRINKING
De Windmolen............27 D3
Uilenspiegel..............28 C4

ENTERTAINMENT
Entrenous................(see 13)
MaZ.......................29 A5
Vinkenzettingen (Sunday Finch
Singing).................30 D3

SHOPPING
't Apostelientje.........31 C3

TRANSPORT
Bike Rental...............32 B6
Bus Station...............33 B6
Bus to City Centre........34 A6
De Lijn Office............(see 34)
Taxi Rank.................35 B6

To Kasteel ten
Berghe (1km)

To Damme (100m);
Damme (5km);
Oostkerke (9km);
Sluis (15km);
Knokke (18km);
Het Zwin (20km)

Dampoort

Handelskom

To Akademisch Ziekenhuis
St-Jan (2km); Lissewege (13km);
De Haan (15km);
Zeebrugge (18km);
Ostend (24km)

To Hertog Jan
(2.5km); Jan
Breydel Stadium
(3km)

To Kasteel
Tillegem (3km);
Kasteel Tudor
(5.5km);
Kasteel van
Loppem (7km);
Kortrijk (48km);
Ypres (49km)

St-Kruis

To Camping
Memling (1.5km);
Antwerp (95km)

Markt

Burg

Koningin
Astridpark

Playground

See Bruges Centre Map (p134)

Begijnhof

Stations-
plein

Train
Station
Etap Hotel
(under construction)

To Ghent (44km);
Brussels (93km)

Isabella of Portugal. Bruges grew fat and at one point the population had ballooned to 200,000, doubling that of London. Flemish art blossomed and the city's artists, known misleadingly as the Flemish Primitives (see p39), perfected paintings that were anything but primitive.

However, the guildsmen's relationship with their distant overlords was tense. A dynastic conflict between the French and Hapsburg empires in 1482 caused rising taxes and restrictions in the guildsmen's privileges. This in turn sparked a decade of disastrous revolts. At one point in 1488, presumptuous Bruges townsmen even dared to imprison the Hapsburg heir Maximilian of Austria for four months on a site that's now the Craenenburg Café (Markt 16). The Hapsburgs took furious retributions, with Bruges forced to demolish its city walls. While on paper the 'Liberty of Bruges' remained as a powerful autonomous district, traders sensed the city's coming demise. The Hanseatic League moved from Bruges to Antwerp and many merchants followed. But most devastating of all, the Zwin gradually silted up so Bruges lost all access to the sea. Despite attempts to build another canal, the city's economic lifeline was gone and the town was left full of abandoned houses, deserted streets and empty canals. Bruges slept for 400 years.

The city slowly emerged from its slumber in the early 19th-century as war-tourists passed through en route to the Waterloo battlefield (p217). In 1892 Belgian writer and poet Georges Rodenbach published *Bruges-la-Morte* (Bruges the Dead), a novel that beguilingly described the town's forlorn air and alerted well-heeled tourists to its preserved charm. Curious, wealthy visitors brought much-needed money into Bruges, and ever since the town has worked hard at renovations and embellishments to maintain its reputation as one of the world's most perfectly preserved medieval time capsules.

Antique Bruges escaped both world wars relatively unscathed and now lives largely off tourism. However, beyond the cute central area, greater Bruges includes a newer sprawl where vibrant manufacturing industries produce glass, electrical goods and chemicals, much of it exported via the 20th-century port of Zeebrugge ('Sea Bruges') to which Bruges has been linked since 1907 by the Boudewijnkanaal (Baudouin canal).

Orientation

Old-town Bruges is neatly encased by an oval-shaped moat that follows the city's medieval fortifications. While the walls are gone, four of the nine 14th-century gates still stand. The city centre is an ambler's dream, its sights sprinkled within leisurely walking distance of its compact centre. The train station is about 1.5km south of the central square (Markt); buses shuttle very regularly between the two, but it's a lovely walk via Minnewater.

Information
BOOKSHOPS
De Reyghere Reisboekhandel (Map p134; ☎ 050-333 403; Markt 12; ☺ 9.30am-noon Tue-Sat & 2pm-6pm Mon-Sat) Well-stocked travel bookshop.

WESTERN FLANDERS

DISCOUNT CARDS
Bruges offers a somewhat bewildering series of passes and multi-tickets. Best value is the **Musea Brugge Pass** (three-days/one-year €15/25 adult, €5/8 child), which gives you free entry to all 15 city-owned attractions. While some of these are barely worth 10 minutes of your time, others are unmissable. Even if you only visit the Belfort and Groeningemuseum, you'll have already saved a euro. Savings are much more marginal with the very comprehensive **Love Bruges City Pass** (48hr/72hr €35/45). It includes the Musea Brugge 15, private attractions like Choco-Story, Diamantmuseum, Frietmuseum and De Halve Maan brewery, a city tour (limited times) and a canal boat ride (before 11am or after 2pm only). You'll also score discounts on bicycle rental, Flanders bus passes and sights in neighbouring towns. It all sounds remarkably generous on paper, but in reality you'll need to be pretty hyperactive to make the most of all that's offered.

It's often better to buy the Musea Brugge pass then get discount rates on the rest (typically 20%) by using a **Bruges Card** (www.brugescard.he) or **Welkom@Brugge Card** (www.welkom-brugge.be). These cards are given away free to guests by most hostels and hotels and are so ubiquitous that simply mentioning them is usually enough to get the discount.

THE BRUGES MATINS, 1302

The precocious wealth and independent-mindedness of Bruges' medieval guildsmen brought political tensions with their French overlords. In 1302, when guildsmen refused to pay a new round of taxes, the French sent in a 2000-strong army to garrison the town. Un-cowed, Pieter De Coninck, Dean of the Guild of Weavers, and Jan Breydel, Dean of the Guild of Butchers, led a revolt that would go down in Flanders' history books as the 'Bruges Matins' (Brugse Metten). Early in the morning on 18 May, guildsmen crept into town and murdered anyone who could not correctly pronounce the hard-to-say Dutch phrase *'schild en vriend'* (shield and friend). This revolt sparked a widespread Flemish rebellion. A short-term Flemish victory six weeks later at the Battle of the Golden Spurs (see p166) near Kortrijk gave medieval Flanders a very short-lived moment of independence.

INTERNET ACCESS
Bauhaus Cybercafe (Map p130; Bauhaus Hostel, Langestraat 145; per hr €3; 🕑 9am-10pm).
Café Mundo (Map p134; ☎ 050-349 744; St-Janshospitaal Bldg, Mariastraat 38; per half/full hr €3/5; 🕑 11am-late Wed-Sun) A real cafe with free wi-fi and internet computers.
Punjeb Call Shop (Map p134; Philipstockstr; per hr €2.50; 🕑 10am-midnight) Call shop.
Teleboutique (Map p130; Predikherenstraat 48; per hr €3; 🕑 10am-9pm Sat-Thu, to 1.30pm Fri)

LAUNDRY
Wassalon (Map p134; Ezelstraat 51)

LEFT LUGGAGE
Train station lockers (per 24hr small/large €3/4)

MEDICAL SERVICES
Akademisch Ziekenhuis St-Jan (off Map p130; ☎ 050-452 111; Ruddershove 10) The city's main hospital has a 24-hour emergency unit.
Apotheek Soetaert (Map p134; ☎ 050-332 593; Vlamingstraat 17; 9am-12.30pm & 2pm-6.30pm Mon-Sat, closed Wed pm) Charming olde-worlde pharmacy.
Doctors on weekend duty (☎ 050-364 010)
Pharmacists on weekend duty (☎ 050-406 162)

MONEY
ATM Post office (Map p134, Markt 5); Fortis Bank (Map p134, Simon Stevinplein 3); Europabank (Map p134, Vlamingstraat 13)
Fintro (Map p134; Vlamingstraat 18; 🕑 8.30am-4.45pm Mon-Fri, 9am-12.30pm & 2-4pm Sat) Offers better commission-free rates for cash than most competitors. Cashing travellers cheques incurs a €2.48 charge (up to €500).

POST
Post office (Map p134; ☎ 050-331 411; Markt 5) Gorgeous building with spires, brick gables and a stone arcade.

TOURIST INFORMATION
There are two offices, both sell extensive €2 guide booklets and €0.50 city maps. They also stock the great map-guide **Use-it** (www.use-it.be), which offers useful local tips on a decent map. It's free but you'll have to ask for it.
Tourist Information counter (Map p130; Train Station; 🕑 10am-5pm Mon-Fri, to 2pm Sat)
Tourist Office (In&Uit Brugge; Map p134; ☎ 050-448 686; www.brugge.be; 't Zand 34; 🕑 10am-6pm Fri-Wed, to 8pm Thu) By day this well-organised office has a useful accommodation booking service (€2.50 fee plus deposit). After hours, there's a 24-hour touch-screen computer outside listing hotel details and availability.

Sights
All appear on map p134 unless otherwise marked.

MARKT
Flanked by medieval-style step-gabled buildings, this splendid open market square is Bruges' nerve centre. Horse-drawn carriages clatter between open-air restaurants and camera-clicking tourists watched over by a verdigris-green **statue of Pieter De Coninck and Jan Breydel**, the leaders of the Bruges Matins (see the boxed text, above). Towering 83m above the square like a gigantic medieval space-rocket is the fabulous 13th-century **Belfort** (Belfry; adult/concession/child €8/6/5; 🕑 9.30am-5pm, last tickets 4.15pm). There's relatively little to see inside, but it's worth the mildly claustrophobic 366-step climb for the fine views. Look out through wide-gauge chicken wire for panoramas across the spires and red-tiled rooftops towards the wind turbines and giant cranes of Zeebrugge. Visitor numbers are limited to 70 at once, which can cause queues at peak times.

The belfry's 47-bell carillon is still played manually on a changing schedule (typically

Wednesdays and weekends). Timings are posted on a signboard in front of the 13th-century **Hallen** (former market halls), which host occasional exhibitions and fairs.

BURG

One short block east of the Markt, the Burg has been Bruges' administrative hub for centuries. It also hosted the St-Donatian Cathedral till 1799, when it was torn down by anti-religious zealots. Perhaps someone should do the same to the **Toyo Ito pavilion**, a geometric contemporary 'artwork' that looks like the entrance to a subterranean car park and currently mars the otherwise lovely square's tree-filled centre.

Turn your back on it to admire the square's southern flank, incorporating three superb interlinked facades. Most eye-catching with its early baroque gabling, gilt highlights and golden statuettes is the **Brugse Vrije** (Burg 11a). It was once the palace of the 'Liberty of Bruges', the large autonomous territory and administrative body that was ruled from Bruges (1121–1794). Much of the building is still used for city offices, but you can visit the former aldermen's room, the **Renaissancezaal** (adult/concession €2/1; 9.30am-12.30pm & 1.30-5pm) to admire its remarkable 1531 carved chimneypiece. Above a black marble fireplace and alabaster frieze, an incredibly detailed oak carving depicts a sword-waving Emperor Charles V (see the boxed text, p27). Charles is flanked by his grandparents, Ferdinand of Aragon and Maximilian of Austria, both of whom sport extremely flattering codpieces.

Next door the beautiful 1420 **stadhuis** (city hall; Burg 12) has a fanciful facade that's second only to Leuven's for exquisitely turreted Gothic excess. It's smothered with replica statues of the counts and countesses of Flanders, the originals having been torn down in 1792 by French soldiers. Inside an audio-guide explains numerous portraits in somewhat excessive detail before leading you upstairs to the astonishing **Gotische Zaal** (Gothic Hall; adult/concession €2/1; 9.30am-5pm Tue-Sun). Few rooms anywhere achieve such a jaw-dropping first impression as this dazzling hall with its polychrome ceiling, hanging vaults, romantically historicist murals and upper frieze of gilt figures.

Basilica of the Holy Blood

The Stadhuis's western end morphs into the strangely invisible **Heilig-Bloedbasiliek** (Burg 5; 9.30-11.50am & 2-5.50pm Apr-Sep, 10-11.50am &

2-3.50pm Thu-Tue, 10-11.50am Wed Oct-Mar). The basilica takes its name from a phial supposedly containing a few drops of Christ's blood that was brought here after the 12th-century Crusades. The right-hand door leads upstairs to a colourfully adorned chapel where the relic is hidden behind a flamboyant silver tabernacle and brought out for pious veneration at 2pm daily. Also upstairs is the basilica's one-room **treasury** (adult/child €1.50/free), where you'll see the jewel-studded reliquary in which the phial is mounted on Ascension Day for Bruges' biggest annual parade, the Heilig-Bloedprocessie (p17).

Downstairs, entered via a different door, is the basilica's contrasting bare-stone 12th-century Romanesque chapel, a meditative place that's almost devoid of decoration.

CENTRAL CANAL AREA

A cute passageway (Blinde Ezelstraat, 'blind donkey street') burrows out of the Burg and crosses the very picturesque canal: don't forget to look behind you! Across the bridge the stone slabs of the colonnaded 1821 **fish market** (Vismarkt; 7am-1pm Tue-Fri) still accommodate fish stalls most mornings, along with trinket sellers later in the day. Several seafood restaurants here back onto pretty Huidenvettersplein, where archetypal Bruges buildings include the old tanners' guildhouse. Don't miss the superb **canal view** (www.360cities.net/image/rozenhoedkaai-brugge) from outside 't Klein Venetie café (itself unremarkable). With the belfry towering above a perfect canal-fronted gaggle of medieval house-fronts, the view is lovely any time. But it's especially compelling at dusk as the floodlights come on. From here canal-side Dijver leads southwest towards Bruges' foremost city museums.

Groeningemuseum

The **Groeningemuseum** (Dijver 12; adult/concession €8/6; 9.30am-5pm Tue-Sun) is Bruges' most celebrated art gallery. While not enormous, the 11 rooms pack in an astonishingly rich collection whose particular strengths are in superb Flemish Primitive and Renaissance works. Gruesomely gory scenes include flaying alive in Gerard David's *Judgement of Cambyses* (1498; room 1) and the multiple tortures of *St George* (room 3) – the saint manages to keep his bright white underpants remarkably unsoiled, nonetheless. In room 2 are much more meditative works including Jan Van Eyck's 1436 radiant, if rather

WESTERN FLANDERS

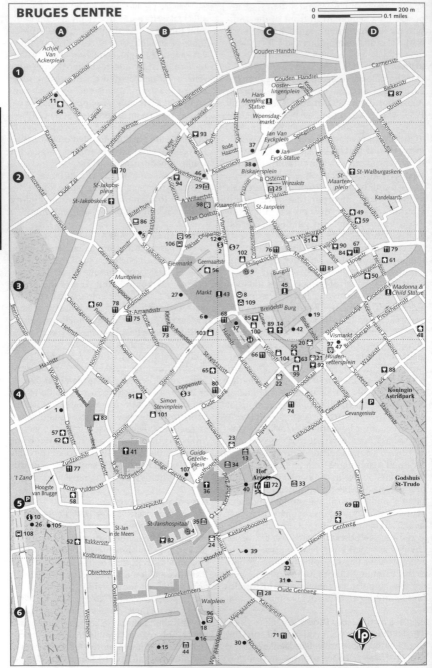

BRUGES CENTRE

0 — 200 m
0 — 0.1 miles

odd, masterpiece *Madonna with Canon George Van der Paele* (1436) and Hans Memling's *Moreel Triptych* where cheeky little details recall scenes from *Blackadder I*. Later artistic genres also get a look in, including a typically androgynous figure by superstar symbolist Fernand Khnopff, plus a surrealist canvas each from Magritte and Delvaux.

With your Groeningemuseum ticket, admission is free to the **Arentshuis** (Dijver 16; adult/concession/child €2/1/free; 9.30am-5pm Tue-Sun), a stately 18th-century patrician house displaying the powerful paintings and etchings of Frank Brangwyn (1867–1956), a Bruges-born artist of British parentage.

Gruuthuse

The **Gruuthuse** (Dijver 17; adult/concession €6/5; 9.30am-5pm Tue-Sun) takes its name from the flower and herb mixture (*gruut*) that used to flavour beer before the cultivation of hops. Its heraldic entrance in a courtyard of ivy-covered walls and dreaming spires is arguably more interesting than the rambling, somewhat unsatisfying decorative-arts exhibits within. The view from the upstairs gallery window into the treasury-apse of the Onze-Lievevrouwekerk is worth a look.

Hof Arents

Behind the Arentshuis, **Hof Arents** (admission free; summer 7am-10pm, winter to 9pm) is a charming little park where a hump-backed pedestrian bridge, **St-Bonifaciusbrug**, crosses the canal for idyllic views. Generally nicknamed Lovers' Bridge, it's where many a Bruges citizen steals their first kiss. Privileged guests staying at the Guesthouse Nuit Blanche (p141) get the romantic moonlit scene all to themselves once the park has closed.

Onze-Lievevrouwekerk

This large, somewhat sober 13th-century **church** (Mariastraat; 🕑 9.30am-4.50pm Mon-Sat, 1.30-4.50pm Sun) sports an enormous tower that's currently 'wrapped' for extensive renovation. Inside it's best known for Michelangelo's serenely contemplative 1504 *Madonna and Child* statue, the only such work by Michelangelo to leave Italy during the artist's lifetime. In the church's apse, the **treasury section** (adult/concession €2/1) displays some splendid 15th- and 16th-century artworks plus the fine stone-and-bronze tombs of Charles the Bold (Karel de Stoute) and his daughter, Mary of Burgundy, whose pivotal marriage dragged the Low Countries into the Hapsburg empire, with far-reaching consequences (see p26).

St-Janshospitaal

In the restored chapel of a 12th-century hospital building with superb timber beamwork, this **museum** (Mariastraat 38; adult/concession/child €8/6/free; 🕑 9.30am-5pm Tue-Sun) shows various historical medical implements and medically themed paintings, but is best known for six masterpieces by 15th-century artist Hans Memling, including the enchanting reliquary of St-Ursula. Your ticket also allows visits to the hospital's restored 17th-century **apotheek** (pharmacy), accessed by an easily missed rear door.

ST-SALVATORSKATHEDRAAL

Stacked sub-towers top the massive central tower of 13th-century **St-Saviour's Cathedral** (Steenstraat; 🕑 2-5.45pm Mon, 9am-noon & 2-5.45pm Tue-Fri, 9am-noon & 2-3.30pm Sat & Sun). In daylight the construction looks somewhat dour, but once floodlit at night, it takes on a mesmerising Escheresque fascination. The cathedral's interior is vastly high but feels oddly plain despite a selection of antique tapestries. The atmosphere isn't improved by ongoing noisy restoration work. Beneath the tower, a glass floor reveals some painted graves, while popping €0.50 into a slot illuminates the tower's hollow interior. There's a passingly interesting **treasury** (adult/concession €2/1; 🕑 2-5pm Sun-Fri) displaying 15th-century brasses and a 1559 triptych by Dirk Bouts.

WALPLEIN

Founded in 1856, **De Halve Maan** (☎ 050-332 697; www.halvemaan.be; Walplein 26) is the last fam-ily *brouwerij* (brewhouse) in central Bruges. Multilingual **guided visits** (admission €5.50; 🕑 11am-4pm Sun-Fri, to 5pm Sat Apr-Oct, 11am-3pm Mon-Fri, to 4pm Sat & Sun Nov-Mar), lasting 45 minutes, depart on each hour. They include a tasting but can sometimes be rather crowded. Alternatively you can simply sip one of their excellent *Brugse Zot* (Bruges Fool, 7%) or *Straffe Hendrik* (Strong Henry, 9%) beers in the appealing brewery *café*.

While Antwerp is now the centre of the diamond industry, the idea of polishing stones with diamond 'dust' was originally pioneered in Bruges. This is the theme developed by the slick **Diamantmuseum** (Diamond Museum; ☎ 050-342 056; www.diamondmuseum.be; Katelijnestraat 43; adult/senior/student €6/5/4; 🕑 10.30am-5.30pm), which also displays a lumpy, greenish 252-carat raw diamond and explains how the catchphrase '*Diamonds are Forever*' started as a De Beers marketing campaign. **Diamond-polishing demonstrations** (🕑 12.15pm) cost €3 extra.

Hidden away off nearby streets are several attractive *godshuizen* (almshouses, see the boxed text, opposite) including the 1713 **Godshuis de Vos** (Noordstraat 2-8), 1654 **Godshuis OLV Zeven Weeën** (Groeninge) and 1330 **Rooms Convent** (Mariastraat 9-21). For the most spacious little oases of calm push the green door and relax in **Godshuis St-Jozef & De Meulenaere** (Nieuwe Gentweg).

BEGIJNHOF AREA

Known in English as the 'Lake of Love', the charming green park around the **Minnewater** really does give this area a romantic quality. In Bruges' medieval heyday, this is where ships from far afield would unload their cargoes of wool, wine, spices and silks.

Bruges' delightful **begijnhof** (admission free; 🕑 6.30am-9pm) originally dates from the 13th century. Although the last *begijn* (opposite) has long since passed away, today residents of the pretty, whitewashed garden complex include a convent of Benedictine nuns. Despite the hoards of summer tourists, the *begijnhof* remains a remarkably tranquil haven. In spring a carpet of daffodils adds to the quaintness of the scene. Just inside the main entrance, **'t Begijnhuisje** (adult/student/senior €2/1/1.50; 🕑 10am-5pm Mon-Sat, 2.30pm-5pm Sun) is a typical *begijnhof* house now converted into an endearing little four-room museum that includes an austere bed-chamber, a well-cloister and a traditional kitchen. Outside the *begijnhof*'s 1776 **gateway bridge** lies a tempting, if predictably tourist-

BEGIJNHOVEN & GODSHUIZEN

In the 12th century, large numbers of men from the Low Countries embarked on Crusades to the Holy Land. Many never returned. Their now unchaperoned women-folk often felt obliged to seek security by joining a religious order. However, joining a convent required giving up one's worldly possessions and even one's name. A middle way, especially appealing to relatively wealthy widows, was to become a *begijn* (*béguine*). These lay sisters made Catholic vows including obedience and chastity, but could maintain their private wealth. They lived in a self-contained **begijnhof** (*béguinage* in French): a cluster of houses built around a central garden and church, surrounded by a protective wall. Land (normally at the outskirts of town) was typically granted by a pious feudal lord, but once established these all-female communities were self-sufficient. Most had a farm and vegetable garden and made supplementary income from lace-making and from benefactors who would pay the *begijnen* to pray for them.

In the 16th century Holland's growing Protestantism meant that most Dutch *begijnhoven* were swept away. In contrast, Spanish-ruled Flanders was gripped by a fervently Catholic counter-reformation that re-shaped the *begijn* movement. Rebuilt *begijnhoven* became more hospice-style institutions with vastly improved funding. From 1583 the Archbishop of Mechelen decreed a standardised rulebook and a nun-like 'uniform' for *begijnen* who at one point comprised almost 5% of Flanders' female population.

A century ago some 1500 *begijnen* remained in Belgium, but as of 2009 only one remains, Marcella Pattyn in Kortrijk (p163). Kortrijk's is one of 14 Flanders *begijnhoven* on the Unesco World Heritage List. Each is beautifully preserved albeit these days lived in by ordinary townsfolk. Most appealing are examples in Diest (p203), Lier (p192), Turnhout (p191) and Bruges (p129).

Looking somewhat similar to *begijnhoven* but usually on a smaller scale are **godshuizen** (alms-houses), typically featuring red-brick or whitewashed shuttered cottages set around a tiny enclosed garden. Originally built by merchant guilds for their members or by rich sponsors to provide shelter for the poor (and to save the sponsors' souls), these days they're great places to peacefully unwind if you dare to push open their usually closed doors. Bruges has a remarkable 46 *godshuizen*.

priced, array of terraced restaurants, lace shops and waffle peddlers.

'T ZAND

This oversized square is part bus station, part bleakly paved promenade lined by hotels and restaurants. Its latter-day **fountain** featuring cyclists and lumpy nudes looks more appealing when floodlit at night. The dominant building is the vast red **Concertgebouw** (☎ 050-476 999; www.concertgebouw.be; 't Zand 34) a concert hall and art space opened in 2002 to celebrate Bruges' year-long stint as the European City of Culture. While some hail its minimalism as proof that Bruges offers more than historical quaintness, it's hard to see much beauty in its brutal rectilinear form. Views from the 7th-floor **Forum+** (adult/child/MB €2/1/free, with Groeningemuseum ticket free; ⏰ 9.30am-4.30pm) gallery-promenade are magnificent though partly interrupted by vertical struts.

CHIPS & CHOCOLATE

Choco-Story (☎ 050-612 237; www.choco-story.be; Wijnzakstraat 2; adult/concession/child €6/5/4; ⏰ 10am-

5pm) is a highly absorbing chocolate museum tracing the cocoa bean back to its role as an Aztec currency. Learn about choco-history, watch a video on cocoa production and sample a praline that's made as you watch (last demonstration 4.45pm).

The **Frietmuseum** (☎ 050-340 150; www.frietmuseum.be; Vlamingstraat 33; adult/concession/child €6/5/4; ⏰ 10am-5pm; closed Christmas–mid-Jan) takes a similar approach, following the history of the potato from ancient Inca gravesites to the Belgian fryer, but the result is somewhat less gripping. The entry fee includes a €0.40 discount-token for the basement **frituur** (fries €2; ⏰ 11am-3pm) that immodestly claims to fry the world's ultimate chips.

ST-ANNA & DAMPOORT QUARTERS

Charming canal-scapes, street scenes and a few minor sights make the centre's little-visited northeastern corner a fine place for random wandering, perhaps en route to the Damme paddlesteamer (p146).

For lovely canal views (best in morning light) look west from outside the *café*

Uilenspiegel (see p144) or, three blocks further north, from the corner of St-Annarei and Blekkersstraat. The latter looks west towards Jan Eyckplein, where the spindly spire of the 15th-century **Poortersloge** (Burghers' Lodge) rises grandly beside the **Oud Tolhuis**. It's now the provincial library, but until the 18th century it was where tolls were levied on goods being brought into the city.

Views across the canal to busy Langerei remain attractive passing a small **lever bridge** (Map p130) that's reminiscent of Amsterdam and a large, underused **seminary** (www.priester worden.be). Free with a St-Janshospitaal museum ticket, **OLV-ter-Potterie** (Map p130; Potterierei 79; adult/concession €2/1; 9.30am-12.30pm & 1.30-5pm) is a smaller historical church-hospital complex. Ring the bell to gain entry and you'll find yet more fine 15th- to 16th-century art. The lushly baroque church section houses the reliquary of St-Idesbaldus and a polychrome wooden relief of Mary breastfeeding baby Jesus. In more prudish later centuries the virgin's nipple received a lacy camouflage, rendering the scene bizarrely impractical.

In Bruges' heyday heavy goods were lifted out of barges using human walking power in contraptions that looked like the recreated historical **treadmill crane** (Map p130) facing *café* Du Phare (see p143). South of here a calm, tree-shaded **towpath walk** links four photogenic **windmills** (Map p130), two of which host tiny, summer-only museum rooms and occasionally have their sails set in motion. The fortified gate-tower **Kruispoort** (Map p130; Langestraat) is an impressive isolated remnant of the former city wall. Directly west is one of Bruges' oddest churches, the 15th-century **Jeruzalemkerk** built by the Adornes family. Supposedly based upon Jerusalem's Church of the Holy Sepulchre, it's a macabre monument with a gruesome altarpiece covered in skull motifs and an effigy of Christ's corpse tucked away in the rear mini-chapel. The black-marble tomb of Anselm Adornes contains only his heart, presumably all that could be carried back to Bruges after he was murdered in Scotland in 1483. To see all of this you'll need to purchase a ticket to the attached **Kantcentrum** (Lace Centre; Map p130; www.kantcentrum.com; Peperstraat 3a; adult/child €2.50/1.50; 10am-noon & 2-6pm Mon-Fri, to 5pm Sat). Its collection of lace covers a decent variety of styles, but disappointingly little attempt is made at educating the novice as to what differentiates them. The centre's main attraction

is that (afternoons only) you can watch bobbin lace being made by informal gatherings of experienced lace-makers and their students. Once you've seen how mind-bendingly fiddly the process is, you'll swiftly understand why handmade lace is so very expensive.

The **Museum voor Volkskunde** (Folklore Museum; Map p130; Balstraat 43; adult/concession €3/2; 9.30am-5pm Tue-Sun) presents 18 themed tableaux illustrating Flemish life in times gone by (a 1930s sweetshop, a hatter's workshop, a traditional kitchen etc). While less engrossing than equivalents in Ghent (p120) or Liège (p250), the setting is an attractive *godshuis* (see p137) and the time-warp museum *café*, De Zwarte Kat, charges just €1.25 for a beer.

Activities
CYCLING
For picturesque cycling routes follow rural canal sides beyond Damme. Oostkerke (9km from Bruges' Dampoort) makes a good short run or head for pretty Sluis just across the Dutch border (15km via canal banks). For simple routes like these use the detailed *Bruges Surroundings* map (available free from Snuffel and Bauhaus hostels). For more complex routes the tourist office sells the *5x Bike Around Bruges* map-guide (€1.50).

Tours
CANAL TOURS
Half-hour **canal cruises** (adult/child €5.70/2.80; 10am-6pm Mar–mid-Nov) start frequently from five central jetties. As you float down Spiegelrei towards the slender turret of the Poortersloge (Jan Van Eyckplein) try imagining that the other tourists are in fact 15th-century Venetian merchants arriving to register their wares at the Oud Tolhuis (left).

HORSE-DRAWN CARRIAGE RIDES
Carriage tours (€35 for up to five people) depart from the Markt and take 35 minutes, including a pit stop at the *begijnhof*. In summer, aim to jump on board between 6pm and 7pm when most day-trippers have left town and Bruges' buildings glow golden in the sun's late rays.

MINIBUS TOURS
City Tour (www.citytour.be; from 10am) runs hourly 50-minute don-your-headphones **city tours** (adult/child €12/7) plus some two-hour trips to Damme. They start from the Markt; pay aboard.

LACED UP

There are two main ways of making lace (*kant/dentelle* in Dutch/French). **Needlepoint lace** (*naaldkant*) uses a single thread to embroider a pattern on a piece of cloth or paper that will eventually be discarded. Originally Italian, the technique was perfected in Brussels and the classic needlepoint stitch is still known as 'corded Brussels'. In contrast **bobbin lace** (*kloskant*) creates a web of interlinked threads using multiple threaded-bobbins meticulously twisted using a maze of hand-placed pins. It's an astonishingly fiddly process, believed to have originated in 14th-century Bruges. Using hundreds of bobbins, some of the finest known handmade samples originated in Binche (p216) while **Chantilly**, an originally French sub-form using black cotton, was for years a noted speciality craft of Geraardsbergen (p167). To save time and avoid errors, 19th-century Brussels manufacturers came up with **cut-thread lace** in which a series of smaller bobbin-lace details are sewn together to create larger pieces. The most typical styles were **Rosaline** where little rose details were often pearl-embroidered, and **Duchesse** with flower-and-leaf motifs. These days much lace-making is, understandably, fully mechanised, but the old handmade craft can still be seen demonstrated at Bruges' **Kantcentrum** (opposite). For more on Belgian lace see www.mbd.be.

Quasimodo (☎ 050-370 470; www.quasimodo.be) runs **Triple Treat tours** (under/over 26yr €45/55; ☽ 9am Mon, Wed & Fri Feb–mid-Dec) visiting Damme, the castle-parks at Loppem and Tillegem (p146), the artists' village of Lissewege (p152) and the Atlantikwall near Ostend (p149), with promises of waffles, beer, chocolate and a picnic lunch thrown in. Quasimodo also runs **Flanders Fields tours** (under/over 26yr €45/55; ☽ 9am Tue-Sun Apr-Oct) to Ypres, Passendale and Hill 60 (p160).

Festivals & Events
Highlights include the Holy Blood procession **Heilig-Bloedprocessie** (www.holyblood.com; ☽ Ascension Day) and the roughly five-yearly Golden Tree pageant (next in August 2012; see p18).

Sleeping
The tourist office's brilliantly comprehensive **accommodation website** (http://hotels.brugge. be/en) helps you filter through a hundred hotels and almost 150 B&Bs, but almost all options can get seriously overbooked from Easter to October and over Christmas. Things get especially tough at weekends when two-night minimum stays are commonly required. Many cheaper B&Bs charge around €10 per room less if you stay more than one night. For self-catering holiday flats click through links on www.brugge.be/internet/en/toerisme/log ies_restaurants/vakantie-woningen.htm.

BUDGET
Camping Memling (off Map p130; ☎ 050-355 845; www. campingmemling.be; Veltemweg 109, St-Kruis; campsites/ caravan €14/25, off season €11.20/20; ☽ year-round; ☞)

Quiet camping ground in St-Kruis where pitch prices assume two adults. Get off bus 11 at Vossensteert and walk back 400m towards Bruges.

Hotel Lybeer (Map p134; ☎ 050-334 355; www.hostel lybeer.com; Korte Vuldersstraat 31; dm/s/d without bathroom from €14/25/50, d with bathroom €60; ☐) The Lybeer has plenty of tatty edges, but few hostels have such a homey feeling nor such congenitally good-humoured staff. It's handily central in a typical Bruges terrace house that's 'just clean enough to be healthy, just dirty enough to be happy', according to a sign at reception.

Snuffel Backpacker Hostel (Map p134; ☎ 050-333 133; www.snuffel.be; Ezelstraat 47-49; dm €15-17, d €36; ☒ ☐) Basic but original rooms with shared kitchen. They're above an unpretentious bar that has occasional live music. Take bus 3 or 13 from the train station.

Bauhaus (Map p130; ☎ 050-341 093; www.bauhaus.be; Langestraat 135; hostel dm/d/tr per person €15/17/19, hotel s/d €28/44, flats per person €25; ☐) One of Belgium's most popular hang-outs for young travellers, this virtual backpacker 'village' incorporates a bustling hostel, apartments, a nightclub, internet cafe and a little chill-out room that's well hidden behind the reception and laundrette section at Langestraat 145. Simple dorms are operated with key cards; hotel-section double rooms have private shower cubicles; bike hire is also available. The bar-restaurant (Sacré Coeur, p143) is excellent except when you're trying to sleep above it. Take bus 6 or 16 from the train station.

't Keizershof (Map p130; ☎ 050-338 728; www. hotelkeizershof.be; Oostmeers 126; s/d €35/44; ☐P☐)

Remarkably tasteful and well kept for this price, the seven simple rooms with shared bathrooms are above a former brasserie-*café* decorated with old radios (now used as the breakfast room). Free parking.

Passage Bruges (Map p134; ☎ 050-340 232; www.passagebruges.com; Dweersstraat 26-28; dm €15, d without/with bathroom €50/65) The *café*-restaurant is inviting but hostel dorms, while attractively appointed, have no keys – making security a real worry. Showers work on an infuriating push-button system. Breakfast not included.

MIDRANGE

Hotel Central (Map p134; ☎ 050-331 805; www.hotelcentral.be; Markt 30; d without bathroom €50-70, with bathroom €60-100) Above a typical tourist restaurant right on the Markt, the eight rooms here have bold two-colour decor. Most have neat shower booths, but only room 9 has that superb view towards the belfry.

B&B Degraeve (Map p130; ☎ 050-345 711; www.bedandbreakfastmarjandegraeve.be; Kazernevest 32; s/d/tw/tr €50/60/70/80; ☾ closed Feb) Two remarkably eccentric guest rooms with shared musical bathrooms are overloaded with religious trinkets and doll-parts. Draped in artificial flowers, the house has a pleasant if slightly out-of-centre location. Bicycle rental costs €6 per day. Try their homemade sweet apple wine (free tasting) and beer (€2).

B&B Gheeraert (Map p134; ☎ 050-335 627, 0473-763 299; www.bb-bruges.be; Riddersstraat 9; s/d/tr €60/70/90; ☒ 🖳 ☎) At the top of a steep spiral staircase, three bright lofty rooms with whitewashed walls, art prints and polished wood floors share a plain lounge/computer room. Two night minimum.

Tine's Guesthouse (Map p130; ☎ 050-345 018; www.tinesguesthouse.com; Zwaluwenstraat 11; s/d/ste €60/70/90; ☒ 🅿 ☎) Offers freshly decorated rooms and use of a kitchen, lounge room, top-billiard table and small patio, while the 'suite' has a roof terrace. Special pluses here are Tine's effervescent hospitality, the great breakfast, free lunch packet, free bicycle hire and station pick-up – very helpful given the somewhat out-of-centre location. There's free street parking.

Hobo B&B (Map p130; ☎ 050-341 465; www.hobo-bedandbreakfast.be; Ganzenstraat 54; s/d €65/70; ☎) Unpretentiously charming, real-home B&B where the Laura Ashley-esque 'Romantic Room' (up some steep stairs) has a private bathroom. The smarter 'B&W' and mildly

nautical 'Blue' rooms have their own showers but share a toilet. Hanging spoons make for original decor in the breakfast room.

B&B Setola (Map p134; ☎ 050-334 977; www.bedandbreakfast-bruges.com; St-Walburgastraat 12; s/d/tr/q €70/80/90/120; ☒ ☎) Pleasant and very central, with three neat, pine-floored rooms ranged round a guest kitchen. The Orange Room has A-frame beams and two ladder-access extra beds.

Baert B&B (Map p134; ☎ 050-330 530; www.bedandbreakfastbrugge.be; Westmeers 28; s/d €70/80) In a 1613 former stable this is one of very few places in Bruges that you'll get a private canal-side terrace (adorably flower decked though not on the loveliest canal section). Floral rooms have bathrooms across the landing; bathrobes are provided. A big breakfast spread is served in a glass veranda, and extras include welcome drink and a pack of chockies.

Hotel Imperial (Map p134; ☎ 050-339 014; www.hotelimperial.be; Dweersstraat 24; d €70-85) Loveable, well-kept eight-room family hotel with floral bedspreads, timber floors, pine- and 1930s-cabinets and photos of old Bruges. A delightful little patio garden forms the focus of the dining room. The helpful, knowledgeable owner keeps cats and finches. Breakfast included.

Hotel Ter Reien (Map p130; ☎ 050-349 100; www.hotelterreien.be; Langestraat 1; internet rates from d/tr/f €79/114/139, peak rates €100/180/200; ☾ reception 8.30am-9.30pm) Eleven of the 26 good value if unexceptional rooms have lovely canal views (€10 supplement), while all are neat and clean with functional plastic bathroom booths.

B&B Dieltiens (Map p134; ☎ 050-334 294; www.bedandbreakfastbruges.be; Waalsestraat 40; s/d/tr €70/80/100) Old and new art fills this lovingly restored classical mansion, which remains an appealingly real home run by charming musician hosts. Superbly central yet quiet.

Hotel Patritius (Map p134; ☎ 050-338 454; www.hotelpatritius.be; Riddersstraat 11; d €80-122; ☾ closed Jan; 🅿 ☎) Enter this proud 1830s townhouse through the tall carriageway and past a little bar-lounge. Up the historic spiral staircase, 16 guestrooms vary quite radically in size and style, some with exposed beams, others mildly chintzy and some recently renovated in bolder style (albeit with oddly kitschy dog portraiture). Despite relatively modest prices there's a decent breakfast and pretty garden, but parking costs extra.

Hotel Egmond (Map p130; ☎ 050-341 445; www.egmond.be; Minnewater 15; low season s/d from €92/98, weekend

€105/115; ⊙ reception closes 6pm; **P** 🛜) First impressions are truly exciting: a peaceful Minnewater park location, a classic step-gabled facade and ancient fireplaces in a medieval-styled lobby. Sadly the guest rooms are a major anticlimax ranging from bland to dowdy.

St-Niklaas B&B (Map p134; ☎ 050-610 308; www .sintnik.be; St-Niklaasstraat 18; s €95-115, d €120-145; 🛜) Room 1 has a clawfoot bath and antique glass panel, but it's the other two rooms' remarkable Pisa-like belfry views that make this welcoming B&B so special.

De Triptiek Maison d'Hôtes (Map p134; ☎ 0498-656 025; www.triptiek.be; Nieuwe Gentweg 57; d €120-145; ✗) One of Bruges' most seductive B&Bs, with three faultlessly manicured rooms, luxuriously piled pillows, well-chosen fabrics and stripped wooden floors. The artistic yet unfussy house is fashioned from three gently modernised 17th-century cottages that contemplate a cherry tree in the small, well-tended garden.

Hotel Bourgoensch Hof (Map p134; ☎ 050-331 645; www.bourgoensch-hof.be; Wollestraat 39; r standard/canal-view from €123/149) Historic, understated family hotel with one of the most spectacular canal views in Bruges. The decor had become pretty dated at the time of research, but there are brand-new owners so things should improve.

B&B Huyze Hertsberge (Map p134; ☎ 050-333 542; www.huyzehertsberge.be; Hertsbergestraat 8; d €140-160) Very spacious and oozing with good taste, this late-17th-century house has a gorgeous period salon decked with antiques and sepia photos of the charming owner's great-great-grandparents (who first moved in here in 1901). The four guest rooms are comfortably grand, each with at least partial views of the tranquil little canal-side garden. Meet Fidèle the 'movie' Labrador.

TOP END

Number 11 (Map p134; ☎ 050-330 675; www.number11 .be; Peerdenstraat 11; d €155-175; 🛜) Featuring the distinctive ceramic works of Martine Bossuyt, this artistic, top-notch B&B, with logoed linens and pralines on the pillow, feels more like an intimate boutique hotel. There's a private salon and courtyard garden for the handful of guests.

our pick **Guesthouse Nuit Blanche** (Map p134; ☎ 0494-400 447; www.bruges-bb.com; Groeninge 2; d €175-195) Pay what you like, nowhere else in Bruges can get you a more romantic location than this fabulous B&B, which started life as a 15th-century tannery. It oozes history, retaining original Gothic fireplaces, stained-glass roundels and some historic furniture, while bathrooms and beds are luxury-hotel standard. Room rates cover the bottle of bubbly in your minibar. Drink it in the fabulous canal-side garden or on 'Lovers' Bridge' in Hof Arents (p135), to which the guesthouse has a unique private entrance. Owner David De Graet is a philosophical artist (below).

Relais Bourgondisch Cruyce (Map p134; ☎ 050-337 926; www.relaisbourgondischcruyce.be; Wollestraat 41-47; d €185-415; ⊙ Mar-Dec) This luxurious little boutique hotel occupies a unique part-timbered

---

DAVID DE GRAEF, FLEMISH ARTIST

Your paintings seem to be full of apocalypse and rebirth I like that. Can I use it?! Yes. I'm an optimist. But it's optimism from the ashes of decadence. My art is full of tenderness but with a vein of cruelty.

Why did you come to Bruges? Bruges is the horn of plenty! It has the advantages of a big city with none of the inconveniences. It's safe. It's clean. No traffic jams. No traffic lights [in the centre]. That's unique for a city of its size. But I also came for the house [Guesthouse Nuit Blanche, above]. Before then my art wasn't always taken seriously. But somehow just owning a house that's this historic changes everything. I must be someone 'serious'. And the house is 'magnetic'. I don't need to put up a gallery sign. If I leave the door open people just can't help themselves – they wander in to look inside. I can't blame them. Before I bought it the place was something rather secretive. Owned by a baron. Black limousines would come and go, the shutters would stay closed. Now I've 'democratised it'. You wouldn't believe it but some of my guests are actually Bruges residents! They simply want a chance to stay in such a mythical building. Churchill visited. The present king and queen avoided the paparazzi by sleeping here the night after their wedding before going on honeymoon. And this is where King Leopold III first met his controversial second wife. So you might even blame this old house for the whole 1950 royal question (p33)!

medieval house that's been tastefully updated and graced with art, antiques, Persian carpets and fresh orchids. A special delight is relaxing in the canal-side lounge while drooling tourists cruise past on their barge tours. Most of the 16 rooms are somewhat small but full of designer fittings, including top-quality Vispring beds, Ralph Lauren fabrics and (in some) Philippe Starck bathrooms.

Relais Ravestein (Map p130; ☎ 050-476 947; www .relaisravestein.be; Molenmeers 11; d rack rate/online discount from €276/138; 🖳) This hip canal-side hotel is a beautiful marriage between classic grandeur and contemporary chic. Exposed beams in the bedrooms vie for attention with jacuzzi baths and rainforest showers. The €500 Bridal Suite has a fabulous canal-view balcony. Off-season deals see prices cut in half.

Kempinski Dukes' Palace (Map p134; ☎ 050-447 888; www.kempinski-bruges.com; Prinsenhof 8; internet discounts €199-723, rack rates €350-990; P ⅀ 🛜) Imposingly tall with a Disney-esque turret, this large-scale five-star hotel partly occupies the Prinsenhof building, Bruges' 15th-century royal palace and the place where Phillip III of Burgundy created the chivalric Order of the Golden Fleece in 1430. It was massively rebuilt in 2008 – some guest rooms retain historical elements, but all the room decor creates a sense of timeless class. The contrastingly modernist bar adds some designer chic, while a giant red poodle gives the art-filled garden a surrealist twist.

Eating

From cosy *estaminets* (taverns) to first-class restaurants – Bruges has all bases covered. For chocolate shops see p145.

Sol y Somba (Map p130; ☎ 050-317 301; http://tapas barsolysombra.be; Langestraat 121; simple tapas from €4; 🕒 6pm-10pm Tue-Sat) Big farmyard tables, candles and the odd barrel are dotted about this unusually spacious tapas-bar, which hosts very occasional flamenco concerts.

Eethuis Aubergine (Map p134; ☎ 050-348 707; St-Amandstraat 25; pastas/panini from €7/6.50; 🕒 11am-10pm Mon-Sat) Aubergine is the most attractive of several relatively inexpensive eateries on this central pedestrian street. While food is decent, staff seem over-worked and tetchy.

Carlito's (Map p134; ☎ 050-490 075; www.carlitos.be; Hoogstraat 21; pizza/mains/lunch from €8/10/12.50; 🕒 noon-2.30pm & 6-10.30) Bright Italian restaurant with white painted woodwork, good service and sensible prices.

De Bron (Map p134; ☎ 050-334 526; Katelijnestraat 82; small/medium/large lunch plate €8.50/9/10.50, soup/organic wine €2/3.30; 🕒 noon-2pm Tue-Sun) Bright, easy-to-miss vegetarian lunch-restaurant serving organic drinks, delicious soups and a multi-item dish-of-the-day where your only choice is the size (vegan options possible). Add soy sauce and sesame to taste.

Ganzespel (Map p130; ☎ 050-331 233; www.gan zespel.be; Ganzenstraat 37; pastas €8.35-12, mains €9.35-17; 🕒 6.30pm-10pm Fri-Sun) A cosy *café*-style front room of a 1705 house is decorated with historic snakes-and-ladders boards and warmed by a log fire in winter. There's a very inexpensive meal-of-the-day or try the specialities, ostrich or *onglet*. Upstairs are three idiosyncratic B&B guest rooms (double €55 to €85), one with musical shower.

our pick **Est Wijnbar** (Map p134; ☎ 050-333 839; estwijnbar.cjb.net; Braambergstraat 7; mains €9.50-12.50, tapas €3.50-9.50, wine per glass €3.50-9; 🕒 4pm-midnight Sun-Thu, noon-2am Fri & Sat) Seductive soft-jazz adds to the delightful atmosphere of this tiny two-tiered wine bar. Part-stripped paint on heavy beams creates a modern feel without detracting from the intimate historical charm of the 1617 Kogge Guildhouse building. Tempting light meal options, seven of them vegetarian,

---

LATE NIGHT, EARLY MORNING

If your stomach demands more than just chips or kebab after 11pm, try the effortlessly elegant, open-kitchened restaurant **Christophe** (Map p134; ☎ 050-344 892; www.christophe-brugge.be; Garenmarkt 34; mains €20-30; 🕒 7pm-1am Thu-Mon), which serves until 1am. Or, before 3am, you could tuck into typical Flemish fare at the cosily historic **'t Gulden Vlies** (Map p134; ☎ 050-334 709; www.tguldenvlies. be; Mallebergplaats 17; 🕒 7pm-3am Wed-Sun).

Most of the restaurants that line the Markt offer breakfasts with a view from €7, but check carefully what's included before sitting down. If you just want coffee and a croissant, the cheapest deal is at chain bakery **Panos** (Map p134; Zuidzandstraat; coffee/croissant €1.60/0.80; 🕒 7am-6.30pm Mon-Sat, 11am-6.30pm Sun) whose Zuidzandstraat branch has plentiful seating upstairs and, unlike most other bakeries, no extra charge for eating in.

include aubergine/pesto pastas, quiches, salads and raclette (Swiss cheese-melt). Coffee (€4.50) comes with three chocolates.

Sacré Coeur (Map p130; ☎ 050-341 093; www.sacrec .be; Langestraat 137; mains €9.80-15, pizzas €7.40-10; ⊙ bar 10pm-very late, kitchen noon-2pm & 6-10pm) One side is the ever-buzzing pub-*café* of the Bauhaus hostel, the other an eccentric dining area adorned with rock-rimmed mirrors and a giant clockface. Food includes hearty, well-cooked local specialities like beef-and-Leffe stew, while a draught Brugse Zot beer is cheaper here than in the brewery! Great value.

Du Phare (Map p130; ☎ 050-343 590; www.duphare. be; Sasplein 2; mains €10-18; ⊙ 11.30am-late Wed-Mon, kitchen 11.30am-3pm & 6pm-midnight) Out-of-centre, blues-jazz tavern serving everything from ostrich stroganoff, to couscous to Thai scampi in a spacious old brick house on a small canal island. Pastas and snacks served all day. Bus 4 stops in front.

In 't Nieuwe Museum (Map p130; ☎ 050-331 222; Hooistraat 42; mains €10-25; ⊙ noon-2pm & 6 10pm Thu-Tue, closed Sat lunch) A slightly out-of-the-way brown *café* eatery offering plate-of-the-day meals for €7.50 and serving veggie burgers, eel dishes, ribs, steaks and creamy *vispannetje* (fish casserole).

De Botellier (Map p134; ☎ 050-331 860; www.debot telier.com; St-Jakobsstraat 63; mains from €16, pasta/veg dishes from €8.80/13.50; ⊙ 11.45am-2pm Tue-Fri & 6.45-10pm Tue-Sat) Decorated with hats and old clocks this adorable little restaurant sits above a wine shop overlooking a delightful handkerchief of canal-side garden. Diners are predominantly local. Reservations are wise.

Ryad (Map p134; ☎ 050-331 355; www.ryad.be; Hoogstraat 32; mains €18-24, lunch menu €10.50; ⊙ noon-2.30pm & 6-10.30pm Thu-Mon) Indian curries supplement the usual couscous and tajines offered by this atmospheric Moroccan restaurant that's heavily perfumed with incense. Upstairs is a cosy cushioned 'Berber' tea lounge.

Bistro Arthies (Map p134; ☎ 050-334 313; www.arthies .com; Wollestraat 10; mains/mussels from €19/21; ⊙ 11.30am-10pm Wed-Mon) Managed by Arthies, an interior designer who looks like a dashingly Gothic Billy Connolly. He uses a projected clock, giant black flower bowls and stylishly whacky lamps to create an ambience that's eccentric yet fashion conscious. There's an all-day €18 menu.

Den Dijver (Map p134; ☎ 050-336 069; www.dijver .be; Dijver 5; mains €19 26, 3-/4-/5-course menu €46/56/73, incl beers €56/68/89; ⊙ noon-2pm & 6.30-9.30pm Fri-Tue) Den Dijver is a pioneer of fine beer cuisine

where you can match the brew you drink with the one the chef used to create the sauce on your plate. But this is no pub: beers come in wine glasses served on starched tablecloths in an atmosphere of Burgundian grandeur. The impressive €20 lunch menu includes *amuse-bouche*, nibbles and coffee.

De Stove (Map p134; ☎ 050-337 835; www.restaurant destove.be; Kleine St-Amandsstraat 4; mains €19-33, menu without/with wine €42/58; ⊙ noon-1.30pm Sat-Tue & 7pm-9pm Fri-Tue) Despite the perennial rave reviews, this calm, one-room family restaurant remains friendly, reliable, inventive and intimate, without a hint of tourist-tweeness.

Saint-Amour (Map p134; ☎ 050-337 172; www .saint-amour.be; Oude Burg 14; mains €25-40, menu without/with wine €60/78; ⊙ noon-2pm & 6.30pm-9.30pm Wed-Sun) Prize-winning chef Jo Nelissen creates culinary magic in the 1548 vaults of this subterranean restaurant.

Sans Cravate (Map p130; ☎ 050-678 310; www .sanscravate.be; Langestraat 159; mains €30-42, menus €52-65; ⊙ noon-2pm Tue-Fri & 7pm-9.30pm Tue-Sat) Bare brick walls, a modernistic fireplace and striking contemporary modern ceramics form a stage for this open-kitchened 'cooking theatre' which prides itself on its gastronomic French cuisine and fresh ingredients.

De Gouden Harynck (Map p134; ☎ 050-337 637; www .dengoudenharynck.be; Groeninge 25; mains €38-45, lunch/3-course/4-course menus €35/74/89; ⊙ lunch & dinner Tue-Sat) Behind an ivy-clad façade, this uncluttered Michelin-starred restaurant garners consistent praise and won't hurt the purse quite as severely as certain better-known competitors.

De Karmeliet (Map p130; ☎ 050-338 259; www .dekarmeliet.be; Langestraat 19; mains €55-95, menus €80-170; ⊙ lunch & dinner; ⊠) Three Michelin stars and prices to match.

QUICK EATS

Het Dagelijks Brood (Map p134; ☎ 050-336 050; Philipstockstraat 21; snacks €5-11; ⊙ 8am-6pm Wed-Mon) Typically inviting, rustic bakery-tearoom of the Pain Quotidien chain (p51), with a big communal table.

Chip vans (Map p134; Markt; ⊙ 10am-3am) Takeaway *frites* (from €2.25) and hot dogs (from €3) sold from two green vans on the Markt.

SELF-CATERING

Proxy/Delhaize (Map p134; Nordzandstraat 4; ⊙ 9am-7pm Mon-Sat) Supermarket.

Smatch (Map p130; Langestraat 55; ⊙ 8.30am-7.30pm Mon-Sat) Supermarket.

WESTERN FLANDERS

Drinking

Tempting terraces line the Markt, while for canal views it's hard to beat the seats outside *café*s **'t Klein Venetie** (p134; Braambergstraat 1) or **Uilenspiegel** (Map p130; Langestraat 2-4). If it's cold, a cosy place for canal-view beers is the semi-medieval-styled cafe within the Hotel Bourgoensch Hof (p141).

De Republiek (Map p134; ☎ 050-340 229; St-Jakobsstraat 36; beer/mojito from €1.90/7.50, meals €12-19; ☿ 11am-late) This youthful local favourite has a modern, back-lit bottle-rack, flickering bowl-candles and a rear summer terrace courtyard. Snack options include tofu-veggie stir-fries, fajitas and tandoori shrimps. DJs weekend nights.

De Garre (Map p134; ☎ 050-341 029; Garre 1; ☿ noon-1am) Nowhere else on the planet serves the fabulous 11% Garre draught beer, which comes with a thick floral head in a glass that's almost a brandy balloon. But that's not all. This hidden two-floor *estaminet* also stocks dozens of other fine Belgian brews including remarkable Struise Pannepot (€3.50; see the boxed text, p49).

Opus Latino (Map p134; ☎ 050-339 746; beer/snacks/tapas from €2.20/8.50/6; ☿ 11am-11pm Thu-Tue) Modernist *café* with weather-worn terrace tables right at the waterside – where a canal dead-ends beside a Buddha-head fountain. Access is via the easily missed shopping passage that links Wollestraat to Burg, emerging near the Basilica of the Holy Blood.

Cafédraal (Map p134; ☎ 050-340 845; Zilverstraat 38; www.cafedraal.be; beer/wine/cocktails from €2.80/5/10, mains €25-48; ☿ 6pm-1am Tue-Thu, to 3am Fri & Sat) Attached to an upmarket seafood restaurant this remarkable aperitif/cocktail bar has an enclosed tree-shaded garden and displays bottles in gilt 'holy' niches. Despite being illuminated by luminous fish and hanging 'hams' it somehow manages to feel suavely classy rather than ridiculous.

B-In (Map p134; ☎ 050-311 300; www.b-in.be; Janshospitaal Bldg, Zonnekemeers; beer/cocktails from €2/7; ☿ 6pm-1am Tue-Sat) Sizeable lounge bar and restaurant targeting a 30s to 40s crowd with DJs spinning mainstream sounds at weekends.

L'Estaminet (Map p134; ☎ 050-330 916; Park 5; beer/snacks/pastas from €1.80/6/8; ☿ 11.30am-11pm Tue-Sun, 4pm-11pm Thu) Behind the new covered veranda you'll find a traditional Flemish *café*-bar with cheap beers, old-style strip-mirrors, weighty beams and an antique Luneville lamp. Inexpensive pub food is available too.

Charlie Rockets (Map p134; ☎ 050-330 660; www.charlierockets.com; Hoogstraat 19; beer €1.80; ☿ 8am-4am) Lively bar in vaguely Hard Rock Café style featuring a big cinema projector, Babyfoot and pool table. Music (live on winter Fridays) plays till late reverberating through the sturdy dormitories (with bunk beds) upstairs (dm/d €17/50).

Herberg Vlissinghe (Map p130; ☎ 050-343 737; www.cafevlissinghe.be; Blekerstraat 2; beer/snacks/pasta from €1.80/3.50/8; ☿ 11am-10pm Wed-Sat, to 7pm Sun) Bruges' oldest *café* has been pouring beers since 1515. Local legend has it that Rubens once painted an imitation coin on the table here and then did a runner. Portraits, lantern-lamps and flat irons lend character.

't Brugs Beertje (Map p134; ☎ 050-339 616; Kemelstraat 5; ☿ 4pm-1am Thu-Tue) One of those perfect beer-bars with smoke-yellowed walls, enamel signs, hop-sprig ceilings and knowledgeable staff to help you choose from a book full of brews.

Vino Vino (Map p134; ☎ 050-345 115; Grauwwerkersstraat 15; ☿ 6pm-late Tue-Sat) Candle-lit bar with beamed ceilings playing blues music and serving inexpensive tapas/snacks. For several other late-night options go round the corner onto Kuiperstraat.

De Windmolen (Map p130; ☎ 050-339 739; Carmersstraat 135; beer/snacks/pasta from €1.80/4.50/8.50; ☿ 10am-late Mon-Thu, to 3am Fri & Sun) Quaint corner *café* with a sunny terrace overlooking one of the St-Anna windmills.

Retsin's Lucifernum (Map p134; ☎ 050-341 650; http://thelucifernum.blogspot.com; Twijnstraat 6-8; admission including drink €3; ☿ 9pm-2am Sat, some Sundays) This former Masonic lodge is draped in flags, scaffolding and body parts. Ring the bell on a Saturday night and hope you're invited inside where an otherworldly candle-lit bar may be serving potent rum cocktails and serenading with live Latin music. Or maybe not. It's always a surprise.

't Poatersgat (Map p134; Vlamingenstraat 82; beers from €2; ☿ 5pm-late) Descend through a concealed hole in the wall into this mood-lit, cross-vaulted cellar serving over 100 Belgian beers to a relatively youthful crowd.

Entertainment

There's live music on winter Fridays at Charlie Rockets (above), blues on alternate Sundays at Du Phare (9pm, Oct-May; p143) and low-key jazz every Sunday night at the loveable Est Wijnbar (Map p134).

Cultuurcentrum Brugge (☎ info 050-443 040, tickets 050-443 060; www.ccbrugge.be) coordinates theatrical and concert events at several venues, including the majestic 1869 theatre **Koninklijke Stadsschouwburg** (Map p134; Vlamingstraat 29), out-of-centre **MaZ** (Map p130; Magdalenastraat 27) and experimental little **Biekorf Theaterzaal** (Map p134; Kuipersstraat 3) in the public-library complex. It's also worth checking www.cactusmusic.be (typically world-music concerts) and seeing what's on at **Concertgebouw** (see p137), which has a program of theatre, classical music and dance.

Entrenous (Map p130; ☎ 050-341 093; www.bauhaus zaal.be; Langestraat 145; ☼ 10pm Fri &/or Sat) A real nightclub in central Bruges…at last.

English Theatre of Bruges (Map p134; ☎ 050-687 945; www.tematema.com; Walplein 23; €5; ☼ five times daily Tue-Sun) The one-man, 30-minute show 'Bruges Abridged' is a comedy and sing-along that takes off of the Bruges holiday experience.

Vinkenzettingen Although there's no set schedule one place that you might get to see the eccentric (if hardly exciting) 'sport' of finch singing is on the suburban St-Anna street of Hugo Verrieststraat (Map p130), early Sunday morning in summer.

Shopping

The main shopping thoroughfares are Steenstraat and Geldmuntstraat/Noordzandstraat, along with linking pedestrianised Zilverpand. There are morning markets on Wednesdays (Markt) and Saturdays ('t Zand).

't Apostelientje (Map p130; ☎ 050-337 860; Balstraat 11; ☼ 9.30am-12.15pm & 1.15-5pm Wed-Sat, 1pm-5pm Tue, 10am-1pm Sun) Bruges overflows with lace vendors but this sweet little 'museum shop' is well off the normal tourist trail and promises all-handmade products. Much of it is antique. See the boxed text, p139.

Mille-Fleurs (Map p134; ☎ 050-345 454; Wollestraat 33) Flemish tapestries (machine-made near Wetteren).

2-Be (Map p134; ☎ 050-611 222; www.2-be.biz; Wollestraat 53; ☼ 10am-7pm) Vast range of Belgian products from beers to biscuits in a snazzy, central location, but prices can be exorbitant. Their 'beer wall' is worth a look, as is the wonderfully located canal-side bar-terrace, where 'monster' 3L draught beers (€19.50) are surely Belgium's biggest.

BEER SHOPS
Several shops offer a vast array of Belgian beers and their associated glasses to take away.

Compare prices carefully and remember that 'standard' brews like Leffe or Chimay will generally be far cheaper in supermarkets.

Bacchus Cornelius (☎ 050-345 338; Academiestraat 17; ☼ 1pm-6.30pm) Better prices than many competitors and some brews chilled for ready consumption.

De Biertempel (Map p134; ☎ 050-343 730; Philipstockstraat 7; ☼ 10am-6pm)

Bottle Shop (Map p134; ☎ 050-349 980; Wollestraat 13; ☼ 10am-7pm)

CHOCOLATE SHOPS
Galler (Map p134; Steenstraat 5)

Chocolate Line (Map p134; Simon Stevinplein) Experiments with startling flavours – the chilli-chocolate works well, wasabi less so. Chocolate body paint costs €7.50, brush included.

Getting There & Around
BUS
Eurolines (☎ 02-274 1350; www.eurolines.be) has buses to London (around €30) departing 5.30pm from the bus station, but tickets must be pre-booked by phone, online or in Ghent. Eurolines has no Bruges ticket office. For **city buses** (single/day-pass €1.60/6; ☼ 5.30am-11pm) you'll save money pre-purchasing tickets (single/day-pass €1.20/5) at the **De Lijn Office** (Map p130; www.delijn.be). Any bus marked 'Centrum' runs to the Markt. To return to the station, the best central stop is **Biekorf** (Map p134).

TRAIN
Bruges' **train station** (☎ 050-302 424) is 1.5km south of Markt. Twice-hourly trains run to Kortrijk (€7, fast/slow 38/51 minutes) and to Brussels (€12.90, 62 minutes) via Ghent (€5.40, 23 minutes). Hourly trains go to Antwerp (€13.60, 80 minutes), Knokke (€3.30, 20 minutes), Ostend (€3.70, 13 minutes) and Zeebrugge (€2.70, 13 minutes) via Lissewege.

For Ypres (Ieper) take the train to Roeselare then bus 95 via Langemark (p161) or 94 via Passendale, Tyne Cot and Zonnebeke (p162), all places you're likely to want to see anyway.

BICYCLE
Bike-rental outfits:
B-Bike (Map p134; ☎ 0499-705 099; Zand Parking 26; per hr/day €4/12; ☼ 10am-7pm Apr-Oct)

Rijwielhandel Erik Popelier (Map p134; ☎ 050-343 262; Mariastraat 26; per hr/half-/full day €4/8/12, tandem per hr/half-/full day €10/17/25; ☼ 10am-6pm Oct-Easter, to 7pm Easter-Sep) Good bicycles for adults and kids, helmets for hire, free map, no deposit.

Train station luggage room (per half-/full day €6.50/9.50, deposit €12.50; 7am-8pm) Must return same day.

CAR
Given central Bruges' nightmarish one-way system the best idea for drivers is to use the large covered **carpark** (per hr/24hr €0.50/2.50) beside the train station. Bargain fees here include a free return bus ticket to the centre for the car's driver and all passengers. Just show your parking ticket when boarding the bus. If you park elsewhere be aware that non-metered street parking still requires you to set your parking disc (maximum stay four hours). Traffic wardens are merciless.

TAXI
Taxis wait on the Markt and in front of the train station. Otherwise phone ☎ 050-334 444 or ☎ 050-384 660.

AROUND BRUGES
By bicycle or car, there's a wealth of tree-lined canals, sweet rural villages and the odd castle all within easy reach of Bruges. Or you could head to the coast via Damme, Dudzele and pretty Lissewege (p151).

Damme
pop 10,900

The historic inland port-village of **Damme** (www. vvvdamme.be) is so super-pretty that in summer it's all too often overwhelmed with cars, cyclists, walkers and boat-loads of day-trippers jostling down the dead-straight 5km of road/canal from Bruges. But don't despair. Drive or cycle another 2km east and you'll quickly leave some 90% of the tourist crowds behind. Then turn south where two canals meet and pick a random spot to admire the soaring rows of wind-warped poplars. Whether reflected in glass-still waters or fog draped on a misty winter's morning, the scene is a magical, visual poem drawn straight from Jacques Brel.

Charming Damme village is little more than a single street plus a main square upon which the fine Gothic **stadhuis** is fronted by a **statue of Jacob Van Maerlant**, a 13th-century Flemish poet who lived and died in Damme. He's buried in the 12th-century **Onze Lieve Vrouwekerk** (Our Lady's Church; Kerkstraat; admission church/tower €0.50/1; 2pm-5.30pm Tue-Sun May-Sep), which was vastly expanded in the village's heyday, only to be partially torn down when things started to wane.

Opposite the stadhuis, a restored patrician's house is home to the **tourist office** (☎ 050-288 610; www.toerismedamme.be; Jacob Van Maerlantstraat 3; 9am-noon & 1-6pm Mon-Fri, 10am-noon & 2-6pm Sat & Sun mid-Apr–mid-Oct, to 5pm mid-Oct–mid-Apr) and the **Uilenspiegel Museum** (adult/concession/family €2.50/1.50/5; same times) recounting the stories of Uilenspiegel, a villain in German folklore but a jester and freedom fighter in Flemish literature.

Damme is full of *café*s and eateries, but you'll find other less tourist-swamped taverns and restaurants along surrounding canal towpaths every kilometre or two. However, many go into semi-hibernation in winter.

The classic if somewhat over-rated way to visit Damme is to take a lazy 35-minute canal trip on the Lamme Goedzak tourist **paddle steamer** (one way adult/senior/child €6/5.50/4.50, return €7.50/6.50/5.50; from Damme 9am-5pm, from Bruges 10am-6pm Easter–mid-Oct). It departs on odd-numbered hours from Bruges' Noorweegse Kaai, reached by bus 4 from the Markt. Alternatively bus 43 (€1.80, 20 minutes) runs every two hours till 3.30pm, April to September only. Or you can cycle.

Castles
There are several attractive castles right on Bruges' doorstep. Moated **Kasteel Tillegem** is now used as district offices and is set in the extensive public parkland of Domaine Tillegembos. Also accessed off Torhoutsteenweg (the N32 road leading south) in Sint-Michiels, the 1904 **Kasteel Tudor** (www.conquistador.be; Zeeweg 147) is backed by the beech-woods of Domein Beisbroek. Phone ahead to check whether **Kasteel van Loppem** (☎ 050-822 245, 0477-280 538; www.kasteelvanloppem.be; Steenbrugsestraat 26, Loppem; adult/child €3.50/1; 10am-noon & 2pm-6pm Tue-Thu & Sat) is open and if its **labyrinth** (€1.25; 2pm-6pm Sat & Sun Apr-Oct) is accessible. Some 2km north of Bruges, **Kasteel ten Berghe** (☎ 050-679 697; www.kasteeltenberghe.be; Dudzeelsesteenweg 311; d weekdays/Fri/Sat €140/160/180; reception from 3pm; P) is a Victorian moated fantasy castle that now forms a romantic boutique hotel. Free parking makes it an ideal base for touring the region by car.

THE COAST
Virtually all of Belgium's 66km coastline is fronted with a superbly wide, hard-sand beach. However, while some remnant sand dunes survive, the coast is predominantly

backed by a succession of bland, concrete-blighted resorts. De Haan, central Nieuwpoort and outer parts of wealthy Knokke-Heist are the only real exceptions. Every settlement offers a wide selection of accommodation, but heavy pre-bookings mean finding a room can still be hard in summer. Out of season many towns feel deserted, but with its regular events and conventions, hub-town Ostend manages to keep a livelier vibe year-round.

Ostend (Oostende)
pop 69,000

Bustling Ostend (Oostende in Dutch, Ostende in French) grew from a fishing village into a fortified port and was ravaged by a four-year siege (1600–1604) as the last 'Belgian' city to refuse Spanish re-conquest. Later it bloomed as one of Europe's most stylish seaside resorts. Most of that style was bombed into memories during WWII when German occupying forces (re)built the remarkable Atlantikwall sea-defences (p149) that are today the town's most fascinating sight. In the post war era Ostend was rebuilt as a grid of entirely unaesthetic apartment blocks – the kings and artists who once lived here wouldn't recognise the place today. Nonetheless its beach is wide, its night-life accessible and its plethora of ho-hum hotels offer ample accommodation for penny-pinching British coach-tours who can't afford nearby Bruges.

ORIENTATION & INFORMATION
The main shopping thoroughfare is pedestrianised Kapellestraat.

ATM (Kapellestraat 77)

Cyber Cafe (☎ 059-250 713; Koningsstraat 7; per hr €2; ☻ 10am-11pm) Internet computers at the back of a tobacconist/bottleshop.

Goffin Exchange (☎ 059-506 828; St-Petrus & Paulusplein 19; ☻ 9.30am-6pm) Changes money without commission, but at far-from-generous rates.

Post office (Marie-Joséplein 11) Has an ATM.

Tourist Office (☎ 059-701 199; www.toerisme-oostende.be, www.dekust.org; Monacoplein 2; ☻ 9am-7pm Mon-Sat & 10am-7pm Sun Jun-Aug, 10am-6pm Mon-Sat & 10am-5pm Sun Sep-May) Gives away great city maps and a full-colour brochure, Soak up the Sea, that's effectively a complete guidebook.

SIGHTS
The tourist office's **City Pass 200% Oostende** (24/48/72hr €12/15/20) gives free entry to all the sights reviewed here. Take at least the 48-hour version if you want to see everything – one day would be extremely rushed. Add just €6 extra to get the summer-only **XL Pass**, which also includes a Franlis sea ride (see p150) and entry to **Earth Explorer** (☎ 059-705 959; www.earthexplorer.be; Fortstraat 128b; adult/concession/child €14.50/12.50/10.50; ☻ 10am-6pm Apr-Sep), a science-based experience near Fort Napoleon with some 50 exhibits to help you 'feel' how the world works.

Beachfront
Ostend is primarily a domestic seaside resort. Along its remarkably wide sandy beach is a spacious promenade with the usual selection of summer seaside entertainments, *kwistax* (pedal car) rentals, ice-cream vendors and shoulder-to-shoulder tea-room restaurants with glassed-in terraces. The main section is mostly overshadowed with 10-storey concrete buildings. An exception is at the very '50s Thermae Palace Hotel, which is flanked by a neo-classical side arcade topped by a striking equestrian **statue of Léopold II**. Below him stand a fawning gaggle of European and African subjects. Ostend's other 1950s landmark, the distinctively boxy **Kursaal** (☎ 059-705 111; www.kursaaloostende.be; Monacoplein), contains a top restaurant, view-*café*, a casino (minimum age 21, passport/ID needed to enter) and a convention centre in whose foyer is a golden **statue**

THE COAST BY TRAIN & TRAM

During July, August and at other peak holiday times, half-price day-return rail tickets called 'Een Dag aan Zee/Un Jour à la Mer' are available from any Belgian station to eight major coastal cities (including De Panne, Knokke and Ostend) plus Veurne. Returning from a different seaside town costs no extra. Given the appalling traffic jams and parking problems on summer weekends, such day trips are an ideal way to sample the coast's modest charms, even if you have a car.

Once you're there, **De Kusttram** (www.delijn.be) coastal trams trundle all the way from Knokke to De Panne/Adinkerke departing every 15 minutes from 5.30am to 11pm. The full route takes just over two hours. Single tickets cost €1.20/2 for a short/long journey while one-/three-day tickets for €5/12 allow unlimited travel on both tram and De Lijn buses.

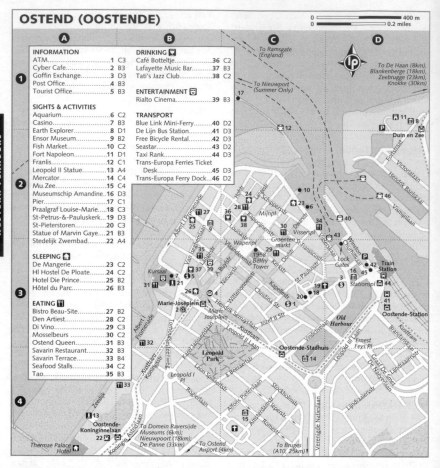

of Marvin Gaye playing a tacky golden piano. Gaye wrote his last hit 'Sexual Healing' while living in Ostend during 1981.

Visserskaai Quarter

It's a pleasant diversion to watch squawking gulls scavenging from beam-netted sole-fishing boats as they unload behind the little **Fish Market** (Vistrap; Visserskaai). The quayside road is backed with wall-to-wall fish restaurants, there's also a tiny **Aquarium** (☎ 059-500 876; Visserskaai; adult/child €2/1; ☑ 10am-12.30pm & 2-6pm Jun-Sep, to 5pm Apr-May, weekends only Oct-Mar), a long **pier** marking the harbour mouth, and two operators offering summer sea excursions.

Near the station, **Museumschip Amandine** (☎ 059-234 301; www.museum-amandine.be; Vindictivelaan 35-Z; adult/child €4/2; ☑ 10am-5.30pm Tue-Sun, 2-5.30pm Mon) was the last Ostend trawler to fish around Iceland (1970s). Visits take you inside, where the crew's bunk room, the fish-freezing room, engine room and bridge are brought alive with wax-work figures and suitable sound effects. You'll also walk beneath the ship, admiring its virile propeller and watching videos about Ostend's fishing industry.

Ostend's most striking historical building is the **St-Petrus-&-Pauluskerk** (Sint-Pietersstraat), with its beautifully ornate twin spires, rose window and a dark neo-Gothic interior. Despite its antique appearance the church only dates from 1905. A stone 'bridge' behind the altar leads into the tiny crown-topped **Praalgraf Louise-Marie**, the 1859 tomb-chapel of Belgium's first queen. The strange octagonal tower behind it is the 1729 **St-Pieterstoren**, a last remnant of a mostly 15th-century church that's since been lost.

Beyond the yacht-filled Old Harbour is the fully rigged, three-masted **Mercator** (☎ 059-705 654; www.zeilschip-mercator.be; Old Harbour; adult/senior/child €4/3/2; ☺ 10am-5.30pm Jul-Aug, times vary low-season), a 1932 sailing ship once used for Belgian navy training purposes. It's now a nautical museum and hosts changing exhibitions.

Art

Ostend's foremost gallery, **Mu.Zee** (☎ 059-508 118; www.kunstmuseumaanzee.be; Romestraat 11; adult/senior/child €6/5/1; ☺ 10am-6pm Tue-Sun), features predominantly local artists. There's a significant collection by symbolist painter Léon Spilliaert (1881–1946) whose most brooding works are reminiscent of Munch's. Hidden away on an intermediate half-floor are sketches and minor paintings by expressionist pioneer James Ensor (1860–1949), but though valuable for Ensor fans they're unlikely to impress the un-initiated. The family house where Ensor lived and worked from 1875 to 1916 now forms the attractive little **Ensor Museum** (☎ 059-805 335; Vlaanderenstraat 27; adult/concession €2/1; ☺ 10am-noon & 2-5pm, closed Tue). Its ground floor is presented as a 19th-century souvenir shop (which it had been in Ensor's time) and sports cabinets full of crustacea, skulls, masks and bizarre fish grafted with demonic faces – elements that appeared in many Ensor paintings. On the 2nd floor is a reproduction of Ensor's chaotic 1888 classic, *The Entry of Christ into Brussels*.

Domein Raversijde

This extensive provincial reserve creates a rare green gap between the apartment towers around 6km west of Ostend. It incorporates several dune and marsh areas, fascinating WWII remnants and a partly reconstructed 15th-century hamlet. These form three distinct but related **museums** (☎ 059-702 285; www.west-vlaanderen.be/raversijde; Nieuwpoortsesteenweg 636; per museum adult/concession €6.50/5.40, three-museum multi-ticket €9.75/8.10; ☺ 2pm-5pm Mon-Fri, 10am-6pm Sat & Sun Apr-early Nov, 10am-6pm daily Jul-Aug, last entry 4pm). Two of them are predominantly outdoors so bring waterproofs. The most gripping is **Atlantikwall**, a remarkably extensive complex of WWI and WWII bunkers, gun emplace-ments and linking brick tunnels created by occupying German forces. Most bunkers are furnished and 'manned' by waxwork figures and there's a detailed audio-guide explanation (albeit sometimes overly concerned with gun calibres). This is one of Belgium's best and most underrated war sites, but you'll need good weather, around two hours and rea-sonable fitness to make the most of the 2km walking circuit.

Beside the Atlantikwall is the **Memorial Prins Karel**, a largely forgettable museum remember-ing King Leopold II's brother Charles who took over as regent following WWII (see p33) then in 1950 retired as an artist to a remark-ably modest basket-weaver's cottage here. By giving his Raversijde Royal Estate to the provincial government, Charles saved this fascinating area from coastal developers.

Around 10-minutes' walk south along footpaths between the marshes is the site of **Walraversijde**, a once-vibrant fishing village that disappeared entirely following the strife of 1600–1604. Today you can visit the ar-chaeological site of the former village along with four convincingly re-built and furnished thatched houses while an audio-guide tells the village's history through the voices of a series of well-acted 1465 characters. An interactive museum then makes sense of why the village died out.

From the Kusttram stop 'Domein Raversijde' you can reach the Atlantikwall via wooden steps leading south up the dune side then following signs (around 150m). If driving note that the only parking is on the Domein's south side at Walraversijde off Nieuwpoortsteenweg where there's a stop for bus 6 back to Ostend.

Fort Napoleon

The impenetrable pentagon of **Fort Napoleon** (☎ 059-320 048; www.fortnapoleon.be; Vuurtorenweg; adult/senior/child €5/4/2; ☺ 10am-6pm Tue-Sun Apr-Oct, daily Jul-Aug, 1pm-5pm Wed-Sun Nov-Mar) is an unusu-ally intact Napoleonic fortress dating from 1812, though there's comparatively little to see inside and the audioguide covers many of the same topics you'll have heard at the Atlantikwall. Drinking at the fortress *café* gets you decent glimpses without paying the entrance fee. The fort is 1.5km across the harbour from central Ostend, but over 3km away by road. Get off the eastbound Kusttram at 'Duin en Zee' then walk 500m northwest passing in front of the 'Earth Explorer' building. Alternatively, in season, take the thrice-hourly **Blue Link mini-ferry**

(☎ 059-502 676; adult/child/bicycle €1.5/1/1; ◷ 10.30am-1pm & 1.45-6pm Sat & Sun Apr-Oct, daily Jul-Aug) then cross the lock gates and walk 1.2km east (bring a map).

ACTIVITIES

Out-and-back sea cruises (45 minutes) are offered by **Franlis** (adult/child €8/5; ◷ hourly 11am-5pm daily Jul-Aug, 1pm-5pm Sat & Sun May, Jun & Sep) and Seastar (see opposite). **Stedelijk Zwembad** (☎ 059-503 838; Koninginnelaan 1; adult/child €3.25/2; ◷ 9am-8pm Mon-Fri, to 6pm Sat & Sun) is a full-sized indoor swimming pool.

SLEEPING

Ostend groans under the weight of hotels with a row along Visserskaai and dozens of big, bland fair-priced options in the central blocks around De Ploate youth hostel. Remarkably few are actually on the seafront. Some hotels close from December to March, while most charge higher rates in summer or at weekends.

HI Hostel De Ploate (☎ 059-805 297; www.vjh.be; Langestraat 82; dm HI members/non-members €18.80/21.80) Some rough edges but superbly central.

Hôtel du Parc (☎ 059-701 680; www.duparcoostende .com; Marie Joséplein 3; low season s/d/tr/q €56/80/95/102, high season €60/96/102/115; ℗) The 1928 art deco building is a classified monument and the ground-floor brasserie is *the* meeting place for local bourgeoisie, but guest rooms, while perfectly neat, lack that nostalgic vibe. Front rooms are airy and pleasant, back ones cramped and dark. Parking costs €14.

Hotel Die Prince (☎ 059-706 507; www.hotel-die prince.be; Albert I Promenade 41; midweek/weekend without view s €54/60, d €66/75, with sea-view s €60/75, d 75/95; ⚲) Die Prince is one of the rare hotels with a beach view. Prices here are modest and the public areas rather swish. Room decor is functional but little two-seat desks allow you to wave-gaze from your window. Breakfast included, wi-fi €5 for two hours.

De Mangerie (☎ 059-701 827; www.mangerie.info; Visserskaai 36; street-/harbour-view d €75/95, ste €115) With dark-wood floors, fine linens and comfy sitting areas, the Mangerie's four wonderfully spacious guest rooms continue the suave designer themes of their tempting fish restaurant downstairs (mains €18 to €25).

EATING

Tearoom-restaurants covering a wide range of styles and prices stand side-by-side along the promenade between Savarin and the Kursaal.

There are plenty more seafood restaurants along Visserkaai.

Di Vino (☎ 0473-871 297; Wittenonnenstraat 2; mains €12.50-17; ◷ 11.45am-2pm & 6.30-10pm Wed-Sun Sep-Jun, daily Jul-Aug) Intimate candle-lit wine-bistro with bottles and corks for decor, rustic furniture and a €10.50 lunch deal that includes wine and coffee.

Den Artiest (☎ 059-808 889; Kapucijnenstraat 13; meals €16-23; ◷ 5pm-3am, kitchen 7pm-2am) Unusually obliging informal brasserie with tables multi-layered in an original fashion around a high central space. Long brass-tube lamps and fun knick-knacks provide atmosphere while ultra-generous meals are barbequed in front of you in the central fire hearth. Highly recommended for drinks-only too. Occasional live music.

Tao (☎ 059-438 373; www.tao-oostende.be; Langestraat 24; mains €16-25, tapas €5-7.50; ◷ 6.30pm-2am) This highly fashion-conscious lounge-restaurant covers the gamut of culinary possibilities from Thai to Belgian to Mexican. There's a long street terrace and an interior whose giant blob-lamps create a trendy-retro mood. Occasional salsa-dance lessons.

Mosselbeurs (☎ 059-807 310; Dwarsstraat 10; mussels €21-25; ◷ noon-2pm & 6-10pm Wed-Sun) The decor, wrapped around a central spiral stairway, is stylish, except for the tacky silver mussel shells twinkling on some wall surfaces. Is the gratuitous meat-slicer displayed in the corner a veiled threat to those who don't pay their bill?

Savarin (☎ 059-313 171; www.savarin.be; Albert I Promenade 75; mains €28-32; ◷ variable) Modern, upmarket seafood restaurant with flashily indulgent decor in black, silver and gold behind a glassed-in veranda. Savarin also has an open-air summer terrace two blocks down the prom backed by neo-classical columns (beer/tapas/mains from €2.50/6/18).

Ostend Queen (☎ 059-445 610; www.ostendqueen.be; 2nd fl, Kursaal bldg, Monacoplein; mains €21-40, 3-/4-course menu €48/58; ◷ noon-2.30pm & 7-10pm Thu-Mon) Take the lift with piped sea-sounds to this suave, modern brasserie for fine seafood and the very best beach views in town. One floor down is a cocktail lounge decked with whacky giant jellyfish lamps. On the ground floor the Huis van Oostende tearoom offers afternoon drinks and snacks (from €6).

Self Catering

Market day is Thursday.

Seafood stalls (kraampjes; Visserskaai; ◷ 9.30am-dusk) Several wagon-stalls sell smoked and cooked fish, surimi snacks, pre-fried calamari rings, little tubs of grey shrimps and plastic bowls of steaming hot *wulloks* (whelks/sea snails) available *natuur* (in salty broth) or *pikant* (spicy).

Spar (Groentenmarkt 1; ⏰ 2pm-6.30pm Mon, 8.30am-6.30pm Tue-Sat, 8.30am-12.30pm Sun) Supermarket.

DRINKING & ENTERTAINMENT

A series of great and varied *café*s and pubs lead north from the Kursaal Langestraat and Van Iseghemlaan and on several of the connecting lanes. Den Artiest, Tao and Bistro Beau-Site (see Eating above) are all great for drinks as well as food.

Bistro Beau-Site (☎ 0486-774 574; Albert I Promenade; coffee/beer/tapas/sandwiches/pasta from €2/1.80/4/4/12; ⏰ 11am-7pm Wed, Thu & Mon, noon-late Sat & Sun) A class apart from anything else on the seafront, this small arty cafe has art deco touches, a big communal farmhouse table, jazz tinkling on the stereo and art books to peruse. Upstairs are window seats with great beach views.

Café Botteltje (☎ 059-700 928; www.hotelmarion.be; Louisastraat 19; ⏰ 11.30am-1am or later Tue-Sun, 4.30pm-1am Mon) Serves around 300 different beers including a dozen on draught in a spacious *café* reminiscent of a British pub.

Lafayette Music Bar (Langestraat 12; beer/cocktails from €1.90/7.10; ⏰ 6pm-3am Tue-Sun) With the mirrored panelling of a traditional *café*, but the black walls and back-lit bottle-racks of a fashion-conscious cocktail bar, Lafayette hits a balance between hip and friendly. Conversation bubbles at candle-lit tables without being drowned out by DJs whose taste is more Parisian jazz or Barry White than drum 'n' bass.

Tati's Jazz Club (☎ 059-433 993; Langestraat 71; ⏰ from 8pm Thu-Sun) Little cellar venue with live jazz.

GETTING THERE & AROUND

Ostend's last car-ferry operator, **TransEuropa Ferries** (☎ 059-340 260; www.transeuropaferries.com), has services to Ramsgate, England, but only for those travelling by motorised vehicle (no foot passengers). Tickets are sold from an office beside the train station, but boat access requires driving a 3km loop east. In summer you can reach Nieuwpoort by boat with **Seastar** (☎ 058-232 425; www.seastar.be; adult/child €13.50/9.50, return €18.50/11.50; ⏰ Jul-Aug) leaving at noon daily plus 4.30pm Saturdays (1½ hours).

At least three trains run hourly from Ostend to Bruges (€3.70, 13 minutes) continuing to Lille via Kortrijk, Antwerp via Ghent or Liège via Brussels.

De Lijn bus 53 runs to Diksmuide (€2, 50 minutes) and bus 6 to Domein Raversijde via Ostend Airport. Bus 68 (hourly, not Sundays) follows route 6 but continues all the way to Veurne (€2, 1¼ hours) via Nieuwpoort and Oostduinkerke-dorp (for the fishery museum). The Kusttram (see the boxed text, p147) is more useful for reaching De Haan and Knokke and stops conveniently close to all of Ostend's main sights. De Lijn has ticket offices at the bus terminal and at Marie Joséplein tram stop.

Free **bicycle hire** (☎ 059-555 669; ⏰ 7.30am-7.30pm Sep-Jun, to 10pm Jul-Aug) is available behind the train station. ID is required, bikes must be returned the same evening.

Ostend to Knokke
DE HAAN
pop 11,700

Prim and proper De Haan (Le Coq) nestles among dunes 12km northeast of Ostend. It's Belgium's most compact and engaging beach resort with belle-époque winding avenues, early 20th-century villas and only a very limited blight of rectilinear apartment-slabs (maximum five-storeys). De Haan's most famous visitor, Albert Einstein, lived here for a few months after fleeing Hitler's Germany in 1933.

Several fanciful half-timbered hotels and a scattering of tasteful eateries, bakeries and shops form an appealing knot around a cottage-style former tram station that houses the **tourist office** (☎ 059-242 135; www.dehaan.be; Koninklijk Plein; ⏰ 10am-noon & 2-5pm Apr-Oct, Sat & Sun only Nov-Mar). The beach is 600m north, beyond a circular park and unusually palatial police station.

In between is the excellent value **La Tourelle** (☎ 059-233 454; www.latourelle.be; Vondellaan 4; s/d/t from €60/67/95; ⏰ Feb-Nov) an adorable family house-hotel in a pale, turreted mansion. It has fresh, dolls-house decor, contemporary four-poster beds, free help-your-self coffee and a great roof-terrace sundeck. Book well ahead to get the tower room (*torenkamer*, €90).

Very close to the beach, **de Coqisserie** (☎ 059-430 043; www.decoqisserie.be; Koninklijke Baan 29; r/loft/apt from €85/125/150, high season €110/150/175) has very stylishly appointed new rooms and luxuriously modern apartments above an appealing new coffee-house restaurant. Save €15 if staying two nights or longer.

WESTERN FLANDERS

In a much-modernised 18th-century farmhouse that's now surrounded by well-spaced suburbia **Hotel Duinhof** (☎ 059-242 020; www.duinhof.be; Leeuwerikenlaan 23; s/d €110/125, summer €130/150; ⏲ reception 9am-8pm; P ⏚ ☎ ☎) is a very relaxing retreat. It's 2km from the beach, but offers guests free bicycle rental, free parking and free use of the sauna complex. Rooms with stripped-wood floors and antique-style furniture overlook a central garden-field with open-air swimming pool. The appealing lounge has a well-stocked honesty bar. Minimum two-night stays at weekends.

Manoir Carpe Diem (☎ 059-233 220; www.manoircarpediem.com; Prins Karellaan 12; s/d/ste from €130/135/220; ⏲ mid-Feb-Dec; ☎) On a knoll set back 400m from the beach, the indulgent Carpe Diem blends architecturally into the surrounding patchwork of tile- and thatch-roofed whitewashed villas. Classical music, oil paintings, aged silverware, log fires and hunting prints create a welcoming atmosphere in the two cosy lounges. Room styles vary, but each is spacious.

BLANKENBERGE

Each summer some of the world's biggest and most fanciful **sandcastles** (www.sculpta.be; Koning Albert-I-laan 115; adult/senior/child €11/9/7; ⏲ 10am-7pm Jul-Aug) are built at unexotic Blankenberge to an annually changing theme.

ZEEBRUGGE

Initially built between 1895 and 1907, Zeebrugge's enormous artificial **harbour** had been in use less than a decade when Allied forces sunk ships to block its entrance, thus preventing German naval use during WWI. Further bombed in WWII, the harbour finally reopened to sea traffic in 1957. Departure terminals for overnight UK-bound ferries to Hull (P&O, Kaai 106) and Rosyth (near Edinburgh, Norfolk Line, Kaai 113) are 2km north of Zeebrugge-Strandwijk tram stop, or 3km from Zeebrugge train station. It's an unpleasant walk. A direct bus to the terminal (€3.50) connecting with the P&O boat departs 7.30pm from Bruges bus station.

A considerable contrast to brutally functional Zeebrugge is the cute little village of **Lissewege** (www.lissewege.be), 4km south, with its pretty whitewashed cottages and oversized brick church. Set in meadows 1.6km north of Lissewege, a sturdy 13th-century barn is the last remnant of the original **Abdij Ter Doest**,

a once powerful abbey ruined during the religious wars in 1569. A smaller abbey farm, rebuilt in 1651, now hosts the very appealing **Hof Ter Doest** (☎ 050-544 082; www.terdoest.be; Ter Doeststraat 4; s/d €110/130, weekend €130/150, mains €13.50-30), complete with a six-room boutique hotel and small hammam in the former stables, a sauna in a wheeled wagon facing the reed-filled canal outside and a tempting restaurant in the main building.

KNOKKE-HEIST
pop 34,000

Knokke is the preferred summer destination for Belgium's bourgeoisie. It's a sprawling place whose renowned nightlife scene caters to a rather insular clique. Architecturally Knokke's monotonous central high-rises look far from elite but there's a plentiful scattering of art galleries and swanky shops while low-rise mansions extend for several kilometres through neighbouring Duinburgen and De Zoute. Fans of surrealist art will burst with frustration at the **Casino Knokke** (☎ 050-630 505; www.partouchecasinos.be; Zeedijk-Albertstrand 509). Its upstairs dining room features an incredible 72m circular mural by René Magritte and, half-hidden in an unused entry hall, there's a superb 1974 Paul Delvaux lit by one of Europe's biggest glass chandeliers. Incredibly, neither is regularly accessible.

HET ZWIN

Around 5km northeast of Knokke, Het Zwin was once one of the world's busiest waterways, connecting Bruges with the sea. However, in medieval times the river silted up, devastating Bruges' economy. The marshy area is now a reserve, a tranquil region of polders, ponds, scrub-forest and mud flats that blush purple with *zwinnebloem* (sea lavender). Migrating swans, ducks and reed geese arrive here seasonally and there are populations of eagle owls and storks. To peruse the area from a distance (for free), walk or cycle to the 'flying' **hare statue**, around 2.5km down the promenade from Knokke's Surfers' Paradise beach bar. The bar is accessed by summer bus 12 (stop Zwinlaan) then by walking up Appelzakstraat and turning right. You can walk back from the hare statue along the beach unless tides are very high.

To walk in parts of the reserve rather than simply looking down on it from the dunes, visit the **Het Zwin Nature Park** (☎ 050-607 086;

www.zwin.be, in Dutch & French; Graaf Leon Lippensdreef 8; adult/child €5.20/3.20; ☺ 9am-5.30pm Easter-Sep, to 4.30pm Oct-Easter, closed Mon Sep-Jun, closed Dec). Rubber boots are essential for much of the year. Click 'luisterwandeling' on their website to download a guided walk (English available) for your MP3 player. Bus 12/13 (hourly in summer, weekends only other times) gets you here.

Ostend to De Panne
NIEUWPOORT

During WWI, the German advance was halted at **Nieuwpoort** when local partisans opened (and later re-opened) the sluice-gates on the Noordvaart canal to flood (and keep flooded) the fields between the IJzer River and the train line. You can see the main sluice-gates on the northeast approach to town where the bridge crosses the IJzer. Beside the site are a pair of **memorials** to the hundreds who died here in WWI, including a particularly ugly yellow-stone rotunda surrounding an equestrian Albert I statue. WWI bombardments devastated the townscape, but from the 1920s the medieval main square was rebuilt including the former 1280 town hall, belfry and a sizeable church. Flanked by stepgabled houses, the scene looks lovely at dusk, thanks to tasteful floodlighting, but by day the over-neat brickwork lacks the apparent authenticity of similar reconstructions in Ypres or Diksmuide.

These days Nieuwpoort is the coast's top sailing centre. The yacht harbour, around 1km north of town, is a memorable mass of masts overlooked by the panoramic Galjeon restaurant. **Zeilexcursies** (www.zeilexcursies.be) and **Magic Sailing** (www.magicsailing.be) sail Nieuwpoort–Ostend–Nieuwpoort by yacht for €60 per person (minimum four) including lunch in Ostend. **AS** (www.as-tian.com) and **Sailors Only** (www.sailorsonly.com) offer yacht charters, **Le Boat** (www.leboat.net) and **Hoseasons** (www.hoseasons.co.uk) rent liveaboard canal/river-boats (from €650/1350 per week in March/July).

Daily in July and August, **Seastar** (☎ 058-232 425; www.seastar.be; Orlenpromenade 2) runs a 90-minute sea cruise to Ostend (adult/child €13.50/9.50), departing 2.30pm from a terminal northwest of town. Their canal barge ride to Diksmuide (adult/child €13.50/9.50, return €18.50/11.50) leaves at 2pm (some days at 10am too), starting from behind the sluices off the Bruges road.

OOSTDUINKERKE

Some 6km further west, Oostduinkerke is famed for its handful of surviving **paardevissers** (www.paardevissers.be), horseback shrimp-fishermen who ride their stocky Brabant horses into the sea dragging triangular nets through the low-tide shallows. These days shrimp catches are minimal and the age-old tradition is maintained essentially as a tourist spectacle (on Astridplein beach). Check the website for a calendar of outings, which only happen around 25 times a year, mostly in July and August.

Oostduinkerke-dorp, the old village centre, is 1.5km inland from the tram stop. Hidden behind the bronze-spired old town hall lies an interesting, state-of-the-art **Fishery Museum** (Nationaal Visserijmuseum; ☎ 058-512 468; www.visserijmuseum.be; Pastoor Schmitzstraat 5, Oostduinkerke; adult/senior/youth €5/3/1; ☺ 10am-6pm Tue-Fri, 2pm-6pm Sat & Sun). Visits walk you through a genuine 19th-century fisherman's cottage, teach about fish quotas and fishermen's superstitions then send you beneath a 1930s fishing smack flanked by aquariums of fish. An accompanying soundtrack of waves and shrieking gulls builds up to a four-minute storm every half hour. While partial explanations are in four languages, fuller audio-guides aren't yet available in English. Veurne–Ostend bus 68 stops nearby.

Halfway between village and coast, **Sint-Niklaaskerk** is an extraordinary 1956 church whose bulky pale-brick tower has an almost medieval look, except for the massive 13m-high crucified Christ hanging on its east wall. Turn east near the church and continue 700m to find the modern, peacefully located **HI hostel De Peerdevisser** (Jeugdherberg; ☎ 058-512 649; www.peerdevisser.be; Duinparklaan 41; HI member/non-member €18.80/21.80).

ST-IDESBALD

Hidden in unexpectedly leafy suburbs, the **Delvaux Museum** (☎ 058 52 12 29; www.delvauxmuseum.com; Delvauxlaan 42; admission €8; ☺ 10.30am-5.30pm Tue-Sun Apr-Sep, Thu-Sun Oct-Dec) occupies a pretty whitewashed cottage that was home and studio to Paul Delvaux (1897–1994), one of Belgium's most famous surrealist artists. Delvaux' penchant for locomotives, skeletons and endless big-eyed nudes doesn't appeal to everyone, but there's something fascinating about his warped take on perspective and his dreamy evocations of the 'poetic subconscious'. This museum shows a wide range of his work, as

WESTERN FLANDERS

well as family memorabilia and the numerous toy trains that decorated his studio. From the Koksijde/St-Idesbald tram stop walk west along the main road towards De Panne, then follow signs inland and left, around 1km total. The museum's garden **café** (beer €2.20 to €3.80, seasonal mussels €19.50 to €22.50) is delightful.

DE PANNE & ADINKERKE
pop 9900

A busy beach resort, **De Panne** (www.depanne.be), started life as a fishing village set in a *panne* (hollow) among the dunes. Here King Léopold I first set foot on Belgian territory in 1831. This event is commemorated by a massively stone-framed **royal statue** that surveys the summer beer stalls and banal apartment towers on the beachfront directly north of De Panne Esplanade tram stop. In 1940, the sand dunes between De Panne and Dunkerque (Dunkirk, France) were the scene of the famous skin-of-their-teeth evacuation that saved a large part of the retreating WWII British army. West of De Panne's central strip, some of those grassy-topped dunes still survive, now forming part of a nature reserve for winter's migratory birds. The sand feels great underfoot, but westward coastal views are marred by the belching smokestacks of Dunkerque.

The classic holiday-maker's way to get around here is by *Kwistax* that weave along the beaches and promenades.

The train station called 'De Panne' is actually 3km inland at **Adinkerke**, with the Kusttram coastal-tram terminating next door. Less than 1km south of the station (and 600m north of the E40 motorway), Adinkerke's shops offer a last chance for chocoholic motorists heading to the channel ports or for bargain-hunting French smokers.

A Kusttram stop between Adinkerke and central De Panne serves **Plopsaland** (☎ 058-420 202; www.plopsaland.be; De Pannelaan 68, Adinkerke-De Panne; adult/under 1m tall/under 85cm €27/6/free), a major kids' theme park based around wonderfully named Belgian TV characters Wizzy, Woppy and Plop the gnome. Their website gives opening dates, times and online discount tickets (€24).

VEURNE
pop 11,900

Delightful little Veurne has an architectural charm that trumps all of the coastal towns put together. Historic spires and towers peep above the picture-perfect Flemish gables that

surround its super-quaint **Grote Markt** (central square). Its 1628 octagonal **belfort**, a Unesco World Heritage Site, rises behind the 17th-century former courthouse building. It now houses a helpful **tourist office** (☎ 058-335 531; www.veurne.be; Grote Markt 29; ☉ 10am-noon & 1.30-5.30pm Apr-Sep, 10am-noon & 2-4pm Tue-Sun Oct-Mar, closed Sun mid-Nov–Mar) whose **stadhuis tours** (adult/child €3/2; ☉ several daily, see blackboard) offer the easiest way to peep inside the 1612 Flemish Renaissance-style **town hall** next door. Across the Grote Markt lies the gabled 1615 **Vleeshuis** and the 15th-century **Spaans Paviljoen** (Spanish Pavilion), Veurne's town hall before being commandeered as a garrison for Spanish officers during Hapsburg rule.

Behind the Grote Markt's southeast corner, the church tower of **St-Niklaaskerk** (Appelmarkt; admission €1.50; ☉ 10-11.45am & 2-5.15pm mid-Jun–mid-Sep) is a bulky 13th-century affair affording good summer views.

Set behind Grote Markt, Veurne's main church is the delicately spired **St-Walburgakerk**, a spacious, heavily buttressed affair containing the much revered relics – the skull of St-Walburga (in a reliquary facing the entrance) and a wooden fragment that was supposedly once part of Jesus' original cross (not displayed). In an attractive small park behind the **Citerne** is a strange crouched brick building converted to barracks during WWII but incorporating the church's abandoned 14th-century west portal.

Near the motorway junction, 2km south of central Veurne, a classical 17th-century farmstead houses the delightful **Bakkerijmuseum** (☎ 058-313 897; Albert I-laan 2, Veurne; adult/senior/child €5/3.50/1; ☉ 10am-5pm Mon-Thu, 2pm-5pm Sat & Sun). The museum comprehensively examines baking, from grain production to *speculaas* moulding. There's also a chocolate statue and barnfuls of milling machines. Explanations are Dutch/French only but a €1 leaflet adds English summaries. Come on Tuesdays to see the baking demonstrations.

Sleeping & Eating

The Old House (☎ 058-311 931; www.theoldhouse.be; Zwarte Nonnenstraat 8; low season s/d/q €50/80/170, high season €60/90/180; ✗ P) Creamy paintwork, indulgently oversized showers, splendid linens and gentle modernism turn this classically styled 1770 mansion into a beguiling boutique hotel, though the cheapest singles are narrow and cramped. There's an original salon-lounge, a stylish bar area and gated free parking. It's a short stroll through the park west of St-Walburgakerk.

our pick **'t Kasteel en 't Koetshuys** (☎ 058-315 372; www.kasteelenkoetshuys.be; Lindendreef 5; d without/with bathroom €99/108; ✗ 🛜) This delightful 1907 red-brick mansion features high ceilings, old marble fireplaces and stripped floorboards, creating a lovely blend of classic and modern, all immaculately kept. There's a very inviting lounge-salon, a garden and terrace and sauna-hammam (extra charge). It's three blocks south of Grote Markt.

Taverne Flandria (☎ 058-311 174; www.taverne-flandria.be; Grote Markt 30; 🕙 10am 10pm Fri Tue, 10am-6pm Wed) One of a wide range of down-to-earth *cafés* on the Grote Markt, the Flandria serves inexpensive pub-meals and a good variety of beers (including Chimay Triple on draught). Their coffee comes with a complimentary thimble of custard-like advocaat – use the spoon.

Au Petit Coin (☎ 0495-249 082; Appelmarkt 1; mains €20-26; 🕙 noon-2pm & 7-10.30pm Thu-Mon) While choice is limited and portions modest, the flavour combinations are truly delicious in this cosy gastronomic delight where the peeling paint is a rustic design feature not a sign of neglect. It's a small medieval house tacked onto St-Niklaaskerk, just southwest of Grote Markt.

Getting There & Around

Veurne's extravagantly spired little train station is 600m east of Grote Markt via Ooststraat. Trains leave half-hourly for De Panne (€1.60, seven minutes) and Ghent (€10.10, 65 minutes) via Diksmuide

(€2.50, 11 minutes). Hourly bus 68 goes to Oostduinkerke-dorp, Nieuwpoort and Ostend. Bus 50 runs to Ypres via Lo and Oostvleteren up to seven times daily.

Wim's Bike Center (☎ 058-312 209; www.wimsbikecenter.be; Pannenstraat 35, Veurne; per day €8.70; 🕙 9am-noon & 1.30pm-6pm Tue-Sat) rents bicycles.

AROUND VEURNE

This pan-flat agricultural area produces some of Belgium's very best beers. The canal-diced scenery of potato- and corn-fields isn't dramatic but back lanes are peaceful and several keyed bicycle routes mesh with the Westhoek cycling guide-map (€6) sold by various tourist offices.

Veurne to Poperinge

The pretty two-street village of **Wulveringem** sports a spooky slate-towered **church**, curious statue-carving **studio** and most notably **Kasteel Beauvoorde** (☎ 058-299 229; www.kasteelbeauvoorde.be; adult/concession/child €5/4/free; 🕙 10am-5.30pm Tue-Sun Jul-Aug, 2pm-5.30pm Thu-Sun Mar-Oct), a moated four-storey mansion-castle. Originally a late 16th-century pleasure-park house with turret added in 1612, its present form dates from a romantic 1875 rebuild by art-collecting local mayor Arthur Merghelynck. The fanciful interiors remain intact and fully furnished, down to the suits of armour, gilded leather 'wallpaper' and recycled monastic choir-stalls used as wood-panelling in the Knights' Room.

Notice the photogenic wooden **post-mill** at **Oostvleteren**'s main crossroads. Four hundred metres east, on Oostvleteren's church square, is **Het Witte Paard** (Oostvleterendorp 1; 🕙 Fri-Mon 11am-10pm), an especially appealing village pub decked with ivy, old bicycles and battered trumpets. They serve their own unique 'Anti-stress' beers (€6.40).

The mythical **Westvleteren Trappist beer** doesn't actually come from nearby Westvleteren village but from the isolated **Abdij Sint-Sixtus** (www.sintsixtus.be/eng/brouwerij.htm), some 4km further southwest via a web of tiny lanes. The architecturally unremarkable abbey and its brewery are closed to visitors, but across the road is the abbey's surprisingly modern *café*, **In de Vrede** (☎ 057-400 377; www.indevrede.be; 🕙 10am-8pm Sun-Thu Apr–mid-Sep, Sun-Wed Oct-Dec & mid-Jan–Mar, closed Easter). This Holy Grail for many international ale-fans is the only place in the world that you can be (virtually) sure of tasting the incomparable Westvleteren 12°, often cited as Belgium's greatest beer. The *café*'s cheese-shop-counter sometimes sells six-packs of the beer or €16.10 beer-tasting sets (four bottles and a Westvleteren beer-glass). However, anyone wishing to purchase a full case must pre-reserve by appointment using the abbey's **'beerphone'** (☎ high toll 070-210 045), preferably calling on the dot of 9am Monday morning. You'll need to give your car number plate and agree a pick-up time (weekday afternoons only, no credit cards!).

Another remarkable beer, chocolatey **Pannepot** (http://struise.noordhoek.com/eng), is one of the Struise range produced at (and when available sold by) the banal-looking **Deca Brewery** (Elverdingestraat 4, 8640 Woesten; ⏲ shop 9.30am-noon & 1-6pm Tue-Fri, to 5pm Sat) in the un-exciting village of **Woesten** on the main Ypres–Veurne road.

Between Oostvleteren and Diksmuide, quaint little **Lo** has a pixie-esque twin-spired **city gate** and a vastly oversized **church**. Graced with a very pretty brick belfry-tower, the photogenic 1566 former **town hall** now houses the good-value **Hotel Stadhuis** (☎ 058-288 016; www.stadhuis -lo.be; Markt 1; s/d/tr from €50/70/105), with atmospheric lobby-restaurant and sauna. The five simple little guest rooms with wooden beamed ceilings and decent bathrooms are accessed off a corridor decorated with antique jugs and basins.

Diksmuide
pop 15,500

Like Ypres, Diksmuide was painstakingly restored after total obliteration in WWI. Though used as a large car park, the resurrected Grote Markt (main square) offers an impressive array of traditionally styled brick gables, two inexpensive hotels, several terraced *cafés* and a romantically towered **city hall**. Set directly behind, the truly vast church has a particularly fine rose window. The tulip-turreted **Boterhalle** hosts a **tourist office** (☎ 051-519 146; http://toerisme .diksmuide.be; Grote Markt 28; ⏲ 10am-noon & 2-5pm).

Pleasure boats are moored attractively at the river port 1km west. Directly beyond rises the unique 1950 **IJzertoren** (☎ 051-500 286; www.ijzertoren .org; IJzerdijk 49; adult/youth/child €7/1/free; ⏲ 10am-5pm, to 6pm Apr-Sep). Built of drab, purple-brown brick and topped with power station–style windows this colossal 84m-high 'peace' tower is at once crushingly ugly and mesmerisingly fascinating. It's set behind the shattered ruins of a 1930 original, whose mysterious sabotage in 1946 remains controversial. The tower is probably Flanders' foremost nationalist symbol. Its 22

floors house a very expansive museum related to WWI and Flemish emancipation. Entry is free on Flemish National Day (11 July) and the Yzerbedevaart nationalist rally is held here on the last Sunday of August, albeit diminished in scale since a split in the movement.

Highly-rated Oerbier is a stealthy dark ale, served at several Diksmuide hostelries including central **'t Gouden Mandeken** (Grote Markt; ⏲ 9.30am-late), which also does excellent seasonal mussels in garlic-cream (*room-look*) for €18.95. Alternatively at weekends, get draught Oerbier at the brilliantly colourful little *café* of its brewery, **De Dolle Brouwers** (☎ 051-502 781; www .dedollebrouwers.be; Roeselarestraat 12B, Esen; ⏲ café 2-7pm Sat & Sun). It's located 3km east in **Esen** village, hidden behind a butcher's shop 100m south of Esen's powerfully oversized church. The beer labels' kooky light-heartedness belies the brewery's murderous WWII history – German troops massacred local men here then locked around 200 women and children in the cellar. At 2pm on Sundays there's a tour in English.

POPERINGE
pop 19,400

For centuries the Poperinge area has produced the quality hops required for Belgium's beer industry. Once the municipal hops weighing-and store-house, the 19th-century Stadsschaal now houses the distinctive smelling **National Hopmuseum** (☎ 057-337 922; www.hopmuseum.be; Gasthuisstraat 71; adult/concession/child €5/4/2.50; ⏲ 10am-6pm Tue-Fri, 2pm-6pm Sat, 10am-noon & 2-6pm Sun, closed Dec-Feb), where you'll learn more about hops than you'd ever want to know. The simple attached pub-*café* serves several local brews and was once home to Dirk Frimout, Belgium's first astronaut. It's two blocks west of the almost-attractive **Grote Markt** where the **tourist office** (☎ 057-34 66 76; www.poperinge.be; Grote Markt 1; ⏲ 9am-noon & 1-5pm Mon-Fri, till 4pm Sat & Sun, closed Sun mid-Nov–Mar) is in the basement of the romantic neo-Gothic **Stadhuis** (built 1911).

Between the two lies an unusually light-hearted WWI attraction, the appealing **Talbot House** (☎ 057-333 228; www.talbothouse.be; Gasthuisstraat 43; adult/senior/youth €8/7/5; ⏲ 9.30am-5.30pm Tue-Sun). Reverend Philip 'Tubby' Clayton set up the Everyman's Club here in 1915 to offer rest and recreation for WWI soldiers regardless of rank. The main 1790 townhouse has barely changed since. The garden is a charming oasis, and visits start with a modest exhibition accessed from Pottestraat where photos, quotes

---

TICKET SAVVY

A €10 combination ticket includes the Hopmuseum and Talbot House and also gives you a €2.50 discount on the excellent In Flanders Fields Museum in Ypres (right).

---

and videos remind visitors of Tubby's sharp gallows humour. End the visit with a free cup of English-style tea in the kitchen. Or you could stay the night in one of the simple **guest rooms** (s/d €28/50, breakfast €6) with shared bathrooms (bookings advised).

There are numerous *cafés* plus five simple hotels around the Grote Markt. But for something special book **Hotel Recour/ Restaurant Pegasus** (☎ 057-335 725; www.pegasus recour.be; Guido Gezellestraat 7; d/ste from €150/325, breakfast/menu €16/65; ❷ ▢). The main 18th-century house has a luxurious lounge, comfortably upmarket restaurant and eight romantic rooms. Individually themed, most feature nostalgic colour combinations, chandeliers, four-poster beds and jacuzzi baths. Junior suite Urania retains an old wooden winch wheel over the bed. A metal walkway above the garden lawn leads to another seven contrastingly modern rooms, each adopting the style of a classic 20th-century designer. The Recour is 100m east of Grote Markt, halfway to the imposing **Sint-Janskerk** (Bruggestraat; ❷ 7.30am-7pm), whose 'miraculous' little virgin-and-child statuette reputedly brought a stillborn child to life in 1479.

Getting There & Away

Poperinge–Ypres takes eight minutes by train (€2), or 18 minutes by bus 60, both hourly. You'll need to pre book for the eccentrically routed Belbus 69 to Westvleteren, Woesten, or Oostvleteren.

YPRES (IEPER)
pop 35,000

Only the hardest of hearts are unmoved by historic Ypres (Ieper in Dutch). In the Middle Ages it was an important cloth town ranking alongside Bruges and Ghent. In WWI some 300,000 Allied soldiers died in the 'Salient', a bow-shaped bulge that formed the front line around town. Ypres remained unoccupied by German forces, but was utterly flattened by bombardment. Incredibly, after the war,

the beautiful medieval core was convincingly rebuilt and the restored Ypres Lakenhalle is today one of the most spectacular buildings in Belgium. Most tourism still revolves around WWI and related themes and the Salient remains dotted with cemeteries, memorials, bunkers and war museums.

Information

British Grenadier (☎ 057-214 657; www.salienttours .com; Meensestraat 5; ❷ 9.30am-1pm, 2-6pm & 7.30-8.30pm) Bookshop specialising in all things WWI-related, plus bookings for battlefield tours. The morning tour (four hours, departs 10am, €35) visits major Salient sites. The 2.30pm short tour (€28) goes to Hill 60 and Bayerwald, a trench complex at which young Adolf Hitler served as a corporal.

Over the Top (☎ 057- 424 320; www.overthetoptours.be; 41 Meensestraat; ❷ 9am-12.30pm, 1.30-5.30pm & 7.30-8.30pm) Similar combination of WWI books, memorabilia and tours (North Salient 9.30am, South Salient 2pm, both €35).

Visitors centre (☎ 057-239 220; www.ieper.be; Lakenhalle, Grote Markt; ❷ 9am-6pm Mon-Fri, 10am-6pm Sat & Sun Apr–Mid-Nov, to 5pm Mid-Nov–Mar) Tourist office for Ypres and surrounds with extensive bookshop.

Sights
LAKENHALLE & MUSEUMS

Dominating the lovely Grote Markt, the enormous, brilliantly reconstructed **Lakenhalle** (cloth hall) is one of Belgium's single-most impressive buildings. Its 70m-high belfry has the vague appearance of a medieval Big Ben. The original version was completed in 1304 beside the Ieperslee, a river that, while now completely covered over, once allowed ships to sail right up to the Lakenhalle to unload their cargoes of wool. These were stored beneath the high gables of the 1st floor, where you'll now find the unmissable **In Flanders Fields Museum** (☎ 057-239 275; www.inflandersfields.be; Grote Markt 34; adult/child/family €7.50/3.50/18; ❷ 10am-6pm Apr-Sep, to 5pm Tue-Sun Oct-Mar, last entry 1hr before closing). No museum gives a more balanced yet moving and user-friendly introduction to WWI history. It's a multisensory experience combining soundscapes, videos, well-chosen exhibits and interactive learning stations at which you 'become' a character and follow his/her progress through the wartime period. Keep your ticket to gain free entrance to three other minor museums: the **Education Museum** (G de Stuerstraat 6a; ❷ 10am-12.30pm & 2-5pm) in St-Niklaaskerk, the one-room **Belle Almshouse Chapel** (Rijselstraat 38; ❷ 10am-12.30pm & 2-6pm Tue-Sun

---

GOOD OLD POPS

During WWI, Poperinge was just out of German artillery range so it became a posting and R&R station for allied soldiers heading to or from the Ypres Salient. English troops who remembered it for its entertainments and prostitutes referred to the town fondly as 'Pops'. But it also had a more sinister side as a place of execution for wartime deserters. Hidden behind a red door in the north side of the Stadhuis you can still see the chilling original **shooting post** and the stone-walled **death cell** (Guido Gezellestraat 1; ☽ 9am-5pm) where deserters spent their last night. Brochures available in the cell explain in some detail the era's injustices accompanied by a soundscape telling of the 1917 execution of 17-year-old soldier Herbert Morris.

Apr-Oct) featuring rare medieval art, and the **Stedelijk Museum** (Ieperleestraat 31; ☽ 10am-12.30pm & 2-5pm Tue-Sun), a decent little gallery set in a 1555 almshouse complex.

Appended to the Lakenhalle's eastern end in 1619, the working **Stadhuis** (admission free; ☽ 8.30-11.45am Mon-Fri) was reconstructed in 1969. There's splendid stained glass in the council chamber. Directly behind, the vast church, **St-Maarten en St-Niklaaskerk**, had been a cathedral until 1797. Post WWI reconstruction has beautifully restored its soaring Gothic interior.

MENIN GATE
Unveiled in 1928, the memorable white-stone **Menenpoort** (Meensestraat) is a huge gateway inscribed with 54,896 names of British and Commonwealth troops lost in the quagmire of WWI, who have no graves. Every evening at 8pm, traffic is halted while buglers sound the **Last Post** (www.lastpost.be), a moving tradition that started in 1928. Every evening the scene is different. The buglers might be accompanied by pipers, troops of cadets, a choir or a military band that marches back to perform in the Grote Markt afterwards. Check the listing calendar posted near the gate's southwest corner. The gate looks especially impressive at night.

RAMPARTS
Ypres is unusual in that it has retained extensive sections of its Vaubanesque city fortifications. These sturdy brick-faced walls line the town's southern moat and are topped by pleasant gar-

dens. The tourist office's free *Ramparts Route* leaflet introduces a dozen historic fortifications that you'll see as you walk 2.6km around the ramparts on walking/cycling paths know as the **Vestingroute**. Several short cuts are possible. Between the 14th-century **Leeuwentoren** (Lion's Tower) and medieval **Rijselpoort** (Lille Gate), the **Ramparts Cemetery** is one of Ypres most attractive military graveyards.

Sleeping

Ypres has a considerable number of mostly unremarkable midrange hotels. For something more exclusive, stay in Poperinge or Kortrijk. Kortrijk also has the nearest youth hostel.

Jeugdstadion (☎ 057-217 282; www.jeugdstadion .be; Bolwerkstraat 1; tent/adult/child €1.50/3/1.50; ☽ mid-Mar–Oct) Camping ground and youth centre 900m southeast of the town centre.

B&B Zonneweelde (☎ 057-202 723; Adjudant Masscheleinlaan 18; s/d €30/50) A charming older lady keeps her lovable time-warp home fastidiously clean. It has a nostalgic scent of years gone by. There's a hotchpotch of furniture and bathroom facilities are shared.

Sultan Hotel (☎ 057-219 030; www.sultan.be; Grote Markt 33) The location is fabulous but corridors are slightly battered, rooms are simple (if fairly neat) and mattresses are somewhat saggy.

Ambrosia Hotel (☎ 0476-467 016; www.ambrosia hotel.be; D'Hondtstraat 54; �﹖) The nine rooms at this reasonably central hotel aren't as hip as the reception might imply. Beds are somewhat soft and attic singles are tiny, but they're all pleasantly new, wi-fi's free and breakfast's included. Check in by 8pm.

B&B Ter Thuyne (☎ 057-360 042; www.terthuyne.be; Gustave de Stuersstraat 19; s/d €60/75; ▯) Three comfortable rooms that are modern but not overly fashion conscious. They're luminously bright and scrupulously clean.

Hotel Regina (☎ 057-218 888; www.hotelregina.be; Grote Markt 45; standard s/d €70/85) Above a velveteen-*café*, the Regina enjoys a perfect location directly overlooking the Lakenhalle. Attempts at 'artistic' decor generally backfire and some rooms use nauseating colour schemes. However, the Ensor room, with old-world timber interior and unbeatable views, is a worthy exception.

Yoaké B&B (☎ 057-203 514; www.yoake-ieper.be/bed home.htm; Tempelstraat 35; d €85) Smart two-room B&B attached to a hip wellness centre.

Albion Hotel (☎ 057-200 220; www.albionhotel. be; St-Jakobsstraat 28; s/d €89/114; ☽ closed Jan; �﹖)

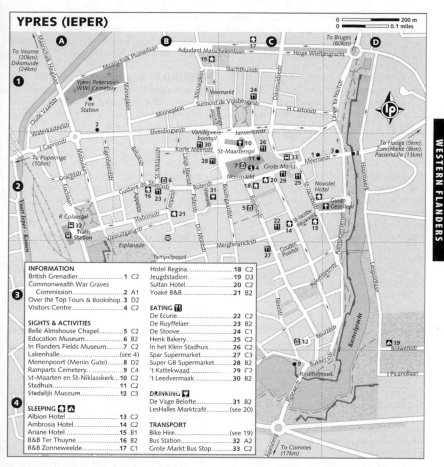

YPRES (IEPER)

Behind the step-gabled yellow-brick facade, the Albion can't quite shake off its past as an office building, despite a pleasant library-lounge area. Rooms have high ceilings and motel-style decor. Wi-fi per hour/day €5/12.

Ariane Hotel (☎ 057-218 218; www.ariane.be; Slachthuisstraat 58; s/d €95/120) In this peaceful, professionally managed larger hotel, two thirds of the rooms are in contemporary design style, the rest taking a more 1990s floral approach. Wartime memorabilia dots the common rooms and the swish restaurant is a popular Ypres institution.

Eating

The Grote Markt hosts a Saturday morning market (so don't park there Friday night).

Henk Bakery (☎ 057-201 417; St-Jakobsstraat; 6.45am-6pm Tue-Fri, 5.45am-7pm Sat, 5.45am-4pm Sun) Fresh bread and pastries to takeaway.

't Kattekwaad (www.frituur-kattekwaad.be; Grote Markt; chips/sauce/beer from €1.60/0.70/1.50; 11am-11pm) Chips and cheap snacks with a perfect Lakenhalle view, served in this unusually well-appointed *friterie*.

't Leedvermaak (☎ 057-216 385; Korte Meersstraat 2; mains €7-17; lunch Wed-Fri & Sun, dinner Tue-Sun) Low-key theatrically themed bistro with very reasonable prices for pastas (€7 to €10), veggie dishes (€7 to €12) and tapas (from €3.50).

our pick De Ruyffelaer (☎ 057-366 006; www.deruyffelaer.be; Gustave de Stuersstraat 9; mains €13-19, menus €22-30; 11.30am-10pm Sat & Sun, 5.30pm-10pm Thu-Fri) Enjoy traditional local dishes, including

WESTERN FLANDERS

chicken in *kriek* (cherry lambic), or rabbit in beer sauce, in an adorable, wood-panelled interior with old checkerboard floors and a brocante decor, including dried flowers, old radios and antique biscuit tins.

In het Klein Stadhuis (☎ 057-215 542; www.kleines tadhuis.be; Grote Markt 32; mains €14.50-24; ☷ 11am-midnight, kitchen 11.30am-2.30pm & 6-11pm) This popular brasserie-cafe has the facade of a quaint medieval guildhall, a great Grote Markt terrace and a somewhat surreal split-level interior. It's good for drinks or delicious, fairly priced meals from steak to mussels (seasonal) to vegetarian moussaka.

De Stoove (☎ 0479-229 233; www.destoove.be; Surmont de Volsbergestraat 12; mains €18-23; ☷ noon-2pm Thu-Tue & 6-9pm Thu-Mon) Fish, steak or seafood served with pared-down minimalist style in a century old townhouse.

De Ecurie (☎ 057-360 367; www.deecurie.be; A Merghelynckstraat 1a; mains €18-22; ☷ 11.30am-2pm & 6.30-10pm Tue-Sat) An intimate former stable-building features antique brick floors and walls decorated with postcards of old Ypres. Franco-Belgian food.

Drinking

De Vage Belofte (☎ 057-215 650; Vismarkt; beer €1.60; ☷ 4pm-late Tue-Sun) A piano hangs on the two-storey inner wall above a row of Champagne bottles, summer tables spill out across appealing Vismarkt and DJs turn the tables Friday and Saturday nights.

LesHalles Marktcafé (Grote Markt 35; beer/coffee/pancakes/mains from €1.60/1.80/2.30/12; ☷ 9am-4am Wed-Mon) Grote Markt grand *café* that's been given a fresh modern twist with a giant lamp and metal clock-face centrepiece. DJs crank things up from 10pm Thursday to Saturday nights.

Getting There & Away

Regional buses leave from outside the train station, most picking up in the Grote Markt (check the direction carefully). Ypres–Menen buses pass through Hooge. Bus 95 runs to Langemark German Cemetery. Rare bus 40 runs to Langemark town via Essex Hill. And you can reach Zonnebeke and Tyne Cot (600m walk) on bus 94 (roughly twice-hourly weekdays, five daily weekends). Both buses 94 and 95 continue to Roeselare where trains connect to Bruges. Bus 20 to Diksmuide (50 minutes) runs five times daily.

Trains run hourly to Poperinge (€2, seven minutes), Comines (€2.40, nine minutes),

Kortrijk (€4.80, 30 minutes), Oudenaarde (€8.10, one hour) and Brussels (€16, 1¾ hours).

Jeugdstadion (p158) rents adult/child bicycles for €10/5 per day.

AROUND YPRES
Ypres Salient

Flanders' WWI battlefields are famed for red poppies both real and metaphorical. From 1914 the area suffered four years of senseless fighting during which thousands of soldiers and whole towns disappeared into a muddy, bloody quagmire. The fighting was fiercest in the 'Ypres Salient', a bulge in the Western Front where the world first saw poison-gas attacks and thousands of diggers valiantly tunnelled underground to dynamite enemy trenches.

These days many local museums have collections of WWI memorabilia, there are dozens of maudlin, beautifully maintained war graveyards, and a surprising number of concrete bunkers, bomb craters and trench sites can be visited (though remember that the originals were muddier, used wood rather than metal supports and had no woodland-shade – virtually every tree had been pummelled into matchwood by artillery fire). There are also a few non-war attractions to lighten the tone.

PLANNING A VISIT

The sites are spread over a vast agricultural area that's scenically pleasant without being especially memorable. So your first chore is figuring out what you really want to see.

Grave searches

If you had relatives killed in the fighting the first step will usually be to work out the location of their grave or memorial. For British and Commonwealth grave lists the **Commonwealth War Graves Commission** (☎ 057-200 118; www.cwgc.org; Elverdingsestraat 82, Ypres; ☷ 8.30am-noon & 1.30-4.30pm Mon-Fri) has an Ypres office. Online resources for other nationalities:

- www.inflandersfields.be/£dodenregister for French and Belgian graves
- www.abmc.gov for American graves
- www.volksbund.de for German graves

Ypres bookshops also offer grave-search help.

General Visits

If you're looking for a specific war-site other than a grave, www.wo1.be is helpful.

If you just want a general taster you might join a half- or one-day tour organised by Over the Top (p157), or, starting from Bruges, Quasimodo (p139). Advance bookings are often necessary.

If organising your own tour by car or bicycle, according to the level of detail you want, there are several specific guides available from bookshops or the visitor centre in Ypres.

- Westhoek-Tourism's excellent *Great War in Flanders Fields* pamphlet is free and readable online at www.tourism flandersfields – click 'Meer Informatie' under the 'Great War' banner for the English version.
- *In Flanders Fields Route* booklet (€2.50) describes a two-day 82km itinerary complete with map and sight information.
- *Major & Mrs Holt's Concise Battlefield Guides to the Ypres Salient* are detailed guides that come in mini (€11) and full (€24) versions offering three- and four-hour touring itineraries plus plenty of historical information. They assume that you'll also buy the accompanying *Battle Map of the Ypres Salient* (€4.95)

to help track down those lesser-known sights.

SELECTED SITES
The following main sites are all keyed to map p161. While a car makes visits much easier and reduces backtracking, buses can get you close to most sites (see opposite).

Cemeteries
Each cemetery is moving for its regimented ranks of headstones. Beside **Essex Farm Cemetery** on the N369, you can still see the concrete first-aid bunker where Canadian doctor John McCrae wrote the famous poem *In Flanders Fields*. The poem, reprinted on an information board here, led to the continuing image of poppies as a symbol of wartime sacrifice. Across the wide canal, hidden amid the vast new wind turbines of a light industrial zone is a restored defence system called the **Yorkshire Trench**.

Four silhouette statues survey the eerie **Deutscher Soldatenfriedhof** beyond the northern edge of Langemark. It's the area's main German WWI cemetery and while smaller than Tyne Cot (see below), it's arguably the most memorable graveyard of the whole Salient. Some 44,000 corpses were grouped together here, up to ten per granite grave slab interspersed by oak trees and trios of squat, mossy crosses. Entrance to the site takes you through a black concrete 'tunnel' that clanks and hisses spookily with distant war sounds, while four short video-montages commemorate the tragedy of war.

Probably the most visited Salient site, **Tyne Cot** is the world's biggest British Commonwealth war cemetery, with 11,956 graves. A huge semicircular wall commemorates another 34,857 lost-in-action soldiers whose names wouldn't fit on Ypres' Menin Gate. The name Tyne Cot was coined by Northumberland Fusiliers who fancied that German bunkers on the hillside here looked like Tyneside cottages. Two such dumpy concrete bunkers sit amid the graves, with a third partly visible through the metal wreath beneath the central white Cross of Sacrifice.

Passendale
The 1917 battles around Passendale (then Passchendaele) left almost 500,000 casualties and made Passendale synonymous with wasted life. These days it's more positively known for cheese, as you can see at the interactive, mildly interesting **Oude Kaasmakerij**

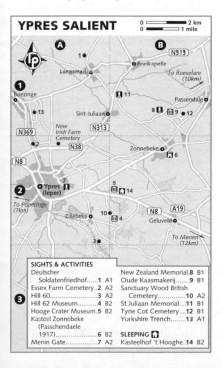

YPRES SALIENT

0 ———— 2 km
0 ———— 1 mile

SIGHTS & ACTIVITIES		
Deutscher	New Zealand Memorial.**8** B1	
Soldatenfriedhof......**1** A1	Oude Kaasmakerij......**9** B1	
Essex Farm Cemetery..**2** A2	Sanctuary Wood British	
Hill 60.........................**3** A2	Cemetery.............**10** A2	
Hill 62 Museum..........**4** B2	St Juliaan Memorial....**11** B1	
Hooge Crater Museum.**5** B2	Tyne Cot Cemetery....**12** B1	
Kasteel Zonnebeke	Yorkshire Trench.......**13** A1	
(Passchendaele		
1917)..................**6** B2	SLEEPING	
Menin Gate................**7** A2	Kasteelhof 't Hooghe..**14** B2	

AT THE CROSSROADS OF WAR

The Ypres Salient was formed by Allied attempts to repel and push back the invading German army before it could reach the strategic North Sea ports in northern France. The area's line of long, barely visible undulations (don't be fooled by names like 'Hill 60') provided just enough extra elevation to make good vantage points and were thus much-prized military objectives. Hundreds of thousands of lives were lost in bid after counter bid to take these very modest ridges. Years of deadlocked trench warfare obliterated local villages and created a barren, merciless landscape of mud and despair. The first battle of Ypres in October and November 1914 basically set the lines of the Salient. After that both sides dug in and gained relatively little ground either way for the remainder of the war despite three other valiantly suicidal battles that would follow. The most infamous of these came in spring 1915 when Germans around Langemark (p161) launched WWI's first poison-gas attack. It had devastating effects not only on the advancing Allied soldiers but also on the Germans themselves. On 31 July 1917 British forces launched a three-month offensive commonly remembered as the Battle of Passchendaele (Passendale, p161), or the 'battle of the mud'. Fought in shocking weather on fields already liquidised by endless shelling, this horrifically futile episode killed or wounded over half a million men, all for a few kilometres of ground. And these modest Allied gains were lost again in April 1918. However, that would be the last German assault. By November the war was over. But the reconstruction of villages and replanting of trees would take years and even now farmers regularly plough up large quantities of unexploded munitions in their fields. Today the green and pleasant farmland is patchworked with 170 cemeteries where row upon row of crosses stand in silent witness to all the wasted life.

(☎ 051-777 005; www.deoudekaasmakerij.be; ☽ 10am-5pm, closed some Mon & Wed mornings), 1.2km west of Tyne Cot. Videos and antique machinery compare old and new cheese-making techniques while a gratuitous naked Cleopatra takes a bath in plastic asses' milk.

Zonnebeke

In the centre of Zonnebeke village is a lake-fronted Normandy chalet-style mansion called **Kasteel Zonnebeke** (www.zonnebeke.be). It was built in 1922 to replace a castle bombarded into rubble during WWI. Its stables host a stylish resto-café while inside there's a tourist information booth and the particularly polished WWI museum **Passchendaele 1917** (☎ 051-770 441; www.zonnebeke.be, www.passchendaele.be; adult/student €5/1; 10am-6pm Mon-Fri, 2pm-6pm Sat & Sun Feb-Nov), which charts local battle progressions with plenty of multilingual commentaries. The big attraction here is descending into its multi-room 'trench experience' with low-lit wooden-clad subterranean bunk rooms and a soundtrack to add war-time atmosphere. Entirely indoors, explanations are much more helpful here than in muddier 'real' trenches elsewhere.

Hooge

In a quaint repurposed chapel on the Ypres–Menen road (N8) is the small but characterful two-room **Hooge Crater Museum** (☎ 057-468 446; www.hoogecrater.com; Meenseweg 467; adult/child €4.50/2; ☽ 10am-5pm Mar-Nov Tue-Sun). Enter between assorted WWI sandbags, rusty rail-sections and field guns. Inside, uniformed mannequins, arms and assorted memorabilia are ranged in venerable old display cases around a life-sized model of a red Fokker triplane. The attached *café* is appealing. Massive explosions detonated beneath German defences by British engineers created the crater for which it's named. The crater now forms a pretty pond 100m east of the museum. Along with some recently re-excavated **trenches**, it lies in the **gardens** (admission €0.50) of the attractive pseudo-Tudor **Kasteelhof 't Hooghe** (☎ 057-468 758; www.hotel kasteelhofthooghe.be; Meenseweg 481; s\d\tr €70/90/120). This is a red-tiled, half-timbered hotel whose 15 rooms are comfortable though not overly luxurious. The screams you hear aren't war related but rather hail from fun-seekers just behind the garden taking high-adrenaline fair-rides in **Park Bellewaerde** (☎ 057-468 686; www.bellewaerdepark.be; Meenseweg 497; adult/child under 1.4m/under 1m €27/23/free; ☽ 10am-6pm Jun-Aug, to 5pm Easter holidays & Wed-Sun May). This could be the place to leave the kids rather than dragging them to too many WWI graveyards.

Hill 62

The family-run **Hill 62 Museum** (☎ 057-466 373; www.ypres-1917.com/hill_62.htm; Canadalaan 26; adult/child

€7.50/5; ◷ 10am-6pm) has a chaotic hotchpotch of WWI helmets, shoes, guns and grenades partly displayed in a surreally ordinary gnome-fronted house. Numerous harrowing war photos are displayed, some in antiquated wooden stereoscopic viewers. The main attempted justification for the hefty entrance fee is an extensive string of 'original trenches' in the woodland garden along with a cross-pinned relic of a bombarded tree. It's 200m beyond the **Sanctuary Wood British Cemetery**, ie around 2km down a dead-end lane from the nearest bus stop (Hooge).

Comines

An administrative curiosity, the commune of **Comines-Warneton** (Komen-Waasten in Dutch, www.villedecomines-warneton.be) is a detached enclave of Francophone Hainaut sandwiched between Flanders and France. Comines town itself is cut in two by the border. Just 150m across the River Lys on the French side stands the very distinctive 1623 **Comines Town Hall**, with a wildly bulbous Unesco-listed belfry tower that was meticulously rebuilt after WWI. It faces the 1922–1938 **St-Chrysole church**, a compulsively hideous attempt at neo-Byzantine grandeur. Nearby on the Belgian side the unexpectedly fascinating **Musée de la Rubanerie** (☎ 056-555 800; adult/child €2/1; ◷ 9am-11.30am & 1.30-4.30pm Tue-Fri, 3pm-4.30pm Sat, 10.30am-noon Sun) celebrates Comines' economic mainstay since 1719, the ribbon-making industry. On weekends, passionately knowledgeable museum staff set the antique machinery in motion and use cunningly devised model mechanisms to explain how they work. Suddenly ribbon looms, bootstrap twisters and zipper functionality all seem remarkably engrossing. But you'll need some spoken French.

The train station, 800m north, has hourly trains to Ypres (€2.40, 9 minutes). Around 2km further northeast **Ice Mountain** (☎ 056-554 540; www.ice-mountain.com; Rue de Capelle 16, Comines; per hr/day incl gear €17.5/48; ◷ 10am-11pm, daily Sep-Apr, Wed-Sun May-Aug) is a year-round artificial ski-slope.

KORTRIJK
pop 74,000

Prosperous Kortrijk (Courtrai in French) is a deeply historical place with several curiosities and atmospheric cafes to seek out. Founded as the Roman settlement of Cortoriacum, the town was a prosperous flax and linen centre, but was severely bombed by the Allies during WWII. Today's very patchy architectural mix lacks the overall charm of many other historic Flemish towns.

Information

Centrale Bibliotheek (☎ 056-277 500; Leiestraat 30; ◷ 11am-6pm Mon-Fri, 10am-4pm Sat). Library with free internet computers and wi-fi.

Tourist office (www.kortrijk.be/toerisme; ◷ 9am-6pm Mon-Fri, 10am-5pm Sat & Sun Apr-Sep, 9am-5pm Mon-Fri, 10am-4pm Sat & Sun Oct-Mar) Within Kortrijk 1302 (see below). Offers maps, listings-brochures and bicycle rental.

Sights

The **Grote Markt** is scarred by insensitive 20th-century constructions, but the restored 1421 **Historisch Stadhuis** building has a fine, ornate facade dotted with stone mini-spires and niche statues. From certain angles the slightly leaning, multi-spired brick **belfort** (belfry) aligns photogenically with the very grand 83m tower-spire of **St-Maartenskerk**. The latter is a mostly 15th-century Gothic church built on the site of St-Eloi's 7th-century chapel. Immediately north, a portal opens to Kortrijk's small but utterly delightful enclosed **Begijnhof** (admission free; ◷ 7am-9pm), a charming cluster of whitewashed old terraced houses on narrow cobbled lanes. See the boxed text, p137, for more info on *begijnhoven*.

Echoing with wistful music the **Onze Lieve Vrouwekerk** (Our Lady's Church; ◷ 7am-7pm Mon-Sat, to 6pm Sun) has a gilt sun-burst altarpiece, heraldic panels in the 1373 St-Catherinekapel and features Van Dyck's 1631 painting *Kruisoprichting* (Raising of the Cross) in the left transept. Poet-priest Guido Gezelle was once pastor here (1872–1889), while in 1302 the church displayed the spurs that gave the Battle of the Golden Spurs its name (see the boxed text, p166). That battle took place on Groeningheveld, now a leafy city park marked by a 1906 pseudo-medieval **gateway** and the triumphant **Groeninge Statue** featuring a woman unleashing the Flemish lion. For much more on the battle visit the modern **Kortrijk 1302** (☎ 056-277 850; Begijnhofpark;

MUSEUM SAVERS

Kortrijk's three major museums are free on the first Sunday of each month. Other days, pay €8 to see all three.

WESTERN FLANDERS

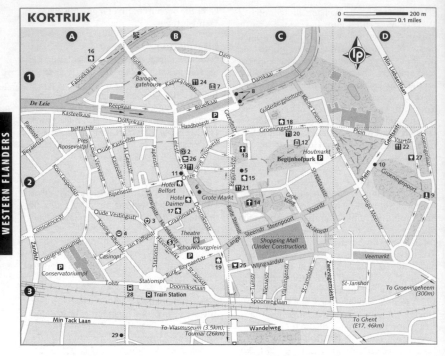

adult/child €6/2.50; 10am-6pm Tue-Sun Apr-Sep, to 5pm Oct-Mar) 'experience'-museum. Despite English-language audio-guide (essential) and multiple video screens, the experience is disappointingly static and rather unsatisfying for non-Flemish visitors. However, the 14-minute movie climax offers the intriguingly self-defeating conclusion that the battle's importance (and thus the museum's, presumably) has been disproportionately over-blown. How Belgian. Easily missed near the start of the 'experience' is a museum section on city arts and history in an old building of the former Groeninge Abbey.

A classical river-facing 1785 mansion retaining Louis XVI gilt interiors hosts the **Broelmuseum** (056-277 780; Broelkaai 6; adult/concession/child €3/2/free; 10am-noon & 2-5pm Tue-Fri, 11am-5pm Sat & Sun) featuring works by major local painters. Don't miss Roelandt Savery's 1604 masterpiece *Plundering of a Village* or Emmanuel Viérin's semi-impressionist scenes of the Begijnhof. The museum garden has a notable orangery. To get here cross a narrow stone bridge guarded by the hefty **Broeltorens**. The last reminders of Kortrijk's medieval

city wall, these twin three-storey stone towers feature machicolations and conical roofs and look magical in night-time floodlights when the backdrop of mediocre apartments is less apparent.

About 3km south of town by bus 13 (every 20 minutes from the train station) is the surprisingly engrossing **Vlasmuseum** (Flax Museum; 056-210 138; www.vlasmuseum.be; Etienne Sabbelaan 4; adult/senior/youth/child €3/2/1/free; 9am-12.30pm & 1.30-6pm Tue-Fri, 2-6pm Sat & Sun, closed Dec-Feb). It takes a Madame Tussaud's approach to explain the processes and development of the flax and linen industries on which Kortrijk's economy was historically based. Some famous Belgians, including Eddy Merckx, were used as models.

Sleeping

Groeningeheem (056-201 442; www.vjh.be; Passionistenlaan 1a; dm/s/d €16.40/25/42; reception 5pm-10pm; P) Friendly but functional HI youth hostel in a former school.

B&B Belle Epoque (0496-255 560; www.lbekortrijk. be; Fabriekskaai 5; d €70-90;) Facing the Leie in an area under extensive regeneration, this narrow step-gabled house is unique – maintaining its original 1907 de Coene–designed mantelpiece, stained glass and exuberant hallway. The rooms are in contemporary classic style each with their own bathrooms albeit on different floors. Free wi-fi.

Center Hotel (☎ 056-219 721; www.centerhotel.be; Graanmarkt 6; s/d/tr €65/75/110) Modern chocolate-toned rooms at reasonable prices above a subtly fashionable bar.

Ibis Hotel (☎ 056-257 975; website www.ibishotel .com; Doorniksestraat 26; weekend/week d €70/80) Central if somewhat generic, the Ibis has a useful 24-hour bar-reception.

B&B Begijnhofkamers (☎ 0486-230 250; a.van hauwere@belgacom.net; Begijnhof 26; week/weekend d €78/85) Guests get a whole homey floor within an archetypal *begijnhof* cottage-house sporting heavy beams and lacy bedspreads. It's in a fabulous location, but make sure you check in before 9pm or the *begijnhof* doors will be shut.

ourpick Hotel Messeyne (☎ 056-212 166; www .messeyne.com; Groeningestraat 17; s/d €120/135; 🖳 📶) In one of Kortrijk's grander historic townhouses (1662), beamed high ceilings and original fireplaces meld beautifully with stylishly contemporary decor. Rooms are immaculate and designer corridors imaginatively feature cacti as art. There's a well-regarded restaurant (closed Sundays), free sauna, garden-facing fitness room and a darkly mysterious little bar-lounge.

Eating

A range of tempting *cafés* line Grote Markt with a couple more on Kapucijnenstr near the Broelmuseum.

Café Rouge (☎ 056-258 603; www.caferouge.be; St-Maartenskerkhof 6a; beer/coffee €2/2.20, snacks €7-14, mains €14-24; ⏰ 11am-9pm Tue-Sun) This bistro's French-style shuttered facade contrasts with

a stylish but unintimidating modern interior. The summer terrace fills a tree-lined pedestrianised square between the Begijnhof and St-Maartenskerk. Great for drinks, meals or afternoon pancakes (from €3.50).

Brasserie de Heeren van Groeninghe (☎ 056-254 025; Groeningestraat 36; snacks/pastas/mains from €3.50/10/13; ⏰ 10am-10pm Thu-Mon) At night flickering lanterns lure you through the carriageway to a part brash *café* bistro, part grand old mansion with high ceilings and original gilt decor (in the grand Marthe de Spiegeleir room). The summer terrace leads through to Kortrijk 1302. Boon Kriek (€2.20) on draught. Reservations wise at weekends.

't Mouterijtje (☎ 056-201 414; Kapucijnenstraat 25a; mains €14-24; ⏰ 5pm-midnight Fri-Tue) Spacious, brightly lit family brasserie in an attractively modernised old house.

Cyrano de Bergerac (☎ 056-252 900; www.cyrano debergerac.be; Vaartstraat 14; mains €18-38, menu €39; ⏰ noon-2pm & 6.30-10pm Tue-Sat) This inviting restaurant has a short, ever-changing menu served in an 18th-century cottage-style interior. It's idiosyncratically decorated with bugles, dripped candle wax and a rooster rampant on the feathered central chandelier. Staff is very obliging.

Drinking

Kortrijks Koffiehuis (☎ 056-217 270; Leiestraat 20; coffee €2; ⏰ 10am-6.30pm Mon-Sat) Coffee shop and cafe whose wonderfully aromatic beans are ground daily in the historic de Coene interior.

Bar Oskar (Vlasmarkt 7; beer €1.50; ⏰ 3pm-5am Tue-Sun) Smokily characterful and rough edged, this student-oriented bar plays trancy music and, along with similar neighbouring places, keeps Vlasmarkt's open terraces lively till the early hours.

Staminee den Boulevard (☎ 0474-993 976; www .denboulevard.be; Groeningelaan 15; ⏰ 6pm-3am; ✗)

WESTERN FLANDERS

BATTLE OF THE GOLDEN SPURS

Flanders' French overlords were incensed by the Bruges Matins massacre of May 1302 (see p132). Philip the Fair, the French king, promptly sent a well-equipped cavalry of aristocratic knights to seek retribution. Outside Kortrijk on 11 July this magnificent force met a ragged, lightly armed force of weavers, peasants and guild members from Bruges, Ypres, Ghent and Kortrijk. Expecting little from their lowly foes, the horseback knights failed to notice a cunningly laid trap. The Flemish townsfolk had previously disguised a boggy marsh with brushwood. Snared by the mud, the heavily armoured French were quickly immobilised and slaughtered, their golden spurs hacked off as trophy souvenirs. It was the first time professional knights had ever been defeated by an amateur infantry and the event became a potent symbol of Flemish resistance. At least that's the way it's remembered thanks to Flanders' first great novel, *De Leeuw van Vlaanderen* (The Lion of Flanders), and to this day 11 July is celebrated as Flanders' 'national' holiday.

Flickering candles and crooning soft jazz create a delightfully cosy atmosphere in this characterful *café* serving draught Chimay (€3.20) among 120 beers. Light snacks available.

Getting There & Around

Trains depart Kortrijk at least hourly for Oudenaarde (€3.90, 20 minutes), Ghent (€6.30, 20 minutes), Ypres (Ieper, €4.80, 30 minutes), Bruges (Brugge, €7, 50 minutes), Brussels (€11.70, one hour) and Lille, France (32 minutes). Change in Mouscron (Moeskroen) for Tournai (Doornik, €4.80, 32 minutes) or in Lichtervelde for Diksmuide (€6.60, 41 minutes) and Veurne (€8.60, 52 minutes).

The tourist office rents bicycles (half-/full day €6/9.50) to be returned before closing. For longer-term rentals there's **Mobiel** (☎ 056-249 910; www.mobiel.be; Bloemistenstraat 2b; city bike hire half-/full day €7/9; ☼ 8.30am-noon & 1.30-6.30pm Mon-Fri, 10am-noon & 1.30-6pm Sat). ID required.

OUDENAARDE
pop 28,000

The little Flemish city of Oudenaarde (Audenarde in French) grew wealthy in the mid-16th century when local weavers switched to tapestry-making. Enormous Oudenaarde wall tapestries, filled with exquisite detail and luminous scenes of nature, nobility or religion, were in great demand by French and Spanish royalty. But by the end of the 18th century wars had caused serious trouble and the tapestry industry all but disappeared.

Oudenaarde's impressive market square is dominated by a gorgeous 1536 **stadhuis** (town hall; Grote Markt), with a crown-topped central belfry-spire. The attached **tourist office** (☎ 055-317 251; www.oudenaarde.be; ☼ 9am-5.30pm Mon-Fri, 10am-5.30pm Sat & Sun Apr-Oct, 9.30am-noon & 1.30-4pm Mon-Fri, 2-5pm Sat Nov-Mar) offers 1½ hour **stadhuis tours** (adult/senior €5/4; ☼ 11am & 3pm Tue-Sun, Apr-Oct) visiting the building's sumptuous historic interior, perusing its famous silverware collection and dawdling interminably in a vaulted basement housing a dozen faded but priceless 16th-century Oudenaarde tapestries. Without a guide only the tapestry room (€3) is accessible, also via the tourist office.

Across the square **St-Walburgakerk** (Sint-Walburgastraat; ☼ 2pm-5pm Tue, Thu & Sat Easter-Oct, Tue-Sun Jun-Aug) is an imposing church cobbled together from a 13th-century chancel and a 15th-century Brabantine-Gothic tower with 49-bell **carillon** (☼ concerts 8.30pm Thu Jul-Aug). Inside are numerous paintings and more tapestries.

Across the road, cycling fans share the sensations and emotions of the classic Tour of Flanders bike race at the modern **Centrum Ronde van Vlaanderen** (☎ 055-339 933; www.crvv.be; Markt 43; adult/concession €7/5; ☼ 10am-6pm Tue-Sun, last entry 5pm).

Walk southeast past the quaint 1499 **Begijnhof** (Achterburg; admission free; ☼ 7am-7pm, to 9pm Jun-Sep), cross the river via the **lift-bridge**, then turn right to find the large **OLV van Pamele** church and remnants of the **Zwartzusterklooster** (Pameleplein), a much-altered 13th-century convent. Or turn left to find the **Huis de Lalaing** (Bourgondiëstraat 9; adult/senior €3/2; ☼ 1.30-5pm Tue-Fri during exhibitions), a rococo-style historic mansion that hosts changing exhibits but is most interesting for the working tapestry design and repair workshops upstairs (included in ticket price).

Three small, decent hotels face off around the Stadhuis. Marginally the most appealing of these is the gently stylish **Hostellerie La Pomme d'Or** (☎ 055-311 900; www.lapommedor.be;

Markt 62; s/d €90/105, mains €10.50-24) where a little decanter of port awaits you in your guest room. Each hotel is above its own appealing brasserie-*café*, but for more refined dining cross the square to **Margaretha's** (☎ 055-210 101; www.margarethas.be; Markt 40; mains €20-28, lunch/dinner menu €25/55, beer/wine/cocktails from €2.80/4.50/8; ⏰ 11.30am-11pm Wed-Mon, kitchen 11.30am-2pm & 6-10pm). This top-notch restaurant, lounge and wine bar has William Morris–style interiors, framed fabrics and a flurry of swords above the medieval fireplace. It occupies a 16th-century house grafted onto what was once a 12th-century fortress tower and was reputedly the childhood home of Charles Quint's illegitimate daughter, Margaret (Margaretha) of Palma, who later became governor of the Spanish Netherlands (1559–1567).

De Carillon (☎ 055-311 409; Markt 49; ⏰ 9am-10pm Tue-Sun) is an endearingly authentic *café* in a stand-alone 17th-century gable-house tacked onto St-Walburgakerk. Local 'abbey' beer Ename Triple is only €2.80 on draught.

Trains from Oudenaarde run twice hourly to Kortrijk (€3.90, 20 minutes), hourly to Ghent St-Pieters (€4, 28 minutes) and Brussels (€8.60, 50 minutes). From the train station turn right then follow Stationstraat and Nederstraat to the Markt, 900m south.

AROUND OUDENAARDE

The hilly area around Oudenaarde is confusingly nicknamed the Flemish Ardennes. If you're driving, the winding route between Oudenaarde and Geraardsbergen is particularly pretty, especially after **Brakel**, where a central roundabout is formed from a surreal stack of rusty bicycles.

Ename

For most Belgians, Ename is associated with an abbey beer brewed by Oudenaarde's **Brouwerij Roman** (www.roman.be), 5km towards Geraardsbergen. Actually Ename itself is now a tiny village 3km northeast of Oudenaarde. But in AD 925 it was one of three main defence posts (with Antwerp and Valenciennes) along the pre-medieval French and Ottonian-German border. Its once vast abbey was demolished following the French Revolution and the field where it stood is now an unfenced **archaeological site** (Lijnwaadmarkt 20) brought to life by a **'TimeScope'** (free; ⏰ 9.30am-4.30pm Apr-Oct) computer interpretation booth. There's also a night-flashing lamp, a piece of installation

art asking visitors in Morse code 'What are you doing here?' Some 600m away beside the millennium-old stone church in Central Ename is the very imaginative museum **PAM Ename** (☎ 055-309 040; www.ename974.org; adult/family €2.50/3.75; ⏰ 9.30am-5pm Tue-Sun) where a 15-minute video and '1000-year feast' talking tableau help explain Ename's unique history.

GERAARDSBERGEN
pop 31,400

Known in French as Grammont, ancient Geraardsbergen has been a 'free city' since 1068 and is famous for having what locals insist is the original **Manneken Pis** (Markt). Find the little pisser beside the stairs leading up to the turreted 1893 town hall. It's on Geraardsbergen's large, sloping main square, which is otherwise mostly undistinguished except for central **St-Bartholomeuskerk** (⏰ 8.30am-6pm Apr-Oct, to 4pm Nov-Mar) with its colourful interior and superb altarpiece. Beside the town hall, the tourist office **De Permanensje** (☎ 054-437 289; www.geraardsbergen.be; Markt; ⏰ 9am-noon & 1.30-4pm, closed some weekends) offers a range of museum-like video introductions to the town's trades and traditions, push-and-sniff buttons to press and a selection of costumes for the Manneken. There are more Manneken costumes across the river in the **Geraardsbergse Musea** (☎ 054-413 783; Kollegestraat 27; adult/child €1.25/0.75; ⏰ 2pm-5pm Tue-Sun Apr-Sep), an old-fashioned 'everything' museum with rooms celebrating matchboxes, cigars, and Geraardsbergen's signature Chantilly black lace.

For cycle-enthusiasts the name Geraardsbergen is inextricably linked with the Muur van Geraardsbergen/Mur de Grammont. One of Belgium's great professional cycling challenges, it's a steep cobbled rise that forms a major highlight of the Tour of Flanders race. The well-signposted Muur leads attractively up from behind the Markt to the **Oudenberg chapel** on a panoramic hilltop.

Just off the main square, eclectic *café* **De Erfzonde** (☎ 054-417 887; Brugstraat 3; ⏰ 8am-6pm Wed-Sun, 8.30am-1pm Mon) has a zany mix of pots and saints and is a great place to sample Geraardsbergen's famous Mattentaart (€1.50), a light, semi-sweet curd-filled pastry.

Trains run hourly to Lessines (€1.70, seven minutes), Ath (€3, 23 minutes), Ghent (€5.50, 50 minutes) and Brussels (€6.60, 80 minutes).

Eastern Flanders

This region's undisputed centre of gravity is dynamic Antwerp, a historic port and diamond-trading city currently basking in a third Golden Age that has made it one of Europe's more unlikely fashion and clubbing centres.

Deeply historic cities on a more manageable scale include increasingly resurgent Mechelen, sweet little Lier and self-confident Leuven, Flanders' leading university town. Lier, Turnhout and lesser-known Diest have arguably Belgium's best *begijnhoven* while offbeat Scherpenheuvel is Catholic Flanders' take on Lourdes. Workaday Hasselt is famed for its *jenever* (Dutch-style gin), Hoegaarden for its white beer and Tienen for its sugar. Between Tienen and appealing Sint-Truiden, tiny Zoutleeuw has a fine town hall and a uniquely splendid church interior. Lovable Tongeren, claiming somewhat questionably to be Belgium's oldest settlement, hosts a famous Sunday antiques market.

As in Western Flanders the historic cores of towns and cities are the main attractions. The countryside lacks dramatic scenery though in the southeastern Haspengouw and Hageland regions you'll find pretty, undulating hillsides greened with orchards and even some vineyards. And as always there are scattered castles to be found lurking in forgotten villages if you look a little closer. Note that for the sake of this guide, 'Eastern Flanders' refers to the eastern half of today's Flanders region, not that of the historic Flanders county. This explains why the province of East Flanders is actually covered in the Western Flanders chapter (see p115).

HIGHLIGHTS

- **Master Class** Rubens (p177) meets avant-garde fashionistas (p177) in Antwerp
- **Gothic Excess** Leuven's ornate stadhuis (p199)
- **Sweet Inspiration** Tienen's Sugar Museum (p205)
- **Cloistered Charm** Lovable *begijnhoven* in Diest (p203), Lier (p192) and Turnhout (p191)
- **Belfry Bonanza** Three towers for the price of one in magical Sint-Truiden (p206)
- **Childhood Nostalgia** The superb toy museum in Mechelen (p195)
- **Wonderful Wit** Hoegaarden's white-beer experience (p205)

- PROVINCES: ANTWERPEN (CAPITAL ANTWERP), LIMBURG (CAPITAL HASSELT), VLAAMS-BRABANT (CAPITAL LEUVEN)
- LANGUAGE: DUTCH

ANTWERP (ANTWERPEN)
pop 455,000

Belgium's second city and biggest port, Antwerp (Antwerpen/Anvers in Dutch/French) is the country's capital of cool, a powerful magnet for mode moguls, club queens, art lovers and diamond dealers. In the mid-16th century it had been one of Europe's most important cities and home to baroque superstar artist Pieter Paul Rubens as you'll be so constantly reminded. Despite many historical disasters thereafter and severe WWII bombings, the city retains an intriguing medieval heart with *café*-filled cobbled lanes, a riverside fortress and a truly impressive cathedral. Today Antwerp's top drawcards are its vibrant fashion and club scenes and the startling visual and cultural contrasts between its close-packed neighbourhoods. This can span vast spectra, from thrilling multicultural melanges to worrying racist backwaters to Hassidic Jewish and gay-friendly quarters, all within a few blocks of each other.

History

A fort was built here during Charlemagne's time (768–814), and was visited by such noted Christian missionaries as St Amand and St Bavo before being destroyed by the Vikings in 836. Antwerp's well-protected port on the wide Scheldt River (Schelde in Dutch, Escaut in French) really came into its own once the Zwin waterway silted up, destroying Bruges' economy and forcing traders to move east. In 1531 the world's first specially built stock exchange opened here and by 1555 Antwerp had become one of Europe's main trading, cultural and intellectual centres, with a population of around 100,000.

But prosperity was ruthlessly cut short when Protestants smashed the city's cathedral in 1566 (a period known as the 'Iconoclastic Fury'). Fanatically Catholic Spanish ruler Philip II sent troops to restore order but 10 years later the unpaid garrison mutinied, themselves ransacking the city and massacring 8000 people (the 'Spanish fury'). After further battles and sieges Antwerp was finally incorporated into the Spanish Netherlands and force-fed Catholicism. Thousands of skilled workers (notably Protestants, Jews and foreigners) headed north to the relative safety of the United Provinces (today's Netherlands).

By 1589 Antwerp's population had more than halved to 42,000. Prosperity passed progressively to Amsterdam, although Antwerp revived somewhat after 1609 with the Twelve Years' Truce between the United Provinces and the Spanish Netherlands. No longer cut off from the rest of the world, trade and the arts flourished anew and the city's printing houses became known throughout Europe. The world's first newspaper, *Nieuwe Tydinghen,* had been invented here by Abraham Verhoeven in 1606.

Then the Treaty of Westphalia, which finally concluded the Dutch–Spanish wars in 1648, struck a massive blow by closing the Scheldt to all non-Dutch ships. Without its vital link to the sea Antwerp was ruined. But Napoleon's arrival, in 1797, changed all of that. The French rebuilt the docks, Antwerp got back on its feet and by the latter 19th century it had become the world's third-largest port, after London and New York. In 1920 Antwerp hosted the Olympic Games and in 1928 construction began on Europe's first skyscraper, the 27-storey Torengebouw (see p177).

During WWII Antwerp's port made it an obvious military target and during German occupation of the city around two-thirds of the Jewish population perished. Starting from the 1960s the city saw a steady influx of foreigners (most visibly North Africans) leading over time to a notable anti-immigrant backlash. In an odd contradiction with the city's growing status as a modern fashion capital during the 1990s, the city showed a darker side when a nationalist-racist party won a significant percentage of votes in local elections.

Orientation

Around the magnificent Antwerpen-Centraal train station lies the frenetic, predominantly Jewish and Indian diamond-trading district. The old city centre of Antwerp, based around the Grote Markt, is 1km west along the grand pedestrianised shopping thoroughfare known as Meir (pronounced 'mare'). St-Andries, the fashionista hub, leads south towards Het Zuid ('t Zuid), one of the top nightlife and museum zones. North of the Grote Markt, 't Schipperskwartier (the sailors' quarter) has a seedy, dog-eared feel about it, with a red-light district based around St-Paulusplaats.

EASTERN FLANDERS

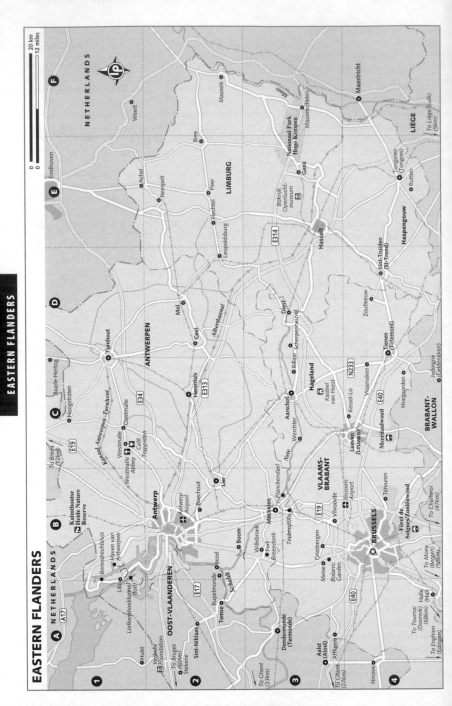

Gentrification is progressing a little further north, where regenerated 19th-century docklands are known as 't Eilandje (Little Island).

Information
BOOKSHOPS
De Slegte (Map pp174-5; ☎ 03-231 66 27; Wapper 5; ⏰ 9.30am-6pm Mon-Sat) Secondhand books.

FNAC (Map pp174-5; ☎ 03-231 20 56; Grand Bazar Mall, Groenplaats; ⏰ 10am-6.30pm Mon-Thu & Sat, 10am-7pm Fri) Events ticketing and a strong travel-guide section.

INTERNET ACCESS
All of the following are on Map pp174-5, have a half-hour minimum usage and also offer long-distance phone calls.

InTouch (St-Jakobsmarkt 90; per hr €1.50; ⏰ 10am-8pm Sun-Fri)

Net@Punt (Annessensstraat 9; per hr €1.50; ⏰ 9am-8pm Mon-Sat)

Phonehouse (de Coninckplein 17; per hr €1.25; ⏰ 10am-8pm Sat-Thu)

LEFT LUGGAGE
Antwerpen-Centraal (small/medium/large per 24hr €3/3.50/4) Lockers at the central train station.

MEDICAL SERVICES
ZNA St-Elisabeth (Map pp174-5; ☎ 03-234 41 11, emergency 03-234 40 50; www.zna.be; Leopoldstraat 26; ⏰ 24hr) Central hospital.

HANDS UP FOR A LEGEND
The name Antwerpen probably derives from a riverside mound (*aanwerp*) where archaeologists found remnants of a Gallo-Roman settlement. But legend offers a marketably colourful alternative starring a giant called Druon Antigoon. A fearsome extortionist, Druon controlled a bend of the Scheldt, forcing passing ship captains to pay a toll. However, the day was saved by Roman warrior Silvius Brabo, who killed the giant, chopped off his hand and chucked it in the river. The place of *hand werpen* (hand throwing) subsequently became Antwerpen. Today *Antwerpse handjes* (Antwerp hands) have become a virtual city trademark that turns up in all manner of guises, from de Koninck beer glasses to chocolates to souvenir trinkets.

MONEY
ATMs (Map pp174-5) KBC Bank (**Eiermarkt**); main post office (**Groenplaats**); post office (**Pelikaanstraat**); Fortis Bank (**Wapper**)

Leo Stevens (Map pp174-5; ☎ 03-232 18 43; De Keyserlei 64; ⏰ 9.30am-4.30pm Mon-Fri) Excellent exchange rates, but handles cash only. Opposite Antwerpen-Centraal station.

TOURIST INFORMATION
Main tourist office (Map pp174-5; ☎ 03-232 01 03; www.visitantwerpen.be; Grote Markt 13; ⏰ 9am-6pm Mon-Sat, 9am-5pm Sun)

Tourist booth (Map pp174-5; Antwerpen-Centraal train station; ⏰ 9am-5.45pm Mon-Sat, 9am-4.45pm Sun)

TRAVEL AGENCIES
Airstop (Map pp174-5; ☎ high toll 070-233 188); Jezusstraat 16)

Connections (Map pp174-5; ☎ high toll 070-23 33 13; Melkmarkt 23)

Sights & Activities
For festivals and events in Antwerp, see p16.

GROTE MARKT
As with every great Flemish city, Antwerp's medieval heart is a classic **Grote Markt** (Market Sq; Map pp174–5). Here the triangular, pedestrianised space features a voluptuous, baroque **Brabo Fountain** depicting Antwerp's hand-throwing toponymic legend (see the boxed text, left). Flanked on two sides by very photogenic **quildhalls**, the square is dominated by an impressive Italo-Flemish Renaissance-style **stadhuis** (town hall), completed in 1565.

There's an unusual chance to explore the city's sewer system through **Het Ruihuis** (Map pp174-5; ☎ 03-232 01 03; www.ruihuis.be; Suikerrui 21; without/with guide €2.50/14.50; ⏰ 9.30am-5.30pm Thu-Tue). Wellington boots are provided but there's no real bag storage so leave any luggage in your hotel. Tours last around three hours.

ONZE LIEVE VROUWEKATHEDRAAL
Belgium's finest Gothic **cathedral** (Map pp174-5; ☎ 03-213 99 51; Handschoenmarkt; adult/concession €5/2; ⏰ 10am-5pm Mon-Fri, 10am-3pm Sat, 10am-4pm Sun) was 169 years in the making (1352–1521). Wherever you wander in Antwerp, its gracious, 123m-high spire has a habit of popping unexpectedly into view and rarely fails to jolt a gasp of awe. The tower is unusually delicate in the way it was crafted, and can be climbed some Wednesdays in summer but only in small groups organised through the tourist

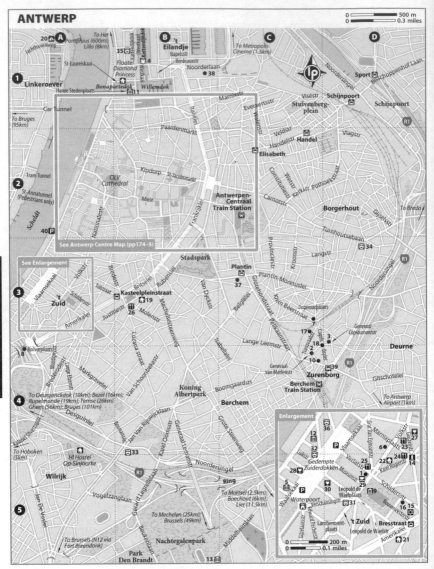

office (book ahead). The cathedral's imposing interior sports later-baroque decorations, including four early Rubens canvases – the celebrated triptych *Descent from the Cross* (1612) is immediately to the right of the central crossing.

The square directly south, **Groenplaats**, was Antwerp's main graveyard until the 18th century. It now hosts a much-photographed 1840 **statue of Rubens** and several popular terrace *cafés*.

FASHION HUNTING

Antwerp is a world leader in the fashion scene (see p42 and p177). Start a visit to the St-Andries 'Fashion District' with **ModeNatie**

SIGHTS & ACTIVITIES		Witte Paleizen	**18** C3	Brasserie den	
Ann Demeulemeester	**1** D5			Artist	**29** D5
De Vier Seizoenen	**2** C4	SLEEPING 🛏️🏠		Den Draak	(see 7)
Euterpia	**3** D3	Bed, Bad & Brood	**19** B3	The Glorious	**30** D5
Flandria Harbour Cruises		Camping De Molen	**20** A1		
(Kaai 14)	**4** B1	Hotel Rubenshof	**21** D5	ENTERTAINMENT 🎭	
FotoMuseum	**5** C5	Mabuhay B&B	(see 7)	Café Hopper	**31** D5
Help U Zelve	**6** D4	Maison Delaneau	**22** D5	Café Local	**32** C5
Het Roze Huis	**7** C3	The Black	(see 21)	deSingel	**33** B4
Hospital	(see 30)			Roma	**34** D3
Justitiepaleis	**8** A4	EATING 🍴		Theatre 't Eilandje	**35** B1
KMSKA	**9** D5	De Biologisch-		Zuiderpershuis	**36** D4
Les Mouettes	**10** C4	Dynamische Bakkerij	**23** D4		
MAS	**11** B1	Lucy Chang's	**24** D5	TRANSPORT	
MHKA	**12** C4	Nero	**25** D5	Avis	**37** C3
Middelheimmuseum	**13** B5	Taverne De Balie	**26** B3	Budget	**38** B1
Neptune Monument	**14** D5			Bus 14 to Airport	**39** D4
Synagogue	**15** D5	DRINKING 🍷🍺		Gedemple	
't Bootje	**16** D5	Atthis	**27** D4	Zuiderdokken	
Twaalf Duivels	**17** C3	Bar Tabac	**28** C5	Free Parking	**40** A2

(Map pp174-5; www.modenatie.com; Nationalestraat 28), a rounded Flatiron-style building. ModeNatie cohosts the Flanders Fashion Institute and a mode museum, **MoMu** (☎ 03-470 27 70; www .momu.be; adult/concession €7/5; ☉ 10am-6pm Tue-Sun), which regularly changing exhibitions. Nearby a similar 19th-century triangular-shaped building hosts Dries Van Noten's Antwerp flagship, **Het Modepaleis** (☎ 03-470 25 10; www.driesvannoten.be; Nationalestraat 16). In an old bank building with a gorgeous stained-glass cupola, **Verso** (Map pp174-5; ☎ 03-226 92 92; http://b2c.verso.be; Lange Gasthuisstraat 11) offers a wide range of designer-ware, cosmetics and accessories, and has a hip *café*. **Walter** (Map pp174-5; ☎ 03-213 26 44; www.waltervan beirendonck.com; St-Antoniusstraat 12) is part shop, part installation art, featuring more designer work from the 'Antwerp Six'.

Stroll on to Lombardenvest, Huidevetterstraat and Schuttershofstraat, a few blocks to the east, but don't miss Kammenstraat for streetwear, retro labels and urban scrawl. Extensive **Fish & Chips** (☎ 03-227 08 24; www. fishandchips.be; Kammenstraat 36-38) is the classic where, accompanied by in-store DJs, shoppers can amuse themselves with a veg juice at the upstairs bar and 'tube-surf' back down. Semi-mythic **Fans** (☎ 03-232 31 72; www.fanssite.be; Kammenstraat 80) nearby has sold punk-ware since the days of the Sex Pistols. More mainstream shops like **Monique Stam** (Map pp174-5; ☎ 03-225 10 76; www.moniquestam.be; Kammenstraat 54; ☉ 10am-6pm) have affordable multibrand collections.

Increasingly, fashion stores are also appearing in 't Zuid, where **Ann Demeulemeester** (Map p172; ☎ 03-216 01 33; www.anndemeulemeester.

be; Verlatstraat 38) has her flagship. In this area **Hospital** (Map p172; ☎ 03-411 89 80; www.hospital -antwerp.com; de Burburestraat 4; ☉ 10am-6.30pm Tue-Sat, 1-6pm Sun) is the latest concept in upmarket fashion retail, a stylishly rebuilt 7m-tall former stable that also displays vintage cars, motorbikes and has an enticing wine-bar/restaurant (The Glorious; p186).

For much more information get the tourist office's *Fashion Walk* booklet (€10), which introduces key designers and contains five self-guided tours. If you want to follow the very latest fashion developments, blog site www.antwerpisthenewparis.com is a good starting point.

MUSEUM PLANTIN-MORETUS

The idea of giving a **museum** (Map pp174-5; ☎ 03-221 14 50; www.museumplantinmoretus.be; Vrijdag Markt 22; adult/youth €6/4; ☉ 10am-5pm Tue-Sun) Unesco World Heritage status might seem odd till you've seen this fabulous place. Once home to the world's first industrial printing works, it has been a museum since 1876. The medieval building and 1622 courtyard garden alone are worth the visit. Highlights include the wonderfully preserved 1640 library, the historic bookshop (room 4), and rooms 11

ANTWERP FOR FREE

Website www.gratisinantwerpen.be lists a daily calendar of free concerts and events. Most major city-run museums are free every day for those under 19 or over 65…and for everyone on the last Wednesday of each month.

EASTERN FLANDERS

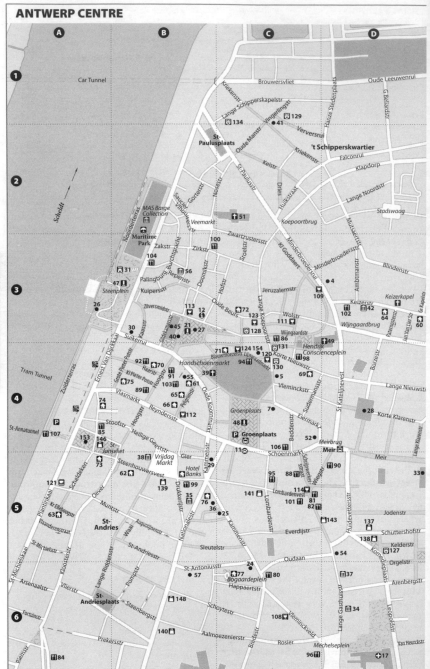

ANTWERP CENTRE

EASTERN FLANDER-
SEASTERN FLANDERS

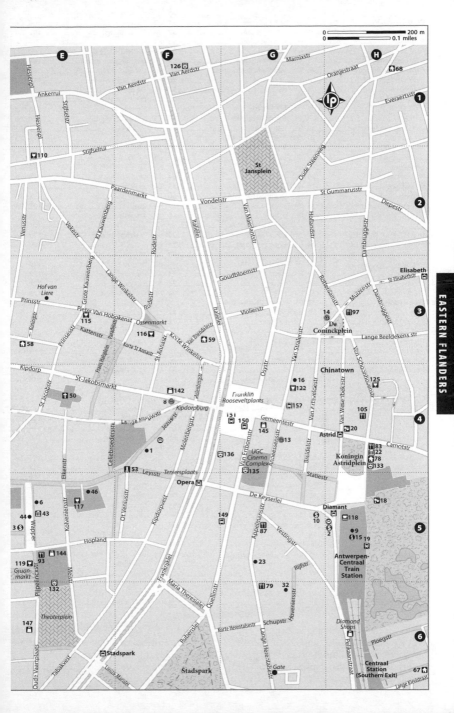

EASTERN FLANDERS

and 21 for their gilt leather 'wallpaper'. Then there's a priceless collection of manuscripts, tapestries and a roomful of ancient printing presses with video explanations of their usage. As in seemingly every major Antwerp museum, the valuable painting collection includes an original Rubens but also, more interestingly, there are examples of books by Rubens' brother that Pieter Paul illustrated and Moretus published.

THE ANTWERP SIX

In the late 1980s, daring, provocative yet wide-ranging shows in London and Paris launched the reputations of half a dozen fashion graduates from Antwerp's Royal Academy (www.antwerp-fashion.be). They've since become known internationally as the 'Antwerp Six'. The group's most commercially prominent figurehead is Dries Van Noten, whose colourful bohemian clothes sell worldwide. Conceptual-artist-cum-designer Walter Van Beirendonck (www.waltervanbeirendonck. com) has created outfits for rock supergroup U2, and merges wild and futuristic clubwear with postmodern ideas about everything from biotechnology to aliens. See his collections at Walter (p173), which also features soft women's wear by Dirk Van Saene.

Now Germany based, Dirk Bikkemberg launched the first fashion-house-designed football boot in 2006 (the €320 kangaroo-leather 'Bix'). In Antwerp find his designs at Verso (p173).

Ann Demeulemeester's timeless designs favour monochromes – often black – while Marina Yee is known for 'reconstructing' garments out of secondhand ware.

True to surrealist expectations the Antwerp six are actually seven. That's if you include 'unofficial' member Martin Margiela, whose very wearable, back-to-school-look fashions are displayed in his whitewashed, unsigned Brussels boutique (p79).

OTHER HISTORIC HOUSES

Several other museum-houses also have priceless art collections. Their medieval styled interiors are also impressive if none quite as stunning as Plantin-Moretus; also, for nonspecialists visiting more than one or two can feel somewhat repetitive.

The lovely 17th-century **Rockoxhuis** (Rockox House; Map pp174-5; ☎ 03-201 92 50; Keizerstraat 10-12; adult/concession €2.50/free; ☺ 10am-5pm Tue-Sun) has another gem of a courtyard garden and displays artworks by Rubens, Jordaens, Van Dyck and Pieter Breughel the Younger.

Restored along original lines, the 1611 **Rubenshuis** (Map pp174-5; ☎ 03-201 15 55; www.rubenshuis.be; Wapper 9-11; adult/youth €6/1; ☺ 10am-5pm Tue-Sun) was built as home and studio by celebrated painter Pieter Paul Rubens (p179). Rescued from ruins in 1937 the building is architecturally indulgent with baroque portico, rear facade and formal garden. The furniture dates from Rubens' era but was not part of the original decor. Ten Rubens canvases are displayed.

A Rubenshuis ticket gets you in free to **Museum Mayer Van den Bergh** (Map pp174-5; ☎ 03-232 42 37; www.museummayervandenbergh.be; Lange Gasthuisstraat 19; adult/concession €4/3; ☺ 10am-5pm Tue-Sun), a simulated 16th-century townhouse actually built in 1904. Its highly prized Van den Bergh art collection includes Breugel's grotesque, Bosch-like *Dulle Griet* (Mad Meg).

Home to a smaller art collection, **Maagdenhuis** (Maidens' House; Map pp174-5; ☎ 03-223 53 20; Lange Gasthuisstraat 33; adult €3; ☺ 10am-5pm Wed-Mon, 1-5pm Sat & Sun) was a 16th- to 17th-century orphanage and child refuge. Notice a few cut playing cards? They were snipped in half when girls were brought to the refuge by impoverished parents unable to feed them: one piece was retained by the parent and the other kept with the child as identification tokens.

HENDRIK CONSCIENCEPLEIN

Rubens turned architect in 1621 to design the facade and tower of the stunning Flemish baroque church **St-Carolus-Borromeuskerk** (Map pp174-5; Hendrik Conscienceplein 6; admission free). A 2009 fire caused considerable damage but the ornate carved confessionals and overwhelmingly huge altarpiece survived. Until restoration is complete you can peek through the door but not enter. The church dominates a pleasant enclosed square honouring celebrated author Hendrik Conscience (1812–83), who revived the notion of writing in Dutch and penned the very influential semihistorical novel *Lion of Flanders* glamorising the 1302 Battle of the Golden Spurs (p166).

MEIR AREA

Completed in 1932, the art deco **Torengebouw** (Map pp174-5; Eiermarkt) was Europe's first skyscraper. Don't imagine the Empire State: its local nickname 'Boerentoren' (Farmers' Tower) mocks the tower's somewhat blunt appearance. Hidden away nearby, the **Handelsbeurs** was the world's first tailor-made stock exchange when built in 1531, but the original burnt down in 1858 and the 1872 replacement is in serious need of repairs.

Antwerp's major pedestrian shopping street, Meir/Leystraat, sports numerous statue-topped

EASTERN FLANDERS

classical and rococo-style buildings, which reach a particular architectural crescendo around the **Van Dyck Statue** (Map pp174–5). Also impressive is the mid-18th-century **Koninklijk Paleis** (Map pp174–5), a palatial building used by Napoleon after 1811 and later by the Belgian royal family. It's currently under renovation.

Do look inside the fabulous **Stadsfeestzaal** (Map pp174–5; www.stadsfeestzaal.com; Kolveniersstraat 7), a shopping mall centred on a magnificent 1908 neoclassical exhibition hall, restored to its full gilt-laden opulence since 2007. For the fully indulgent Stadsfeestzaal experience sit atop a two-storey champagne glass and sip bubbles in the Laurent Perrier Champagne Bar (p186).

THE RIVERFRONT AREA

On a waterside knoll, **Het Steen** (Map pp174–5; Steenplein) is a dinky but photogenic castle from 1200 AD occupying the site of Antwerp's original Gallo-Roman settlement. Outside is a humorous **statue of Lange Wapper**, a tall folkloric 'peeping Tom' figure showing off his codpiece to two diminutive onlookers. The castle's maritime museum has closed (pending an eventual move to MAS, p180) but for now the misnamed **Maritime Park** remains. That's actually a long, open-sided wrought-iron shed displaying a collection of historic barges.

Popular raised riverside promenades were originally built nearby in the early 20th century so that townsfolk could view the exotic cargoes arriving from the Congo. The southern promenade, **Zuiderterras**, leads down to St-Jansvliet, ringed by lively restaurants and an access point for the 572m-long **St-Annatunnel**, a pedestrian link to the undeveloped Linkeroever (Left Bank), worth the stroll for excellent waterfront panoramas once you emerge.

VLEESHUIS

One block inland, layered red-and-white stonework makes the striking 1504 **Vleeshuis** (Butchers' Guildhall; Map pp174–5; ☎ 03-233 64 04; www.museumvleeshuis.be; Vleeshouwersstraat 38-40; adult/concession €5/3; ❧ 10am-5pm Tue-Sun) look like rashers of bacon. Its permanent Klank van de Stad exhibition displays musical instruments specifically related to Antwerp. The idea is interesting but the reality is less impressive than the Brussels equivalent (p82).

STATION QUARTER

With its neo-Gothic façade, vast main hall and splendidly proportioned dome, the extraordinary 1905 **Antwerpen-Centraal train station** (Map pp174–5) was recently rated by *Newsweek* as one of the world's five most beautiful.

The surrounding area is highly multicultural, with a different atmosphere every few blocks. Sleazy peepshows rub shoulders with grand century-old buildings, a two-street Chinatown and the world's main diamond exchanges.

Antwerp Zoo

Splendid animal statues and striking big-cat mosaics welcome visitors to world-famous **Antwerp Zoo** (☎ 03-202 45 40; www.zooantwerpen.be; Koningin Astridplein 26; adult/senior/child €18.50/14.50/13.50; ❧ opens 10am, last entry 3.45-6pm according to season). Although one of the world's oldest zoos (founded 1843), many enclosures in the 10-hectare site are state-of-the-art while older ones are being upgraded. The zoo's breeding program has an international reputation. Save money with a combi-ticket if you're also visiting nearby **Aquatopia** (Map pp174–5; ☎ 03-205 07 40; www.aquatopia.be; Koningin Astridplein 7; adult/senior & child €13.85/9.50; ❧ 10am-6pm, last entry 5pm), a professional and extensive child-friendly aquarium experience. Check out its jolly website for free children's-ticket offers.

The Diamond Quarter

These days 94% of diamonds are worked in India but Antwerp craftspeople still cut most bigger, high-value gem diamonds and an astounding 80% of all the world's uncut diamonds are still traded in Antwerp. With a turnover of €23 billion, diamonds represent around 8% of Belgium's exports by value. The remarkably unassuming **diamond district** (www.awdc.be) lies immediately southwest of the station, with Antwerp's four dour diamond exchanges on Hoveniersstraat and Rijfstraat. These high-security if entirely unexotic pedestrianised streets are also home to Indian banks, specialist transportation companies and the industry's governing body **HRD Antwerp** (Diamond High Council; Map pp174–5; www.hrdantwerp.be; Hoveniersstraat 22). Though now Indian dominated, historically the diamond business was mainly the domain of Orthodox Jews, whose black coats, broad-rimmed hats and distinctive long hair-curls remain an iconic sight around here. Diamond and gold shops on Appelmansstraat, Vestingstraat and Hoveniersstraat aren't glitzy but do often offer retail prices around 30% below high-street jewellers. There are further

PIETER PAUL RUBENS

Even if his signature plump nudes, muscular saints and gigantic ultra-Catholic religious canvases aren't your artistic cup of tea, it's hard to visit Antwerp without stumbling on at least a couple of attractions related to the city's superstar artist, Pieter Paul Rubens (1577–1640). Perhaps the most entertaining is the annual **Rubens Market** (Grote Markt; ☉ 15 Aug) with market stalls staffed by salesfolk in foppish 17th-century costumes. Well, some of them, anyway.

Rubens was born in Siegen, Germany, where his parents had temporarily fled to escape religious turmoil in Antwerp. They returned home a decade later and by the age of 21 Rubens had become a master painter in Antwerp's Guild of St-Lukas. In 1600 he became court painter to the Duke of Mantua and travelled extensively in Italy and Spain, soaking up the rich Renaissance fashions in art and architecture. When his mother died in 1608, Rubens returned to Antwerp, built a city centre house-studio (Rubenshuis, p177) and worked on huge religious canvases and portraits of European royalty. He was joined by contemporaries such as Antoon (Anthony) Van Dyck and Jacob Jordaens; the studio's output was staggering.

In the 1620s Rubens also took on diplomatic missions, including a visit to London, where he was knighted by Charles I.

For his family tomb Rubens painted *Our Lady Surrounded by Saints,* which included portraits of his father, his wives and himself in the role of St George. It's in a small chapel behind the high altar of the aristocratic, partly Gothic **St-Jacobskerk** (Map pp174–5; Lange Nieuwstraat 73; adult/concession €3/2; ☉ 2-5pm Mon-Sat Easter-Oct, 9am-noon Nov-Easter).

Rubens canvases grace many Antwerp museums and churches with key works shown at KMSKA (below), Rockoxhuis (p177) and Onze Lieve Vrouwekathedraal (p171) as well as in Brussels' superb Musées Royaux des Beaux Arts (p82).

Tourist offices sell three different walking-tour booklets (€4) for discovering Antwerp in Rubens' footsteps.

shops on the Antwerpen-Centraal station arcade beside Pelikaanstraat.

Learn all about diamond history, processing and allure at the well explained **Diamantmuseum** (Diamond Museum; Map pp174-5; ☎ 03-202 48 90; Koningin Astridplein 19-23; adult/concession/child €6/4/free; ☉ 10am-5.30pm Tue-Thu), which also has changing jewellery 'treasure shows' and live gem-polishing demonstrations.

You can see similar polishers at work along with a much more cursory (but free) diamond introduction at **Diamondland** (Map pp174-5; ☎ 03-229 29 90; www.diamondland.be; Appelmansstraat 33a; admission free; ☉ 9.30am-5.30pm Mon-Sat year-round, 10am-5pm Sun Apr-Oct), which is essentially a friendly, zero-pressure lure to get visitors into a diamond salesroom.

'T ZUID

KMSKA

Topped with winged charioteer statues, this monumental 1890 **art gallery** (Koninklijk Museum voor Schone Kunsten; Royal Museum of Fine Arts; Map p172; ☎ 03 238 78 09; www.antwerpen.be/cultuur/kmska; Leopold de Waelplaats; adult/concession/child €6/4/free, last Wed of the month free; ☉ 10am-5pm Tue-Sat, 10am-6pm Sun) is a grandiose neoclassical masterpiece. Almost all the Belgian greats are represented, from Van Eyck and Van der Weyden through Matijs, Rubens and Van Dyck, to Ensor, Wouters and Magritte. Three large 1480 Memling works are under restoration as you watch in room T.

As of 2011 the whole museum is due for a massive renovation and may be closed for years.

Other Galleries

Contemporary art fans should check out whether the curious **M HKA** (Museum van Hedendaagse Kunst Antwerpen; Map p172; ☎ 03-238 59 60; www.muhka.be; Leuvenstraat 23) has reopened after its long-term renovation. Another renovated warehouse houses **FotoMuseum** (Map p172; ☎ 03-242 93 00; www.fotomusuem.be; Waalsekaai 47; adult/concession €6/4; ☉ 10am-5pm Tue-Sun), which features imaginative, regularly changing exhibitions. An oddity of the permanent collection is a giant wooden slide-viewing contraption but, overall, it is not as inspiring as Charleroi's equivalent (p222).

Architectural Sights

Zurenborg (p180) has the city's main concentration of art nouveau architecture but

EASTERN FLANDERS

fine examples in 't Zuid include the wonderful metal-framed, picture-fronted **Help U Zelve** (Steiner School; Map p172; Volkstraat 40) and cute **'t Bootje** (Map p172; Schildersstraat) with its little ship-shaped balcony. Around the corner is a strikingly palatial neo-Moorish **synagogue** (Bouwmeesterstraat).

The incredible **Neptune Monument** (Map p172; Marnixplaats) commemorates with heavy chains (a design feature in this city) the closure of the River Schelde, which caused Antwerp such economic harm before 1795.

Antwerp's 21st-century **Justitiepaleis** (law court; Map p172; Bolivarplaats) is a massive, airy construction topped with gleaming titanium 'sails'. Like a spiky cousin to the Bilbao Guggenheim, it's very striking, yet somehow fails to be either memorable or truly beautiful. Trams 8 and 12 terminate on a vast windswept square out the front but there's little to see inside.

'T SCHIPPERSKWARTIER & 'T EILANDJE
Between St-Paulusplaats and Verversrui in the sailors' quarter ('t Schipperskwartier) is Belgium's largest **red-light district** (Map pp174–5). It's a functional, quietly seedy affair servicing itinerant sailors and lacking the touristic patina of its Amsterdam equivalent. Its appropriate name, Oude Manstraat (Old Man St), sets the tone. Just south of here, the 1517 **St-Pauluskerk** (St Paul's Church; Map pp174-5; Veemarkt; admission free; 2-5pm May-Sep) has retained a resplendent baroque interior despite a series of fires.

Further north, 't Eilandje is a flourishing former dockland area where **MAS** (Museum aan de Stroom; Map p172; ☎ 03-206 09 40; www.mas.be) is a lumpy modernist tower whose panorama platform should offer great city views once it opens (circa 2011). Museum exhibits will cover Antwerp's history from its earliest beginnings to recent times along with the collections of the National Maritime and Ethnographic Museums.

ZURENBORG
Handily near Berchem train station, elegant Zurenborg is a largely residential area famed for its rich belle époque, neoclassical and art nouveau house facades mostly built between 1894 and 1914. Roofs and towers are spiked with onion tops or witches' hats, wrought-iron balconies, bay windows, slate tiles, stained glass and mosaic. Many houses were only spared demolition in the 1960s thanks to vocal protests by artists. Tram 11 runs right along Cogels-Osylei, where numbers 50, 55 and 80 are all exquisite art nouveau buildings. The area's focal point is a small roundabout flanked by the **Witte Paleizen** (White Palaces; Map p172); their grand facades are considered to resemble chateaux in France's Loire Valley. Other gems:

De Vier Seizoenen (The Four Seasons; Map p172; cnr Waterloostraat & Generaal Van Merlenstraat) Fine mosaic work.
Euterpia (Map p172; Generaal Capiaumontstraat 2) Greek neoclassical with a door handle resembling an Olympic torch.
Les Mouettes (The Seagulls; Map p172; Waterloostraat 39) More art nouveau swirls.
Twaalf Duivels (Twelve Devils; Map p172; Transvaalstraat 59 & 61) A timber facade gives way to 12 wooden devils who leer at passers-by.

MIDDELHEIM
Middelheimmuseum (Map p172; ☎ 03-828 13 50; www.middelheimmuseum.be; Middelheimlaan 61; admission & parking/audio guide free/€3; opens 10am Tue-Sun year-round, last entry Oct-Mar 4.30pm, Apr & Sep 6.30pm, May 7.30pm, Jun & Jul 8.30pm) is a handsomely landscaped 27-hectare sculpture park containing more than 300 works by sculptors including Rik Wouters, Rodin and Henry Moore. Take bus 17 (direction Wilrijk Universitair Ziekenhuis) 4km south from Antwerpen-Centraal to Beukenlaan, then walk 500m east.

Tours
Diamond Bus (adult/concession/child €11/10/6; hourly departures 10.30am-4.30pm Apr-Oct, 10.30am-3.30pm Sat & Sun Nov-Mar) Six-stop hop-on hop-off double-decker bus with multilingual commentary. Starts from Antwerpen-Centraal train station; buy ticket (valid 24 hours) on board.
Flandria (Map pp174-5; ☎ 03-231 31 00; www.flandria.nu; Steenplein 1; office 9.30am-5.30pm Mon-Fri, ticket kiosk 11am-4.30pm Mon-Fri, 10am-5pm Sat & Sun Jul-Aug) Riverboat excursions on the Scheldt (50 minutes; departing 11.30am, 1pm, 2.30pm & 4pm daily July to August, weekends only September; adult/concession €5/3) depart from Steenplein and afford alternative views of the city skyline. For harbour cruises see p190.
Peerdentram (Map pp174-5; Grote Markt; tour €5; from noon Apr-Oct) Hourly 40-minute tours of the old city in an old-fashioned double-decker coach drawn by two stocky Brabant horses.
Rent A Bike (p189) Can organise various guided cycle tours.
Segwaytour (Map pp174-5; www.belgium-segwaytour.com; Tourist Office, Grote Markt; tour €35; 11am, 2pm & 4pm Jun-Sep) Two-hour, 17-site tour on a stand-up

---

GAY & LESBIAN ANTWERP

Antwerp's vibrant LGTB scene is widely diffused around town, with relevant places usually flying rainbow flags. Tourism Antwerp produces the useful multilingual map-guide *Gay Antwerpen* while Friends Gaymap (www.gaymap.info) is available free from gay/lesbian bookshop-cafe **Boekhandel 't Verschil** (Map pp174–5; ☎ 03-226 08 04; Minderbroedersrui 33; noon–6pm Wed-Sun).

In Zurenborg, **Het Roze Huis** (Map p172; ☎ 03-288 00 84; www.hetrozehuis.be; Draakplaats 1) is an umbrella organisation for LGTB groups and home to the popular bar/venue **Den Draak** (www.dendraak.be; noon–2am Tue-Sun).

The rather stark 't Zuid bar **Atthis** (Map p172; ☎ 03-216 37 37; www.atthis.be; Geuzenstraat 27; 8.30pm–late Fri & Sat) is the meeting place for Belgium's longest-running lesbian group.

In a historic 16th-century warehouse, **Café Hessenhuis** (Map pp174–5; ☎ 03-231 1356; Falconrui 53; 10am–late) is a popular *café* whose cool, modern interior attracts a trendy mixed clientele by day and mostly gay men by night. Stylish *café*-brasserie **Popi Café** (Map pp174–5; ☎ 03-238 15 30; Plantinkaai 12; from noon) hosts a gay/mixed crowd, and appealing Café Confiture (p186) is gay-oriented. A huddle of less wholesome drinking spots give Van Schoonhovenstrat, north of Antwerpen-Centraal station, its nickname **Vaseline St** (Map pp174–5).

On Saturdays Red & Blue (p187) hosts Antwerp's hottest nightclub for gay men: friendly and unthreatening. For a full-on fetish experience, **Boots** (Map pp174–5; ☎ 03-231 34 83; www.the-boots.com; Van Aerdtstraat 22; 10.30pm–late Fri & Sat) has rooms devoted to fulfilling almost every imaginable sexual fantasy. Its detailed dress code (see website) includes compulsory shoes for those otherwise arriving naked!

There are several inexpensive gay lodgings with shared bathrooms. Colourful **Mabuhay B&B** (Map p172; ☎ 0477-62 62 81; www.mabuhay.be; Draakstraat 32; s/d €45/55) is handy for Den Draak. Simple **B&B 2000** (Map pp174–5; ☎ 03-234 12 10; http://guestrooms.happygays.be; Van Boendalestraat 8; s/d €44/59;) occupies a fairly central 1869 townhouse. Exclusively gay **G8 B&B** (Map pp174–5; ☎ 0477-62 62 81; www.g8.be; Trapstraat 20) has a four-bed 'encounter' dorm. Very central Katshuis (below) and Emperor's 48 (p182) are gay-friendly.

---

motorised trolley contraption. No children; maximum passenger weight 113kg; book ahead online.

Sleeping

Antwerp offers a marvellous range of B&Bs. These are extensively listed on www.gastenkamersantwerpen.be, which typically includes availability data. Central chain hotels (not reviewed) include an Ibis, a Radisson and a Hilton with a lovely facade looking somewhere between a Parisian department store and a Budapest station.

BUDGET

The dreary HI hostel Op-Sinjoorke is 3km south of the centre but a new one should open in 2011 with inner garden, rooftop terrace and much better location on Bogaardeplein.

Camping De Molen (Map p172; ☎ 03-219 81 79; Jachthavenweg, Thonetlaan; adult/child/car/tent/caravan €2.50/1/1/1.25/2.50; mid-Mar–Oct) Pleasantly sited campground on the Linkeroever (Left Bank) of the Scheldt River handy for the Sint-Anna 'beach'. Take bus 36 to Gloriantlaan/Huygenstraat.

Den Heksenketel (Map pp174–5; ☎ 03-226 71 64; www.heksenketel.org; Pelgrimstraat 22, dm €17;) Stairways and walls are unashamedly rough in this atmospheric, fabulously central if rather chaotic hostel. Bunk beds are decent in the three mixed-sex bunk-dorms but there are no lockers, and toilets are in somewhat short supply. Sheets and a haphazard DIY breakfast are included. There's no lock-out but when the wonderful little folk-music *café* downstairs is closed (Monday and Tuesday), finding reception staff can be challenging. Towels are €1 each.

Katshuis (Map pp174–5; ☎ 0476-20 69 47; www.katshuis.be; Grote Pieter Potsraat 18 & 19; s/d/tr €30/45/70) This is a pair of quiet, superbly central B&Bs without the breakfast – instead there's help-yourself coffee and a luxuriously late 2pm checkout. Stairs are steep and rooms vary but while none are overly polished, some have microwave, chandeliers and wooden beams and all are excellent value. Check in is from 4pm: phone ahead to arrange arrival time.

Hotel Rubenshof (Map p172; ☎ 03-237 07 89; www.rubenshof.be; Amerikalei 115-117; s/d/tr without bathroom

€33/52/69, with bathroom €55/76/93) Rooms are ropey, worn and approximately clean, with paper-thin pillows. However, prices are modest and the free breakfast is served in a fabulous art nouveau dining room adjoining a partly gilded neorococo salon, once the Antwerp second home of Belgium's cardinals. Take tram 12 to Bresstraat.

Etap Hotel (Map pp174-5; ☎ 03-202 50 20; www.accorhotels.com; Lange Kievitstraat 145; tr €45; 🛜) Missed the last train out? This generic chain hotel is an ideal, inexpensive fallback, with 24-hour reception and an acceptance of credit cards. Breakfast €7 extra.

Hotel Postiljon (Map pp174-5; ☎ 03-231 75 75; www.hotelpostiljon.be; Blauwmoezelstraat 6; s/d with shared toilet from €45/60, with private toilet from €65/75; 🛜) This simple but neat little family hotel right beside the cathedral features partly stained-glass windows and free wi-fi. Breakfast costs €10.

Hotel Scheldezicht (Map pp174-5; ☎ 03-231 66 02; www.hotelscheldezicht.be; St-Jansvliet 2; s/d/tr with shared bathroom from €50/70/90; 🕐 reception 7am-10pm; 🖳) While certainly not luxurious, this sweetly old-fashioned hotel has an atmospheric reception/breakfast room displaying old biscuit tins and B&W photos. Floors are irregular, mattresses slightly saggy and most rooms share toilets, but the decor has been recently spruced up and the location is superb.

MIDRANGE
Bed, Bad & Brood (Map p172; ☎ 03-248 15 39; www.bbantwerp.com; Justitiestraat 43; s/d/f minimum 2 nights €60/70/85; 🕽 🖳) BB&B has squeaky wooden floors, high ceilings, some old-fashioned furniture and a remarkable spaciousness for a B&B in this price range. Get off trams 12 or 24 at the vast Gerechtshof (former courthouse) with its verdigris statues of justice.

Diamonds and Pearls (Map pp174-5; ☎ 03-289 39 95; www.hoteldap.com; Pelgrimstraat 26; d €70-120; 🕽 🛜) Supercentral, this five-room B&B-style 'hotel' is fabulous if you get room 1 (antique furniture, oak-board floor) or 2 (balcony, brick-tile floor). However, rooms 3 and 4 have horribly stain-splattered carpets while 5 is a bizarre three-level annex.

B&B Emperor's 48 (Map pp174-5; ☎ 03-288 73 37; www.emperors48.com; Keizerstraat 48; s/d/apt €60/80/150; 🕽 🖳) Stylish, low-lit B&B in an 1878 townhouse. Walls feature works by respected photographer Bart Michielsen (www.bartmichielsen.net), including several male torsos that stop somewhat short of homoeroti-

cism. Gay-friendly but heterosexual guests are welcome.

Park Inn (Map pp174-5; ☎ 03-202 31 70; www.antwerpen.parkinn.be; Koningin Astridplein; d/business/ste from €83/124/159; 🕽 🛜) Strikes a great balance between fashion and comfort; the sparkling-clean new rooms are suffused with light and come with Nespresso-maker and free wi-fi. Guests get free use of the swimming pool at the plush nearby Radisson. The location is handy for the station and zoo but it's not Antwerp's most salubrious neighbourhood.

Aandekeizer B&B (Map pp174-5; ☎ 03-225 22 96; www.aandekeizer.be; Keizerstraat 62; s/d €110/125; 🕽) This lavish B&B pairs new if classical wallpapers with restored antique furniture and tasteful oriental features with beautifully equipped new bathrooms. For breakfast the delightful Dutch hosts usher you into their remarkable museum-quality private lounge or library.

Hotel Matelote (Map pp174-5; ☎ 03-201 88 00; www.matelote.be; Haarstraat 11; d/ste from €120/190) Full designer fashion brings white-on-white rooms to a 16th-century building in a magnificently central yet peaceful location. Breakfast (€10) is served at exclusive restaurant Gin Fish (p185).

Hotel Rubens (Map p185; ☎ 03-222 48 48; www.hotelrubensantwerp.be; Oude Beurs 29; r from €120; 🕽 🛜) Proud not to follow minimalist designer trends, the reliable 36-room Rubens consciously maintains its classical if somewhat 1980s partly floral decor. Guests are greeted with Chocotoffs and a glass of port or sherry on arrival. 'Atmosphere' rooms glow fanciful colours at turn-down. It's just a stone's throw from the Grote Markt.

The Black (Map p172; ☎ 03-298 42 98; www.hoteltheblack.be; Amerikalei 113; d €125-175; 🕐 check-in 2-7pm Mon-Sat, 2-3pm Sun) Four stylishly appointed, black-and-white rooms are unashamedly sexy, with a claw-foot bath forming a performance stage at the foot of the bed. It's run B&B style so don't expect a hotel-style reception.

Other helpfully central B&Bs:
Big Sleep (Map pp174-5; ☎ 0474 84 95 65; www.intro04.be/thebigsleep; Kromme Elleboogstraat 4; s/d/t €55/80/105) Appealing, well-located, one-room B&B with salon, lounge and wood-decked courtyard.
B&B Le Patio (Map pp174-5; ☎ 03-232 76 61; www.lepatio.be; Pelgrimstraat 8; d/tr €95/120; 🕐 reception 6-7pm, closed Aug; 🕽 🖳) 'English' cottage decor and an old beamed breakfast room.

M0851 (Map pp174–5; ☎ 03-297 60 66; www.m0851 .be; Nationalestraat 19; d €120-130) Design-oriented rooms above a leather fashion-accessory shop.

B&B Siddartha (Map pp174–5; ☎ 03-232 97 44; www. bazarbizar.be; Steenhouwersvest 18; d/tr/f €129/172/226) Two colourful rooms decorated using items from the associated Asian gift shop on the ground floor.

TOP END

Hotel 't Sandt (Map pp174–5; ☎ 03-232 93 90; www.hotel -sandt.be; Zand 17; s/d from €180/200, weekend €150/170; P ✗ ☎) Only the TV screens are flat in this full-facility hotel, which melds three historic buildings into one harmonious whole. Some rooms have period curiosities (beams, pulley wheels etc) and light neocolonial touches. The cheaper 'duplex' rooms have wrought-iron stairs up to bed. Wi-fi per hour/day €5/10; parking €16; breakfast included.

Maison Delaneau (Map p172; ☎ 03-216 27 85; www. maisondelaneau.com; Karel Rogierstraat 20; d €180-500; ✗ ☎) Black floors, all-white decor and modernist slit fireplaces create a design-perfect boutique hotel experience where every room comes with an oversized rainforest shower. The basement is an exclusive 200-sq-metre spa complex. White pebbles turn the garden into a work of art.

ourpick **Hotel Julien** (Map pp174–5; ☎ 03-229 06 00; www.hotel-julien.com; Korte Nieuwstraat 24; r €190-275; ✗ ✗ ▣) Very discreet boutique house-hotel exuding a tastefully understated elegance and subtle modernist style. A reception area that feels like a designer's office leads to a library and unique dining room with faceted ceiling and long, aged wooden table where breakfast (free) is served. Rooms in greys and whites have DVD players and fresh orchids, some with exposed beams or old brick-tile floors.

De Witte Lelie (Map pp174–5; ☎ 03-226 19 66; www. dewittelelie.be; Keizerstraat 16-18; r €245-525; ✗ ✗ ☎) Delightful scents of fresh lilies and ground coffee welcome you into this exclusive house-hotel combining a trio of renovated 16th-century mansions and a central courtyard. The 11 luxurious rooms are predominantly white, some with mouldings and exposed beams. The new owners are gradually introducing brighter colours and semiretro design features with rather mixed results. Breakfast (€25) is taken in a big communal kitchen. Wi-fi and (limited) minibar are free.

Eating

The choice is staggering in all price categories. **Out in Antwerp** (www.outinantwerp.be) has a handy restaurant search function sorted by food type and price range.

QUICK EATS

Exki (Map pp174–5), Le Pain Quotidien (Map pp174–5) and Lunch Garden all have central branches; these chains are described on p51.

Danku (Map pp174–5; Koningin Astridplein 11; snacks €1.50-2; 🕙 10am-8pm Mon-Sat) Hip 'eco' fast food where nothing's over €2, not even the freshly squeezed OJ or cheese-pesto quesadillas.

Frituur No 1 (Map pp174–5; Hoogstraat 1) Fine, if pricey, fries (€3) available virtually all night.

Pazzi per la Pizza (Map pp174–5; Keizerstraat 2; wine/ panini/pasta from €2.70/3.40/8; 🕙 8am-6pm Mon-Sat) In a stark interior behind an iron-framed art nouveau facade, precooked, reheated real Italian food is sold by weight to eat in or takeaway. There are student and takeaway discounts, and veggie options.

CHOCOLATES & SWEETS

Sweet tooth? Whether or not you choose to play tourist by buying Antwerp diamond- and hand-shaped choccies, wandering Schrijnwerkersstraat/Korte Gasthuisstraat takes you past numerous top chocolatiers (Map pp174–5) and specialist bakeries, including Goosens, Godiva, Neuhaus, Burie (Map pp174–5; famed for intricate marzipan and chocolate sculptures) and Philip's Biscuits (*speculaas* specialist). Pensioner-friendly tea-room cafe **Désiré de Lille** (www.desire delille.be; Schrijnwerkersstraat 14-18; 🕙 9am-8pm) is far from hip but it's widely reputed for its waffles (century-old recipe; €3.50), pancakes (€2.50) and beignets (fried dough-balls; €4.90).

Del Rey (Map pp174–5; www.delrey.be; Appelmansstraat 5-9; per kg €58; 🕙 9am-6.30pm Mon-Sat Sep-Jul) *Degustation* salon of a top-rate confectioner where coffee (€4.15) comes with a praline and a biscuit.

RESTAURANTS
City Centre

Tempting options line Pelgrimstraat, Grote Pieter Potstraat, Oud Koormarkt and Hoogstraat, with a few more hidden in the medieval alleys in between. There's more around the cathedral, down Korte Nieuwstraat and the cobbled lanes around Hendrik Conscienceplein. Suikerrui is the street for mussels.

Eetcafé 't Goe Leven (Map pp174–5; ☎ 03-231 18 11; Hoogstraat 34; tapas/paella/pasta €5/5/8; 🕙 11am-11pm

HORTA ON THE MOVE

Of all the buildings created in the short flowering of art nouveau, the 1899 Maison du Peuple by maestro architect Victor Horta (p89) was among the most celebrated. A daring glass-vaulted structure full of Horta trademarks, it was designed as an entertainment venue for the masses and built not in Antwerp but on Place Vandervelde in Brussels. Sadly, like so many buildings of its genre, it was eventually abandoned and in 1965, despite an international outcry, was dismantled and replaced by a bland 26-storey tower. The original plans to reassemble the Maison du Peuple elsewhere were quietly shelved.

Over 20 years passed, during which many sections simply rusted away in a field. Fortunately some other fragments had been more carefully warehoused. These eventually featured in a 1988 Ghent exhibition and a competition was launched to find the best way to incorporate them into a new building. The result, finally opened in 2000, was Antwerp's **Grand Café Horta** (Map pp174-5; ☎ 03-203 56 60; www.grandcafehorta.be; Hopland 2; snacks €10-14, mains €14-28, 3-course beer menu €35; ⏱ from 9am, kitchen 11am-10pm Sun-Thu, 11am-11.30pm Fri & Sat).

Sun-Fri, 11am-1am Sat, kitchen noon-9pm) Halfway between brown bar and *grand café*, this place has a big chandelier and cosy creeper-shaded rear terrace. Service is charming and fair-priced tapas come in starter-sized portions.

Lombardia (Map pp174-5; www.lombardia.be; Lombardenvest 78; light meals €6.20-17; ⏱ 8am-6pm Mon-Sat) It's peace, love and (organic) food at this health-food shop-*café* with a pun-loving menu of snacks to suit vegans and special diets, and an appealing summer street terrace. Veggie meal-of-the-day is €12.50.

La Cuisine (Map pp174-5; ☎ 03-226 42 71; St-Pieter-&-Paulusstraat 7; mains €7-8.50, 3-course menu €8.50; ⏱ noon-2.30pm & 4-7pm Mon-Sat mid-Sep–mid-Jun) Bargain eatery run by youth learning the trade.

Berlin (Map pp174-5; ☎ 03-227 11 01; Kleine Markt 1-3; mains €10-18; ⏱ 10am-1am; 🖘) Spacious brasserie serving drinks and simple bistro fare. Free wi-fi.

Sombat Thai (Map pp174-5; ☎ 03-226 21 90; Vleeshuisstraat 1; mains €12-17.50; ⏱ 6-11pm Sun-Tue; 🖳) Very refined Thai restaurant in a fantasy Flemish castle-style building with spacious candle-lit interiors, jazz-toned music and high ceilings covered in oriental parasols. MSG-free.

Hungry Henrietta (Map pp174-5; ☎ 03-232 29 28; Lombardenvest 19; mains €14-24; ⏱ noon-2pm & 6-9pm Mon-Fri) Lunch with hip fashion designers in this black-walled, black-tabled little restaurant whose six-item Belgo-French menu changes daily.

Le Zoute Zoen (Map pp174-5; ☎ 03-226 92 20; http://sites.resto.com/lezoutezoen; Zirkstraat 15; mains €14-29; ⏱ closed Sat lunch & Mon) Wax-piled candelabras, teak cabinets full of knick-knacks and items of funky glassware create an inviting, atmospheric ambience. Try bass in saffron,

Antwerp stew in De Koninck beer–sauce or a vegetarian pasta.

Zuiderterras (Map pp174-5; ☎ 03-234 12 75; www.zuiderterras.be; Ernest van Dijckkaai 37; mains €15-27; ⏱ 9am-midnight Mon-Thu, 9am-1am Fri-Sun, kitchen noon-10pm) This modern landmark restaurant epitomises Antwerp's contemporary architectural poise. Enormous plate-glass windows provide superb river views and summer tables fan out along the walkway. It's a superb place to be dazzled by sunset rays over respected contemporary cuisine, but you'll usually need to book ahead.

De Peerdestal (Map pp174-5; ☎ 03-231 95 03; Wijngaardstraat 8; mains €16.50-52; ⏱ 11.30am-3pm & 5-10pm) One of many restaurants in this atmospheric cobblestone quarter, Peerdestal sports glass chandeliers and an almost life-sized two-piece horse sculpture amid the timber beams. Horse appears on the menu too but there's also Madeira-steak, sole, ribs and (predictably pricey) lobster.

Het Vermoeide Model (Map pp174-5; ☎ 03-233 52 61; Lijnwaadmarkt 2; beer €2.25, mains €17-25; ⏱ 4-10pm Tue-Sun) Within this very atmospheric if somewhat touristy medieval house-restaurant the rooms are full of exposed brickwork and there's live piano music on some winter weekends. But the 'secret' surprise is a steep, creaky staircase leading up to a little roof terrace for which reservations are essential in summer. The menu includes steaks, ribs, *waterzooi* (€17.50) and seasonal mussels in calvados.

De Kleine Zavel (Map pp174-5; ☎ 03-231 96 91; www.kleinezavel.be; Stoofstraat 2; mains €23-30; ⏱ noon-2.30pm & 6-11pm Wed-Sun) Bistro-style decor and an informal atmosphere belie this restaurant's high gastronomic standing for fusion cuisine with an accent on fish and

Mediterranean flavours. The €34 lunch menu includes wine.

Sir Anthony Van Dyck (Map pp174-5; ☎ 03-231 61 70; www.siranthonyvandijck.be; Oude Koornmarkt 16; mains €34, 4-course menu €47; ◷ lunch & dinner Mon-Sat) Innovative Flemish cuisine served in a secretive location in the Vlaeykensgang, a tiny, cobbled 16th-century alley. Calm, upmarket decor; booking virtually essential.

Gin Fish (Map pp174-5; ☎ 03-231 32 07; Haarstraat 9; 4-course menu without/with 1/2-bottle wine €65/83; ◷ 6.30pm Tue-Thu, 7pm & 9pm Fri & Sat; ✆) Seeking closer customer contact, celebrated chef Didier Garnich relinquished his Michelin-starred restaurant to set up this unique eatery where most of the guests sit at a dining-shelf around his open kitchen. The fixed-arrival-time meal will be fish-based but beyond that it's all a surprise according to Didier's whims and the market-fresh ingredients on offer. Bookings are essential.

Station Quarter

Cheap dining options abound north of Antwerpen-Centraal station: on slightly dodgy Van Artveldstraat alone you'll find African, Himalayan, Filipino, Thai and Indian *cafés* all within a block.

Kubus Permeke (Map pp174-5; www.casvzw.eu; De Coninckplein 25; beer/sandwiches/mains/menu from €1.70/2.30/8.30/10; ◷ 10am-8.30pm Mon-Fri, 10am-2.30pm Sat & Sun) Architecturally interesting glass cube where a city-run project provides inexpensive food and drinks aimed at low-income families. Anyone can go, though, and presentation and quality are much higher than you might anticipate.

Aahaar (Map pp174-5; ☎ 03-226 00 52; Lange Herentalsestraat 23; buffet €9; ◷ noon-3pm & 6-9.30pm) Unpretentious place for inexpensive, 100% vegan/vegetarian Jain Indian buffets including five mains, two sweets and rice.

't Zuid

De Biologishch-Dynamische Bakkerij (Map p172; Volkstraat 11; coffee/cake from €1.90/2.80; ◷ 8am-6pm Mon-Sat, 10am-6pm Sun) Invitingly rejuvenated olde-worlde bakery-cafe serving scrumptious tart-slices, mostly veggie snacks, and breads made from spelt.

Dansing Chocola (Map pp174-5; ☎ 03-237 19 05; Kloosterstraat 159; coffee/breakfast €1.80/13, mains €10-15; ◷ 10am-1am; kitchen closes 10pm) Order drinks, tajines, pastas or salads to a White Stripes soundtrack in this creeper-fronted *eetcafé*

(pub serving meals) with funky mismatched lamps, tattooed staff, pavement terrace and ceiling-mouldings painted marble-green.

Lucy Chang's (Map p172; ☎ 03-248 95 60; www.lucychang.be/antwerpen; Marnixplaats 16; mains €12-20; ◷ noon-midnight) With aged floorboards, bamboo touches and unthreateningly hip interior design, this is a welcoming 't Zuid address for wok dishes and coconut-based curries. A heated terrace faces Neptune.

Nero (Map p172; ☎ 03-292 65 00; www.bars serienero.be; Leopold de Waelplaats 34; ◷ 7.30am-late Mon-Fri, 8.30am-late Sat & Sun) Vertical striplamp clusters, stacked wine bottles as decor and throbbing beats that grow louder as the evening progresses accompany a street terrace that's as popular for breakfast coffees as for Thai fish or calamari snacks served till midnight.

LATE NIGHT

Taverne De Balie (Map p172; Justitiestraat 67; beer/meals from €1.70/8.50; ◷ 24hr) If hunger strikes at 4am, head for this entirely unremarkable *café*-bar, which serves *pintjes*, lasagne and steaks all night.

K Zeppos (Map pp174-5; Mechelseplein; beer/meals from €1.90/9.50; ◷ 11am-2am, kitchen till midnight) Good brasserie food served at a friendly, fashionable *eetcafé* that pays homage to classic children's TV character Kapitein Zeppos It's the most appealing (if earliest-closing) on Mechelseplein, a square that's famed for its late-night bars.

SELF-CATERING

Spar (Map pp174-5; Van Schoonhovenstraat 21; ◷ 8am-7pm Tue-Fri, 9am-6pm Sat & Sun) Supermarket in a wrought-iron former market hall.

Super GB (Map pp174-5; Groenplaats; ◷ 8.30am-8pm Mon-Sat) Supermarket in the basement of the Grand Bazar shopping centre.

Drinking

Excellent terrace *cafés* are scattered liberally, especially around the cathedral area and KMSKA. If you still want a drink after 3am try Bar Tabac (p186), Kassa 4 (p186) or head for Mechelseplein. To sound like a local order a *bolleke* (literally 'little bowl') and receive a glass of De Koninck, Antwerp's favourite brown ale. If you're dehydrated head for the old-fashioned handle-turned **drinking fountain** (Map pp174-5; Korte Gasthuisstraat; free).

See p181 for lesbian- and gay-preferred drinking spots.

CITY CENTRE

The choice is utterly astonishing.

Oud Arsenaal (Map pp174-5; ☎ 03-232 97 54; Pijpelincxstraat 4; draught lager/Westmalle €1.60/2.50; ☾ 9am-10pm Mon & Wed-Fri, 9am-7.30pm Sat & Sun) Congenially old-fashioned *bruin café* attracting grizzled elderly locals with exceptionally reasonable beer prices, brew-of-the-month and guest ales.

De Vagant (Map pp174-5; ☎ 03-233 15 38; www. devagant.be; Reyndersstraat 21; ☾ noon-late) More than 200 *jenever* (€2.20 to €7.50) are served in this bare-boards local *café* or sold by the bottle across the road from its *slijterij* (bottle-shop), which resembles an old-style pharmacy.

't Elfde Gebod (The 11th Commandment; Map pp174-5; Torfbrug 10; beers €2.20-5.20, snacks €5-10.50; ☾ noon-midnight) This ivy-clad medieval masterpiece has an astounding interior decked with angels, saints, pulpits and several deliciously sacrilegious visual jokes. Good if pricey sandwiches (€8.50), and St-Bernardus triple on draught (€3.80).

Bierhuis Kulminator (Map pp174-5; ☎ 03-232 45 38; Vleminckveld 32; ☾ 8pm-midnight Mon, 11am-midnight Tue-Fri, 5pm-late Sat) Classic beer-pub boasting 700 mostly Belgian brews, including notably rare 'vintage' bottles laid down to mature for several years like fine wine.

Café Confituur (Map pp174-5; www.cafeconfituur.be; Minderbroedersrui 38; coffee/snacks/pastas/dinner-salads from €2/5.50/9.50/12; ☾ 11am-midnight Wed-Sun, kitchen 11am-9pm) Black and scarlet decor on traditional architecture gives this gay-friendly *café* a modern twist. Watch trams rumble by from the terrace.

And there are so many more:

Den Engel (Map pp174-5; Grote Markt 3; ☾ 11am-2am Mon-Sat, noon-1am Sun) Historic guildhall pub with fabulous cathedral views from the terrace.

De Kat (Map pp174-5; Wolstraat 22; beer from €1.80; ☾ noon-late) Unpretentious *bruin café* where you could try Elixir d'Anvers (€3.30), a saccharin-sweet, bright-yellow liqueur made in Antwerp since 1863 and reputed to aid digestion – Louis Pasteur awarded it a diploma in 1887.

Highlander (Map pp174-5; www.cafehighlander.com; Pieter Van Hobokenstraat 2; ☾ 11am-late Tue-Fri, 2pm-late Sat) Tartan curtains and dozens of whiskey bottles add a curious twist to this otherwise typical historic *café*.

Laurent Perrier Champagne Bar (Map pp174-5; Stadsfeestzaal; champagne per glass €11; ☾ 10am-7.30pm) Kitschy indulgence sipping bubbles in and from a champagne glass within the incredibly ornate Stadsfeestzaal (p178) Two-for-one happy-hour 4pm to 6pm weekdays.

Pelikaan (Map pp174-5; Melkmarkt 14; ☾ 11am-late) Lively smoky brown *café*.

Something Els (Map pp174-5; ☎ 03-231 26 14; Oude Beurs 58; ☾ 1-8pm Tue-Sat) Workshop for drinks and leather… Unusual but nothing kinky!

STATION QUARTER

Le Royal Café (Map pp174-5; Antwerpen-Centraal station; coffees/beers/sandwiches from €2/2/2.30; ☾ 7am-9pm Mon-Fri, 8am-9pm Sat & Sun) Sumptuous gilt-work, marbled walls and a 15m-high ceiling must make this one of the world's most majestic station buffets. Yet a coffee-and-croissant breakfast costs only €2.50. Toilet €0.40.

Kassa 4 (Map pp174-5; Ossenmarkt; ☾ 10am-6am) Student-oriented *bruin café* with tables spilling onto a pedestrianised square and fierce competition for those 33cl beer glasses, refilled for the same price as a 25cl *pintje*.

Pushkin (Map pp174-5; Van Stralenstraat 16; beers €2; ☾ 4pm-2am Mon-Fri, noon-2am Sat & Sun) Pseudomedieval half-timbered bar run by Russians.

'T ZUID

Take your pick from numerous terraced bar-restaurants on Leopold De Waelplaats or another strip on Waalsekaai.

Bar Tabac (Map p172; www.bartabac.be; Waalsekaai 43; draught beer €1.90-2.40; ☾ 8pm-7am Wed-Sun) Wonderfully unpretentious, low-lit one-room bar that tries hard not to try hard. The decor could be from a 1960s rural French grocery. Cheap beers include wonderful Westmalle Dubbel on draught. If you prefer smoother lounge-style bars there's half a dozen close by.

Brasserie den Artist (Map p172; ☎ 0477-22 50 00; Museumstraat 45; beer/coffee/champagne €2.20/2.20/9, breakfast/snacks/meals from €7.50/8.20/16; ☾ 8.30am-midnight Mon-Sat, 8.30pm-noon Sun) Marble table-tops, teardrop lamps and ornate chandeliers adorn this appealing if slightly overrenovated *grand café*.

The Glorious (Map p172; ☎ 03-237 06 13; www. theglorious.be; De Burburestraat 4a; wine per glass from €5, mains €16-22, menu €35; ☾ 10am-2am Tue-Sat, 1-6pm Sun, kitchen noon-2.30pm & 6-11pm) Reflecting the poutingly stylish fashion boutique that it fronts, this intimate, dark-toned wine-bar/bistro is a place 'to be seen' without entirely breaking the bank.

Entertainment

Extensive, if all in Dutch, **Week Up** (www.weekup. be) is available from tourist offices and many *cafés*. In summer check out www.zva.be.

Tickets for concerts, opera, theatre and dance performances can be bought from FNAC (p171) or **Prospekta** (Map pp174-5; ☎ 03-203 95 86; Grote Markt 13; ⏰ 10am-6pm Tue-Fri, noon-5pm Sat), which shares a guildhall with the tourist office.

CINEMAS

As for anywhere in Belgium, **Cinenews** (www .cinenews.be) tells you what film's playing where and gives detailed cinema location details.

Roma (Map p172; ☎ 03-235 04 90; www.deroma .be; Turnhoutsebaan 286) In the predominantly Moroccan suburb of Borgerhout, this classic 1928 cinema has been meticulously restored by enthusiastic volunteers. Offbeat films screen mostly Monday to Wednesday but there's also folk dancing and a variety of concerts. Trams 10 and 24 stop in front.

LIVE MUSIC

Buster (Map pp174-5; ☎ 03-232 51 53; www.busterpodium .be; Kaasrui 1; ⏰ 8pm-late usually Wed-Sat) Varied program of jazz, blues jams, rock'n'roll and stand-up comedy, often without cover charge. At various other addresses on the same street there's a karaoke room, a piano bar, an R&B *café* and a pub with occasional live Irish music.

De Muze (Map pp174-5; ☎ 03-226 01 26; Melkmarkt 15; beers from €1.80, from €2.30 during concerts; ⏰ 11am-4am) Very appealing triple-level *café* with an Escher-like interior hosting great live jazz from 10pm Monday to Saturday (but not Wednesday or Thursday in summer).

De Rots (Map pp174-5; ☎ 03-234 08 94; www.de-rots .be; Melkmarkt 11; ⏰ 11am-11pm Mon-Thu, 11am-3am Fri & Sat, 2-11pm Sun) Red-walled rock bar with regular metal, thrash and psychobilly concerts.

Café Hopper (Map p172; ☎ 03-248 49 33; www. cafehopper.be; Leopold de Waelstraat 2; ⏰ 10.30am-2am) Popular little *café* with live jazz sessions most Sunday afternoons (4pm, free), Monday evenings (free but drink prices rise €0.50) and some other weeknights (cover charge varies).

NIGHTCLUBS

Antwerp's club scene begins with smooth lounges featuring in-house DJs and ends with high-octane house parties. Track down clubs, one-off parties and festivals using **Noctis** (www.noctis.com), **Partyguide** (www.partyguide. be), **TheClubbing** (www.theclubbing.com) or fliers from Fish & Chips (see p173).

Café d'Anvers (Map pp174-5; www.cafe-d-anvers.com; Verversrui 15; admission €10; ⏰ 11pm-7.30am Thu-Sat) Lurid scarlet interiors reflect the red-light-district setting. On Friday nights in July and August, Free Vibes features new, resident and visiting DJs without cover charge.

Café Local (Map p172; www.cafelocal.be; Waalsekaai 25; members/nonmembers €9/10, beers/shots €2.50/5; ⏰ from 10pm Wed, Thu, Sat & Sun) Deservedly popular nightclub with surprise free snacks handed out randomly and an imaginative Mexican trading-post themed bar-island. On Paradise Saturdays deck chairs and palm fronds appear. Thursday student nights are free, Wednesdays are formal (collared shirts required), and on the first Sunday of each month the music takes a salsa-merengue turn. Several nearby lounges and music bars on Waalsekaai and Luikstraat also crank up the music till the wee hours.

Red & Blue (Map pp174-5; ☎ 03-213 05 55; www. redandblue.be; Lange Schipperskapelstraat 11; beers €2.50; ⏰ 11pm-7am Thu-Sat, 2-11.30pm Sun) Great dance venue with decent sized yet still intimate dance floor plus a small sitting area behind a wall of Absolut Vodka bottles. Thursday's free TGIT (www.thankgoditsthursday.be) is a 'student night', on Fridays a mixed crowd grooves to house music (€10), Saturday sees a celebrated gay night and Sundays feature classic '70s-style disco (€10).

Big out-of-town clubs include **Carré** (www .carre.be), on the N12 in Willebroek, **La Rocca** (www.larocca.be), towards Lier, **Illusion** (www.illu sionxl.be), between Lier and Duffel, **Highstreet** (www.highstreet.be), in Hoogstraaten and **Trix** (www.trixonline.be), a Borgerhout club/concert venue where artists from Snoop Dogg to Uriah Heep played during 2009.

THEATRE, DANCE & OPERA

deSingel (Map p172; ☎ 03-248 28 28; www.desingel.be; Desguinlei 25) Two concert halls offering a highly innovative program of classical music, international theatre and modern dance.

Bourlaschouwburg (Map pp174-5; ☎ 03-224 88 44; www.bourlaschouwburg.be; Komedieplaats 18) Beautiful 1830s theatre with a rounded facade topped by statues of muses, composers and writers.

Theater 't Eilandje (Map p172; ☎ 03-234 34 38; www .koninklijkballetvanvlaanderen.be; Westkaai 16) This grey

1990s venue is the (non-exclusive) home base of the Royal Flanders Ballet.

Vlaamse Opera (Map pp174-5; ☎ 03-202 10 11; www.vlaamseopera.be; Frankrijklei 1) A stunning 1907 opera house with sumptuous marbled interior and a majestic facade that's sadly diminished by the 1960s monstrosity built next to it.

Zuiderpershuis (Map p172; ☎ 03-248 01 00; www.zuiderpershuis.be; Waalsekaai 14; tickets €10-20) This cultural centre lays on an impressive calendar of music, dance, theatre and workshops from mostly non-Western cultures at least thrice weekly. There's a popular attached *café*.

Koningin Elisabethzaal (Map pp174-5; ☎ high toll 0900 260 00; www.elisabethzaal.be; Koningin Astridplein 23-24) Shows range from the Chippendales to Kodo drummers, Diana Kraal to the Flanders' Philharmonic Orchestra (www.defilharmonie.be).

Het Paleis/Stadsschouwburg (Map pp174-5; ☎ 03-202 83 60; www.hetpaleis.be, www.stadsschouwburgantwerpen.be; Theaterplein 1) This twin theatre/show venue occupies an ugly 1980 eyesore commonly nicknamed the Bunker.

Shopping

Pedestrianised Meir is shopper-central but for a more intimate, exclusive experience head to the so-called Quartier Latin, a small cluster of streets either side of Huidevettersstraat, notably Schuttershofstraat and Korte Gasthuisstraat (west of Theaterplein). See p178 for diamonds and gold.

ANTIQUES & BRIC-A-BRAC

Many of Antwerp's renowned antique shops are found on Steenhouwersvest, Schuttershofstraat, Komedieplaats and Leopoldstraat. Operating since the 16th century, **Vrijdag Markt** (Map pp174-5; 6-11am Fri) is the city's oldest 'antique' flea market, selling everything by auction (in fast Dutch). *Brocante* (bric-a-brac) traders have taken over Kloosterstraat and Oever (south of St-Jansvliet) and supply the weekly **Rommelmarkt** (Map pp174-5; St-Jansvliet; 7am-3pm Sun).

COMIC STRIPS

Both of the following stock English-language comics:

Mekanik Strip (Map pp174-5; ☎ 03-234 23 47; www.mekanik-strip.be; St-Jakobsmarkt 73; 10am-6.30pm Mon-Fri, 11am-6pm Sat)

Stripwinkel Beo (☎ 03-233 25 36; www.stripwinkel beo.be; Oude Vaartplaats 16; 10am-6.30pm Tue-Sat, 10am-2pm Sun)

FASHION & ACCESSORIES

See p172 for major boutiques.

Véronique Branquinho (Map pp174-5; ☎ 03-233 66 16; www.veroniquebranquinho.com; Nationalestraat 73) Zen-interior flagship store.

Louis (Map pp174-5; ☎ 03-232 98 72; Lombardenstraat 4) Has newer 'big' name designers like Raf Simons, Bernhard Willhelm and Jurgi Peersons.

Coccodrillo (Map pp174-5; ☎ 03-233 20 93; Schuttershofstraat 9a) No-frills shoe boutique that's an Antwerp institution.

Episode (Map pp174-5; ☎ 03-234 34 14; Steenhouwersvest 34a) Vintage clothes with bottom-line prices.

Labels Inc (Map pp174-5; ☎ 03-232 60 56; Aalmoezenierstraat 4) Cut-price end-of-line designer wear including pieces by Belgium's big names.

Delvaux (Map pp174-5; ☎ 03-232 02 47; Komedieplaats 17) Classical Belgian leather handbags and accessories since 1829.

Nico Taeymans (Map pp174-5; ☎ 03-231 82 18; Korte Gasthuisstraat 23) Noted Antwerp jewellery designer.

Olivier Strelli (Map pp174-5; ☎ 03-231 81 41; Hopland 6) Fashions by Belgium's mad hatter.

Pardaf (Map pp174-5; ☎ 03-232 60 40; Gemeentestraat 8) Huge townhouse full of secondhand clothes.

Getting There & Away

AIR

Four kilometres southeast of the city centre in Deurne, very limited **Antwerp airport** (☎ 03-285 65 00; www.antwerpairport.be) offers **CityJet/VLM** (www.cityjet.com) flights to Manchester and London City, with connections to Jersey.

BUS

Eurolines (Map pp174-5; ☎ 03-233 86 62; www.eurolines.be; Van Stralenstraat 8; 9am-6pm Mon-Fri, 9am-3.30pm Sat) international buses start from near its office. **De Lijn** regional buses use a variety of stops including many around Franklin Rooseveltplaats, notably for the 410 to Turnhout via Westmalle.

CAR RENTAL

Avis (Map p172; ☎ 03-218 94 96; www.avis.be; Plantin-Moretuslei 62)

Budget (Map p172; ☎ 0800 155 55, 03-213 79 60; www.budget.be; Noorderlaan 32)

TRAIN

The gorgeous main train station, **Antwerpen-Centraal** (Map pp174-5; ☎ 03-204 20 40) is an attraction in itself (see p178). In addition to high-speed, prebookable Thalys trains there are also hourly 'regular' services to Amsterdam (from €30.20). Both take around two hours via Schiphol Airport (€27.80, 110 minutes) but a new high-speed service is due to start in 2011.

Domestic services:

Destination	Fare (€)	Duration (min)	Frequency (per hr)
Aarschot	5.90	45	2
Bruges	13.60	70	1
Brussels	6.60	35-49	5
Ghent	13.60	50	2
Hasselt	10.50	65	1
Leuven	6.60	45	2
Liège ('Luik')	15.40	125	1
Lier	2.50	15	2
Mechelen	3.50	15	2
Ostend	16.70	95	1

Many trains also pick up from Antwerpen-Berchem station.

Getting Around
TO/FROM THE AIRPORT
Bus 14 takes 20 minutes to Antwerp from Quellinstraat (two blocks west of Antwerpen-Centraal) and just five minutes from outside Antwerpen-Berchem station.

Taxis cost about €10.

BICYCLE
Antwerp is cycle friendly but double lock your bike as theft is common. Barnacled to the side of the cathedral, **Rent A Bike** (Map pp174-5; ☎ 03-290 49 62; www.antwerpbikes.be; Lijnwaadmarkt 6; ☺ 9am-6pm) rents cycles from €6/8.50 per half-day/24 hours.

CAR & MOTORCYCLE
Accessible 24-hour paid parking is centrally available beneath Groenplaats. For free parking, use the southern end of the riverside quay; enter opposite Fortuinstraat, 800m south of Grote Markt. When it's not used for festivities, there's also free parking in 't Zuid on the Gedempte Zuiderdokken, the huge square between Vlaamsekaai and Waalsekaai.

Often jammed with traffic, the Antwerp 'Ring' is very unforgiving: signs aren't always very clear and if you take the wrong turn it's virtually impossible to find an easy way back to the highway. The name 'ring' is misleading too: a proposed €2.5 billion linking viaduct

that was due to close the loop was rejected by citizens in a 2009 referendum.

PUBLIC TRANSPORT
The same tickets are valid for all buses, trams and *premetro* (underground trams), which operate from about 6am to midnight. *Nachtlijn* (night buses) operate weekends only.

De Lijn's has several **ticket/information kiosks** (☎ 0702 202 00, high-toll; www.delijn.be; ☺ typically 8am-4pm Mon-Fri), notably at *premetro* stations Diamant (below Antwerpen-Centraal station) and slightly northwest at Franklin Rooseveltplaats. These offer free city-transport maps, and tickets prepurchased here cost €1.20 (one-hour single), €5 (*dagpas* – one-day multiticket) or €8 (10-journey *lijnkaart*). You'll pay around 35% more if buying tickets onboard.

Premetro trams 2, 3, 5 and 15 run underground along the main drag from Diamant to Groenplaats and beneath the Scheldt River to Linkeroever. For 't Zuid, tram 8 from Groenplaats and Zuid-bound bus 23 from Franklin Rooseveltplaats stop outside KMSKA.

TAXI
Taxis wait at Groenplaats, outside Antwerpen-Centraal and on Koningin Astridplein but are otherwise relatively hard to find. Call **Antwerp Taxi** (☎ 03 238 38 30; www.antwerp-tax.be; €2.75 plus per km €1.60) well ahead to book a ride. Between 10pm and 6am an extra €2 is added to fares.

AROUND ANTWERP
Antwerp Port
Beautiful it ain't. But its sheer jaw-dropping scale makes driving through **Antwerp Port** (www.portofantwerp.com) an unforgettable experience. The world's fourth-largest port complex (Europe's second after Rotterdam), it's a surreal modern maze of cranes, loading yards, container stacks, docks, pipes, rail lines, warehouses and petrochemical refineries. These stretch to the Dutch border, all neatly spaced amid the remnants of grassy polder fields. When the vast Kanaldok (port extension) was built (1956–66), seven villages were bulldozed to make space. Of most, just an isolated church tower or windmill remains.

The two-street village of **Lillo** (www.lillo krabbevanger.be), population 40, has been preserved within a Scheldt-side former star-fort. In extraordinary contrast to the light-industrial surroundings, Lillo's tiny village square comes quaintly to life with terraced *café*s on sunny Sunday afternoons, when you can also visit Lillo's moving and unexpectedly extensive **Poldermuseum** (☎ 03-569 98 73; www.poldermuseum -lillo.be; Tolhuisstraat 10-16; adult/senior/child €1.50/1/0.50; ⊙ 1-6pm Sun & national holidays, Easter-Sep). Amid seemingly endless old tools and clogs, photos and exhibits show life before the great transformation that created the port. There's even a fully recreated local pub interior.

Flandria Harbour Cruises (Map p172; ☎ 03-231 31 00; www.flandria.nu; Kaai 14) offers short (adult/ concession €10/8; 1½ hours; 11.30am Friday to Sunday, daily July to August) and long (adult/concession €12/10; 2½ hours; 2.30pm Friday to Sunday Easter to November, daily May to September) harbour tours starting from 't Eilandje, north of the city centre, and going as far as Boudewijnsluis/Delwaidedok, respectively. The ticket booth opens half an hour before departure. No prebookings except for groups.

With a car you could stop at **Het Pomphuis** (☎ 03-770 86 25; www.hetpomphuis.be; Siberiastraat; mains €21-25; ⊙ 10am-10.30pm Mon-Sat, noon-10pm Sun), a strikingly monumental restaurant-brasserie-bar in a 1920 pumphouse 3km north of central Antwerp. It's close to the route to Lillo.

Verbeke Foundation

The mind-bending **Verbeke Foundation** (☎ 03-789 22 07; www.verbekefoundation.com; Westakker, Stekene; adult/senior/student/child €8/7/6/free; ⊙ 11am-6pm Thu-Sun) pushes the boundaries of contemporary art with a warehouse-sized exhibition-gallery and an overgrown farmyard dotted with 'sculptures', railway-sleeper constructions, a decomposed horse-corpse and the odd broken car wash. In two installation pieces you, as a 'hotel' guest, become part of the art. On an island in a fishpond, one 'room' **CasAnus** (d incl breakfast €120) is a massively oversized reconstruction of the human rectum by Dutch sculptor Joep Van Lieshout (www.at eliervanlieshout.com). Graciously, the simple small-bedded interior is clean and white with a curtained-off toilet and shower. There's no bathroom anywhere near Kevin Van Braak's **Campingflat II** (per person €15): four tents vertically stacked on a metal scaffold, each with little seating areas.

To find the foundation take the A11 Antwerp–Bruges highway to junction 11, then from the northern exit roundabout

follow 'Hellestraat/Koewacht' signs 600m further west.

Antwerp to Ghent

The main city en route is historic **Sint-Niklaas** (www.sintniklaas.be), where Belgium's largest Grote Markt features a baroque church dedicated (predictably enough) to St Nicholas, whose half-saint, half-Santa statue also adorns the square. By car from Antwerp, a more circuitous route takes you through **Bezel**, whose tall-steepled church is closely ringed by superb *café*-restaurants occupying picturesquely traditional Flemish buildings. A crenellated gateway leads through to parkland where the town's odd castle-mansion stands partly on stone stilts above its river moat.

Nearby, mostly lacklustre **Rupelmonde** (population 3000) is famed as the birthplace of Mercator (aka Gheert Cremer), the famous cartographer whose lopsided map projection convinced generations of schoolkids that Africa was no bigger than Greenland. Mercator's generously bearded green-copper statue stands before Rupelmonde's picturesque baroque church. A block south is an unusual if overrenovated example of a historic **tidal mill** (adult/child €1.25/0.60; ⊙ 1-5pm Tue-Sun Easter-Oct, from 11am some weekends). Mill tickets also let you peruse the four-storey Graventoren, a diminutive brick tower (remnant of the town's former castle) that now houses mannequin scenes depicting events in Mercator's life.

Swinging back to Sint-Niklaas you'll pass through **Temse** (Tamise in French), whose Gemeenthuis (now hosting a tourist office) is a fairy-tale 1905 fantasy of dainty turrets in an otherwise largely unremarkable Scheldt-side town.

Antwerp to Holland

A perfectly good highway links Antwerp to Amsterdam via historic Breda and fascinating Utrecht. Should you prefer to avoid motorways, there are two minor Belgian attractions along the slow route to Breda. Scenery is mostly ho-hum.

WESTMALLE

Numerous beer fans stop at the N12 roadside **Café Trappisten** (☎ 03-312 05 02; www.trappisten.be; Antwerpsesteenweg 487), a modern restaurant-bistro where you can sip Westmalle's famous Trappist beers while glimpsing (through trees and across a field) the discreet **Westmalle**

Abbey (closed to visitors), where it's brewed. Antwerp–Turnhout bus 410 stops outside twice-hourly.

HOOGSTRATEN
pop 18,600

The N14 Malle–Breda road rumbles right past the fabulous **belfry** of Hoogstraten's **St-Katherinakerk** (admission free; ☼ 11am-4pm Tue-Sat Sep-Apr, 11am-5pm Tue-Sat May-Aug). It's an enormous 105m-tall red brick edifice fascinatingly picked out with dots of white-stone detail. Originally dated 1550, it was spitefully dynamited by retreating WWII German troops in 1944, but meticulously rebuilt between 1950 and 1958. Next door the matching 1534 stadhuis is also eye-catching and hosts a helpful **tourist office** (☎ 03-340 19 55; www.hoogstraten.be; ☼ 9am-noon & 1-4pm Mon-Fri, from 10am weekends). Another 250m north lies the modest, Unesco-listed **begijn-hof**, whose peaceful atmosphere is marred by road noise. To find truly delightful rural calm continue another 1.2km north, turn right opposite the bus depot and follow Molenstraat 600m past the **Salmmolen** windmill to **Laermolen** (admission free), a small, thatched 14th-century watermill in an idyllic location. It's still functioning but only grinds four times a month (second and fourth Sunday of each month at 2pm plus the following Tuesday at 7.30pm).

TURNHOUT
pop 40,000

Founded as an 11th-century hunting retreat for the Hertog (Duke) of Brabant, today Turnhout doesn't offer the immediate visual appeal of many other Flemish cities. However, hidden behind big wooden gates at Begijnstraat 61 is one of Belgium's loveliest **begijnhoven** (admission free; ☼ 7am-10pm). Around a long narrow garden set with grotto, church and religious statues, its tiled brick houses sport lanterns and matching shutters and prettily flank a single loop of cobbled street. There's even a sheep-mown lawn area, behind which is the superb **Begijnhof Museum** (☎ 014 42 12 48; Begijnhof 56; adult/concession €2.50/1.50; ☼ 2-5pm Tue-Sat, 11am-5pm Sun). Entering the perfectly preserved kitchen feels like you've walked straight into a Flemish Primitive painting. Turnhout's last *begijn* only died in 2002 and the museum's many treasures are all genuinely local. To get the full, fascinating insight, cross your fingers that that day's (volunteer) guide speaks English. 'Harry' is particularly brilliant.

En route from the Grote Markt catch a framed glimpse of Turnhout's impressive, moated **castle**, now used as the courthouse. The **tourist office** (☎ 014 44 33 39; www.tram41.be; Grote Markt 44; ☼ 9am-4.30pm Mon-Fri, 1-4pm Sat & Sun) sells €5 discount combi-tickets should you wish to visit all of Turnhout's museums. This deal includes the Begijnhof Museum and the intriguing **Speelkaartmuseum** (☎ 014 41 56 21; Duivenstraat 18; adult/concession €2.50/1.50; ☼ 2-5pm Tue-Sat, 11am-5pm Sun), celebrating Turnhout's role as the world's second largest producer of playing cards. It displays a range of antique industrial machines used in card creation, including a vast steam-powered drive wheel.

Sleeping & Eating

Hotel Terminus (☎ 014 41 20 78; Grote Markt 72; s/d/tr from €50/78/114) On the square's southwest corner, the Terminus has creaky uneven floors and tiny bathroom-booths but there's a lift and breakfast's included: fair enough value given the location.

Turnout City Hotel (☎ 014 82 02 02; www.turnhoutcity-hotel.be; Stationsstraat 5; s/d €120/130, weekends €90/100) The best of three options around the train station, this unusual place was professionally converted from a railway depot. Tidy, well-appointed rooms have plug-in internet, kettle and free coffee and wine. Some overlook the rail tracks, others have open terraces at the streetside.

Hostellerie Ter Driezen (☎ 014 41 87 57; www.ter-driezen.be; Heretalsstraat 18; s/d €127/157) This 18th-century former mayor's house has a wonderfully alluring fireside lounge and dining room that both ooze historical warmth. The delicate garden topiary is also impressive, though the bedrooms, while large, aren't quite to the same exacting standards. It's 150m south of Grote Markt, en route to the Speelkaartmuseum.

Beauregart (☎ 014 55 87 95; www.beauregart.be; Grote Markt 46; beer €1.90-3.30, snacks €3.60-9.80, meals €7.50-17; ☼ 10am-midnight) With modern purple chairs, bright blue walls and lugubrious giant lamps, this very hip bar-restaurant and chill out covers all bases but is only one of a truly incredible range of terrace *cafés* on Turnhout's Grote Markt, an architectural mish-mash that faces a gigantic central brick church. For cosier, more upmarket dining follow the medieval alley that tunnels beneath Grote Markt 29. For pitas and internet follow Otterstraat east.

In den Spytighen Duvel (☎ 014 42 35 00; www.spytighenduvel.be; Otterstraat 99; ☼ 2pm-1am) Beer-pub with over 150 choices.

Getting There & Away

The train station is 700m west of Grote Markt along Merodelai. Trains run twice hourly to Lier (€5.50, 35 minutes) and hourly to Antwerp (€7, 50 minutes). Buses pick up near both the station and Grote Markt, with hourly 460 going to Baarle-Hertog (below), 430 to Hoogstraten and 450 to Tilburg in the Netherlands. Bus 410 runs twice hourly to Antwerp (80 minutes) via Westmalle (32 minutes).

LIER

pop 32,800

Another of Flanders' overlooked gem towns, compact Lier is ringed by a circular waterway and the green Vesten, a rampart walkway where the city walls once stood. Archetypal historic facades line the **Grote Markt**, where a tall, elfin-spired 1369 belfry gives character to the refined **stadhuis**. In its basement an obliging **tourist office** (☎ 03-800 05 05; www. toerismelier.be; Grote Markt 57; ☒ 9am-12.30pm & 1.30-5pm, closed weekends Nov-Mar) hands out excellent free maps and suggestions for walks. Don't miss the especially charming **begijnhof**, a Unesco site that's one of Belgium's loveliest and most extensive. Enter via Schapenkoppenplein, Begijnhofstraat or Vesten. Distinctive, if less photogenic, are the brick **almshouses** (Godshuis; Begijnhofstraat 24).

The **Stedelijk Museum** (☎ 03-800 03 96; Florent Van Cauwenberghstraat 14; adult/child €1/0.50; ☒ 10am-noon & 1-5pm Tue-Sun) is a delightful three-room art gallery featuring two Breughels (Pieter the Younger) and several well-chosen locally relevant historic canvases. For an extra €0.50, a combi-ticket includes the **Timmermans-Opsomerhuis** (☎ 03-800 05 55; Netelaan 6; adult/child €1/0.50), featuring works by renowned local artists: notice Isidoor Opsomer's 1900 painting of Jesus in Lier! Upstairs the focus is on writer Felix Timmermans (1886–1947), whose 1916 novel *Pallieter* recast Lier-folk as life-loving Bohemians: they'd previously been dismissively nicknamed *Schapekoppen* (sheep-heads) for their short-sighted medieval decision that the town host a sheepmarket rather than Flanders' first great university.

Lier's most iconic monument is the photogenic **Zimmertoren** (☎ 03-800 03 95; www.zimmer toren.com; Zimmerplein; adult/child €2.50/1.50; ☒ 9am-noon & 1.30-5.30pm Tue-Sun), a partly 14th-century tower incorporating a fanciful 1930 timepiece that's eccentrically overendowed with dials, zodiac signs and a globe, on which Congo remains Belgian. Figures on the south side perform bell-striking duties every hour. Horology specialists might enjoy going inside to see the mechanisms, slow-moving video explanations, and a pavilion displaying a second 1935 astronomical Wonder Clock. With 93 dials, the latter is undoubtedly superclever but not particularly attractive to nonspecialists; the 'world's slowest moving' mechanism isn't exactly dynamic and the audioguide's stentorian commentary can be baffling for those of a less scientific mind.

Stand on the Aragonstraat bridge for a beautiful perspective-framed view of **St-**

A MEDIEVAL BAARLES-UP

Belgium's knack for the surreal takes an astonishing geographical twist at the visually unremarkable town of **Baarle-Hertog** (http://english.baarledigitaal.org). Aficionados of geo-political oddities might notice that this Belgian village (population 2330) is totally surrounded by Dutch territory. On closer inspection the situation is even more complex. On the face of it, Baarle-Hertog and **Baarle-Nassau** (Netherlands) effectively form one intermeshed town. But legally the former consists of 22 miniature Belgian enclaves, within which there are another eight exclaves of the Netherlands. It's the world's messiest border-jigsaw.

All this stems from a bizarre 1198 agreement in which the Duke of Breda (later Nassau) was given the village of Baarle, but did *not* receive the surrounding farmland, which was jealously guarded by the Hertog (ie Duke) of Brabant for its then-valuable agricultural tax revenues.

Today the main fun of a visit is nabbing the southernmost table on the terrace of **Hotel Den Engel** and sipping a drink with one foot either side of the delineated border-line. The hotel is directly north of the Belgian side's oddly spired Sint-Remigiuskerk church and its far-from-thrilling one-room museum of monumental candles.

Bus 460 runs from Turnhout to Baarle hourly. Dutch bus 132 (www.bba.nl) continues Baarle–Tilburg–Breda. By car there's a pleasantly rural (if easily missed) lane from Hoogstraten.

Gummaruskerk (Kardinaal Mercierplein; ☺ 10am-noon & 2-5pm Mon-Sat). This huge stone-buttressed Gothic church commemorates Lier's sainted founder, a nobleman from King Pepin's French court who died here in 775. The church tower was re-capped by an 18th-century rococo cupola after being struck by lightning. Its interior features an ornate stone altar screen and some fine artworks, but its celebrated 16th-century stained-glass windows have been temporarily removed for long-term restoration.

Sleeping

The town centre's two poorly signed hotels are both easy to miss. A third is (controversially) under construction: a historic brick terrace beside Gevangenenpoort is being converted. There's a Best Western out towards Aarschot and the tourist office lists various B&Bs.

Hof van Aragon (☎ 03-491 08 00; www.hofvanaragon .be; Mosdijk 1-6; s/d from €72/87; ☏) The riverside setting, medieval outer walls and elements of original beamwork look initially appealing but in several places stair carpets, wallpaper and lamps need attention, and some mattresses are pretty thin.

Hotel Florent (☎ 03-491 03 10; www.hotelflorent .be; Florent Van Cauwenberghstraat 45; s/d/ste €95/110/150) Built in 2004, the three-storey red brick mansard architecture is forgettable but rooms have modern interiors that nominally conform to Antwerp design book norms.

Eating & Drinking

Bakeries sell *Liers vlaaike*, archetypal fat pastries made with syrup, cinnamon and flour. The town's sharply acidic trademark beer, Caves, is a strong-smelling brown ale that doesn't appeal to everyone's taste.

Grote Markt, Eikelstraat and Zimmerplein are lined with places to eat and drink. Or there are these closer and more-inspired options.

De Oude Komeet (De Comeet; ☎ 03-293 69 07; Florent Van Cauwenberghstraat 16; beers/snacks/mains from €1.90/5.20/9.20; ☺ 11am-late Thu-Mon) Gilt cherubs hold wooden beams, and a contemporary wrought iron chandelier sits above the fireplace. In summer drink or eat in the 'garden', where the rubble of a demolished building has been softened by a creeper and is overlooked by a rotund Confucius.

De Nieuwe Schapestal (☎ 03-489 02 20; www. schapestal.be; Koning Albertstraat 3; mains €14-21; ☺ noon-2pm & 6-10pm Thu-Mon) Bracketed by purple walls

and wire-wool ceiling, tuck into scampi in coconut and red curry, vegetarian couscous or a 12-dish Persian mezze. Across the road is appealing artists' *café* 't Goed Voorbeeld.

De Fortuin (☎ 03-480 29 51; www.defortuin.be; Timmermansplein 7; mains €14.50-45.50, menu €32.50; ☺ 11.30am-10pm) Tourist-oriented and somewhat pricey but you get to sit on an open river barge or within a beautiful historic shuttered barn with original timbers. It specialises in brochettes, with wok dishes also available.

't Hiernumaals (Grote Markt 28; beers from €1.70; ☺ 7pm-late Mon-Fri, 8pm-late Sat) Atmospheric brown bar in the alley that leads to Mister 100 (a famous billiard lounge). It can get rowdy on Saturday nights.

't Kruisken Drankhuis (Kardinaal Mercierplein 3; ☺ noon-late Thu-Tue, 2pm-late Wed) This 1498 house facing St-Gummaruskerk has been a pub since 1839. Eccentric clockmaker Louis Zimmer of Zimmertoren fame used to lubricate his mental flywheels with a daily *jenever* or two here. There's a convivial terrace and the tasty €7.50 spaghettis are generous.

Getting There & Away

Useful buses departing from the northern corner of Grote Markt include the 297 to Antwerp-Rooseveltplaats (45 minutes, every 10 to 20 minutes), 550 to Mechelen's Veemarkt (36 minutes, hourly) and 556 to Mechelen-Nekkerspoel (37 minutes, hourly). From the **train station** (☎ 03-229 55 03), 1km northeast of the Grote Markt, trains run thrice-hourly to Antwerp (€2.50, 20 minutes), and hourly to Diest (€6.30, 30 minutes), Leuven (€6.30, 44 minutes) via Aarschot (€4.20, 25 minutes), and Brussels (€6.30, 40 minutes) via Mechelen (€2.90, 16 minutes).

MECHELEN
pop 77,000

With Belgium's sturdiest cathedral, a superb central square and a scattering of intriguing museums, Mechelen (Malines in French) is one of Flanders' most underrated historic cities. It's true that the uncountable churches and baroque house-fronts are all too often interspersed with banal postwar architecture. And the canals generally lack Bruges' prettiness. But on summer weekends, when Bruges gets packed with tourists, business-oriented Mechelen offers discounted rates in some inspirational accommodation choices.

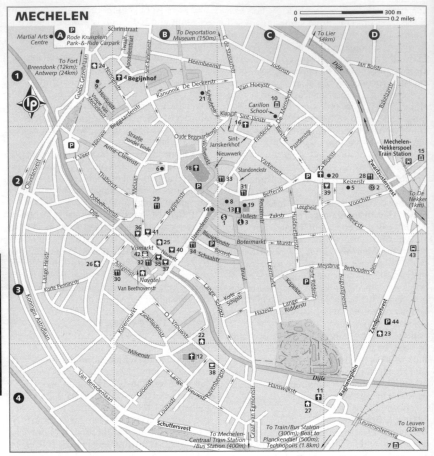

EASTERN FLANDERS

History

Converted to Christianity by 8th-century Irish evangelist St-Rombout, Mechelen became and has remained the country's religious capital. In 1473 Charles the Bold chose Mechelen as the administrative capital of his Burgundian Low Countries, a role maintained after his death by his widow, Margaret of York. Margaret's step-granddaughter Margaret (Margriet) of Austria (1480–1530) later developed Mechelen's court into one of the most glamorous of its day. Science, literature and the arts thrived, and many elaborate buildings were constructed. When Margaret died, in 1530, her ultrapowerful nephew Charles Quint (p27) moved the capital to Brussels. Mechelen's star faded though the city regained the historical spot-light very briefly in May 1835 when continental Europe's first train arrived from Brussels.

Information

Connection Cafe (Keizerstraat 60; internet per hr €1; ☺ 11am-10pm Sat-Thu) Inexpensive internet and phone centre.

UiT In Mechelen (☎ 015 22 00 08; www.tourism mechelen.be; Hallestraat 2; ☺ 9.30am-4.30pm Mon-Fri, 9.30am-3.30pm Sat & Sun Oct-Mar, closes one hr later in summer) This central tourist office gives away simple free maps and sells better ones (€0.50), the Geogids Mechelen city-history guide (€3.75) and the colourful, more practical booklet *Streetwise Mechelen* (€5). The website is brilliantly comprehensive.

Use-It (www.use-it.be) Brilliant free Mechelen guide-map available from the youth hostel or to download.

Sights

GROTE MARKT

A fine array of **baroque house-fronts** lead up IJzerenleen, beyond the **Schepenhuis**, a castle-style fantasy building that became Mechelen's parliament from 1473, and into the splendid **Grote Markt**. At the square's eastern side, the remarkable **stadhuis** started life as the 14th-century Cloth Hall and had its northern flank later rebuilt as a devil-may-care festival of stone flamboyance. Dominating the square and the whole city is the vast **St-Romboutskathedraal** (Grote Markt; admission free; ⏰ 8.30am-6pm). This robust cathedral features a Van Dyck crucifixion on the right as you enter and dozens more fine artworks below the stained glasswork of the apse. But by far the most notable feature is the gigantic, 97m-high **tower** (adult/senior/child €7/5/3.50; ⏰ last entry 4.30pm). You'll need at least 40 minutes return for the strenuous climb (over 500 steps) and double that to see and listen to everything covered by the audio guide. As well as brilliant views from the new rooftop viewing platform (unsheltered, so avoid it in heavy rain), highlights include the human treadmill once used to bring up building materials, plus the impressive 49-bell **carillon**, which rings out across town, most notably in summer's hour-long **Carillon Concerts** (⏰ 8.30pm Mon Jun–mid-Sep). Mechelen also boasts the world's most prestigious school of campanology.

KEIZERSTRAAT

West of Veemarkt (originally Mechelen's animal market) several fine churches face off along Keizerstraat where the municipal theatre, **Stadsschouwburg** (Keizerstraat 3), occupies the stone-fronted former palace of Margaret of York. Margaret was the diplomatically brilliant sister of English King Richard III, whose marriage to Charles the Bold of Burgundy enraged the French. Much respected, she became the de facto dowager ruler of Burgundy's Low Countries from Mechelen. Her step-granddaughter Margaret of Austria didn't like the decor of the place so moved across the road to her own palace in 1506. That's now the city's step-gabled **Courthouse** (admission free; ⏰ 8.30am-12.30pm & 1.30-4pm Mon-Fri) and, despite many subsequent alterations, it maintains a gorgeous courtyard garden where Charles Quint would have played as a boy.

TOY MUSEUM

With 7000 sq metres of toys, games, dolls, teddies and pastimes the wonderful **Speelgoedmuseum** (☎ 015 55 70 75; www.speelgoedmuseum.be; Nekkerstraat 21; adult/child €7/5; ⏰ 10am-5pm Tue-Sun) has lots to keep the kids busy. Meanwhile, adults can peruse the history of toys, walk inside a 'Breugel' painting and get maudlin over the nostalgic range of playthings, from Meccano to Lego, toy soldiers to Airfix kits and working train sets. The museum backs onto Mechelen-Nekkerspoel train station.

CHURCHES

The history of Belgium's religious capital has left Mechelen overloaded with fine **churches** (⏰ mostly 1-5pm Tue-Sun, 1-4pm Tue-Sun Nov-Mar), including the splendidly restored **Begijnhofkerk** with its controversial portrait of God-the-father, the enormous **OLV-over-de-Dijle** with an original Rubens, 1677 **St-Petrus & Pauluskerk** and the under-repair **St-Janskerk**. The dome-crowned **OLV-Hanswijkbasiliek** has an unusual if rather grubby circular interior with superb Paradise Lost pulpit, brilliant 1690 carved

EASTERN FLANDERS

confessionals and an octagonal floor-stone commemorating the pope's 1985 visit. But its main treasure is the Hanswijk Madonna statuette dating from 988 and still the centrepiece of Mechelen's greatest religious pageant (p16).

Several other churches have been imaginatively repurposed, including one as a hotel and another as the **Cultuur Centrum Mechelen** (☎ 015 29 40 00; www.cultuurcentrummechelen.be; Minderbroedersgang 5), one of several city venues for exhibitions and music.

REFUGES
Being the home of Belgium's Catholic primate (archbishop), Mechelen hosted abbots from wealthy monasteries in medieval times who would come to consult him and, thus, required city residences. Known as 'refuges', some such residences became grand affairs, including the beautiful, brick-spired 1484 **Tongerlo Refuge** (Schoutestraat 7). This has been home to **De Wit Royal Manufacturers** (☎ 0475 52 29 05; www.dewit.be; adult/child €6/2; ☽ tour starts 10.30am Sat Jan-Jun & Aug–mid-Dec), tapestry makers and repairers, since 1889. On Saturday mornings it's possible to join a 1½-hour tour to see contemporary tapestry work in action, but the tour might not be in English. Group tours possible by arrangement (€100).

BEGIJNHOF
Unlike many classic versions elsewhere, Mechelen's **begijnhof** (www.groot-begijnhof-meche len.be) is now simply an area of old-city lanes ,but several such streets are flower-strung and charming. The junction of Schrijnstraat and Twaalf-Apostelenstraat is particularly attractive while the pretty Hoviusstraat frames a startlingly discordant view of the old **Het Anker brewery** (see p198; www.hetanker.be), whose brasserie tasting room is currently under renovation.

TOWN MUSEUM
The **Museum Hof van Busleyden** (☎ 015 20 20 04; www.stadmechelen.be; Frederik De Merodestraat 65; admission free; ☽ 10am-5pm Tue-Sun) is Mechelen's municipal museum, full of works by local artists (notably Rik Wouters and Willem Geets) and samples of the city's historic crafts (furniture, lace and gilded leather 'wallpaper'). It's set in the splendid high-Gothic-style mansion that was once home to Hieronymus van Busleyden, a humanist cohort of Erasmus and Thomas More. The

1505 brick building looks especially magnificent from the south courtyard and its tall spire contains a carillon used for practice by the campanologists of the world-renowned Carillon School.

DEPORTATION MUSEUM
The **Joods Museum van Deportatie en Verzet** (Jewish Museum of Deportation & Resistance; ☎ 015 29 06 60; www.cicb.be; Goswin de Stassartstraat 153; admission free; ☽ 10am-5pm Sun-Thu, 10am-1pm Fri) movingly tells the story of Jewish persecution in WWII Belgium while in the brick-vaulted basement there are harrowing photos demonstrating the stark fate of 28 convoys sent to the concentration camps. Only 1400 returned. The museum building itself, once the Dossin Barracks, was used by the Nazis as a deportation centre from 1942.

TRAIN MUSEUM
De Mijlpaal (The Milestone; ☎ 015 41 22 13; Leuvensesteenweg 30; admission €5; ☽ 2-6pm Sat May, Jun & Sep) is a railway museum commemorating Europe's first train ride (5 May 1835) and partly housed in an 1837 loco works. Bus 3 stops nearby.

Tours
V-Zit (www.v-zit.be), in conjunction with the tourist office, organises bicycle rental (€12; book ahead), guided walks and cycle rides plus 45-minute afternoon **boat tours** (adult/child €6/4; ☽ Sat & Sun Apr-Oct, Tue-Sun Jun-Sep) along Mechelen's waterways, departing every hour on the half hour between 1.30pm and 5.30pm from Haverwerf.

Sleeping
HI Hostel De Zandpoort (☎ 015 27 85 39; www .mechelen-hostel.com; Zandpoortvest 70; members dm/s/d €18.80/33/46; ☽ check-in 5-10pm; ⓟ ☒ ▢) Spic-and-span modern youth hostel whose breeze-block walled rooms all have decent private bathrooms. Bring your own towel and padlock for the small safety lockers. Lock-out 11am to 5pm; free parking.

Muske Pitter (☎ 015 43 63 03; www.muskepitter.be; Hanswijkstraat 70; s/d €47/64) Unpretentious rooms attached to a local tavern that's handy for the main train station. Breakfast included, bicycle parking available.

Hotel Carolus (☎ 015 28 71 41; www.hetanker.be; Guido Gezellelaan 49; weekend s/d €74/78, weekday €78/97; ⓟ ☲) Motel-style rooms in a partly creeper-covered house whose main curiosity is a summer terrace overlooking stacked beer-casks in the historic Het Anker brewery.

B&B Dusk till Dawn (☎ 015 41 28 16; www.dusk tilldawn.be; Onze-Lieve-Vrouwestraat 81; d €120-130) An age-old grey handle rings the doorbell at this delightful two-room B&B in an 1870s townhouse once owned by the Lamot brewing barons. Subtle colours and discerning modern decor reign while the bar/smoking room adopts some art nouveau touches. Guests can use the peaceful garden.

Martins' Paterhof (☎ 015 46 46 46; www.martins -hotels.com; Karmelietenstraat 4; d weekend/weekday from €137/187; ❄ ⊛ ⓫) An awesome rose window and religious mosaic usher you into this phenomenal 1867 Franciscan monastery church, totally reworked into a fabulously stylish hotel. All but the cheapest ('cosy') rooms maintain original design elements, from column-tops to stained-glass windows, most dramatically in room 528. The meeting/breakfast room features the renovated altar. Check for internet bargains.

ourpick **Hotel Vé** (☎ 015 20 07 55; www.hotelve.com; Vismarkt 14; s/d from €158/184, weekends & holidays from €84/98) Designed with impeccable contemporary taste, this former fish-smokery building imaginatively uses the former chimney as its stairwell, tar-painted to prevent smells but retaining curious original pulley-wheels and adding artistic creations fashioned from old invoice papers. Even the smallest rooms are spacious and the location is slap bang among the city's most popular *cafés*.

Eating

Mechelen's agricultural specialities include *witloof* (endives) and especially *asperges* (asparagus), prominent on restaurant menus mid-April to late June. For pitas and cheap takeaways look along Befferstraat, east of Grote Markt.

D'Afspraak (☎ 015 33 17 34; Keizerstraat 23; meals €4.20-18.50; ❄ 11am-10pm Wed-Sun) A lamp fashioned from wine bottles and a crate hangs from the high ceiling of this traditional low-key *café*. Great value pub food is served with unexpected aplomb, notably the goat's-cheese *(geitenkaasje)* salad (€11) or the garnished pesto-mozzarella-garlic grilled baguette (€4.70). Delicious.

Toko Karachillio (☎ 0478 45 30 02; www.tokokarachillio. be; IJzerenleen 35; light meals €8-16.50; ❄ 11am-10pm Mon-Sat, 4.30-9pm Sun) Lime green lamps and deliber-

ately paint-chipped tables give an informal yet trendy feel to this chatty *café* serving a range of tapas, wraps, pastas and Flemish standards with a modern twist. Try typically Belgian ham-wrapped endives in cheese sauce for €10. Tearoom menu is from 2pm to 6pm; reservations advised for dinner; lounge bar upstairs.

't Nieuw Werk (☎ 015 34 53 40; www.nieuwwerk. be/UK; Nieuwwerk 11; lunch/dinner mains from €9/13.50, menus €19/38; ❄ noon-3pm Mon-Sat, 6-10pm Thu-Mon) Grills, fish, salads and speciality pastas served at summer tables that spill onto a convivial little 'hidden' square within easy earshot of the cathedral carillon.

De Graspoort (☎ 015 21 97 10; www.graspoort.be; Begijnenstraat 28; mains €12-24; ❄ noon-2pm Tue-Fri, 6-10pm Tue-Sat) Eclectic, 'real fusion' food with Italian, Thai, Japanese and Greek influences, served beneath heavy timber ceilings or at tables that spread beneath a vine-draped outside space at the end of an easily missed alley. Many vegetarian options on request.

Grand Café Lamot (☎ 015 20 95 30; www.grand cafelamot.be; Van Beethovenstraat 8; mains €13.50-20.50; ❄ 9am-10pm) Perched in a contemporary glass cube, the cathedral tower rising above lamp-lit Vismarkt across the river, you nibble anything from teriyaki veggies to €20 mussels. It's above the Lamot Heritage Centre in a repurposed former brewery, whose giant copper brewing vat still remains as incidental decor. Snacks and drinks served on the waterside terrace downstairs.

De Kok & De Proever (☎ 015 34 60 02; Adegemstraat 43; mains €19-25; ❄ lunch Mon-Fri, dinner Mon-Sat) Candle-lit white furniture, maroon linen and timber floors create a romantic interior behind a 17th-century facade. The French-Belgian cuisine includes recipes using sauces made with *speculaas* spice and local beers.

D'Hoogh (☎ 015 21 75 53; www.dhoogh-restaurant. be; Grote Markt 19; mains/menus from €34/55; ❄ noon-2.30pm Wed-Fri, 7-9.30pm Wed-Sat) Dress formally for a highly refined culinary experience in a historic house that radiates upmarket class yet is not as excruciatingly expensive as many Michelin-starred restaurants.

Drinking

The riverside quarter around Vismarkt/ Nauwstraat is a compact but appealing nightlife zone with a *café*-bar for virtually any taste. A favourite for years, **De Gouden Vis** (☎ 015 20 72 06; Nauwstraat 7) has art nouveau features and a refreshing unpretentiousness that

---

BEER & HISTORY

All around town *cafés* serve Het Anker–produced beers (p196), many named with Mechelen's curious history in mind. **Maneblusser**, its sneakily drinkable, well-built 6% blond, literally means 'moon extinguisher'. That's been a self-mocking nickname for Mechelen townsfolk since 1687 when cloud-diffused moonlight above the cathedral tower was mistaken for a cathedral fire.

Pass over the somewhat citrussy **Margriet** (named for the city's feisty 16th-century ruler Margaret of Austria) in favour of a **Gouden Carolus**, commemorating the golden coinage of Charles Quint (p27). Gouden Carolus 'Classic' is a rich 7.5% dark beer. Lesser known variants include 9% Tripel (a sturdy, cellar-aged blond) and 8% Ambrio, a unique brown ale loosely based on a 1433 recipe said to have been Charles' favourite tipple.

Slightly cloudy, with a mildly spiced acidic edge, Gouden Carolus **Hopsinjoor** is a hoppy pun on Op-Sinjoorke, a lewdly cackling folkloric antimascot whose reputation for wife-beating was traditionally punished by tossing him in the air during annual parades. The theft of the original 1647 mannequin was once the cause of aggro between Mechelen and Antwerp but he's now safely retired to room 9 of the Museum Hof van Busleyden (p196). There's a 'flying' **Op-Sinjoorke statue** outside the stadhuis.

---

draws an eclectic crowd. Next door, fluttering brewery fliers and ethereal music greet beer-connoisseurs to **Den Stillen Genieter** (Nauwstraat 9; 🕙 8pm-4am) with its phenomenal list of some 400 brews. **Café Den Akker** (Vismarkt) and less historic **Café Popular** (Vismarkt) have summer seating spilling onto the square, as does **t' Ankertje aan de Dijle** (Vismarkt 20; 🕙 4pm-late Mon-Fri, 11.30am-late Sat & Sun), whose lovely medieval facade hides a slightly contrived 'olde' atmosphere that's an inexpensive showcase for Het Anker's local beers. **Mille** (☎ 015 63 09 63; www.mille-mechelen. be; Nauwstraat 10; 🕙 restaurant 5.30-11pm Wed-Sun, club 10pm-4am Thu-Sat) is more fashion-conscious and turns into a nightclub after hours.

De Zondvloed (☎ 015 64 03 79; www.dezondvloed. be; Onze-Lieve-Vrouwestraat 70; 🕙 10am-6pm Mon-Sat) Good coffee served with Proust's 'most literary of cakes' (a Madeleine) in this delightfully calm, 2nd-floor bookstore coffee shop.

D'Hanekeef (☎ 015 20 78 46; Keizerstraat 8; 🕙 9am-4am Mon-Sat, noon-3am Sun) Retaining its traditional patterned floor tiles and heavy wooden beams, Mechelen's 'oldest pub' is ideal for low-key beery conversations with newspaper-reading locals. The place started life as the chicken-farmers' exchange, hence all the cocks on the recently modernised walls.

Getting There & Around

From the bus station and adjoining Mechelen-Centraal train station it's 1.3km to the Grote Markt (take buses 1 to 5). From Mechelen-Centraal, hourly trains run to Leuven (30 minutes), Turnhout (55 minutes) via Lier (15 minutes) and (for now) to Amsterdam (€33.60,

145 minutes) via Schiphol Airport (€31.20, 129 minutes). Fast/slow trains take 15/28 minutes to Brussels and 17/33 minutes to Antwerp, each running up to thrice hourly. Slow trains also stop in handier Mechelen-Nekkerspoel.

Bus 681 to Brussels Airport, 532 to Aarschot and 560 and 561 to Lier pick up briefly just north of the Zandpoortvest Car Park, which offers cheap (one hour/10 hours €1/2.50) and relatively central parking.

Rent bicycles (€8 per day) from **De Nekker** (☎ 015 55 70 05; www.denekker.be; Nekkerspoel-Borcht 19; 🕙 8am-10pm Mon-Fri, 9am-9.30pm Sat & Sun) – a vast provincial sports/recreation centre and pay-to-enter lake-beach 1km east of Mechelen-Nekkerspoel station.

AROUND MECHELEN
Technopolis

Designed for kids and teenagers but fascinating for those of all ages, Belgium's best **science museum** (☎ 015 34 20 00; www.technopolis.be; adult/senior/child €10.50/9.50/8; 🕙 9.30am-5pm) has dozens of hands-on activities to entertain and engage an enquiring mind. Especially popular are the variety of simulator rides and the set of levers that allow you to lift a full size car. Allow at least two hours. Technopolis is 1.8km south of town at junction 10 (Mechelen-Zuid) of the E19 motorway, ideal if you're driving from Brussels to Antwerp. From Mechelen station take bus 282, every half hour on weekdays.

Fort Breendonk

'HALT! Those who cross this line will be shot' declares a welcoming sign in Gothic German script. Built in 1906 as an outlying defence post for Antwerp, **Breendonk Fort** (☎ 03-886 75 25; www.breendonk.be; Brandstraat 57, Willebroek; adult/senior/child €6/5/5; ☯ 9.30am-5.30pm, last visit 4.30pm) became an infamous Nazi concentration camp in WWII. Its low-slung concrete structure is still eerily surrounded by barbed wire fences and fronted by herringbone guard huts. Visits take you through torture rooms, cells and dark dank corridors accompanied by sixteen videos and a two-hour audioguide relating harrowing personal tales of those who (just) survived. And of those who didn't. Even in summer, this place chills to the bone.

The fort is just off the A12 Antwerp–Brussels highway at junction 7 in Willebroek (12km west of Mechelen). Buses 260 and 460 take 90 minutes from Brussels' Gare du Nord. Willebroek station, a 20-minute walk away, is on the hourly Leuven–Mechelen–St-Niklaas line. Bring an umbrella on wet days.

LEUVEN
pop 89,800

Intimate and lively, Leuven (Louvain in French) is an ancient capital, a prominent brewing centre and Flanders' oldest university town. In term time some 25,000 students give the city an upbeat, creative air. The picturesque central core is small enough that you could easily see the sights in a short day trip, but characterful pubs and good-value dining could keep you here for weeks.

In&Uit Leuven (☎ 016 20 30 20; www.leuven.be/toerisme; Naamsestraat 1; ☯ 10am-5pm Mon-Sat) is the tourist office, located around the side of the stadhuis. **Staatopdekaart** (http://leuven.staatopdekaart.be) has a useful interactive online info-map. **Namaste Communication** (Brusselsestraat; internet per hr €1.50; ☯ 8am-8pm Sun-Fri), opposite Ibis Hotel, offers internet access and discounted telephone calls.

Sights
GROTE MARKT
Far and away Leuven's most iconic sight is the incredible 15th-century **stadhuis** (Grote Markt; ☯ tours at 11am & 3pm Mon-Fri, 3pm Sat & Sun Apr-Sep, 3pm daily Oct Mar). This flamboyant late-Gothic structure is an architectural wedding cake overloaded with terraced turrets, fancy stonework and colourful flags. Added in the mid-19th

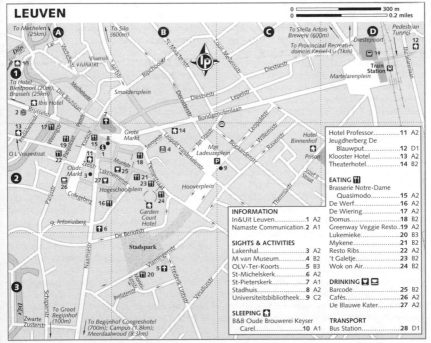

Hotel Professor..............11	A2
Jeugdherberg De	
Blauwput..................12	D1
Klooster Hotel..............13	A2
Theaterhotel................14	B2

EATING 🍴
Brasserie Notre-Dame	
Quasimodo..............15	A2
De Werf.....................16	A2
De Wiering.................17	A2
Domus........................18	A2
Greenway Veggie Resto..19	A2
Lukemieke...................20	B3
Mykene......................21	B2
Resto Ribs..................22	A2
't Galetje...................23	B2
Wok on Air.................24	B2

INFORMATION
In&Uit Leuven................1	A2
Namaste Communication.2	A1

SIGHTS & ACTIVITIES
Lakenhal.......................3	A2
M van Museum..............4	B2
OLV-Ter-Koorts............5	B3
St-Michielskerk..............6	A2
St-Pieterskerk...............7	A1
Stadhuis......................8	A2
Universiteitsbibliotheek....9	C2

DRINKING 🍺
Barcode.....................25	B2
Cafés.........................26	A2
De Blauwe Kater..........27	A2

SLEEPING 🛏
B&B Oude Brouwerij Keyser	
Carel.......................10	A1

TRANSPORT
Bus Station................28	D1

THE KUL

Within a century of being founded in 1425, the Katholieke Universiteit van Leuven (KUL) had become one of Europe's most highly regarded universities. It attracted famous academics and freethinkers, such as the cartographer Mercator (p190), Renaissance scholar Desiderius Erasmus, and the father of anatomy, Andreas Vesalius.

In response to suppression by French and Dutch rulers during the 18th and 19th centuries, the university became a bastion of Flemish Catholicism and these days is still at the heart of Flemish thinking.

The looting and destruction of the university by German troops in August 1914 horrified the world and was a signal that WWI had ushered in an entirely new attitude to war.

Language issues came once more to a head in the late 1960s, when Flemish students protested the absence of lectures in their mother tongue. Violent riots in 1968 eventually forced the French-speaking section to set up a separate Francophone campus in the purpose-built new town of Louvain-la-Neuve (p220), southeast of Brussels. Splitting the library collection took until the 1980s.

---

century, a phenomenal 236 statues smother the exterior, each representing a prominent local scholar, artist or noble from the city's history. Incredibly, the stadhuis survived relatively unscathed during the numerous wars that devastated the rest of town. In WWII a bomb scoured part of the facade but miraculously failed to explode. The interior is less dramatic but does feature a few sculptures by Constantin Meunier (see p89), who once had a workshop on Minderbroedersvest.

Across the square, **St-Pieterskerk** (Grote Markt; ☾ 10am-5pm Mon-Fri, 10am-4.30pm Sat, 2-5pm Sun, closed Mon mid-Oct–mid-Mar) is another late-Gothic structure. Construction started in 1425 but unstable subsoil forced the builders to abandon a planned 170m-high tower, giving the northwest facade a distinctly unfinished look. The interior boasts an elaborately carved stone rood screen, baroque wooden pulpit and a treasury (Schatkamer) featuring two priceless triptychs by Leuven-based Flemish Primitive artist Dirk Bouts (c 1415–75). One of these, Bouts' 1464–67 masterpiece, *Het Laatste Avondmaal,* curiously sets Jesus' last supper in a typical Flemish Gothic dining hall. The panels' lively history has seen them 'lost' several times, including being carted off to Germany during WWII where they saw the war out in a salt mine.

UNIVERSITY BUILDINGS

Dominating Monseigneur Ladeuzeplein is the imposing **Universiteitsbibliotheek** (University Reference Library; http://bib.kuleuven.be; Monseigneur Ladeuzeplein 21), a very grand Flemish Renaissance style palace, above which soars a Scandinavian-style brick tower topped with a three-storey octagonal stone cupola. The library was convincingly rebuilt after WWI with the charity of 400 American universities, having been infamously put to the torch along with much of the city by the German occupation force in August 1914. It was rebuilt once again after WWII.

The university's official headquarters is within the **Lakenhal** (Cloth Trading Hall; Naamsestraat), a large but less than memorable 14th-century stone building with many an empty statue-niche.

OTHER SIGHTS

M van Museum (☎ 016 22 69 09; www.mleuven.be; Leopold Vanderkelenstraat 28; ☾ 10am-6pm Tue & Wed, Fri-Sun, 10am-8pm Thu) is a state-of-the-art six-storey gallery opened in September 2009 to house a priceless collection of mostly 15th- to 18th-century religious art along with contemporary works and high profile exhibitions.

Secured behind large walls, the cobblestone **Groot Begijnhof** is a Unesco World Heritage site south of the city centre. Originally founded in 1232, most of the houses today date from the 17th century, when around 300 Beguines lived here. The restored, somewhat sober houses are now a university residential quarter. **St-Jan de Doperkerk** (☾ 1.30-4.30pm Tue-Sun Apr-Sep), the *begijnhof's* Gothic church, hides an elaborate baroque interior.

Much of Leuven's historic townscape was obliterated in the world wars, but other eye-catching baroque churches survive, including **St-Michelskerk** (Naamsestraat; ☾ 1.30-4.30pm Tue-Sun) and **OLV-Ter-Koorts** (Vlamingenstraat). There's also a sprinkling of 18th-century well-posts to spot.

The famous, highly automated **Stella Artois Brewery** (www.breweryvisits.com; Vuurkruisenlaan; adult/child €6/free; ☺ Tue-Sat, reservation only) can be visited but you'll need to book online through the website. Unless you're in a group choose 'last minute' and find a slot according to the flagged language of any available tour.

Sleeping

As well as places listed there are three lower-midrange hotels facing the train station, a central Ibis and a Novotel in the strongly perfumed area near Stella Artois Brewery. De Werf (p202) has cheap rooms.

Jeugdherberg De Blauwput (☎ 016 63 90 62; www.vjh.be; Martelarenlaan 11a; dm/d €18.80/46; ✖ 🖥 ♿) Modern HI-hostel (nonmembers pay €3 extra) with spunky decor and good vibes. Rooms have ensuite showers and toilets, there's a good bar, courtyard and internet access (per hour €2). Access it via the more northerly of the train station's two main platform tunnels.

Hotel Professor (☎ 016 20 14 14; Naamsestraat 20; s/d €65/80) The eight ensuite guestrooms are slightly musty but considerably better than you'd fear from the access passageway and creaky stairs. Check in at the central but rather mundane cocktail bar downstairs (open till 1am).

Hotel Biestpoort (☎ 016 20 24 92; www.hotelbiestpoort.be; Brusselsestraat 110; d weekend/weekday from €70/85; ☺ reception 3-10pm Mon-Sat) Purple maroon walls in poky rooms with small bathroom booths are hardly impressive but the place is usefully central.

Theaterhotel (☎ 016 22 28 19; www.theaterhotel.be; Bondgenotenlaan 20; d €90-125; ☺ reception 7am-11pm; ✖ 🛜) Opposite Leuven's grand 1866 theatre, pleasant if unremarkable rooms lead off bright red corridors, one of which sports an incongruous hanging canoe. Breakfast (included) is served in a high-ceilinged dining room with old mouldings and modern sculptures.

our pick **B&B Oude Brouwerei Keyser Carel** (☎ 016 22 14 81; www.keysercarel.be; Lei 15; s/d €105/120) The sturdy streetside facade doesn't prepare you for this veritable gallery in a grand mansion whose oldest section dates from 1595. The best of three well-appointed rooms has a four-poster bed, private sauna (extra charge) and views of the extensive family garden, which incorporates a 1940 wartime

bunker and the most extensive surviving remnant of Leuven's 1120 city wall. The delightful owners keep lovable dogs.

Klooster Hotel (☎ 016 21 31 41; www.martins-hotels.com; Onze Lieve Vrouwstraat 22; d cosy/charming/exceptional €245/285/370, internet specials from €99; ✖ 🖥 🛜 ♿) Peaceful, central and suavely atmospheric, this 39-room boutique hotel occupies a partly 16th-century building that had been home to Emperor Charles Quint's secretary and was later a convent. Understated coffee-cream furnishings work well with the antique brickwork, beamwork and simulated fires in pricier rooms. A nearby historic mansion is being converted to create an extra 60-room annex.

Eating

Pedestrianised Parijsstraat and Muntstraat offer a nonchalant mix of eateries and *café*s for all tastes and pockets. There are many options around the stadhuis, €5 pizza-places up Naamsestraat and various oriental options on Tiensestraat. Student customers ensure long hours and decent prices at many places.

Greenway Veggie Resto (☎ 016 30 97 35; www.greenway.be; Parijsstraat 12; mains €5-9.50) Delicious, well-priced vegetarian Thai curries, meat-free pastas and organic veg-burgers will tempt even the most confirmed carnivore to forget flesh in this neat if simple eatery with its calming woodland photo-mural.

Domus (☎ 016 20 14 49; Tiensestraat 8; beer/snacks/mains from €2/3.40/7; ☺ 9am-1am Tue-Sun, kitchen 11.30am-10.30pm) Redolent of a rambling old-English country pub, this appealing, bright and relatively calm brewery-*café* has heavy beams and rough-plastered part-brick walls generously adorned with photos, paintings and assorted knick-knacks. It's great for sandwiches, fair-priced meals or one of its own brews: try Nostra Domus, a gentle but balanced 5.8% amber beer.

Brasserie Notre-Dame Quasimodo (☎ 016 22 37 62; Grote Markt 11; sandwiches/pastas/mains from €2.70/4.60/7.90; ☺ 9.30am-1.30am) You can forgive the disappointing interior given its wide range of inexpensive food that's available all day and much of the night. It has a terrace right beside the stadhuis (partly shaded with a classic piece of wrought-ironwork).

Lukemieke (☎ 016 22 97 05; www.lukemieke.be; Vlamingenstraat 55; mains €8-10; ☺ noon-2pm & 6-8.30pm Mon-Fri) This casual vegetarian eatery with garden terrace is hidden in a residential street facing Stadspark.

De Werf (☎ 016 23 73 14; www.dewerf-leuven. be; Hogeschoolplein 5; snacks €4, mains €9-13; ☺ 9am-midnight Mon-Fri) Road signs, lanterns and creeper-draped frontage add character to this student favourite whose tables spill across the road towards a quiet tree-lined square. It uses kitchen roll for serviettes and pink plastic tumblers for drinks. Guestrooms from €35.

De Wiering (☎ 016 29 15 45; www.dewiering.be; Wieringstraat 2; mains €6-16.50; ☺ 11.30am-late, kitchen noon-11pm) An intriguing display of rusty railings, a moped and a dangling ladle entices one into this multi-levelled cafe-resto decorated with old clocks, accordions, dolls and pipes. Cosy for a drink or 'grandma's Flemish food'.

Resto Ribs (☎ 016 23 62 13; www.resto-ribs.be; Parijsstraat 26; mains €9-19; ☺ noon-11pm Mon-Sat, noon-10pm Sun) Brown paper tablecloths, old enamel signs, hardboard panelling and original floor tiles create the congenial feel of an old-fashioned *café* in rural France. Popular for skewered meats, pastas and afternoon tapas.

Wok on Air (☎ 016 62 47 83; Tiensestraat 62; mains €8.50-12; ☺ noon-3pm Mon-Sat & 6-10.30pm daily) Stylishly simple bright white and lime-green student eatery where you sit at a modern Japanese-style bar to watch the Chinese chef wok-up noodle specials, soups (from €4) or gyoza. No credit cards.

Mykene (☎ 016 23 75 23; www.mykene.be; Muntstraat 44; mains €9-25; ☺ noon-2.30pm & 5.30-10pm) A delightful range of eateries spill tables onto the cosy flag-decked medieval alley called Muntstraat (www.muntstraat.be). Mykene is one of the more intriguing, its decor an odd mix of contemporary art, historic rafters, a wax-dripping candelabra and the stone arches of a former cloister. Tapas and garnished jacket potatoes supplement classic Belgian options.

't Galetje (Tiensestraat 44; per scoop €1.10; ☺ 11am-11pm Apr–mid-Nov) Delicious takeaway ice creams.

Drinking

At night the wall-to-wall *café*-bars on Oude Markt literally hum until the wee hours. Just pick the music and ambience that appeals. Domus and de Wiering (p201) are also good drinking options.

De Blauwe Kater (☎ 016 20 80 90; Hallengang 1; beers €1.90-4.50; ☺ 7pm-2am) This delightful little jazz/blues bar serves around 100 different beers and stages free live performances most Monday nights in term time (October to June).

Barcode (Muntstraat 22; beer/shisha from €1.90/7; ☺ 11am-3am; ☺) Hip, high-ceilinged music lounge-bar whose suspended swing seats are popular for puffing on fruity shisha (hubble-bubble) pipes.

Getting There & Around

Leuven's modern **train station** (☎ 016 21 21 21) is 800m east of the Grote Markt. Trains run four or five times hourly to Brussels (€4.80, fast/slow 24/36 minutes), twice to Mechelen (€4, fast/slow 22/29 minutes), Diest (€4.80, fast/slow 24/32 minutes), Brussels airport (€5.35, 16 minutes) and Liège (€9.90, fast/slow 34/54 minutes). There's an hourly slow train to Antwerp (€6.60, 65 minutes) via Lier (€6.30, 45 minutes) but it's often faster to go via Mechelen.

Eurolines (www.eurolines.be) international coaches and **De Lijn** (☎ 016 31 37 37) buses use the bus station beside the train station. Buses 1 and 2 shuttle to Grote Markt for €1.60/2 purchased ahead/aboard. A *dagkaart* (day card) costs €5/6.

Jeugdherberg De Blauwput (see p201) rents **bicycles** (€10 per day, deposit €150).

LEUVEN TO HASSELT

Travelling by car you could easily see this route's main sites in a day, but a better idea is to sleep in intriguing Diest (opposite), then return via Tongeren (p206) and Tienen (p204).

Aarschot
pop 26,900

Largely bypassed by tourism, Aarschot nonetheless has a gentle charm, its vast, distinctive bulb-spired Demer-Gothic central **church** sporting a vast candelabra chandelier behind the altarpiece. The very limited remnants of Aarschot's **begijnhof** look particularly charming during the magical **Sint-Rochusverlichting** (☺ dusk-midnight 15 Aug), when the town's electric lamps are extinguished and replaced by twinkling candles.

You can spoil yourself relatively inexpensively by putting up at **Kasteel van Nieuwland** (☎ 016 56 58 46; www.kasteelvannieuwland.be; Domein Nieuwland 6; s/d/ste from €85/99/200; ℗ ☺), a peaceful chateau built by an 1860s brewery baron on the southwest edge of town.

Horst Castle

Sat in a reflective moat, the picture-perfect medieval **Kasteel van Horst** (☎ 016 62 33 45; www. erfgoed-vlaanderen.be/kasteelvanhorst; St-Peters-Rode; adult/

concession/child €4/3/free; ⊙ 2-5pm Mon, Wed & Sun) is as spectacular as Beersel Castle (p113) with the bonus of a delightful rural setting. The lovely, contemplative **grounds** (admission free; ⊙ 10am-6pm) and drawbridge-facing *café*-restaurant **Streekgasthof Wagenhuis** (☎ 016 62 35 84; www .traiteurdienst-horst.be; ⊙ 11.30am-11.30pm Wed-Mon), tucked away at the back of Sint-Pieters-Rode village, 7.5km south of Aarschot, make a visit worthwhile even when the castle interior is closed. But you'll need wheels and a good map to get here.

Scherpenheuvel

In the 14th century a wooden statue of the virgin was attached to a solitary oak tree that had once been the centre of pagan worship. A boy who attempted to remove the statue was struck down with paralysis, a somewhat spiteful 'miracle', for which the spot became venerated. By 1609 a stream of pilgrims had funded a unique seven-sided baroque **basilica** (⊙ 7.30am-7.30pm May-Aug, 7.30am-6.30pm Sep-Apr) whose domed exterior is distinctively dotted with gilded stars. Countless pilgrims still come to Scherpenheuvel from all over Belgium, particularly in May and on summer weekends, to pray for healing miracles and to pay homage to the minuscule Virgin statuette ensconced beneath a stylised tree-sculpture over the altarpiece.

An attractive circle of wooded parkland around the basilica features shedfulls of burning candles lit by the faithful. Albertusplein, the surrounding arc of road, is dotted with *cafés*, restaurants and seasonal hut-shops peddling all manner of religious trinkets. Off-season, try the shop **Grote Bazar** (Albertusplein 14; ⊙ 9.30am-6pm) to stock up on memorable Lourdes-style Catholic kitsch.

If it's open do look inside the little park building marked 'Info-Tourist'. That's in fact a 1632 **well-house** (restored 1819) containing a rare human treadmill that was used to drag water barrels up 62m.

Scherpenheuvel is about 6km west of Diest, accessible by hourly Diest–Aarschot bus 35.

Diest

pop 22,500

From 1499 to 1794 the ancient town of Diest was a domain of Orange-Nassau Princes, today's Dutch ruling family. The town retains a considerable scattering of fine old architecture, albeit much of it brutally interrupted by

bland modernity. The attractive, oddly shaped Grote Markt is dominated by the huge 1533 **St-Sulpitius Church** (museum admission €1.25; ⊙ 2-5pm Tue-Sun Jul-Aug, Sun only mid-May–mid-Sep) built in two colours of stone that seem oddly thrown together. It's worth taking 10 minutes to peruse the vaulted basement of Diest's fine 18th-century **stadhuis**, next door, where the appealing little **Stadsmuseum** (☎ 013 35 32 09; Grote Markt 1; admission €1.50; ⊙ 10am-noon & 1-5pm) elegantly displays a selection of chalices and reliquaries (no English explanations).

A block east and then south you'll find the **tourist office** (☎ 013 35 32 74; www.toerismediest. be; Felix Moonsstraat 2a; ⊙ 10am-noon & 1-5pm) on a pedestrian street corner facing a pair of half-timbered facades. It dispenses useful maps and suggests town walks. But what really makes Diest worth a stop is its wonderful 1252 **St-Katharinabegijnhof**, arguably Belgium's most charming *begijnhof* (p137). Featuring a 14th-century church and a few artists' studio-galleries, this picturesque village-within-a-village retains an aura that's charmingly authentic and well repays an idle wander. At its heart lies a suitably medieval-styled hostelry, the high-ceilinged **Gasthof 1618** (☎ 013 67 77 80; www.gasthof1618.be; Kerkstraat 8; snacks €3-8, mains €8-23; ⊙ 11am-11pm, closed Mon Oct-Apr), whose manorial atmosphere is all the more believable once the candles and central wood fire are lit. Try the seasonal *Diestse kruidkoeck* (€3.50), a pancake made with tansy (a herb known locally as *boerenwormkruid*), washed down with draught La Trappe (the one Trappist beer that isn't Belgian). St-Katharinabegijnhof's splendid baroque portal is at the eastern end of Begijnenstraat, a 10-minute stroll east of the Grote Markt. Start down Koning Albertlaan, with its 1346 **Lakenhalle**, chunky medieval **super-gun**, indulgently spired **post office** and several appealing facades above the shop fronts. Then dogleg past the 1288 **OLV Church** (⊙ 9.30am-4pm), built of eroded coffee-brown sandstone.

SLEEPING & EATING

B&B Catalpa (☎ 013 31 14 39, 0494 81 63 99; www.bbdiest. be; Schaffensesteenweg 55; s/d/tr €35/50/75) Charming Marthe Tonet invites guests into her lovely 1900 house, with its high ceilings and 1940s furniture. The triple room in the eaves has a private shower but toilets are shared in what's very much a family home. Breakfast is taken on the garden-view veranda. It's two blocks

EASTERN FLANDERS

north of OLV Church passing the highly photogenic Ezeldijkmolen watermill.

The Lodge (☎ 013 35 09 35; www.lodge-hotels.be;
Refugiestraat 23; s/d €85/120, ste from €110/155; ☒ ☐)
Diest's most charming hotel partly occupies
a turreted stream-side mansion that was originally a medieval abbot's retreat. Peaceful yet
central (just 200m north of Grote Markt),
the 20 rooms are attractively furnished with
a refreshingly uncluttered elegance.

La Bas (☎ 013 32 30 32; www.labasdiest.be; Koning
Albertstraat 11; mains €10; ☹ from 11am-/8am-/9am-6pm
Tue/Wed/Thu-Sat, 2-6pm Sun) Ultramodern *café* with
striking black-and-scarlet decor and an in-
scrutable Buddha surveying the rear terrace.
Good for breakfasts (Wednesday to Saturday)
and light healthy cuisine.

Brasserie The Lodge (☎ 013 32 76 76; Michel
Theysstrat 6; mains €8.50-31; ☹ 11am-10pm Mon-Fri, 5.30-
10pm Sat, noon-10pm Sun) Same name as and near
The Lodge, but a separate establishment in an
alluring historic house with old-meets-new
decor and a sizeable orangery-style veranda.
Game dishes are available in season; bookings
wise at weekends.

GETTING THERE & AWAY
Brussels–Leuven–Tongeren and Antwerp–
Lier–Liège trains (both hourly) stop in
Diest, taking 11 minutes from Aarschot
and 15 minutes from Hasselt. To find the
Grote Markt (1.3km south) turn left out of
the train station, veer right (crossing the
Demer onto Weerstandplein) then continue
down Statiestraat and Demerstraat. Bicycles
can be hired from the **Provinciedomein Halve
Maan** (☎ 013 31 15 28; per day €7), 600m south of
the *begijnhof.*

Hasselt
pop 69,100
Nowhere in Belgium has a more palpable
sense of comfortable prosperity than Hasselt,
the bustling capital of Limburg province.
But, while the cosmopolitan townsfolk are
amply provided for with state-of-the-art
entertainment and sports facilities, tasteful
shops and excellent restaurants, the predomi-
nant architectural landscape is functionally
20th century.

Hasselt celebrates its fame as Belgium's
unofficial *jenever* capital with the **Nationaal
Jenevermuseum** (☎ 011 23 98 60; www.jenevermuseum.
be; Witte Nonnenstraat 19; adult/concession €3/1; ☹ 10am-
5pm daily Jul-Aug, Tue-Sun Sep-Dec & Feb-Jun, closed weekend

mornings in winter, last entry 4pm), housed in a beautifully restored, still-active 19th-century distillery. Visits conclude with a free sample shot.
The city centre's north–south pedestrianised
spine (Koning Albertstraat/Hoogstraat/
Demerstraat) passes 200m to the west.

Three blocks south, Demerstraat passes the
well-signed tourist office, **In&Uit Hasselt** (☎ 011 23
95 40; www.hasselt.be; Lombaardstraat 3; ☹ 9am-5pm Mon-
Fri, 10am-5pm Sat). A block further is the most impressive of Hasselt's several fine churches, the
1520 **St-Quintinuskathedral** (Fruitmarkt; ☹ 9.30am-
5pm), with its very distinctive octagonal-
spired belfry. Within 50m the delightful **B&B
't Hemelhuys** (☎ 011 35 13 75; www.hemelhuys.be;
Kemelrijk 15; s/d weekday €80/95, weekend €100/110) sits
on one of the city's few really quaint corners,
has soothing modern decor, a garden, a comfy
common lounge and five rooms worthy of a
boutique hotel. About 1km west is the **train
station** (☎ 011 29 60 00), with trains once or twice
hourly on the Brussels–Leuven–Tongeren and
Antwerp–Lier–Liège routes.

Around Hasselt
Between Hasselt and Genk lies a vast series of
provincial parks and woodlands. These incorporate a splendid **arboretum** (admission free) and
one of Europe's largest open-air museums,
the 60-hectare **Bokrijk Openluchtmuseum** (☎ 011
26 53 00; www.bokrijk.be; adult/concession/youth €10/8.50/1,
half-price from 4pm; ☹ 10am-6pm Apr-Sep). The latter
offers a nostalgic look at Flanders' past, with
over 100 original old buildings, including village churches, townhouses, farmhouses, windmills and an ancient *herberg* (pub) that have
been dismantled then reassembled here since
1958. Local people dressed in traditional garb
bake bread and tend veggie gardens, evoking
the village life of yesteryear. Hourly Genk–
Hasselt trains (10 minutes, hourly) stop 500m
south of the southern entrance but hourly bus
1 from Hasselt is more convenient (Monday
to Saturday only). By car there's a still more
convenient alternative entrance beside the
19th-century mansion-castle, **Kasteel Bokrijk**.
Parking costs €3.

LEUVEN TO TONGEREN
Tienen
pop 32,000
Known as Belgium's sugar capital, Tienen
(Tirlemont in French) has a liberal scattering
of medieval buildings, including two spectacularly vast churches. The market square

lacks the perfection of those in some other Flemish cities but its solid 1846 **militia-house** (Grote Markt 6) is well worth visiting for both the **tourist information office** (☎ 016 80 57 38; 🕑 10am-5pm Tue-Sun) and the superb **Suikermuseum** (Sugar Museum; ☎ 016 80 56 66; www.erfgoedsitetienen.be; adult/senior/youth/child €5/4/4/free; 🕑 10am-4pm Tue-Sun), one of Belgium's most inspired museums. Interactive, witty and surrealistically metaphorical presentations include a postnatal hospital ward for sugar beets, a cartoon encounter with Queen Bee and a 'painting' gallery with a talking Napoleon. Suddenly sugar lumps seem fascinating. Finish the visit in the attached *café* where local apple cake (€2.20) marries well with Tienen's sour, unfiltered 'duck' beer, *Tiense Kweiker Tripel*.

Alpha Hotel (☎ 016 82 28 00; www.alphahotel.be; Leuvensestraat 95; s/d/tr €82/94/106) is a staid but handily located accommodation choice 500m northwest of Grote Markt, 200m before the train station.

For more appealing accommodation, those with a car should head 4km up the N223 towards Aarschot (p202). In rural Vissenaken, **De Schutting** (☎ 016 89 73 75; www.deschutting.be; Romeinsebaan 108, Vissenaken; s/d/q €50/60-80/100) offers nine good-value, new rooms with elements of historic furniture. It's in converted 19th-century stables attached to a 1663 farmhouse; there's a shared kitchen, BBQ patio and honesty bar. Jovial host Geert can arrange horse rides but only for experienced riders.

Hoegaarden
pop 6400

Home of the world-famous, eponymous white beer, Hoegaarden was an autonomous county until feisty 10th-century Countess Alpaïdis cunningly ceded her lands to the Prince Bishops of Liège. This made Hoegaarden a disconnected enclave surrounded by, but independent from, medieval Brabant. In the 18th century such enclaves enjoyed tax-free status, jump-starting dozens of breweries in Hoegaarden. After Liège's independence was quashed in 1795, Hoegaarden lost its tax advantage and the breweries progressively closed down, until finally revived in the latter 20th century.

Hoegaarden today is mostly a fairly glum small town but its cute little central square (Gemeenteplein) features a metal-framed bandstand, behind which rises Belgium's 'largest rococo church', the 1759 **Sint-Gorgoniuskerk**.

To see its splendid twin-staired wooden pulpit and cherub-topped organ, request the key from the facing **tourist office** (☎ 016 76 78 43; www.hoegaarden.be; Houtmarkt 1; 🕑 10am-5pm) in front of the delightful **Tuinen van Hoegaarden** (☎ 016 76 78 43; www.detuinenvanhoegaarden.be; Kappitelpark, Houtmarkt 1; admission free; 🕑 10am-9pm). Those 16th-century formal gardens lead down from a lovely wisteria-fronted *café*-terrace to the contrastingly contemporary little **Garden of Eden** (admission free; 🕑 10am-5pm).

Beer fans will make a beeline for the **Old Hoegaarden Brewery** ('t Wit Gebrow; ☎ 016 76 74 33; www.twitgebrouw.be; Stoopkensstraat 24; adult/child €6/free; 🕑 10am-8pm Wed-Sun), a slick, interactive museum experience celebrating the iconic white beer. Buy tickets from the attached 19th-century **Kouterhof brasserie-restaurant** (www.kouterhof.be) and return afterwards for a free beer and souvenir glass. (The modern brewery, about 1km further east, doesn't usually offer visits.)

In a 1636 brick house, charming **Herberg-brouwerij Nieuwhuys** (☎ 016 81 71 64; www.nieuwhuys.be; Ernest Ourystraat 2; beers €1.50-4, wine €2.60, snacks €2.80-11.80; 🕑 5pm-late Thu-Sat, 3pm-late Sun) produces mellow Alpaïde stout (€2.60) in its own microbrewery. That's visible through a glass floor-plate in its brilliantly pitched, jazz-toned pub-*café*.

Bus 360 (Tienen–Jodoigne/Geldenakel) departs from Zijdelingsestraat outside Tienen station, taking 15 minutes to Hoegaarden.

Zoutleeuw
pop 8100

Once one of Brabant's seven pre-eminent 'free-cities', sleepy little Zoutleeuw (Leau in French) fell into decline along with the medieval cloth-making industry from the 15th century. Despite terrible floods (1573), fires (1676), Spanish occupation (1578) and French looting (1701), two great historic structures survived remarkably well. The **tourist office** (☎ 011 78 12 88; www.zoutleeuw.be; 🕑 10am-noon & 2-4pm Tue-Fri, also 1-5pm Sat & Sun Apr-Sep) lies within one: the intriguing composite Town Hall/Vleeshalle/Lakenhalle building, whose majestic pre-Raphaelite murals can be perused for free along with a small archaeological exhibition.

Across the road, Zoutleeuw's main attraction is **St-Leonarduskerk** (admission €1.50; 🕑 2-5pm Tue-Sun Easter-Sep), topped with a fanciful tower reminiscent of a galleon's crow's nest. Miraculously, given Zoutleeuw's turbulent history, the interior of this huge Gothic church was the only significant example in all of Belgium to escape untouched during the religious turmoil and invasions of the 16th to 18th centuries. Its magnificent statuary thus offers a unique insight to pre-Iconoclastic church design.

Within two minutes' walk on the central square are a trio of appealing places to eat and drink. Tienen–Sint-Truiden bus 23 runs hourly through Zoutleeuw.

Sint-Truiden
pop 38,300

A soaring trio of historical towers gives the extensive **Grote Markt** of Sint-Truiden (St-Trond in French) a fairy-tale feel that easily justifies an hour or two of your time. The 7th-century relics of local saint, St-Trudo, which made the town a major medieval pilgrimage centre, are housed in the 1854 **Onze Lieve Vrouwekerk** (Grote Markt), behind which a seven-storey, 11th-century tower is all that remains of the former **St-Trudo Abbey**. Come here at 5pm any summer Sunday to relive one of St-Trudo's miracles! The most eye-catching tower is the slender 1606 **belfry** attached to the peach-vermillion painted **Stadhuis** (partly 13th century), whose remarkably versatile carillon can even ding-dong the Beatles' 'Ob-la-di Ob-la-da'. Opposite, the **tourist office** (☎ 011 70 18 18; www.toerisme-sint-truiden.be; Grote Markt) might entice you to visit various museums around town.

Marred with several new constructions, the **Sint-Agnesbegijnhof**, 1km northeast of the centre via Plankstraat, is not one of Belgium's loveliest *begijnhoven*. But it is unique in retaining a *begijn*-farmstead, and its lopsided 1258 **church** (admission free; ☺ 10am-noon & 1.30-5pm) is renowned for its gruesome medieval mural of St Agatha's martyrdom. While here, visit the **Festraets Studio** (☎ 011 68 87 52; Begijnhof 24; admission free; ☺ hourly 9.45am-3.45pm Mon-Fri except 12.45pm Tue-Fri, 2.45pm & 3.45pm Sat & Sun), home to what is billed as the 'world's biggest astronomical clock' (6m high, 4 tonnes).

Cicindria Hotel (☎ 011 68 13 44; www.cicindria-hotel. be; Abdijstraat 6; s/d from €75/100) is a central, sparklingly clean if rather cramped, new hotel just 200m north of Grote Markt. The reception booth is hidden upstairs.

Much more appealing are the four spacious and beautifully appointed rooms above the stylish, great-value restaurant **Belle Vie** (☎ 011 68 70 38; www.belle-vie.be; Stationstraat 12; r €60-90), whose

charms aren't immediately evident from the outwardly severe brick facade. It's 700m west of the Grote Markt (via Stapelstraat), just 150m before the train station.

Just off Grote Markt, tucked behind the church, **Nieuwscafe** (☎ 011 70 28 50; www.nieuwscafe. be; Heilig Hartplein 5; mains €7-16) is a suavely modern brasserie-restaurant (five vegetarian options) with a bar area that's ideal for coffee sipping and newspaper reading by day. On 'Loving Saturday' nights the *café* becomes a popular nightclub.

Bus 23a runs to Tongeren, bus 23 goes to Tienen via Zoutleeuw.

TONGEREN
pop 29,500

Proudly claiming to be Belgium's oldest town, likeable Tongeren (Tongres in French) was a prosperous 2nd-century Roman settlement on the Cologne–Bavay road. By the 4th century it had become one of the Low Countries' earliest Christian bishoprics, but in 1677 it was catastrophically torched by Louis XIV's French troops. Today the compact city is remarkable for retaining several sections of Roman-era city walls and has an inventive modern **Gallo-Roman Museum** (☎ 012 67 03 30; www.galloromeinsmuseum.be; Kielenstraat 15; adult/family/concession/child €7/15/5/1; ☺ 9am-5pm Tue-Fri, 10am-6pm Sat & Sun).

Medieval and Roman remnants are visible in the little archaeological site outside the elegant **Onze Lieve Vrouwebasiliek** (Basilica of Our Lady; ☺ 10am-noon & 1.30-5pm). This mostly 14th- to 16th-century church marks the supposed first place north of the Alps where the Virgin Mary was worshipped. Every seven years its venerated 1479 walnut Madonna statue is piously paraded round town (next in July 2016) in the large-scale if very staid **Kroningsfeesten** (www.kroningsfeesten.be) procession.

One of Tongeren's pleasantly sedate attractions is lingering in a terrace *café* facing the iconic **statue of Ambiorix**, a local tribal chieftain who led a brief 54 BC revolt against Julius Caesar's early Roman rule. Ambiorix (loosely represented by Beefix in the classic Asterix cartoons) had been largely forgotten till the 1830s, when newly founded Belgium was in need of national heroes. A handy nearby **tourist office** (☎ 012 39 02 55; www.tongeren.be; Stadhuisplein 9; ☺ 8.30am-noon & 1-5pm Mon-Fri, 10am-4pm Sat & Sun) gives away comprehensive map-guide pamphlets and rents bicycles.

Three blocks south and west is a small web of pretty backstreets that once formed Tongeren's **begijnhof**. The scene looks especially gorgeous at dusk viewed across a small canal when walking between the chunky stone **Moerenpoort** (medieval city gate-tower) and the brilliantly located HI youth hostel, **Begeinhof** (☎ 012 39 13 70; www.vjh.be; St-Ursulastraat 1; dm member/nonmember €18.80/21.80; 🖥 👤), a low-slung barn of a place with functional six-bed dorms set behind a busy, fair-priced brasserie-*café*.

Eburon Hotel (☎ 012 23 01 99; http://eburonhotel.be; De Schiervelstraat 10; d comfort/select from €70/100; 🔆 🛜) offers Tongeren's most appealing accommodation, stylishly oozing designer modernist style yet set within a partly 12th-century convent complex that has been dramatically transformed into a shopping, dining and hotel complex. There's a wine bar in the vaulted historic cellars. Prices vary greatly according to demand.

For something much more traditional, eat at the superquaint **Herberg De Pelgrim** (☎ 012 23 83 22; Brouwerstraat 9; mains €12-19; 🕑 11am-11pm Wed-Sun), a 1632 step-gabled house beside the 13th-century Begijnhofkerk church in the loveliest corner of the *begijnhof*. Spare ribs are the speciality.

Tongeren has a fair sprinkling of antique shops (most closed Mondays and Tuesdays) and on Sunday mornings the town hosts a famous **antique and brocante market** (Veemarkt; 🕑 from 5am Sun).

The bus/train station is 400m west of the centre. Hourly trains depart for Hasselt (€3.70, 20 minutes), Liège (€3.80, 30 minutes) and Sint-Truiden (via Hasselt; €5.70, 45 minutes). Bus 23A goes direct to Sint-Truiden (€2.50, 35 minutes).

Hainaut &
Brabant Wallon

There's much more to western Wallonia than initially meets the eye. While townscapes here lack the magic of Bruges or Ghent, the area hosts some of Belgium's craziest and most unmissable annual festivals, including the Mons 'Doudou' (p214), Ath's giants' parade (p18) and Lessines' penitents' procession (p16). Binche's renowned carnival (p216) had such a historic reputation for excess that it gave the English language the term 'binge'. On Brussels' southern fringe, the world-famous Waterloo Battlefield is one of Belgium's most popular tourist draws. Tournai and Nivelles sport Belgium's finest Romanesque churches. And with your own wheels there are many offbeat attractions to seek out, from unique canal-workings to the beers of Silly, along with some magnificent chateaux and the particularly haunting abbey ruins at Aulne and Villers-la-Ville.

Once-vibrant Charleroi and La Louvière are often associated with industrial decay but beyond Charleroi's slag heaps lies some very pretty, undulating farmland. This area lacks the name recognition of the Ardennes but is often more instantly attractive if you prefer patchworks of woodland over blanket forests. If it is forests you're after, head south into the Botte du Hainaut, which, though partly in Namur province, is covered for convenience in this chapter. Be aware that accommodation is thin on the ground in that southern quarter so advance planning might be wise in summer if you're not taking day trips.

HIGHLIGHTS

- **Architectural Insight** Romanesque transforms into Gothic in Tournai's iconic cathedral (p210)
- **Carnival Capers** Binge with the Gilles of Binche (p216)
- **The mud that changed history** The battlefield of Waterloo (p216
- **Photo Finish** The world-class photography museum (p222) near Charleroi
- **Time Stopped Still** The evocative Cistercian abbey ruins at Villers-la-Ville (p220) and Aulne (p223)
- **Dragon Slayers** Mons' Le Doudou (p214), one of Belgium's most raucous, mesmerising traditional festivals
- **Steam Blower** Brasserie à Vapeur (p212) comes to life one Saturday a month at Pipaix

★ Waterloo

★ Tournai
★ Pipaix

★ Villers-la-Ville

Mons ★

★ Charleroi

Binche ★
Aulne

- PROVINCES: HAINAUT (CAPITAL MONS), BRABANT WALLON (CAPITAL NIVELLES)
- LANGUAGE: FRENCH

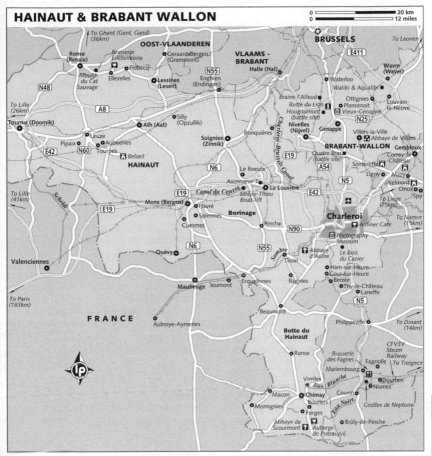

TOURNAI

pop 67,300

Enjoyable Tournai (pronounced tour-*nay*, Doornik in Dutch) has Wallonia's most memorable Grand Place and one of Belgium's finest cathedrals. Inhabited since ancient antiquity (visit Archeosite, p212, to learn more) it grew to prominence as the Roman trading settlement of Tornacum, and was the original 5th-century capital of the Frankish Merovingian dynasty. Clovis, the most celebrated Merovingian king, was born here in 465 and while he soon decamped to Paris, he left Tournai as the region's spiritual centre. Autonomous from France as of 1187, the city retains two towers (St-Georges and Prends-Garde) from the first 1202 city wall and a curi-

ous fortified bridge (Pont des Trous) from the wall's later expansion. In 1513 Tournai was conquered by Henry VIII of England and the town even sent a parliamentary representative to London before being sold back to France in 1519. Just two years later it was swallowed by the Hapsburg-Spanish empire. Tournai found renewed wealth as a centre for tapestry-making (in the 16th century) and porcelain manufacture (in the 18th century) but was devastated in 1940 by WWII fire-bombing. While the cathedral largely survived, almost all other historic buildings had to be painstakingly restored. Restoration was so complete that the lovely Grand Place now looks somewhat more medieval that it had done before the war.

Information

Internaute (☎ 069 84 67 43; Rue du Château 63; per hr €2.40; 10am-midnight Mon-Fri, 1.30pm-1am Sat) Funky internet bar.

Office du Tourisme (☎ 069 22 20 45; www.tournai .be; Vieux Marché aux Poteries 14; 8.30am-5.30pm Mon-Fri, 10am-noon & 2-5pm Sat, 2.30-6pm Sun) A 23-minute movie (in English; €3.50) traces Tournai's history.

Post office (Rue St-Martin 25)

Sights

Tournai's gorgeous triangular **Grand Place** is ringed with *cafés* in fine gable-fronted guildhouses merrily flying heraldic banner flags. Kids play in 'dare-you' fountains between the gilt-detailed **Halle-des-Draps** (Cloth Hall) and Belgium's oldest belfry, the 72m-high Unesco-listed **Beffroi** (adult/concession €3.50/1; 9.30am-12.30pm & 2-5.30pm Tue-Sun, to 5pm Nov-Feb, last entry 45 min before closing).

At sunset, or when artfully illuminated at night, the scene is at its most beautiful viewed from near **Église St-Quentin**, a hefty Romanesque church with a striking red-tiled roof. From here a classic cluster of five grey stone towers seem to float above the square. These trademark features of Tournai's skyline are the spires of the remarkable if sober **Cathédrale Notre-Dame** (Our Lady's Cathedral; Pl de l'Évêché; admission free; 9.30am-noon & 2-5pm Apr-Oct, 10am-noon & 2-4pm Nov-Mar), another World Heritage Site. Damaged by a freak 1999 tornado, the cathedral is likely to remain a vast building site until around 2016. However, for all the scaffolding inside, the interior remains a fascinating textbook example of evolving architectural styles, from the magnificent Romanesque nave through a curious bridging transept into an early Gothic choir whose soaring pillars bend disconcertingly out of line. The wood-panelled little Chapelle St-Louis features large canvases by Rubens and Jacob Jordaens and there's plenty more 'treasure' in the **trésor** (admission €2; 9.15-11.45am Mon-Fri & 2-5.45pm daily).

Multilingual signboards around town introduce numerous other local curiosities, though appeal is patchy beyond the immediate historical centre.

MUSEUMS

The city's **museums** (9.30am-12.30pm & 2-5.30pm Wed-Mon Apr-Oct, 10am-noon & 2-5pm Mon, Wed-Sat, 2-5pm Sun Nov-Mar) each charge adult/concession €3.50/2, but various multiticket options exist and all museums are free the first Sunday of the month.

An angel in a gas mask points surreally at the door of the **Musée des Beaux-Arts** (☎ 069 22 20 43; Enclos St-Martin), whose impressive art collection is housed in an airy gallery designed by art-nouveau maestro architect Victor Horta. Rogier Van der Weyden (aka Roger de la Pasture) – Tournai's best-known artist and an exponent of the Flemish Primitive style – is well represented along with local stars Louis Gallait (1810–87) and Roméo Dumoulin (1883–1944), but you'll also find Pieter Breughel the Younger, Jacob Jordaens and even French Impressionist Edouard Manet.

The **Musée du Folklore** (☎ 069 22 40 69; Réduit des Sions) is a rabbit warren of fascinating city-relevant relics. Facing Tournai's palatial 1830s **Hôtel de Ville** (Town Hall) on the site of the former St-Martin's Abbey, is Belgium's oldest **Natural History Museum** (☎ 069 33 23 43; Cour d'Honneur), featuring a tropical greenhouse with carnivorous plants.

Musée de la Tapisserie (Tapestry Museum; ☎ 069 84 20 73; Place Reine Astrid) and **Musée d'Histoire et des Arts Décoratifs** (☎ 069 84 37 95; Rue St-Martin 50b) showcase decorative arts produced by the city's classic industries, tapestry and porcelain respectively.

Sleeping

Camping de l'Orient (☎ 069 22 26 35; campingorient@ tournai.be; Rue Jean Baptiste Moens 8; campsite per adult/ child/tent €3/2.50/2.50) Part of a lakeside swimming complex 2km southeast of the train station by bus W.

HI Hostel (Auberge de Jeunesse; ☎ 069 21 61 36; www .laj.be; Rue St-Martin 64; members dm/s/d €16.40/33/48; reception/check-in 5-10pm) Pleasant, friendly hostel with kitchen and an unexpectedly good breakfast included (served from 7.45am to 9.30am). It's five minutes' walk from the Grand Place or a bus 4 hop (direction Baisieux) from the train station.

our pick **B&B Mme Daniel** (☎ 0472 38 69 72; fdaniel @skynet.be; Rue des Soeurs Noires 35; s/d €45/60;) This personal homestay option has airy new loftsuites with great mattresses and kitchenettes, a floral room featuring well-used classical furniture and a slightly Bohemian ground floor with access to the delightful semiwild garden. Family art and knick-knacks, as well as the loveable Shetland sheepdog, create a

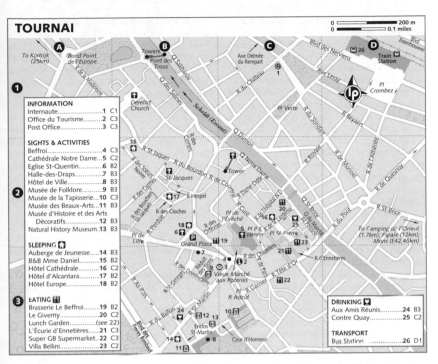

TOURNAI

0   200 m
0   0.1 miles

INFORMATION
Internaute........................1 C1
Office du Tourisme...........2 C3
Post Office.......................3 C3

SIGHTS & ACTIVITIES
Beffroi............................4 C3
Cathédrale Notre Dame...5 C2
Eglise St-Quentin.............6 B2
Halle-des-Draps...............7 B3
Hôtel de Ville...................8 B3
Musée de Folklore...........9 B3
Musée de la Tapisserie....10 C3
Musée des Beaux-Arts.....11 B3
Musée d'Histoire et des Arts
Décoratifs...................12 B3
Natural History Museum.13 B3

SLEEPING
Auberge de Jeunesse......14 B3
B&B Mme Daniel..............15 B2
Hôtel Cathédrale............16 C2
Hôtel d'Alcantara............17 C3
Hôtel Europe...................18 B2

EATING
Brasserie Le Beffroi.........19 B2
Le Giverny......................20 C2
Lunch Garden.............(see 22)
L'Écurie d'Ennetières.......21 C3
Super GB Supermarket....22 C3
Villa Bellini.....................23 C2

DRINKING
Aux Amis Réunis.............24 B3
Contre Quay...................25 C2

TRANSPORT
Bus Station 26 D1

---

truly homely atmosphere in this house dating back to 1673 that has neither a sign nor a buzzer at the entrance: ring the archaic handle-bell at the green door but phone ahead to arrange your arrival time. Limited English spoken.

Hôtel Europe (☎ 069 22 40 67; www.europehotel .be; Grand Place 26; s/d €50/65) Eight bland rooms above a bamboo-tropical rum bar in a pseudo-medieval house located right on the Grand Place.

Hôtel d'Alcantara (☎ 069 21 26 48; www.hotel alcantara.be; Rue des Bouchers St-Jacques 2; s/d from €84/94) Tournai's most appealing hotel looks regal from outside, with pleasant sitting areas and a pretty garden terrace. Inside, the decor takes a quite unexpected turn, some of the 17 rooms (each different) experimenting only semi-successfully with '70s-retro elements and odd ceiling materials. Rooms at the rear suffer from road noise. The main staircase is conceptual art, service is obliging and wi-fi costs €5.

Hôtel Cathédrale (☎ 069 21 50 77; www.hotel cathedrale.be; Place St-Pierre 2; standard/executive €94/105; ✗) Fifty-one small, passably comfortable

rooms with oddly uncoordinated designs and some other minor niggles.

Eating

Brasserie Le Beffroi (☎ 069 84 83 41; www.brasserie lebeffroi.be; Grand Place 16; beer/salads from €1.70/10.50; ☽ 10am-midnight, kitchen 11am-11pm) The most traditional of numerous Grand Place *cafés*, Le Beffroi offers a spacious terrace, fair prices and several vegetarian-friendly salads.

L'Écurie d'Ennetières (☎ 069 21 56 89; www.ecurie dennetieres.be; Ruelle d'Ennetières; mains €12-17, 3-course menu €30; ☽ noon-2pm & 6.30-10pm) Affordable Belgo-French cuisine served in a high-ceilinged room with exposed brick walls and aged marionettes hanging from hefty wooden beams.

Villa Bellini (☎ 069 23 65 20; Place St-Pierre 15; mains €9-14; ☽ noon-1.15pm & 7-10.30pm Wed-Mon) This attractive pizzeria's front room is a former 1940s pharmacy and retains the appealing interior and dozens of old wooden medicine drawers. Thin-crust pizzas are well renowned and calzones are enormous, but our four-cheese pasta was unpalatable. The back dining rooms lack atmosphere; try to get a table in the front room.

Le Giverny (☎ 069 22 44 64; Quai du Marché au Poisson 6; mains €20-26, menu €32-83; ✆ closed Mon, lunch Sat & dinner Sun) This calm, refined French restaurant with professional service occupies an old bakery partly retaining the old pattern-tiled floors. Despite chandeliers, high ceilings and white pressed tablecloths the atmosphere isn't intimidating. Reservations are essential.

Super GB (Rue Tête d'Or 669; ✆ 8am-8pm) supermarket has a cheap **lunch garden** (✆ 9am-9pm Mon-Sat, 11.30am-9pm Sun) cafeteria that's good if you just want to stoke the stomach.

Drinking

Terrace *cafés* ring the Grand Place with more on Place St-Pierre and particularly on the riverside, where things stay lively later.

Contre Quay (Quai du Marché au Poisson 16; ✆ 3pm-late) Lugubrious tear-drop lamps, UV glow and insistent music makes this a youth favourite amid several similar nearby options.

Aux Amis Réunis (☎ 069 55 96 59; Rue St-Martin 89; ✆ 10am-10pm Mon-Fri, 11am-midnight Sat) Enticing old-fashioned locals' pub dating from 1911 with art nouveau touches, ceramic beer-taps and a table for playing the archetypal Tournai game called *jeu de fer*, in which players cue metal discs towards a series of pegs and gates.

Getting There & Away

Tournai's train station, 900m northeast of the Grand Place, has services twice-hourly to Mons (€6.60, fast/slow 23/43 minutes) and Brussels (€11.70, fast/slow 61/73 minutes), hourly to Lille-Flanders (€6, 25 minutes) in France. Change in Mouscron for Kortrijk (€4.80, 32 minutes total).

TOURNAI TO MONS

You'll need a car and decent map to find the following.

Pipaix

Started in 1785 and 'modernised' in 1895, the tiny **Brasserie à Vapeur** (☎ 069 66 20 47; www .vapeur.com; Rue du Maréchal 1, Pipaix) is now Belgium's last traditional steam-operated brewery. This wonderfully authentic family enterprise sometimes experiments with curious flavours (pumpkin, fig leaves), and also produces semi-sour Saison Pipaix and celebrated Vapeur Cochonne, whose bare-breasted cartoon-pig

labels have been censored in the US. Taste the beers across the road at rustic *café* **Cense** (small/regular beer €1/2; ✆ 10am-6pm Wed-Sun) or visit on the first Saturday of each month (9am to 11.30am) to observe the brewery's whizzing flywheels and experience the saunalike heat of the brewing process. On brewing days simply lift the latch of the brewery's side door to enter. Or better, make a reservation in advance to stay on for a tempting beer-influenced buffet lunch (€30) of ham, cheese, freshly baked beer-bread and endless ale. Sunday **brewery tours** (€6; ✆ 11am Sun Apr-Oct, in French) also include beer tasters but are less interesting since the machinery is silent.

Aubechies

pop 400

Giving a fascinating visual picture of prehistoric human lifestyles, Aubechies' **Archeosite** (☎ 069 67 11 16; www.archeosite.be; adult/child €7/3.50; ✆ 9am-5pm Mon-Fri year-round, plus 2-7pm Sun Jul & Aug) has used local archaeological evidence to build a 'village' of dwellings and workshops representing Neolithic, bronze age and Gallo-Roman eras, plus a somewhat less convincing Roman temple. Come on a summer Sunday afternoon when craftsmen in period costume demonstrate cottage industries of times gone by.

Facing Aubechies' barrel-vaulted 1077 church, **Taverne St-Géry** (☎ 0475 31 61 34; ✆ 6-10pm Fri-Sun) is one of rural Belgium's most authentic village pubs. It's a whitewashed farm-style place whose interior walls incorporate Roman pottery finds and an original stable trough. It serves a good yet inexpensive range of local beers and cheeses.

Belœil

Sitting in an artificial lake within a vast manicured park, the **Château de Belœil** (☎ www.chateau debeloeil.com; adult/child €8/4; ✆ 1-6pm daily Jul & Aug, Sat & Sun only Apr-Jun & Sep) is a regal country palace-house, immodestly seeing itself as the Belgian Versailles. Inside it's packed with classical furniture and portraiture relevant to the princes 'de Ligne', whose scion Eugène de Ligne (1804–80) turned down the chance to be Belgian king in 1831. An audioguide explains things in detail but the interior somehow lacks the majesty of Modave (p233) and has a fair share of rucked carpets and peeling ceilings. It's free to approach the grand entrance courtyard.

ATH

Ath (www.ath.be) was founded around 1160 by Baldwin IV of Hainaut and his dour 12th-century fortress-keep (the **Tour de Burban**) is still standing 150m west of the **Grand Place**. Hidden in the attic of Ath's modest early 17th-century **town hall** (Grand Place) is the friendly two-room **Musée National des Jeux-de-Paume** (☎ 0475 47 40 19; www .museenationaldesjeuxdepaume.be; adult/child €2.50/free; 🕑 2.30-6pm Sun Apr-Sep), which celebrates the typical Walloon game of *balle-pelotte* (see p46). Tucked behind Rue de Brantignies 10, **Église St-Martin** has an unusual slate tower-spire and an outdoor wooden crucifixion scene.

Ath's main source of fame throughout Belgium is for its **Procession of the Giants** (p18), held in late August. If you miss the big weekend, you can learn more at the **Maison des Géants** (☎ 068 26 51 70; www.maison desgeants.be; Rue de Pintamont 18; adult/senior/student €5/4.50/4; 🕑 10am-noon & 1-6pm Tue-Fri, 2-6pm Sat & Sun Apr-Sep, 10am-noon & 1-5pm Tue-Fri Oct-Mar) in a grand old mansion opposite the castle-style tower of **Église St-Julien**. While the giants' story is professionally told (in English by request), you're effectively locked into an hour-long series of multimedia presentations. For most casual visitors 15 minutes would be enough.

Ath's train station, 400m south of the Grand Place, is on the Brussels–Tournai line.

LESSINES

The main reason to visit the rather lacklustre hometown of René Magritte (born at Rue Magritte 10) is for the spooky Good Friday penitents' procession (see p16). Nonetheless if you're passing by during the weekend consider visiting the **Hôpital Notre-Dame de la Rose** (www.notredamealarose.com; adult/senior/student/child €7.50/6.50/6/3.50; 🕑 2-6.30pm Sat & Sun Apr-Oct, Tue-Sun Jul & Aug, last entry 5.45pm), founded in 1242. It's Belgium's only medieval convent-farm-hospital complex to have survived reasonably intact, albeit now in the midst of a massive reconstruction project. Where complete, interiors feel rather over-renovated and far less interesting than Burgundy's equivalent Hospices de Beaune. Still, the rich collection of religious art includes a curious 16th-century painting showing Jesus with a female breast (audioguide item 52), the collection of historical medical implements is intriguing and the bird-beaked plague-doctor in his leather cape (item 88) is unforgettable.

AROUND LESSINES
Ellezelles

For a village with little real charm, Ellezelles makes a valiant effort to attract tourists with tales of witches and comically preposterous claims of being Hercule Poirot's 'birthplace'. A 6km trail, **Le Sentier de l'Étrange**, encourages visitors to walk into the pretty rolling countryside seeking out rather silly latter-day 'sculptures'. Fortunately Ellezelles does have one of the region's most appealing hotels, **Au Couvent des Collines** (☎ 068 26 40 50; www.couvent -des-collines.be; Ruelle des Ecoles 25; d €98-116; 🕑 closed Sun), in a tastefully converted 1830 convent. In a farmhouse setting 1km northwest, **Brasserie Ellezelleoise** (Rue Guinamont 75; beer €3; 🕑 11am-8pm) is an endearing brewery-pub creating and serving Quintine 'witch' beer and 'Hercule' stout, playing on the Poirot theme. **Moulin du Cat Sauvage** is an attractive roadside post-mill halfway to Ronse (Renaix).

ENGHIEN
pop 12,000

Behind the old-town core of charming Enghien (Edingen in Dutch) lies the lovely **Parc d'Enghien** (adult/concession/audioguide €3/2.50/2; 🕑 10am-6pm Apr-Oct, 10am-6pm Jul & Aug, 10am-5pm Sat & Sun Nov-Mar). Originally set out in the 17th century by the Dukes of Arenberg, the park incorporates vast stands of woodland, fountains, statues, a tiny 'Chinese' pavilion, a topiary garden, a pondside terrace-*café* and the mansion-castle **Château Empain** (closed to the public). Views here are beautiful, with a foreground of flowers, a tree-flanked fortified chapel-tower mid-distance and the Salisbury-style spire of St-Nicholas Church poking up behind. Enter the park through the **tourist office** (☎ 023 97 10 22; www.enghien-edingen.be; Park 5), which is a one-minute walk from the main square via a stone arcade-arch. Within the arch you'll also find the hidden entrance to the upmarket Belgo-French restaurant **La Cuisine de Mon Père** (☎ 023 95 49 18; Grand Place 30; lunch/dinner menu €15/34; 🕑 noon-2pm & 6.30-10pm). Of three wonderfully authentic local *cafés* around the central square, **Le Rembrandt** offers the widest beer menu, but all serve excellent local brew, the full-strength Double Enghien. Despite the name, the beer's actually brewed 9km west in **Silly** (Opzullik in Dutch), a humdrum town of 8000 people worth driving through if only to photograph the town sign or to buy a crate of talking-point Silly Pils from the **brewery**

(☎ 068 55 16 95; www.silly-beer.com; Rue Ville Basse 2; ☯ 8am-noon & 1.30-5pm Mon-Fri).

MONS
pop 91,200

Calling all dragon slayers. Once a year Mons (Bergen in Dutch) riotously comes to life during the Lumeçon (below), which reaches its boisterous culmination on one of Wallonia's finest Grand Places. At other times you'll find a scattering of interesting minor attractions and the hilltop spires look enticing from afar, but the few local historical structures are interspersed with dowdy streetscapes. Many museums are free to enter on the first Sunday of each month.

History

Mons developed around the site of a Roman *castrum* (fortified camp). For centuries it was the capital of the powerful county of Hainaut until 1436 when that was incorporated into Duchy of Burgundy. To some Brits, Mons is remembered for the Angels of Mons, a legend that arose in 1914 based around a host of heavenly archers. During WWII the American liberation campaign had its first victory here. Since 1967 Mons has been home to the Supreme Headquarters of the Allied Powers in Europe (Shape), which employs some 8000 American and NATO officials and is based 5km north of town.

Information

Maison du Tourisme (☎ 065 33 55 80; www.pays demons.be, in French; Grand Place 22; ☯ 9.30am-6.30pm) Free glossy booklets introduce Mons' numerous minor attractions. Ask to see the 15-minute video introduction to the town (available in English).

Sights & Activities

The most visually arresting building on the *café*-lined **Grand Place** is the splendid 15th-century **Hôtel de Ville** (Town Hall), next to the tourist office. On the front-left flank of its gateway portal it's become customary to score a wish by stroking the head of a tiny iron **monkey** (Singe du Grand Gard), though traditionally such a practice was only supposed to work for women hoping to get married or pregnant within the year. The gateway leads to a pretty area of courtyard garden. Interesting lanes climb from the square's northwest side to the hilltop site of Mons' original fortress. That's long gone but through a modest gateway chapel you'll find the 80m-tall World Heritage–listed baroque **beffroi** (belfry), a 17th-century marvel billowing with black-and-gold mini-domes. By 2011 the belfry should be open to visits but till then the surrounding garden (admission free) is still worth the climb for fine views across the city rooftops.

Descending to the west, **Collégiale Ste-Waudru** (www.waudru.be; Place du Chapitre; ☯ 9am-6pm) is a 15th-century church of huge proportions. Inside is the fanciful 1782 **Car d'Or**, the gilded, cherub-festooned chariot used to carry the magnificent golden **reliquary** of Ste-Waudru during Le Doudou. The reliquary otherwise hangs above the altar. Displays in the small **treasury** (adult/child €2.50/1.25; ☯ 1.30-5pm Tue-Sat, 1.30-6pm Sun) include Ste-Waudru's shroud and a sword-slashed skull – supposedly

---

LE DOUDOU

Known locally as Le Doudou, the incredible Unesco-listed festival **La Ducasse** (www.ducassedemons .be) sees the remains of Ste-Waudru (a 7th-century female miracle worker and the city's patron) raucously paraded around town in the **Procession du Car d'Or**. Then at lunchtime on the Grand Place, an insistent drum beat and cycling chant accompanies the **Lumeçon**, a mock battle pitting good against evil in the form of St-George versus a 9.4m-long wickerwork dragon. Lesser characters include 18th-century soldiers, St-George's sidekicks – the Chinchins – and a gang of devils helping out the dragon. If you dare, join the crowd surging forward to grab hairs from the 200kg-dragon's tail as it flails around wildly. But beware that while thrilling, getting anywhere close can be potentially hazardous given the life-threatening squeeze of the crowd.

Purloining a dragon hair is supposed to augur a spell of good luck. In June 2009 high-level discussions aimed at forming a new government coalition started rather light-heartedly when Elio di Rupo (the Mayor of Mons, as well as leader of Belgium's Francophone Socialist Party) handed out strands of Doudou dragon tail to fellow party leaders to give negotiations a superstitious helping hand.

that of sainted Merovingian King Dagobert II. For some conspiracy theorists, Dagobert's murder in AD 675 is considered to have been an attempt to put an end to the 'Jesus bloodline'.

OTHER MUSEUMS
If you're a fan of exotic gilded clocks, dazzling porcelain and silver coffeepots from the 1775 to 1825 period, check out the rich collection at the sumptuous three-room **Musée François Duesberg** (☎ 065 36 31 64; Rue de la Houssière 2; admission €5; ☼ 2-7pm Tue, Thu, Sat & Sun). It's in the converted former national bank building between Ste-Waudru's and the train station. Septuagenarian collector-curator Baron Duesberg brims with such passionate enthusiasm you might mistake him for Louis de Funès.

BAM (Musée des Beaux-Arts; ☎ 065 40 53 24; Rue Neuve 8; adult/concession €8/5; ☼ hours vary) is a discordant new glass cube offering lavish changing exhibitions of late 20th-century art. It's one block northwest of the Grand Place.

Sleeping & Eating
Central Mons is stuffed with good and good-value restaurants while a great range of informal *cafés* line the Grand Place and Marché aux Herbes. Decent accommodation options are contrastingly few. Several of the limited options are in the area around the train station that, despite some revamping, is far from salubrious.

Auberge de Jeunesse du Beffroi (☎ 065 87 55 70; www.laj.be; Rampe du Château 2; members dm/d/q €18.60/46/64; ☼ reception/check-in 5-8pm; ☒ ☐) Just before the base of the belfry, this modern, well-equipped HI hostel has an attractive tiered design making good use of the sloping terrain. Advance reservations are essential in the low season.

Hôtel Infotel (☎ 065 40 18 30; www.hotelinfotel .be; Rue d'Havré 32; s/d/tr from €73/75/90; P ☎) This boxy hotel has generic motel-style furnishings but it's just footsteps from the Grand Place. Parking and internet is free, breakfast is €10.

Hôtel St James (☎ 065 72 48 24; www.hotel stjames.be; Place de Flandre 8; s/d €73/80; P ☎) Mons' most characterful choice gives a refined old brick-and-stone house a trendy two-tone makeover. Behind the main building, via a handkerchief of garden, a newer, equally fashionable rear section has road noise. It's just across the ring-boulevard, 10 minutes' walk east of the Grand Place via Rue

d'Havré. Free parking and wi-fi, breakfast is €12.

La Vie est Belle (☎ 065 56 58 45; Rue d'Havré 39; mains €6.50-17, 4-course menu €15; ☼ noon-3pm Tue-Sun, 6-11pm Tue-Sat) This family-style restaurant is superb value for homestyle Belgian food that's filling rather than gourmet (think meatballs, mashed potatoes, rabbit or mussels), and the naive puppet-models adorning the decorative mirrors add character.

Sel & Sucre (☎ 065 59 05 07; www.sel-et-sucre.be; Rue de Nimy 6; 3-course lunch/dinner menu from €20/35; ☼ lunch Tue-Sun, dinner Tue-Sat) Modern little restaurant just off the Grand Place coloured in deep maroon tones and noted for the chef's spontaneous cuisine.

Getting There & Around
Mons' **train station** (Place Léopold) and neighbouring **TEC bus station** (☎ 065 38 88 15) are 700m west of the Grand Place via Rue des Clercs. Trains run twice hourly to Brussels (€8.60, 55 minutes), Charleroi (€5.90, fast/slow 30/50 minutes) and Tournai (€6.60, fast/slow 23/43 minutes).

Free public minibuses shuttle every 15 minutes from Monday to Saturday between 7am and 9pm between the train/bus station and the Grand Place.

AROUND MONS
Spiennes
If you thought any old rock was enough for men during the stone age, think again. In fact they were so particular that they'd dig many metres down through levels of inferior quality flints to get to the good stuff. See for yourself at the **Spiennes Neolithic flint mine** (☎ 065 35 34 78; Rue du Point du Jour; www.minesdespiennes.org; adult/child €2.50/1.25; ☼ 10am-4pm 1st Sun of month Mar-Nov), one of Unesco's least visited World Heritage Sites. Visitors get to touch real and imitation Neolithic tools before being harnessed and taken down what appears to be a manhole on an 8m vertical ladder. Underground you'll see workings that were carved out more than 6000 years ago with interesting, very personal explanations (one guide speaks some English). The small but fascinating site is hidden behind an unmarked metal shed on a hillside above Petit-Spiennes where tracks signed 'Minières' peter out. Driving back down there's a gorgeous view of Mons' spires across the fields. Private visits are possible by arrangement (minimum fee €30).

Driving from Mons to Spiennes, notice the extraordinary, shattered castle in **Havré**, a moated roadside affair where three corner towers look like 19th-century mill-houses while the contrasting fourth retains its stone structure and bulbous spire.

Canal Craft

The Bruxelles–Charleroi Canal was built in 1832 to carry coal to the capital. In its first form the canal required 55 locks, two aqueducts and a tunnel, and the journey averaged three days. This has now been reduced to one day, in part by the installation of the 1.4km-long **Inclined Plane** at Ronquières, a 1968 contraption like a gigantic slope-sliding bath. It's strangely mesmerising to watch it trundling oh-so-slowly into action.

Even more dramatic is the 2002 **Strépy-Thieu Boat-lift** (Ascenseur Strépy-Thieu; ☎ 078 05 90 59; info .strepy_thieu@hainaut.be; adult/senior/child €5.50/5/2.50; ☉ 9.30am-6.30pm Feb-Nov, last entry 5pm), the world's tallest ship lift, raising or lowering a counterbalanced pair of gigantic 'baths' through some 73 vertical metres. Visually the gigantic concrete mechanism isn't beautiful, but its scale is awesome, as was the sum of money it cost to build (more than €150 million). Visits allow you to look down on the engine room from the

6th-floor exhibition hall. There's also an inexpensive view-*café*, and you can see a 35-minute multilingual video on the lift's construction and eight imaginative, five-minute presentations celebrating 'Belgian Genius' culminating in a cartoon-strip quiz staged in a mock schoolroom. On Sunday you can **ride** (adult/senior/child €5.50/5/3.50; ☉ 11.30am, 1.45pm, 3.15pm, 4.45pm, Sun, May–mid-Sep) in a boat up or down the lift. Combination tickets save around 20%.

Prebooked tours with **Rivertours** (www.river tours.be; adult/child €18/14; ☉ 9am Sat & Sun, May-Sep) add a cruise down the canal, followed by a sightseeing bus ride past the four Unesco-listed **historic ship-lifts** (near La Louvière) that Strépy-Thieu replaced.

Strépy-Thieu is accessible on bus 30 from La Louvière. The lift head can be briefly glimpsed while driving the Tournai–Brussels motorway eastbound. Look south just west of the Le Roeulx junction.

Binche
pop 32,000

Historic Binche once sported an opulent palace-castle of Mary of Hungary, sister of mighty Charles Quint (see the boxed text, p27). That's long gone but the town still maintains sections of historical city walls,

---

CARNIVAL DE BINCHE

Binche lives for its Unesco-listed **carnival** (www.carnavaldebinche.be; ☉ 8 Mar 2011, 21 Feb 2012). Although preparatory events occur for several weeks before, the festival culminates on Shrove Tuesday, by which stage houses have battened down the hatches, shops have metamorphosed into impromptu bars and woefully insufficient portable toilets have been installed to cope with the miraculous trans-substantiation of beer into urine.

Unlike at 'normal' carnivals you won't see multifarious musical floats rolling around town. In Binche the undisputed stars of the show are the Gilles, stomping male figures who all dress alike in clogs and thickly straw-padded suits decorated with heraldic symbols, scarlet piping, jingling bells and white shoulder ruffs. The Mardi Gras ceremonies have two main parts, each tumultuously drunken yet oddly solemn at the same time. In the morning each 'brotherhood' of Gilles clomps its rhythmic way to the town hall, then briefly don spooky green-eyed masks while performing a time-honoured stomp and shaking sticks to ward off evil spirits.

After a lunchtime lull, up to a thousand Gilles march across town in one vast shuffling slow-motion parade wearing their enormous ostrich-feather headdresses (weather permitting). Each carries a wicker basket of oranges. Oranges are lobbed intermittently into the heaving crowd and at observers who cheer on from those windows that haven't been protectively boarded up. Don't even think of hurling one back, however tempting it might be – the Gilles-thrown oranges are metaphorical blessings. Despite appearances, the carnival is a serious celebration, taking months of preparation and involving strict rules of conduct. The rituals surrounding it date back hundreds of years and the Gilles' finery is thought to be an interpretation of the elaborate, Inca-inspired costumes worn by courtiers at a world-famous feast held here by Mary of Hungary to honour Emperor Charles V in 1549.

has a scruffily attractive main square and a sizeable 17th-century church (Collégiale St-Ursmer). For most of the year the town has a rather grey and slightly forlorn look. But all that changes for a week of carnival festivities that are one of the world's most unusual (see the boxed text, opposite). If you're anywhere near during Mardi Gras, Binche is an absolute must. Otherwise, get a feel for what it's about at the **Musée International du Carnaval et du Masque** (☎ 064 33 57 41; www.musee dumasque.be; Rue St-Moustier 10; adult/concession/child €6/5/3.50, free 1st Sun of each month; ☒ 9.30am-4.30pm Tue-Fri, 10.30am-4.30pm Sat & Sun).

GETTING THERE & AWAY

Mons–Binche bus 22 (€3.25, 40 minutes) runs around every 40 minutes. At carnival time, however, impossible traffic makes the train (€4.40, 40 minutes) much more sensible. From Binche's delightful wrought-iron-framed station, trains bound for Louvain-la-Neuve run hourly via Halle and Brussels (€8.60, 59 minutes). Change in La Louvière (€2.20, 12 minutes) for Charleroi or Mons.

WATERLOO BATTLEFIELD

Tourists have been swarming to Waterloo's battlefield sites ever since 1815 when one of Europe's bloodiest battles caused 32,000 deaths and changed the course of history by marking a final defeat for Napoleon. Before visiting, do remember that a battlefield is, after all, just a field. Having said that, this battlefield area encompasses a vast, attractive patchwork of gently undulating crop land crowned by a dramatic battle landmark and dotted with a plethora of memorials and museums. For the full experience come during one of the battle re-enactments, usually held on the weekend nearest the battle's anniversary (18 June); see p17.

Beware that the main battlefield site is some 5km south of central Waterloo town, with other sites spread considerably further.

Sights & Activities
LION HAMLET

The most tangible battlefield attractions are clumped around the **visitor centre** (☎ 023 85 19 12; www.waterloo1815.be; Route du Lion; ☒ 9.30am-6.30pm Apr-Sep, 10am-5pm Oct-Mar). From here you can access Waterloo's most visually arresting

sight, the **Butte du Lion** (Lion's Mound; Route du Lion; adult/child €6/4), a 40m grassy cone of artificial hill that rises steeply to a massive bronze lion. It commemorates William of Orange (later King William II of the Netherlands), who was wounded on this spot while co-commanding Allied troops. Building the impressive mound took two years, and was made by women who carted up soil in individual baskets. It's well worth climbing the 225 steps to survey the battlefield's deceptively minor undulations that so fooled Napoleon's infantry.

The Butte ticket also includes entry to the charmingly old-fashioned if slightly damp-worn **Panorama de la Bataille** (Battleground Panorama), created back in 1912. From its elevated gallery you check out a circular action-packed painting of the battle scenes across a three-dimensional foreground littered with fallen helmets, broken down fences, dead horses and the odd corpse – models, naturally. The partly labelled scene is 110m in circumference and made atmospheric by a rumbling soundtrack of battle cries, bagpipes, cannon fire and thundering hooves.

If you buy a **Hameau du Lion Pass** (adult/concession/child €8.70/6.50/5.50) instead of the standard Butte ticket, it also allows you access to the visitor centre's interesting **battle presentation**, shown every 20 minutes, which starts with a wordless, low-tech audiovisual introduction to the key sites, then follows with 20 minutes of highlights from Sergei Bondarchuk's lavish 1970 movie re-creation of the battle (filmed in Russia at astonishing expense using over 15,000 Soviet troops as extras).

The pass ticket also throws in entry to the small **Musée de Cire** (Wax Figures Museum) across the road. Despite some original costumes, the waxworks itself is largely forgettable but it's housed in a sturdy, traditional building originally constructed in 1821 as a tavern-hotel-museum to cater to Napoleonic war veteran-tourists. Its former function continues in much of the building where the **Bivouac de l'Empereur** (☒ 10am-7pm; beer €2.30-4.30, mains €9.50-23) retains painted brick arches, heavy wooden beams, sepia photos, battle pictures, army standards and original memorabilia, much of it picked up from the battlefield itself over generations. Log fires burn in big open hearths as you join the throng at gingham-clothed tables for an unpretentious lunch or a well-chilled glass of floral Waterloo 7 beer (€3.50).

OTHER BATTLEFIELD SITES

Die-hard battlefield fans can visit a whole series of other battle-related sites, though be prepared for long walks or various driving hops. Alternatively, the Lion Hamlet visitor centre organises 45-minute **battlefield tours** (adult/child €5.50/4.40) including commentaries taking keener visitors to several outlying 1815 sites on an old Bedford truck-bus. Its **Pass+Tour ticket** (adult/concession/child €12/9/7) combines the tour and Hameau du Lion Pass.

Hougoumont

Had Napoleon broken through here early in the battle everything would have turned out differently. It's a classic fortified farm with a miniature chapel around 20 minutes' walk southwest of the lion, but the site is currently undergoing substantial restoration and can't be entered.

Plancenoit

In 1815 a crucial sideshow battle between French and Prussian armies engulfed

---

THE BATTLE OF WATERLOO: A SIMPLIFIED HISTORY

After a disastrous invasion of Russia and having lost the decisive 1813 Battle of Leipzig, legendary French emperor Napoleon Bonaparte seemed finally defeated. Several European governments were heartily relieved and had him imprisoned on the island of Elba. Yet on 1 March 1815 he escaped, landed in southern France and with remarkable speed managed to muster a huge following army. The European powers promptly declared war and chose Brussels as the point at which to form a combined army. However, in the days before railways it could take weeks to march an army into place. Napoleon knew that time was of the essence. If he could meet either army individually, Napoleon's 124,000 men would outnumber roughly 106,000 Anglo-Dutch-Hanoverian troops or an approaching army of 117,000 Prussians. But he had to strike fast before the two combined.

On 16 June Napoleon struck the Prussians at Ligny (p221), where Blücher, the Prussian commander, was wounded and the Prussian army appeared to have been put to flight. Napoleon then turned his attention to British commander Wellington, whose troops were assembling at Waterloo, a carefully chosen defensive position just south of Brussels.

At sunrise on Sunday 18 June the two armies faced off. Due to heavy overnight rain, the start of the battle was delayed to allow the soggy ground to dry out. The French attack started mid-morning with a pincer movement to the west focusing on a farm at Hougoumont (above) that was vital for the defence of Wellington's right. The assault took far longer than anticipated, fatally slowing Napoleon's game plan. Meanwhile, by 1pm, the French had word that the Prussian army was not routed after all. Indeed it had regrouped and was now moving in fast. Napoleon detached a force to meet it and for several hours battle raged at Plancenoit (above), depriving Napoleon of crucial manpower on the main battlefield.

At 2pm a massive wave of French infantry marched shoulder-to-shoulder towards Wellington's left flank. However, thousands of allied musketeers had been cleverly hidden in long, three-deep rows behind a ridge-top hedge (along what is now the rural lane, Route de la Marache). Here they were invisible to the French infantry, who had to slog uphill through the mud. Invisible that is until suddenly, at the very last minute, they rose row by row to unleash volleys of musket fire into the terrified ranks of Frenchmen, whose close-knit formations compounded the difficulty of escape.

After this chaotic debacle, the French cavalry was sent in to charge Wellington's centre. However, the well-trained allied infantrymen formed defensive squares in which the bayonets of their muskets collectively turned groups into impenetrable 'hedgehogs' of spikes. The musketeers couldn't reload and shoot at the cavalry. But the cavaliers, armed mostly with sabres, couldn't finish off the squares either. The result was somewhat of a stalemate. For Napoleon the situation was becoming ever more urgent given the steady approach of the main Prussian force. Napoleon ordered his Imperial Guards, the army's best soldiers, to break through Wellington's centre. It was a desperate last-ditch effort – the guards had to slog uphill through mud churned up by the cavalry's previous attempt and were mown down by the opposing infantrymen from their protected high-ground position.

Around 8.15pm Wellington led a full-scale advance, the French fell into full retreat and Napoleon fled, abandoning his damaged carriage at Genappe with such haste that he didn't even have time to remove its cache of diamonds. He officially abdicated a week later and spent the rest of his life in exile on St Helena.

WATERLOO REPLAY

Hundreds or even thousands of costumed 'soldier' enthusiasts gather each year on a weekend close to 18 June to re-create scenes from the classic battle. Before the action begins, it's fascinating to visit their encampments (French 'army' at the Dernier Quartier Général de Napoléon, below; Allies at Hougoumont, opposite), where, apart from all the cars and bottled beers, living conditions approximate the 1815 original. You'll need a prebooked grandstand ticket (www.waterloo1815.be) to watch the main battle re-enactment on a field south of Lion Hamlet (p217). It's an incredible visual spectacle regularly punctuated with musket fire, thumping cannon shots and cavalry sorties circling around infantry squares. However, events don't play out historically and understandably the unpaid soldier-enthusiasts see little fun in playing dead, so the result is a little unfocused and just a tad dissatisfying. A much less publicised and arguably even more exciting second reconstruction is held at Plancenoit (opposite), typically one night before the main spectacle. The battle starts in a field on the northern edge of the village, where the action can be hard to see as there's no raised viewing platform. However, one feels more in the thick of things and all the more so once the action spills off the field and into the village centre. Best of all it's free.

this pleasant country village 6km east of Waterloo. There's a hidden Gothic-black Prussian memorial 500m north of the village's steeply sloped central square, where the dramatic finale of a local battle reconstitution is best watched from the comfort of local pub terrace, **Le Gros Vélo** (☎ 026 33 17 46; Place de Plancenoit 22; Saint-Joseph abbey beer €3; 🕑 10am-10pm Fri-Wed, kitchen closed Wed). Bus 36 connects to Braine-l'Alleud station.

Dernier Quartier Général de Napoléon

The isolated farmhouse complex where Napoleon breakfasted the morning of the battle now forms a small **museum** (☎ 023 84 24 24; Chaussée de Bruxelles 66, Vieux-Genappe; adult/child €2/1; 🕑 10am-6.30pm Apr-Oct, 1-5pm Nov-Mar). It's 4km south on the Waterloo–Genappe road, accessible by the somewhat infrequent Charleroi-bound bus 365.

WATERLOO TOWN

pop 29,000

Around 5km north of the battlefield, the middle-class suburban town of **Waterloo** (www.waterloo-tourisme.be) was a small village when Wellington slept here before and after the battle. The inn he stayed at is still partly a pub, the rest forming the modest but well laid-out **Musée Wellington** (☎ 023 54 78 06; www.museewellington.be; Chaussée de Bruxelles 147; adult/concession/child/Brusselscard €5/4/2/free; 🕑 9.30am-6.30pm Apr-Sep, 10am-5pm Oct-Mar). Exhibits of interest range from battle plans to the prosthetic leg of Lord Uxbridge. It's at Waterloo's central crossroads opposite a distinctive church with yet more battle memorials. Bus W stops outside.

Getting There & Around

TEC bus W (Map pp72–3) runs every 30 minutes from Ave Fonsny at Brussels-Midi to Waterloo town, and continues past Lion Hamlet to Braine-l'Alleud train station. You'll generally save money buying a multistop day card (€6). If coming by train from Charleroi or Nivelles, Braine-l'Alleud is more convenient than awkwardly located Waterloo station but you'll still need to backtrack on bus W to reach the sights. The tourist office opposite Musée Wellington in Waterloo town rents bicycles for solo exploration.

NIVELLES

pop 24,100

Ancient Nivelles (Nijvel in Dutch) sports one of Belgium's most unusual and impressive churches, the 11th-century **Collégiale Ste-Gertrude** (Grand Place; 🕑 9am-5pm Mon-Sat, 2-5pm Sun). It was once attached to one of Europe's foremost abbeys, founded in 648. Its first abbess, Gertrude, was a great-great aunt of Charlemagne, and was later sainted for her miraculous abilities including rat-catching (which warded off plague) and devil-snaring (which saved the mythical Knight of Masseik from losing a Faustian bargain). The church building is 102m long with a soaring multi-level western facade topped with a squat octagonal tower flanked by turrets. Watch the southern turret on the hour to see its life-sized 350kg gilt statue strike the clock bell with a hefty hammer.

The interior's enormous Romanesque arches are unadorned stone, but notice the 15th-century wooden chariot that's still used to carry Ste-Gertrude's silver *châsse* (casket) during Nivelles' greatest procession, the Tour Sainte-Gertrude. The current *châsse* is an inventive 1982 replacement for the magnificent 84kg gold-and-silver original, smashed apart by a 1940 German bombing raid that also destroyed the church's Gothic spire.

Fascinating and detailed two-hour **guided tours** (€5; 2pm daily, plus 3.30pm Sat & Sun) in French get you access to the crypt, the tower gallery and the pretty cloister for photogenic views. You're then shown archaeological diggings that reveal five earlier church-mausoleum sites, and the grave of Charlemagne's first wife Himeltrude, whose 1.85m skeleton can be seen reflected by a well-placed mirror.

English-language tours (€30 per group) can be organised through the **tourist office** (☎ 067 84 08 64, 22 04 44; www.tourisme-nivelles.be; Rue de Saintes 48; 8.30am-5pm) around 200m southeast of the church. Staff can also suggest several walks, though Nivelles' patchy townscape lacks much visual drama.

Sleeping & Eating

Nivelles' one hotel, **Nivelles Sud** (☎ 067 21 87 21; www.hotelnivellessud.be; Chaussée de Mons 22; s/d €71/86; 🖭 P), is a large, relatively upmarket motel 1.2km west behind a shopping centre at the motorway intersection.

The eastern edge of Grand Place has a wide selection of fun *café*-restaurants. A touch more refined than most, **L'Union** (☎ 067 21 81 27; Grand Place 27; snacks €3-9.50, beers €1.90-3.50; 9.30am-11pm) is widely reputed for its *tarte al djote* (€8.90), a unique Nivelles' speciality that's somewhere between pizza and quiche but flavoured with fragrant green chard. Smaller, much cheaper takeaway versions cost just €1.30 at the brilliant historic bakery-shop **Le Chant du Pain** (Rue du Géant 1; 7am-7.30pm Mon-Sat), 150m east of the Grand Place via Rue de Namur.

For a good selection of cosy eateries – including weekday sandwich shops, an upmarket Indian and two hip Franco-Belgian restaurants – stroll along the Rue de Bruxelles that exits the main square just next to the Palais de Justice building.

Getting There & Away

The Grand Place is a 15-minute walk from Nivelles' train station via Rue de Namur. Hourly Brussels–Charleroi fast trains take 20 minutes in either direction. Nivelles–Brussels commuter trains are vastly slower.

WAVRE-OTTIGNIES-GEMBLOUX

Walibi & Aqualibi

Adrenaline-packed big-scale rides are the trademark of **Walibi & Aqualibi** (Map p209; ☎ 010 42 15 00; www.walibi.be; Blvd de l'Europe 100, Wavre; adult/senior/child €31/28/27; Apr-Oct), a combined theme park and water park off the E411 Brussels–Namur highway. Check the website for opening dates and closing times. At the time of research these parks were closed for renovation. Ottignies–Leuven trains stop twice hourly at Bierges-Walibi station, around 800m from the park entrance.

Louvain-la-Neuve

In the chaos of 1968 the Francophone university faculties of KUL (p200) were violently driven out of Leuven. Louvain-la-Neuve was purpose-built to give them a new home. Set amid hilly woodlands, most buildings here are archetypal 1970s collegiate. However, one major attraction is the inventive 2009 **Hergé Museum** (☎ 010 48 84 21; www.museeherge.com; Rue du Labrador 26; adult/student/child €9.50/7/5; 10am-6pm Tue-Sun, last entry 5pm), celebrating the multitalented creator of comic-strip hero Tintin (opposite). The museum's unique architecture alone is worth the visit: an abstract glass-and-concrete boat-shaped creation filled with multistorey geometrical forms slashed through with a central 'light chasm' filling the structure with intriguing angles and views. While this creates an audacious mass of empty space, the exhibition is nonetheless extensive and engaging. Highlights of the museum include numerous models, pictures and source materials assembled by the artist to ensure the accuracy of his sketches, and you can also listen to 1½ hours of audio-guided commentary or watch a 20-minute video. Note the original triptych portrait of Hergé by Andy Warhol, for whom Tintin was a cited influence. The gift shop sells Tintin albums in numerous languages.

The museum is a short walk from the bus and train stations. Ultraslow direct trains take 1¼ hours to Bruxelles-Central (hourly) but you'll generally save 20 minutes by changing onto an express in Ottignies (nine minutes). TEC-Rapido bus 3 runs six times daily (35 minutes, Monday to Friday) to Braine-l'Alleud via Waterloo Mont-St-Jean, 1.5km from Waterloo's battlefield site.

Villers-la-Ville

Nestled in a pretty wooded dell lie the extensive, ivy-clad ruins of the **Abbaye de Villers** (☎ 071 88

TINTIN

Quiff-headed boy-reporter Tintin is Belgium's most iconic comic-strip character. Tintin's adventures involve a beloved and humorous team of misfits, including dog Snowy, crusty companion Captain Haddock and half-deaf Professor Calculus, fan of a malaprop or two. Despite some criticism of racial stereotyping, the Tintin comic books have been translated into more than 50 languages and still sell more than two million copies a year. Blistering barnacles! And that's more than two decades after the death of creator Georges Remi, whose pen name Hergé comes from his reversed initials, RG, pronounced in French. A stunning new Hergé museum opened in Louvain-la-Neuve in 2009 (opposite) and Tintin sales are likely to increase further still in 2011 when the character returns in a DreamWorks movie, *Secret of the Unicorn*, guided by Steven Spielberg and Peter Jackson.

---

09 80; www.villers.be; adult/concession/child €5/4/2; ☺ 10am-5.30pm Apr-Oct, 10am-4.30pm Wed-Mon Nov-Mar). Once one of Belgium's biggest monastic complexes, Villers was never rebuilt after the destructive onslaught of 1794 when French revolutionaries stirred up a nationwide anti-religious fervour that led to the sacking of virtually every such institution. To add insult to injury a railway line was built through the site in the 1850s. Visitors can also make out the foundations of a brewery, kitchen and old warming room – in its day the only part of the complex to have winter heating. A few times a year, the gigantic, shattered church makes an atmospheric venue for outdoor concerts or Shakespearean dramas.

Across the road from the ruins the **Taverne du Moulin** (☎ 071 87 68 65; www.moulindevillers.be; Rue de l'Abbaye 55; ☺ 10am-11pm Tue-Sun) gets mixed reviews for its meals, but is ideal for a coffee, cake or drink in an old stone-vaulted mill house after you've visited the ruins.

Villers-la-Ville train station (on the Ottignies–Charleroi line) is 1.6km south of the abbey entrance. Exiting the train station, turn left, continue to a T-junction then turn right and follow the main road to the ruins.

Gembloux
pop 22,000

Forgettable Gembloux is worth a five-minute stop to glimpse its dour five-storey Unesco-listed belfry, whose two-level spire seems to be holding up a dark-timber umbrella. The sombre structure is best viewed across the town's main square from the attractively turreted 1589 **Maison du Bailli** (now the town hall). Around 300m up the Grand Rue, big wooden gates lead into the enclosed lawns of a stately **former abbey** that now houses Gembloux's agricultural university. Beside the gates is a pair of underworked tourist offices, which seem sweetly surprised to find that any tourists actually bother to drop in. On the triangular 'square' opposite is the unpretentious terrace *café* **Estaminet** (☎ 081 61 57 57; Place St-Guibert 6; mains €12-20; ☺ 11am-11pm Mon-Fri, 10am-6pm Sun), with an interior curious for incorporating a chunk of 12th-century city wall behind the bar.

Castle Villages

Back in the 13th century the borderland between the county of Namur and the Duchy of Brabant lay close to Gembloux, and the region's villages are still dotted with minor medieval castles. For day-tripping Brussels motorists this area offers one of the easiest ways to get out into attractive rolling hills, but without wheels the sights don't really justify the complex trips by public transport and long walks from the region's stations.

Around 5km southwest of Gembloux, the pretty hamlet of **Corroy-le-Château** hides its partly 13th-century **castle** (adult/child €7/4; ☺ 10am & 2pm Sat & Sun May-Sep) in thick private woodlands so you can only see its squat barrel-shaped stone towers on visiting days. The furnished interior has secret wall-passages to the chapel, along with an original Van Dyck and an intriguing latter-day family-portrait ceiling, but the full 1¾-hour tour is far too long.

The village of **Sombreffe** is less appealing than Corroy but its **castle** (www.lechateaudesombreffe .be) has a particularly fine quiver of variously shaped towers. The central keep is private but you can enter the central courtyard.

The next village southwest is **Ligny**, where the whole course of European history would have changed had Napoleon's pre-Waterloo battle with Blücher's Prussians proved more conclusive (see the boxed text, p218). Battle fans can visit Ligny's rather sparse five-room **Musée Napoléon** (☎ 071 88 89 51; www.ligny1815.org; Centre Général Gérard, Rue Pont-Piraux 23; adult/senior/child €4/3/2; ☺ 2-5pm Thu-Sun Apr-Oct).

HAINAUT & BRABANT WALLON

There are fortified farms in nearby **Balatre** and **Tongrinne**. A 13th-century stone tower 1km south of **Mazy** forms part of the delightful **Golf de Falnuée** (☎ 81 63 30 90; www.falnuee.be; Rue Emile Pirson 55, Mazy), whose golf course spreads like emerald-green baize towards unspoilt wooded ridges. The scene is idyllic viewed from its **restaurant-café** (mains €11-18; ☑ 10am-4pm Tue-Sun Nov-Mar, 9am-10pm daily in summer) in vaulted former castle stables above which are 10 decent new motel-style **guestrooms** (s/d/ste €70/80/140) sporting elements of modern art. Breakfast is €10. There's also a wellness centre (end of par 5).

Around 500m south of Falnuée towards the little watermill village of **Onoz**, look left across the rail tracks to see the mighty fortress of **Mielmont** rising high on a crag amid the trees. At the western edge of **Spy**, a 10-minute walk through pretty woodland zigzags down to a very modest (and unfenced) cliff-cave that's one of Belgium's best-known **Neolithic sites**.

CHARLEROI
pop 200,600

Until the 1960s this region's coalfields were the main force behind Belgium's economy. These days the main reason that travellers transit bedraggled Charleroi is to make use of the ultracheap flights offered from its international airport. However, there's a certain demonic grandeur in the city's massive rust-chimneyed steelworks rising like an industrial Frankenstein amid the now-landscaped slag heaps. And while the cityscape is dominated by gruesome concrete, a few art nouveau and art deco exceptions can be found using a pamphlet from the **tourist office** (☎ 071 31 82 18; www .charleroi.be, www.paysdecharleroi.be; ☑ 9.30am-5pm Mon-Fri) at the main train station, Charleroi-Sud.

On the main square, **L'Église St-Christophe** (Place Charles II) is a bizarre church whose historic baroque frontage and rear altarpiece have been spliced with a 1956 dome and an extraordinary two-storey golden mosaic of the apocalypse, designed in a dazzling Klimt-goes-Roman style. The art deco **town hall** (Hôtel de Ville, Place Charles II) is entered from the rear of the building beneath a monumentally ugly 1936 belfry. You might be permitted to climb the tower for sweeping views if you ask nicely in French at the small, rather specialist **Jules Destrée Museum** (☎ 071 86 11 38; admission free; ☑ 9am-5pm Tue-Fri) hidden away on the 3rd floor.

Across Place du Manège is the stern 1956 **Palais des Beaux-Arts** (www.pba.be; Place du Manège

1) theatre building, behind which you'll find the airy new **Musée des Beaux-Arts** (Fine Art Museum; ☎ 071 86 11 34; www.charleroi-museum.be; admission free; ☑ 9am-5pm Tue-Fri, 10am-6pm Sat). The museum has an excellent art collection, including works by James Ensor, Rik Wouters, Paul Delvaux, René Magritte and Impressionist Anna Boch, though space seriously limits the number of works that can be shown at any one time.

Charleroi's cultural highpoint is its avant-garde dance company, **Charleroi/Danses** (www .charleroi-danses.be), which performs at **Les Écuries** (☎ 071 20 56 40; Blvd Pierre Mayence 65c), as well as in Brussels (see p109) and abroad.

Charleroi-Sud train station is a quick walk from Place Charles II, passing twin statues by 19th-century master Constantin Meunier. Trains run every 30 minutes to Brussels (€8.60, 50 minutes), Mons (€5.90, fast/slow 30/48 minutes) and Nivelles (€4.20, 20 minutes).

AROUND CHARLEROI
Charleroi Airport

Around 6km north of the city, **Charleroi airport** (www.charleroi-airport.com) is Belgium's main hub for budget airlines, notably Ryanair. **L'Elan** (www.voyages-lelan.be) runs direct buses to/from a stop near Brussels Midi station roughly every half an hour (single/return €13/22, one hour, last northbound 11.30pm, first southbound 4.30am). Allow ample extra journey time during rush hour. Buy tickets in the terminal at counter 1 or pre-purchase online.

If you're heading anywhere except Brussels, start with the TEC 'Aeroport' bus (www.info tec.be; €2.50, 18 minutes) to Charleroi-Sud train station. It runs twice hourly on weekdays, hourly at weekends. Save money by purchasing a combined bus-rail ticket before leaving the airport (maximum fare €11 to anywhere in Belgium).

The nearest of eight mostly generic airport accommodation options is the Etap Hotel which, while physically very close to the terminal, is actually 1.4km away by circuitous road. The cheapest is a Formule1, with shared toilets.

Photography Museum

The prize-winning **Photography Museum** (☎ 071 43 58 10; www.museephoto.be; Ave Paul Pastur 11, Mont-sur-Marchienne; adult/senior/student/child €6/4/3/free; ☑ 10am-6pm Tue-Sun) is Europe's biggest and possibly its most impressive, with an engrossing collection of historic, contemporary and artistic prints. Don't miss the area upstairs above the cloister dealing with air-brushing, tricks-of-the-trade and optical illusions. Particularly intriguing is a little curtained room in which you effectively stand within a giant pin-hole camera. Although most labels are only in French, the ideas are generally self-explanatory. The museum occupies the modernised and rebuilt shell of a staid 19th-century convent building right at the centre of dreary Mont-sur-Marchienne, 3km south of Charleroi by regular bus 70.

Airliner Café

One of Belgium's weirdest café-bars, **Air US Café** (☎ 071 48 69 00; www.airuscafe.com; Gilly; beers/cocktails/ paninis/pastas from €2.40/6.70/5.20/8; ☒ 2pm-late Mon-Fri, 11am-late Sat & Sun) started life as a 1985 Nigeria Airways Airbus 310. The plane is now parked incongruously 3km northeast of central Charleroi (Metro Gazomètre) where Chaussée de Montigny (N572) passes over the N90. Pilot-uniformed waitresses serve margaritas at business-class airliner seats or on an open terrace on the wing. Various themed parties take place after 9pm, including salsa, karaoke, singles nights and male strip shows.

Le Bois du Cazier

This sizeable **industrial museum-complex** (☎ 071 88 08 56; www.leboisducazier.be; Rue du Cazier 80, Marcinelle; adult/child €6/4; ☒ 9am-5pm Tue-Fri, 10am-6pm Sat & Sun) features plenty of old machines (some operational) in a converted mine site where a horrific underground accident killed 262 miners of 10 nationalities back in 1956. A gripping 15 minute multilingual video commemorates that loss and reflects on how it forced the improvement of industrial safety standards. The ticket also includes entry to an industrial museum celebrating Charleroi's former glories as a centre for the steel, glass and coal industries, the **Glass Collection** (☒ closed 12.30-1.45pm) with items dating back as far as 3000 years, and the **Ateliers** (☒ closed 1-2pm), workshops offering varying demonstrations of bronze craft, glass-blowing etc. Allow at least two hours for a visit, three if you do the landscaped walk up the old slag heaps. Bus 52 (10 minutes) runs hourly from Charleroi-Sud train station but not on Sundays.

Aulne

As impressively ruined as the Villers-la-Ville abbey, but much lesser-known, the **Abbaye d'Aulne** (☎ 0471 48 86 18; admission €5; ☒ 11am-6pm daily Jul & Aug, Wed-Sun Apr-Oct) was founded in 671 on the site of a ruined Roman villa. Its giant, 18th-century incarnation survived barely 50 years before being smashed by the French in 1794. Visiting the shattered remnants is a powerful experience, and includes an extensive (if rather slow-moving) audioguide, available in English. It's possible to peep into much of the site for free by walking around the rear wall to the **brasserie-taverne** (☎ 071 56 20 73; www.valdes ambre.be; ☒ 2-8pm Fri-Sun, daily during holiday periods), which overlooks the main area of ruins. The brasserie brews its own Blonde des Pères beer (€3.10), served here in earthenware chalices.

Aulne has no public transport (except school buses) so you'll need your own wheels. The surrounding scenery of the wooded Sambre valley is appealing, and the abbey makes a nice detour if driving to Thuin.

Thuin

One of Wallonia's quainter towns, old Thuin (pronounced 'twa') is a picturesque huddle of partly medieval streets occupying a narrow ridge that peers down on the wooded Sambre River. The town's historical centrepiece is its Unesco-listed **beffroi** (belfry; admission €3; ☒ 11am-5pm Tue-Sun Apr-Sep, 10am-4pm Sat & Sun Oct-Apr), a 1639 stone bell-tower topped with five slate spires and numerous gilded baubles. Apart from the (loud!) bells and old/new clock mechanisms, the tower is empty and one climbs (with audioguide) up newly installed metal steps and steep ladders for the fine regional views. Start a visit in the **tourist office** (☎ 071 59 54 54; www .thuin.be; Place Albert 1er 2; ☒ 9am-5pm), which has free town maps suggesting a hilly 20-minute stroll through the town's 'hanging' (ie steeply terraced) gardens – though they are somewhat overgrown and far from Babylonian.

Thuin train station is across the river far below the old city. If driving, consider heading 6km south to the archetypal village of **Ragnies**, where a magnificent, superbly renovated former farm-castle now hosts the **Distillerie de Biercée** (☎ 071 50 00 50; www.distilleriedebiercee .com), creators of numerous types of local eau-de-vie (plum brandy) including classic P'tit Peket. Taste a shot (€2) at its wonderfully appointed **café** (☒ 11am-7pm Tue-Sat, 11am-9pm Sun Apr-Sep) decked with old enamel signs and winding copper piping. Or, if time permits, take a one-hour **distillery tour** (€6.50; ☒ 3pm) including samples.

BOTTE DU HAINAUT

Shared by Hainaut and Namur provinces, this undulating mixture of farms, woodlands and castle villages is more immediately pretty than the thickly forested Ardennes, yet oddly it's far less touristed. As with much of Wallonia no single site individually justifies the trip but if you're driving, stringing together half a dozen brief stops makes for a fabulous day out. Much of the limited accommodation here is in *gîtes* (www.gitesdewallonie.be) that usually require one-week stays and advanced booking. Even for B&Bs advance bookings are virtually essential both due to high occupancy and because owners might not otherwise be there when you pass by.

Castle Villages

The N5 dual-carriageway is fast and straight but the area's back lanes wind through a series of vaguely intriguing castle villages.

Ham-sur-Heure's streamside 12th-century castle was returreted to splendid effect in 1900 and is now the town hall. Pretty **Cour-sur-Heure** has an archetypal fortified farm. Noted for its Notre-Dame de Grâce pilgrimage (www.notre damedegrace.be), **Berzée** has a castle that's a curious architectural mishmash on a hill towards Rognée. In central **Thy-le-Chateâu** the castle's turreted grey-stone walls match the church, which was largely rebuilt after WWII bombing. **Laneffe** would be lovelier if the thundering N5 didn't cut right through. The **Ferme-Château de Laneffe** (☎ 071 65 58 32; www.ferme -chateau-laneffe.com; Grand-Route 45; d/tr/ste €70/92/193) offers four well-appointed rooms tucked into the timber eaves of a classic castle-farm. The suite sleeps five. Should you arrive by horse, hay and tethering options are available.

Philippeville

Between 1659 and 1815 Philippeville was an ultrafortified enclave of France completely encircled within the Holy Roman (and later Hapsburg) Empire. Today the pentagonal street layout only hints at the town's unique history but the main square, once the central courtyard of the vast fortress, has several appealing historic buildings, *cafés* and a **tourist office** (☎ 071 66 23 00; http://users.swing.be/tourisme .philippeville; Rue des Religieuses 2; ☼ 1-5pm Jul & Aug). The latter organises fascinating (though slow-moving, and only in French) 90-minute guided walks through the fort's 16th-century **souter-rains** (subterranean passageways; tour & video €3; ☼ 1.15pm

& 2.45pm Jul & Aug), of which more than 10km remain. Above ground don't miss the little **Chapelle des Remparts**, a unique chapel fashioned from the fortress' former gunpowder store.

Mariembourg

Mariembourg was once a highly important citadel-fortress guarding the border of the Spanish Low Countries. Its capture by the French in 1555 was a major blow to the Spaniards, who hurriedly built Philippeville to replace it (only to lose that too a century later).

Mariembourg retained its powerful wall-bastions until 1852 when they were removed as proof of Belgium's pledged neutrality. Today there's not a stone of them left but the street plan still follows that of the original citadel, fanning out from a charming tree-dappled main square that sports a fine 1584 church. Most visitors come to Mariembourg for the **CFV3V Steam Train** (☎ 060 31 24 40; http://cfv3v.in-site -out.com; Chaussée de Givet; single/return €7/11) that runs through charming scenery to Treignes (38 minutes). The website has a calendar of colour-coded timetables; steam *(vapeur)* trains run at least once on yellow, green, purple and brown dates departing at 2.20pm, returning 3.40pm. If you miss it there are several locomotives and carriages on view from the car park, or you can watch incoming trains from the *café*. The steam-train station is 800m southeast of the town centre and main train station, at which trains stop roughly hourly between Charleroi (€6.60, 45 minutes) and Couvin (€1.60, seven minutes).

Beer lovers who can't wait for Chimay might wish to stop 1km south of Mariembourg towards Nismes at the **Brasserie des Fagnes** (☎ 060 31 15 70; N939; ☼ 10am-9pm daily Jul & Aug, 11am-7.30pm Tue-Fri, 10am-9pm Sat & Sun Sep-Jun). Fronted with a silly fake windmill device, this working mini-brewery it's undoubtedly tourist-oriented but its interesting beer museum is free to check out and the pleasant tavern serves its own sturdy, well-balanced Super des Fagnes brews.

Couvin

pop 13,500

Modest **Couvin** (www.couvin.be) is the area's biggest town with a selection of eateries on noisy Place Général Piron. The old town's quieter central knoll of austere grey-stone buildings has a passing appeal. On the busy main road towards the train station, **Au Milieu de Nulle Part** (☎ 060 34 52 84; Rue de la Gare 10; s/d €60/70; mains €15-22; ☼ bistro lunch

& dinner Wed-Sun) offers sober B&B rooms with garden and river views. It's attached to the delightful L'Absinthe bistro decorated with wine bottles, barrels and dried hydrangeas.

The Charleroi–Philippeville–Mariembourg–Couvin route is served by hourly trains and occasional bus 451.

Nismes

Nearby **Nismes** (www.viroinval.be) makes an attractive base with a pretty river neatly dividing the old church from a fanciful neogothic **castle** (now the town hall) set amid extensive public parkland. Behind the church you'll find the basic **Café du Barrage** (☎ 060 31 11 25; www.cafe-au-barrage.be; Rue de l'Église 2; beer €1.50-3, meals €6-15; ☻ 10am-10pm), where you can rent **mountain bikes** (VTT; per half/full day €11/15). A great though somewhat hilly ride takes you past Nismes decaying historic mills to **Dourbes**, where there are kayaking opportunities and an utterly shattered castle ruin. From there continue over a steep wooded hill to **Fagnolle**, possibly Wallonia's most perfectly preserved stone village, though there's nothing whatever to do there unless a game of *balle-pelotte* is underway on the central square. Cycle back to Nismes via Mariembourg (opposite).

For fine dining at decent prices, Nismes cosiest option is **La Bonne Auberge** (☎ 060 31 10 90; Rue Bassidaine 20; ☻ 11am-3pm & 6-9pm) where you can enjoy trout dishes from €10 in a tasteful if stylistically mixed interior. They also offer ensuite *chambres d'hôtes* **rooms** (s/d €42.70/61, €52/75 weekends).

Grottes de Neptune

If you've seen the caves at Han (p236) or Hotton (p245), this modest **cave system** (☎ 060 31 19 54; Route de l'Adugeoir 24; adult/child €8/5; ☻ tours every 45 min 11am-5.15pm Apr-Sep, Sat & Sun only Oct-Mar) is likely to be underwhelming. Nonetheless, while stalagmites are sparse, the visit culminates with a low-ceilinged boat ride down the underground Eau Noire River plus a musical light-and-water show in a subterranean cascade pool. The entrance to the site is 3km north of Couvin, 500m east of the N5.

Hitler's HQ

For a few months in 1940 the Nazi leader commanded Western Front operations from deep forest near **Brûly-de-Pesche**, 8km south of Couvin. The modest concrete **Abri d'Hitler** (☎ 060 37 80 38; adult/child €4/3.50; ☻ 10.30am-5pm Tue-Sun Easter-Sep) bunker can be visited, along with two pavilions that house some explanatory displays.

Chimay
pop 9700

At the heart of this archetypal castle town is a compact Grand Place spilling forth terraced *café* tables in summer and overshadowed by the looming presence of an extravagantly spired 16th-century church. Directly west through a stone archway is the 15th-century **Château de Chimay** (☎ 060 21 44 44; www.ville-de-chimay.be; Rue du Château 18; admission €7; ☻ tours 10am, 11am, 3pm & 4pm Easter-Oct) with a bulbous dome spire of its own. To fully appreciate the castle's massive stone bulk, walk around its base on the lanes that descend steeply to the river valley. The castle, once home to Chimay's powerful medieval rulers (the De Croy family), was gutted by fire in 1935 but faithfully rebuilt. Visits are by one-hour guided tour.

Chimay's world-famous Trappist beers are actually brewed in the austere 1850 **Abbaye de Scourmont** (www.scourmont.be), 7km south of Chimay (4km beyond Bourlers). The brewery doesn't allow visitors but you can enter the abbey **church** (☻ 7am-8pm) or stroll in the fragrant coniferous forest park opposite. To sample the beer head 1.2km back towards Bourlers, where **Auberge de Poteaupré** (☎ 060 21 14 33; www.chimay.com; Route de Poteaupré 5, Bourlers; d winter/summer €65/75, beers €1.75-2.50, mains €8-19; ☻ restaurant noon-2.30pm & 6.30pm-9pm daily Easter–mid-Sep, Sat plus some lunches mid-Sep–Easter) is the abbey's official watering hole. Its artistically presented €10 'degustation' gets you a taster of abbey cheeses, the three classic beers plus the unique (if hardly memorable) Chimay Spéciale Poteaupré, a cloudy, low-strength draught-only ale that's available absolutely nowhere else.

In Chimay town, the delightful **Petit Chapitre** (☎ 060 21 10 42; Place du Chapitre 5; d/ste €80/100; ☻ reception/check-in 3.30-6.30pm) offers a charming B&B experience in a turreted, wisteria-draped building full of antiques and flamboyant furnishings. It's directly behind the church, with a tiny flower-decked front terrace.

Chimay's cramped **Camping** (☎ 060 51 12 57, 0476 99 85 80; Allée des Princes 1; caravan/tent & car/tent & bike/extra adult/extra child €15/11/7/5/2.50 ☻ Apr-Oct) is 700m west of the centre and is overlooked by multistorey apartments.

Bus 60/1 runs from Couvin to Chimay (€1.50, 40 minutes) 10 times daily, 109a runs to Charleroi (80 minutes) via Beaumont.

The Ardennes

If you're looking for outdoor activities, fresh air and greenery, head for Belgium's southeastern corner. Here you'll find meandering rivers, dramatic cave systems, forested hills and deep valleys hiding stone villages and ancient castles. There's even skiing a few days a year, though don't expect rugged mountains. Some attractions are accessible by train and bus but to really appreciate the rural highlights you'll need a car or strong cycling legs. The Ardennes biggest fans tend to be Dutch and Flemish motorists for whom the region's rather modest contours are a novelty. English-speaking visitors are comparatively rare, so you'll find it useful to speak at least a little French or Dutch in this region. Read Timing It Right (p233) before setting out.

Pleasant Namur, Wallonia's unlikely capital, sports a vast military citadel and a fair sprinkling of museums. The cave systems at Rochefort, Han-sur-Lesse and Hotton are Belgium's three most remarkable and each has its own distinct character. Durbuy, Coo, La Roche-en-Ardenne and Bouillon are all good bases for kayaking, mountain biking and other outdoor adventures. Castles abound: La Roche-en-Ardenne and Bouillon sport looming crusader-era ruins, Modave's chateau has a sumptuous interior, while the views of Jehay's moated magnificence are hard to top.

Industrial and parochial, mighty Liège is Wallonia's biggest city. It takes a little understanding but offers loads of unexpected discoveries under its grimy exterior. Spa is indeed the original spa town while Stavelot, Malmédy and Eupen burst with revelry during their fabulous carnivals.

HIGHLIGHTS

- **Sinuous Semois** Random riverside rambles culminating in Belgium's most spectacular viewpoint at Rochehaut (p240)
- **High Spot** Hiking in the Hautes Fagnes' unique moorland landscape (p261)
- **Paddle Power** Kayaking adventures from La Roche-en-Ardenne (p244) or Coo (p255)
- **Getting Deep** Descending towards the centre of the earth at Hotton (p245) and Rochefort (p236)
- **Trappist Treasure** The Abbaye Notre Dame in Orval (p241)
- **Crusader Connections** The spooky castle ruins at Bouillon (p238)
- **Carnival Celebrations** Laetare festivities in Stavelot (p256)
- **Scratch the Surface** The hidden attractions of grimy Liège go way deeper than its sexy new station (p248)

- PROVINCES: LIÈGE (CAPITAL LIÈGE), LUXEMBOURG (CAPITAL ARLON), NAMUR (CAPITAL NAMUR)
- LANGUAGES: FRENCH & GERMAN

THE ARDENNES

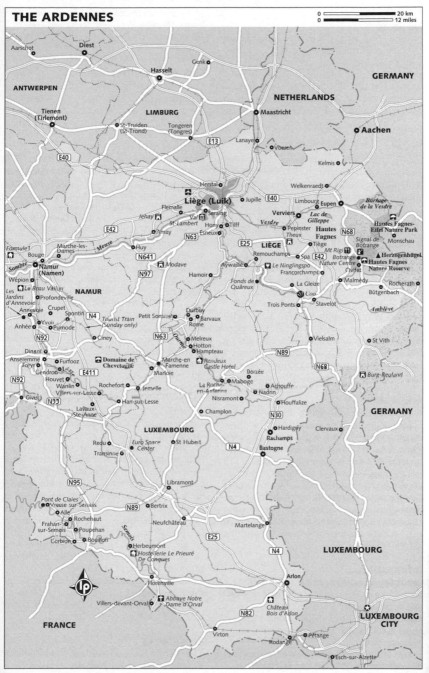

THE ARDENNES

0 — 20 km
0 — 12 miles

Aarschot

Diest

Genk

GERMANY

Hasselt

ANTWERPEN

NETHERLANDS

Tienen (Tirlemont)

LIMBURG

Maastricht

Aachen

St-Truiden (St-Trond)

Tongeren (Tongres)

E40

E13

Lanaye

Voeren

Kelmis

Herstal

Welkenraedt

Liège (Luik)

Jupille

E40

Limbourg

Eupen

Barrage de la Vesdre

Flémalle

Seraing

Verviers

Lac de Gilleppe

Jehay

Val

St-Lambert

Hony

Tilff

Vesdre

Pepinster

Theux

Hautes Fagnes

N68

Signal de Botrange

Hautes Fagnes-Eifel Nature Park

E42

Amay

Esneux

N63

LIÈGE

Tiège

Botrange Nature Centre

Monschau

Formule1

Marche-les-Dames

Bouge

Meuse

Huy

N641

Modave

E25

Remouchamps

Spa

E42

Mt Rigi

Herzogenhügel

Hautes Fagnes Nature Reserve

Ovifat

Sombre

Namur (Namen)

N97

Aywaille

Le Ninglingspo

Francorchamps

Malmedy

Rocherath

Wépion

Hamoir

Fonds de Quareux

La Gleize

Les Jardins d'Annevoie

Le Beau Vallon

Profondeville

NAMUR

Coo

Stavelot

Bütgenbach

Annevoie

Crupet

Spontin

N4

Petit Somme

Durbuy

Barvaux

Trois Ponts

Amblève

Anhée

Yvoir

Purnode

Ciney

N63

Rome

Ourthe

Melreux

Hotton

Vielsalm

St Vith

Dinant

Anseremme

Furfooz

Domaine de Chevetogne

Marche-en-Famenne

Hampteau

N89

N68

Freyr

Gendron

E411

Rendeux Castle Hotel

Borzée

Maboge

Achouffe

Burg-Reuland

Houyet

Wanlin

Rochefort

Jemelle

Marloie

La Roche-en-Ardenne

Nadrin

Givet

N95

Villers-sur-Lesse

Han-sur-Lesse

Nisramont

Houffalize

GERMANY

Lavaux-Ste-Anne

Champlon

N30

LUXEMBOURG

Hardigny

Clervaux

Redu

Euro Space Center

St Hubert

Rachamps

Trausinne

N4

Bastogne

Libramont

N95

Pont de Claies

Vresse sur Semois

N89

Bertrix

Alle

Rochehaut

Neufchâteau

Martelange

N4

LUXEMBOURG

Frahan-sur-Semois

Poupehan

E25

Corbion

Bouillon

Semois

Herbeumont

Hostellerie Le Prieuré De Conques

LUXEMBOURG CITY

Florenville

Arlon

Villers-devant-Orval

Abbaye Notre Dame d'Orval

N82

Château Bois d'Arlon

FRANCE

Virton

Pétange

Rodange

Esch-sur-Alzette

THE ARDENNES

NAMUR

pop 106,200

Namur (Namen in Dutch) commands the confluence of the Meuse and Sambre Rivers with a vast former military citadel that was one of Europe's mightiest fortresses right up until WWI. Beneath lies a gently picturesque old-town core that has much to discover if you look behind the slightly grubby exterior.

History

Namur's history is inevitably interwoven with that of its fortress. Celts then Romans had military camps here, and in the Middle Ages the counts of Namur built a well-protected castle on the craggy rocks overlooking the river junction. Strengthened under Spanish rule in the 1640s, the castle was captured by the French in 1692 then redesigned as a text-book fortress by Louis XIV's renowned military engineer Vauban. Razed and rebuilt again thereafter, by WWI the fortress was considered impregnable, yet it fell within three days of the German invasion. In WWII Namur suffered again, with heavy bombing causing extensive damage. The citadel continued in military use right up until 1977, when Belgian army paratroopers finally packed up and left the it to a generation of tourists.

Orientation

Namur's main shopping street, Rue de l'Ange/Rue de Fer, leads from the train station area to the town's nominal heart, Place d'Armes. West of here a small ancient quarter of narrow pedestrian lanes is full of tempting eateries. The citadel is directly across the river Sambre. The town of Jambes lies across the Meuse, Bouge (site of the annual grand fire) is 3km east and Wépion straggles several kilometres southwest down the Meuse's western riverbank beyond the Youth Hostel.

Information

Centre Gay & Lesbien de Namur (☎ 081-228 552; Rue des Brasseurs 13; ◷ 10am-5pm Tue-Fri) Functional LGTB information office.

CyberCenter (☎ 081-226 249; Rue Godefroid 1; internet per 15 mins/hr €0.50/1.50; ◷ 9am-11.30pm) Internet and photocopies.

Tourist Office (☎ 081-246 449; www.namurtourisme .be, www.mtpn.be; ◷ 9.30am-6pm; Sq Léopold) Has a free brochure *La Citadelle: Visites & Balades,* a map showing five self-guided citadel walking tours. There are additional information booths at Terra Nova and on the Esplanade.

Sights & Activities

THE CITADEL

Dominating the town, the mighty **Citadelle de Namur** (www.citadelle.namur.be; admission free) covers a whole craggy hilltop with ramparts, tunnels and sections of grey outer wall. Don't expect medieval fripperies: this vast 19th-century structure was an active fortress until 1977. But the site is nonetheless compelling and offers some terrific views especially from the *café* Le Panorama (p231) and from a section known as **Château des Comtes**, where the two-room dungeon, the **Logis Comtal** (admission €2; ◷ 10am-6pm Jul-Aug, 10am-5.30pm Sep-Jun), is an all-in-French history museum that's barely worth the entry fee.

The citadel's central section is a former barracks called **Terra Nova** (☎ 081-654 500; Rte Merveilleuse 64; ◷ 11am-6pm). This is the starting point for **Citadel walking tours** (€5; ◷ 10.30am Apr-Sep) and visits into the **souterrains** (adult/concession €5/4; ◷ 11.30am, 12.30pm, 3.30pm & 4.30pm Apr-Sep, plus 11.30am some weekends low season), a network of dripping underground tunnels. A little **tourist train** (◷ 11am-5pm Apr-Nov) tours the citadel's widespread viewpoints and minor attractions starting on the hour from Terra Nova and five minutes earlier from the Esplanade car park.

Citadel access for pedestrians is on the steep sloping Rampe Verte from Rue des Moulins or via a stairway from Place St-Hilaire. By car use Rte Merveilleuse from behind the 1911 **casino building** (www.casino denamur.be, www.hotelbeauregard.be). Parking spaces are easier to find on the Esplanade than at Terra Nova or outside **Parfumerie Guy Delforge** (☎ 081-221 219; www.delforge.com; 10am-5.30pm Mon-Sat, 2pm-6pm Sun), a perfume maker who fills an old stone house with floral aromas and classical music. It offers perfume laboratory tours on Saturdays at 3.30pm (€3.50).

An hourly minibus (€1) shuttles between the main tourist office and Terra Nova or use bus 3 (also hourly) then stroll down from the Château de Namur (p231).

CITY CENTRE

The pedestrianised central square, Place d'Armes, has been brutally marred by a

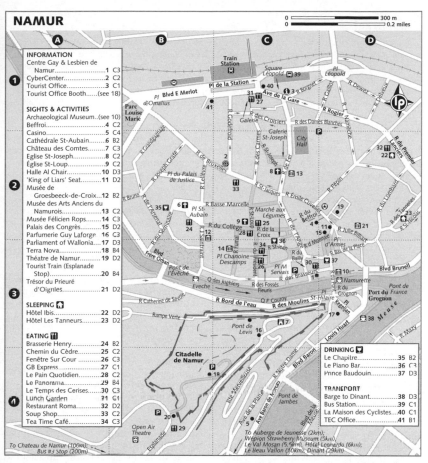

NAMUR

INFORMATION
Centre Gay & Lesbien de
  Namur...........................1 C3
CyberCenter..................2 C1
Tourist Office.................3 C1
Tourist Office Booth......(see 18)

SIGHTS & ACTIVITIES
Archaeological Museum..(see 10)
Beffroi...........................4 C2
Casino..........................5 C4
Cathédrale St-Aubain......6 B2
Château des Comtes.......7 C3
Eglise St-Joseph............8 D3
Église St-Loup................9 C2
Halle Al Chair.................10 C2
'King of Liars' Seat..........11 D2
Musée de
  Groesbeeck-de-Croix...12 B2
Musée des Arts Anciens du
  Namurois....................13 C2
Musée Félicien Rops.......14 C3
Palais des Congrès..........15 D2
Parfumerie Guy Laforge...16 C3
Parliament of Wallonia....17 D3
Terra Nova....................18 B4
Théâtre de Namur...........19 D2
Tourist Train (Esplanade
  Stop)..........................20 B4
Trésor du Prieuré
  d'Oignies....................21 D2

SLEEPING
Hôtel Ibis......................22 D2
Hôtel Les Tanneurs.........23 D2

EATING
Brasserie Henry..............24 B2
Chemin de Cèdre............25 C2
Fenêtre Sur Cour 26 C3
GB Express....................27 C1
Le Pain Quotidien...........28 D2
Le Panorama.................29 B4
Le Temps des Cerises......30 D2
Lunch Garden................31 C1
Restaurant Roma............32 D2
Soup Shop....................33 C2
Tea Time Café................34 C3

DRINKING
Le Chapitre....................35 B2
Le Piano Bar..................36 C3
Prince Baudouin.............37 D3

TRANSPORT
Barge to Dinant..............38 D3
Bus Station....................39 C1
La Maison des Cyclistes...40 C1
TEC Office.....................41 B1

To Chateau de Namur (100m);
  Bus #3 Stop (200m)

To Auberge de Jeunesse (2km);
Wepion Strawberry Museum (5km);
Le Val Mosan (5.5km); Hôtel Leonardo (6km);
Le Beau Vallon (10km); Dinant (29km)

1980s concrete department store. However, it still features the elegant stone-and-brick **Palais des Congrès** (www.namurcongres.be) conference centre, rebuilt in the 1930s with war reparations from Germany (the German army having torched the whole square in 1914). Behind lies the Unesco-listed **beffroi** (belfry; Rue du Beffroi), a medieval stone fortress tower on which a clock spire was plonked in 1733. Facing the fine sandstone facade of the 1868 **Théatre du Namur** (☎ 081-226 026; www.théatredenamur.be), a statue of the beloved local composer Nicolas Bosret hides a tiny **stone seat**. This is where the 'King of the Liars' (Roi des Menteurs) is crowned during the amusingly drunken Fêtes de Wallonie festivities (see p19).

Although far from being the region's biggest city, Namur proudly hosts the **Parliament of Wallonia** (☎ 081-231 036; http://parlement.wallonie .be; Rue Notre Dame 1; ❂ group tours by arrangement 10am, 11am, 2pm, 3pm, 4pm Mon-Fri), housed in a former hospice beside the River Meuse. The chamber is decidedly undramatic and visits are generally limited to preorganised groups, but if you turn up at the right moment you just might be able to attach yourself to one of those. Bring ID.

Museums
In a very fine 1753 former abbot's house, the **Musée de Groesbeeck-de-Croix** (☎ 081-248 720; Rue Saintraint 3; adult/concession €3/1.50; ❂ 10am-12.30pm & 1.15-5pm Tue-Sat) displays decorative arts in

---

MOSAN ART

While 'Mosan' could refer to anything from the Meuse Valley, Mosan art is generally associated with superb Romanesque chalices and crosses of copper, bronze, gold and brass made in the ancient Diocese of Liège. Eleventh-century Huy (p233) was initially at the forefront of such metallurgical developments, with a Huy goldsmith thought to be the creator of the fabulous Mosan font now displayed in Liège's Église Collégiale St-Barthélemy (p251). However, the craft soon became so firmly associated with Dinant (p235) that one form of fine copperwork remains known today as *Dinanderie*.

One of the last great exponents of Mosan metalwork was Brother Hugo d'Oignies, cofounder of a priory at Oignies east of today's Charleroi. His late 12th-century masterpieces mirror the stylistic transition from Romanesque to Gothic and his elaborate creations were used to hold religious relics including a supposed rib of St Peter brought back from crusades in the Holy Land. Hugo perfected the use of filigree for decorative features and was an early European experimenter with *niello*, in which a dark copper-alloy inlay highlights delicate lines etched onto a gold or brass background.

Fine examples are exhibited in Namur's Trésor du Prieuré d'Oignies (below), with more Mosan art on display in Liège at both the Musée de la Vie Wallonne (p250) and Grand Curtius (p251).

---

23 beautifully furnished rooms around a formal courtyard garden. Don't miss the 18th-century kitchen.

The intriguing little **Trésor du Prieuré d'Oignies** (Treasury of the Priory of Oignies; ☎ 081-254 300; Rue Julie Billiart 17; admission €2; ☣ 10-11.30am & 2-4.30pm Tue-Sat) is a one-room hoard of priceless Mosan chalices, crosses and reliquaries (see the boxed text, above) hidden away within a modern working convent. Ring the easily overlooked bell to be taken on a guided tour. When Oignies priory was sacked by antireligious French Revolutionaries the treasures were whisked away and hidden by walling them up in a farmhouse. In 1818 they were passed to the Sisters of Our Lady in Namur, whose convent was bombed flat during WWII. Fortunately the treasure had been wisely buried at the outbreak of war and survived the bombing.

Opposite the tall, red baroque frontage of the 1655 **Église St-Joseph**, an 18th-century mansion hosts the interesting **Musée des Arts Anciens du Namurois** (Museum of Ancient Art; ☎ 081-220 065; Rue de Fer 24; adult/senior/child €3/1.50/free, audioguide €2; ☣ 10am-6pm Tue-Sun), displaying old artworks from the region, including religious pieces, more Mosan metalwork and paintings by 16th-century artist Henri Blès. Entry fees rise during temporary exhibitions.

The **Musée Félicien Rops** (☎ 081-776755; www.musee rops.be; Rue Fumal 12; adult/concession €3/1.50, audioguide €2; ☣ 10am-6pm Tue-Sun, daily Jul & Aug) is devoted to 19th century artist Félicien Rops (1833–98), born a few streets away at Rue du Président 33. His penchant was for illustrating erotic lifestyles and macabre scenes.

The 1590 **Halle Al Chair**, one of the only medieval buildings to have survived Namur's continual historical war-pummellings, now houses an **Archaeology Museum** (☎ 081-231 631; Rue du Pont; adult/concession €3/1; ☣ 10am-5pm Tue-Fri, 10.40am-5pm Sat & Sun).

Churches

Baudelaire reputedly described the **Église St-Loup** (Rue du Collège) as a 'sinister and gallant marvel'. It's a remarkable 1777 baroque church whose interior, viewed through a locked glass doorway, has unusual purple-marble columns, black-stone arches and complex tracery all across the ceilings.

The Italianate neoclassical **Cathédrale St-Aubain** (Pl St-Aubain; ☣ 8.30am-4.45pm Tue-Fri, to 7.30pm Sat, 9.30am-7.30pm Sun) could use a good hot bath but its domed interior remains breathtaking if only for its gigantic scale.

WÉPION

Grand early 20th-century turreted homes give a sedate grandeur to this riverside village-suburb that's synonymous with strawberries in any Belgian mind. In summer, green hut-kiosks peddle soft fruit and a little **Strawberry Museum** (Musée de la Fraise; ☎ 081-462 007; www.museedelafraise .be; Chaussée de Dinant 1037; ☣ 2pm-6pm Easter-Oct) sells strawberry beer (€1.70), strawberry liqueurs and strawberry jams. To avoid heavy traffic on the main N92 (Chaussée de Dinant), stroll the parallel riverside towpath, a walking and cycle path that gives great views across the river to the magnificent private **Château de Dave**.

Sleeping

City centre accommodation is limited but if you've got wheels there's ample choice along the Meuse Valley and in country villages beyond. There's a cheap Formule1 Motel (p284) 6km north in the Rhisnes-Suarlée industrial zone at junction 12 (Namur Ouest) of the E42 motorway. The nearest campsites are 7km away. Advance bookings are wise.

CITY CENTRE

There's an inexpensive option opposite the station and functional rooms above the casino if all else is full.

Hôtel Les Tanneurs (☎ 081-240 024; www.tanneurs .com; Rue des Tanneries 13; s €40 200, d €55-215, breakfast €10; ✖ 🖳) Brilliantly fashioned out of a renovated 17th-century tannery, this unique hotel unites modern comfort with historical charm. It's a complex warren of 30 rooms, each totally different. Some are double-level affairs with show-off jacuzzis while others have rambling rooftop views. The cheapest rooms are very small and less atmospheric but great value.

Hôtel Ibis (☎ 081-257 540; H3151@accor.com; Rue du Premier Lanciers 10; d Fri-Sun/Mon-Thu/festivals €69/79/95; 🛜) Opposite the striking crenellated gateway of a former 1885 army garrison (now a car park), this fresh new hotel has good value, if generic, rooms and a welcoming nautically themed bar-reception area. Wi-fi per hour/day €4.50/9.90.

Château de Namur (☎ 081-729 900; www.chateau denamur.com; Ave de l'Ermitage; s/d/tr/ste from €100/ 130/170/200) Crowning lovely gardens at the top of the citadel park, this 29-room hotel looks at first glance like a believable tower-fronted castle. However, while it's peaceful, the building is actually a 1930s caprice with corridors that are somewhat institutional and room decor that falls well short of stylish.

OUT OF TOWN

Auberge de Jeunesse (HI Hostel; ☎ 081-223 688; www .laj.be; Rue Félicien Rops 8; members dm/s/d €18.80/33/46; 🕑 8am-11pm mid-Mar–mid-Oct; ✖ 🖳) This pleasant hostel partly occupies the attractive redbrick riverfront mansion that was once a studio of artist Félicien Rops (see opposite). Annoyingly there's only one room-key per dormitory. The hostel is around 10 minutes' walk south along the riverbank from the ca-

sino or accessible on either bus 3 or bus 4, which both run hourly from the station.

our pick **Le Beau Vallon** (☎ 081-411 591; Chemin du Beau Vallon 38; without bathroom s/d €40/50, with bathroom s/d €56/60; Ⓟ) Set in well-kept lawns with a private chapel, this utterly charming rural *chambres d'hôtes* occupies a 1650 stone farmstead maintaining original floorboards, banisters and fireplaces. Rooms have a sunny 'English-cottage' decor and the hosts are delightful. Take the N92 south, turning east 2.3km south of Wépion's Carrefour Supermarket, and it's 1.1km up a tiny lane starting beside Da Laora restaurant.

Hôtel Leonardo (☎ 081-460 811; hotel.beauregard@ skynet.be; Chaussée de Dinant 1149, Wépion; d €59-155; Ⓟ 🛝) Rather than disguise the hotel's late '70s college-style design, the Leonardo harnesses it semisuccessfully with light-touch retro decor. The real pluses here are the calm riverside location, sauna and inside-outside swimming pool. It's just south of Wépion's big Carrefour Supermarket. Prices vary radically by date.

Eating

Tea Time Café (☎ 0496-524 422; Rue St-Jean 35; 🕑 8.30am 5.30pm Tue-Sat) Tiny, stylish yet inexpensive sandwich shop/tearoom with a street terrace in summer.

Brasserie Henry (☎ 081-220 204; Pl St-Aubain 3; mains €11-22; 🕑 noon-midnight Sun-Thu, noon 1am Fri & Sat) In a stately 200-year-old building this high-ceilinged *grand café* is great for a calm, casual beer (€1.80) and also serves fair-priced Belgian food, including seasonal mussels, till late.

Fenêtre Sur Cour (☎ 081-230 908; www.exterieurnuit .be; Rue du Président 35; mains €12-22; 🕑 lunch & dinner Mon-Sat) Modern art complements the refined grandeur of neat tablecloths, chandeliers and partly stained-glass windows. Reliable Belgian dishes include *ris de veau* (kidneys) or *gratinade St-Jacques* (scallops au gratin).

Restaurant Roma (☎ 081-226 624; www.restaurant roma.be; Rue du Premier Lanciers 8; mains €7.50-18; 🕑 noon-2.30pm & 6-11pm) Modern decor, stylishly presented pastas and decent fresh-baked pastas in a location that's somewhat off-beat but very handy for those sleeping at the Ibis.

Le Panorama (☎ 081-655 871; Citadelle; snacks/mains/ sundaes from €6.10/10.50/4.60; 🕑 9am-10pm) High in the citadel, this bell-spired pavilion sports a recently modernised *café* with spectacular views of the Meuse and the wooded valley that extends attractively beyond the apartment blocks of Jambes. Views from the spacious terrace are even better for that eagle's perch feeling. The kitchen stays open all day.

Le Val Mosan (☎ 081-460 026; www.levalmosan.be; Rue Adrien de Prémorel 29, Wépion; mains €10-17; ☽ noon-10pm Tue-Sat, kitchen closed 2pm-7pm) Down in Wépion village the attraction of this *café*-resto is the peaceful riverside setting with veranda seating and an oblique view of the palatial Château de Dave. Trout from €11.50. From the Strawberry Museum continue 400m south then head 100m east towards the river.

Le Temps des Cerises (☎ 081-225 326; www.cerises.be; Rue des Brasseurs 22; mains €18-24; ☽ noon-2.30pm Tue-Fri & 6-10.30pm Tue-Sat) The food is authentic Walloon and French, the cosy restaurant a slightly twee pastiche of gingham, scarlet-framed mirrors and customer-signed wall-graffiti.

Chemin du Cèdre (☎ 081-262 515; http://sites .resto.com/lecheminducedre; Rue St-Loup 4; mains €9.50-18, lunch €9.50; ☽ noon-2.30pm & 6-10.30pm) Luscious Lebanese fare served in a splendid historic mansion given more than a hint of fashionably modern style.

QUICK EATS
Lunch Garden has branches in both Namur and Wépion and there's a central Le Pain Quotidien (see p51).

Soup Shop (☎ 081-657 500; www.soup-shop.com; Rue de Bruxelles 35; mains €4-9; ☽ noon-6pm Mon-Sat) Crepes, soups and quiches from an appealing self-service shop-restaurant.

Drinking
The cobbled streets around Place Chanoine Descamps and the nearby tree-lined Place du Marché aux Légumes (with its ornate historic pump-well) make up the town's liveliest quarter.

Le Piano Bar (☎ 081-230 633; Pl du Marché aux Légumes 10; beers €1.60) Grungy bar with cheap beers and free live music on many Friday and Saturday nights from 10pm.

Prince Baudouin (Rue de Marechovelette 15; beers/ sandwiches/salads from €1.80/2.50/8.50; ☽ 8am-8pm) Archetypal if slightly downmarket mirror- and wood-panelled *café* with central street terrace facing Place d'Armes. Snacks served all day.

Le Chapitre (Rue du Séminaire 4; beers from €2.70; ☽ 5pm-1am Sun-Fri, 5pm-2am Sat) At this convivial and charmingly rustic beer-pub, available brews are listed on a lengthy blackboard menu. The Chapitre 'house beer' (€3.30) is a well-formed, highly drinkable blonde.

Getting There & Away

BOAT
At 10am on Sundays (mid-July to late August), **Bateaux Meuse** (www.bateaux-meuse.be; Blvd Baron Louis Huart) runs a 3¾-hour boat service to Dinant (adult/child €16/14, return €22/18) passing rocky cliffs, forested hillsides, chateaux and distinctive turreted riverfront mansions. It departs Dinant for the return leg at 3.30pm. Daily in July and August, boats leave Namur at 3pm for Wépion (adult/child €8/6, 1¾ hours).

BUS
TEC (☎ 081-253 555; www.infotec.be; Pl de la Station; ☽ 7am-7pm) local and regional buses start from either Place de la Station or the nearby bus station.

CAR & BICYCLE
At the train station, cars can be rented from **Budget** (☎ 081-830 110; ☽ 9am-12.30pm & 1.30-5.30pm Mon-Fri). Bikes can be hired from **La Maison des Cyclistes** (☎ 081-813 848; www.maisonsdescyclistes.be; Pl de la Station 2b; per half day/full day/weekend €7/9/14; ☽ 2pm-6pm Mon-Fri, 9.30am-noon & 12.45-6pm Sat & Sun May-Oct only). A flat riverside cycle path runs much of the way to Yvoir, avoiding the busy N92 road.

TRAIN
Behind a stately stone facade, Namur's train station has futuristic glass elevator tubes that seem designed for a spaceship. Regional connections include the following:

Destination	Fare (€)	Duration (min)	Weekday Frequency
Brussels	8.10	62	2 per hr
Charleroi	5.10	31 or 44	2 per hr
Jemelle	8.10	41	1 per hr
Libramont	11.70	62	1 per hr
Liège	8.10	45	2 per hr
Luxembourg City	29.20	120	1 per hr
Marloie	7.40	35	1 per hr
Mons	10.50	70	2 per hr

Getting Around
City buses start from near the train station. Routes 4, 21, 30 and Dinant-bound 34 pass near the youth hostel and cross Wépion. Convoluted bus route 3 links the youth hostel and the Château de Namur hourly.

At weekends in July and August, riverboats link five central jetties shuttling three times an hour for €0.50 per stop (eg €2 for the four-stop trip Eveche to Jambes).

NAMUR TO LIÈGE
Huy
pop 20,100

Straddling the Meuse, halfway between Namur and Liège, Huy (pronounced 'wee'), was one of northern Europe's first chartered cities (1066) and a rich early metallurgical centre within the Prince Bishopric of Liège. Today, those sights that survived WWII are interesting and striking without being really beautiful. Don't be intimidated by the gigantic, doomsday cooling towers of Tihange nuclear power station 3km east of town.

Central Huy is 1.5km south of its train station. Beside the main Meuse River bridge, **Collégiale Notre-Dame** (☑ 9am-noon & 2-5pm) is a vast rectilinear church in heavily Gothic style. It looks rather unfinished, but has a fine rose window and a celebrated treasury (under restoration). In a turreted brick building next door, the **Tourist Office** (☎ 085-212 915; www.pays-de-huy.be; admission free; ☑ 8am-6pm Mon-Fri, 10am 6pm Sat & Sun) organises one-hour Meuse **cruises** (adult/child €4/3.50; ☑ 2pm, 3pm & 4.30pm Tue-Sun Jul-Aug, Sat & Sun only Sep) departing from a jetty opposite. Both are overshadowed by Huy's indomitable stone **fortress** (adult/child €4/3.50; ☑ 9-11.30am & 1-3.30pm Mon-Fri, 11am-5pm Sat & Sun Apr-Sep, 11am-6pm daily Jul-Aug), climbed in around six minutes via a zigzag path starting 400m further southwest along the riverside. The oppressively dour structure dates from 1818 and was used by German forces in WWII as an interrogation centre.

Two blocks southeast of the church, largely unrefined *café*-bars line the **Grand Place**. A tiny alley beside the attractive 1766 **town hall** leads into cobbled Place Verte, where you'll find sharp-spired **Église St-Mengold** and the 16th-century **Maison Nokin**. Mysterious Rue des Frères Mineurs continues east between high, ancient walls, emerging beside the town's main museum, **Musée communal** (☎ 085-232 435; Rue Vankeerberghen; admission free; ☑ 2-4pm Tue-Fri, to 6pm Sat & Sun). It is set in a building that was 'recycled' from a priory after the French Revolution. Bricked up church windows are still obvious and the exhibition rooms are set around an atmospheric 1669 cloister.

Many other historical features are folded into Huy's architectural fabric making it intriguing to wander within the knot of alleys that form the city's small central core.

River-facing **Hotel du Fort** (☎ 085-212 403; www.hoteldufort.be; admission free; ☑ 8am-6pm Mon-Fri, 10am-6pm Sat & Sun) offers clean but dated rooms. It's just beyond the fort path, before the old railway bridge. For a selection of restaurants wander pedestrianised Rue Griange directly south from Grand Place.

Namur–Huy–Liège trains run twice hourly. Expresses take 19 minutes Huy–Liège but only the slowest local service (44 minutes, hourly) stops in both Amay and at handily central Liège-Palais station.

Around Huy
MODAVE

Few of Belgium's numerous castles have an interior to beat the memorable **Chateau de Modave** (☎ 085-411 369; www.modave-castle.be; adult/senior/student/child €7.50/6.50/4/free; ☑ 10am-5pm Tue-Sun Apr–mid-Nov). The most astonishing (if discoloured) of the well-preserved 1673 stucco ceilings is the incredible heraldic relief that covers the entrance hall. You can glimpse that for free while accessing the vaulted subterranean **café** (☎ 085-233 583; beers/coffees/cakes/snacks from €2.20/2.20/3/4.50; ☑ 11am-4pm Tue-Sun Apr–mid-Nov). But doing the whole audioguide visit (50 minutes) shows you another 20 majestically furnished rooms plus a lead-lined stone-cut bath, a remarkable bed-alcove and the one balcony (room 7) from which you can really appreciate the castle's strategic perch on a 60m high cliff above a pretty rural stream (curiously the source of Brussels' drinking water). You'd never guess this from the castle's level main frontage, which comprises classical

TIMING IT RIGHT

To appreciate the Ardennes region's rural villages and scenic byways you'll need a careful sense of timing. In July and August and on any sunny weekend the hotels and hub villages tend to get overloaded. Yet by October many attractions and go into virtual hibernation. So midweek in June and September is generally the ideal time to go. In winter the Ardennes can be snow-draped when Brussels is only mildly cold. That's great if you want to ski (mostly cross-country) but beware that the infamously crash-prone E411 highway gets dangerously icy. Driving that road on any holiday-season Friday night (southbound) or Sunday (northbound) you'll need a good thick book to read in the traffic jams.

THE ARDENNES

French gardens, an extensive grey-stone fortified farm and a pair of 800m grand avenues leading from Modave village. Modave is 13km south from Huy via the N641. Ciney-bound bus 126a passes by 10 times on weekdays (20 minutes from Huy). By car, numerous attractive rural lanes invite further exploration en route to Hamoir and Durbuy (p246).

JEHAY
In the golden glow of late afternoon, **Château de Jehay** (☎ 085-82 44 00; www.chateaujehay.be; Rue du Parc 1, Jehay; castle/park only €5/2.50; ⌚ 2-5pm Tue-Fri, 11am-6pm Sat & Sun Apr-Sep) is undoubtedly one of Wallonia's most photogenic sights. Like a gingerbread fantasy, this turret-spiked 1550 castle is a fabulous confection of alternating brick and stone rising from an extensive tree-ringed moat. Nine rooms are furnished while outbuildings house changing exhibitions. Jehay is around 6km north of **Amay**, a mostly humdrum town whose partly 11th-century church, **Église Saint-Georges et Sainte-Ode** has an unusual triple-spired portal tower.

Nine times daily Huy–Amay–Liège bus 85 stops just 100m from the castle, taking 30 minutes from Huy or 55 minutes from Liège.

NAMUR TO DINANT
Wépion (p230) and **Profondeville** are attractive. At Annevoie **Les Jardins d'Annevoie** (☎ 082-679 797; www.annevoie.be; Rue des Jardins 37; adult/child €7.80/5.20; ⌚ 9.30am-5.30pm Apr-Oct, till 6.30pm Jul-Aug) are classical gardens laid out in 1758 around the manor house of Charles-Alexis de Montpellier. It's a delightful mix of French, Italian and English styles incorporating plenty of fountains and tree-lined waterways. Four B&B rooms are available in an associated cottage.

Yvoir
pop 8600
A narrow road bridge crosses the Meuse at Annevoie, passing the Fitevoye Rocks (popular with climbers) en route to **Yvoir** (www .paysdevalles.be). Yvoir's modestly cute central square offers a good chance of seeing locals play *balle-pelotte* (see p46) at 3pm on either Saturdays or Sundays in summer. About 1km south near Yvoir's train station, **Li P'tit Passeû** (adult/child return €1/0.90; ⌚ 10am-8pm) is a rope-drag boat that regularly nips across to the **Ile d'Yvoir** (www.iledyvoir.com), a small river island where you can rent boats or kayaks for €5/30 per hour/day.

Crupet
pop 450
Driving east from Yvoir (initially past unsightly quarries) brings you through some lovely rolling countryside to little Crupet. Its extremely picturesque streamside **Château des Carondelet** is a moated 13th-century tower-house that looks especially photogenic in morning light. High above, beside the village's stone church, is an amusingly kitschy Catholic rock-pile **grotto** and a little sculpture gallery. Four *café*-restaurants serve signature trout dishes, but customer service often ranges from sloppy to downright rude. Fortunately, 3km west near Ivoi village, there's an excellent alternative in the delightful **Chateau de la Poste** (☎ 081-411 405; www.chateaudelaposte.be; Ronchinne 25, Maillen; d €68-115; P ⓦ). A total facelift in 2009 has brought modernist colours and humorous twists to the decor of this grand 19th-century castle-hotel set in 42 hectares of rolling parkland. Originally built by a Ghent industrialist, the

---

ACTIVE ARDENNES

Several of the main tourist honeypot towns offer a range of adventure sports. The choice is widest in Durbuy (p246) and Coo (p255) but the former has very limited public transport while the latter, despite sporting a handy train station, has very limited accommodation. That makes either slightly awkward for those without a car. Good alternatives include La Roche-en-Ardenne (p244) and Bouillon (p239), which are more appealing hubs than the comparatively accessible kayaking points at Yvoir (above), which has limited facilities, and Anseremme (opposite), south of Dinant. It's generally worth calling ahead to check what's available before setting off, especially for kayaking on smaller rivers where water levels are sometimes too low for paddling. While many operators claim to offer rafting, few rivers are high enough until around November, by which time the experience will be a very chilly one.

Virtually every local tourist office sells a great selection of hiking and mountain-biking maps.

castle later became a royal residence for King Leopold II's daughter Princess Clémentine, who had caused an infamous diplomatic problem by falling inconveniently in love with Napoleon's grand nephew. Today the hotel offers great-value rooms and numerous activities for kids and adults: Wii, cinema, pool table and baby foot are free, mountain-bike rental costs extra. Nonresidents can drop in for a drink or meal – particularly appealing when the imaginative log fire gets going on the upper terrace. Note that despite the official address, the hotel is nearer to Crupet than to Maillen village.

Dinant
pop 12,700

Viewed across the river from near the **tourist office** (☎ 082-222 870; www.dinant.be; Ave Cadoux 8; ⏰ 8.30am-7pm Mon-Fri, 9.30am-7pm Sat, 10am-6pm Sun), Dinant forms a distinctly photogenic scene. Seen from here the vast, unadorned 1818 **citadel** (☎ 082-223 670; www.citadelledinant .be; Le Prieuré 25; adult/child €7/5.40; ⏰ 10am-6pm Apr-Oct, 10am-5pm Sat-Thu Nov-Mar, weekends only in Jan) looms menacingly on its clifftop perch, high above the town's centrepiece church, the distinctive bulbous-spired **Église Notre-Dame** (Pl Reine Astrid; admission free; ⏰ 10am-6pm). It's interesting for a few minutes. However, the town is squeezed claustrophobically against the cliffside. Parking is awkward, traffic is heavy and the crowded streets are perfumed with diesel fumes and chip fat. Vaguely lost-looking tourists try to stretch the experience by jostling into overcrowded restaurants or taking the cable-car to the citadel, which is sparse on sights albeit offering toe-curlingly vertical views. Many escape by cruising down the River Meuse to **Anseremme** (50 min return; adult/child €6/4.50; ⏰ every 30min 10am-1.30pm & 5-6pm Apr-Oct) or **Freÿr** (1¾ hr return; adult/child €10/8; ⏰ 2.15pm May-mid-Sep). Freÿr's riverside renaissance chateau boasts very impressive formal gardens.

Attractive but rarely open, the 15th-century **Leffe Abbey** (☎ 082-222 377; www.abbaye-de-leffe.be; Place de l'Abbaye 1; admission free; ⏰ 3-4pm Wed, Sat & Sun Jun-Aug) is an active religious community 1km north of central Dinant. Opposite the modest **abbey church** (admission free; ⏰ 6am-7pm) there's a little **Leffe Beer Museum** (⏰ 1pm-6pm Fri-Sun Apr-Oct) catering to those who'd prefer to overlook the inconvenient fact that famous Leffe beer (www.leffe.com) is actually brewed in Leuven.

> ### UNLUCKY DINANT
> From the 12th century, Dinant was a major centre for a form of Mosan copper- and brass-work that's still known today as *dinanderie*. However, most craftsmen fled after August 1466, when the town was virtually destroyed by the forces of Burgundian King Charles the Bold. Why did Charles attack? Because some Dinant townsfolk had dared to call him a bastard. Naming the Bishop of Liège as his illegitimate dad didn't help either. History repeated itself in WWI when around 10% of the population was executed and much of the town razed in retaliation for resisting the German occupation.

Dotted about town you'll notice many a saxophone motif. That's a celebration of Dinant's most famous scion, Adolphe Sax, who was born here in 1814 and patented the instrument in 1846. But this and numerous other musical inventions (some displayed in Brussels' Old England Building, p82) did not gain Sax great wealth and he died penniless in 1894 after a decade of legal wrangles.

Getting There & Away
Bus 433 links Namur to Dinant via Yvoir and Dave (across the river from Wépion). Route 431 runs Namur–Spontin via Purnode, not to be confused with 43/1 which runs Dinant–Ciney. Flat riverside bike paths trace much of the castle-dotted Namur–Yvoir–Dinant route (28km) though some sections join the busy main road. You could return to Namur by hourly train from Yvoir (30 minutes) or Dinant (37 minutes), but remember that bikes add €5 to the fare. For Crupet you'll really need a car.

LESSE VALLEY
The 89km Lesse River winds through pretty oak woods, limestone hills and agricultural meadows before joining the Meuse at Anseremme south of Dinant. At Han-sur-Lesse the river tunnels underground forming the magnificent but very commercial caves that are the region's biggest tourist draw. If Han's endless summer crowds annoy you, Rochefort offers better accommodation and has a great cave system of its own.

The region's vast array of accommodation, minor museums, parks and activities are explained in detail on www.valdelesse .be and www.haute-lesse-tourisme.be plus in widely available free brochures that include street maps of Han, Rochefort and other major villages.

Infrequent Dinant–Libramont local trains stop at Anseremme, Gendron and Houyet. From Jemelle on the Namur–Luxembourg railway line, bus 29 runs hourly to Han (€1.50, 15 minutes) via Rochefort (€1.20, seven minutes). For the rest of this area you'll need wheels. Both Lavaux-Ste-Anne and the Euro Space Centre are handily placed at junctions of the E411.

Anseremme

Summer kayaking is especially popular (indeed sometimes overly crowded) on the Lesse between Anseremme and Gendron (12km, three hours) and Houyet (22km, five hours). In Anseremme, **Ansiaux** (☎ 082-213 535; www .ansiaux.be; Rue du Vélodrome 15) organises kayaks, transfers and mountain-bike hire.

Han-sur-Lesse
pop 900

Han is basically two streets of mediocre hotels and inexpensive tourist restaurants serving the summer hordes who arrive in coachloads to visit Belgium's most famous caves, the **Grottes de Han** (☎ 084-377 213; www.grotte-de-han .be; Rue Lamotte 2; adult/child €12/7; ☿ 10am-4pm Apr-Oct, hours vary midsummer & low season, check website). The guided visits (English often available) start after a 10-minute ride in charmingly rickety open-sided tramcars. They culminate with a four-minute sound-and-light show in a 20m-high cave that also hosts occasional theatrical performances. In between you stroll through a succession of impressive subterranean galleries, each well endowed with stalactites and especially fine *draperies* (beautiful translucent 'curtain' formations). The walk is 2km, but gradients and steps aren't especially challenging. Dress appropriately (13°C) and allow at least two hours (plus however long it takes to board the tram). May to August departures are every half-hour (except 12.30pm) from the ticket office opposite Han's grey-stone central church. Low-season departures are approximately hourly.

To keep you in town, Han's **Super-Combiticket** (adult/concession/child €18.90/16.90/11.90) throws in three other attractions with the cave visit. The cursory geological museum (Musée du Monde

Souterrain) and flashy but ultimately pointless 3D **Speleogame** (☿ every 20 min from noon) are mere filler. But the enjoyable 75-minute **Safari** (☿ approximately half-hourly) is worthwhile. Sitting on partly covered truck-wagons, you're driven several kilometres past and through woodland and meadow enclosures stocked with wolf, lynx, bison, eagle-owls, Przewalski's horses and other rare European fauna. The scenery is very pretty and viewpoint stops include one where the Lesse disappears into the hillside. However, commentary is not in English and, in summer, predeparture queues can be annoyingly long.

One block from the church, the **Gîte d'Étape** (☎ 084-377 441; gite.han@gitesdetape.be; Rue du Gîte d'Étape 10; adult/child/infant €16.10/13.20/7.65) offers hostel accommodation with €1.50 discounts for HI members (€4 supplement if you don't have your own sleeping bag). There are two central campsites and half a dozen unexciting hotels.

Rochefort
pop 12,000

The childhood home of tennis superstar Justine Henin, Rochefort makes a pleasant regional base for exploring the Lesse Valley. Almost everything is conveniently strung along one long main street known variously as Rue de Behogne, Place Roi Albert 1er and Rue Jacquet. This rises gently from an imposing statue-fronted church, passes the **tourist office** (☎ 084-345 172; www.valdelesse.be; Rue de Behogne 5; internet per hr €1; ☿ 8am-5pm Mon-Fri, 9.30am-5pm Sat & Sun, to 6pm summer weekdays) and continues to the sporadically open **Château Comtal** (☎ 0496-617 145; Rue Jacquet; adult/child €2/1.50; ☿ 2am-4pm on occasion), combining a 12th-century fortress ruin and a spired 18th-century mansion-castle.

Many shops and *cafés* sell Rochefort's famous Trappist beer, but the **Abbaye de St-Rémy**, where it's brewed (3km north), is closed to the public. Rochefort's main attraction is the **Grotte de Lorette** (☎ 084-212 080; Drève de Lorette; adult/concession/child €7.95/6.75/4.95; ☿ 10.30am-4.30pm Mar-Oct), about 500m southeast of Rue Jacquet via Rue St-Gervais (well signed). This cave system has fewer stalactites than Han and handling the 626 relatively steep steps is more physical. However, the small-group visits give a vastly more personal experience. Some geologically fascinating strata have signs of plate-tectonic movement, the half-lit stairways give a magical hint of the main cave's great vertical depth (65m) and there's a memorable revelation of its full majesty at the end of a visit during an atmospheric light show. Look for the sorcerer! Tours (mostly in French) taking over an hour depart every 90 minutes (minimum two guests), or every 45 minutes mid-July to August. A combination ticket (adult/concession/child €16.70/15/11.20) includes both *grottes*, Han and Lorette.

The tourist office sells walking and cycling maps, notably the 1:25,000 scale *Rochefort et ses Villages* (€7.50). About 200m downhill from the church, **Cycle Sport** (☎ 084-213 255; Rue de Behogne 59; rental per morning/afternoon/full day €10/15/20; ⏱ 9.30am-noon & 1.30-6.30pm Tue-Sat, 9.30am-noon Sun) rents bicycles, ideal for cycling the **RAVel** (www.ravel.wallonie.be) path to Houyet along a cemented former railway.

SLEEPING & EATING

Gîte d'Étape 'Le Vieux Moulin' (☎ 084-214 604; www .giterochefort.be; Rue du Hableau 25; adult/youth/child €14.60/11.70/7.65, membership/sheets €4/4) Pleasant riverside hostel. Zigzag down from the square beside the tourist office, cross the park and it's the crab-red building directly across the footbridge to the right.

L'Ôdace (☎ 084-444 169; www.lodace.be; Pl Albert Ier 30; s/d/ste €65/85/100; ⏱ restaurant closed Mon & Thu) Four newly redecorated rooms and a suite continue the retro-trendy vibe of the stylish tapas/wine bar downstairs.

Hôtel Le Vieux Logis (☎ 084 21 10 24; www.levieux logis.be; Rue Jacquet 71; s/d/tr/q €71/80/103/126) Facing the chateau, with shutters and window boxes on its stone facade, this atmospheric but unpretentious old place has lashings of antique furniture and wooden panelling plus an almost medieval courtyard garden. Up creaky stairs, the 10 rooms have period furniture but very dated bathrooms.

B&B Le Vieux Carmel (☎ 084-445 341; Rue Jacquet 61; d €75-85) Once part of a 17th-century convent, the stone-floored guest lounge features a boar's head and a roaring fire in winter (the 'Ardennes TV'). Most intriguing of the five rooms is 'Denise' with its uncurtained claw-foot bathtub on the old floorboards facing the bed. 'Charlotte' and smaller 'Helena' are less magical.

Hôtel La Malle Poste (☎ 084-210 986; www.malle poste.net; Rue de Behogne 46; s/d/ste from €80/110/170; Ⓟ Ⓢ) Enter through a 17th-century coaching inn that houses the hotel's indulgent La Caleche Restaurant (closed Wednesday and

Thursday), above which are two particularly impressive suites featuring metal four-poster beds. A stone tunnel, complete with 8000-bottle wine collection, links to a subterranean swimming pool and sauna, above which large rooms are new yet classical and feature jacuzzi baths. Built into old eaves, the cheapest, smaller 'Cocher' rooms have revealed stone- or brickwork and a more Ardennaise decor. Lovely garden.

Bella Italia (☎ 084-221 520; Rue de Behogne 50; pizza & pasta €6.50-12.50; ⏱ 11.45am-3pm & 6-11.30pm) This restaurant's decor is entirely forgettable but the great-value light-crust, wood-oven pizzas wash down beautifully with a Rochefort 8 (€3). A dozen other restaurants in various styles conveniently line the main street.

Lavaux-Ste-Anne

Visible west of the E411 motorway (junction 22a, 10km from Han), **Chateau Lavaux-Sainte-Anne** (☎ 084-388 362; www.chateau-lavaux. com; adult/senior/child €6.50/6/4.00; ⏱ 9am-5.30pm, 9am-7pm Jul-Aug) is a photogenic 1450 moated fortress that was converted into a lordly mansion in 1634. The four towers come with machicolations and bell-shaped domes while rooms are relevantly furnished and display various exhibits from local crafts to hunting trophies. Castle views from the three-pond wetland, **Zone Humide** (adult/child €5/3), are pleasant but hardly worth the fee. To enjoy a sneaky view into the castle and its formal garden without paying the ticket, have a drink in the courtyard brasserie (opens 11am).

Attached to the village's other brasserie-*café*, the loveable **B&B 4 Lunes** (☎ 084-388 426; www.les4lunes.be; Rue du Chateau 1b; d €70; ⏱ Feb-Dec) combines modern decor and elements of exposed brickwork.

On the main square, **Lemonnier** (☎ 084-388 883, 0477-196 651; www.lemonnier.be; Rue Lemonnier 82; d €95-125; ⏱ Thu-Mon) has nine bright, fresh rooms, a memorably contemporary garden, superstylish sitting room and a renowned restaurant. Breakfast is €12.

Redu

At junction 23 of the E411 don't be alarmed to see the 'skeleton' of a space shuttle diving towards you. It's a model that attracts families to the excellent highwayside **Euro Space Center** (☎ 061-656 465; www.eurospacecenter.be; adult/child €11/8; ⏱ 10am-7pm Jul-Aug, 10am-6pm various other dates, see website, last entry 2hrs before closing). Visits include a 75-minute series of movies and gadgets followed by a five-minute simulator ride. For €4 extra a bungee-style contraption offers the sensation of moon walking at one-sixth Earth's gravity. Outside (no ticket necessary) there's a labyrinth-quiz and a solar system built to scale.

Around 3km west, little **Redu** (www.redu-village dulivre.be) is Belgium's equivalent of Hay-on-Wye, a village full of secondhand and antiquarian bookshops. Most books sold are in French, though timber-framed **De Eglantier & Crazy Castle** (☎ 061-656 615; Rue de Transinne 34; ☺ 11am-6pm) has a selection of English volumes. On the first Saturday of August, Redu's **nuit-du-livre** sees bookstalls open all night with fireworks popping at midnight. Two of the village's numerous tavern-*café*-restaurants offer inexpensive guestrooms.

ST-HUBERT
pop 5700

If you're cutting across country between Redu (or Rochefort) and Bastogne you'll pass through an area that's still rich with deer and wild boar. At its heart, **St-Hubert** (www.saint-hubert-tourisme.be) bills itself as the 'European Capital of Hunting & Nature'. For the gun-averse, the agreeable town's main sight is the rather spooky **Basilique des Saints-Pierre-et-Paul** (☎ 061-612 388; Pl de l'Abbaye; ☺ 9am-6pm Apr-Oct, 9am-5pm Nov-Mar), a grey stone slab of a church with a netting-draped late-Gothic interior and particularly fine 1733 oak choir stalls. The latter are topped by cross-headed stags reflecting the legend of St-Hubert (see the boxed text, right), whose grave here made the former Abbey of Andange into a major pilgrimage site from the 9th century. On St-Hubert's day (early November) the square outside the church is host to one of Belgium's weirder religious ceremonies as priests bless a menagerie of pet dogs, along with their owners' bread!

BOUILLON
pop 2200

This highly likeable little castle town occupies a tight loop of the pretty Semois River. Slouching like a great grey dragon high on the central rocky ridge, its unmissable focus is the **Château de Bouillon** (☎ 061-466 257; Rue du Château; adult/senior/child €5.90/5.10/4.30; ☺ 10am-6.30pm Jul-Aug, earlier closing Mar-Jun & Sep-Nov, weekends only Dec-Feb), Belgium's finest feudal castle

> ### HUNTING HUBERT
>
> Hubert, a local 7th-century count, was about to bag a stag when Christ appeared between the creature's antlers imploring him to embrace a religious life. Understandably baffled, the count put down his weapon and let the beast flee. Moved by the vision he subsequently gave up his worldly goods and took to the forest, where he lived as a hermit. Hubert has since become the patron saint of hunting, a rather odd choice considering that his 'miracle' had been to spare the stag.

ruin. It harks back to 988 and the days of Godefroid (Godefroy) de Bouillon, whose name you'll hear a lot in these parts (see the boxed text, opposite). Although later expanded by France's great military engineer Vauban, the castle still sums up everything you might wish for in a dark-age castle – dank dripping passageways tunnelling into the hillside, musty half-lit cell rooms, rough-hewn stairwells and many an eerie nook and cranny to discover. To really get the heebie-jeebies take a night-time **torchlight tour** (€5.90 plus €2 for the flaming torch; ☺ 10pm Tue-Sun mid-Jul–mid-Aug & some other dates). Daytime entry in summer includes the open-air bird show **Spectacle de Fauconnerie** (☺ 11.30am, 2pm & 3.30pm daily Mar-Oct, Sat & Sun only in winter), which sees trained 'wig-snatching' owls, hawks and eagles swooping low over spectators' heads.

From the northeast corner of the castle car park, steps descend to the **Musée Ducal** (☎ 061-464 189; www.museeducal.be; Rue du Petit 1; adult/child €4/2.50; ☺ 10am-6pm Easter-Sep, 10am-5pm Oct–mid-Nov), which is spread over two historic houses and incorporates an antique metal smithy. Very varied displays highlight Godefroid de Bouillon's life, the First Crusade, the local metallurgy industry and local artist Albert Raty (1889–1970).

Wind down from here past the town hall, a little cinema and the mustard-yellow stone **church** to *café*-dotted Grand Rue. Across **Pont Liège** (the central bridge), a riverside lane to the right leads quickly to the **tourist office** (Maison du Tourisme; ☎ 061-465 211; www.bouillon-tourisme.be; Quai des Saulx 12; ☺ 9am-6pm, to 5pm winter), which sells useful hiking maps (1:25,000). Behind in the same 17th-century former convent building is Bouillon's flashiest attraction, the

Archéoscope Godefroid de Bouillon (☎ 061-468 303; www.archeoscopebouillon.be; Quai des Saulx 14; adult/child €6/4.50; ☺ from 10am, last entry 4pm, 5pm or 5.30pm depending on season, closed Jan & winter weekday mornings), designed to bring Godefroid's story to life for 21st-century folk. Visits start every 35 minutes with a multilingual film, after which you walk through the screen into a darkened space moodily showing off a replica of Godefroid's Jerusalem tombstone. Beyond are interesting displays dealing with crusades, castles and convent life.

A **combination ticket** (adult/senior/child €13.90/ 11.80/9.60) is available for the castle, Musée Ducal and Archéoscope.

Activities

The tourist office sells excellent walking and cycling maps that are great for exploring the extensive oak and beech forests surrounding Bouillon. The gently flowing Semois River meanders beautifully through umpteen S-bends offering relaxed and peaceful kayaking with fewer 'traffic jams' than on the Lesse south of Dinant. **Semois Kayaks** (☎ 0475-247 423; www.semois-kayaks.be; Rue de Libehan 6; ☺ Easter-Sep) organises kayak trips around the Tombeau de Géant (see p240) to Poupehan (15km) and on from Poupehan to Frahan-sur-Semois (5km). **Les Epinoches** (☎ 061-256 878; www.kayak-lesepinoches. be; Faubourg de France 29; ☺ Easter-Oct) takes you by minibus to Dohan (14km) or Saty (7km) then lets you kayak back. In Alle, 20km west down the Semois, **Récréalle** (☎ 061-500 381; www .recrealle.be; Rue Léon Henrard 16, Alle-sur-Semois; ☺ Easter-Sep) offers quad biking, climbing, kayaking and more.

Sleeping & Eating

Camping Halliru (☎ 061-466 009; Rte de Corbion 1; campsites per adult/child/site €3/1.50/4.50; ☺ closed Oct-Mar) One kilometre south of town along the river

HI Hostel (Auberge de Jeunesse; ☎ 061-468 137; www. laj.be; Rte du Christ 16; members dm/s/d €18.80/33/46; ☺ low season by reservation only, closed Jan) Perched on the ridge opposite the castle with views over the whole town. From the bus station turn left, follow Rue des Champs to the T-junction, turn right and wind up into Rte du Christ. From central Bouillon, take a short cut up stairs near Place St-Arnould.

B&B Adam (☎ 061-467 156; guyadam10@scarlet.be; Rue du Brutz 10; tw without bathroom €30) Three homely *chambres d'hôtes* rooms in an utterly charming 17th-century family cottage backing onto a crooked snicket that short cuts up to the castle. The kitchen, replete with homemade jams, is an almost museum of rustic style. Breakfast costs €3.

Hôtel Panorama (☎ 061-466 138; www.panorama hotel.be; Rue au Dessus de la Ville 23; s/d/executive/ste €70/90/110/130; ✂) The exterior looks like a dated Swiss ski hotel but inside the decor is modern and well chosen and virtually every room shares in the fabulous view that gives the place its name. Meals are available (mains €21, three-course menus €30 to €42). The terrace is ideal for a summer drink. Another hotel and two decent B&Bs share the same ridge road.

Hôtel de la Poste (☎ 061-465 151; www.hotelposte .be; Pl St-Arnold 1; s/d/luxe/ste from €64/98/138/158; ✂) Creaky stairs, uneven floors and purple-brown marble walls adorn this pleasantly old-fashioned hotel, which hosted Napoleon

---

GODEFROID DE BOUILLON

At the heart of Brussels' busy Place Royale stands a statue of Godefroid de Bouillon. This 11th-century crusader is seen as one of Belgium's ancient heroes, though the actions of his army would receive few medals today.

Born in 1060, Godefroid (Godfrey in English) was 36 when he sold the ducal castle of Bouillon to the prince-bishop of Liège, using the money to lead one of three 'Christian' crusader armies across Europe to the Holy Land. Well before meeting their supposed Muslim foes, Godefroid's army of around 60,000 seriously degenerated in both number and ethics, slaughtering thousands of Jews in towns across Germany soon after setting off.

It took three years to reach Jerusalem. Godefroid's soldiers breached the city walls on 15 July 1099 and proceeded to massacre an estimated 40,000 Muslims and Jews. According to a contemporary account, six months after the orgy of slaughter the streets still reeked of rotting bodies. Victorious Godefroid was offered the title 'King of Jerusalem' but settled instead for 'Defender of the Holy Sepulchre'. He died a year later in Jaffa, near today's Tel Aviv, but his brother Baldwin reigned on, keeping the Holy Land 'Belgian' for several more years.

III back in 1870. Rooms have been recently redecorated in calm brown tones. Luxe versions have brilliant corner-wrap windows, but cheaper doubles suffer some road noise and beds can be saggy. The location is wonderfully central – above a panelled brasserie-restaurant (mains €21, three-course menus €30 to €42) by the Pont de Liège.

La Ferronnière (☎ 061-230 750; www.laferronniere .be; Voie Jocquée 44; d without/with view from €90/110, tr/q €145/165) This charming ivy-clad mansion, 500m northeast of centre, is decorated in a fresh, lightly classical style. The unique feature is a beautifully maintained little garden and dining-terrace (menus €35 to €65, Monday to Saturday) with a perfectly framed if somewhat distant castle view.

La Vieille Ardenne (☎ 061-466 277; Grand Rue 9; mains €12-17, menus €21-27; ⓨ lunch & dinner, closed Wed Sep-Jun) Beer steins dangle from the beams of this compact, traditional Ardennes-style *café*-eatery and summer tables overflow onto neighbouring pavements. Fair-priced trout and quail are served along with seasonal *gibier* (game) dishes in October and November. Sample *Brasserie de Bouillon*'s local historically themed beers here or buy them by the bottle from a shop across the street.

Getting There & Away

Bus 8 (50 minutes) runs six times daily to Bouillon from Libramont on the Namur–Luxembourg railway line. Buses stop at both Quai du Rempart near central Pont de Liège and at the bus station at the southern end of town above Pont de France.

You can drive up to the castle entrance via Rue du Château or take a four-stop **tour 'train'** (adult/child €5/2.50; ⓨ 10.15am-6pm) from the Pont de Liège, but on foot the relatively gentle climb takes only 10 minutes and there are stairway short cuts from both Rue du Moulin and Blvd Heynen (next to the tennis court near Pont de la Poulie).

AROUND BOUILLON
Semois Valley

Either side of Bouillon, the Semois River forms eccentric loops flanked by vividly green waterside meadows that are swiftly swallowed in steeply rising wooded valley sides. At their best the scenes are delightful, though many riverside meadows are marred by a summer overload of camping and caravan sites.

For information about exploring by kayak, see p239. By car, get a good map and follow winding roads that rollercoaster between streamside and plateau-top villages. The most celebrated panoramic viewpoint is called the **Tombeau du Géant**. But a more accessible and even more impressive alternative is at **Rochehaut**, a village that sits high above a perfect river-curl enfolded in deep green forests. Views peer down onto the attractive little 'dead-end' hamlet of **Frahan-sur-Semois**, to which there's a steep footpath and pedestrian bridge but no direct road.

Another place where the riverine scene remains pristine is around the unique, low-slung **Pont de Claies**, a very rare surviving example of a rickety, once-typical footbridge, simply constructed by placing hazel-weave onto log-stilts embedded in the river. The bridge is hidden away 500m from the church in quaint **Laforêt** hamlet, 1km from the 18th-century Pont St-Lambert bridge in regional centre **Vresse-sur-Semois**. Vresse hosts a fortress-like 1786 stone church-tower and, rather incongruously, a reconstruction of Belgium's first steam locomotive, 1835 'Le Belge', which would seem better parked in the train museum (p196) in Mechelen. Vresse's tourist office occupies a former hotel that was once a retreat for artists and thinkers including surrealist poet Jean Cocteau. Next door, **Cap Semois** (☎ 061-501 354; ⓨ Easter-Sep) rents mountain bikes (€25 per day) and organises kayak trips to **Bohan** (€28).

East of Bouillon, there are further Semois panoramas from lanes around **Herbeumont**, a relatively large village featuring a perched stone fortress site that's considerably more ruined than Bouillon's but still imposing from certain angles.

SLEEPING & EATING

There are hotels and *chambres d'hôtes* in virtually every village in this area, though you might still struggle to find space on summer weekends without reservations.

Au Franco Belge (☎ 061-500 464; Rue Albert Raty 121, Vresse-sur-Semois; s/d without bathroom €45/55, with bathroom €49/69) Basic but inexpensive rooms above an unpretentious Vresse taverne-restaurant.

Hostellerie de la Semois (☎ 061-500 033; www.hostel leriedelasemois.be; Rue Albert Raty 63, Vresse-sur-Semois; d €77) Half-timbered hotel that's supposedly 150 years old but renovated to look much newer, albeit by no means contemporary.

While room decor isn't thrilling, the overall effect is warmer and more appealing than most other Vresse options.

Auberge de la Ferme (☎ 061-461 000; www.auberge delaferme.be; Rue de la Cense 12, Rochehaut; s/d/ste from €70/100/280; ☒ closed Jan) Occupying a large proportion of Rochehaut's cottages, the rambling auberge offers great-value rooms in a wide variety of sizes and styles. The restaurant-reception is decked with rural antiques and is invitingly warm if just a little contrived (menus €30 to €60). Rochehaut's very best views are a 20-second walk away.

Hostellerie Le Prieuré De Conques (☎ 061-411 417; www.conques.be; Rue de Conques 2, Conques; s/d from €105/124) Originally a medieval outpost of Orval Abbey, this whitewashed historic farmstead is now a 12-room gastro-hotel (dinner menu €36). Rooms are very comfy, if not quite as splendid as the immaculate lawns and characterful lounge bar might suggest. It's 2km southeast of Herbeumont towards disappointing Florenville.

Orval

Built of glowing golden sandstone, the highly photogenic **Abbaye Notre Dame** (☎ 061-311 060; www.orval.be; adult/senior/child €4.50/4/2.50, ☒ 9.30am-6.30pm Jun-Sep, to 6pm Mar-May & Oct, 10.30am-5.30pm Nov-Feb) is most famous for its Orval Trappist beer. A Cistercian monastery since 1132, the complex had barely finished a total rebuild when, in 1793, it was wrecked, looted and reappropriated (like all Belgium's monasteries) by antireligious French Revolutionary soldiers. Rebuilding only restarted in the late 1920s, partly funded by specially surcharged commemorative postage stamps. The evocative **ancient ruins** were left to one side and can still be visited along with an 18th-century **pharmacy-room**, medicinal herb garden and a small **museum** located in part of the labyrinthine vaults. There's also a simple audio-visual portrayal of monastic life that screens hourly on the hour/half-hour in Dutch/French. If Catholic philosophy grips you and your French is good enough, it's possible to sleep in the monastery for two to seven days (prearrangement essential) as part of a **spiritual retreat** (hotellerie@orval.be; per night €35), during which you're encouraged to join in the daily cycle of prayers. Bring your own bed linen.

The abbey's famous brewery is closed to visitors (except the second weekend of September) but you can buy samples of the

> **SOMETHING FISHY AT ORVAL**
>
> When Orval's Abbey (left) was founded by Italian monks in 1070, they chose the site of a then-recent miracle. Widowed Countess Mathilda of Tuscany had been admiring the beautiful spot when her wedding ring slipped from her finger into a local stream. Racked with despair she prayed to the Virgin Mary who, it was believed, summoned a fishy search party to retrieve the ring. Centuries later, as you'll notice from any Orval beer bottle, a trout carrying a golden ring remains the monastery's logo.

monastery's wares at the reception shop. The monastery is 700m up the N840 from the N88 junction marked by a hostellerie with a pleasant terrace and views of a minor castle. Halfway between is Orval's official abbey tavern, the unrepentantly traditional **Auberge de l'Ange Gardien** (☎ 061-311 886; ☒ 11am-8pm, last food 7pm). As well as snacks and 'normal' Orval Trappist beer it also serves Orval 'trois-cinq' (€2.40), a lighter, bitter monastery beer that's available nowhere else.

Around 3km south on the N840 lies the unusually charming yet untouristed village of Villers-devant-Orval, where **Domaine du Vieux Chateau** (☎ 061-320 271; www.hotelduvieux chateau@skynet.be; Pl du Moulin 7, Villers devant Orval; s/d with toilet €40/50, with bathroom €45/55; ☒ closed late Sep & late Feb) is a friendly 14-room family hotel. It sits in a sizeable area of grassy farm-park incorporating the minimal remnants of an historic castle that was mostly obliterated in 1940 bombing. The better rooms are built into the eaves with good new showers. Given the friendly welcome, free breakfast and honest pricing one can forgive the odd patch of peeling wallpaper.

ARLON
pop 25,800

If you're driving to Luxembourg, the south Ardennes' regional capital Arlon (Aarlen in Dutch) makes a good quick pit stop. First settled as a Roman trading post, the town's small central core retains a medieval street plan (but not appearance), spiralling almost imperceptibly up to a central hilltop. Here was once a powerful fortress of which only the sturdy stone foundation platform remains. That's now crowned by a modest but distinctive

church (Église St-Donat) and offers unexpectedly inspiring views. The **Maison du Tourisme**
(☎ 063-219 454; www.arlon-tourisme.be; Rue des Faubourgs
2; ⏱ 8.30am-5pm Mon-Fri, 9am-4pm Sat & Sun) is just off
Arlon's main square, Place Léopold.

The **Tour Romaine** is a tiny if curious subterranean fragment of Roman stonework
reached by a little tunnel-passage just off
Arlon's far-from-grand Grand Place. Show
yourself in having borrowed the key (€0.50
per person) from the barman at next door **Café
L'Albi** (Rue du Marché au Beurre; ⏱ 8am-10pm Mon-Sat,
2-9pm Sun). Many more valuable mementoes
of Arlon's Roman and Merovingian history
are displayed in the rich, but rather static,
Musée Archéologique (☎ 063-212 849; www.ial.be; Rue
des Martyrs 13; adult/child €4/1; ⏱ 9am-noon & 1.30-5.50pm
Tue-Sat mid-Sep–mid-Apr, Tue-Sun mid-Apr–mid-Sep). A
combination ticket (€6) also allows you to visit
the attractively furnished **Maison Gaspar** across
the road, whose most notable attraction is a
fine 15th-century altarpiece.

Château Bois d'Arlon (☎ 063-233 441; Rte de Virton
354, Toernich; d/ste from €125/175) has 10 rooms/suites
in an 1898 castle set amid woodland and lawns
that sweep down to a pond, 6km southwest of
Arlon on the N82.

Arlon's train and bus stations are a 10-
minute walk south of Place Léopold. Hourly
trains stop here between Brussels (€19.40, 2¾
hours) and Luxembourg (€10.40, 20 minutes).
For Libramont, twice-hourly expresses take
30 minutes but local trains (1½ hours) loop
round via Rodange and Virton. For Bastogne
take bus 3 to Martelange then bus 2.

BASTOGNE
pop 14,400
During WWII's Battle of the Bulge, Bastogne
was encircled and heavily bombarded by
German forces but refused to capitulate. Over
65 years later, the town retains many wartime
reminders and its main square – a car park
adorned with a Sherman tank – is named Place
McAuliffe for the famous 'Nuts!' general (see
the boxed text, opposite). The circular, glass-
walled building here is a helpful **tourist office**
(Maison du Tourisme; ☎ 061-212 711; www.paysdebastogne
.be; Pl McAuliffe; ⏱ 9am-6pm mid-Jun–mid-Sep, 9.30am-
12.30pm & 1-5.30pm mid-Sep–mid-Jun). Bastogne's
main shopping thoroughfare, Rue du Vivier/
Rue du Sablon, leads 800m northeast to Place
St-Pierre, around which sit a mask-towered
stone **church**, the lonely little **Porte de Trèves**
gate-tower and a former seminary building

hosting one of Belgium's most affecting WWII
museums, **J'avais 20 ans en '45** (☎ 061-502 002; http://
212.166.19.20/20ansen45/eng/presentation.php; adult/child
€6.50/5; ⏱ 10am-6pm, last entry 5pm). The main attractions here are the dozens of eyewitness
video-tales retold by citizens and ex-soldiers
shedding nuanced light on the WWII era –
from rationing to collaboration to treatment
of enemy soldiers. Keep the entry ticket to get
a €1.50 discount at **Bastogne Historical Centre**
(☎ 061-211 413; www.bastognehistoricalcenter.be; Colline
du Mardasson; adult/senior/child €8.50/7/6 incl audioguide;
⏱ 10am-5.30pm Mar-Dec), a more standard war
museum full of uniforms, weapons, a couple
of dioramas and a cinema playing a 25-minute
documentary using real wartime footage. It's
another 1.5km northeast at Mardasson, a gentle hill topped by a large **American War Memorial**
shaped as a circle within a five-pointed star.
Its sombre grey pillars are inscribed with the
names of the American states and a narrative
of the battle. A cavelike chapel-crypt beneath
features Protestant-, Catholic- and Jewish-
themed mosaics by Fernand Léger.

Right on Bastogne's main square, the
warm, friendly **Hôtel Collin** (☎ 061-214 888; www
.hotel-collin.com; Pl McAuliffe 8; s/d/tr €67/85/105) is a well-
kept family hotel with a pseudo art nouveau
cafe and a Mediterranean styled restaurant.
Motorists wanting something more peacefully
rural might prefer **B&B Ferme de la Hé** (☎ 061-535
938; www.bedandbreakfastbastogne.nl; Hardigny 29; d €70).
This delightful *chambres d'hôtes* has two de-
signer-rustic guestrooms in a self-contained
converted barn across a neat yard from the
Dutch owners' former farmhouse. It's 600m
north of picturesque little Hardigny village,
11km northeast of Bastogne via the N30 or
4km east of the E25 motorway's junction 52
via Rachamps.

Two curious eateries lie a stone's throw
from Place McAuliffe. **Pullman Wagon-Resto**
(☎ 061-211 085; Rue de Neufchâteau 1A; takeaway chips/
sauce €1.70/0.50, sit-down meals €7.50-16; ⏱ 11.30am-3pm
Fri-Wed & 5.30pm-9pm Fri-Tue) is a *friterie*-diner in
the adapted body of a postwar Chausson bus
chassis. More stylishly appointed **Wagon Léo**
(☎ 061-211 441; www.wagon-leo.be; Rue du Vivier 4; mains
€8.90-26.50; ⏱ 11.30am-9.30pm Tue-Sun) partly occupies a 1940s tram carriage with wooden-inlay
walls. One block further northeast on Rue du
Viver, Rue Lamborelle is a dreary short street
featuring a handful of initially unappealing
bars and *cafés*. However, the furthest of these,
Brasserie Lamborelle (☎ 061-218 055; Rue Lamborelle

BATTLE OF THE BULGE

Widely nicknamed the Battle of the Bulge, the Battle of the Ardennes was one of the fiercest land confrontations of WWII. In September 1944, both Belgium and Luxembourg had been liberated by American troops after four years of German occupation. However, the Allies then pushed on into the Netherlands and France, leaving relatively few soldiers to defend the forested Ardennes. Hitler, sensing this weakness, ordered a counter-attack in the depths of winter. The Von Rundstedt Offensive ploughed through the hills and valleys of northern Luxembourg and into Belgium forming a 'bulge' in the Allied line. It was a desperate attempt to capture the Antwerp and the River Meuse ports to block supplies and paralyse the Allied advance. Hitler's army got within sight of Dinant (p235) but failed to break through.

During this invasion, the town of Bastogne was surrounded but its defenders, the American 101st Airborne Division, kept fighting. When offered an opportunity to surrender, their commander General Anthony McAuliffe gave the curt, much-quoted response – 'Nuts!' His troops held out until early January, when Allied reinforcements managed to drive Nazi forces back through snowy Luxembourg into Germany. By the end of the battle in January 1945, nearly 80,000 Americans, 100,000 Germans and numerous Belgian and Luxembourg civilians had died. Meanwhile many Ardennes villages including La Roche-en-Ardenne, Houffalize and St-Vith had been bombed to rubble. Memorials to this tragic Christmas are numerous across the region. Bastogne and Luxembourg City have large military cemeteries (see p269) and there are dozens of poignant museums, most memorably in Bastogne, Diekirch (p279) and La Roche-en-Ardenne (below).

19; beers/snacks from €1.80/3; 🕙 11am-1am Tue-Sun), has an appealing interior, real fire in winter and a selection of around 120 beers. Their 'house brew' Airborne (€3.80) is a well-balanced 7.5% brown beer served in a novel ceramic cup shaped like a helmet.

Bus 163b runs every two hours to Libramont (45 minutes) on the Brussels–Arlon–Luxembourg railway line. Monday to Saturday, hourly buses into Luxembourg run to Ettelbrück (one hour) via Wiltz (25 minutes).

OURTHE VALLEY

The picturesque River Ourthe has twin sources that converge south of castle-topped La Roche-en-Ardenne. La Roche, along with painfully quaint Durbuy, is one of the Ardennes most popular spots for organising a wide range of outdoor activities.

La Roche-en-Ardenne
pop 4200

If you're arriving from the west, La Roche makes a sudden dramatic appearance with its evocative ancient fortress ruins crowning the town's central knoll above a tight curl of the verdant Ourthe Valley. Floodlit on a foggy night the scene is especially memorable viewed from Rue du Chalet, the N833 Hotton road forking south and east at the Hotel du Chalet and descending towards Place du Bronze.

From this square, La Roche's main street leads north across the Ourthe, and is variously called Rue Purnalet, Place du Marché, Rue de l'Église and Rue Châmont – all within 500m. Within this short space you'll pass the town hall, the castle-access steps, the post office, two ATMs, the **tourist office** (☎ 084-367 736; www .la-roche-tourisme.com; Pl du Marché 15; internet access per hr €5; 🕙 9am-7.30pm Jul-Aug, 9.30am-5pm Sep Jun), three adventure-sports operators, the church and the main museum. And, naturally, plenty of shops selling La Roche's signature smoked hams. Where Rue Châmont becomes Rue de Cielle, veer left on Ave du Hadja and cross the river again to find the bus station.

SIGHTS

La Roche's picture-postcard 11th-century **castle ruins** (Château Féodal; ☎ 084-411 342; www .chateaudelaroche.be; adult/child €4/2.50; 🕙 10am-6.30pm Jul-Aug, 11am-5pm Apr-Jun & Sep-Oct, 1-4pm Mon-Fri & 11am-4.30pm Sat & Sun Nov-Mar) look best from a distance, but the site makes for steep, pleasant strolls and in July and August you could spot a ghost at 10pm! The ruins sometimes close if conditions become too icy.

The collection at the **Musée de la Bataille des Ardennes** (☎ 084-411 725; www.batarden.be; Rue Châmont 5; adult/child €6.40/3.20; 🕙 10am-5.15pm Wed-Sun Apr-Dec, weekends only Jan-Mar) displays waxwork scenes, maps, and the odd video provides a competent, if unsophisticated, explanation of La

Roche's involvement in the Battle of the Bulge (see the boxed text, p243). During those two snowy weeks of 1944–45, 114 villagers perished and 90% of La Roche's buildings were flattened. The personal remembrances of local women are especially poignant.

From the northeast corner of Place du Bronze, Rue Rompré leads east to **Grès de la Roche** (☎ 084-411 878; www.gdlr.be; Rue Rompré 28; adult/senior/child €5/4.50/3.50; ☽ 10am-noon & 1.30-5pm Tue-Sun Apr-Oct, weekends only Feb, Mar, Nov & Dec, closed Jan). This imaginative rural museum takes you on a half-hour audioguided tour (no short cuts) around a former earthenware workshop, introducing kiln-firing methods and the local usages of the pottery produced, and incorporating press-and-sniff 'smellevision' buttons. One scene depicts medieval life in La Roche castle. After the pottery, take another 10 minutes to learn all about ham smoking, one of La Roche's main cottage industries.

Around 800m south of Place du Bronze off the road to Hives, don't miss the charming **Moulin de la Strument** (☎ 084-411 380; www.strument.com; Petite Strument 62; audioguided tour €3.75; ☽ 10am-5pm Sat & Sun Feb-Dec, daily Jul-Aug) a 19th-century watermill whose original three-storey workings have been meticulously restored. Guests at the lovely attached hotel can visit for free.

For a short steep stroll start beside the church on Rue Trou Bourbon and take the footpath that hugs the northern flank of the castle ruins up to the spired stone cube of **Chapelle Ste-Marguerite**. The chapel glows spookily on misty nights. Around 2km further up this winding lane you'll reach **Le Parc à Gibier** (☎ 084-311 015; www.parcagibierlaroche.be; Plateau Deister; adult/child €4.50/2.50; ☽ 10am-5pm Easter-Oct, 10am-7pm Jul & Aug, weekends only Nov-Easter), one of several similar animal parks in the Ardennes showing off deer, wolves and wild boars.

ACTIVITIES

The winding Ourthe passes through steep wooded valleys with lovely meadows. Not all are overrun by caravan parks and the river makes for appealing **kayaking** when water is high enough (far from certain in summer). Most options drop you at Nisramont (25km, €20) or Maboge (12km, €15) to paddle back to La Roche. Brandsport offers La Roche to Hampteau (19km, €19), 2km before Hotton (opposite).

Kayaking-cycling combos (€28) are also possible. **Mountain bikes** (VTT) can be hired

(€17/24 per half/full day) and the tourist office sells maps detailing good cycling and hiking routes. Several hiking trails converge at the hamlet of Borzée but beware that Borzée's 'Panorama Terrace' is a distinct disappointment in an ugly 1970s architectural carbuncle.

For those with extensive experience, **horse riding** is organised by Domaine des Olivettes (below). Reservations are essential, usually several weeks ahead.

Operators

Adventure activity operators include the following:

Ardenne Aventures (☎ 084-411 900; www.ardenne-aventures.be; Rue du Hadja 1) Three branch offices in town offer kayaking, rafting, mountain bikes and quad bikes.

Brandsport (☎ 084-411 084; www.brandsport.be; Pl du Marché 16; ☽ 9.30am-6pm Sat & Sun) Kayaking and mountain bikes from La Roche plus shooting, caving, climbing and a forest 'rope course' from its main farm-style base in Mierchamps village, where it offers clients simple group accommodation (€15 per person with your own sleeping bag).

Les Kayaks de l'Ourthe (☎ 084-368 712; Rue de l'Église 35) Near the tourist office.

SLEEPING

Numerous options offer rooms for about €60 to €80 around the main street but better choices tend to be slightly further removed from the centre.

Domaine des Olivettes (☎ 084-411 652; www.lesolivettes.be; Chemin de Soeret 12; dm first/subsequent night €17/12, s with shower/bath, €60/70 d €70/90) This hotel/hostel/equestrian centre has 10 slightly rough-edged en suite rooms above a hunting-themed lounge but is notable for offering some of the Ardennes' only dormitory accommodation, in a separate section above the stables. Bring your own sleeping bag or pay €6 extra for bedding (limited availability). It's high on a hill around 1km southeast of the centre (turn first right off Rue Rompré heading east from Place du Bronze).

Le Vieux La Roche (☎ 084-412 586; www.levieuxlaroche.com; Rue du Chalet 45; s/d €30/43) Simple, unpretentious, great-value family B&B. Five guestrooms share two toilets but have private shower booths. Rear rooms avoid road noise.

Villa le Monde (☎ 0497-218619; www.villalemonde.com; Rue du Nulay 9; s/d/tr/q €56/70/101/128; ☏) This super four-room B&B is run by a young multilingual Dutch couple who reflect their love of travelling and music in the room names and decor. Castle views are awesome from 'Jack Johnson' and even better from their airy bar-lounge, where you could try to qualify for 'Gnome University'. The B&B is 200m south of Pl du Bronze towards Bastogne. Free wi-fi.

Les Genêts (☎ 084-411 877; www.lesgenetshotel.com; Corniche de Deister 2; s/d €70/82) Seven re-painted, if not restyled, rooms in warm colours are set above a cosily old-fashioned lounge with grandfather clock, cacti and sweeping views down towards the river and obliquely across to the castle. The hotel's restaurant (mains €16.80 to €23.10, menus €22 to €40) is closed on Thursdays.

Moulin de la Strument (☎ 084-411 380; www.strument. com; Petite Strument 62; s/d/ste €77/85/91, camping per person/tent/caravan €2.5/8.50/8.50, shower/electricity €2/2.50; P 🛜) The town's most charming hotel (closed January) and campsite (open Easter to October) are nestled next to a babbling stream in a secluded, wooded valley 800m south of Place du Bronze. Attached to the 19th-century mill museum (opposite), the eight well-appointed hotel rooms have gleaming new bathrooms.

EATING & DRINKING
Numerous presentable but unremarkable eateries dot the main street and Place du Bronze, while in between both a Chinese restaurant and a brasserie sit beside the bridge and offer great castle views across the river.

L'Ancienne Poterie (☎ 084-411 878; Rue Rompré 28; beers/snacks/mains €1.80/5-9/12-19; 🕙 11am-5.30pm, Tue-Sun, main meals 11.30am-2.30pm only) The town's most atmospheric restaurant-*café*, attached to the Grès de la Roche pottery museum, features interior beams and curious fuel-ports where firewood was once loaded to heat the kilns. Try the house beer and a €5 taster plate of home-smoked hams.

Maison Bouillon et Fils (☎ 084-411 880; Pl du Marché 9; sandwiches/taster plates €2.75/9.50; 🕙 salon 11am-6pm Wed-Mon, shop 8.30am-6.30pm) Where but in the Belgian Ardennes would a butcher's shop have its own tasting salon? With lacy lamp shades, gingham tablecloths and plenty of smoked meat, it's a local classic. The sandwiches (*tartines*) arrive with a dish of pickles, good washed down with a shot of Prunalet, the local plum liqueur.

Il Castello (☎ 084-457 999; www.ilcastello.be; Rue Châmont 24; pizzas/wine from €8/2; 🕙 noon-3pm & 5.30-9pm Tue-Sun) The interior's entirely neutral but the fresh, thin-crust Sicilian-style pizzas are very hard to beat.

Vieux Moulin (☎ 084-411 380; www.strument .com; Petite Strument 62; mains €14-22; 🕙 Fri-Sun Feb-Dec, daily Jul-Aug) Downstairs at Moulin de la Strument, this restaurant specialises in game dishes (from October) but also serves drinks and snacks.

GETTING THERE & AWAY
Hourly trains on the Brussels–Namur–Luxembourg rail line stop at Marloie, from where bus 15 (30 minutes) connects to La Roche at least six times daily on weekdays, twice at weekends. Check www.infotec.be for timetables. As ever in the Ardennes, you'll need your own wheels to really explore the scenic back roads.

Hotton
Hidden beneath partly wooded hills 1.7km southwest of Hotton is one of Belgium's most impressive cave systems. These **Grottes de Hotton** (☎ 084-466 046 Apr-Nov, 083-688 365 Dec-Mar; www.grottesdehotton.com; Chemin de Spéléoclub; adult/child €9/6; 🕙 last tour 5pm Jul-Aug, last tour 4pm Apr-Nov, 2pm & 3.30pm Sat & Sun only Dec-Mar) boast several delightful sculpted grottoes sporting collections of pretty stalagmites and some weird 'eccentrics' (mini stalactitelike concretions that form corkscrews or protrude horizontally against all scientific logic). However, the real highlight is descending a former siphon through upturned vertical strata and emerging into a dramatically narrow, 37m-high subterranean chasm. It's very impressive. While the experience lacks the commercialism of Han, guided visits (at least 80 minutes) can drag on excessively and aren't necessarily available in English. Tours depart at least hourly in midsummer but relatively rarely (according to demand) in other months. Call in the morning for the day's exact departure times. Dress for 12°C temperatures and be prepared for 580 steps.

If coming by bus, get off in Hotton village and nip across the bridge to the **tourist office** (☎ 084-466 122; www.si-hotton.be, www.cir-ourthe.be; 🕙 10am-6pm Jul-Aug, 10.30am-5pm Tue-Sun Sep-Jun) to get an area map.

There are two intriguing accommodation options in Hampteau, 2km south of Hotton towards La Roche. **La Vielle Ferme** (☎ 084-466 764; Rte de la Roche 33, Hampteau; s/d without bathroom €40/55, with bathroom €50/70) is a supercute half-timbered historic farmhouse that's now an informal restaurant with four simple rooms, plus two more

---

ELFY BEER

Despite the silly elves and gnomes on the labels, **La Chouffe** (www.achouffe.be) brews some of the Ardennes' best beers, especially its beautifully balanced blonde with a perfectly pitched hint of acidity. The name is a mild pun on **Achouffe**, the pretty Ourthe Valley village where it's brewed. Achouffe's striking post-code 6666 suggested the name for another of the brewery's speciality ales. Hidden behind the little factory building, Achouffe's **brewery café** (☎ 061-289 455; 🕐 10am-9pm Thu-Mon, daily Jul-Aug) smells a little of school dinners, but allows you to taste several fine brews in driver-friendly *galopin* (180ml sampler-size glasses), while perusing the inox brewing vessels through a large glass window. Brewery visits (€7.50 including a souvenir glass) run frequently at weekends but most are in Dutch and not for drop-in guests; contact the brewery (visitebrasserie@ hotmail.com) well in advance to book a slot with an existing group tour. Note that you'll need to drive a car since the bottling site is 4km away in Fontenaille and transport isn't provided (though two beers are – how very Belgian!).

---

comfortable ones in a 20th-century timber pavilion behind. Across the river, **Chateau d'Héblon** (☎ 084-466 573; www.chateauheblon.be; Rue d'Héblon 1, Hampteau; ste €130) is an 1887 stone mansion whose idyllic streamside setting and homely lounges are more the attraction than its large and personable, but rather dated, suites.

Every two hours trains on the Jemelle–Esneux–Liège line stop at Melreux from which **TEC** (www.infotec.be) bus 13 runs to La Roche via Hotton seven/five times daily on weekdays/weekends.

Durbuy
pop 400

'The world's smallest town' – that's how Durbuy sells itself. While Hum in Croatia might dispute the claim, the memorable soubriquet certainly helps to keep Durbuy's photogenic cobblestone alleys and restaurants well filled with weekenders and summer tourists. At its heart is a fairly modest riverside **castle** (private) that dates from 1756, the medieval original having been destroyed under Louis XIV of France. Behind are many quaint greystone buildings, the odd half-timbered hall plus almost as many hotels and gallery-shops. On crowded summer weekends the village becomes one big amusement park. At other times it reverts to being the picturesque little village that it always was.

On the main square, the very professional **tourist office** (☎ 086 21 24 28; www.durbuyinfo.be; Pl aux Foires 25; 🕐 9am-5pm Mon-Fri, 10am-6pm Sat & Sun Sep-Jun, 9am-6pm Jul-Aug) has an ATM and plenty of suggestions for other attractions to keep you in town (topiary garden, jam-maker, microbrewery, free diamond museum, horse-cart rides etc).

ACTIVITIES
Durbuy Adventure (☎ 086-212 815; www.durbuyadven ture.be) offers a bewildering range of outdoor activity options at several different locations around Durbuy, plus at Barvaux (opposite) and Rome, a small settlement in between, where they have a carting course, a quarried hillside offering climbing adventures and a lake offering 'waterballs', where kids get 10 hilarious minutes in a walk-on-water plastic bubble. **Le Petite Merveille** (☎ 086-211 608; www .lpm.be) also offers kayaking, mountain biking and a range of climbing-based activities. Both companies rent mountain bikes, do bike-kayak combos and have sales agents/ booths in central Durbuy during weekends and midsummer. Prebooking is wise even out of season.

SLEEPING & EATING
The tourist office offers very comprehensive listings for a dozen hotels, as many B&Bs and around 30 restaurants. Prebooking is wise at weekends and midsummer, but finding a room midweek in low season for €60 should be easy.

Camping Le Vedeur (☎ 086-210 209; Rue Fond de Vedeur; camping per person/car/caravan €3/3/15, tent €3-7; mid-Apr–mid-Oct) Recently revamped riverside camping ground.

Hôtel Victoria (☎ 086-212 300; www.hotel-victoria .be; Rue des Recollectines 4; d Mon-Thu from €80, Fri-Sun from €100) In this brilliantly central, ivy-clad 18th-century building, the time-worn wooden steps are as creaky as ever but there's now a fashion-conscious resto-*café* and the guestrooms have been reworked in contemporary shades of apple and plum. Some retain exposed timber beams.

Le Clos des Recollets (☎ 086-212 969; www.clos
desrecollets.be; Rue de la Prévôté 9; s/d/tr/f €80/95/122/150;
☽ Thu-Mon) While the 14 comfortable rooms
don't win prizes for decor, they're scattered
around three delightful interconnecting half-
timbered houses and the overall atmosphere
is charming. The alluring restaurant (menus
€29 to €49; open 7pm to 11pm Friday to
Tuesday and 4pm to 6.30pm Sunday) serves
reliable French cuisine and in summer you
can dine outside on an intimate tree-lined
square.

Le Sanglier des Ardennes (☎ 086-213 262; www
.sanglier-des-ardennes.be; Rue Comte d'Ursel 14; d Mon-Thu
€110, Fri-Sun €150) Durbuy's classic address, this
celebrated hotel appeals to older couples who
linger in the indulgent lounge-bar receiving
libations from smartly waistcoated waiters.
Guestrooms featuring old furniture and occasional hat-boxes suggest a certain Edwardian
restraint. Breakfast costs €15. The restaurant features trout, steaks and game dishes
(October to Christmas), while the informal
summer *café* section has plastic tables right
by the riverside. Three other hotels in town
are co-owned.

B&B Au Milieu de Nulle Part (☎ 0476-418 821;
www.aumilieudenullepart.com; Rue des Recollectines 5;
d/ste €125/180; ☽ Fri-Sun) This gorgeously rustic B&B on Durbuy's quaintest pedestrianised alley offers subtle decor, old lamps and
five artistically designed rooms, each with
different furnishings.

La Canette (☎ 086-212 668; Rue Eloi 1; 2-course
menu €27; ☽ 7-11pm Fri, Sat, Mon & Tue, noon-7pm Sun)
Enticing old-town restaurant whose particular
delight is its narrow *café*-bar section decorated
in typical old-time style.

Le Fou du Roy (☎ 086-210 868; Rue Comte d'Ursel
4; lunch €21, 2-/3-course menu €29/35; ☽ Wed-Sun) Le
Fou du Roy is a cosy upmarket restaurant in
the castle's former concierge quarters, featuring a decor of clocks in one room, modern-
meets-farmyard in another as well as a
tiny triangular handkerchief of summer
garden terrace.

GETTING THERE & AWAY
If you don't want to drive, walk or cycle
from Barvaux (right), check times carefully
with **TEC** (☎ 081-253 555; www.infotec.be) for
the rare Barvaux–Durbuy buses (15 minutes),
which run up to six times daily in July and
August but weekends only or not at all in
other months.

Around Durbuy
BARVAUX
pop 1200
The nearest train station to Durbuy is some
4km east at Barvaux on the Liège–Jemelle
line. From the station walk 800m downhill to
central Barvaux and cross the river bridge to
find Barvaux's tourist office and the clustered
seasonal offices of Durbuy Adventure (opposite), **Ardennes Promotion** (☎ 0475-607 089; www.pvka
.be) and two other kayaking agents. All can rent
you a bicycle to get you to Durbuy or possibly
drive you there if you want to paddle back.

While Barvaux itself isn't gorgeous, it's famous for its remarkable **Labyrinth** (www.lelabyrinthe
.be; adult/child €8.50/6.50; ☽ 10.30am-7.30pm Jul-Sep, last entry
5.30pm), an extensive maze of maize whose design
is different each summer. Allow a few hours to
visit. Avoid during or after heavy rain.

PETITE SOMME
About 4km west of Durbuy, the attractive
hamlet of Petite Somme sports a particularly
photogenic **castle** (Château de Petite Somme)
behind an open floral lawn. The 13th-century
structure has appealing neogothic additions,
while the interior mixes beautifully restored gilt
mouldings with vividly coloured wall paintings
of Vedic deities watched over by enthroned
Prabhupada statues. The decor makes sense
since this is home to **Radhadesh** (☎ 086-322 926;
www.radhadesh.com), headquarters of Belgium's
Hare Krishna community. Visitors are welcome to use the site's architecturally bland
vegetarian restaurant (samosa/thali €3/12; ☽ noon-8pm
Tue-Fri Apr-Oct, 11am-8pm Sat & Sun year-round) but need
to join somewhat overlong **guided tours** (adult/child
€6/3; ☽ several daily in Dutch, 3.30pm in French, 4pm Sat & Sun
in English) to visit inside the castle, see the temple
room, climb the tower and watch a 15-minute
video on Krishna consciousness.

Esneux
pop 13,000
While still scenically pleasant, the Ourthe
Valley road gets increasingly busy along the
river's more northerly reaches. However, if
you're driving this way look up as you cross the
central river bridge in Esneux. Peeping through
hilltop trees high above you should spy the remarkable 1905 **Chateau de Fy** (private, no public
access), whose fairy-tale tower is said to have
been the inspiration for scenes in Walt Disney's
Sleeping Beauty. Disney had apparently seen a
photo of Fy snapped by a WWII soldier.

LIÈGE

pop 194,000

At first glance Wallonia's largest city has a miserably glum look that gets even worse in its soul-crushing industrial suburbs. However, it doesn't take much scratching to discover an entirely different Liège, a living architectural onion with layer upon layer of history lying just beneath the disfigured surface. Proudly free-spirited citizens are disarmingly friendly and no Belgian city bubbles with more joie de vivre. Love it or loathe it, Liège is quirky, unique and oddly compulsive.

History

The site of a former Roman villa overlooking the River Meuse was transformed into a humble chapel in AD 558. The revered bishop of Tongeren-Maastricht, St-Lambert had come here to pray in 705 when set upon and murdered by enemies from an opposing clan. Lambert's successor developed a church to commemorate the foul deed, and this site rapidly became associated with miracles. Pilgrims arrived from far and wide, including the great Frankish emperor Charlemagne. Their generous donations allowed the development by 1015 of St-Lambert's Cathedral, then one of the greatest in northern Europe. Meanwhile in 980 Liège had become the capital of a huge principality ruled by prince-bishops. Wielding both religious and secular powers, these 'mini-popes' incredibly managed to maintain their (somewhat reduced) territory's independence for almost eight centuries. Initially their rule was remarkably enlightened. Personal liberties were enshrined here centuries before such freedoms were accepted in surrounding feudal Europe. Comparative broad-mindedness plus access to monastic translations of Arabic scientific texts (purloined during the crusades) gave Liège and its dependencies (including Huy, Dinant and Hasselt) a technological edge in the development of local industries from metallurgy to distillation. Early 17th-century Liège businessmen were major exporters of arms and gunpowder. However, by the late 18th century the prince-bishopric had become a clumsy anachronism and economic gripes led to the 1789 Révolution Liégeoise. After a complex tussle, the prince-bishops were definitively ousted on the third attempt and Liège townsfolk voted in 1793 to demolish the city's fabulous St-Lambert's Cathedral, by then a symbol of the hated former rulers. Swiftly thereafter Liège was occupied and annexed by revolutionary France.

Post Waterloo (1815), the territory passed to the Dutch king, who sold the former prince-bishops' now purposeless Seraing summer palace to an English industrialist, John Cockerill. Suddenly Liège was swept into a new dynamic industrial age. Local steel and, especially, glass production proved world class, powering a vast period of growth in both the city and its industrial satellite towns of Herstal and Seraing (p254).

Germany's 1914 attack on the city marked the first major battle of WWI. This saw Liège become the world's first city to suffer a campaign of aerial bombing, courtesy of newfangled Zeppelin airships. The city's massively expensive ring of 1890 fortresses proved no match for Germany's advanced munitions. However, by holding out for twelve days, Liège's brave defenders gave the rest of Europe just enough time to prepare a defence from Germany's westward march. The grateful French presented shattered Liège with the *Légion d'Honneur* medal, while Parisian coffee-shops honoured the city by renaming a classic Viennese-style dessert as Café Liègeoise. The name has stuck.

As with most of Europe's heavy-industrial towns, Liège's fortunes slumped after the 1970s and while a much diminished steel industry still survives, the city's periphery is dotted with the rusty remnants of a more prosperous past.

Orientation

Strikingly empty-looking Place St-Lambert forms the city's central gateway. Historic buildings lead east via attractive Place du Marché to patchily grand Rue Hors Château, behind which fascinating alleys and stairways back onto a very steep hillside leading up (north) to the former citadel that's now a park topped by a hospital. South of Place St-Lambert is the commercial centre, while across the River Meuse is the island of **Outremeuse** (www.fgfw .be/rlom), whose straight-faced working-class residents consider it a 'Free Republic'.

Information

Alliage (☎ 04-223 6589; http://alliage.be; Hors Château 7; ⏱ 9am-5pm Mon-Fri & 7-9pm Fri) Gay and lesbian association. Click 'agenda' on their website for listings of upcoming events.

LIÈGE

0 ——— 300 m
0 ——— 0.2 miles

Ⓐ   **Ⓑ**   **Ⓒ**   **Ⓓ**

❶

INFORMATION
Alliage...1 C3
ATM...2 A4
Connections.....................................3 B5
easy@phone.....................................4 C4
easy@phone.....................................5 D5
easy@phone.....................................6 C4
FNAC..7 B4
Maison du Tourisme.........................8 B4
Moneytrans.......................................9 C4
Office du Tourisme..........................10 D3
Post Office.......................................11 C5

❷

SIGHTS & ACTIVITIES
Archéoforum....................................12 B4
Cathédrale St-Paul...........................13 B5
Église Collégiale St Barthélemy.......14 D3
Église St-André................................15 C3
Église St-Gérard..............................16 D3
Former Church of St-Antoine...........17 C3
Grand Curtius..................................18 D3

Hôtel de Ville.................................19 C4
Montagne de Bueren.......................20 C3
Musée d'Ansembourg......................21 D3
Musée de la Vie Wallonne..............22 C3
Musée de l'Art Wallon.....................23 D3
Musée Tchantchès............................24 D6
Palais des Princes Évêques..............25 B3
Sélys-Longchamps Mansion.............26 A4
Simenon Birthplace (Plaque)...........27 C4
Tchantchès Pilot Sculpture..............28 C3
Underground Stream........................29 C3

SLEEPING
Hôtel Hors Château..........................30 D3
Hôtel Les Acteurs.............................31 A5

EATING
Au Point de Vue..............................32 B4
Café Classico...................................33 D4
Enoteca...34 A4
La Fondue Royale............................35 D5

Le Bistrot d'en Face.........................36 C4
Le Brasilia..37 A5
Nun's...38 C3

DRINKING
Café Le Petit Bougnat.....................39 D5
La Maison du Pékèt.........................40 C4
Le Pot au Lait..................................41 B5
Taverne à Pilori...............................42 C3

ENTERTAINMENT
Caroline Music................................43 B5
Chez Bouldou..................................44 A5
Cinema Churchill.............................45 B5
Les Olivettes....................................46 C4
Opéra Royal de Wallonie................47 B4

TRANSPORT
La Maison des Cyclistes...................48 C4
Liège-Opera Bus Stand....................49 B4
Pl St-Lambert Bus Stand..................50 B4

THE ARDENNES

ATMs (Rue des Dominicains, Rue du Pot d'Or)
easy@phone (per hr €1; Central Rue Léopold 14;
☉ 9.30am-8pm Thu-Tue; Central Rue Léopold 25;
☉ 9am-8pm Sun-Fri; Outremeuse Rue Puits-en-Sock 51;
☉ 9am-8pm Sun-Fri) Cheap internet and phone calls at
three handy locations.
FNAC (☎ 04-232 7111, ticket sales 04-232 7112;
www.fnac.be; Rue Joffre 3; ☉ 10am-6.30pm Mon-Sat)
Books, maps and reservations for concerts and theatre
performances.
Moneytrans (Rue Ferdinand-Hénaux 7; ☉ 9.30am-
7.30pm Mon-Sat) Moneychanger.
Tourist offices (www.liege.be; Maison du Tourisme
☎ 04-237 9292; Pl St-Lambert 32; ☉ 9am-6pm
Jun-Sep, 9.30am-5.30pm Oct-May; Office du Tourisme
☎ 04-221 9221; Féronstrée 92; ☉ 9am-5pm Mon-Fri,
10am-4.30pm Sat, 10am-2.30pm Sun)
Post office (Rue de la Régence 26; ☉ 9am-5pm Mon-
Fri, 9am-noon Sat)

Sights & Activities

PLACE DU MARCHÉ & AROUND
Now used as a courthouse, the vast but rather
drab **Palais des Princes-Évêques** (Palace of the
Prince-Bishops) dominates dismally windswept Place St-Lambert. However, immediately east lies Liège's charming, if modestly
sized, original main square, Place du Marché,
sporting a fine row of traditional house fronts,
street cafes and a pair of very elegant well-
fountains. Between the trees, a cartoonesque
Tchantchès (see the boxed text, p252) pilots his
little metal aeroplane while the 1719 **Hôtel de
Ville** (city hall) glows lugubriously in its blood-
red spotlights. Behind the square rises the unusual dome of inaccessible **Église St-André**, shaped
like a Teutonic knight's pointed helmet.

Two blocks north, in an adapted convent-
cloister building, the imaginative, modern
Musée de la Vie Wallonne (Museum of Walloon Life;
☎ 04-223 6094; www.viewallonne.be; Cour des Mineurs;
adult/senior/child €5/4/3; ☉ 10am-5pm Tue-Sat, 10am-
4pm Sun) takes visitors on a fascinating amble
through the region's past, exploring everything from 12th-century Mosan metalwork
(see the boxed text, p230) to 1960s room
interiors. Videos and exhibits chart the region's incredible 19th-century industrial
growth then give a depressing roll call of 20th-
century demise. Fun, quirky exhibits include
a bedpan hidden within 'books'. Temporary
exhibitions are housed in the Baroque **former
church of St-Antoine**.

Nearby a dead-end alley-stub, continuing
from the north end of Rue Mere Dieu, disap-

LIÈGE PASS

These one-/two-day passes (€12/18) allow
free entry to 12 attractions, including all
those reviewed here. They also allow one
free Simenon audioguide tour (see the
boxed text, opposite) and offer discounts on
Meuse cruises. Available at tourist offices.

pears into a short unlit tunnel. Bring a torch
and continue to the tunnel's dark end to see
the emerging channel of an **underground stream**
(temporarily) guarded by a very spooky family
of long-necked fox-faced statues.

Rue Hors Château, running east from here,
sports many historic buildings. The scene
could look very appealing were their facades
cleaned up as beautifully as that of the splendid baroque **Église St-Gérard** (Rue Hors Château 23).
Several tiny medieval passageways burrow
beneath the house fronts into hidden yards,
above which the partly wooded citadel hill
rises very steeply. If you climb the 373 vertiginous steps of **Montagne de Bueren** then turn
right, you'll find a hilltop **war memorial** and city
panorama point behind which are the grassy
5m-tall brick bastions of the **former citadel** in
a partly wooded park. It's less strenuous to
climb the narrow side stairways that lead past
Nun's (p253) into the gated **Terraces des Minimes**
(admission free; ☉ 9am-6pm). Formerly the terraced
fruit gardens of a series of religious orders,
this is now a lovely hillside park-garden with
great views that survey the incredible chaos
of Liège's rooftops.

MAJOR MUSEUMS
Three of Liège's most important museums are
conveniently huddled between Féronstrée and
the Meuse. All three are free to enter on the
first Sunday of each month, as is **Mamac** (☎ 04-
343 0403; www.mamac.be; Parc de la Boverie; adult/conces-
sion €5/3; ☉ 1-6pm Tue-Sat, 11am-4.30pm Sun), Liège's
contemporary art museum.

From outside, the **Musée de l'Art Wallon**
(☎ 04-221 9231; Rue St-Georges; adult/senior/child €5/3/
free; ☉ 1-6pm Tue-Sat, 11am-4.30pm Sun) is a 1980s
concrete travesty. Within, however, clever
design creates a spiral of gallery spaces ideal
for viewing the museum's excellent collection of paintings by French-speaking Belgians.
The scope ranges from fine medieval canvases
by Lambert Lombard and Pierre Paulus to
surrealist works by Paul Delvaux. Particular

strengths are century-old images of industrial Wallonia. Constantin Meunier's *La Coulée à Ougrée* has an almost Soviet-realist feel while Cécile Douard's inspired *Le Terril* portrays worker-women struggling hopelessly up a metaphorical slag heap.

The splendid **Grand Curtius** (☎ 04-221 6817; www .grandcurtiusliege.be; Féronstrée 136; adult/senior/child €5/3/ free; ☻ 10am-6pm Wed-Mon) uses the thoroughly renovated mansion of a 17th-century Liège entrepreneur to unite four formerly independent museum collections. It then makes a very ambitious stab at explaining the whole historical development of visual and decorative arts from prehistoric stone chippings to art nouveau pianos, while also interweaving the tales of Liège artists and industries. The result can be somewhat bewildering and disparate, but there's an incredible wealth of treasures to discover and you'll need a couple of hours to do it justice, even without the more detailed audioguide (included) or temporary exhibitions (extra).

Much less time-consuming is the beautiful **Musée d'Ansembourg** (☎ 04-221 9402; Féronstrée 114; adult/child €5/3/free; ☻ 1-6pm Tue-Sat, 11am-4pm Sun), less a museum than a magnificently furnished 1755 Regency mansion retaining original stucco ceilings and some gilded leather 'wallpaper'. Highlights include four original 17th-century Oudenaarde tapestries, but explanations are very cursory so you could easily see all 18 rooms in around 20 minutes.

CHURCHES

Each prince-bishop, it's said, wanted to found his own church. So it's hardly surprising that Liège is utterly packed with religious architectural masterpieces, many left half-forgotten. Most eye-catching is **Église Collégiale St-Barthélemy** (Pl St-Barthélemy; adult/senior/child €2/1/0.50; ☻ 10am-noon & 2-5pm, closed Sun morning), a large Rhenish-style church with twin Saxon-style towers whose cream and cerise exterior has been so well restored it looks almost like a film set. The church houses a famous 1118 baptismal font that's one of the world's most celebrated pieces of Mosan art. Probably created by Renier of Huy, the great brass bowl was rescued from a chapel of St-Lambert's Cathedral when that cathedral was demolished in 1793. It rests on oxen figures and is adorned with five baptismal scenes, elaborately described in a video screened nearby. To glimpse the font for free, peer through the long, narrow slit window in the church's western end.

In the city centre, **Cathédrale St-Paul** (www .cathedraledeliege.be; Pl de la Cathédrale; admission free; ☻ 8am-5pm) has soaring Gothic vaults, a colourfully patterned ceiling and fine stained-glass windows. Its slickly presented three-storey **Trésor** (Treasury; ☎ 04-232 6132; www .tresordeliege.be; adult/concession €5.50/4.50; ☻ 2-4.30pm Tue-Sun) guards many of the other artworks, vestments and chalices rescued from St-Lambert's in 1793. The most extraordinary item is the jewel-studded gold-and-silver reliquary of St-Lambert. In the form of a life-sized bust, it contains what's supposedly Lambert's skull (though six other Lambert skulls also exist!) and is encrusted with intricate tales from the saint's life. Computer screens help explain relevant history and the audioguide (included) gives even more information. Don't throw away your ticket: it'll gain you free entrance to the Archéoforum.

ARCHÉOFORUM

Destroyed following the Revolution Liégeoise (see p248), the greatest church of them all, St-Lambert's Cathedral, is now a mere scattering of foundation stones invisible beneath bleak Place St-Lambert. These archaeological

---

GEORGES SIMENON – LARGER THAN FICTION

Liège-born author Georges Simenon (1903–89) did nothing by halves. His famous character Inspector Maigret appeared in no less than 76 different crime-busting novels yet that's barely a quarter of Simenon's astoundingly prolific tally. While writing he could churn out a book on average every 11 days yet still had time to move house 33 times and to bed an incredible 10,000 women. Well, the latter's his own immodest estimate. His second wife claims it was 'only' 1200.

Diehard Simenon fans can visit 28 places loosely related to the writer's youth and career using the tourist office's multilingual brochure, *Sur les traces de Simenon*, or their **audioguide tour** (€6, two hours). One of very few of places that actually has any tangible visible reference to Simenon is the brass **plaque** marking his birthplace at Rue Léopold 24.

diggings, along with remnants of an earlier Roman villa, can now be visited in the atmospherically (if sometimes impractically) underlit **Archéoforum** (☎ 04-250 9370; www.archeoforumdeliege.be; Pl St-Lambert; adult/concession €5.50/4.50; ☼ 11am-5.15pm Tue-Sun). Visits include a 15-minute computer-simulated 'tour' of the original cathedral plus a video documenting the farcical 20th-century history of the site (both in English). Note that Archéoforum entry is free if you first visit the Trésor at Cathédrale St-Paul (p251) or pay full price at Grand Curtius (p251), so keep those tickets. But vice versa doesn't work.

MONT ST-MARTIN

Once magnificent former canons' mansions line Mont St-Martin, which climbs steadily to the large 16th-century grey-stone **Basilique St-Martin** (☎ 04-223 6774; Mont St-Martin; ☼ 2-5pm Jul-Aug), occasionally used as a venue for classical music concerts. Specific sights are limited but stairways such as Their-le-Fontaine, descending from the ridgetop, provide fascinating hunting grounds for higgledy-piggledy townscapes interspersed by unexpected chunks of tower or city wall.

LIÈGE-GUILLEMINS STATION

Around 2km south of centre, Liège's main train station is an incredible 2009 icon designed by master architect Santiago Calatrava. Its bold white sweeping curves create a unique modernist structure that looks like a vast glass-and-concrete manta ray.

Sleeping

The historic **Sélys-Longchamps mansion** (Mont St-Martin 9) is scheduled to be converted into a luxurious Crowne Plaza (www.crowneplaza liege.be) hotel during 2010 but the site looks very, very far from finished.

Auberge de Jeunesse (☎ 04-344 5689; www.laj .be; Rue Georges Simenon 2; members dm/s/d €18.80/33/46;

⊠ 🖳) This modern HI hostel in Outremeuse is a focus for the boisterous 15 August events (see Festival Outremeuse, p18). Free organic breakfast, internet €1.50 per hour. Call ahead if planning to check in after 6pm. From Liège-Guillemins station take bus 4 to Place St-Lambert then bus 18 to Place Léopold.

Hôtel Les Acteurs (☎ 04-223 0080; www.lesacteurs .be; Rue des Urbanistes 10; s/d/tw/tr €45/66/73/83) This personable 16-room hotel has 24-hour reception and a congenial little *café*. En suite toilet-shower booths are tiny in some rooms, very cramped singles lack natural light and 'double' beds are narrow. Nonetheless the triple rooms are generously sized and the overall atmosphere is pleasant. Relatively central, breakfast included.

Husa Couronne (☎ 04-340 3000; www.hotelhusa delacouronne.be; Pl des Guillemins 11; d €65) The unexpectedly stylish Couronne has design features worthy of a top hotel. The location is far from central but it's ideal for catching an early train from the astonishing new Liège-Guillemins station right in front. Room sizes vary considerably without affecting the price. Breakfast €6 to €15.

Hôtel Hors Château (☎ 04-250 6068; www.hors-chateau .be; Rue Hors Château 62; s/d/ste €78/95/125) Brilliantly located in the city's historical quarter, the nine rooms combine fashionable modern design with bare antique brickwork and old beams. Call ahead to arrange arrival times (especially on Sundays when the restaurant is closed) as reception isn't permanently manned and is inaccessible in a gated access-way till you get your key. Breakfast €12, free internet.

Ramada Plaza (☎ 04-228 8111; www.ramadaplaza -liege.com; Quai St-Léonard 36; low/high season d €89/250; 🛜) The lobby of this outwardly unremarkable six-storey business hotel feels mildly dated and corridors are neutral, but the comfortable rooms were very appealingly redesigned in 2009. The rear section offers a total surprise

---

TCHANTCHÈS

Liège's mascot and oldest 'citizen' is a big-nosed wooden puppet called Tchantchès. He was supposedly born between two cobblestones in the city's 'free' Outremeuse quarter on 15 August 760. His miraculous arrival is an oft retold humorous tale that's a thinly disguised Biblical satire. However, unlike the baby Jesus, Tchantchès has a penchant for getting riotously drunk on *pékèt* (Walloon *jenever*) and head-butting people. Still, beneath such minor flaws, he's good-hearted and much loved, typifying the free spirit of the Liègois. If you speak decent French it's worth hearing his 'life story' retold at the **Musée Tchantchès** (☎ 04-342 7575; www.tchantches.be; Rue Surlet 56; admission €3; puppet shows 2.30pm Wed & 10.30am Sun Jun-Sep).

with breakfast room, bar and meeting rooms all tucked into the beautiful brick vaulting of a former convent. Front rooms have river views but face a noisy multilane boulevard. Pleasant garden, free internet, wi-fi in lobby.

Eating

The tourist office publishes a comprehensive dining advertorial guide *Liège Gourmande*. There are plenty of midrange choices in and around the Place du Marché and a curious variety on the sometimes daunting little pedestrianised streets leading off Rue Pont d'Avroy. In Outremeuse, Rue Roture is an old cobbled alley lined with sweet little restaurants, while Rue Surlet has pitta shops and groceries.

Café Classico (☎ 04-250 6955; Rue Hors Château 122; beer/sandwiches/tapas from €1.60/3.50/4; ⏰ 8am-midnight Tue-Fri, 5pm-2am Sat, 11am-2am Sun, kitchen noon-3pm & 6-10pm) This Spanish bar with design touches and a big Osborne bull is surprisingly stylish for such an inexpensive *café*.

Le Brasilia (☎ 04-222 1919; Rue Pont d'Avroy 44; mains €9-15; ⏰ 24hr) If you want something more than a pitta kebab at 4am it might be worth braving the Brasilia's cheesy mirror-and-lantern nautical interior.

Le Bistrot d'en Face (☎ 04-223 1584; www .lcbistrotdenface.be; Rue de la Goffe 10; mains €9.80-19; ⏰ noon 2.30pm & 7-10.30pm Wed-Sun, closed Sat lunch) Typical Liégeois and rural French food served in a 16th-century building with classic bistro-style decor.

Au Point de Vue (☎ 04-223 6482; www.brasserie -aupointdevue.be; Pl Verte 10; mussels €16.50-25, mains €12-28; ⏰ 8am-midnight, kitchen till 10pm) Busy, informal brasserie serving French and Liégeois food in a 1652 brick house or a street terrace with an oblique (if traffic-blighted) view of the neoclassical opera building.

La Fondue Royale (☎ 04-342 6423; Rue Roture 68; fondue €12.20-21; ⏰ 6.30-10.30pm Thu-Tue) This cute fondue place occupies a half-timbered 14th-century house, one of half-a-dozen appealing minirestaurants on the most attractive alley in Outremeuse.

Nun's (☎ 04-222 1069; www.nuns.be; Impasse des Ursulines 18; mains €13-19, beer/champagne €3.50/10; ⏰ noon-2pm Wed-Fri & Sun, 6.30-10pm Wed-Sun) In the hidden 18th-century remnants of a *begijnhof*, Nun's restaurant-bar-lounge has a delightful summer-terrace garden, a fashion-conscious champagne bar and a two-part restaurant. The French section is rather brash

but there is a more interesting modern Thai section upstairs.

Enoteca (☎ 04-222 2464; www.enoteca.be; Rue de la Casquette 5; 2-/3-/4-course menus €19/21/23; ⏰ lunch Mon-Fri, dinner Mon-Sat) Widely respected for serving reliable, fairly priced Italian food using fresh ingredients, all prepared before your eyes in the white-tiled open kitchen.

Drinking

Tiny lanes around the Rue du Pot d'Or are boisterous till very late but can feel intimidating. The Place du Marché area is less edgy.

Taverne à Pilori (☎ 04-222 1857; Pl du Marché 7; beer/pékèt/meals from €1.80/1.80/8.50; ⏰ 9am-last customer) The most traditional of the many terraced *cafés* facing the city hall on lovely Place du Marché.

La Maison du Pékèt (☎ 04-250 6783; www.maison dupeket.be; Rue de l'Épée 4; ⏰ 10am-2am) This lively, multiroomed *café* with bare-brick antique walls has tables sprawling onto a little square behind the Hôtel de Ville. It's a classic place to sample various types of *pékèt* (Walloon *jenever*; dry/fruit €1.80/2.80). Wines and beers are also served.

Café Le Petit Bougnat (Rue Roture 17; pékèt/beer €1.50/1.60; ⏰ 5pm-late Tue-Sun) Wonderfully genuine local rustic *café* with rough floors, candles in bottles and the perfect terrace on Outremeuse's sweetest square. Expect mayhem all around here on 15 August.

our pick **Le Pot au Lait** (☎ 04-222 0584; www .potaulait.be; Rue Sœurs de Hasque; internet per hr €2; ⏰ 10am-2am Mon-Sat, 2pm-2am Sun; 🛜) Down an alley of Gaudiesque bike stands and psychedelic murals, Liège's wackiest pub-*café* is a spacious, trippy mix of TV-faced dolls, cows peeping through palm foliage, and rampant fish heads. Free wi-fi, draught La Chouffe €2.30.

Entertainment

Caroline Music (☎ 04-223 6889; www.carolinemusic.be; Rue de l'Université 28) sells tickets for gigs across Belgium, including those in nearby Verviers.

Opéra Royal de Wallonie (☎ 04-221 47 20; www .orw.be; Rue des Dominicains 1) Wallonia's main opera house.

Cinema Churchill (☎ 04-223 4107; www.grignoux.be; Rue du Mouton-Blanc 18) Three-screen cinema with a grand stained-glass facade shows most films in their original language with French subtitles. Consult the central column of their website's 'agenda' for the upcoming schedule.

Chez Bouldou (www.cafe-bouldou.be; Rue Tête de Bœuf 15; ☽ from 7pm Mon-Sat) High-spirited *café* with a large central bar and cellar. Come for concerts, (Wednesdays and Sundays), jams (Thursdays), piano bar (Tuesdays) or join jolly crowds bopping to familiar oldies on DJ Saturdays. No cover charge.

Les Olivettes (☎ 0498-470 450; www.lesolivettes.eu; Rue Pied du Pont des Arches 6; ☽ from 8pm Fri & Sat, 11am Sun) In the days of Jacques Brel *Café Chantants* were common – smoky pubs where crooner, pianist and accordionist sang for their beer. Today Les Olivettes is an ultra-rare, authentic survivor, its *pékèt*-supping audience even more geriatric than the performers. Unique, no cover, expect plenty of interaction.

Getting There & Away

The most central train station is relatively minor **Liège-Palais**. Direct trains from Diest (€9.90, 80 minutes), Hasselt (€7.40, one hour) and Tongeren (€4.20, 35 minutes) stop here as do a few daily services to Luxembourg City via Coo, Trois Ponts, Vielsalm and Clervaux. From Aachen, Antwerp, Brussels, Lier and Verviers only the slowest regional trains stop in Liège-Palais, so for these destinations it's usually faster to hop two stops (six minutes) south to the principal train station, extraordinary **Liège-Guillemins** (☎ 02-528 2828), and switch to an express. Trains for Eupen (€6.40, 45 minutes) and Maastricht (€8.50, 30 minutes) stop only at Liège-Guillemins, as do high-speed Thalys (www.thalys.com) trains on the Brussels–Aachen–Cologne route (seven daily) and ICE services on the Brussels–Cologne–Frankfurt line. Remember to prebook way ahead to get decent fares on high-speed services.

Eurolines (☎ 04-222 3618; www.eurolines.be; Rue des Guillemins 94) international buses leave from Rue du Plan-Incliné next to Liège-Guillemins train station. **TEC** (☎ 04-361 9444; www.infotec.be) bus 85 to Huy via Jehay castle (p234) and Amay starts hourly from **Place St-Lambert**. Huy-bound bus 9 passes near the Val St-Lambert glassworks in Seraing after 35 minutes and bus 65 runs to Remouchamps (80 minutes, up to 13 daily), both picking up at **Liège-Opera** bus stand.

Getting Around

Buses 1 or 4 link Liège-Guillemins to central Place St-Lambert. For a taxi call **Liège Taxi** (☎ 0800-322 00). **La Maison des Cyclistes** (☎ 04-222 9954; www.provelo.org; Rue de Gueldre 3; ☽ 3-6pm Mon-Fri,

closed Tue & Thu Nov-Apr) rents bicycles (per hour/day/week €3/12/48). ID required; €175 deposit for longer rentals.

For parking information see www.liege centre.com/officiel/index.php?page=213.

AROUND LIÈGE

Seraing

pop 62,000

If you thought Charleroi was Belgium's ugliest city you haven't seen Seraing. Once at the forefront of Belgium's industrial revolution, its rusty steel plants and timewarp brick tenements now have a fascinating ghastliness, amid which the former summer palace of the prince-bishops still stands most incongruously. This became the headquarters of the region's original steelworks, founded in 1817 by English entrepreneur John Cockerill, whose statue now fronts the nearby Georgian-style town hall. Some 4km west along the quay, the Seraing's one compelling attraction is the world-famous **Val St-Lambert Glassworks** (see the boxed text, opposite), which has occupied a former monastery site since 1826. Once the planet's leading glassmaker, its workforce has dwindled from 5000 in 1900 to barely 60 today, but it still manages to create lead-crystal masterpieces with almost 19th-century tools. The company allows **visits** (☎ 04-330 3800; www.cristalpark.com; Rue du Val 245; adult/senior/child €12/10/6; ☽ 10am-5pm), which start in the former abbot's 'chateau' with a 20-minute film. You can peruse some extraordinary glass sculptures and take a 40-minute high-tech glass-discovery 'experience' involving a simulated 'balloon ride' and descent into an Egyptian tomb. That's all very imaginative (though slow moving and in rather garbled English), but the main part of a visit is the unique chance to see a master glass-blower in action during an hour-long guided workshop tour (in French and Dutch only) departing at 10am, 11.30am, 2pm and 3.30pm. It's all amiably haphazard and well worth experiencing while the opportunity lasts.

AMBLÈVE VALLEY

The River Amblève (Amel in German) curls west and north through pretty wooded hills from the Eastern Cantons (p260) via appealing Stavelot (p256) to join the River Ourthe south of Esneux (p247). The mixed woodland and meadow scenery has a bucolic charm and side valleys offer many walking, cycling and

---

CRYSTAL CREATIONS

In much of Asia, Belgium's fame relies far less on its beer and chocolate than its glassware. Nineteenth-century Maharajahs loved the stuff and barely an Indian palace exists that doesn't sport at least a couple of Belgian crystal chandeliers. The most famous name is Val St-Lambert from Seraing, whose production peaked before WWI. Although some 90% of its production was sent for export, distinctive two-colour cut-glass pieces remain prized possessions in many a Belgian home. These days, however, most such manufacture has shifted to places with lower labour costs, while changing tastes have also posed a challenge for surviving designers. Should you want pieces of classic Belgian glassware it's ironically often cheaper to buy antique items, especially if you don't need a full set. (Some Brussels shops are specialists, see p109.)

---

driving excursions. Be aware, however, that the scenes are pleasant rather than truly dramatic and that the main valley itself is slightly marred by a railway track.

As usual you'll value your own wheels to explore the mildly attractive side lanes, but trains run every two hours on the Liège–Luxembourg line stopping in Coo, Trois Ponts (for Stavelot) and Aywaille, from which bus 42a (www.infotec.be) shuttles along the N633 up to seven times daily (four times Saturdays, twice Sundays) via Remouchamps, Ninglingspo, La Gleize and Trois Ponts. A few buses continue south to **Vielsalm**, famous for its blueberries and the curious 29 July Macrâles night (see p18).

Remouchamps

In the shadow of a soaring motorway viaduct, the pleasant if generally forgettable village of **Remouchamps** (www.ourthe-ambleve.be) has a central tourist office beside which is the entrance to **Les Grottes du Remouchamps** (☎ 04-360 9070; www .grottes.be; Rue de Louveigné 3, Remouchamps; adult/senior/child €11/9.50/8; ☒ 10.15am-4pm Feb-Nov daily, Dec-Jan weekends only). This famous cave system lacks the dramatic depth of Rochefort (p236) and its stalactites aren't a patch on those of Han (p236) but 85-minute tours culminate in a remarkable 700m punt down a half-lit underground river. Mind your head, bring a plastic bag to cover wet boat seats and dress for 12°C temperatures: nothing too smart as you'll descend a narrow 1912 spiral staircase that can be a little muddy. Tours depart once a group of around 20 has assembled. That can be very fast in high season but might take an hour or two in winter.

Ninglingspo

A popular series of gentle hikes follow the trickling Ninglingspo stream up through rustling woodlands from the parking lot beside cheap, unappealing café-bar **Le Ninglingspo**

(☎ 04-384 4429; s/d €30/60; ☒ daily Easter-Aug, Fri-Sun Sep-Easter) on the N633 500m east of Nonceveux. The easiest walk is a 15-minute stroll to the **Cascades de la Chaudière** waterfall. Around 5km further south beside the N633, cross beneath the railway to see the river splashing through rocky rapids known as the **Fonds de Quareux**.

La Gleize

A century ago bored Belgian Queen Henrietta-Marie used to ride her horse across the hills from Spa to this modest village with its 12th-century Romanesque church. The stables and an associated half-timbered house where she'd arrive have recently been converted into one of the region's best value accommodation options, **Aux Écuries de la Reine** (☎ 080 785 799; www.ecuries.be; s/d/tr/q €55/72/90/120, high season €62/84/111/148; ☒ ☒). There's a lovely sloping garden, outdoor swimming pool and a range of recently modernised rooms with rustic beams. Check in across the road at the appealing café-restaurant **Le Vert de Pommier** (mains €9-24; ☒ 11.30am-9pm Thu-Tue summer, Fri-Mon winter), decorated with sepia portraits and Walloon sayings. Two-night minimum stay most weekends.

Coo

In the 18th century, monks from Stavelot's abbey (p256) created an oxbow lake on the Amblève by cutting a short-cut river channel at the tiny hamlet of Coo. Cascading down 15m

---

BOOK AHEAD

The whole Ardennes region gets busy in summer: booking ahead is highly advised in high season, especially around Spa, Stavelot and Malmédy. During carnival or the Belgian Grand Prix you'll need to plan months in advance.

this forms Belgium's tallest waterfall. Cupped in a pretty woodland valley, the scene is charming at dusk once the hoards of day-trippers have gone home. Meanwhile, by day, if you can stand the summer crowds, Coo makes a useful starting point for all manner of outdoors activities, mostly organised through **Coo Adventure** (☎ 080-689 133; www.coo-adventure.com; Petite-Coo 4). Possibilities include mountain-bike rental, kayaking, paintball, shooting, caving, quad biking, 'dropping' (an orienteering exercise where you're dumped at a random location with a map and have to find your way back), white-water rafting (water-level dependent, often best November to February) or even test-driving a Ferrari (€85 for 15 minutes). It's well worth phoning ahead to check availability of any activity.

Opposite the waterfall is **Plopsa Coo** (☎ 080-684 265; www.plopsa.be; person over/under 1m/under 85cm tall €22/6/free; ☺ see website), a kids' amusement park with 17 summer activities including a *bobluge* (hillside bobsled-style ride), labyrinth, bumper cars, minigolf and a cable car that rumbles up the hillside for pleasant views.

Camping de la Cascade (☎ 080-664 312; www .camping-coo.be; per site €6-9, per person €3-4.50) lies in expansive riverside meadows 300m from the waterfall. Washrooms are basic. For now Coo has only one hotel, the riverside **Val de La Cascade** (☎ 080-684 980; www.valdelacascadecoo.be; Petit-Coo 1; s/d/ tr/q €71/80/93/116), a family-style affair with dated '70s bathrooms and sorry attempts at artwork, though most rooms do have private balconies. However, there's plenty more choice 7km away in Stavelot and Coo's convivial terraced *café*-restaurant **Le Baron** (☎ 086-389 661; www.le-baron.be; Petit Coo 6), which plans guestrooms.

Coo's railway station is just 400m from the waterfall, towards Trois Ponts.

Stavelot
pop 6600
Set amid gentle slopes with appealing glimpses of surrounding lush green hills, little Stavelot is the Amblève Valley's most attractive and historic town. Architecturally it offers a loveable mix of grey-stone, tile-fronted and half-timbered 18th-century houses, many leading off along narrow lanes from Place St-Remacle, the central cobblestone square. Hanging amid the town's flower baskets you'll see many decapitated heads with long red Pinocchio-style noses. These represent the *Blancs Moussis*, white-caped figures who are the mainstay of Stavelot's unique carnival, **Laetare** (www.laetare-stavelot.be; ☺ 4th Sun of Lent); see

also p16. Their disguises reputedly date back to the 16th century when the principality's prince abbot forbade local monks from taking part in festivities. Stavelot's turbulent history has long revolved around such scheming prince abbots, whose territory of Stavelot-Malmédy enjoyed periods of virtual independence like that of Liège. You can learn lots more through audioguides, photos and videos in the big, red-painted **Abbaye de Stavelot** (☎ 080-880 878; www .abbayedestavelot.be; Ave Ferdinand Nicolay; adult/concession €7.50/6; ☺ 10am-6pm) that dominates the lower town behind the archaeological fragments of a once-gigantic stone church. The abbey entrance fee also includes interesting temporary exhibitions and an impressive collection of racing cars and motorbikes illustrating 100 years of motor racing. Upstairs a two-room submuseum introduces Guillaume Apollinaire (1880–1919), the French poet, art critic and champion of Picasso. Youthful Apollinaire had stayed in Stavelot one summer while his mum gambled in Spa. Presumably she lost, as they left without paying their hotel bill! The abbey's cash desk doubles as a **tourist office** (☎ 080-862 706; http://tour isme.stavelot.be; ☺ 10am-1pm & 1.30-5pm) and the gift shop sells a useful selection of maps and guides for cycling and hiking in the pretty local region. A useful 7km walk heads west to Coo (see p255) via the peaceful hamlet of Ster. **Ardennes Cycling** (☎ 0476-471740; Pl St-Remacle) rents bicycles.

SLEEPING & EATING
Central Stavelot has several appealing hotels and B&Bs, while **Auberge St-Remacle** (☎ 080-862 047; www.auberge-stavelot.be; Ave Ferdinand Nicolay 9; s/d/tr/q €37/50/75/100) has budget beds with shared bathrooms above a noisy abbey-facing bar. Breakfast €7. The closest campsite is the very basic **Camping de Challes** (☎ 080-862 331; sites per adult/child/tent/car/ caravan €5/2.50/1/1.50/2; ☺ Apr-Oct), 2km east in a lovely tree-shaded meadow at Challes.

Hostellerie La Maison (☎ 080-880 891; www.hotel lamaison.info; Pl St-Remacle 19; s/d Mon-Thu €70/97, Fri-Sun €75/105) In a distinguished townhouse above a classy restaurant (two-/three-/four-course meals €31/37/47) on Stavelot's main square, La Maison's rooms come with old-board floors, period furniture and old fireplaces. Walls are in fresh contemporary colours, but some ceiling paintwork is chipped and the tiny bathrooms feel like afterthoughts.

Hôtel/Restaurant Mal-Aimé (☎ 080-862 001; Rue Neuve; 3-course meal €25; ☺ restaurant dinner Fri-Sun, lunch Sun & sporadically on some other days) This eccentric delight has comfortable, if ultraminimalist, modern rooms (single/double for €80/90) above one of the Ardennes most special eateries. If you can stand the absurdly slow service, the three-course meals are astonishing feats of top cuisine at bargain prices. Sunday meals are four-course 'surprises'. The dining room is smothered in Bohemian quotes, poems and massed pictorials relevant to Apollinaire who did a runner from this very place in 1909. The remarkable stained-glass frontage looks best at breakfast (free to guests).

Hôtel d'Orange (☎ 080-862 005; www.hotel-orange .be; Devant les Capucins 8; s/d/tr/f €85/98/121/135, summer weekends €113/136/148/160; 🖳) Run by the same family since 1795, this 17-room hotel has gilt mirrors, old beams, somewhat parochial bird-and-flower patterned wallpaper, rebuilt bathrooms and plenty of communal sitting space. From Place St-Remacle walk 200m east along mostly picturesque Rue Haute past the incongruous Spa supermarket.

ourpick Dufays (☎ 080-548 008; www.bbb-dufays.be; Rue Neuve 115; d midweek/weekend €116.50/126.50) This exquisitely restored 200-year-old stone building offers six lavish B&B rooms, each with a special character. All are delightful but the art deco decadence of 'Années 30' and the tasteful on-safari brilliance of the 'Africa Room' (great balcony views) are particularly memorable.

GETTING THERE & AWAY

From Trois Ponts train station, bus 745 runs roughly hourly to Stavelot (10 minutes, 6km) continuing to Malmédy (p260). Up to seven times daily bus 294 runs Trois Ponts–Stavelot–Verviers (70 minutes) via Francorchamps and Tiège, where you can change for Spa. Two direct buses to Spa (30 minutes) run weekdays only: bus 744 departs Stavelot at 12.45pm, bus 750 at 4.03pm.

SPA

pop 10,500

Europe's oldest health resort, Spa is *the* original spa from which the English word derived (see boxed text, p258). At the town's heart is a grand trio of neoclassical buildings: the currently disused original 1862 **bathhouse**, the 1908 **Exhibition Halls** and the 'world's first' **casino** (☎ 087-772 052; www.casinodespa.be; Rue Royale 4; ⏲ 11am), originally built in 1770. To gamble or simply to admire the casino's muralled ceilings you'll need to be over 21 years of age, have your passport handy and apply for a temporary (free) membership pass. Behind the casino, the 1885 neo-Romanesque **Church of St-Remacle** is reminiscent of a mini Tournai cathedral. Currently under long-term reconstruction, the nearby octagonally spired **Pouhon Pierre-le-Grand** was the site of Spa's original springs, renamed for Peter the Great, the Russian tsar whose visit to Spa in 1717 helped popularise the resort.

A series of central *café*-brasseries with terraced tables beneath fine shady trees face the casino complex, but the scene is needlessly marred by the endless traffic clogging the intermediate Rue Royale. Directly west in a picturesque Léopold II–era pavilion is the **tourist office** (☎ 087-795 353; www.spa-info.be; Pl Royale 41; ⏲ 9am-6pm Mon-Fri, 10am-6pm Sat & Sun Apr-Sep, to 5pm Oct-Mar), backing onto a wrought-iron

---

CAVING IN

Wallonia has numerous visitable *grottes* (cave systems). Each has its attractions and each is incredibly different, though guides do tend to give the same basic spiel: you'll soon be an expert on stalactite spaghetti and carbonate concretions if you visit a few. Our speleological favourite five:

- Grotte de Lorette (p236) at Rochefort – remarkable depth
- Hotton (p245) – great grottoes and a fabulously vertical subterranean chasm
- Han-sur-Lesse (p236) – undeniably lovely if annoyingly commercial
- Remouchamps (p255) – for the underground river ride, not the concretions
- Neptune (p225) – for the friendly personal welcome more than the stalactites

It's worth remembering that subterranean temperatures will be around 12°C year-round (9°C at Rochefort). After an hour or so that starts to feel uncomfortably cold if you've arrived in only a T-shirt, or uncomfortably warm if you've come excessively bundled up on a snowy winter's day. Since all visits are by fixed-route guided tours, you can't simply 'escape' if you start to sweat or shiver so think ahead.

marketplace where Sunday morning flea markets are held. This leads into **Parc de Sept Heures**, a lovely park that in summer features minigolf, pétanque and pony rides (€4). The park's north side slopes very steeply up through splendid beech woods. A state-of-the-art new funicular (€1 per person) climbs the slope in futuristic glass-cube pods taking cure-seekers up to Spa's most iconic attraction, the 21st-century ridgetop **Thermes de Spa** (☎ 087-772 560; www.thermesdespa.com; Colline d'Annette et Lubin; 🕒 10am-9pm). Fronted by a circular glass facade, this is a top-rate wellness centre offering a wide variety of saunas, hammams and hydrotherapy pools (three hours/one day costs €17/21). Numerous other beauty treatments are available by prearrangement.

While Belgium's King Leopold II was playing colonial domination in Congo, his feisty Hungarian-born queen avoided the boredom of Brussels by moving to Spa and riding her horses across the Ardennes. **Villa Royale Marie-Henriette** (☎ 087-774 486; Ave Reine Astrid 77; adult/child/concession €3/1/2; 🕒 2-6pm Jul-Sep, 2-6pm Sat & Sun mid-Mar–Jun & Oct-Dec), the 1862 Napoleon III–style former hotel where she stayed, is now a minor museum. The stables include a series of horsy exhibits and an old forge, while the main building features old Spa water bottles and laquerware boxes produced as early souvenirs to sell to spa-goers. It's 500m west of the tourist office. Opposite, a short diagonal spur road branches southwest to the train station. Behind the station, millions of bottles of Spa's famous water are still bottled annually at **Spa Monopole** (☎ 087-794 111; www.spa.be, in Dutch & French; Rue Auguste Laporte 34; 🕒 9am-5pm Mon-Fri), where a public gallery overlooks the factory's production floor. It's a 15-minute walk from the tourist office.

Sleeping & Eating

Spa has a dozen hotels and several B&Bs. Cafes, snack shops and restaurants abound.

Camping Parc des Sources (☎ 087-772 311; www.campingspa.be; Rue de la Sauvenière 141; tent/caravan/shower from €12.90/17.50/1; 🕒 Apr-Oct; 🖳) Suburban campsite around 1.5km towards Francorchamps.

La Tonnellerie (☎ 087-772 284; www.latonnellerie.be; Parc des Sept Heures; beer/coffee/pastas/mains from €2/2/14/18; 🕒 lunch & dinner Fri-Tue) Tucked delightfully into the central park, this chalet-style half-timbered building looks at first glance like a typical tourist *café*. However, behind the casual terrace tables there's a relatively sophisticated restaurant above which are fair-priced

guestrooms (doubles €80 to €110) with burlap-matted floors, rustic elements and modern colour schemes. Each is named for a wine.

RadissonBlu Palace Hotel (☎ 087-279 700; www.radissonblu.com; Pl Royale 39; midweek s/d €110.90/131.80, weekend €155.90/176.80, internet rates from €86/94) If you've come for spa soaks, this modern, upper-market chain hotel is the obvious choice, with discounts on the Thermes and a dedicated funicular car operating direct from the hotel so you can get there in your dressing gown. Fair-sized rooms have free wi-fi, kettle and sepia photos of old Spa. There are superb town views from the small top-floor fitness room. Note that the quite separate, manorial-style RadissonBlu Balmoral is 2km east of town.

Getting There & Away

Spa is the terminus of a spur line off the Liège–Aachen line. Hourly trains from Verviers-Central (€2.80, 25 minutes) run via Theux, which sports a medieval castle. For Liège (€4.80, 55 minutes) change trains in Pepinster.

Direct buses run twice daily to Stavelot, but there's more choice if you change in Tiège. Near the Villa Royale Marie-Henriette and Match Supermarket, **Sidi Sports** (☎ 087-221 197; www.sidisports.be; Ave Reine Astrid 71B; 🕒 9am-6pm Wed-Mon) rents bicycles (per half-day/day/weekend €15/22/34). The tourist office sells regional walking/cycling maps.

AROUND SPA

Starting from outside the Casino, **Spa Promenades** (☎ 0475-542 033; adult/child €6/4; 🕒 9.30am-6pm Jun-Sep) runs 40-minute tourist trains on varying circuits that might sweep past some of Spa's outlying springs, or perhaps past the town's grander homes and two suburban castles.

About 2km east of town, **Lac de Warfaaz** is a pleasant pleasure-lake where you can ride pedalos or lounge at waterfront *cafés*. In the forest en route there's an indoor/outdoor pair of swimming pools with waterslides. In winter there are several cross-country skiing tracks and a small alpine run at **Pistes de Ski du Thier des Rexhons** (☎ 087-773 028; www.spaski.be; Rte de Bérinzenne, Nivezé), around 6km south of town.

Between Stavelot and Spa, **Circuit Spa-Francorchamps** (☎ 087-293 700; www.spa-francorchamps.be; Rte du Circuit 55) is Belgium's foremost motor-racing circuit and cited by many F1 drivers as their favourite course. Set in hilly part-woodland it includes significant climbs and a dramatic 150° bend near the main paddock, which is 500m west of **Francorchamps village**. Hotels here will likely be booked out years ahead for Belgium's Formula 1 Grand Prix. At that time traffic can be gridlocked as far away as Liège. The circuit also hosts other races most weekends between April and mid-October, several of which are free to spectators (see website for dates and invitation downloads).

VERVIERS
pop 52,800

Nestled into the Vesdre River valley, 20km east of Liège, sprawling Verviers was already a cloth town in the 15th-century but became an international centre for industrial wool processing in the early 1800s. Its star has since dimmed but amid the postindustrial decline the town retains some patchily genteel corners and two cloth factories still operate, one processing cashmere, the other producing baize for billiard tables. Students come from around the globe to attend wool courses at the town's industrial college and tourists can understand more at the excellent **Centre Touristique de la Laine et de la Mode** (☎ 087-355 703; www.verviersima.be; Rue de la Chapelle 30; adult/concession/child €6/4.50/3; ☉ 10am-5pm Tue-Sun), occupying a 19th-century former wool-processing mill. An audioguide details Verviers' rise and fall and explains the well-preserved equipment, from old wool combs to mechanical spinners to local technological inventions.

Other large pieces of historical textile-factory equipment have been imaginatively repurposed as items of street art all around town. One such piece lies two short blocks south on an attractive strip of tree-lined riverbank, where a recently part-gentrified row of historic houses hosts the new **tourist office** (☎ 087-355 703; www.paysdevesdre.be; Rue Jules Cerexhe 86; ☉ 9.30am-5pm Tue-Sun). They give away guide brochures detailing the various fine fountains that give Verviers its nickname 'City of Water'. The office is around 600m northwest of Verviers-Central train station. However, the city's modern heart is further east, around the parallel squares Place Verte and Place du Martyr. While neither are architecturally memorable, walking there from Verviers-Central station (500m, head northeast) takes you past the chalet entrance to Parc Harmonie with its art nouveau features, a once-magnificent, somewhat unkempt theatre, plus a decent scattering of superb early 20th-century buildings. Another 400m east of Place Verte, cobbled lane Mont du Moulin descends photogenically past ivy-draped and half-timbered buildings from Place du Marché, where the stately town hall faces a road sign pointing the way to Bradford (775km).

Two blocks north, the **Musée des Beaux-Arts et de la Céramique** (☎ 087-331 695; Rue Renier 17; adult/concession/child €2/1/free; ☉ 2-5pm Mon, Wed & Sat, 3-6pm Sun) houses a small but high-quality collection of paintings from the 14th to 19th centuries and some remarkable ceramics. Also nearby, the less interesting **Musée d'Archéologie et de Folklore** (☎ 087-331 695; Rue des Raines 42; adult/concession/child €2/1/free; ☉ 2-5pm Tue & Thu, 9am-noon Sat, 10am-1pm Sun) occupies a fine Louis XV-style townhouse and has a renowned lace collection.

Sleeping & Eating

Hôtel des Ardennes (☎ 087-223 925; www.hoteldesardennesverviers.be; Pl de la Victoire 15; s/d without bathroom €38/50, with bathroom €48/60) Above a cosily small 1900s-style brasserie featuring hunting trophies, brass piping and the odd stained-glass panel are good-value rooms with floral bedspreads and 1930s furniture in some. Loveable in its way and very handy for Verviers-Central train station.

Hotel Verviers (☎ 087-305 656; www.hotelverviers.be; Rue de la Station 4; d standard/superior €95/100) This landmark 100-room hotel occupies a beautifully repurposed 1891 former station, whose grand brick structure is attractively floodlit from below at night. The restaurant and bustling brasserie have a fashionable feel but aren't dauntingly exclusive, while guestrooms strike a fine balance between modern design and midrange functionality. Superior rooms are duplexes with steps up to the bed area. Free wi-fi, breakfast €13.

Hostellerie Lafarque (☎ 087-460 651; www.hostellerie -lafarque.com; Chemin des Douys 20, Pepinster; d/ste €160/250; ✆ Thu-Mon only, closed Jan) Occupying a 20th-century half-timbered wool-baron's mansion 5km west of Verviers, this genteel Relais-et-Chateaux hotel features a Michelin-starred restaurant.

Eating & Drinking

Verviers offers some excellent-value dining and its pubs are remarkably friendly places. Speaking some French will help.

La Boule Rouge (☎ 087-333 950; Pont St-Laurent 10; pastas €7.20-9, mains €10-21, mussels €16-19; ✆ 10am-midnight Mon-Sat, 5pm-midnight Sun) Popular rustic-style *café* with a half-timbered frontage, a wide range of beers and food that's good and inexpensive. It's between Place Verte and Place du Martyr.

Eau 1725 (☎ 087-301 525; €18-20; ✆ noon-2pm Thu-Tue & 6-11pm Thu-Mon) The most tempting of a sedate row of river-facing brasseries and restaurants that flank the tourist office, Eau 1725 offers an imaginative combination of French and Greek cuisine served in a tastefully updated 18th-century townhouse with extra seating in an atmospheric brick-vaulted cellar room.

Le Quay des Artistes (☎ 087-785 013; Rue Xhavée 92; mains €14-22; ✆ 11am-2.30pm Sun, Mon & Wed-Fri, 6.30-10.30pm Wed-Sun, closed Tue) This classic corner brasserie facing the theatre has had a suave makeover and offers an impressive range of Belgo-French food. Good for a calm drink too.

Jean-Philippe Darcis (☎ 087-339 815; Rue Crapaurue 121; ✆ 10am-6pm Tue-Sat, 10am-1pm Sun) The tearoom of one of Belgium's foremost *chocolateries*, famed also for his macaroons. It's between Place Verte and Place du Marché.

Paradise Café (☎ 0484-773 796; Rue du Manège 14; ✆ 11am-late Wed-Mon) Tucked behind the theatre, this totally unpretentious locals' *café* occupies a brilliant 1890s architectural masterpiece with Moorish-style windows and matching mirror panels. English is spoken.

Entertainment

Spirit of 66 (☎ 087-352 424; www.spiritof66.be; Pl du Martyr 16) Known to locals as 'le Sixtysix', this is one of Belgium's foremost venues for superb live music, notably in the blues-rock genre. They have a deserved reputation for finding and re-presenting half-forgotten former greats whose star has passed…rather like Verviers itself.

Getting There & Away

On the Liège–Aachen mainline, Verviers-Central train station has a compact, but soaring, historical entranceway retaining the original wrought-iron ticketing *guichets*. Trains bound for Eupen, Welkenraedt and Spa also stop at marginally more central Verviers-Palais, 300m southeast of Place Verte. TEC bus 294 (seven times daily) to Stavelot via Malmédy and bus 390 to Rocherath via the Botrange Nature Centre (around five times daily) both leave from Verviers-Central station.

AROUND VERVIERS

If you're driving to Eupen, don't miss the short detour from Dolhain to the unusually well preserved hill-citadel village of **Limbourg**, with an oversized church and extraordinarily uneven cobblestone in its long, photogenic main square.

THE EASTERN CANTONS

The Ost Kantonen, Belgium's German-speaking 'Eastern Cantons', is best known for the Haute Fagnes area of moorlands that lies between the pleasant towns of **Eupen** (www.eupen-info .be) and **Malmédy** (www.eastbelgium.com). Both hold world-class carnivals (see p16) and Eupen is Belgium's most Germanic town, though otherwise neither are particular attractions in themselves. The area's history is intriguing. Stavelot-Malmédy had been a semi-independent codiocese since AD 650 and stayed a distinct ecclesiastic enclave (later coruled with Liège) until the prince abbotric was abolished following the French Revolution. When the region was carved up post-Waterloo (1815), Stavelot remained attached to the Netherlands but Malmédy, Eupen and St-Vith were given to Prussia and subsequently became part of Germany. The Netherlands and Prussia couldn't agree who'd get a then-valuable zinc mining settlement now known as **Kelmis**, which became 'Neutral Moresnet' and remarkably survived as one of Europe's least-known semi-independent states until invaded by Germany in 1914. After WWI, the whole Eastern Cantons area was ceded to Belgium under the 1919 Treaty of Versailles. But 20 years later Germany claimed them back and men from these towns were forced to fight alongside soldiers of the Reich throughout WWII. In 1945, Americans liberated the towns and they were handed to Belgium once more. Today this 854 sq km area has its own German-speaking **parliament** (www.dgparlament.be) housed in an 1812 mansion in Eupen, though French remains very widely used across the region, especially in Malmédy.

Hautes Fagnes

These 'High Fens', Hohes Venn in German, are one of Belgium's most popular places for bracing day-hikes and, snow obliging, for *langlauf* (cross-country) skiing. It's also the country's largest nationally protected reserve, an environmentally unique upland plateau of swampy heath and sphagnum peatbogs surrounded by considerable stands of woodland. The 4000-hectare reserve is a haven for wild boars, roe deers, lyrebirds, hen harriers and black grouse, though you're far from certain to see any. Botanical curiosities include *Drosera rotundifolia* (a carnivorous sundew plant) and *Trientales europaea* (Wintergreen Chickweed), a rare seven-petalled flower that features as the reserve's logo.

Don't be misled: the scenery isn't spectacular and the region is often wet, misty and shrouded in low cloud. But if you're suitably prepared this can add to the mesmerising quality of the area. A special feature are sections of footpath made of wooden boarding laid across the marshy peat that allow you to observe the special environment without causing damage or sinking into it.

Access is generally from one of four main car parks, each with its lonely restaurant, ski-hire facilities and walking-path maps.

- **Mt Rigi** (☎ 080-444 844; www.mont-rigi.be; beer/pasta/schnitzel/trout from €1.90/7/15/16; ☻ 10.30am-7pm), a chalet-style restaurant with a sizeable parking area at the junction of the Eupen–Malmédy and Eupen–Bütenbach roads. Food is good value, big windows survey the fenland and it has a welcoming feel despite the noose-dangling figure leering malevolently from the facade. Start here for the well-signed **Fagne de la Polleûr** loop walk, a 4km circuit of boardwalks with useful interpretive panels about relevant wildlife and plants.

- **Baraque Michel** (☎ 080-444 801; beer/pasta/schnitzel/trout from €1.60/7/15/16; ☻ noon-7pm), a typical Ardennes-style restaurant adorned with hunting trophies and serving its own beer. It's 1.5km north of Mt Rigi.

- **Signal de Botrange**, Belgium's highest point (694m), is an unremarkable feature marked with a 1954 **stone tower** (admission free; ☻ 10-6pm) that has all the charm of a fire-station lookout. To climb it, find the door within the attached restaurant building. Beside is a helpful English-speaking **tourist office** (☎ 080-447 300; ☻ 10am-3pm Tue-Fri, 10am-4pm Sat & Sun) who offer hiking-route suggestions, sell detailed walking maps and are the first people to contact for snow-condition reports in winter. It's 1.5km south of Mt Rigi.

- **Botrange Nature Centre** (☎ 080-440 300; www.botrange.be; Rte de Botrange 31; ☻ 10am-6pm), the park's main information centre, is 300m west of the Eupen–Bütenbach road, 1km south of Signal de Botrange (2km north of Ovifat). It's a modern log building with a notable central fireplace beneath a funnel chimney. An attached **museum** (adult/child €3/1.20) explains the Hautes Fagnes' evolution through a geological 'time tunnel', including the impact humans have had on the landscape through sheep grazing, logging and peat extraction (peat heated local houses right up until the 1960s). The idea is good but the 50-minute audioguide is slow paced, latter sections aren't in English and nor is the 25-minute movie.

Reinhardstein

At the southern edge of **Ovifat**, the first village south of the Hautes Fagnes, an idyllic little streamside lane descends 500m from a small car park to the **Château de Reinhardstein** (www.reinhardstein.net; Chemin de Cheneux 50, Ovifat). Originally built in 1354 and restored to archetypal fortress appearance in 1969, the castle can only be visited by **guided tour** (in French or Dutch; adult/senior/child €6/4.80/4.80) departing at 11am or 2.30pm on certain dates (check website). But even when closed, it's well worth the short stroll to admire the sturdy exterior framed by mature trees.

You can also catch a very brief castle glimpse from 'above' when driving between Malmédy and **Robertville**, where there's a popular forest-rimmed reservoir lake and several hotel-restaurants.

> **WALKING THE FAGNES**
>
> A hiker's first purchase should be the 1:25,000 scale *Hautes Fagnes Carte des Promenades* map (€7), which shows dozens of options. It also marks the reserve's various zones. In unlabelled areas you're free to wander. In B-zones you may walk without a guide but must not stray from marked path. C-zones can be partially visited but only with **guided walks** (3-/6-hr walk per group €45/60; Apr-Nov only) preorganised through the tourist office or nature centre. D-zones are closed completely.
>
> Note that there are plenty of other delightful walks in the woodland valleys surrounding the main Fagnes. One easy, pleasant stroll is from Longfaye village to the **Cascade du Bayhon**, a modest but pretty 9m-high waterfall that tumbles into a pool cupped by mossy forest.

Sleeping & Eating

OVIFAT

Gîte d'Étape (☎ 080-444 467; gite.ovifat@gitesdetape .be; Rue des Charmilles 69; dm under/over 26yr €12/15 plus €4/1.50 for sheets/membership) Handy for walkers or skiers, this 109-bed hostel is roughly halfway between Reinhardstein and the Botrange Nature Centre.

MALMÉDY

Book months ahead for the carnival or Belgian Grand Prix weekends.

Hôtel Albert Premier (☎ 080-330 452; www.hotel -albertpremier.be; Pl Albert Ier 40; s/d €70/90, mains €15-25;) Six acceptably clean, if slightly dated, bedrooms above a nearly tasteful midrange restaurant on the town's main square. There are many stairs to climb, especially for the top rooms set in pine-clad eaves.

Hôtel La Forge (☎ 080-799 555; Pl St-Géréon 7; s/d €65/80, mains €8-15; closed Tue) Behind an unpromising facade lies a friendly, if thoroughly local, *café* that has reinvented itself by sprouting convincingly designed art nouveau motifs. Art nouveau also strongly influences the breakfast room, while the 12 guestrooms above are recently rebuilt and feature Toulouse-Lautrec prints. One has a water bed and most have brand new bathrooms. Breakfast is included and cheap authentic meals are available.

EUPEN

Gîte d'Étape (Eupener Jugendherberge; ☎ 087-553 126; www.gitesdetape.be; Judenstrasse 79; dm under/over 26yr €11.70/14.60 plus €4/1.50 for sheets/membership; reception 5-10pm) A hilltop location at the southern edges of town gives this well-kept, if slightly old-fashioned, hostel some lovely sweeping views over rolling forested hills. The bar serves beers at just €1.20.

Pension Zum Goldenen Anker (☎ 087-743 997; Marktplatz 13; s/d with shared toilet €50/60) Survivable rooms are not quite as awful as you'd fear from the sauerkraut-perfumed corridors and the cheap, dowdy, smoke-filled *café* (meals €3.50 to €7.20) beneath. Just two doors from the tourist office, its one real plus is a very central location opposite the St-Nikolaus Kirche (Eupen's monumental church with distinctive copper-green spires). German is spoken, but little French and no English.

our pick Julévi B&B (☎ 0478-493 236; www.julevi .be; Heidberg 4; s/d/q €70/95/165;) A charming, English-speaking couple have transformed this 1869 linen-merchant's house into a stylishly comfortable retreat featuring quality box-spring mattresses, fluffy monogrammed towels and a delightful guest lounge with honesty bar. It trumps most hotels and there's even a little verandah, garden and library. From the train station walk two blocks south to Werthplatz then turn left. The B&B is beside the steps that climb to the leafy Heidbergpark.

Getting There & Away

Eupen's train station (*Bahnhof* in German) is served by hourly trains from Liège-Guillemins (€6.30, 45 minutes) and Verviers (€3.20, 20 minutes). Ovifat and the main Fagnes hub-restaurants are accessible by Rocherath-bound bus 390 from Verviers (€3.60, 30 minutes, five daily, three at weekends) or by St-Vith–bound bus 394 from Eupen (€3.60, 20 minutes, three daily).

From Trois Ponts near Stavelot on the Liège–Luxembourg railway line, bus 745 runs hourly to Malmédy (€1.60, 20 minutes), arriving at Rue de la Gare, which is a few minutes' walk from Malmédy's central Place Albert Ier.

Luxembourg

Which European nation, just 84km long, rates amongst the world's three richest countries? Remarkably, given its rural character, the answer is Luxembourg. That's some achievement given its destruction during WWII, a sad history remembered in war museums across the country, most memorably in Diekirch. The country's economic miracle started with steel but is now based particularly on banking – Belgians joke that visitors only go there to get their money out. In reality, the Grand Duchy's villages make popular getaways for Belgian and Dutch weekenders who walk the forest tracks, dine in auberges and motorbike along the winding country lanes.

But don't leave Luxembourg City to the bankers and Eurocrats. There's a fairy-tale quality to its Unesco-listed historic core, dramatically perched on a once-impregnable cliff top. From this promontory the city overlooks valleys and gorges that were for centuries the key to its defence. Below lie the atmospheric old neighbourhood of Grund and the up-and-coming nightlife zone of Clausen. The capital effortlessly counterpoints historic palaces with state-of-the-art museums; timeless old *cafés* with the glass towers of Kirchberg; down-at-heel (if very safe) station-area backstreets with chic boutiques; 1970s hotels with dazzling Michelin-starred restaurants.

This chapter covers the country anti-clockwise from the capital via the southwest and Moselle wine country to the Müllerthal and Northern (Ardennes) regions. Here, amid verdant hills, the Grand Duchy's most beguiling villages each form attractive huddles beneath medieval castles.

HIGHLIGHTS

- **Precipitous Promenade** Europe's 'most beautiful balcony', Luxembourg City's Chemin de la Corniche (p266) and the scenic descent to the Grund (p268)
- **Wartime Memories** Diekirch's Musée National d'Histoire Militaire (p279)
- **Drinking & Dining** *Cafés,* bars and restaurants (p271) in Luxembourg City's quaint Îlot Gourmand and Grund quarters
- **Enchanted Forests** Hiking into the Müllerthal woodlands from Echternach
- **Medieval Magic** Castles of Vianden (p280), Beaufort (p278), Bourscheid (p279) and Larochette (p276)
- **History comes to life** Luxembourg City's fascinating Musée d'Histoire de la Ville de Luxembourg (p268)
- **Wine Divine** Sparkling tasters in the Moselle Valley (p274)
- **Digging Deep** Descend into an iron ore mine at Rumelange (p274)

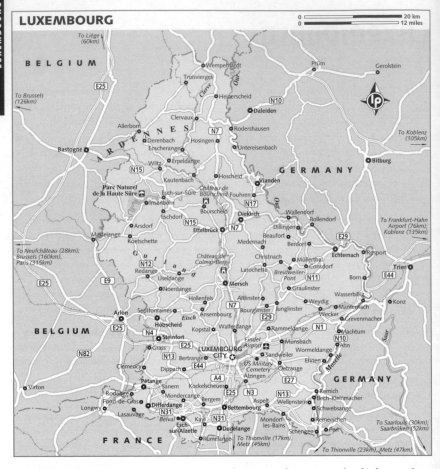

LUXEMBOURG CITY

Population: 85,000

Tell your Belgian friends that you're nipping off for a banking weekend and they'll guess you're Luxembourg bound. What might surprise them, however, is the fun you'll have when you get here, except on Sunday, of course, when the city falls asleep.

History

The foundations of today's city took root in 963 when Sigefroi (Siegfried), count of the Ardennes, built a castle on a rocky spur that's now known as the Bock. From 1354 the region was an independent duchy, which at one point expanded to include Metz in the south and Limburg to the north. Conquered by Burgundy in 1443, the duchy was later incorporated like proto-Belgium into the Hapsburg empire (p26). The city's remarkable fortifications proved particularly impressive during the French revolutionary wars, although not quite good enough to survive a seven-month French siege in 1792–3. After Waterloo in 1815, Luxembourg was declared a Grand Duchy under the Dutch king. Its status caused considerable discussion after Belgian independence, with the Grand Duchy eventually split in two following the 1839 Treaty of London. Strategically important Luxembourg City remained capital of the Dutch part but was garrisoned by Prussian troops – a fact that steadily became a bone of contention between France and Germany. In 1867 a possible war

---

LOCAL LINGO

Though it's long been an everyday language, Letzeburgesch was only proclaimed Luxembourg's national tongue in 1984. Meanwhile almost all Luxembourgers also speak French and German, with many more fluent in English. Useful Letzeburgesch vocabulary includes *moiem* (hello), *eddi* (goodbye), *gudd* (good/delicious) and *schein* (beautiful). Thank you is *'merci'*, but with a stressed first syllable unlike in French.

---

was defused by declaring Luxembourg neutral in a second Treaty of London and by dismantling many of the city's historic fortifications. The demolitions were expensive and took over a decade but provided plentiful stone for a new construction boom.

When the Dutch King William III died in 1890, his daughter Wilhelmina became queen of the Netherlands. However, by Luxembourg's then-current 'Salic' rules of succession, only males could rule the Grand Duchy. This quirk resulted in Luxembourg's previously nominal independence actually becoming a reality, and thus Luxembourg City emerged as a fully fledged European capital.

Germany occupied the city during both world wars. Liberated in September 1944 it was used as one of the allied command centres at the end of WWII for the Battle of the Ardennes (p243). Until 1981 a part-time EEC (now EU) parliament was based here and, although it's since left, Luxembourg City's shiny glass Kirchberg area is still host to several major EU organisations including the European Investment Bank and European Court of Justice.

Orientation

The Unesco-listed Old Town sits high above the gorges of the Alzette and Pétrusse rivers. Below the Bock fortifications an elevator on Plateau du St Esprit offers the easiest pedestrian access to the picturesque Grund river-valley quarter. Luxembourg's iconic, if thoroughly unattractive, modern Red Bridge (Pont Grand-Duchesse Charlotte) takes traffic high across the Alzette and historic Pfaffenthal district to Kirchberg, the modern EU quarter. The main train station, Gare Centrale, is south of the centre in a dreary area that is slightly sleazy by Luxembourg

standards, but is therefore good value for accommodation and is only a few stops by bus from the Old Town.

Information

BOOKSHOPS
Librairie Ernster (☎ 22 50 77 1; Rue du Fossé; ⏰ 9am-6.30pm Mon-Fri, to 6pm Sat)

INTERNET ACCESS
Cyber Beach (34 Place Guillaume II; ⏰ 8am-8pm)
Cyber Mina (38 Rue Ste-Zithe; per hr €2; ⏰ 9am-9pm Mon-Fri, from noon Sat & Sun)
Phone House (47 Rue de Strasbourg; per hr €2.50; ⏰ 1-9pm)

INTERNET RESOURCES
Luxpoint (http://luxpoint.rtl.lu) Useful multilingual links arranged thematically.

LAUNDRY
Quick Wash (31 Rue de Strasbourg; per 5kg service/self-service €12/10; ⏰ 8.30am-6pm Mon-Sat)

LEFT LUGGAGE
Luggage lockers (Gare Centrale; per day €2-4; ⏰ 6am-9.30pm) Far north end of platform 3, inaccessible at night.

MEDICAL SERVICES
Zitha Klinik (☎ 49 77 61; www.zitha.lu; 36 Rue Ste-Zithe; ⏰ 7am-7pm Mon-Fri) Central clinic where you can see a doctor without an appointment

MONEY
Almost every second building in Luxembourg City is a bank. There are ATMs inside Gare Centrale, outside the main post office and at Luxembourg airport.

POST
Main Post Office (25 Rue Aldringen; ⏰ 7am-7pm Mon-Fri, to 5pm Sat)

TOURIST INFORMATION
Luxembourg City Tourist Office (☎ 22 28 09; www.lcto.lu; Place Guillaume II; ⏰ 9am-6pm Mon-Sat, from 10am Sun) Free city maps, walking-tour pamphlets and event guides.
Luxembourg National Tourist Office (☎ 42 82 82 20; www.ont.lu, www.visitluxembourg.lu; Gare Centrale; ⏰ 9am-6pm Mon-Sat, 9.30am-12.30pm & 1-5.30pm Sun) City and national information.

TRAVEL AGENCIES
Sotour (☎ 46 15 14-1; 15 Place du Théâtre; ⏰ 9am-6pm Mon-Fri, to noon Sat).

LUXEMBOURG

Sights

The Old Town has some fine old buildings, contrastingly modern museums and wonderful concentrations of cafes and top restaurants. Meanwhile, the Grund area lies way below at the base of a truly dramatic fortified escarpment and actually 'feels' older. Meandering steeply between the two largely pedestrianised areas is one of the city's greatest pleasures.

OLD TOWN

The neoclassical **Hôtel de Ville** (City Hall; Place Guillaume II) was largely constructed from the stones of an old monastery. Containing Luxembourg's most revered idol and the graves of the Grand Dukes (in the crypt), the **Cathédrale Notre Dame** (Cathedral of Our Lady; Blvd Roosevelt; ☺ 10am-noon & 2-5.30pm) is most notable for its unusually elongated black spires. Government edifices surround Place Clairfontaine while the most loveable knot of old streets lies behind the Palais Grand-Ducal. Photogenically a-twitter with little pointy turrets, this 1573 **Royal Palace** (17 Rue du Marché-aux-Herbes) has been much extended over the years. It now houses the Grand Duke's office with parliament using its 1859 annex. For a brief period in summer the palace opens for gently humorous 45-minute **guided tours** (tours €7; ☺ variable, Mon-Sat mid-Jul & Aug), which deal mostly with the Duke's family history. From the very medieval-gothic dining room, the palace's interior style morphs into sumptuous gilded romanticism upstairs. Tours must be pre-booked via the Luxembourg City Tourist Office. With only 40 tickets available per tour you'd be well advised to book a few hours ahead, especially for the one daily tour in English (typically 4pm). Other tours (in French, German and Dutch) are somewhat less heavily subscribed.

RAMPARTS, VIEWPOINTS & TUNNELS

For lovely views walk the **Chemin de la Corniche**, a pedestrian promenade hailed as 'Europe's most beautiful balcony'. It winds along the course of the 17th-century city ramparts to the **Bock**, the clifftop site of Count Sigefroi's once-mighty fort. Fortifications were mostly destroyed between 1867 and 1883 following the Treaty of London, but there's a great panorama and beneath lie the mildly intriguing **Bock**

Casemates (adult/child €1.75/1; ☺ 10am-5pm Mar-Oct). This honeycomb of damp rock galleries and passages was mostly carved out between 1737 and 1746. They've been used for everything from bakeries to slaughterhouses to garrisons and, despite being partly sealed after 1867, there remain an estimated 17km of tunnels that sheltered up to 35,000 locals during the WWII bombardments.

Visible below the Bock, though requiring quite a circuitous walk to reach from here, are the hefty fortifications of the **Wenzelsmauer** (Wenceslas Wall) which bridges the Alzette to the big Neumünster Abbey (p268) and climbs behind towards a trio of tower remnants dating back to 1050.

OLD TOWN MUSEUMS

Two state-of-the art museums offer imaginative exhibitions. Multilevel spaces have been created by digging deep into the rocky ground beneath.

MNHA

The **National Museum of History and Art** (Musée National d'Histoire et d'Art; ☎ 47 93 30 1; www.mnha.lu in French; Marché-aux-Poissons; adult/family/LC €5/10/free; ☺ 10am-5pm Tue-Sun, till 8pm Thu) occupies a startlingly modern building with a glass atrium. Ten floors sweep you somewhat unevenly from Gallic tomb chambers to modern art via Jan Breughel, Cézanne, Picasso and Luxembourg's Expressionist artist Joseph Kutter (1894–1941). On level 3 look out for a small watercolour of Luxembourg City by William Turner and a drawing of Schengen castle by Victor Hugo.

LUXEMBOURG CITY

0 _____ 200 m
0 _____ 0.1 miles

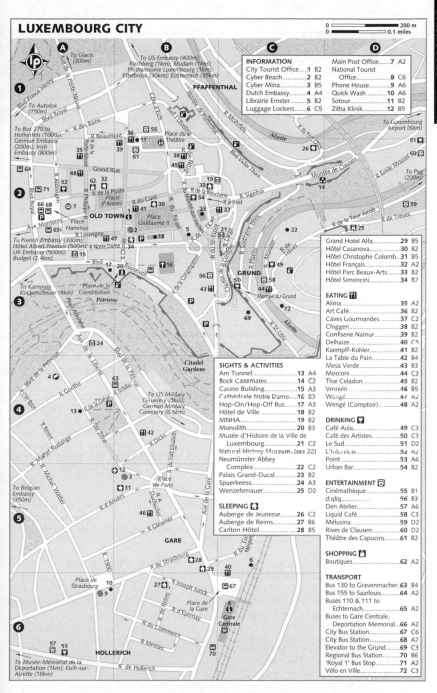

INFORMATION
City Tourist Office........1 B2
Cyber Beach................2 B2
Cyber Mina.................3 B5
Dutch Embassy............4 A4
Librairie Ernster........5 B2
Luggage Lockers........6 C5
Main Post Office.......7 A2
National Tourist
  Office.................8 C6
Phone House.............9 A6
Quick Wash.............10 A6
Sotour..................11 B2
Zitha Klinik...........12 B5

SIGHTS & ACTIVITIES
Am Tunnel..................13 A4
Bock Casemates............14 C2
Casino Building...........15 A3
Cathédrale Notre Dame.....16 B3
Hop-On/Hop-Off Bus........17 A3
Hôtel de Ville............18 B2
MNHA......................19 B2
Monolith..................20 B3
Musée d'Histoire de la Ville de
  Luxembourg..............21 C2
Natural History Museum.(see 22)
Neumünster Abbey
  Complex.................22 C2
Palais Grand-Ducal........23 B2
Spuerkeess................24 A3
Wenzelsmauer..............25 D2

SLEEPING
Auberge de Jeunesse.......26 C2
Auberge de Reims..........27 B6
Carlton Hôtel.............28 B5
Grand Hotel Alfa..........29 B5
Hôtel Casanova............30 B2
Hôtel Christophe Colomb...31 B5
Hôtel Français............32 A2
Hôtel Parc Beaux-Arts.....33 B2
Hôtel Simoncini...........34 B2

EATING
Alima.....................35 A2
Art Café..................36 B2
Caves Gourmandes..........37 C2
Chiggeri..................38 B2
Confiserie Namur..........39 B2
Delhaize..................40 C5
Kaempff-Kohler............41 B2
La Table du Pain..........42 B4
Mesa Verde................43 B3
Mosconi...................44 C3
Thai Celadon..............45 B2
Vesuvio...................46 B5
Wengé.....................47 A2
Wengé (Comptoir)..........48 A2

DRINKING
Café Aula.................49 C3
Café des Artistes.........50 C3
Le Sud....................51 D2
L'Interview...............52 A2
Point.....................53 A6
Urban Bar.................54 B2

ENTERTAINMENT
Cinémathèque..............55 B1
d:qliq....................56 B3
Den Atelier...............57 A6
Liquid Café...............58 C3
Mélusina..................59 D2
Rives de Clausen..........60 D2
Théâtre des Capucins......61 B2

SHOPPING
Boutiques.................62 A2

TRANSPORT
Bus 130 to Gravenmacher...63 B4
Bus 155 to Saarlouis......64 A2
Buses 110 & 111 to
  Echternach..............65 A2
Buses to Gare Centrale,
  Deportation Memorial...66 A2
City Bus Station..........67 C6
City Bus Station..........68 A2
Elevator to the Grund.....69 C3
Regional Bus Station......70 B6
'Royal 1' Bus Stop........71 A2
Vélo en Ville.............72 C3

LUXEMBOURG'S ROYALS

Dutch monarchs wore a second crown as Grand Dukes of Luxembourg from 1815 until 1890. When Dutch King William III died, his only surviving offspring became the Netherlands' Queen Wilhelmina. However, by Luxembourg's then-unreformed Salic Laws, its crown could not pass to a woman. Thus Adolph of Nassau took over as duke. His descendants rule to this day. In 1907, changes to the hereditary rules allowed Marie Adélaïde to become grand duchess, but perceptions of her pro-German stance in WWI meant she was persuaded to abdicate after the war. Thus, remarkably, the Grand Duchy put its royal family up for referendum in 1919. The result was a resounding 'yes' and Marie Adélaïde's younger sister Charlotte took the throne. Never again has their existence been questioned and today their presence remains a welcome symbol of stability and prosperity.

The current Grand Duke Henri met his wife Maria Teresa, then a Cuban-born commoner, while at university in Geneva. Their continued public acceptance is due in part to their relative 'normality'. Although they live in a castle (the 1911 Château Colmar-Berg), their kids go to ordinary schools, and it's quite possible to bump into a prince at the movies or to see the grand duchess out shopping.

Musée d'Histoire de la Ville de Luxembourg

The remarkably engrossing and interactive **Luxembourg City History Museum** (☎ 47 96 30 61; www.musee-hist.lu in French; 14 Rue du St-Esprit; adult/concession/child/LC €5/3.70/free/free; 🕙 10am-6pm Tue, Wed & Fri-Sun, to 8pm Thu) hides within a series of 17th-century houses, including a former 'holiday home' of the Bishop of Orval. The bottom levels reveal the Old Town's rocky geology, there's a lovely garden and an open terrace offers great views. Don't miss the circular, room-sized reproduction painting of the Marché aux Herbes in 1655.

PLACE DE LA CONSTITUTION

Towering above this leafy triangular 'square' is a **monolith** topped by a wreath-bearing golden maiden commemorating Luxembourg's WWI dead. Behind are several **viewpoints** overlooking lawns and gardens, perched on Vauban bastions as the valley falls away to the Pétrusse River. South across the canyon on the far side of Pont Adolphe, the eye-catching copper-spired tower is that of the 1909 Spuerkees building (opposite).

Visible west beyond busy Blvd Roosevelt is the misnamed 1882 **Casino Building** (☎ 22 50 45; www.casino-luxembourg.lu; 41 Rue Notre-Dame; adult/concession/child/LC €4/3/free/free; 🕙 11am-6pm Wed & Fri-Mon, to 8pm Thu), once a grand society-mansion in which the great Hungarian composer-virtuoso Franz Liszt gave his last concert. Now the building is used as an interesting exhibition space for contemporary and installation art.

GRUND

The main joy is cafe-hopping while strolling the pedestrian lanes down from the Old Town and on over to Clausen past the big, renovated **Neumünster Abbey complex** (☎ 26 20 52-1; 28 Rue Münster; 🕙 11am-6pm), which sports a glass-covered exhibition space, performing arts venue and brasserie. Kids might enjoy the family-oriented, interactive **Natural History Museum** (☎ 46 22 33-1; www.mnhn.lu; 25 Rue Münster; family/adult/child/LC €9/4.50/3/free; 🕙 10am-6pm Tue-Sun).

KIRCHBERG PLATEAU

EU institutions including the Court of Justice and European Investment Bank sit on a hilltop new-town area. The architecture is brutally modern: blue-glass towers and harsh steel-strut art that, with the area's relative lack of people, create a surreal futuristic cityscape. Luxembourg City Tourist Office's booklet *Art & Architecture in Public Space* (€0.50) includes a map, photos and 41-point suggested walk here. The most popular attraction here is **Mudam** (Musée d'Art Moderne Grand-Duc Jean;

SCHUMAN NOT SCHUMANN

In Brussels and Luxembourg you'll find streets, buildings and even a train station named for Robert Schuman. Note the single 'n'. Born in Luxembourg, this Schuman was a 20th-century French statesman and key instigator of European integration... not Schumann the 19th-century German composer.

☎ 45 37 85 22; www.mudam.lu; 3 Parc Dräi Eechelen; adult/concession/LC €5/3/free; ☒ 11am-6pm Thu-Mon, to 8pm Wed), Luxembourg's new Modern Art Museum. Open since 2006, the magnificent glass-roofed gallery was created by Chinese-American architect Ieoh Ming Pei (of Louvre pyramid fame). Its turreted modern centrepiece and glass wings sit in studied counterpoint to the recently rebuilt historic **Fort Thüngen** (www.in-visible.lu/fort/). The museum's collection includes everything from photography to fashion, design and multimedia. Take bus 120, 125, 165, 192 or 194 two stops northbound from 'Royal 1' near Place Hamilius (or four stops from Gare Centrale).

SOUTH OF THE CENTRE
Spuerkeess
In a dramatic, century-old, castle-style building, **Spuerkeess** (www.spuerkeess.lu; 1 Place de Metz), the state savings bank, hosts an intriguing **Bank Museum** (☎ 40 15 59 03; admission free; ☒ 9am-5.30pm Mon-Fri) tracing 140 years of tradition and innovation in banking, from piggy banks to ATMs and bank robbers. It's also behind the unusual, underground **Am Tunnel** (☎ 40 15 24 50; 16 Rue Ste-Zithe; admission free; ☒ 9am-5.30pm Mon-Fri, 2-6pm Sun) art gallery. Carved 350m through the Bourbon plateau in tunnels originally designed to link bank buildings, it hosts temporary exhibitions and a permanent display on Edward Steichen, the man behind Clervaux's *Family of Man* (p283).

Musée-Mémorial de la Déportation
Thousands of Luxembourgers were deported during Germany's WWII occupation of Luxembourg, and 1200 of the country's 3700 Jewish population perished. The train station where their harrowing journey began is now the small **Deportation Memorial Museum** (☎ 48 32 32; Gare de Hollerich, 3a Rue de la Déportation; ☒ 9-11.30am & 2-4pm Mon-Thu). Take bus 18 from Place Hamilius Quay 6 (six stops) or Hotel Alfa (three stops).

MILITARY CEMETERIES
Over 5000 WWII US war-dead, including General Patton, are remembered at the moving **US Military Cemetery** (☎ 43 17 27; www.abmc.gov/cemeteries/cemeteries/lx.php; 50 Val du Scheid, Hamm; ☒ 9am-5pm). Wall maps detail the main events that were to blame, notably the liberation of Luxembourg and subsequent Battle of the Ardennes (p243). Rows of white crosses and

---

GAY & LESBIAN LUXEMBOURG
Luxembourg's national LGTB organisation, **Rosa Lëtzebuerg** (www.gay.lu), has a useful website and publishes a monthly what's-on newsletter in French and German. Find a copy at the gay and lesbian information centre, **Cigale** (☎ 26 19 00 18; www.cigale.lu; 60 Rue des Romains; ☒ 1-5pm Mon-Tue, to 6pm Thu), east of Gare Centrale. A small **Luxembourg Pride** festival is held in mid-June.

---

stars are marked with US and Luxembourg flags. White-stone pylons commemorate the soldiers whose bodies were never found. It's 4km from Luxembourg City. Bus 15 departs for Hamm from outside Grand Hotel Alfa (which was itself used as General Bradley's HQ during the Ardennes campaign), but that leaves you 20 minutes' walk short of the cemetery on the wrong side of the motorway.

A vast, sombre **German Military Cemetery** (Cimetière Militaire Allemand; ☒ 9am-5pm; Sandweiler) is 1.5km further east near the N2 Remich road, 10 minutes' walk from Sandweiler Kontrollstatioun bus stop (bus 194 from Royal 1).

Tours
The Luxembourg City Tourist Office runs two excellent two-hour guided walks. The **City Promenade tour** (adult/child €7/3.50; ☒ in English 1pm) covers the Old Town. **Wenzel Walk** (adult/child €8/4; ☒ in English 3pm Sat) winds through the upper and lower towns, through fortifications and along nature trails.

Two tour-bus options depart from the Place de la Constitution. The seven-stop double-decker **Hop-On/Hop-Off Bus** (☎ 23 65 11; www.sightseeing.lu; family/adult/child €35/14//, 30% discount with LC; ☒ 9.40am-5.20pm Apr-Sep, 10.30am-4pm Oct-Mar) runs every 20 minutes (30 minutes in winter) visiting the Old Town, Mudam, a Kirchberg shopping mall and the train station. The **Pétrusse Express** (family/adult/child €27/8.50/5; ☒ Apr-Oct) is a one-hour toy-train tour through the Grund and parks of the Pétrusse and Alzette valleys.

Sleeping
In great contrast to the city's cutting-edge dining scene, many (but not all) accommodation options range from dated to distinctly dowdy, even some with supposedly multistar ratings. Midweek many seem dauntingly

over-priced, but you can save up to 70% on printed rates by making internet bookings for summer weekends.

BUDGET

Camping Kockelscheuer (☎ 47 18 15; www.camp -kockelscheuer.lu; 22 Route de Bettembourg; campsites per adult/child/tent €3.75/2/4.50; ☼ Easter-Oct, reception closed noon-2pm & 10.30pm-7am) Pleasantly sited between a forest and a sports centre 4km southwest of the city. Take bus 5 from Gare Centrale or Place Hamilius.

HI Hostel (Auberge de Jeunesse; ☎ 22 68 89; luxem bourg@youthhostels.lu; 2 Rue du Fort Olizy; members dm/s/d €17.60/29.60/45.20; ⓟ ☒ ◨ ⓰) Modern, no-fuss rooms (maximum six beds) share showers that sandblast, a store-room for bicycles and a very inexpensive restaurant-*café*. It's a steep walking descent from the Old Town or five minutes' walk from 'Clausen Plateau Altmunster', a stop on bus 9, 14 and CN1 routes from Gare Centrale.

There are other HI youth hostels at Bourglinster (17km, p276) and Larochette (28km, p276), both conveniently accessible on Luxembourg–Diekirch buses (number 100, hourly except Sundays), plus at Remerschen (p276) and Hollenfels (23km, p283).

Auberge de Reims (☎ 48 62 45; 17 Rue Junck; s/d/tr with shared bath €35/40/45) If saving money is really all that matters, there are several inexpensive options like this one in a noisy little area of bars and peep shows. It's just a short walk from the train station.

MIDRANGE & TOP END

Hôtel Christophe Colomb (☎ 40 84 14-1; www.christophe -colomb.lu; 10 Rue d'Anvers; s/tw/tr from €75/85/95; ☒ ⓰) The neatest of several bland options on Rue d'Anvers, Christophe Colomb's base prices are fair value, though rates can rise considerably with demand. A lift accesses the 24 largely unadorned motel-style rooms equipped with safe, minibar and small but clean shower room. Breakfast is included, all-day wi-fi costs €4 and parking is €10.

Hôtel Casanova (☎ 22 04 93; www.hotelcasanova. lu; 10 Place Guillaume II; s/d €95/130) The location is fabulously central and the 16 rooms are neat and sunny if lacking any real style. Confusingly, the same place sometimes calls itself Hotel Vauban.

Carlton Hôtel (☎ 29 96 60; www.carlton.lu; 9 Rue de Strasbourg; s/d/tr Mon-Thu €110/125/135, r Fri-Sun from €85; ◨ ⓰) This atmospheric 1920 building

retains original staircases and floral stained-glass windows, but the rooms have been fully upgraded and corridors are given a special touch with conical torch-style lamps. Wi-fi in foyer and lounge.

Hôtel Français (☎ 47 45 34; www.hotelfrancais.lu; 14 Place d'Armes; s/d Mon-Fri €110/140, Sat & Sun €95/120; ◨) Handily central hotel offering 24 somewhat small but presentable rooms above a popular brasserie.

our pick Hôtel Simoncini (☎ 22 28 44; www.hotel simoncini.lu; 6 Rue Notre Dame; s/d/tr/ste midweek from €135/160/185/200, weekend €110/120/145/160; ⓰) Far and away the most contemporary option in the city centre, the foyer is a modern-art gallery and the smart, bright rooms have slight touches of retro-cool. Free wi-fi.

Hôtel Albert Premier (☎ 44 24 42 1; www.albert1er. lu; 2a Rue Albert 1er; d Mon-Thu €155-310, Fri-Sun €105-250; ☒ ◨) This swish boutique hotel offers 10 rooms in indulgent 'Old English' style and 30 new ones in an altogether more sleek, minimalist modern style. Weekend deals including dinner and/or massage are great value. Breakfast costs €18.

Grand Hotel Alfa (☎ 49 00 11-1; www.mercure.com; 16 Place de la Gare; d rack rate/internet discount from €220/160, summer weekends from €65; ☒ ☒ ◨ ⓰) Behind the imposing 1936 facade, rooms have been re-built in the typical international style of the Mercure chain. They're over-priced at rack rate but an incredible bargain if you score a weekend summer-package rate. The breakfast buffet (€18) includes smoked salmon and self-squeezed orange juice, and is taken in the ground-floor brasserie, a fabulous art deco gem.

Hôtel Parc Beaux-Arts (☎ 26 86 76-1; www. parcbeauxarts.lu; 1 Rue Sigefroi; ste Fri-Sun from €180, Mon-Thu from €407; ☒ ◨ ⓰) Exuding understated luxury, the city's most charming hotel comprises a trio of 18th-century houses containing 10 gorgeous suites. Each features original artworks by contemporary artists, oak floors, Murano crystal lamps and a fresh rose daily. Seek out the 'secret' lounge hidden away in the original timber eaves.

Eating

For intimate and original dining options hunt around in the alleys and passages collectively nicknamed 'Îlot Gourmand' directly behind the Royal Palace. There are interesting alternatives in Grund and the revamped Clausen area. Daily in summer (yes, even

Sundays), tables spill merrily onto the leafy Place d'Armes, with everything from burger chains to classy seafood on offer, including chain Mexican and buffet Chinese options. Inexpensive but characterless places for Asian food are scattered along Rue de Strasbourg in the train station area. For extensive restaurant listings consult www.resto.lu

La Table du Pain (www.tabledupain.lu; 37 Ave de la Liberté; ☽ 7am-6pm Mon-Fri) Convivial bakery-cafe with wooden furniture and a good range of breakfast options, baguette sandwiches (takeaway/eat-in from €2.40/6) and big salads (from €12).

Kaempff-Kohler (18 Pl Guillaume; ☽ 8am-6.30pm Mon-Fri, to 6pm Sat) Gently exclusive 1922 patisserie-*traiteur* with cafe seating on the city's central square.

Confiserie Namur (www.namur.lu; 27 Rue des Capucins; ☽ 11.30am-6pm Mon, from 8.30am Tue-Sat) Tea room serving moreish cakes, chocolates and ice cream.

Vesuvio (☎ 48 79 12; 5 Rue Duchscher; mains €7.90-15.50; ☽ 11.45am-2pm & 6pm-11pm) With its copper lanterns and artificial wooden crossbeams, this reliable if rather stereotypical Italian restaurant serves pizzas and pastas that mere mortals can afford. Open Sundays.

ourpick Chiggeri (☎ 22 82 36; www.chiggeri.lu; 15 Rue du Nord; restaurant mains €22-35, 4-/6-course menu €45/72; ☽ noon-2pm & 7.30-10pm Tue-Sun; café mains €14-21, lunch plate €9.80; ☽ 10am-1am Sun-Thu, to 3am Fri & Sat) In a historic turreted building or on its super summer terrace, Chiggeri offers a whole range of varied dining and drinking experiences. Downstairs there's a boisterous brasserie-*café* and a Moroccan-themed lantern-room. At the top of a long, ragged staircase, a classy yet congenially relaxed restaurant with Afro-Aboriginal decor elements has an extraordinary wine list that was certified as the world's longest by Guinness World Records in 2008.

Art Café (☎ 26 27 06 52; www.goeres-group.com/restaurants-bars/bar-art-cafe.php; 1a Rue Beaumont; light meals from €10; ☽ 10am-9pm Mon-Sat) A colour-infused lounge-cafe and piano-bar, complete with theatrical velvet decor and an appealing rear terrace. Good for sandwiches, salads and wok dishes.

Caves Gourmandes (☎ 46 11 24; www.caves-gourmandes.lu; 32 Rue de l'Eau; mains €15-32, lunch/dinner menus from €15/35) Slightly upmarket French and Basque food served in caves dug out of old-town rock centuries ago.

Thai Celadon (☎ 47 49 34; 1 Rue du Nord; mains €18.50-24; ☽ closed Sun & lunch Sat) Excellent Thai food served in an appealingly minimalist Old Town mansion with dark timber floors and white walls with photos of Thai Royals and subtle little neo-colonial flourishes.

Mesa Verde (☎ 46 41 26; 11 Rue du St-Esprit; mains €19.80-25; ☽ lunch Wed-Fri, dinner Tue-Sat, closed lunch Aug; ✗) Exotic and imaginative both in the colours of its psychedelic-carnival decor and the eclectic influences in its imaginative vegetarian and seafood cuisine.

Mosconi (☎ 54 69 94; www.mosconi.lu; 13 Rue Münster; mains/menus from €25/68; ☽ lunch Tue-Fri, dinner Tue-Sat) Exquisite if predictably pricey Italian restaurant with two Michelin stars. It has an idyllic if tiny riverside terrace with the Old Town's cliff face soaring above. Reservations and formal dress essential.

Wengé (☎ 26 20 10 58; www.wenge.lu; 15 Rue Louvigny; mains €25-30; ☽ noon-2.30pm & 7-10pm Mon-Sat) This top-notch yet relatively casual restaurant has hip, shiny-black interiors and a few tables that spill onto the pedestrianised street in summer. They also have a patisserie and tea room, while takeaway sandwiches (€2.70 to €5) are sold from their 'comptoir' on Rue Philippe II (open 8am to 6.30pm).

SELF-CATERING
Alima (Ave de la Porte-Neuve; ☽ 8.30am-8.30pm Mon-Fri, 8am-6pm Sat) Old Town supermarket.

Delhaize (Place de la Gare; ☽ 7am-8pm Mon-Fri, to 6pm Sat, to noon Sun) Supermarket near Gare Centrale.

Drinking
The Old Town, Grund and Clausen are the top drinking spots, with a few more hidden in the unpromising area of Hollerich. Luxembourg-brewed beers include Bofferding, Diekirch, Mousel and Simon Pils.

L'Interview (☎ 47 36 65; 19 Rue Aldringen; beer/coffee from €2.40/2; ☽ 7.30am-1am) Mirrors and wood panelling make this wonderfully unpretentious *café* look like an old-timers' hang-out. But the evening's pumping, well-chosen music caters predominantly for a pre-party student-age crowd. Superb cappuccinos. A restaurant hidden upstairs serves 'world' cuisine.

Le Sud (☎ 26 47 87 50; Rue Émile Mousel, Rives de Clausen; ☽ noon-1am Tue-Fri, 6pm-3am Sat) Panoramic top-floor bar for great views above a top-notch French restaurant. In the lift-hall downstairs you walk 'through' a copper brewing still that's been cut in two.

Urban Bar (www.urban.lu/urbancity.html; 6 Rue de la Boucherie; beers/mojito/snacks from €2.50/8/9.50; ☾ noon-1am) One of several closely huddled hip bar-*cafés* in the Old Town drawing cosmopolitan crowds with lots of English spoken. The waves of '70s-retro foam panelling look like ceilings for a Star Trek space-pod.

Point (48 Rue de Hollerich; ☾ 10pm-6am) Alternative grungy youth-pub that opens when others are closing. Flashier drinking places are hidden away at no 42.

Café des Artistes (☎ 46 13 27; 22 Montée du Grund; ☾ evenings Tue-Sun) In this lovable, atmospheric *café*, every inch of wall and ceiling is covered with posters old and new. There's a spurious lamp post and an old piano that bursts into life with folk tunes whenever the mood's right.

Café Aula (www.aula.lu; 1 Rue de Trèves; ☾ 5pm-1am Mon-Fri, from 7pm Sat, from 8pm Sun) This smoky, unpretentious, traditional-style *café* has rough floors and little surrealist jokes on the walls.

Pyg (☎ 42 08 60; www.pyg.lu; 19 Rue de la Tour Jacob; ☾ 4pm-1am Sun-Thu, to 3am Fri & Sat) Moody little panel-walled bar with much more character than most Euro-Irish pubs.

Entertainment

Summer weekends are packed full of festivals and events. A particular highlight is the mid-July **Blues and Jazz Rallye** (www.bluesjazzrallye.lu) when the streets of Grund and Clausen fill with crowds and live bands till 3am. To find out what's happening consult weekly English-language magazine *352 Luxembourg News* or websites www.nightlife-mag.lu and www.rave.lu. Ticket agencies include **Luxembourg Ticket** (☎ 47 08 95-1; www.luxembourgticket.lu) and **E-Ticket** (www.e-ticket.lu).

CINEMA

For mainstream movies **Cinenews** (www.cinenews.lu) tells you what's on where. The **Cinémathèque** (☎ 29 12 59; 17 Place du Théâtre; adult/concession €4/2.80) shows golden oldies and cult classics at 6.30pm and 8.30pm plus an open-air film at 10pm in summer in the courtyard of nearby Théâtre des Capucins – great atmosphere.

LIVE MUSIC

Most big-name acts perform at either **Kulturfabrik** (www.kulturfabrik.lu) or **Rockhal** (www.rockhal.lu), both in Esch-sur-Alzette,

Luxembourg's second-largest town, 25 minutes away by train.

d:qliq (☎ 26 73 62; www.dqliq.com; 17 Rue du St-Esprit; ☾ 5pm-1am Tue-Sat, to 3am Fri) A small, graffiti-chic, Old Town bar with a varying program of DJs and live, lesser-known bands at weekends (and also some Wednesdays), typically in the electro or house genres. Chill-out area upstairs. There's usually no cover charge.

Liquid Café (☎ 22 44 55; www.liquid.canalblog.com; 17 Rue Münster; ☾ 5pm-1am Mon-Fri, from 8pm Sat & Sun) Atmospheric Grund pub-*café* where two rough-walled antique houses have been knocked together and straddled by a central horseshoe of bar. Live jazz Tuesdays, blues gigs Thursdays.

Den Atelier (☎ 49 54 66; www.atelier.lu; 56 Rue de Hollerich; ☾ generally from 7pm Thu-Sat) Looking like a glum factory, this venue for local and visiting groups is on an unpromising-looking main road about 500m west of Gare Centrale. There's a gaggle of unexpectedly stylish bars hidden nearby at no 42.

NIGHTCLUBS

The scene is in the recently repurposed former Mousel brewery complex at **Rives de Clausen** (www.rivesdeclausen.com), where half a dozen themed bar-resto-clubs stand shoulder to shoulder, including **Verso** (www.verso.lu), Life Bar, **Rock Box** (www.rockbox.lu), very contemporary Ikki and curious safari-themed King Wilma with its skeletal wooden centrepiece. They're all side by side and far from hidden away, so just wander by and see which suits. A shuttle-bus, running till 4am, brings revellers back to the train station via Glacis park-and-ride, and Place Hamilius.

Mélusina (☎ 43 59 22; www.melusina.lu; 145 Rue de la Tour Jacob; cover €8; ☾ 11pm-dawn Fri & Sat) Friendly, ever-popular dance spot set behind a well-perched restaurant terrace. Free entry in summer.

THEATRE, OPERA & DANCE

For an easy overview, consult www.theatres.lu.

Philharmonie Luxembourg (☎ 26 32 26 32; www.philharmonie.lu; 1 Place de l'Europe) Stunning new glass oval across the Red Bridge in Kirchberg that hosts jazz, classical and opera. Bus access as for Mudam (p268).

Grand Théâtre de la Ville de Luxembourg (☎ 47 96 39 00; 1 Blvd R Schuman; tickets €15-25, opera €25-65)

State-of-the-art performing-arts complex featuring an impressive line-up of international dance, opera and theatre.

Théâtre des Capucins (☎ 47 08 95-1; 9 Place du Théâtre) A small venue and open-air courtyard behind Art Café for reviews and summer film screenings.

Shopping

There are department stores on Grand Rue, while Rue Philippe II features boutiques including Kenzo, Hermes, Vuitton and Celine, with the Bonn Frères furniture store occupying the lovely 1855 building at number 9.

Getting There & Away

For details of Luxembourg's unique one-price domestic transport ticket system see right. **Mobility** (www.mobiliteit.lu) and www.autobus.lu both provide comprehensive transport details.

For flights see p297. **Eurolines** (www.eurolines.com) has three buses a week to both Brussels (four hours) and Amsterdam (8½ hours) from Quay 8 at the **regional bus station** (Place de la Gare). However, as they have no Luxembourg office you'll need to call the Brussels office (☎ 0032 2-274 1350) to make the compulsory bookings. Shorter hop-on bus connections to Germany include Hahn Airport (see Getting Around, right) from the regional bus station, and Saarlouis (bus 155, 85 minutes, every two hours), Bitburg (bus 401, 1¼ hours) and Trier (bus 118, one hour) from around Place Hamilius. Other long distance buses pick up from a variety of central points.

Prebookable TGV high-speed trains to Paris (125 minutes) run via Thionville (19 minutes) and Metz (40 minutes). CRE trains to Nancy (1½ hours) also go via Thionville (25 minutes) and Metz (46 minutes). Hourly trains run to Brussels (€33.20, three hours) via Arlon (€10.40, 20 minutes) and to Lille via Namur and Tournai. Every two hours there's a service to Liège via Clervaux. For Germany trains run hourly to Trier (€8.40, 50 minutes), several continuing to Koblenz (€32, 130 minutes). Twelve trains a day run to Basel, Switzerland, via Strasbourg.

Direct domestic trains run hourly to Wiltz (65 minutes) and to Diekirch (30 minutes), both via Ettelbrück.

Getting Around
TO/FROM THE AIRPORTS

For Luxembourg Airport take bus 16 from Gare Centrale via Kirchberg or bus 9 from Place Hamilius via Clausen. Both run every 10 to 15 minutes weekdays, every half-hour Sundays (€1.50, 20 minutes). Airport-bound buses start at 5.40am, last return is at 10.58pm (9.58pm Sunday). For Frankfurt-Hahn airport, **Flibco buses** (www.flibco.com; advanced/last-minute booking €5/17) take two hours departing from Regional Bus Station Quay 1 almost around the clock.

BICYCLE

Vel'oh (☎ 800 61100; www.veloh.lu; ⏲ 24hr) has a network of 43 automated short-term bicycle rental stands (25 equipped with subscription facilities). The system works much as Villo! in Brussels (see p111), with each first-half-hour rental free to subscribers. Digital signboards tell you how many bicycle return-spaces remain at neighbouring stations. You can download station details to your iPhone.

Vélo en Ville (☎ 47 96 23 83; 8 Bisserwée; per half-/full day €12.50/20; ⏲ 10am-noon & 1-8pm Apr-Oct) rents bicycles for children and adults, and can suggest interesting cycle routes.

CAR

The cheapest open-air car park is Glacis, 800m northwest of Place d'Armes. Convenient underground car parks include Place Hamilius (accessed via Rue Aldringen) or the 24-hour parking under Place Guillaume II.

Car-rental agencies:

Autolux (☎ 22 11 81; 33 Blvd Prince Henri)

Budget (☎ 44 19 38; 300 Route de Longwy)

CITY TRANSPORT

Detailed maps of bus routes are available on www.topographie.lu. Buses (including No 8) run every few minutes between the train station and the Place Hamilius city-bus stand then continue to a wide variety of destinations. If you don't have a Luxembourg Card (p266), pre-purchase a ticket or pass at information offices inside the Gare Centrale or underneath Place Hamilius. Tickets are good for all city and national transport (see p307). Most buses operate 5.30am to 10pm but on Friday and Saturday nights there's also a limited **night bus service** (☎ 24 89 24 89) every 15 or 30 minutes until about 3.30am.

AROUND THE GRAND DUCHY

Wherever you go by public transport within Luxembourg the price is the same, €1.50 for up to two hours, €5 for the day (see p307 for conditions). With the highly recommended Luxembourg Card (p266) it's entirely free, as is entry to virtually all the sights reviewed in this chapter.

SOUTHWEST LUXEMBOURG

Don't be fooled by Southwest Luxembourg's poetic moniker, *Le Pays des Terres Rouges* (The Land of the Red Rocks). That's a euphemism for the rust-coloured iron ore that made the heartland of Luxembourg's steel industry. Today money is being poured back in, but Luxembourg's second-largest city, **Esch-sur-Alzette**, is unlikely to become a tourist attraction any time soon.

Six kilometres southeast of Esch-sur-Alzette, **Rumelange** is worth visiting for its **Musée National des Mines** (☎ 56 56 88; www.mnm.lu; Carreau de Walert, Rue de la Bruyère; adult/concession/child/LC €8.50/7/5/free, train-ride only adult/child €4.50/2.50; ☒ 2-6pm Thu-Sun Apr-Jun & Sep & Tue-Sun Jul & Aug, last visit 4.30pm). Once a suitably sized group has assembled (around twice an hour), you're taken by mineral-train into the iron-ore mine and shown a collection of old and new mining machinery with photos that tell the industry's tale. Bring warm clothes and allow 1½ hours for the adventure. From Luxembourg City, bus 197 (26 minutes) runs to Rumelange every half hour on weekdays.

At **Pétange** (50 minutes from Luxembourg City by Rodange-bound trains), the cute steam-powered **Train 1900** (☎ 58 05 81; www.train1900.lu; adult/child €7/4; ☒ Sun May-Sep) connects to an intriguing industrial park at **Fond-de-Gras** (www.fond-de-gras.lu). Steam-train buffs can continue from here on the mineral-line **Minièresbunn** (☎ 50 47 07; http://minieresbunn.kohle-und-eisen.de; adult/child return €5/3; ☒ Sun May-Sep) to Lasauvage, possibly with a stop at an underground workshop in the 1.4km tunnel section. Departures at 2.55pm, 3.05pm and 4pm. Both trains operate on summer Sundays only.

MOSELLE VALLEY

Welcome to one of Europe's smallest wine regions. The wide Moselle River forms the border with Germany, its steeply-rising hillside banks covered with seemingly endless vineyards. In summer the scene turns a beautiful emerald green and the slopes are so neatly clipped they look combed. All along the riverside from Schengen to Wasserbillig you'll find a succession of villages and winery towns on both the Luxembourg and German sides. None are visually outstanding, but **Ahn** and hillside **Wellenstein** are picturesque. Some 23km southeast of the capital, the region's hub is **Remich**, a pleasant town favoured by locals for indulgent lunches, riverside promenades and family splashes in the open-air swimming pool.

Wine Tasting

Excellent *crémants* from the Moselle vineyards give Luxembourg the fizz and pop that keeps it buzzing throughout the summer. Along with fruity Rivaners and balanced Rieslings, it's tasting these wines that makes touring Luxembourg's 'Wine Route' so convivial. Winery visits typically start with a video of production techniques, then walk you through the vast stainless-steel fermentation and storage tanks while explaining the *méthode traditionelle* by which Champagne-style wines get fizzy. Given Veuve Cliquot's laborious original method of *remuage* (turning bottles by hand to remove yeast sediment), it's not surprising that bubbly was once so expensive. However, these days clever machinery can twirl 500 bottles at a time. Each visit ends with a tasting, often quite indulgent. If you want to cut to the

---

WHY SO RICH?

Little Luxembourg is famous for its 157 banks. But it also has a business-friendly tax regime that encourages inward investment, the development of new industries and the relocation of old ones (eg tyre-making). Although the coal and iron industries declined in the 20th-century, Luxembourg City is still a metallurgical heavyweight as the HQ of ArcelorMittal, the world's largest steel company. And why do most visitors come here? To fill up with petrol. Petrol taxes are low (hence the roughly 20% discount over neighbouring countries), but they're far from insignificant and provide another big earner for the treasury.

chase and taste without visiting, each winery has a tasting room where you can sample for free, albeit with an implied obligation to buy at least a bottle or two. Such purchases needn't be expensive with bottles of Ebling white starting at just €3.20.

The following is just a selection of winery operations you can visit. Most visits take over an hour and won't always start the moment you arrive so allow plenty of time or, horror, you'll miss the tasting. Be aware that most wineries are major industrial concerns so don't expect family farmhouse-chateaux. Nonetheless, each has its own attraction.

REMICH

About 1.5km north of Remich's bus terminal, **St Martin** (☎ 23 69 97 74; 53 Route de Stadtbredimus; tour €3.50, with LC free; ☺ 11am, 1pm & 3pm Tue-Sun Apr-Oct) ages its rather acidic *crémants* in wine *caves* that really are caves – cool damp tunnels hewn right into the rock face. Bus 450 Remich–Grevenmacher stops out front.

WORMELDANGE

Arguably the Grand Duchy's best *crémant* come from **Caves à Crémant Poll-Fabaire** (☎ 76 82 11; www.pollfabaire.lu; 115 Route du Vin; tours €2.50; ☺ 2pm-4.30pm, shop 7am-5pm Mon-Fri, 10.30am-8pm Sat), a large salmon-coloured winery complex with an art-deco look on the northern edge of Wormeldange. You might need to call ahead for a tour here (one-glass tasting included, three more for €3.95). Otherwise don't panic – you'll sample the very same bubbly at the Caves des Vignerons in Grevenmacher (see right).

GREVENMACHER

The wine route's largest town, workaday Grevenmacher has the area's two oldest

wineries. On the riverside just beyond the bridge to Germany, **Caves Bernard-Massard** (☎ 75 05 45-1; www.bernard-massard.lu; 8 Rue du Pont; tour adult/child/LC from €4/2.50/free; ☺ 9.30am-6pm Apr-Oct) is an especially grand establishment whose winery feels more like a grand hotel. Probably Luxembourg's best-known producer of Luxembourg sparkling wine, their slick, humorously presented tours take only 20 minutes, departing with great frequency and led by smartly dressed guides. Tour prices vary according to the number of varieties you want to sample afterwards in a delightfully genteel *café* whose open summer terrace has river views (albeit across a busy road).

In an altogether more banal setting 1km north, the vast **Caves des Vignerons** (☎ 23 69 66-1; www.vinsmoselle.lu; 12 Rue des Caves; tour €2.50; ☺ 7am-noon & 1-6pm Mon-Fri May-Aug, from 10am Sat) wine cooperative offers much more personal visits that start, more or less on demand, with a 15-minute video and culminate with particularly generous tastings of both whites and bubbles. Its shop sells fruity Rivaner from €3.26 a bottle.

SLEEPING & EATING

There are hotels dotted all along the wine route, with a particular concentration in Remich. However, the most appealing is **Bamberg's** (☎ 76 00 22; bamberg@pt.lu; 131 Route du Vin; s/d €65/90, mains €21-29; ☺ Wed-Mon), a distinguished little hotel with a wood-panelled old-world restaurant, in the riverside hamlet of **Ehnen**. A few doors away from Bamberg's is a **Wine Museum** (Waïmusee; ☎ 76 00 26; 115 Route du Vin; adult/child/LC €3.50/1.50/free; ☺ 9.30-11.30am & 2-5pm Tue-Sun Apr-Oct) housing a vast collection of old wine-making equipment. It's definitely worth visiting when free with a Luxembourg Card.

CRUISING THE MOSELLE

The riverboat **Princess Marie-Astrid** (☎ 75 82 75; www.moselle-tourist.lu) makes summer trips up and down the Moselle. While doubtless popular with pink-rinse grannies on lunch-club cruises, hop-on/hop-off fares are also available when space allows. Check the timetable on the website ahead of time as there's only one run daily in each direction and both destination and starting points vary. Example fares include Remich to Schengen (one way/return €5/7.50), and Grevenmacher to Trier, Germany (€8/12).

If you just want a quick float-by view of the vineyards, **Navitours** (☎ 75 84 89; www.navitours.lu; adult/child/dog €7/4/1; ☺ 11.15am, noon, 12.35pm, 1.20pm, 2pm, 3.15pm & 4.30pm Mar-Oct) does regular one-hour return cruises from Remich sailing about halfway to Schengen (minimum 15 passengers required).

GETTING THERE & AWAY

CFL bus 175 from Luxembourg's regional bus station runs twice hourly to Remich (except Sundays). From Remich, hourly bus 450 runs via Ehnen (13 minutes) to Grevenmacher (28 minutes, not Sundays). From Grevenmacher, buses run at least hourly to Echternach (40 minutes) on three routes: via Wecker (bus 474, not Sundays), Manternach (bus 475, not Sundays) or Wasserbillig (bus 485) where there's a train station on the Luxembourg–Trier–Cologne mainline.

The Far Southeast

Around 20km southeast of Luxembourg City, **Mondorf-les-Bains** (www.mondorf.lu) is Luxembourg's premier spa town and gambling centre. Beyond, in the Grand Duchy's southeastern corner, lies the peaceful Moselle-side village of **Schengen**. Goethe and Victor Hugo both once stayed in the ivy-draped 1779 castle-tower. If the name sounds oddly familiar that's because the village was where Eurocrats signed a 1985 treaty leading to passport-free travel within most of Western Europe (except the British Isles), a zone now known as the Schengen Area.

At **Remerschen** 2.5km north, there's a fabulous new **youth hostel** (☎ 26 66 73-1; remerschen@ youthhostels.lu; 31 Wäistrooss; dm/s/d €18.20/30.20/46.40; ☽ 5pm-10am) where all rooms come with private bathroom. It's easy stumbling distance from the 1948 **Caves du Sud** (☎ 23 66 48 26; 32 Wäistrooss; ☽ 10am-9pm Tue-Sun), a four-storey winery building with a boat-shaped bar ideal for tasting wines (white/bubbles from €1.30/3.30).

Zenn-bus 185 runs Remich–Remerschen–Schengen–Mondorf approximately hourly Monday to Saturday.

MÜLLERTHAL

Perfect real estate for hobbits and pixies, Müllerthal's most intriguing corners are cut with narrow, mossy ravines, crystal-clear creeks and strange rock formations. But to reach these hidden corners you'll need to hike into the sighing woodlands west of historic Echternach, a curious town of Roman ghosts and waving-handkerchief dances. Peddle there through castle villages or paddle down the Sûre.

Bourglinster
pop 180

Worth a quick stop en route to Larochette, Bourglinster's 18th-century **baroque castle** sits within the shattered ruins of a bigger 12th-

century fortress destroyed by a 1684 French attack. The main hall is closed to visitors but side wings contain two classy restaurants and the courtyard is used for Shakespearean productions during the local **festival** (www.bourglin sterfestival.lu; ☽ early Jul). Across the grassy dry moat are studios for artists, book-binders and ceramics craftspeople.

All this is tucked away just three minutes' walk above the village square. On the main road, the **Bourglinster Youth Hostel** (☎ 26 78 07 07; www.youthhostels.lu; 2 Rue du Gonderange; dm/s/d €18.20/30.20/46.40; ☽ 5pm-10am) occupies an outwardly classical 1761 house whose interior has one historical staircase but is otherwise fully contemporary, with mostly six- and eight-bed bunk-dorms. The village has two simple *café*-bars.

Larochette
pop 1850

Two modest rivers cut a dramatic gash in a woodland plateau and little Larochette fell in. Hemmed between their banks and the rapidly narrowing rock walls, the village's sturdy slate-roofed houses struggle vainly to crawl up and out of the valley but most remain prostrated beneath the dramatic cliff-top ruins of its medieval **castle** (☎ 83 74 97; Route de Mersch; adult/child €2/1; ☽ 10am-6pm Easter-Oct). From the village centre it's accessed by steep stairway paths or by a much gentler 2km double-back road (start off towards Mersch). Up close the site seems less complete than it appears from below but exploring the castle lawns, wall-stubs and stairways is nonetheless compulsive. The four-storey 1385 keep is especially worth climbing for the toe-curling view from its hanging wooden box-window. You can also peep into the dungeon or the endlessly deep well shaft. There's often an art exhibition on show.

There's a pleasant **HI Hostel** (Auberge de Jeunesse; ☎ 83 70 81; www.youthhostels.lu; 45 Rue Osterbuer; members dm/s/d €18.20/30.20/46.40; ☽ Mar-Dec; ☒) 400m north of the town centre, plus half a dozen somewhat lacklustre and old-fashioned hotels along the main Grevenmacher–Diekirch road. Somewhat better than most, albeit on a busy road corner, the **Grand Hôtel de la Poste** (☎ 87 81 78; 11 Pl Bleech; s/d from €60/80) features some wrought ironwork and has a guest room in which US General Patton reputedly once slept. Around 200m north, the **Hôtel Résidence** (☎ 83 73 91; www.hotelresidence.lu; 14 Rue de Medernach; s/d/tw/tr

€67/80/84/116; ☻ Mar-Nov) has some slightly modernist touches to its lounge. Rooms are contrastingly ordinary but some have castle views if you don't mind the road noise.

Hourly bus 100 stops in Larochette between Diekirch (20 minutes) and Luxembourg City (one hour).

Echternach
pop 5100

A fine base for hiking and biking, Echternach also sports Luxembourg's prettiest town square and its holiest basilica-church. On Whit Tuesday the **Sprinprozession** has nothing to do with sneezing though it does see many townsfolk whipping out their hankies (see p16).

Site of a 1st-century Roman villa, Echternach passed to the Merovingian kings who in turn presented the area to Northumbrian missionary St-Willibrord who founded a church here in AD 698. Amongst Ripon-born Willibrord's many 'miracles' was the fact he wasn't beaten to death by the angry guardians of pagan temples that he vandalised in the name of his God.

By the time of Willibrord's death in 739, Echternach had become a thriving royal monastery. Its scriptorium came to be one of northern Europe's most influential and its basilica-church was rebuilt in fine Romanesque style in 1031. A vast Benedictine abbey developed around the basilica and a town around that. After the French invasion of 1794, however, the church was sacked and the abbey used as a porcelain factory. Though rebuilt in 1862, the basilica was bombed to rubble during WWII, which severely damaged much of the town. Nonetheless, Willibrord's relics slept peacefully in the crypt and today the complex has been rebuilt.

SIGHTS
Town Centre

Charming, cafe-filled Rue de la Gare climbs very gently from the bus station to the **Place du Marché**. The delightful town square's pinched waist is given character by the distinctive **Denzelt**, a modestly sized former law court building dating originally from 1520 though the arcade, statues and little corner turrets that give it its current neogothic appearance date from an 1895 rebuild.

A half-block east is the **tourist office** (☎ 72 02 30; www.echternach-tourist.lu; Parvis de la Basilique;

☻ 10am-12.30pm & 2-5pm Mon-Fri Sep-Easter, 10am-5.30pm Easter-Aug) on a pedestrianised courtyard facing the revered neo-Romanesque **basilica** (☻ 9.30am-6.30pm). The post-war reconstruction has created a dark and sombre affair with 1950s stained-glass windows but the vaulted **crypt** still contains the highly venerated relics of St Willibrord in a primitive stone coffin covered by an elaborate white-marble canopy.

Reconstructed 18th-century abbey buildings spread back from the basilica almost to the tree-lined banks of the Sûre. Just behind the main church, the **Musée de l'Abbaye** (☎ 72 74 72; adult/child/LC €3/1.50/free; ☻ 10am-noon & 2-6pm Easter-Jun & Sep-Oct, 10am-6pm Jul & Aug) occupies the vaulted basement that once formed the abbey's famous scriptorium. You'll see ancient codex copies, Merovingian sarcophagi and a video of the Sprinprozession (St-Willibrord Pageant, p16) through the ages – most movingly in 1945 when the town still lay in utter ruin.

Stroll through the gateway in the Abbey's north arcade to peek through wrought-iron gates at the splendid 1736 **Orangery** set in formal French-style gardens, or head east between the tennis courts to the 1761 rococo **Pavilion** where you can enjoy pleasant river views from the balcony.

Roman Villa

If the mosaic floor in the Musée de l'Abbaye whetted your appetite for Roman remains, you might want to investigate the **Villa Romaine** (☎ 26 72 09 74; 47 Rue des Romains; adult/child/LC €3/1.50/free; ☻ 11am-6pm Tue-Sun Jul & Aug, 11am-1pm & 2-5pm Tue-Sun Easter-Jun & Sep-Oct). With virtual imaging depicting life in Roman days, the site incorporates ruins including that of the Roman villa excavated in 1975 during the creation of the reservoir lake (today a popular boating and recreation area). It's 1km from town off Route de Luxembourg.

ACTIVITIES

Marked **hiking trails** start from near the town's bus station. A board listing possible routes gives brief descriptions plus estimated times (from one to four hours). One of the best, the 'E1' (2½ hours), winds up via Troosknepchen and Wolfsschlucht, also known as the **Gorge du Loup**, a sheer-sided, moss-covered canyon flanked by dramatic sandstone formations. With stamina you could continue hiking from there to the village of **Berdorf** which has a **tourist office** (☎ 79 06 43; www.berdorf.lu; 7 An der Laach;

(⊙ 8am-noon & 1-5pm Mon-Fri) and bus connections back to Echternach or Luxembourg City.

Flat riverside **bicycle** paths trace the Sûre River all the way to Diekirch (27km), south into the Moselle Valley and along a former railway line to Luxembourg City. The youth hostel (see below) rents bicycles (half-/full day €8/15) and has a state-of-the-art indoor 14m **climbing wall** (adult/concession/hostel guests €5/2.50/free; ⊙ 6-10pm Tue, Wed & Fri). **Kayakers** could take the hourly bus 500 to Dillingen (opposite) and paddle back.

SLEEPING & EATING

Echternach has a plethora of hotels but many lack much in the way of imagination or style. Virtually all have their own restaurants.

Camping Officiel (☎ 72 02 72; 5 Route de Diekirch; campsites per adult/child/tent €5/3/6; ⊙ Apr–mid-Oct; ⊠) Just 200m from the bus station, this camping ground has tennis courts and a children's playground.

HI Hostel (Auberge de Jeunesse; ☎ 72 01 58; www .youthhostels.lu; Rue Grégoire Schouppe; members dm/s/d €18.20/30.20/46.40; ⊠ ▣ ⬤) Often full with children's groups, this modernist hostel is next to a lake some 2km out of town. Hop off bus 110 (Luxembourg City–Echternach) at the fire station stop (Centre de Secours) and walk 1km towards Rodenhof/Roudenhaff.

Hôtel du Commerce (☎ 72 03 01; www.hotel commerce-echternach.lu; 16 pl du Marché; s/d/tr/q from €51/73/109/130; ⊙ Apr–mid-Nov; ⊜ ⬤) Although it has a facade facing the main square, most rooms are strung out along a side road. While none has much style, prices are reasonable, there's a fitness room and a particularly attractive enclosed garden in which to unwind. Free wi-fi.

Hôtel de la Sûre (☎ 72 94 40; www.hoteldelasure. lu; 49 Rue de la Gare; s/d/tw/tr from €60/70/75/90; ⊜) Above a steakhouse and hip street-*café*, this hotel supplements its standard offerings with better, modern rooms (d €110) featuring pale fabrics and subtle wall decor lightly signed with a gilded hummingbird motif. Some have a jacuzzi.

Hostellerie de la Basilique (☎ 72 94 83; www .hotel-basilique.lu; 7 Place du Marché; s/d/tr €106/156/222; ⊙ Apr–early-Nov; ⬤ ⊠ ⊜ ⊠) A lounge with raffia-tied twigs and decorative amphorae sets the tone in this stylishly suave 14-room delight. It hits the perfect balance between historical charm and relaxed designer simplicity, all in a wonderfully central location.

Medieval Towers (www.echternach-tourist.lu; per week €450-650) Small sections of Echternach's former city walls are still visible incongruously set amid suburban houses. Four of the wall's medieval towers have been imaginatively converted into tourist accommodation, each sleeping four to six people. However, they're only available for weeklong stays and should be booked way ahead via the tourist office (there are photos and details on the website).

Café de Philo'soff (31 Rue de la Gare) There are dozens of appealing *cafés* along this bustling street but the wisteria-draped Philo'soff is a particularly wonderful little art-nouveau gem. Or was – it's currently closed for renovations but hopefully won't be unduly altered by the time you get there.

GETTING THERE & AWAY

Echternach–Luxembourg City buses run direct (number 110, 45 minutes, hourly Monday to Saturday) and daily via Berdorf (number 111, hourly). Except Sundays, 13 daily buses run Echternach–Beaufort–Larochette (40 minutes), including the 414. Bus 401 runs to Bitburg, Germany (40 minutes) every hour or two.

Around Echternach

SCHIESSENTÜUMPEL

This much-photographed little waterfall, crossed by a decorative stone footbridge, is hidden in pretty forests between Müllerthal village and Breidweiler-Pont on the CR121, around 12km southwest of Echternach. As always in this area, it's a great spot for walking.

BEAUFORT
pop 2000

Across a pretty, part-wooded valley behind **Beaufort village** (www.beaufort.lu) lie a pair of castles. One's a standard residential château, but that's hidden behind the very imposing five-storey ruins of a medieval stone **fortress** (☎ 83 60 02; adult/concession/child/LC €3/2/0.50/free; ⊙ 9am-6pm Apr-Oct). Once the site of a Roman camp, the latter expanded from 12th-century origins and despite being bombed during WWII's Battle of the Bulge (p243), there's plenty left to climb.

Buses 502 and 505 from Diekirch drop you in the upper village near the distinctive town hall (Mairie) and **Église St-Michel**, a steep-spired church with four odd corner-spirelets. From here the castle is 600m west, descending steeply past the sweet old fire station.

There's plenty of scope for hiking and biking. Walking suggestions and **bicycle rental** (half-/full day €7.50/15) are available from the reception booth at **Camping Plage** (☎ 83 60 99; www .campingplage.lu; 87 Grand Rue; camping per adult/child/ tent €5.50/3/6.50, plus electricity €2.50, hikers' huts d/tr/q €47/51/55, with heating €51/55/59, booking fee €10; ☒), which doubles as a tourist office. Nonguests can use its heated open-air swimming **pool** (adult/child €3.50/2.20; ☒ 10am-7pm Jul-Aug) and winter **ice-skating rink** (adult/child €3.50/2.20; ☒ mid-Nov–Mar). It's 700m north of the church beside the road to Reisdorf/Eppeldorf.

There's a small, chalet-style **HI Hostel** (Auberge de Jeunesse; ☎ 83 60 75; www.youthhostels.lu; 6 Rue de l'Auberge; dm/s/d €16.20/28.20/42.40; ☒ Feb-Dec; ☒) in the village centre.

The vine-draped **Auberge Rustique** (☎ 83 60 86; www.aubergerustique.lu; 55 Rue du Château; s/d €52/74, snacks €8-10.50, mains €16.50-27.50) would overlook the castles but for a curtain of trees. It offers eight rooms with bright new bathrooms above a lovable country pub-restaurant whose speciality is trout.

DILLINGEN

Beside an antique one-lane bridge at the Wies-Neu Camping in Dillingen, **Outdoor Freizeit** (☎ 86 91 39; www.outdoorfreizeit; 10 Rue de la Sûre; ☒ 9am-4pm) offers sedate canoe and kayaking trips on the Sûre River to Echternach, which can be combined with cycling routes or a bus-back option.

NORTHERN LUXEMBOURG

The Grand Duchy's northernmost region is an extension of Belgium's Ardennes, with winding, fast-flowing rivers cut deep through green tablelands. The main draws are accessible Clervaux, pretty Esch-sur-Sûre and, most notably, dramatic Vianden. Between here and Luxembourg City is Gutland (literally 'Goodland'), a heavily farmed area whose towns are relatively nondescript. The main rail hubs are in Diekirch and forgettable Ettelbrück.

Ettelbrück

The main square in Ettelbrück is called Place Patton in honour of US Third Army general George S Patton who led a liberating US force into town on Christmas Day 1944. He famously noted that 'No bastard ever won a war by dying for his country. He won it by making the other poor dumb bastard die

for his.' However, by December 1945 Patton himself was dead following a car accident in Germany. In an unlikely residential street, the little **General Patton Museum** (☎ 81 03 22; www .patton.lu; 5 Rue Dr Klein; adult/child/LC €5/3/free; ☒ 10am-5pm Jun–mid-Sep, 2-5pm Sun mid-Sep–May) has a plaster copy of the Patton statue that you'll see at Ettelbrück's city fringe (the Diekirch road) and displays some interesting fallen chunks of WWII aircraft. Otherwise, its selection of wartime photos, ammunition and helmets is considerably less impressive than similar collections in Diekirch.

Château de Bourscheid

Viewed from the N27 or from the CR438 8km north of Ettelbrück, this splendid **castle ruin** (☎ 99 05 70; www.bourscheid.lu; adult/senior/child/ LC €5/4/3/free; ☒ 9.30am-6pm Apr-Oct, 11am-4pm Nov-Mar) is surely the nation's most dramatic. As you get closer, the degree of degradation is much clearer but it's still very interesting to clamber about the wall stubs. Admission includes a remarkably extensive 90-minute audioguide and there's a trio of somewhat odd 'visuella' slide presentations to ponder en route. Don't miss climbing the rather squat, 12th-century, square keep for classic turret-framed views over the forested river-bend below.

Bus 545 from Ettelbrück stops in the Bourscheid village, where there's a simple hotel. From the village, the lonely castle is a steep 1.8km descent to the southwest. After visiting you can descend another winding 2km to the N27 and return to Ettelbrück on bus 550 from a junction overlooked by the smart if less-than-obliging Vieux Moulin Hotel. Tucked behind that is a camp ground and an appealing water-powered brasserie good for a river-view drink or a basic meal in the vaulted arches while awaiting the bus.

Diekirch
pop 6000

Of all the many WWII museums commemorating the Battle of the Ardennes, Diekirch's **Musée National d'Histoire Militaire** (☎ 80 89 08; www. nat-military-museum.lu; 10 Rue Bamertal; adult/child/LC €5/3/ free; ☒ 10am-6pm Apr-Nov, from 2pm Dec-Mar) is the most comprehensive and visual. What was once a brewery building is now packed full of WWII equipment, vehicles and memorabilia, while numerous well-executed mannequin scenes illustrate the suffering and hardships of the battles fought in the thick snows of Christmas 1944.

The museum is 200m north of *café*-ringed Place de la Libération in Diekirch's somewhat attractive pedestrianised town centre, where there's a **tourist office** (☎ 80 30 23; http://tourisme .diekirch.lu; ⊗ 9am-noon & 2-5pm Mon-Fri, 2-4pm Sat Sep-Jun, 9am-5pm Mon-Fri, 10am-4pm Sat & Sun Jul-Aug) and the slate-spired **Église St Laurent** (⊗ 10am-noon & 2-6pm Easter-Oct) built on the foundations of a 1500-year-old Roman hall whose heating system can be vaguely discerned in the crypt. A museum of Roman mosaics from a villa site nearby is currently under reconstruction until 2012 (estimate).

Two minutes southwest on the town's modest inner 'ring road', the one-room **Brewery Museum** (☎ 26 80 04 68; www.diekirch.cc; 20 Rue de Stavelot; adult/child/LC €5/3/free; ⊗ 10am-6pm) celebrates Diekirch Beer, the Grand Duchy's best-known lager. The rather elevated ticket price also allows you to peruse a modest car collection in the same building. Neither are gripping.

One block north of Place de la Libération, **Hotel Au Bon Séjour** (☎ 26 80 47 15; www.hotel-beausejour .lu; 12 Rue Esplanade; s/d from €55/65) looks less than inviting at first glance. However, the dark corridors lead to unexpectedly bright, freshly renovated rooms, which are good value if nothing flashy.

It's 700m from the co-habiting train and bus stations to Place de la Libération: head east past the big brewery complex then swing north. Direct trains arrive hourly from Luxembourg City (30 minutes) or you could do a train-bus combination (37 to 47 minutes) via Ettelbrück (10 minutes). Bicycles can be hired from **Rent-a-Bike** (☎ 26 80 33 76; nordstad@cig. lu; 27 Rue Jean l'Aveugle; per half-/full day €10/15; ⊗ 10am-5pm Apr-Oct) on the parallel street behind (west of) the car museum.

Vianden
pop 1600

Palace, citadel or fortified cathedral? At first glance it's hard to tell just what it is that towers so grandly amid the mists and wooded hills above historic little Vianden. In fact it's a vast slate-roofed castle complex whose impregnable white stone walls glow golden in the evening's floodlights, creating one of Luxembourg's most photogenic scenes. Vianden's appealing old town is essentially one road, the cobbled Grand Rue that rises

700m to the castle gates from a bridge across the River Our. Here you'll find a **tourist office** (☎ 83 42 57 1; www.tourist-info-vianden.lu; 1a Rue du Vieux Marché; ⊗ 8am-6pm Mon-Fri, 10am-2pm Sat Apr-Aug, 9am-noon & 1-5pm Mon-Fri Sep-Mar), with newer sections of town following the riverbanks in either direction.

On weekend afternoons in summer, Vianden can get overloaded by noisy fleets of motorcycle tourists. But get up early and you'll have the whole town largely to yourself.

HISTORY

One of the region's first 'cities', Vianden (Veianen in Letzeburgesch) gained its charter way back in 1308 and developed as a major leather and crafts centre. Its craftspeople had formed their own guilds by the late 15th-century, by which stage the county of Vianden had become part of the greater Nassau lands. In the 1790s, like the rest of Luxembourg, Vianden was swallowed by revolutionary France but after 1815 when the French withdrew, a large part of the county was given to Prussia. Vianden itself was left an impoverished backwater cut off from its traditional hinterland. Trade died off and many townsfolk were forced to seek work as travelling minstrels. Meanwhile the Dutch king who'd been handed the town saw little use in its gigantic, hard-to-heat castle. In 1820 he sold it to a scrap merchant who stripped out and flogged any marketable building materials. What remained of the castle fell into ruin despite occasional attempts to shore up the walls. It was not until 1977, when the Grand Ducal family formally gave the castle to the Luxembourg State, that long-term restoration finally went ahead. The result was spectacular and the castle has since formed not only a tourist magnet but also the backdrop set for movies such as 1999's *Shadow of the Vampire*.

SIGHTS & ACTIVITIES
Castle

The famed **château** (☎ 83 41 08-1; www.castle-vianden .lu; adult/concession/child/LC €5.50/4.50/2/free; ⊗ 10am-4pm Nov-Feb, to 5pm Mar & Oct, to 6pm Apr-Sep) is entered through a modern exhibition hall, portcullis gate and up stairs into a vaulted hall full of pikes and armour. The crypt displays plans and models of the castle's various incarnations while some later rooms are furnished in medieval style, including the kitchen and hall 13 with its great fireplace and in-wall cupboards. The 'little palace' shows photos of celebrity visitors from Mikhail Gorbachev to John Malkovich.

Chairlift

The **télésiège** (☎ 83 43 23; 39 Rue du Sanatorium; adult/child return €4.50/2.25, one way €2.75/1.50, with LC free; 🕑 10am-6pm Easter-Oct, closed Mon Easter-May & Oct) whisks you up a forested hill from the lower bank of the river at the end of Rue Victor Hugo. You get off at an open-air *café* from which it's possible to walk down to the castle entrance through forested tracks in around 20 minutes.

Grand Rue

Meandering down from the castle, a narrow lane leads left between Grand Rue 106 and 108 towards an isolated 1603 **belfry** standing on a little ridge-outcrop. It's closed to visitors but from its base there are fine views across town (albeit not of the castle). A little stairway path brings you back to Grand Rue emerging between numbers 58 and 60. Alternatively retrace your route to find the sweet little **Musée Veiner** (☎ 83 45 91; 96-98 Grand Rue; adult/child/LC €3/1.50/free; 🕑 11am-5pm Tue-Sun Easter-Oct) in two knocked-together old houses, one maintaining and displaying its full 19th-century decor, the other partly retaining its 1950s incarnation as a bakery. Upstairs there are some exhibits on the town's history (little in English).

Grand Rue's most attractive section is a square called **Place de la Resistance** where the town hall stands astride a small spring. There's an attractive **church** (Grand Rue 53) and an easily missed alley beside Hotel Heintz leading to a pretty **cloister** that was once at the heart of the 1248 Trinitarian Monastery.

Grand Rue reaches the river at a historic bridge across which is the **Maison de Victor Hugo** (☎ 26 87 40 88; www.victor-hugo.lu, in French; 37 Rue de la Gare; adult/child/LC €4/2.50/free; 🕑 11am-5pm Easter & Jul-Aug, 11am-5pm Sat & Sun May-Jun & Sep-Oct). This was home to author Victor Hugo in 1871 for three months of his 19-year exile from France. That was long enough for him to get the Vianden castle architect fired when Hugo volubly complained that reconstruction work was not up to scratch. Even if you're not excited by its manuscripts and sketches, the house's windows offer some of the very best castle views available. Opposite the house, the Victor Hugo bust is by Rodin.

SLEEPING & EATING

Camping de l'Our (☎ 83 45 05; www.camping-our -vianden.lu; 3 Route de Bettel; adult/child/campsite €4.50/2/5; 🕑 closed Nov-Easter) Pleasant camping ground draped along the riverbank south of town.

HI Hostel (Auberge de Jeunesse; ☎ 83 41 77; www. youthhostels.lu; 3 Montée du Château; members dm/s/d €17.50/29.50/45; 🕑 closed late Dec-early Jan; ✖) Standard hostel within an archetypal shutter-fronted Vianden mansion close to the château entrance. Before you lug your bags 1km up from the bus station be aware that reception is closed between 10am and 5pm.

Hôtel Victor Hugo (☎ 83 41 60; www.hotel-victor -hugo.lu; 1 Rue Victor Hugo; s/d €52.50/70; 🕑 closed Dec-Easter) Attached to a potentially noisy bar with a tree-shaded summer terrace beside the main bridge, this hotel has a warren of reasonably priced rooms that are brighter than many of the alternatives nearby.

our pick **Auberge Aal Veinen** (☎ 83 43 68; www. hotel-aal-veinen.lu; 114 Grand Rue; d €80; 🕑 mid-Jan–mid-Dec, kitchen noon-3pm & 6-10pm Wed-Mon) Eight newly refitted guest rooms (plus a simple €60 single) manage to feel remarkably stylish and well-appointed considering they've been seamlessly inserted into an ultra-quaint barrage of ancient dark-wooden beamwork. This is most apparent downstairs in the ground floor restaurant, which is partly built into the living rock.

Hôtel Heintz (☎ 83 41 55; www.hotel-heintz.lu; 55 Grand Rue; s/d from €41/66, Sat €61/81; 🕑 Easter-Oct, restaurant 6-7.30pm) The Heintz was once the brewery-inn of the Trinitarian monks (see left) and, while by no means monastic today, it retains a lovely olde-worlde *café* (often closed). Grandfather clocks and historical knick-knacks decorate landings between fine old staircases, while guestrooms have been recently repainted and updated with modern art albeit maintaining elements of older furniture. After a pre-prandial drink in the tiny strip-garden, adjourn for a superb trout-in-butter dinner (€15) at the hotel restaurant. But don't be late!

Hôtel Oranienburg (☎ 83 41 53-1; www.hoteloranien burg.com; 126 Grand Rue; s/d/ste from €55/84/130; 🕑 Easter–mid-Nov) Sedate, well-kept family hotel with old beams, creaky stairs, stained-glass elements and a peachy-floral feel to the very middle class dining room. Some rooms are updated, other flouncily floral and there's a games room for kids hidden away on the 3rd floor.

Lajolla Lounge (☎ 061-52 56 55; www.lajollalounge .com; 35 Rue de la Gare; beers €2.50-4; snacks €6.80-12, mains

LUXEMBOURG

€11.50-23.50; ☼ 10am-10pm) The *café*-restaurant is unusually fashion conscious for rural Luxembourg, but the real attraction is drinking or dining on summer tables that spill out along the riverside behind the Victor Hugo house. There are views up to the castle.

GETTING THERE & AROUND

Bus 570 runs twice hourly weekdays and 13 times on Sundays between Vianden and Diekirch (17 minutes). Bus 663 to Clervaux leaves at 9.15am, 10.45am, 2.45pm and 6.15pm. Bike rental is available (for the super-fit!) from **Location de Vélos** (☎ 26 87 41 57; Pavillion de la Gare; half-/full day €10/14; ☼ Jul-Aug) at the bus station.

Esch-sur-Sûre
pop 240

The tiny village of Esch-sur-Sûre wraps around a knoll that's virtually surrounded by an emerald-green loop of the Sûre River valley. Topped by a modest AD 927 castle tower, the scene is one of Luxembourg's prettiest. However, apart from admiring it from various angles there's not a lot to do here; fishing is popular. Or you could seek inspiration at an old cloth factory 400m west of the village. That's now a **museum** (☎ 89 93 31-1; 15 Route de Lultzhausen; adult/child €2/1.25; ☼ 10am-noon & 2-6pm Mon-Tue & Thu-Fri, 2-6pm Sat & Sun Jul-Aug, 10am-noon & 2-5pm Mon-Fri, 10am-noon Sat Sep-Jun) whose displays include an impressive collection of old textile looms. It doubles as information centre for the **Parc Naturel de la Haute Sûre** (www.naturpark-sure.lu), promoting local produce and environmentally aware leisure in the attractive surrounding region. Further west is a long reservoir lake overlooked by a **Youth Hostel** (☎ 26 88 92-01; lultzhausen@youthhostels .lu; HI members dm/s/d €19.20/31.20/48.40) offering kayak and canoe rental, 5km from Esch in Lultzhausen village.

In summer you'll need to book well ahead for **Camping Im Aal** (☎ 83 95 14; www.camping-im-aal. lu; campsites per adult/child/tent €5/2.50/5; ☼ Feb-Dec) set in its own curl of green riverside valley 800m east of Esch towards Wiltz.

Occupying an ever larger percentage of the village's cottages, **Hôtel-Restaurant de la Sûre** (☎ 83 91 10; www.hotel-de-la-sure.lu; 1 Rue du Pont; s/d from €46/66; ☼ Feb–mid-Dec; ✗) has a wide variety of rooms dotted here and there. All are relatively fresh and polished, which can be quite a surprise when, as at their 'Logis de Chevalier' building, you enter through heraldically embellished passageways. Fascinating

room 41 has a bed hung on wires from the ceiling. Check in at the bar-restaurant at the top of the village core, where you can also rent bicycles (per hour/day/week €5/22/123) and arrange for your baggage to be forwarded to your next hotel.

The one real plus of the **Hôtel Beau-Site** (☎ 83 91 34; www.beau-site.lu; 2 Rue de Kaundorf; d €96-130; ☼ Mar-Dec) is its riverside terrace. Viewed from here, the castle knoll is reflected in the Sûre's calm black waters behind a stone bridge. Some rooms have the views too, but the decor lacks style and the corridor carpets are getting ragged.

From Ettelbrück (40 minutes) bus 535 runs hourly on weekdays, five times on Sundays. From Wiltz bus 618 (25 minutes) runs seven times daily Monday to Saturday.

Wiltz
pop 4600

Sweeping up a partly wooded hill, Wiltz' very limited historic centre is largely hidden behind trees, and from below the whole town looks pretty banal. However, those trees hide a Renaissance **town hall** and a rather stately **château** (☎ 95 74 44) whose grounds and amphitheatre come to life during the impressive **Wiltz Festival** (p16; www.festivalwiltz.online.lu; ☼ Jul). The château also hosts the **tourist office** (☎ 95 74 44; siwiltz@pt.lu; ☼ 10am-6pm Jul-Aug, 10am-noon & 2-5pm Mon-Fri, 10am-noon Sat Sep-Jun) through which one gains entry to the appealing **Brewing Museum** (with/without audioguide €3.50/2.50, with LC without audio guide free), with an attractive oversized bottle collection, make-believe bar and, downstairs, working minibrewery (tastings cost €1.50 extra). There are no written explanations for those who forgo the audioguide.

The decent **HI Hostel** (Auberge de Jeunesse; ☎ 95 80 39; www.youthhostels.lu; 6 Rue de la Montagne; members dm/s/d €17.50/29.50/45; ☼ Jan–mid-Nov, closed early Feb & late Apr; ✗ &) is a 700m climb above the château, itself around a 900m climb south from the train station (significantly further by car).

Superbly handy for the château and festival is the **Hotel au Vieux Château** (☎ 95 80 18; www. hotelvchateau.com; Grand Rue 1; s/d €60/70, breakfast €15) but down in the valley below, Wiltz' most engaging accommodation is **Aux Anciennes Tanneries** (☎ 95 75 99; www.auxanciennestanneries. com; 42a Rue Jos Simon; s/d from €79/106; ☼ check-in 2-9pm, restaurant 11.30am-2pm daily, 6.30-9pm Sun-Fri; ✗). In a renovated tannery across a stream, the rooms hit a great balance between modern and designer rustic, with some sporting jacuzzis. Breakfast is included and meals are good value both in the vaulted restaurant and on the streamside terrace.

Wiltz–Luxembourg City trains (one hour) run hourly via Ettelbrück. For Clervaux change at Kautenbach or take hourly bus 630 (35 minutes) from the Lycée du Nord (not Sundays). The tourist office can arrange **bicycle rental** (half-/full day €8/15, deposit €30) with advance notice.

Clervaux
pop 1800

Attractive Clervaux is a sloping tongue of land wrapped into a deep wooded curl of the Clerve River. Dominating this little central plateau is the 1910–1913 neo-Romanesque **Church of Saints Côme & Damien** (☉ 8am-6pm), whose dark, twin towers are spired with diamond facets in typical Saxon style. In front of the church is the very distinctive form of Clervaux's whitewashed **castle**, a photogenic, fully rebuilt replica of the 12th-century original razed in WWII.

Within the castle there's a **tourist office** (☎ 92 00 72; www.tourisme-clervaux.lu; ☉ 9.45-11.45am & 2-6pm Jul-Aug, 9.45-11.45am & 1-5pm Sep-Oct, 2-5pm Mon-Fri Easter-Jun) and a trio of museums (combined admission adult/child €7/3.50), though the only one most visitors come to see is the famous **Family of Man** (☎ 92 96 57; adult/child/LC €4.50/2.50/free; ☉ 10am-6pm daily Jul-Aug, Tue-Sun Easter-Dec, Sun only Dec-Easter) photography exhibition. Gifted to Clervaux in 1964 from New York City, the collection comprises 273 black-and-white, mid-20th-century photos from 68 countries interspersed with wise sayings and quotations. It was conceived as a 'mirror of the essential oneness of mankind' and is thought provoking, though quite how this became a Unesco World Heritage Site is mystifying. Photography fans might prefer the more dynamic, up-to-date photography museum near Charleroi (p222).

The red-tiled spire of the 1909 **Benedictine Abbey of St Maurice** (☎ 92 10 27) pierces the forest skyline on the hill behind town, accessible by a 1km track from the castle. The Abbey's monks are widely known for their Gregorian chants, which you can hear during **mass** (☉ 10.30am & 6pm Mon-Fri, 5pm Sat & Sun). The Abbey also houses a permanent exhibition, **The Monastic Life** (☉ 9am-7pm).

Sleeping & Eating

Camping Officiel (☎ 92 00 42; www.camping-clervaux. lu; 33 Rue Klatzewée; campsites per adult/child/tent €5.30/2.50/5.50; ☉ Easter-Oct; ☒) Just 200m from the town centre this campsite has plenty to keep kids happy including a heated pool, table tennis and a playground.

Hôtel Koener (☎ 92 10 02; www.koenerclervaux.lu; 14 Grand Rue; d/tr from €52/62; ☉ mid-Mar–Nov; ☒) The classiest of four hotels huddled around the pedestrian street that rings the castle's base, the Koener offers a considerable yet lightly expressed grandeur. Many rooms come with jacuzzi and there's a spa complex with a small indoor pool. Back rooms might suffer some road noise.

Café-Restaurant du Vieux Château (☎ 92 00 12; 4 Montée du Château; snacks €6-14, mains €11-21; ☉ Wed-Mon) Tucked in the castle's outer courtyard, this terraced *café* serves drinks, simple meals and snacks, including *craji* (pizza-ettes; €6).

Getting There & Away

Clervaux's train station is 800m north of town up the N18. Hourly trains run to Luxembourg City (52 minutes) via Ettelbrück (26 minutes). Bus 663 to Vianden (45 minutes) via Rodershausen departs at 8.30am, 10am, 2pm and 5pm.

WESTERN LUXEMBOURG

If you're driving between Arlon (p241) and Ettelbrük, consider following the Eisch Valley. Peaceful lanes wind through thick woodlands and pass several castles, both crumblies and mansion-style châteaux. Sturdy ruins peep out between the trees above the pretty if over-tidy village of **Septfontaines**. The grand château at **Ansemborg** allows visitors to admire the statuary and geometric topiary in its attractive **formal gardens** (admission free; ☉ 10am-1pm & 3-7pm). At a sharp bend just beyond, a steep, narrow side lane climbs 1.5km to the mighty medieval castle of **Hollenfels**. Across the moat-bridge lies the dramatically located **Hollenfels Youth Hostel** (Auberge de Jeunesse; ☎ 30 70 37; www.youthhostels.lu; 2 Rue du Château; dm/s/d €17.50/29.50/45; ☒).

The route emerges onto Luxembourg's central north–south highway near **Mersch** whose main street, Place St-Michel, has a rather stately air with pastel-coloured house fronts, a twin-towered Italianate church, dragon statue and modest four-storey castle whose peach-walled gatehouse hosts the tourist office.

Directory

CONTENTS

ACCOMMODATION

Accommodation listings in this book are ordered by price from camping sites and budget hostels (mostly under €20) through B&Bs and midrange hotels (from €60) to top-end options costing over €140 for a double room.

Availability varies markedly by season and area. May to September occupancy is very high (especially at weekends) along the coast, in Bruges and in the resort areas of rural Luxembourg and the Ardennes. However, those same weekends you'll find hotels cutting prices in business cities like Brussels, Antwerp, Kortrijk, Mechelen and Luxembourg City.

For upper-range hotels, online bookings can often save money. Arriving without a booking, tourist offices can usually reserve local accommodation for you if availability remains. The service is often free or asks a deposit that is deducted from your room rate.

Beware that some rural hotels quote accommodation prices 'per person' assuming double occupancy, with 40% supplements for single use. National taxes are invariably included but several towns add a small additional *stadsbelasting/taxe de séjour* (city tourist tax), which might add a euro or two to the tally. At most B&Bs and some hotels, reductions for longer stays are fairly common while some places demand a minimum two- or three-day stay, especially at key times of year.

Many options include breakfast. For those staying two days or more, many hotels (especially in rural areas) offer *demi-pension* (half-board) deals including breakfast and a set lunch or dinner – often fair value but with limited choice of menu. Some popular places in touristy areas of the Ardennes will only rent rooms on summer weekends on a *demi-pension* or *pension complète* (full board) basis. Grander rural getaways increasingly offer *weekend gastronomique* options, accommodation plus various meals that are often high-end, four-course affairs.

Hotels that accept pets usually charge around €3 to €10 per night for the service.

Technically visitors need to show their passport when checking into accommodation, though this is only half-heartedly enforced.

B&Bs

B&Bs (*gastenkamers* in Dutch, *chambres d'hôtes* in French) are increasingly prevalent in both rural and urban Belgium, but very thin on the ground in Luxembourg.

B&B standards can vary from unpretentious homestays to luxury boutique hotels. Breakfast is generally (but not always) included at a communal table – a great way to interact with the owners and other guests. Many are run by vibrant hosts whose enthusiasm for the job can be seen in characterful interiors and thoughtful decor. The best B&Bs offer a level of charm and refinement that trumps all but the very finest top-end hotels.

PRACTICALITIES

- Electrical appliances need a two round-pin adaptor. The supply is 220V, 50Hz.

- Keep up to date with *The Bulletin* (www.thebulletin.com), Belgium's invaluable English-language newsweekly or Luxembourg's equivalent *Luxembourg News 352*.

- Top newspapers include *De Standaard* (in Dutch), *Le Soir* (Francophone) and *Grenzecho* (Germanophone) in Belgium, *Lëtzebuerger Journal* in Luxembourg.

- Radio-wise the BBC World Service is available (648 kHz AM). For contemporary music choose Studio Brussel (in Dutch) or Pure FM (in French), whose jingles make the astonishing assertion that 'Good music makes good people'. Klara (in Dutch) and Musiq3 (in French) play classical music and occasional jazz. Classic21 (in French) is great for classic rock and Sunday-night boogie-blues. Radio frequencies vary by area (see www.radioinvlaanderen.info, www.rtbf.be).

- Flemish TV channels include TV1 (news and sport), VTM (soaps and game shows) and Ketnet/Canvas (documentaries/foreign films). Francophone Belgium is split between La Une and RTL for general news and sport but French channels are also popular, ARTE being especially good for nonmainstream films and documentaries. In Luxembourg RTL broadcasts nightly in Letzeburgesch.

- DVDs should be set on Region 2, and videos on the PAL system.

- Use the metric system for weights and measures. Decimals are indicated with commas and thousands with points (full stops).

You'll generally need to pre-book and arrange a mutually agreeable arrival time. Also be prepared for stairs as elevators are usually nonexistent.

Camping, Caravan Parks & Hikers' Huts

Camping and caravanning facilities are plentiful especially in the Belgian and Luxembourg Ardennes, but sites are often sardined with permanent trailers. Typical rates are compounded from per person, per car and per site fees.

Useful websites:

Camping Flanders (www.camping.be) Camping-ground finder for Flanders.

Camping Wallonia (www.campingbelgique.be) Extensive by-commune camping-ground listings for Wallonia.

CampingGid (www.campinggids-belgie.nl) Customer feedback on Belgian campsites (in Dutch).

Camprilux (www.camping.lu) Camping-site federation for the Grand Duchy.

Nudist Belgium (www.naturisme.be) Links to Belgium's eight campsites where clothing's an encumbrance.

HIKERS' HUTS

Known as *trekkershutten* in Flanders and *wanderhütten* in Luxembourg, these small four-person wooden **cabins** (d/tr/q from €37/41/45) come with basic cooking facilities but charge extra for electricity or heating usage. Maximum stay is four nights. They're mostly attached to campsites or provincial recreation parks, with many along Flanders Cycle Route (p287). In Luxembourg, where they're within walking distance of one another, consult www.trekkershutten.nl. For Belgium download the brochure via www.vlaanderen-vakantieland.be/trekkershutten

Gîtes & Apartments

Especially in southern Wallonia, a good family option is to rent an apartment or especially a holiday home called a *gîte* (*landelijk verblijf* in Dutch, or *gîte rural* in French). Generally you'll rent by the week with prices varying vastly by season, number of occupants and house standards. Some are on farms, others in castles, converted stables or historic buildings. There is often an extra cleaning charge of around €60. Wallonia tourism produces a thick booklet of choices and the following websites can prove helpful.

Belsud (www.belsud.be) *Gîtes* in Wallonia.

Gîtes de Wallonie (www.gitesdewallonie.be) Its website's map feature is especially helpful and also shows rural B&Bs.

Luxembourg National Tourist Office (www.visitluxembourg.lu) Publishes a good brochure entitled *Holiday Apartments Farm & Rural Holidays*.

Vlaamse Federatie voor Hoeve & Plattelandstoerisme (www.hoevetoerisme.be)

DIRECTORY

Don't confuse a *gîte* with a *gîte d'étape* (below), which in Belgium is essentially a hostel, albeit often limited to group bookings.

Hostels & Gîtes d'Étapes

Hostels (*jeugdherbergen* in Dutch, *auberges de jeunesse* in French) generally charge from €12 to €25 for a dorm bed. Those that seem cheapest usually charge extra for bedding, evening the playing field if you don't have a sleeping bag. While breakfast is often included, towels almost never are and you'll need your own soap. In Hostelling International (HI) hostels, non-members pay €3 extra per night (though after six nights you'll get a one year International Guest Card assuming you've kept all six 'stamps'). A few hostels operate midsummer only, some others close during winter. Some have a lock-out policy, typically between around 11am and 5pm. Bring your own padlock if you want to use some hostel lockers.

HOSTEL ORGANISATIONS

Centrale des Auberges de Jeunesse Luxembourgeoises (Map p267; ☎ 26 27 66 40; www.youthhostels .lu; 2 Rue du Fort Olisy, Luxembourg City) Luxembourg's HI hostels.

Gîtes d'Étape (☎ 02-209 0300; www.gitesdetape. be) Aimed primarily at school kids, most of its properties are only for youth groups (typically minimum 20 people) with fees as low as €6 per person per night, to which a one-off cleaning fee (typically €60) is added. More usefully there are also five *gîtes d'étapes* in the Ardennes that operate exactly like youth hostels and for which HI members are waived the €1.50 temporary membership fee. Bring your own sleeping bag or pay €4 extra for sheets.

Les Auberges de Jeunesse (Map pp68-9; ☎ 02-219 56 76; www.laj.be; Rue de la Sablonnière 28, Brussels) Francophone Belgium's HI hostels.

Vlaamse Jeugdherbergcentrale (Map pp174-5; ☎ 03-232 72 18; www.jeugdherbergen.be, in Dutch; Van Stralenstraat 40, Antwerp) Flanders' HI hostels.

Hotels

The Benelux classification system awards stars for facilities (elevators, room service, dogs allowed etc) so don't assume that such classification necessarily reflects quality or price.

It's unlikely that you'll find a hotel room (*kamer* in Dutch, *chambre* in French) for under €40/50 single/double, even with shared bathroom facilities. Midrange hotels typically charge between €70 and €130 for a double room. Check-in time is rarely before 2pm, check out around 11am.

Prices vary somewhat to fit demand. At weekends and in summer prices fall (sometimes dramatically) in business cities like Brussels, Antwerp and Luxembourg. However they rise in tourist places like Bruges, the coastal towns and the Ardennes resorts. It's also worth checking hotel websites for last-minute and advance-purchase deals.

Top-end hotels usually offer private parking. This can be a boon in city centres where parking space is limited but you won't necessarily save much money as most hotels still charge guests around €10 to €20 for 24 hours.

Some smaller hotels are effectively just rooms above a restaurant and when the restaurant's closed there'll be no receptionist unless you pre-arrange an arrival time.

Hospitality Exchanges

For those wanting personal homestay experiences, **Couchsurfing** (www.couchsurfing.org) currently has around 6000 hosts in Belgium.

Motels

If you're driving and don't mind drearily banal locations in outer suburbs, industrial parks or at motorway junctions, you can often get a comparatively inexpensive bed in one of several motel chains. Check their websites for details and maps of how to find them (not always obvious):

- **Campanile** (www.louvrehotels.com/hotel/en/belgium .htm) Fair standard rooms but prices vary considerably by date, often giving massive savings for advance-purchase weekend stays.
- **Etap** (www.etaphotel.com) Simple but with bathroom ensuite. Four Belgian sites cost from €39 per triple, breakfast included.
- **Formule1** (www.hotelformule1.com) Eight branches at motorway junctions. They have minimal staff and only a wash basin ensuite (toilets and showers shared), but rooms are typically clean and rarely cost more than €40 for a triple. Use a credit card or online booking reference to access when the place is unstaffed. Formule1 is part of the Accor Group (www .accorhotels.com), whose higher-class, decent value Ibis hotels are numerous in Belgium.

ACTIVITIES
Cycling

Cycling is a major local passion whether as transport, speed-sport or off-roading by mountain-bike (*terreinfiets* in Dutch, *VTT/ vélo tout-terrain* in French). Bike helmets are not a legal requirement and are rarely worn, except by competition cyclists. At night bicycle lamps are compulsory. Secure your bicycle carefully as bike theft flourishes, especially in Flanders where even two locks and chains can't guarantee 100% safety if you leave it too long. Beware that mopeds are also allowed on bike paths.

BELGIUM

On weekends it's the norm to see troupes of cyclists of all ages whizzing around country lanes clad in fluorescent lycra gear or pulled up for a drink at their favourite wayside pub.

In flat Flanders bikes are an everyday means of travel and relaxation, so dedicated cycle lanes are commonplace on roadsides and drivers are (relatively) accommodating though strong winds can prove discouraging. **Cycle Network Flanders** (www.fietsroute.org) is an incredibly extensive and well-marked web of bicycle routes using cyclepaths and minor lanes for which keyed maps and booklets are available in local tourist offices. The **Great Flanders Route** (www.groteroutepaden.be, in Dutch) is over 800km and its site sells the multilingual book *Topogids Vlaanderen Fietsroute* (€8.50) compiling 61 detailed 1:50,000 route maps and relevant accommodation options. Alternatively there's a downloadable version for your Garmin GPS.

Wallonia's networks of cycle paths, **RAVel** (www.ravel.wallonie.be) and **Randovelo** (www.randovelo. org) often use canal or river towpaths and former railway tracks rebuilt with hard surfaces. Randovelo sells a range of guide maps.

Bikes can be taken on a Belgian train on payment of a supplement (€5/8 one-way/all day) to the passenger fare (see p305). One-day bicycle hire is available from various train stations (consult www.b-rail.be for addresses) and using short-hop city-schemes like Villo (p111) or Veloh (p273). For longer hires it's usually preferable to use private operators. Most bike-rental shops also do repairs.

LUXEMBOURG

Luxembourg is criss-crossed by numbered bicycle paths (*pistes cyclables*). Some cross hilly country and require considerable fitness, whereas PC3 winds gently along the Moselle and Sûre Rivers. Echternach-Diekirch and Remich-Grevenmacher are particularly nice stretches. Locally available guidebook *40 Cycle Routes,* published by Éditions Guy Binsfield, describes 40 selected cycle tours with topographical maps and track descriptions. Bikes can be rented in most major tourist centres, helmets are not compulsory and for €1.50 you can bring your bicycle on a Luxembourg train.

Hiking

Crossing Belgium you'll find various longdistance footpaths called *sentiers de grande randonnée* (GR, www.grsentiers.org) along with countless shorter trails for afternoon rambles. Most are well signposted and keyed to topographical hiking maps sold by tourist offices, which can offer plenty of advice to walkers. In flat Flanders hiking routes typically follow countryside bicycle paths where you must be careful to give way to cyclists. Landscapes are more inspiringly hilly in the Ardennes region of southeast Belgium and rural Luxembourg. Notably the 160km-long 'Transardennaise' footpath links two of the region's best outdoor activity hub towns, La Roche-en-Ardenne (p243) and Bouillon (p238). Most hiking routes are pleasant rather than spectacular, passing through forests patchworked with agricultural land and occasionally fording streams. For something a little different locals flock to the open moorlands of the Hautes Fagnes (p261). Many paths can get surprisingly busy in July and August.

Other great starting points for hikes include Rochefort (p236), Vianden (p280) and Echternach (p277), around which paths weave up, down and around gorgeous sandstone gorges hidden deep within the forests. Simple overnight accommodation for ramblers is available in much of Luxembourg and Flanders in specially conceived hikers' huts (p285).

The excellent multilingual *182x Luxembourg* published by Éditions Guy Binsfield describes 182 of Luxembourg's most charming hikes ranging from 2km to 17km. On the internet, check www.walking.lu and www.europaventure.be.

Billiards

While snooker and pool are widely popular (see www.bbsa.be), Belgium also has its own distinctive forms of billiards (*biljart* in

Dutch, *billard* in French). Championed by its own federation FRBB/KBBB (www.kbbb.be), three-ball billiards uses a table without holes, the aim being not to pot the balls but to use one ball to hit the other two.

Elsewhere you might notice pool-style tables with two goal-holes guarded by rubber-wrapped metal 'mushrooms', and a cross of eight more such 'mushrooms' in the middle. Known variously as *Topbiljart, Billard à Bouchon* or *Golfbiljart* (www.ngbvzw.be, in Dutch), learning its rules can be a great way to meet beery locals in smoky back-street *cafés*.

Belgium is a world leader in billiard ball manufacture (www.saluc.com).

Boating
In summer pleasant short river cruises are popular on the Meuse from Namur (p228), along the Moselle from Remich (p275) in Luxembourg and between Diksmuide and Ostend (p150). Sea cruises and short, splashy excursions into the waves by amphibious WWII-era DUKW (p154) are possible from various seaside towns. By advanced arrangement you can charter yachts and canal boats from Nieuwpoort. From Brussels, **Rivertours** (www.rivertours.be) organises a selection of summer excursions by water and rents river boats. Short tourist boat rides are an ever popular way to view the gorgeous urban canals of Bruges (p129) and Ghent (p138).

Canoeing & Kayaking
Three picturesque rivers in Belgium's Ardennes region offer sedate but popular kayaking sections. In summer, assuming water levels are high enough (always call canoeing agencies ahead to check), each attracts hoards of Flemish and Dutch holidaymakers so you won't be alone. The Lesse, south of Dinant, is the 'wildest' of the trio but also the busiest and even here you shouldn't expect rapids of any magnitude. The main alternatives are the pretty Semois around Bouillon (p239) and the Ourthe between Durbuy (p246) and La Roche-en-Ardenne (p243).

In Luxembourg, canoeing is possible from Diekirch (p279).

Chess
Many smoky *cafés* have chess sets available for clients but the easiest place to find worthy competition amongst total strangers is Brussels' classic Le Greenwich (p104).

Golf
For links and addresses of Belgium's numerous golf courses, consult the website of the **Royal Belgian Golf Federation** (www.golfbelgium.be/clubs.html).

Horse Riding
Experienced riders can join equestrian adventures from La Roche (p244) but should make arrangements well in advance.

Rock Climbing
The most popular area for rock climbers in Belgium is along the Meuse River around Namur and Dinant. Belgium's escarpments are generally high-quality limestone, while Luxembourg has hard sandstone cliffs. Chris Craggs' 1994 Cicerone guide *Selected Rock Climbs in Belgium & Luxembourg* is often available second-hand from internet bookshops.

Skiing
This isn't the Alps. There are few major slopes and no ski resorts. Nonetheless, when the Ardennes gets sufficient snowfall Belgian TV stations give detailed reports and the E411 rapidly fills up with wannabe skiers hurrying south before it all melts again. Most such skiing is cross-country on woodland tracks as around Eupen (www.ternell.be). See www.wallonie-tourisme.be for a comprehensive listing. A few downhill pistes exist including **Mont Des Brumes** (☎ 080-785 413; www.montdesbrumes.be; ⏰ 10am-6pm, snow allowing) between Spa and Stavelot (850m-long red-slope, no snowboards) and a slope near Ovifat (p262). There's also an all-year artificial indoor slope near Comines (p163).

HEALTH CARE
World-class health and dental care is readily available (see www.xpats.com/practical-a-to-z/medical-matters) and Belgium's doctor-patient ratio is Europe's best. To find a Brussels doctor who speaks your language **MGBRU** (www.mgbru.be) is a useful resource, though oddly the site's not in English. Elsewhere hotels and tourist offices might be able to assist. The English-language **Community Help Service** (☎ 02-648 4014; www.chsbelgium.org) is also very helpful for information and offers mental health and crisis support. Following a consultation, doctors' bills are generally payable immediately in cash, so visit an ATM beforehand. At a hospital (*ziekenhuis/hôpital* in Dutch/French) bills

DIRECTORY

are more often payable with cards. **Healthcare Belgium** (☎ 02-773 6154; www.healthcarebelgium.com) is an English-language information service organised by a grouping of 11 major Belgian hospitals aimed mainly at helping foreigners understand the benefits of coming to Belgium for hospital-based treatments.

For minor self-limiting illnesses you might save a doctor's fee by asking advice at a pharmacy *(apotheek/pharmacie)*. Pharmacies usually sport a green cross or the snake-and-rod symbol of Aesculapius (ancient Greco-Roman god of medicine). Most are open from about 8.30am to 7pm Monday to Friday plus Saturday mornings. At night or weekends a limited number stay 'on duty' *(wachtdienst/ de garde* in Dutch/French) but charge higher prices. The duty roster will be displayed in local pharmacy windows and online at www. fpb.be/fr/dutychemist.html for Brussels, www.pharmacie.lu/service_de_garde for Luxembourg and www.pharmacie.be (French, click *Services de garde*) or www.apotheek. be (Dutch, click *Wachtdiensten apothekers*) for Belgium.

BUSINESS HOURS

Restaurants generally open for lunch from noon until 2.30pm while dinner's typically served from 6.30pm to 10pm. Gastronomic restaurants with multi-course menus might have 'last orders' at 9pm while brasseries have more fluid hours, usually serving till 11pm and possibly staying open until midnight or 1am with at least a limited menu. Bars and *cafés* open when they want and in some cases close only when the last barfly drops.

Shops in both countries are open from 10am to 6pm or 6.30pm, Monday to Saturday, some closing for lunch, especially in smaller towns. Tourist-oriented shops often open Sundays then close Mondays. Sunday opening is also common in chains of convenience stores while night stores *(nachtwinkel* or *magasin de nuit)* work dusk till dawn.

Banks open from 8.30am or 9am and close between 3.30pm and 5pm Monday to Friday. Some close for an hour at lunch, and many also open Saturday mornings. Larger post offices open at 9am, closing at 6pm or 7pm Monday to Friday, noon Saturday. Smaller branches close at 5pm, have a lunch break and rarely open at all on Saturdays. In this guide, we've provided business hours when they differ from these norms.

CHILDREN

For most attractions, reduced-price child tickets apply to those under 12 years old, though occasionally eligibility is judged by height. Train travel in Belgium is free for under-12s so long as they're accompanied by an adult and the journey starts after 9am. Accommodation options don't usually charge for toddlers, while for children many hotels can provide an extra bed for around €15 (very variable). Without local contacts it's generally awkward to find a babysitter. In Brussels you can arrange student babysitters to come to your hotel or B&B through **ULB Job Service** (☎ 02-650 2171). Book at least a day ahead. If staying a while in Flanders you could organise babysitters by joining family-oriented organisation **Gezinsbond** (☎ 02-507 8966; www.gezinsbond.be; annual membership €30). Baby cots are available in many B&Bs, hotels and even some hostels, but it's worth reserving ahead as most places stock only one or two. Nappy-changing facilities are only patchily available: try the female toilets at branches of hamburger chain Quick if you're stuck. Breastfeeding in public is acceptable though not commonly seen.

Travelling by car, children under 1.35m must legally travel in a child's safety seat. Most car-rental firms have such safety seats for hire if you pre-book well ahead. Theoretically taxis too should provide a seat if you book in advance. Lonely Planet's *Travel with Children* offers plenty of useful advice.

Sights & Activities for Children

The countries have numerous decent-sized theme parks, including Walibi (p220), Plopsaland (p153) and Park Bellewaerde (p162). For child entertainment with an educational angle it's hard to beat the Euro Space Center (p237), Antwerp Zoo (p178) or fascinating Technopolis (p198) at Mechelen.

In the Ardennes most tourist hub-towns offer summertime cycling, kayaking and a range of kid-friendly options: Durbuy (p246) is especially well set up. *Family Guide* (www .familyguide.lu) is a remarkably detailed resource-book for Luxembourg suggesting around 700 activities, trips and contacts.

CLIMATE CHARTS

Belgium and Luxembourg share a generally mild, maritime climate characterised by many days of grey and/or rainy weather. Winters can have brief harsh spells but like much of

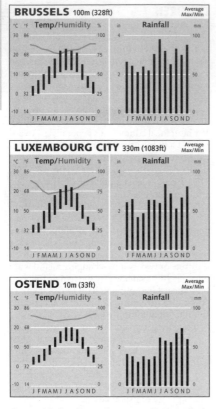

the world, the climate has proved increasingly erratic and unpredictable over recent years. Temperatures dipped to record lows (below -20°C) for a few freak nights in 2008. Then again, the summer of 2009 was the sunniest in recent memory, leading jokers to quip that global warming might not be such a bad thing after all. For more on local weather conditions and suggestions on when to go, see p13.

CUSTOMS

For goods purchased *outside* the EU, duty-free allowances apply to tobacco (200 cigarettes, 50 cigars or 250g of loose tobacco), alcohol (1L of spirits or 2L of liquor with less than 22% alcohol by volume; 2L of wine) and perfume (50g of perfume and 0.25L of eau de toilette). For *duty-paid* items bought at normal shops within other EU countries, allowances are far more generous: 800 cigarettes, 200 cigars or 1kg of loose tobacco; 10L of spirits (more than 22% alcohol by volume), 20L of fortified wine

or aperitif, 90L of wine or 110L of beer; and unlimited quantities of perfume.

DANGERS & ANNOYANCES

While the rate of violent crime is comparatively low, pick-pocketing and petty theft does occur. Leaving valuables on view in a car is unwise, even when you're in the vehicle yourself. Belgium has recently been suffering over 6000 annual cases of *sac-jacking*: the smashing of a passenger-side window to grab your bag while you're stuck immobilised at a red light or a city traffic jam. Late at night, cautious locals prefer to avoid the Brussels-Charleroi train and Brussels' Rue Neuve. Beware that Belgian driving is infamous and drink-driving rules are widely flouted (see p301). As one merrily sozzled motorist told us, 'If I wasn't drunk, I'd be too scared to drive here'.

Restaurants in both countries are legally required to be smoke-free.

Despite hefty fines that nominally apply to owners of a pooch that poops where it shouldn't, dog mess on city streets remains a niggling irritant.

DISCOUNTS

Museums and sights typically offer small discounts to seniors (ie those over 65, sometimes over 60) and, especially in Flanders, give bigger discounts to 'youth' (ie those under 26). Accompanied children (under 12) generally pay even less or go free. Students with an ISIC (International Student Identity Card) might, but won't always, qualify for the 'concession rate' (usually the same as seniors). Bigger Belgian cities offer discounted passes to a selection of municipally owned sights and many have one day a week where key museums are free. The Luxembourg Card (p266) offers exceptional value for visits to the Grand Duchy.

EMBASSIES & CONSULATES

Foreign ministry websites give up-to-date visa information and embassy addresses abroad:
Belgium (www.diplomatie.be)
Luxembourg (www.mae.lu)

Embassies & Consulates in Brussels
Australia (Map pp68-9; ☎ 02-286 0500; www.austemb.be; Rue Guimard 6)
Canada (Map pp66-7; ☎ 02-741 0611; http://belgium.gc.ca; Ave de Tervuren 2)

France (Map pp68-9; ☎ 02-548 8711; www.ambafrance
-be.org; Rue Ducale 65)
Germany (Map p86; ☎ 02-787 1800; www.bruessel
.diplo.de; Rue Jacques de Lalaing 8-14)
Ireland (Map p86; ☎ 02-235 6676; www.embassy
ofireland.be; Chaussée d'Etterbeek 180)
Luxembourg (Map p86; ☎ 02-735 5700; http://brux
elles.mae.lu; 7th fl, Ave de Cortenbergh 75)
Netherlands (Map pp66-7; ☎ 02-679 1711; www
.nederlandseambassade.be; Ave Herrmann-Debroux 48)
New Zealand (Map pp72-3; ☎ 02-512 1040; www
.nzembassy.com; 7th fl, Sq de Meeûs 1)
UK (Map p86; ☎ 02-287 6355; http://ukinbelgium.fco
.gov.uk/en; Rue d'Arlon 85)
USA (Map pp68-9; ☎ 02-508 2111; http://belgium
.usembassy.gov; Blvd du Régent 27)

Embassies & Consulates in Luxembourg
Belgium (off Map p267; ☎ 25 43 25-1; fax 45 42 82; 4
Rue des Girondins)
France (off Map p267; ☎ 45 72 71; www.ambafrance
-lu.org; 8 Blvd Joseph II)
Germany (off Map p267; ☎ 45 34 45-1; www.luxem
burg.diplo.de; 20-22 Ave Émile Reuter)
Ireland (off Map p267; ☎ 45 06 10-1; www.embassy
ofireland.lu; 28 Route d'Arlon)
Netherlands (Map p267; ☎ 22 75 70; www.paysbas.lu;
6 Rue Ste-Zithe)
UK (off Map p267; ☎ 22 98 64; http://ukinluxembourg.
fco.gov.uk; 5 Blvd Joseph II)
USA (off Map p267; ☎ 46 01 23; http://luxembourg.
usembassy.gov; 22 Blvd Emmanuel Servais)

FESTIVALS & EVENTS
Throughout the year there are religious pro-
cessions, music and film festivals and more
than a few bizarre folkloric events. See p16.

FOOD
Throughout this guide, restaurants have
been ordered by price, from least expensive
to most expensive. See p47 for details on
what to expect.

GAY & LESBIAN TRAVELLERS
Attitudes to homosexuality are pretty laid-
back in both Belgium and Luxembourg, with
Belgium a world leader in equal rights for
gays and lesbians. Same-sex couples have
been able to wed legally in Belgium since
2003 and since 2006 have the same rights
enjoyed by heterosexual couples, including
inheritance and adoption. Belgium celebrates
national anti-homophobia day on May 17.
The age of consent in both countries is 16.

Details of gay and lesbian organisations appear in boxed texts under Brussels
(p108), Antwerp (p181), Ghent (p124)
and Luxembourg City (p269) or under
'Information' for Liège and Namur.

HOLIDAYS
Public Holidays
New Year's Day 1 January
Easter Monday March/April
Labour Day 1 May
Ascension Day 40th day after Easter (always a Thursday)
Pentecost & Whit Monday 7th Sunday & Monday
after Easter
Luxembourg National Day 23 June (Luxembourg
only)
Flemish Community Day 11 July (Flanders only)
Belgium National Day 21 July (Belgium only)
Assumption Day 15 August
Francophone Community Day 27 September
(Wallonia only)
All Saints' Day 1 November
Armistice Day 11 November (Belgium only)
Christmas Day 25 December

School Holidays
Belgium 1 July to 31 August; one week in November; two
weeks at Christmas; one week around Carnival; two weeks
at Easter; one week in May.
Luxembourg Mid-July to mid-September; first week
in November; two weeks around Christmas; one week at
Carnival; two weeks at Easter; one week at Ascension.

INSURANCE
A travel-insurance policy to cover theft,
loss and medical problems is a good idea.
Worldwide travel insurance is available at
www.lonelyplanet.com/travel_services. You
can buy, extend and claim online anytime,
even if you're already on the road.

INTERNET ACCESS
Internet cafes are reasonably plentiful in major
cities, often associated with private telephone
centres. As these tend to cater predominantly
to immigrant communities, they're not always located handily for the tourist quarters.
There's also public internet access in some
libraries, hostels, hotels, *cafés* and tourist offices. For those carrying a suitably equipped
laptop, wi-fi is increasingly prevalent in hotels and is free for at least 30 minutes at 65
branches of burger-chain McDonalds (www
.mcdonalds.be, wwwmcdonalds.lu).
    See p15 for useful websites.

LEGAL MATTERS

Police in both countries usually treat tourists with respect and many officers, particularly in Flanders and in Luxembourg, speak fluent English. In both countries you are legally required to carry either a passport or a national identity card at all times. A photocopy should suffice if you don't want to carry your passport for security reasons. Should you be arrested you have the right to ask for your consul to be immediately notified.

In Luxembourg City you can seek free legal advice at the **Service d'Accueil et d'Information Juridique** (☎ 22 18 46; Côte d'Eich).

MAPS

Most tourist offices have decent city plans (often free) and stock for-purchase maps of the surrounding region. Proper road maps are essential for driving or cycling.

If you're driving on bigger roads, a map like Michelin's fold-out Belgium/Luxembourg map (No 716, scale 1:350,000) should suffice and it includes a town index and enlargements of Brussels, Antwerp and Liège.

IGN (Institut Géographique National; www.ngi.be), Belgium's national cartographic institute, publishes a superbly comprehensive range of much more detailed topographic maps, including a complete atlas of Belgium at 1:50,000 scale (€44.95), detailed hiking and cycling maps and DVDs for trekkers explaining routes and including a series of waypoint coordinates you can export direct to your GPS.

De Rouck (www.derouckgeomatics.com) publishes 1:100,000 provincial maps (€7.95) and A5-sized provincial atlases ranging from 1:16,000 to 1:32,000 (€21.95).

Luxembourg cartographers **Geoline** (www.mdi-geoline.lu) produce various city plans, maps and an atlas for the Grand Duchy.

Various online map systems exist. Michelin's www.viamichelin.co.uk is reliable and includes route-choice and distance calculators between any two chosen points.

MONEY

Both Belgium and Luxembourg use the euro (€), which has the same value in all euro-zone countries: see the inside front cover or www.oanda.com for approximate exchange rates. There are eight euro coins (one, two, five, 10, 20 and 50 cents, and one and two euros) and seven euro notes (five, 10, 20, 50, 100, 200

> **OF AGE**
>
> The minimum legal ages in Belgium and Luxembourg:
>
> - drinking alcohol – 16 in Belgium, 17 in Luxembourg
> - driving – 18
> - marriage – 18
> - sexual intercourse – 16 (both heterosexual and homosexual)
> - voting – 18

and 500 euros) but for security purposes, few shops accept notes over €50. For information on local costs, see p13.

Major credit cards are widely accepted. The chip-and-pin system is prevalent rather than using antiquated, less-secure signature-slips, but most expect four-figure PIN-codes (newer ATMs accept six-figure PINs). Certain supermarkets only accept Belgian-issued debit cards while, conversely, most restaurants only want credit cards. For smaller purchases (under €10), many Belgians use an electronic 'purse' called Proton.

Moneychangers

Banks charge comparatively small commission rates but in some cases will only perform currency transactions (especially with cash travellers cheques) for their own clients. Exchange bureaux (*wisselkantoren* in Dutch, *bureaux de change* in French) are usually faster, more conveniently located and open longer, but the buy-sell rate split is generally worse and there's sometimes a hefty commission on top, especially those at airports and stations.

Automated teller machines (ATMs) accepting MasterCard and Visa are widely available though in bigger city centres they may be 'hidden' within bank buildings. There are ATMs at the main international airports.

Tipping

In restaurants, wait staff are properly paid. For exceptional service locals just might leave a small token (perhaps two or three euros) but generally tipping is not expected. A possible exception is in highly touristed areas like central Bruges or at expat hang-outs in Brussels where staff have become happily accustomed to the strange, unsolicited generosity of foreigners. Despite heavy hints from airport cabbies, tipping is not required in taxis either. You will however need to have some small change ready at public toilets, where the attendant will absolutely expect/demand around €0.40 and will likely cause a rumpus if you don't pay up. In old-fashioned cinemas, you are effectively required to tip €1 to the oddly pointless attendant who shows you to your seat.

PHOTOGRAPHY & VIDEO

If you're running out of memory on your digital camera, you can generally burn your photos onto CD at photo labs or, less frequently, at internet cafes. If using film, winter's dull and often overcast conditions make higher-speed film (eg 200 ISO) worth considering. Lonely Planet publishes a useful *Travel Photography* guide. As with all electronic equipment don't forget to bring the correct transformer plugs for your chargers.

POST

In Belgium (www.post.be), *prior* (priority) standard-sized letters under 50g cost €0.59/0.90/1.05 to domestic/EU/non-EU addresses. You'll save 10% by slower *non-prior*. In reality delivery times are very variable whichever you choose. In Luxembourg (www.pt.lu), standard-sized letters cost €0.70/1/1.40 to domestic/EU/non-EU addresses if under 50g, or only €0.50/0.70/0.90 if under 20g. Beware that non-standard letter rates are up to 200% more so check dimensions carefully, eg most British-sized Christmas cards are too big for standard rates.

In Belgian addresses, the street number follows the street name. In Luxembourg the order is reversed. Both countries use a four-digit postal code in front of the city or town name (B-1000 Brussels, for example, the 'B' standing for the country, ie Belgium). 'PB' *(postbus)* or 'BP' *(boîte postale)* means Postal Box.

SHOPPING

Belgium's specialities are chocolate (p52), beer (p48) and lace (p139). Antwerp is famous for diamonds (p178) and avant-garde designer fashions (p172), though Brussels has its own quirky fashion scene (p79). Antiques are popular buys in Brussels (p109), as well as in the Flemish town of Tongeren (p206). With expensive purchases like diamonds or antiques you can often claim the 21% VAT back if you live outside the EU.

Markets selling food, clothing and miscellaneous goods set up on a weekly basis in most Belgian towns, often on Sunday mornings as with La Batte (which takes over Liège's Quay de la Goffe) or Brussels' Marché du Midi (p84). Bric-a-brac *(curiosa/brocante)* flea markets and car-boot sales *(braderie)* are also very popular, notably on Brussels' Place du Jeu-de-Balle (daily, p84) or Antwerp's centuries' old Vrijdagmarkt (Fridays, p188). Bargaining, while not generally customary in Belgium, is worth trying at flea markets.

TELEPHONE & FAX

The international country codes are ☎ 32 for Belgium and ☎ 352 for Luxembourg. To telephone abroad, dial the international access code ☎ 00. For an international operator, call ☎ 1324 in Belgium, ☎ 12410 in Luxembourg.

In Belgium and Luxembourg dial the full number (always quoted including the area code). Regular domestic calls between landlines in both countries are charged at the same rate regardless of distance but they are metered (unlike local calls in North America) so don't expect to talk endlessly for a flat charge.

Non-standard charges apply to the following prefixes:

- 0472 to 0479, 0482 to 0489 and 0492 to 0499 (mobile phones)
- 070 (up to €0.30 per minute) Many transport companies have such toll-lines
- 078 (normal call rates but with a €0.56 connection fee)
- 0800 (toll free)
- 0900 and 0901 (€0.50 per minute)
- 0901 to 0904, 0906 and 0907 (up to €2 per minute)
- 0905 (€2 flat-rate call)
- 0909 (up to €31 per minute; beware!)

Numbers should be dialled in their entirety from within each country. From abroad you drop the initial 0 on Belgian numbers then add the international access code plus 32 for Belgium.

Calling Belgium's national/international directory assistance (☎ 1207/1405) costs a whopping €1.25/3. You can make free online Yellow Pages searches in English with http://goldenpages.truvo.be (Belgium) and www.edituspro.luxweb.com (Luxembourg).

In Luxembourg call ☎ 016/017 for enquiries and ☎ 80 02 00 to make collect calls.

Phone boxes are increasingly rare and few accept coins: generally you'll need a credit card, Proton-card or stored-value phonecard (available from post offices, telephone centres, news-stands etc). Using discount scratch-code pre-payment cards can give considerable savings over standard dial rates for international calls, while many private telephone centres offer internet phone possibilities.

Mobile phones use the GSM system like most of the world except Japan and North America. Getting a local pre-paid SIM card is generally painless and inexpensive. Belgian providers **Proximus** (www.proximus.be), **Mobistar** (www.mobistar.be) and **Base** (www.base.be) each have their pros and cons. In Luxembourg choose between **Tango** (www.tango.lu), **LuxGSM** (www.luxgsm.lu) and **Vox** (www.vox.lu).

Faxes can be sent and received from most private phone-internet shops.

TIME

Both countries run on Central European Time. Clocks move forward one hour for daylight-saving time between the last Sunday in March and the last Sunday in October. The 24-hour clock is used.

TOILETS

Public toilets in Belgium and Luxembourg are few and far between and generally charge fees of €0.30 to €0.50. It's common to use the facilities in fast-food restaurants or cafes though it's obviously polite to buy something while you're there.

TOURIST INFORMATION

Almost every town and village has its own tourist office. Whether called *dienst voor toerisme* or *toeristische dienst* (in Flanders), *maison du tourisme, office du tourisme* or *syndicat d'initiative* (in Wallonia and Luxembourg), all use the easily identifiable white-on-green 'i' symbol. Tourist offices can provide sheaves of brochures, sell detailed walking/cycling maps and can usually book accommodation and arrange guided tours on your behalf.

The following umbrella organisations publish vast numbers of free themed brochures on their regions.

Toerisme Vlaanderen (www.visitflanders.com) Flanders.
Office de Promotion du Tourisme (OPT; www.belgique-tourisme.net) Wallonia.

Brussels International (www.brusselsinternational.be; p76) Brussels.
Luxembourg National Tourist Office (www.ont.lu; p265) Luxembourg.

Belgian Tourist Offices Abroad

Belgium has tourist offices in the following countries, most with separate offices for Flanders and Wallonia:
Canada (Office du Tourisme Wallonie-Bruxelles; ☎ 418-692 4939; www.belgique-tourisme.qc.ca; bureau 525, 43 Rue de Buade, Québec, Québec G1R 4A2)
France Flanders (Flandre Belgique; ☎ 01 56 89 14 42; www.tourismebelgique.com; 6 Rue Euler, F-75008 Paris); Wallonia (Office Belge du Tourisme Wallonie-Bruxelles; ☎ 01 53 85 05 20; www.belgique-tourisme.be; Blvd St-Germain 274, F-75007 Paris)
Germany (Belgien Tourismus Wallonie-Brüssel; ☎ 0221-277 590; www.belgien-tourismus.de; Cäcilienstrasse 46, D-50667 Köln)
Netherlands Flanders (www.toerismevlaanderen.nl); Wallonia (Belgisch Verkeersbureau Wallonië & Brussel; ☎ 023-534 4434; www.belgie-toerisme.be; Postbus 2324, NL-2002 CH Haarlem)
UK Flanders (Tourism Flanders-Brussels; ☎ 020-730 777 38; www.visitflanders.co.uk; 1a Cavendish Sq, London W1G 0LD); Wallonia (Belgian Tourist Office Brussels-Wallonia; ☎ 020-7531 0390; www.belgiumtheplaceto.be; 217 Marsh Wall, London E14 9FJ) To order brochures call ☎ 0800-95 45 245.
USA (Belgian Tourist Office; ☎ 0212-758 8130; www.visitbelgium.com; 220 East 42nd St, Suite 3402, New York, NY 10017)

Luxembourg Tourist Offices Abroad

The Luxembourg National Tourist Office has offices in the following countries:
Belgium (Map p86; ☎ 02-737 5600; Ave de Cortenbergh 75, Brussels; ☼ 9am-5pm Mon-Fri)
UK (☎ 020-7434 2800; www.luxembourg.co.uk; Sicilian House, Sicilian Ave, London WC1A 2QR)
USA (☎ 212-935 88 88; www.visitluxembourg.com; 17 Beekman Pl, New York, NY 10022)

TRAVELLERS WITH DISABILITIES

A 2000 law obliges architects to ensure that new buildings, including hotels and shops, are built in a 'disabled-friendly' way. Slowly increasing numbers of public buildings are thus sprouting lifts and/or ramps, but with numerous buildings that are centuries old, such additions are not always easy to incorporate. Out on the street, wheelchair users must often contend with uneven cobblestones, rough pavements and steep kerbs. Access to metro and train stations often involves steps or escalators, though the transport companies are slowly providing better disabled access, notably to newer Brussels trams and Flanders buses.

In all cities and many big towns, larger hotels can usually accommodate travellers in wheelchairs as can official HI hostels in Brussels, Antwerp, Bruges, Namur, Tongeren and Tournai.

Limited attempts have been made to assist the visually impaired with Braille plaques, though these tend to be poorly maintained so the text becomes illegible after a year or two. Some arts outfits run special tours for the visually impaired, eg Antwerp's KMSKA (p179) on the last Wednesday of each month (book ahead).

Some useful organisations:

Accessible Travel Info Point (Map p/0; ☎ high-toll 070-233 050; www.accessinfo.be; Rue du Marché aux Herbes 61, Brussels) Information for Flanders.

Adapth (☎ 43 95 58 1; www.adapth.lu) Keeps a comprehensive French-language database relating to disability issues in Luxembourg.

Info-Handicap (☎ 36 64 66 1; www.welcome.lu; 65 Ave de la Gare, Luxembourg City) Publishes *Guide du Handicap*, listing useful services and organisations.

Mobility International (www.miusa.org)

Taxi Hendriks (☎ 02-752 9800) Brussels' taxi company specialising in minibus services for disabled people. Book a few days in advance.

VISAS

Belgium and Luxembourg have no special entry requirements for EU, EEA or Swiss citizens. Citizens of Australia, Canada, Israel, Japan, New Zealand and the USA do not need visas for tourist visits of less than three months. Other nationals must have a visa. Check details on Ministry of Foreign Affairs websites of Belgium (www.diplomatie.be) or Luxembourg (www.mae.lu) and start well ahead – as with any Schengen-area visa, processing requires considerable preparation and paperwork. Fees vary by nationality.

WOMEN TRAVELLERS

Today women are prominent in politics and society but Belgium's strong Catholic background once kept women's issues on the back burner and attitudes considered sexist in the UK are still generally shrugged off as unremarkable here. Abortion was only legalised in Belgium in 1990, causing a national drama as the pious King Baudouin temporarily stood down rather than sign the law.

Solo women should encounter few problems while travelling in either Belgium or Luxembourg though the usual warnings apply. It's advisable not to wander alone late at night, especially in the rather seedy red-light districts that are usually near train stations such as at Brussels-North and Mons.

Useful emergency contacts:

Helpline (☎ 02-648 4014) Twenty-four-hour help- and crisis-line based in Brussels.

SOS Viol (☎ 02-534 3636) Rape crisis-line in Brussels.

Waisse Rank (☎ 40 20 40) Women's crisis organisation in Luxembourg City.

Transport

This chapter gives the nuts and bolts about getting to and around Belgium and Luxembourg. Flights and some rail tickets can be booked online through www.lonelyplanet.com/bookings.

GETTING THERE & AWAY

Given you have suitable identification/passport and necessary paperwork (p295), there are no special annoyances entering or travelling around Belgium or Luxembourg.

AIR

Useful Airports

In this age of internet bargains, finding the cheapest route to Belgium and Luxembourg involves researching an incredible matrix of possibilities. While Brussels and Charleroi airports are pretty well connected and Luxembourg has its own airport, it can sometimes save time and/or money to use regional airports or those in France, Germany or the Netherlands, many of which are well linked to Belgium and/or Luxembourg by high-speed train or bus. However, beware that the cheapest high-speed train fares are unchangeable –

THINGS CHANGE...

The information in this chapter is particularly vulnerable to change and our suggestions should be regarded as pointers, not a substitute for your own careful, up-to-date research.

---

a major headache if your plane arrives late. Note that 'flights' sold by KLM ex-Antwerp or by Air France ex-Brussels start with a train ride not an aeroplane so don't mistakenly turn up at the respective Belgian airport or you'll blow your connections. Websites generally give up-to-date listings of the airlines that operate from each airport.

Amsterdam Schiphol (AMS; www.schiphol.nl) A major European air hub, with direct high-speed train links to Antwerp (1¾ hours) and Brussels (2½ hours).

Antwerp (ANR; www.antwerpairport.be) Limited flights but CityJet/VLM connects to London and Manchester.

Brussels (BRU; www.brusselsairport.be) Belgium's main international airport (see p110). Well connected to Europe and Africa, plus some direct flights to North America and Asia.

Charleroi 'Brussels-South' (CRL; www.charleroi-airport.com p222) Belgium's main hub for low-cost Wizzair (http://wizzair.com) and Ryanair (www.ryanair.com) is 55km south of Brussels near Charleroi.

Frankfurt Airport (FRA; www.frankfurt-airport.de) Germany's main air hub now has direct high-speed ICE train links to Brussels (advance/last-minute booking €39/103, three hours) via Liège (€39/90, two hours).

Frankfurt Hahn Airport (HHN; www.hahn-airport.de) A Ryanair budget-airline hub, linked by hourly airport buses to Luxembourg City (www.flibco.com; advance/last-minute booking €5/17, two hours).

Köln-Bonn Airport (CGN; www.koeln-bonn-airport.de) Low-cost connections across Europe with Air Berlin (www.airberlin.com) and Germanwings (www.germanwings.com). It's a short train-ride from Cologne (Koeln-HBF) where there are high-speed rail links to Liège-Guillemins (€15 to €33, 65 minutes) and Bruxelles-Midi (€15 to €46, 2¼ hours).

Liège (LGG; www.liegeairport.com) and **Ostend** (OST; www.ost.aero) Major cargo hubs but passenger services are mostly limited to charters on Thomas Cook Airlines (www.thomascookairlines.com) and Jetairfly (www.jetairfly.com).

Luxembourg (LUX; www.lux-airport.lu, www.aeroport.public.lu) Luxembourg's international airport.

Paris-Charles de Gaulle (CDG; www.aeroportsdeparis.fr) Linked to Bruxelles-Midi by TGV high-speed train (€25-71, 98 minutes) but **Paris-Orly** (ORY) is contrastingly awkward to reach, with no direct public transport from Belgium.

Airlines
BRUSSELS

Airlines flying into Brussels:

airBaltic (BT; www.airbaltic.com) Connections to Scandinavian, Baltic and ex-Soviet destinations via Riga (Latvia).

CLIMATE CHANGE & TRAVEL

Climate change is a serious threat to the ecosystems that humans rely upon, and air travel is the fastest-growing contributor to the problem. Lonely Planet regards travel, overall, as a global benefit, but believes we all have a responsibility to limit our personal impact on global warming.

Flying & Climate Change

Pretty much every form of motor travel generates carbon dioxide (the main cause of human-induced climate change) but planes are far and away the worst offenders, not just because of the sheer distances they allow us to travel, but because they release greenhouse gases high into the atmosphere. The statistics are frightening: two people taking a return flight between Europe and the US will contribute as much to climate change as an average household's gas and electricity consumption over a whole year.

Carbon Offset Schemes

Climatecare.org and other websites use 'carbon calculators' that allow jetsetters to offset the greenhouse gases they are responsible for with contributions to energy-saving projects and other climate-friendly initiatives in the developing world – including projects in India, Honduras, Kazakhstan and Uganda.

Lonely Planet, together with Rough Guides and other concerned partners in the travel industry, supports the carbon offset scheme run by climatecare.org. Lonely Planet offsets all of its staff and author travel.

For more information check out our website: lonelyplanet.com.

Air Lingus Air Transat (AC; www.aircanada.ca) Canada via Toronto or Montreal.
American Airlines (AA; www.aa.com)
BMI (BD; www.flybmi.com) British destinations.
British Airways (BA; www.britishairways.com) World destinations via Heathrow
Brussels Airlines (SN; www.brusselsairlines.com) The biggest Belgian carrier.
CityJet (WX/VG; www.cityjet.com) Flights from Antwerp.
Continental Airlines (CO; www.continental.com) North America via Newark.
Easyjet (U2; www.easyjet.com) Budget flights to Berlin, Geneva, Lyon, Milan and Nice.
Ethiopian Airlines (ET; www.ethiopianairlines.com)
Hainan Airlines (HU; http://global.hnair.com) Direct flights to China.
Etihad (EY; www.etihadairways.com) Asia and Australia via Abu Dhabi.
FlyBe (BE; www.flybe.com) Various smaller British airports via Southampton or Manchester.
Jet Airways (9W; www.jetairways.com) Direct links to North America and India, indirect connections to much of Asia.
KLM (KL; www.klm.be) Global connections via Amsterdam.
Lufthansa (LH; www.lufthansa.be) Global connections via Frankfurt or Munich.
Turkish Airlines (TK; www.thy.com) Many Asian and Middle Eastern destinations via Istanbul.
United Airlines (UA; www.unitedairlines.be)

LUXEMBOURG

Airlines flying into Luxembourg:
British Airways (BA; www.britishairways.com)
Iceland Express (5W; www.icelandexpress.com) Keflavik with connections to New York.
KLM (KL; www.klm.lu)
Lufthansa (LH; www.lufthansa.lu)
Luxair (LG; ☎ 24 56 42 42; www.luxair.lu) Luxembourg's national carrier. Flies to European destinations including Barcelona, Berlin, Dublin, Geneva, Rome and Paris.
SAS Scandinavian Airlines (SK; www.flysas.com)
Swiss International Air Lines (LX; www.swiss.com)
TAP Portugal (TP; www.flytap.be)

Tickets

Most airlines websites and all no-frills carriers now sell their own tickets online but sometimes you can get better deals through online booking agencies or specialist travel agents. **Kayak** (www.kayak.com) is a great fare-comparison tool. Sign up to get date-flexible options and email alerts of price fluctuation graphs over time.

Some other addresses to try:
Airstop (www.airstop.be) Belgium.
Air Brokers International (www.airbrokers.com) USA, round-the-world.
Cheap Tickets (www.cheaptickets.com)
Connections (www.connections.be) Belgium.
Ebookers (www.ebookers.com)

TRANSPORT

Expedia (www.expedia.ca, www.expedia.com, www
.expedia.fr)
JustFares (www.justfares.com) USA.
My Travel (www.mytravel.com) UK.
Orbitz (www.orbitz.com)
STA Travel (www.statravel.com, www.statravel.co.uk)
Trailfinders (www.trailfinders.co.uk) UK.
Travel (www.travel.com.au) Australia.
Travel CUTS (www.travelcuts.com) Canada.
Travelocity (www.travelocity.ca) Canada.
Webjet (www.webjet.com.au) Australia.

Australia, New Zealand & Asia

Many routings involve transferring via a
European hub (London, Paris, Amsterdam or
Frankfurt) though very good alternatives from
Brussels include Etihad via Abu Dhabi or Jet
Airways via Delhi, Chennai or Mumbai.

Europe

When juggling to find the best fares, be very
careful to double-check the small print. Some
budget airlines charge hefty extra fees for
baggage and Ryanair even charges supplements to those who fail to check in online.
It's always worth comparing flights with
mainstream airlines, especially if a slightly
higher fare saves you a long trek to a distant
airport. Don't forget to compare with trains
too if you're coming from neighbouring
countries. Be aware that high-speed train
fares, just like air tickets, are often inflexible
and tend to get more expensive the later you
leave the bookings.

UK & IRELAND
Flight possibilities to/from Brussels:
- Bristol on Brussels Airlines
- Dublin on Air Lingus
- East Midlands on BMI
- Edinburgh on BMI
- Leeds-Bradford on BMI
- London Gatwick on Brussels Airlines
- London Heathrow on BMI or British
  Airways
- Manchester on Brussels Airlines or
  FlyBe
- Southampton on FlyBe
- Newcastle on Brussels Airlines

To/from Luxembourg City:
- Dublin on Luxair
- London City on Luxair
- London Gatwick on British Airways

Budget airline Ryanair flies to Dublin,
Edinburgh, Prestwick and Shannon from
Charleroi (p222) and to Dublin, Edinburgh, and
London-Stansted from Frankfurt-Hahn (two
hours' bus-ride from Luxembourg City).
   CityJet flies to London City and Manchester
from Antwerp. Connections are possible
to Jersey.

USA, Canada & Mexico
North American destinations served directly
from Brussels:
- JFK and Chicago on American
- JFK and Atlanta on Delta
- JFK and Toronto on Jet Airways
- Montreal on Air Transat
- Newark on Continental
- Washington-Dulles on United
- Cancun, Mexico on Jetairfly charters

Alternatively consider flights via Amsterdam,
London, Frankfurt or Paris CDG (on Air
France starting with a train ride from Bruxelles-
Midi that's included in the ticket price).
   From Luxembourg, budget airline Iceland
Express offers competitive fares on advance
purchase tickets to JFK via Keflavik.

LAND
Belgium and Luxembourg are connected to
neighbouring countries by excellent toll-free
motorways, international buses and trains
both high speed (prebooking compulsory) and
'ordinary' (pay-and-go but seats not assured).
If approaching from the southeast by vehicle
fill your petrol tank in Luxembourg, where
fuel prices are among the lowest in Western
Europe. Except in exceptional circumstances
there are no border controls at crossings into
or between Belgium and Luxembourg.

France
BUS
From Paris, **Eurolines** (☎ France 0892-899 091; www.
eurolines.fr) coaches depart from the Gallieni bus
station (eastern terminus of metro line 3). They
run up to 12 times daily to Bruxelles-Nord (€13
to €26, four hours) via Mons or Gent (or 3¼
hours direct) plus six times daily to Antwerp (€15
to €28, 4¾ to 5½ hours). Several weekly overnight buses run seasonally from major Belgian
cities to Bayonne, Chamonix, Limoges, Lyon,
Marseille, Nantes, Perpignan, Toulouse and
many more French destinations. See www.euro
lines.be.

INTERNATIONAL BUSES

Eurolines (www.eurolines.eu) is a Europe-wide consortium of coach operators whose nonsmoking buses are fairly comfortable with reclining seats, air-conditioning and on-board toilets. Tickets must be pre-purchased, not paid aboard. Numerous European destinations are served at least weekly (often daily) from Brussels and Antwerp with many routes also allowing pick-ups in Ghent, Liege, Bruges, Mons and/or Luxembourg though some of these destinations have no ticket office, meaning that you'll need to prebook through a different office. Fares vary enormously (eg Brussels–Prague €9 to €57) but are generally cheapest booked online at least two months ahead, when you'll save the €3 booking fee. Those under 26 or over 60 save 10%, kids under 12 save 50%. Save 25% more on certain routes by purchasing a discount card. Several passes allow jump-on jump-off travel at will but seats are according to availability. Note that while Eurolines has services to Luxembourg, they have no Luxembourg office so you'll have to have prebooked a return or call the Brussels sales office for a phone booking.

Most other international buses are operated by Eastern European and North African companies and are primarily aimed at citizens of those countries. For Morocco most ticket offices and departure points in Brussels are around Metro Lemonier on Ave de Stalingrad. Eastern European buses typically start from Rue Cardinal Mercier beside Brussels' Gare Central, eg **Eurobus** (☎ 02-527 5012; www.eurobus.pl, in Polish; Rue de la Montagne, Brussels; ⏰ 9am-6pm), which operates daily via Antwerp to Katowice (€80, 17 hours) with numerous onward connections across Poland and beyond. **AtlasSib** (www.atlassib.be) runs weekly to Romania.

TRAIN

Hourly **Thalys** (www.thalys.com) high-speed trains (p300) link Paris-Nord via Lille (Rijsel in Dutch) to Bruxelles-Midi (1½ hours). Tickets cost €86 full fare but as little as €29 booked well ahead online. Several daily services continue to both Antwerp (125 minutes) and Liège (2½ hours).

Eight daily **TGV** (www.sncf.com) services from Bruxelles-Midi run to Roissy Charles de Gaule (a Paris Airport) and on to Marne-la-Vallée (for Eurodisney, 1¾ hours) but not to central Paris. At least one such TGV continues to each of the following French destinations: Avignon (4½ hours), Bordeaux (5½ hours), Cannes (seven hours), Carcasonne (7½ hours), Lyon (four hours), Marseilles (five hours), Nice (7½ hours), Perpignan (7½ hours), Poitiers (3¾ hours) and Toulouse (8¼ hours). Several daily TGVs link Paris-Est directly to Luxembourg City (€70, 2¼ hours). Alternatively change in Metz.

Only pre-reserved high-speed trains link Belgium and Paris directly. If you can't get a seat it's possible to travel unreserved on 'ordinary' trains as far as Lille. Lille-bound services run hourly from Kortrijk and Tournai, several times daily from Antwerp (via Ghent) and Herstal (via Liege and Mons). However, once you reach Lille, you'll still need a reserved seat to take the TGV to Paris. A tedious but completely unreserved route if you're desperate would be the eight weekday trains from Charleroi to Jeumont, then from Jeumont head for Paris-Nord (€31.20, 2¼ hours) connecting at either Aulnoye-Aymeries or Mauberge.

One daily Swiss-railways train links the three 'Euro cities' Brussels, Luxembourg and Strasbourg, then continues to Basel and Chur.

Germany

BUS

Deutsche Touring/Eurolines (☎ Frankfurt 069 790 350; www.touring.de) has buses from several German cities to Brussels via Antwerp or Liege. Overnight options include the daily Berlin–Hannover–Antwerp–Brussels service (11 hours, daily) and twice weekly Munich–Frankfurt–Brussels (13½ hours).

From Frankfurt-Hahn airport to Luxembourg City **Flibco** (www.flibco.com) buses run ten times daily (one-way €17, 1¾ hours).

TRAIN

Deutsche Bahn (www.bahn.de) operates the German railway system. Competition between Thalys and Deutsche Bahn's ICE trains can result in bargain fares on the Cologne–Liège–Brussels route (2¼ hours). Compare fares on www.b-rail.be. Annoyingly, however, return fairs limit you to one or other company.

To Luxembourg City, DB trains run from Trier (€8, 50 minutes) and Koblenz (€32, 2¼ hours). Frankfurt–Luxembourg (four hours)

HIGH-SPEED TRAINS

High-speed, limited-stop international trains operate on several key routes. They aren't operated by NMBS/SNCB so rail passes give only partial discounts and reservations are compulsory. Tickets are sold at a few major Belgian railway stations, company websites and www.b-rail.be. Massive discounts are usually available if you book an unchangeable/non-refundable return trip well in advance (but not more than three months ahead). Travellers aged 12 to 26 get a 50% discount and seniors a 30% reduction but only on full-price fares.

High-speed operators:

Thalys (www.thalys.com; ☎ Belgium 070-667 788; France 0892-353 536; Germany 01805-215 000; Netherlands 0900-9296) Main routes Brussels–Liege–Aachen–Cologne (6 daily), Paris–Brussels–Antwerp–The Hague–Rotterdam–Schiphol–Amsterdam. July and August, weekend-only trips include Antwerp–Brussels–Valence–Avignon and Antwerp–Brussels–Marseilles (5¾ hours).

Eurostar (www.eurostar.com) Brussels–Lille–London, several times daily

ICE (www.db.be) Brussels–Liège–Aachen–Cologne–Frankfurt (3¼ hours, three daily) via Frankfurt airport (three hours)

TGV (www.sncf.com) Various French routes but not central Paris

changing in Koblenz costs €59.40/49.50/19 full/discount/IC-bargain.

Netherlands

BUS
Eurolines (☎ 020-560 8788; www.eurolines.nl) operates daily buses from various Dutch cities to destinations in Belgium and Luxembourg. Fares vary substantially according to season, advance booking and offers. Sample destinations from Amsterdam include Antwerp (2½ hours, six daily), Brussels (3½ hours, six daily), Bruges (4¾ hours, three daily) and Luxembourg City (8½ hours, daily).

TRAIN
From Amsterdam, Thalys trains run five times daily to Brussels (advance-purchase/full-fare €19/51, 161 minutes) via Schiphol Airport, The Hague, Rotterdam and Antwerp (€19/45, two hours). There are also hourly 'standard' IC trains (€30.20/36.60, 126/168 minutes to Antwerp/Brussels), also stopping at Mechelen and Bruxelles-Central; no reservations are required and railcards are valid but that can mean standing-room only. Expect everything to change once the FYRA (www.fyra.com) high-speed express starts running Brussels–Amsterdam in just 1¾ hours from around 2011.

BOAT
Viking (www.vikingrivercruises.com) and **AMA** (www.amawaterways.com) do 10-day spring riverboat packages cruising Amsterdam to Bruges and back via Ghent and Antwerp.

UK

BUS
Eurolines (www.eurolines.be ex-Belgium, www.eurolines.co.uk ex-UK) connects various Belgian destinations to/from London's Victoria coach station, including Bruxelles-Nord (four daily) and Antwerp (three daily). Both take 8½ to 10 hours according to channel crossing method and cost £19/€21 to £40/€45 one-way depending on demand and available promotions.

CAR, MOTORCYCLE & FERRY
There are three direct Belgium to UK car-ferry services but most drivers link the countries via the French ports of Calais or Dunkerque (Dunkirk) – these are both less than an hour's motorway-drive west of Ostend. Fares and schedules vary enor-

---

TRAIN OR PLANE FROM THE UK?

The answer obviously depends on your exact departure and arrival points. But from central London to central Brussels, Eurostar trains (see opposite; just under two hours from London-St Pancras to Bruxelles-Midi) will generally beat flying (50 minutes) as check-in time is only half an hour for the train, there's no wait for baggage reclaim, and the stations are more central than the airports – very significantly so if you're using Stansted or misleadingly named 'Brussels South', which is actually 55km south of Brussels near Charleroi.

mously according to seasonal demand. It's best to check the websites and play around with return dates.

Useful contacts:

Eurotunnel (☎ Belgium 070-223 210, UK 08705-353 535; www.eurotunnel.com) Drive-on transporter trains take vehicles (fare usually includes up to five passengers) through the Channel Tunnel between Folkestone and Calais. Departures up to four times hourly. The journey takes 35 minutes but check-in takes around 30 minutes more.

Norfolk Line (www.norfolkline.com/ferry) Thrice-weekly sailings from Zeebrugge (p152) to Rosyth, near Edinburgh, Scotland (☎ UK 0208-127 8303; 20 hours) and several daily crossings Dunkerque–Dover (☎ UK 0208 127 8303).

P&O (☎ Belgium high toll 070-700 774, UK 0871-645 645; www.poferries.com) Regular Dover–Calais ferries plus overnight sailings Hull–Zeebrugge (14 hours, p152).

TransEuropa Ferries (☎ Belgium 059-340 260, UK 01843-595 522; www.transeuropaferries.com) Thrice-daily ferries Ostend–Ramsgate (four hours). One-way fares for cars/motorbikes are €35/53 in winter, €63/85 midsummer, passengers included. No pedestrians carried.

TRAIN

High-speed passenger trains between London-St Pancras and Bruxelles-Midi are operated by **Eurostar** (www.eurostar.com) up to ten times daily (two hours). Reservations are compulsory and full-fare standard/first-class costs £179/260 but vast discounts are available for fixed-departure tickets, especially those booked months ahead (from €51/124 one-way, £59/175 return). Eurostar tickets usually include free travel to/from any Belgian train station so long as you connect without undue delay. Booking is possible online, from major stations and within Belgium via www.b-rail.be (tickets by post). There are further discounts for youths, seniors and children (four to 11 years travelling with an adult). Under fours travel free.

GETTING AROUND

BICYCLE

Bicycles can easily be hired in many cities and at the Belgian railway stations listed on www.b-rail.be/nat/E/common/renting stations/index.php or www.fietspunten.be. Taking a bicycle on a Belgian train adds €5 to the one-way fare, or €8 for one day's travel nationwide. For more on cycling in both countries, see p287. Bike helmets are

not a legal requirement for cyclists and are generally ignored by adults. The Belgian website www.veloroutes.be offers download-able route suggestions (in local languages) for numerous cycle-friendly routes organised by region.

BOAT

A wide range of summer river and canal tour-rides are available through **RiverTours** (www.rivertours.be) and **Brussels By Water** (www .brusselsbywater.be) while various boat excursions are possible from Ostend and especially Nieuwpoort (p153). See p154 for fun-rides in an amphibious DUKW. In Luxembourg, **Navitours** (www.navitours.lu) offers pleasure cruises on the Moselle from Remich.

BUS

Bus transportation is generally organised to complement the efficient rail network (p305). The helpful Belgian Railways website www.b -rail.be also gives useful bus suggestions where that's the logical choice for your route. For Luxembourg, comprehensive bus timetables are available on www.sales-lentz.lu/mob ilitaetswelt/horaires.

Bus services are generally most frequent on school-days, less so on Saturdays. On Sundays services are scant to non-existent on some routes. Also be aware that rural journeys are often slow and circuitous in order to visit villages en route.

Flanders' bus and tram networks are operated by **De Lijn** (☎ high toll 070-220 200; www.delijn.be), whose tickets are slightly cheaper when pre-purchased from a supermarket, newsagency or De Lijn information/ticket kiosk. A €12 pass allows three days' bus travel anywhere in Flanders. Rural 'Belbus' routes operate only by phoning a booking to the local bus station.

In Wallonia, **TEC** (☎ 081-321 711; www.infotec .be) buses charge between €1.30 and €3.50 according to the number of zones travelled or €6.50 for all-day travel. To save around 15% on single fares get a 'Carte Inter', which has stored-value credit (minimum €6). 'Telbus' rural routes only operate if booked a day ahead on ☎ 061-53 1010.

For Luxembourg's single-fare bus-rail ticketing system see p305.

CAR & MOTORCYCLE

Belgium's motorway system is extensive, toll-free and mostly illuminated at night – an

TRANSPORT

TRANSPORT

expensive source of national pride though one that's under threat from budget cuts in 2010. Locals tend to flout the motorway speed limit (120km/h, ie 10km/h lower than neighbouring France) and while radar speed-traps exist, local radio stations merrily report their locations to help save drivers the inconvenience of getting ticketed. Speed drops dramatically at rush hours, when traffic often grinds to a halt on the ring roads around Brussels and Antwerp. The E40 to the coast is usually crammed with beach-goers on sunny weekends. Some minor roads are cobbled and uneven, others seemingly under almost constant repair resulting in a frustrating plethora of diversions (marked quite unsatisfactorily by bright orange signs). Roads in Luxembourg are contrastingly excellent, surprisingly so considering the topography's constant undulations.

The aggressive Belgian driving style can take a little getting used to. Although required to by law, Belgian drivers rarely stop at pedestrian crossings: pedestrians beware! And boozy locals are frighteningly blasé about getting behind the wheel while quite patently hammered, resulting not unpredictably, in a statistically high level of crashes by European standards. Drivers in Luxembourg seem somewhat less pugnacious.

Signs
Outside bilingual Brussels, place names can cause considerable confusion. Some towns have entirely different names in Dutch and French so, for example, driving to Mons from Kortrijk you'll need to follow signs to 'Bergen' until you cross into Wallonia. Returning, follow 'Courtrai' until reaching Flanders! Even certain cities in neighbouring countries have French and Dutch variants. See the boxed list, below. Although there's a similar variation between place names in Luxembourg, the familiar French form is usually signed rather than the Letzeburgesch variant.

Automobile Associations
Foreign visitors belonging to their country's automobile club might receive free membership. Nonmembers will pay call-out fees.
Automobile Club de Luxembourg (☎ 45 00 45-1, 24hr roadside assistance 42 60 00; www.acl.lu) Luxembourg's motoring club.
Touring (Map pp68–9; ☎ 02-233 2211, 24hr assistance 070-344 777 toll-call; www.touring.be; Rue de la Loi 44, Brussels) Belgium's biggest motoring club.

ALTERNATIVE PLACE NAMES
Frequently, road signs in Belgium give only the Dutch or French rendering of town names. Some key ones to be aware of:

English	Dutch	French
Aachen* (D)	Aken	Aix-la-Chapelle
Antwerp	Antwerpen*	Anvers
Bruges	Brugge*	Bruges
Brussels	Brussel*	Bruxelles*
Courtrai	Kortrijk*	Courtrai
Jodoigne	Geldenaken	Jodoigne*
Köln*/Cologne (D)	Keulen	Cologne
Leuven/Louvain	Leuven*	Louvain
Lille (France)	Rijsel	Lille*
Mechelen/Mechlin	Mechelen*	Malines
Namur	Namen	Namur*
Nivelles	Nijvel	Nivelles*
Mons	Bergen	Mons*
Paris (France)	Parijs	Paris*
Roeselare	Roeselare	Roulers
The Hague (N)	Den Haag*	La Haye
Tournai	Doornik	Tournai*
Trier* (D)	Trier	Trèves
Veurne	Veurne*	Furnes
Ypres	Ieper*	Ypres

*=name as used locally, (D)=Germany, (N)=Netherlands

ROAD DISTANCES (KM)

	Antwerp	Bouillon	Bruges	Brussels	Ghent	Hasselt	Kortrijk	La Roche	Liège	Luxembourg City	Mechelen	Mons	Namur	Ostend	Tournai
Bouillon	202														
Bruges	113	270													
Brussels	47	155	115												
Ghent	58	115	55	60											
Hasselt	75	160	188	80	133										
Kortrijk	106	240	44	92	48	172									
La Roche	175	67	243	113	188	110	213								
Liège	115	105	205	90	173	40	182	70							
Luxembourg City	262	107	330	200	275	200	300	108	140						
Mechelen	24	180	123	25	68	81	116	138	110	225					
Mons	112	170	114	65	92	145	70	143	140	230	88				
Namur	112	90	180	65	125	70	150	63	60	150	90	80			
Ostend	138	295	25	140	80	220	59	253	230	355	148	129	205		
Tournai	131	215	69	75	73	155	25	188	185	275	141	45	125	84	
Ypres	134	268	57	120	76	200	28	241	210	328	144	98	178	45	53

VAB (☎ 24hr assistance 070-344 777 toll-call; www.vab .be) Flanders' motoring association.

Bring Your Own Vehicle

If you're driving your own car into Belgium and Luxembourg, in addition to your passport and driving licence, you must carry vehicle registration (proof of ownership) and insurance documents (see p304). All cars should also carry a first-aid kit, warning triangle and reflective jacket. A fire extinguisher should be accessible to the driver (not just in the boot).

Driving Licence

Be aware that if you're under 18 you can't drive legally in Belgium even if you have a valid licence in your home country. Otherwise, visitors from EU countries can use their home licences while non-EU citizens officially need an International Driving Permit to drive in Belgium or Luxembourg. These are usually issued effortlessly by the motoring association in your home country for a small fee (one photo required) on the presentation of your ID and valid licence. International Driving Permits are typically valid for one year. Note that by 2012 a planned new Europe-wide system of drivers licences might change the rules.

Fuel

For now diesel is around €0.30 per litre cheaper than petrol in Belgium though new taxes proposed for 2010 might level the prices. Note that diesel is *diesel* in Belgian French, not *gazole* as in France. *Mazout* is cheaper diesel used for domestic heating and also the nickname for a beer-and-cola shandy but it's illegal to use for powering your vehicle.

At night and on Sundays most petrol stations look closed but will still dispense fuel using pin-coded credit/debit-card readers.

Luxembourg's fuel prices are among the lowest in Western Europe. While the gap has closed somewhat in recent years, you'll still pay around €0.20 less per litre than in Belgium (€0.10 for diesel). Luxembourg does well out of 'petrol tourism' despite criticism that it causes unnecessary CO_2 emissions, and the Luxembourg tourist office even bothers to advertise the current prices (www.luxembourg.co.uk/faq.html#petrol).

TRANSPORT

Car Hire

Renting a car is pretty pointless if you simply want to visit Bruges, Ghent, Antwerp and Brussels: you'll spend more time finding parking than actually driving anywhere. However, in rural Belgium having a car will transform your experience as many of the country villages, moated castles and rural cave-sites are infuriatingly awkward to reach by public transport.

For renting, foreign drivers will need to show their passport or ID card as well as their driving licence, and a credit card. Most rental companies require drivers to be aged 23 or over and to have been driving for at least one year. Generally car rentals allow you to visit any of the other Benelux countries without insurance worries but check conditions.

The usual tips apply: check whether insurance, collision-damage waiver, liability insurance and unlimited kilometres are included. If they're not double-check what costs you might be liable for. Remember that weekly rental rates are generally vastly better value than rates of one or two days and that there's often a hefty surcharge when renting from airports or stations.

You'll generally save money by organising rental reservations at least a few days in advance. When shopping for good prices, there are several tricks, including quoting frequent flyer memberships and pre-emptively signing up to car rental email listings for bargain offers and member discounts. With multinational rental companies you can sometimes find surprisingly significant differences between prices quoted on various sub websites (eg xxxx.com, xxxx.co.uk, xxxx.be), so try a few if you're mathematically adroit enough to juggle the matrix of currencies, different mileage conditions and insurance variations.

Some rental companies:

Avis (www.avis.be) 21 Belgian locations.

Budget (www.budget.be, www.budget.lu) 15 Belgo-Luxembourg locations.

Europcar (www.europcar.com/car-BELGIUM.html) 28 Belgian locations.

Hertz (www.hertz.be)

Sixt (www.sixt.com/car-rental/belgium)

CAMBIO

Cambio (www.cambio.be; membership from €33 plus €4 per month, deposit €150) is a car-share system designed for folks that need occasional short-duration hires (for longer usage, car hire is usually cheaper). Cambio cars are parked all over Belgium. Members book usage online, open the car with their member's smart card and are debited around €0.33 per km plus €2 per hour for usage, petrol included. Two years previous driving experience is required.

LEASING

Visitors who are not EU residents but plan to drive for more than three weeks in Europe should investigate car-leasing programs such as **Peugeot Eurolease** (www.eurolease.com.au, www.eurolease.co.nz) and **Renault Eurodrive** (www.renault-eurodrive.com). These leases generally provide you with a new car, unlimited kilometres and insured freedom to visit most countries of Western and Central Europe, but most assume you'll start in France and may charge a supplement for pick-up/drop-off in the Benelux. Organise things well in advance.

Insurance

Motor-vehicle insurance with at least third-party cover is compulsory throughout the EU. Your home policy may or may not be extendable to Belgium and Luxembourg; it's a good idea to get a Green Card from your home insurer confirming that you have the correct coverage.

Road Hazards

Most Belgian city centres are devilishly laced with frustratingly complex one-way systems. Trams have priority, and beware of passengers disembarking onto the street. Also, be conscious of cyclists. Although cyclists often have separate bike lanes, the chances of a collision

---

LOOK RIGHT!

One peculiarity that horrifies Anglo visitors and ensures them adrenaline-pumped journeys is the *voorrang van rechts/priorité à droite* (give way to the right) law, applicable in Belgium, Luxembourg and most of continental Europe. By this rule, if a junction is not otherwise marked, cars darting out from right-hand side streets have right of way over vehicles on the main road. The rule is no longer applicable at roundabouts and is suspended anywhere where a major highway is marked with a white-rimmed yellow diamond sign. But in towns it applies all too regularly. So always look right.

increase at intersections when vehicles are turning right and drivers fail to notice that a cyclist has come alongside the car on the cycle path. And remember the 'give way to the right' rule (see the boxed text, opposite.

Road Rules

Standard international road signs are in use but the 'give way to the right' law takes a lot of getting used to (see the boxed text, opposite). Driving is on the right, and the speed limit is 50km/h in built-up areas, 90km/h outside urban centres and 120km/h on motorways (130km/h in Luxembourg). Seat belts are compulsory in the front and rear. The widely flouted blood-alcohol limit is 0.05%, which could mean two strong beers and you're over the limit. That's stricter than in the UK, USA and Ireland, which allow 0.08%.

HITCHING

Hitching is never entirely safe and Lonely Planet doesn't recommend it. Obviously travellers who decide to hitch are taking a small but potentially serious risk. Those who do choose to hitch will be safer travelling in pairs. Remember to let someone know where you are planning to go. It's illegal to hitch on motorways in Belgium and Luxembourg but if you can reach a motorway service area, asking politely for a ride can prove reasonably successful (assuming you're bags aren't too big). The challenge is finding a good starting point: try http://hitchwiki.org/en/Belgium for pointers.

Paid hitches can be organised through **EuroStop** (www.taxistop.be; per 100km €3) and **LuxStop** (www.luxstop.8m.com; per 100km €5) which matches travellers with drivers, mostly for long-distance international rides.

LOCAL TRANSPORT

The major cities in both countries have efficient and reliable bus networks. Trams are also used in some Belgian cities, and Brussels and Antwerp also have metro systems and a *premetro* (trams that run underground for part of their journey). Public transport services generally run until about 11pm or midnight in major cities, or until 9pm or 10pm in towns.

Taxis are metered and tips are not required. While you'll often find taxis waiting outside airports and major train stations, elsewhere you'll usually need to phone for one (ideally an hour or two ahead). Trying to flag down passing cabs is about as hopeless as hitching for submarines. Good luck.

TRAIN

A rail network map is shown on p306. For a more detailed version see http://hari.b-holding.be/Hafas/folders/map_en.htm. Trains in both countries have 1st- and 2nd-class compartments, both completely nonsmoking.

Belgium

In 1835, Belgium's Brussels-Mechelen railway line was the first in continental Europe. There's a copy of the first loco at Vresse-en-Semois (p240), Mechelen's railway yards have their own, rarely open museum (p196) and there are enthusiast-run steam railways starting from Mariembourg (p224).

Today **Belgian Railways** (NMBS/SNCB; ☎ 02-528 2828; www.b-rail.be) has a dense network, especially in Flanders. Station logos, originally designed by art nouveau architect Henri Van de Velde, are a 'B' in an oval.

Seniors (ie those aged over 65, including visitors) pay only €5 for a return 2nd-class trip anywhere in Belgium. Exclusions include weekday trips starting before 9am or weekend

---

BELGIUM'S TOP STATIONS

Train stations can be architectural masterpieces in their own right. Our favourites:

- Liège-Guillemins (p254) – a jaw dropping 21st-century triumph. Take the gratifying opportunity to employ that most indulgent of French adjectives, 'époustouflant'

- Antwerpen-Centraal (p178) – vast, belle époque marvel. Don't miss the buffet

- Binche (p216) – seems rather forgotten but features some delicate wrought ironwork

- Gent-St-Pieters (p128) – romantic historicist murals inside, a stylised castle style turret outside

- Schaerbeek – once grand, now a rather forlorn suburban Brussels stop

- Luxembourg City – sports a tower like a Danish cathedral

Verviers-Central, Veurne and De Panne (Adinkerke) are notable too.

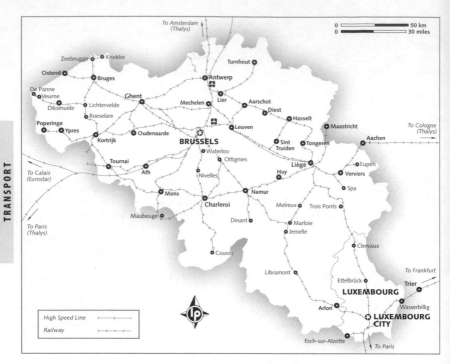

trips during mid-May to mid-September. Children under 12 travel for free when accompanied by an adult, again provided the journey starts after 9am.

If travelling with a pet, the pet needs a €2 ticket unless it's carried in an approved (and closed) basket. Transporting a bicycle adds €5 to a single ticket or pay €8 to take it on any number of train trips during one day. Note that some stations including Bruxelles-Central don't allow bicycle transportation.

Tickets should be prepurchased at ticket offices or machines, though annoyingly most of the latter only accept Belgian-issue debit cards. Unless the station where you alight has no ticketing facilities, buying once aboard will incur a €3 surcharge (if you actively seek out the conductor) or €12.50 (if they think you were trying to cheat). Standard return tickets cost twice a single but there are special discount day-trip options (see right), special weekend-return fares and the following passes:

- **Go Pass/Rail Pass** Allows ten one-way trips anywhere in Belgium (except to/from border stations) and permits transfers en route but not stopovers (ie you're

supposed to take the first feasible connection). Before getting aboard you must write into the space provided the start and end stations plus the date. Valid one year, the pass is not limited to one person

DISCOUNTED DAY TRIPS

Belgian Railways offer discounted packages to certain mainstream destinations, known as B-Dagtrips/B-Excursions in French/Dutch. You get a 2nd-class day-trip rail ticket, selected admission fees and possibly even a complimentary drink. As the total price is typically less than a normal return train ticket, the admission is effectively free. However, only certain destinations and dates apply. Although the full listing is only available in Dutch and French, do try to look up the excursion's code number on www.b-rail.be/php/bexcursions before heading to the ticket office. Otherwise you'll infuriate a queue of waiting commuters while the ticket agent rustles interminably through a brick-thick manual.

so you could, for example, write in the same details four times over and use the ticket for a group of four people. Passes cost €50/73 (2nd class) for those under/over 26 years old.

■ **Key Card** A similar card allowing 10 short-hop rides (typically 15km maximum) for €17. Website http://hari.b-holding .be/infsta/StationDetailSearch.aspx lists exactly which destinations are valid from any chosen starting point station. All of the following would be OK: Antwerp–Lier, Lier–Mechelen, Mechelen–Vilvoorde, Vilvoorde–Brussels, Brussels–Waterloo, Waterloo–Nivelles. As with the Rail Card you must fill in the date, start station and end station for each ride before boarding. However, no transfers are permitted so if you change trains you'll need to fill in a second line on the pass. Valid six months.

Luxembourg

Luxembourg's joint railway-bus network is co-ordinated by **CFL** (☎ 24 89 24 89; www.cfl.lu). There are just two main ticket types, both allowing unlimited travel on any public transport within the country (except to/from border-crossing points). From the time you date-stamp it, a €1.50 *kuurzzäitbilljee* (*billet courte durée*) ticket is valid two hours while a €5 *dagesbilljee* (*billet longue durée*) is valid all day and until 8am the next morning. Prepurchase your ticket at an office or train station or pay a €1.50 supplement once aboard. Upgrading to first class costs just €0.80 extra.

The excellent Luxembourg Card (p266) gives free bus and train travel plus discounted admissions to numerous sights, as explained on p301. Use http://mobiliteitszentral.hafas.de to find the best bus or train connection.

TRANSPORT

Language

CONTENTS

WHAT LINGO WHERE?
Belgium

Belgium's population is split between Dutch-speaking Flanders (*Vlaanderen* in Dutch) in the north, French-speaking Wallonia (*la Wallonie* in French) in the south, and the small German-speaking region, known as the Eastern Cantons, based around the towns of Eupen and St Vith in the east. Brussels is officially bilingual though French has long been the city's dominant language.

You may hear people calling the Dutch spoken in Belgium 'Flemish', thereby underlining the cultural identity of the Flemish people. In reality, grammar and spelling rules of Dutch in Belgium and Dutch in the Netherlands are the same, and 'Flemish', or *Vlaams* as it's known, is not a separate language in itself.

If you spend any time travelling around Belgium, you'll have to get used to switching between Dutch (*Nederlands*) and French (*français*). Flanders in the north is Flemish and therefore Dutch-speaking. Visitors' attempts to speak French here are generally considered culturally insensitive and ill-informed, especially in less tourist-oriented cities such as Leuven and Hasselt. English, on the other hand, is considered neutral and much more acceptable – many Flemish speak English fluently and are very accommodating when it comes to speaking to foreigners. In Brussels, French is the main day-to-day language, so it's fine to speak in French, though English is widely spoken so tourists can get by with English most of the time. In Wallonia far fewer people speak English, and once you get away from major cities or tourist centres you'll need some French to get by. The people in the Eastern Cantons tend to be fluent in both German and French and may also speak some English. If you're unsure of which language group someone comes from, it's probably best to stick to English until you've sussed it out. For more on the underlying tensions between the Dutch- and French-speaking communities in Belgium, see The Linguistic Divide, p36.

Belgium's linguistic divide may cause some confusion, particularly if crossing between Flanders and Wallonia. For example, when driving from Antwerp, the sign you're following to Bergen (the Flemish name) will disappear and Mons (French) will appear – you'll need to know both the Flemish and French names for a city in order to keep up with road signs. The same goes for reading timetables and signboards at train stations. With the exception of Brussels, these are written in the local language only, hence you may start your journey scanning a timetable to 'Courtrai' and end up needing to look out for a station sign displayed 'Kortrijk'. For a list of alternative place names, see p302.

Luxembourg

Luxembourg has three official languages: French, German and Letzeburgesch. Unlike in Belgium, these languages live together harmoniously. Most Luxembourgers are fluent in all three as well as in English, which is widely spoken in the capital and by younger people around the countryside.

Letzeburgesch is most closely related to German and was proclaimed the national tongue in 1984. Luxembourgers speak Letzeburgesch to each other but generally switch to French when talking to foreigners.

The Grand Duke and government ministers address the nation in Letzeburgesch and debates in parliament are usually carried out in the national tongue. However, French is the official language of government announcements, laws, legislation and the judiciary. Street names and road signs tend to be in French and Letzeburgesch, and the press is predominantly in German and French.

A couple of Letzeburgesch words often overheard are *moien* (good morning/hello), *äddi* (goodbye) and *wann ech gelifft* (please). Like French speakers, Luxembourgers say *merci* for 'thank you'. A phrase that might come in useful is *schwatzt dir Englesch?* (pronounced 'schwetz dear anglish'), which means 'Do you speak English?'.

DUTCH

Dutch nouns come in one of three genders: masculine, feminine (both with *de* for 'the') and neuter (with *het* for 'the'). Where English uses 'a' or 'an', Dutch uses *een,* regardless of gender.

There's a polite and an informal version of the English 'you'. Generally, the polite form *u* is used with people you don't know well and older people, rather than the informal *je*.

For more extensive coverage of the language, pick up a copy of Lonely Planet's *Dutch* phrasebook.

PRONUNCIATION

Pronunciation guides are included with all Dutch phrases in this chapter. Below is a key as to how to pronounce the various sounds. If you simply read our pronunciation guides as if you were reading English, however, you should have no problems being understood. Note that the stressed syllables in words are in italics in our pronunciation guides.

Vowels

Most vowels have a long and a short version; the distinction is important as it can distinguish the meaning of some words.

a	as the 'u' in 'run'
aa	as the 'a' in 'father'
aw	as in 'saw'
e	as in 'bet'
ee	as in 'see'
eu	as the 'u' in 'nurse'
ew	**ee** pronounced with rounded lips
ey	as the 'e' in 'bet', but longer
i	as in 'hit'
o	as in 'pot'
oh	as the 'o' in 'note'
oo	as in 'zoo'
öy	similar to the sound of 'er-y' in 'her year' (without the 'r' sound)
u	as in 'put'
uh	a neutral vowel, as the 'a' in 'ago'

Consonants

Most consonants in Dutch are pronounced the same as their English counterparts. A few distinctive sounds:

kh	as the 'ch' in the Scottish *loch*
r	trilled
zh	as the 's' in 'pleasure'

ACCOMMODATION

I'm looking	*Ik ben op zoek*	ik ben op zook
for a ...	*naar een ...*	naar uhn ...
campsite	*camping*	kem·ping
guesthouse	*pension*	pen·syon
hotel	*hotel*	ho·tel
youth hostel	*jeugdherberg*	yeukht·her·herkh
I'd like (a) ...	*Ik wil graag*	ik wil khraakh
	een ...	uhn ...
bed	*bed*	bet
double room	*tweepersoons-*	twey·puhr·sohns·
	kamer	kaa·muhr
room with a	*kamer met*	kaa·muhr met
bathroom	*badkamer*	bat·kaa·muhr
room with	*kamer met*	kaa·muhr met
two beds	*twee bedden*	twey be·duhn
single room	*eenpersoons-*	eyn·puhr·sohns·
	kamer	kaa·muhr
to share a	*bed op een*	bet op uhn
dorm	*slaapzaal*	slaap·zaal

LANGUAGE

How much is it per ...?	Hoeveel is het per ...?	hoo·veyl is huht puhr ...
night	nacht	nakht
person	persoon	per·sohn

Do you have any rooms available?
Heeft u een kamer vrij? heyft ew uhn *kaa*·muhr vrey
May I see the room?
Mag ik de kamer zien? makh ik duh *kaa*·muhr zeen
Where is the bathroom?
Waar is de badkamer? waar is duh *bat*·kaa·muhr

CONVERSATION & ESSENTIALS

Hello.	Dag./Hallo.	dakh/ha·loh
Goodbye.	Dag.	dakh
Yes.	Ja.	yaa
No.	Nee.	ney
Please.	Alstublieft. (pol)	als·tew·bleeft
	Alsjeblieft. (inf)	a·shuh·bleeft
Thank you	Dank u/je	dangk ew/yuh
(very much).	(wel). (pol/inf)	(wel)
Thanks.	Bedankt.	buh·dangt
You're welcome.	Graag gedaan.	khraakh khuh·daan
Excuse me.	Pardon.	par·don
	Excuseer mij.	eks·kew·zeyr mey
I'm sorry.	Sorry./Excuses.	so·ree/eks·kew·zuhs
See you soon.	Tot ziens.	tot zeens

How are you?
Hoe gaat het met hoo khaat huht met
u/jou? (pol/inf) ew/yaw
I'm fine, thanks.
Goed, bedankt. khoot buh·dangt
What's your name?
Hoe heet u/je? (pol/inf) hoo heyt ew/yuh
My name is ...
Ik heet ... ik heyt ...
Where are you from?
Waar komt u waar komt ew
vandaan? (pol) van·daan
Waar kom je waar kom yuh
vandaan? (inf) van·daan
I'm from ...
Ik kom uit ... ik kom öyt ...

DIRECTIONS

Where is ...?
Waar is ...? waar is ...
Can you show me (on the map)?
Kunt u het mij tonen kunt ew huht mey *toh*·nuhn
(op de kaart)? (op duh kaart)
Could you write the address, please?
Kunt u het adres kunt ew huht a·*dres*
opschrijven alstublieft? op·skhrey·vuhn als·tew·*bleeft*

How far is it?
Hoe ver is het? hoo ver is huht
How do I get there?
Hoe kom ik er? hoo kom ik uhr
Go straight ahead.
Ga rechtdoor. khaa rekht·*dohr*
Turn left.
Ga naar links. khaa naar lings
Turn right.
Ga naar rechts. khaa naar rekhs
at the corner
op de hoek op duh hook
at the traffic lights
bij de verkeerslichten bey duh vuhr·*keyrs*·likh·tuhn
What street/road is this?
Welke straat/weg is dit? *wel*·kuh straat/wekh is dit

by bicycle	met de fiets	met duh feets
by bus	met de bus	met duh bus
by train	met de trein	met duh treyn
on foot	te voet	tuh voot

north	noord	nohrt
south	zuid	zöyt
east	oost	ohst
west	west	west

behind	achter	akh·tuhr
close	dichtbij	dikht·bey
far (from)	ver (van)	ver (van)
here	hier	heer
in front of	voor	vohr
near (to)	dicht bij	dikht bey
next to	naast	naast
opposite	tegenover	tey·khuhn·oh·vuhr
there	daar	daar

SIGNS – DUTCH	
Dames	Women
Gesloten	Closed
Heren	Men
Informatie	Information
Ingang	Entrance
Inlichtingen	Information
Kamers Vrij	Rooms Available
Niet Toegelaten	Prohibited
Open	Open
Politiebureau	Police Station
Uitgang	Exit
Verboden	Prohibited
Vol	Full/No Vacancies
WC's/Toiletten	Toilets

EMERGENCIES – DUTCH

I'm lost.
Ik ben de weg kwijt.   ik ben duh wekh kweyt
There's been an accident.
Er is een ongeluk   uhr is uhn *on*-khuh-luk
gebeurd.   khuh-*beurt*
Leave me alone!
Laat me gerust!   laat me khuh-*rust*
Help!
Help!   help

Call …!	*Haal …!*	haal …
a doctor	*een doktor*	uhn *dok*-tuhr
the police	*de politie*	duh po-*leet*-see

EATING OUT

For a food and drink glossary, see p53.

A table for two, please.
Een tafel voor twee,   uhn *taa*-fuhl vohr twey
alstublief.   als-tew-*bleeft*
Do you have a menu in English?
Hebt u de kaart   hept ew duh kaart
in het Engels?   in huht *eng*-uhls
What's the speciality here?
Wat is hier de   wat is heer duh
specialiteit?   spey-sya-lee-*teyt*
I'd like (the dish of the day).
Ik had graag   ik hat khraakh
(de dagschotel).   (duh *dakh*-skhoh-tuhl)
I'd like the set menu.
Ik neem het dagmenu.   ik neym huht *dakh*-muh-new
I'm a vegetarian.
Ik ben vegetariër.   ik ben vey-khey-*taa*-ree-yuhr
The bill, please.
De rekening, alstublief.   duh *rey*-kuh-ning als-tew-*bleeft*

HEALTH

Where is the hospital?
Waar is het ziekenhuis?   waar is huht *zee*-kuhn-höys
I need a doctor.
Ik heb een dokter nodig.   ik hep uhn *dok*-tuhr *noh*-dikh
I'm ill.
Ik ben ziek.   ik ben zeek

I'm …	*Ik ben …*	ik ben …
asthmatic	*asthmatisch*	ast-*maa*-tis
diabetic	*suikerziek*	*söy*-kuhr-zeek

I'm allergic	*Ik ben allergisch*	ik ben a-*ler*-khis
to …	*voor…*	vohr …
antibiotics	*antibiotica*	an-tee-bee-*o*-tee-ka
nuts	*noten*	*noh*-tuhn
penicillin	*penicilline*	pey-nee-see-*lee*-nuh

antiseptic	*ontsmettings-middel*	ont-*sme*-tings-mi-duhl
aspirin	*aspirine*	as-pee-*ree*-nuh
condoms	*condooms*	kon-*dohms*
contraceptive	*anticonceptie-middel*	an-tee-kon-*sep*-see-mi-duhl
diarrhoea	*diarree*	dee-a-*rey*
nausea	*misselijkheid*	*mi*-suh-luhk-heyt
sunscreen	*zonnebrandolie*	*zo*-nuh-brant-oh-lee
tampons	*tampons*	*tam*-pons

LANGUAGE DIFFICULTIES

Do you speak English?
Spreekt u Engels?   spreykt ew *eng*-uhls
How do you say … in Dutch?
Hoe zeg je …   hoo zekh yuh …
in het Nederlands?   in huht *ney*-duhr-lants
I (don't) understand.
Ik begrijp het (niet).   ik buh-*khreyp* huht (neet)

NUMBERS

0	*nul*	nul
1	*één*	eyn
2	*twee*	twey
3	*drie*	dree
4	*vier*	veer
5	*vijf*	veyf
6	*zes*	zes
7	*zeven*	*zey*-vuhn
8	*acht*	akht
9	*negen*	*ney*-khuhn
10	*tien*	teen
11	*elf*	elf
12	*twaalf*	twaalf
13	*dertien*	*der*-teen
14	*veertien*	*veyr*-teen
15	*vijftien*	*veyf*-teen
16	*zestien*	*zes*-teen
17	*zeventien*	*zey*-vuhn-teen
18	*achttien*	*akh*-teen
19	*negentien*	*ney*-khuhn-teen
20	*twintig*	*twin*-tuhkh
21	*eenentwintig*	*eyn*-en-*twin*-tuhkh
22	*tweeëntwintig*	*twey*-en-*twin*-tuhkh
30	*dertig*	*der*-tuhkh
40	*veertig*	*veyr*-tuhkh
50	*vijftig*	*veyf*-tuhkh
60	*zestig*	*zes*-tuhkh
70	*zeventig*	*zey*-vuhn-tuhkh
80	*tachtig*	*takh*-tuhkh
90	*negentig*	*ney*-khuhn-tuhkh
100	*honderd*	*hon*-duhrt
1000	*duizend*	*döy*-zuhnt
2000	*tweeduizend*	*twey*-döy-zuhnt

LANGUAGE

SHOPPING & SERVICES

What time does it open/close?
Hoe laat opent/sluit het?   hoo laat *oh*·puhnt/slöyt huht

I'd like to buy ...
Ik wil graag ... kopen.   ik wil khraakh ... *koh*·puhn

How much is it?
Hoeveel is het?   hoo·*veyl* is huht

May I look at it?
Mag ik het zien?   makh ik huht zeen

I don't like it.
Ik vind het niet leuk.   ik vint huht neet leuk

Do you take credit cards?
Accepteert u   ak·sep·*teyrt* ew
kredietkaarten?   krey·*deet*·kaar·tuhn

more	*meer*	meyr
less	*minder*	*min*·duhr
bigger	*groter*	*khroh*·tuhr
smaller	*kleiner*	*kley*·nuhr

I'm looking	*Ik ben op zoek*	ik ben op zook
for a/the ...	*naar ...*	naar ...
bank	*de bank*	duh bangk
bookshop	*een boeken-*	uhn *boo*·kuhn·
	winkel	win·kuhl
department	*een groot-*	uhn khroht·
store	*warenhuis*	*waa*·ruhn·höys
pharmacy	*een apotheek*	uhn a·po·*teyk*
laundry	*een wasserette*	uhn wa·suh·*re*·tuh
market	*de markt*	duh markt
nightshop	*een nachtwinkel*	uhn *nakht*·win·kuhl
post office	*het postkantoor*	huht *post*·kan·tohr
public toilet	*een openbaar*	uhn *oh*·puhn·baar
	toilet	twa·*let*
supermarket	*een supermarkt*	uhn *sew*·puhr·mart
tourist office	*het toerisme-*	huht too·*ris*·muh·
	bureau	bew·roh

TIME & DATES

What time is it?	*Hoe laat is het?*	hoo laat is huht
It's (two) o'clock.	*Het is (twee) uur.*	huht is (twey) ewr
When?	*Wanneer?*	wa·*neyr*
in the morning	*'s morgens*	smor·khuhns
in the afternoon	*'s middags*	smi·dakhs
in the evening	*'s avonds*	saa·vonts
yesterday	*gisteren*	*khis*·tuh·ruhn
today	*vandaag*	van·*daakh*
tomorrow	*morgen*	mor·khuhn

Monday	*maandag*	*maan*·dakh
Tuesday	*dinsdag*	*dins*·dakh
Wednesday	*woensdag*	*woons*·dakh
Thursday	*donderdag*	*don*·duhr·dakh
Friday	*vrijdag*	*vrey*·dakh
Saturday	*zaterdag*	*zaa*·tuhr·dakh
Sunday	*zondag*	*zon*·dakh

January	*januari*	*ya*·new·aa·ree
February	*februari*	*fey*·brew·aa·ree
March	*maart*	maart
April	*april*	a·*pril*
May	*mei*	mey
June	*juni*	*yew*·nee
July	*juli*	*yew*·lee
August	*augustus*	aw·*gus*·tus
September	*september*	sep·*tem*·buhr
October	*oktober*	ok·*to*·buhr
November	*november*	no·*vem*·buhr
December	*december*	dey·*sem*·buhr

TRANSPORT

When does	*Hoe laat*	hoo laat
the ... leave?	*vertrekt ...?*	vuhr·*trekt* ...
When does	*Hoe laat*	hoo laat
the ... arrive?	*komt ... aan?*	komt ... aan
boat	*de boot*	duh boht
bus	*de bus*	duh bus
plane	*het vliegtuig*	huht *fleekh*·töykh
train	*de trein*	duh treyn

Where is the ...?	*Waar is ...?*	waar is ...
airport	*de lucht-*	duh *lukht*·
	haven	haa·vuhn
bus stop	*de bushalte*	duh *bus*·hal·tuh
train station	*het trein-*	huht treyn·
	station	sta·*syon*
tram stop	*de tramhalte*	duh *trem*·hal·tuh

I'd like a ...	*Ik wil graag ...*	ik wil khraakh ...
ticket.		
1st-class	*eerste klas*	*eyr*·stuh klas
2nd-class	*tweede klas*	*twey*·duh klas
one-way	*een enkele*	uhn *eng*·kuh·luh
	reis	reys
return	*een retour-*	uhn ruh·*toor*·
	ticket	ti·ket

cancelled	*geannuleerd*	khuh·a·new·*leyrt*
delayed	*vertraagd*	vuhr·*traakht*
first	*eerste*	*eyr*·stuh
last	*laatste*	*laat*·stuh
platform	*spoor/perron*	spohr/pe·*ron*
number	*nummer*	*nu*·muhr
ticket office	*loket*	*loh*·ket
timetable	*dienst-*	*deenst*·
	regeling	rey·khuh·ling

I'd like to hire	*Ik wil graag een*	ik wil khraakh uhn
a/an ...	*... huren.*	... *hew*·ruhn
bicycle	*fiets*	feets
car	*auto*	*aw*·to
motorbike	*motorfiets*	*mo*·tuhr·feets

FRENCH

Note that there are certain formalised differences between the French language used in Belgium and in France, such as some numbers.

For a more in-depth guide to the language, get a copy of Lonely Planet's *French* phrasebook.

PRONUNCIATION

Most sounds in French are similar to their English counterparts. Read the pronunciation guides, included next to the French phrases in this section, as if they were English, keeping in mind the following few distinctive French sounds. Remember to add a light stress on the final syllable in a word.

Vowels

Most vowels have a long and a short version; the distinction is important as it can distinguish the meaning of some words.

a	as the 'u' in 'run'
ai	as in 'aisle'
air	as in 'fair'
ay	as in 'say'
e	as in 'bet'
ee	as in 'see'
er	as in 'her' (without the 'r' sound)
ew	**ee** pronounced with rounded lips
o	as in 'pot'
oo	as in 'zoo'

A characteristic feature of French is the use of nasal vowel sounds. Pronounce them as if you're trying to make the sound through your nose rather than your mouth – the effect is similar to the silent '-ng' ending in English (eg in 'singing'). In our pronunciation guides, nasal vowel sounds are represented with the symbols **om**, **on**, **ong**, **um**, **un** and **ung**.

Consonants

ng	as in 'sing'
ny	as in 'canyon'
r	pronounced from the back of the throat while constricting the muscles to restrict the flow of air
zh	as the 's' in 'pleasure'

BE POLITE!

An important distinction is made in French between *tu* and *vous*, which both mean 'you'; *tu* is only used when addressing people you know well, children or animals. If you're addressing an adult who isn't a personal friend, *vous* should be used unless the person invites you to use *tu*. In general, younger people insist less on this distinction between polite and informal, and you will find that in many cases they use *tu* from the beginning of an acquaintance.

GENDER

All nouns in French are either masculine or feminine and adjectives take different forms to reflect the gender of the noun they modify. The feminine form of many nouns and adjectives is indicated by a silent **e** added to the masculine form, as in *ami* and *amie* (the masculine and feminine form of 'friend').

In the following phrases both masculine and feminine forms have been indicated where necessary. The masculine form comes first and is separated from the feminine by a slash. The gender of a noun is also often indicated by the preceding article: *le/un/du* (m) or *la/une/de la* (f) for 'the/a/some'; or one of the possessive adjectives: *mon/ton/son* (m) or *ma/ta/sa* (f) for 'my/your/his/her'.

ACCOMMODATION

I'm looking for a ...	*Je cherche ...*	zher shersh ...
campsite	*un camping*	un kom·peeng
guesthouse	*une pension (de famille)*	ewn pon·syon (der fa·mee·ler)
hotel	*un hôtel*	un o·tel
youth hostel	*une auberge de jeunesse*	ewn o·berzh der zher·nes
I'd like (a) ...	*Je voudrais ...*	zher voo·dray ...
room with a bathroom	*une chambre avec une salle de bains*	ewn shom·brer a·vek ewn sal der bun
room with a double bed	*une chambre avec un grand lit*	ewn shom·brer a·vek un gron lee
room with two beds	*une chambre avec des lits jumeaux*	ewn shom·brer a·vek day lee zhew·mo
single room	*une chambre à un lit*	ewn shom·brer a un lee
to share a dorm	*coucher dans un dortoir*	koo·sher don zun dor·twa

LANGUAGE

How much is it per ...?	Quel est le prix par ...?	kel e ler pree par ...
night	nuit	nwee
person	personne	per·son

Do you have any rooms available?

Est-ce que vous avez des chambres libres?	e·sker voo·za·vay day shom·brer lee·brer

May I see it?

Est-ce que je peux voir la chambre?	es·ker zher per vwa la shom·brer

Where is the bathroom?

Où est la salle de bains?	oo e la sal der bun

CONVERSATION & ESSENTIALS

Hello.	Bonjour.	bon·zhoor
Goodbye.	Au revoir.	o·rer·vwa
Yes.	Oui.	wee
No.	Non.	no
Please.	S'il vous plaît.	seel voo play
Thank you.	Merci.	mair·see
You're welcome.	Je vous en prie.	zher voo·zon pree
	De rien. (inf)	der ree·en
Excuse me.	Excusez-moi.	ek·skew·zay·mwa
Sorry.	Pardon.	par·don

What's your name?

Comment vous appelez-vous? (pol)	ko·mon voo·za·pay·lay voo
Comment tu t'appelles? (inf)	ko·mon tew ta·pel

My name is ...

Je m'appelle ...	zher ma·pel ...

Where are you from?

De quel pays êtes-vous? (pol)	der kel pay·ee et voo
De quel pays es-tu? (inf)	der kel pay·ee e·tew

I'm from ...

Je viens de ...	zher vyen der ...

DIRECTIONS

Where is ...?

Où est ...?	oo e ...

Can you show me (on the map)?

Pouvez-vous m'indiquer (sur la carte)?	poo·vay·voo mun·dee·kay (sewr la kart)

Could you write it down, please?

Est-ce que vous pourriez l'écrire, s'il vous plaît?	e·sker voo poo·ryay lay·kreer seel voo play

Go straight ahead.

Continuez tout droit.	kon·teen·way too drwa

Turn left/right.

Tournez à gauche/droite.	toor·nay a gosh/drwa

at the corner

au coin	o kwun

at the traffic lights

aux feux	o fer

---

behind	derrière	dair·ryair
far (from)	loin (de)	lwun (der)
in front of	devant	der·von
near (to)	près (de)	pray (der)
opposite	en face de	on fas der

EATING OUT

For a food and drink glossary, see p53.

A table for two, please.

Une table pour deux, s'il vous plaît.	ewn ta·bler poor der seel voo play

Do you have a menu in English?

Est-ce que vous avez la carte en anglais?	es·ker voo za·vay la kart on ong·lay

What's the speciality here?

Quelle est la spécialité ici?	kel a ler spay·sya·lee·tay ee·see

I'd like the dish of the day.

Je voudrais avoir le plat du jour.	zher voo·dray a·vwar ler pla dew zhoor

I'd like the set menu.

Je prends le menu.	zher pron ler mer·new

I'm a vegetarian.

Je suis végétarien/ végétarienne. (m/f)	zher swee vay·zhay·ta·ryun/ vay·zhay·ta·ryen

I'd like to order the...

Je voudrais commander...	zher voo·dray ko·mon·day ...

The bill, please.

La note, s'il vous plaît.	la not seel voo play

HEALTH

Where is the hospital?

Où est l'hopital?	oo e lo·pee·tal

I need a doctor.

J'ai besoin d'un médecin.	zhay ber·zwun dun mayd·sun

I'm ill.

Je suis malade.	zher swee ma·lad

I'm ...	Je suis ...	zher swee ...
asthmatic	asthmatique	zas·ma·teek
diabetic	diabétique	dee·a·bay·teek
epileptic	épileptique	zay·pee·lep·teek

EMERGENCIES – FRENCH

I'm lost.
Je me suis égaré/e. (m/f)   zhe me swee·zay·ga·ray
There's been an accident.
Il y a eu un accident.   eel ya ew un ak·see·don
Leave me alone!
Fichez-moi la paix!   fee·shay·mwa la pay
Help!
Au secours!   o skoor

Call ...!	Appelez ...!	a·play ...
a doctor	un médecin	un mayd·sun
the police	la police	la po·lees

I'm allergic	Je suis	zher swee
to ...	allergique ...	za·lair·zheek ...
antibiotics	aux antibiotiques	o zon·tee·byo·teek
nuts	aux noix	o nwa
peanuts	aux cacahuètes	o ka·ka·wet
penicillin	à la	a la
	pénicilline	pay·nee·see·leen

antiseptic	l'antiseptique	lon·tee·sep·teek
aspirin	l'aspirine	las·pee·reen
condoms	des préservatifs	day pray·zair·va·teef
contraceptive	le contraceptif	ler kon·tra·sep·teef
diarrhoea	la diarrhée	la dya·ray
nausea	la nausée	la no·zay
sunblock cream	la crème solaire	la krem so·lair
tampons	des tampons	day tom·pon
	hygiéniques	ee·zhen·eek

LANGUAGE DIFFICULTIES

Do you speak English?
Parlez-vous anglais?   par·lay·voo ong·lay
How do you say ... in French?
Comment dit-on   ko·mon dee·ton
... en français?   ... on fron·say
I understand.
Je comprends.   zher kom·pron
I don't understand.
Je ne comprends pas.   zher ner kom·pron pa

NUMBERS

0	zéro	zay·ro
1	un	un
2	deux	der
3	trois	trwa
4	quatre	ka·trer
5	cinq	sungk
6	six	sees
7	sept	set
8	huit	weet
9	neuf	nerf
10	dix	dees

11	onze	onz
12	douze	dooz
13	treize	trez
14	quatorze	ka·torz
15	quinze	kunz
16	seize	sez
17	dix-sept	dee·set
18	dix-huit	dee·zweet
19	dix-neuf	deez·nerf
20	vingt	vung
21	vingt et un	vung tay un
22	vingt-deux	vung·der
30	trente	tront
40	quarante	ka·ront
50	cinquante	sung·kont
60	soixante	swa·sont
70	septante	se·tont
80	quatre-vingts	ka·trer·vung
90	nonante	no·nont
100	cent	son
1000	mille	meel

SHOPPING & SERVICES

I'd like to buy ...
Je voudrais acheter ...   zher voo·dray ash·tay ...
How much is it?
C'est combien?   say kom·byun
May I look at it?
Est-ce que je peux le voir?   es·ker zher per ler vwar
I don't like it.
Celu ne me plaît pas.   ser·la ner mer play pa

Can I pay	Est-ce que je peux	es ker zher per
by ...?	payer avec ...?	pay·yay a·vek ...
credit card	ma carte de	ma kart der
	crédit	kray·dee
travellers	des chèques	day shek
cheques	de voyage	der vwa·yazh

more	plus	plew
less	moins	mwa
bigger	plus grand	plew gron
smaller	plus petit	plew per·tee

I'm looking	Je cherche ...	zhe shersh ...
for a/the ...		
bank	une banque	ewn bonk
hospital	l'hôpital	lo·pee·tal
market	le marché	ler mar·shay
police	la police	la po·lees
post office	le bureau de poste	ler bew·ro der post
public phone	une cabine	ewn ka·been
	téléphonique	tay·lay·fo·neek
public toilet	les toilettes	lay twa·let
tourist office	l'office de	lo·fees der
	tourisme	too·rees·mer

TIME & DATES

What time is it?
Quelle heure est-il?   kel er e til
It's (eight) o'clock.
Il est (huit) heures.   il e (weet) er
It's half past (eight).
Il est (huit) heures et demie.   il e (weet) er e day·mee

in the morning	*du matin*	dew ma·tun
in the afternoon	*de l'après-midi*	der la·pray·mee·dee
in the evening	*du soir*	dew swar
yesterday	*hier*	yair
today	*aujourd'hui*	o·zhoor·dwee
tomorrow	*demain*	der·mun
Monday	*lundi*	lun·dee
Tuesday	*mardi*	mar·dee
Wednesday	*mercredi*	mair·krer·dee
Thursday	*jeudi*	zher·dee
Friday	*vendredi*	von·drer·dee
Saturday	*samedi*	sam·dee
Sunday	*dimanche*	dee·monsh
January	*janvier*	zhon·vyay
February	*février*	fayv·ryay
March	*mars*	mars
April	*avril*	a·vreel
May	*mai*	may
June	*juin*	zhwun
July	*juillet*	zhwee·yay
August	*août*	oot
September	*septembre*	sep·tom·brer
October	*octobre*	ok·to·brer
November	*novembre*	no·vom·brer
December	*décembre*	day·som·brer

TRANSPORT

At what time	*À quelle heure*	a kel er
does the ...	*part/arrive ...?*	par/a·reev ...
leave/arrive?		
boat	*le bateau*	ler ba·to
bus	*le bus*	ler bews
plane	*l'avion*	la·vyon
train	*le train*	ler trun
I'd like a ...	*Je voudrais*	zher voo·dray
ticket.	*un billet ...*	un bee·yay ...
1st-class	*de première*	der prem·yair
	classe	klas
2nd-class	*de deuxième*	der der·zyem
	classe	klas
one-way	*simple*	sum·pler
return	*aller et retour*	a·lay ay rer·toor
platform	*le numéro*	ler new·may·ro
number	*de quai*	der kay
the first	*le premier* (m)	ler prer·myay
	la première (f)	la prer·myair
the last	*le dernier* (m)	ler dair·nyay
	la dernière (f)	la dair·nyair
ticket office	*le guichet*	ler gee·shay
timetable	*l'horaire*	lo·rair
train station	*la gare*	la gar
I'd like to hire	*Je voudrais*	zher voo·dray
a/an ...	*louer ...*	loo·way ...
bicycle	*un vélo*	un vay·lo
car	*une voiture*	ewn vwa·tewr
motorbike	*une moto*	ewn mo·to

Also available from Lonely Planet:
Dutch and *French* phrasebooks

Glossary

See p53 for a list of culinary terms. Nl/Fr after a term signifies Dutch/French.

abdij/abbaye (Nl/Fr) – abbey
apotheek (Nl) – pharmacy
ARAU (Fr) – Atelier de Recherche et d'Action Urbaine (Urban Research & Action Group)
auberge de jeunesse (Fr) – youth hostel

balle-pelotte – Belgian ball game (see p46)
bakker/bakkerij (Nl) – baker/bakery
barouches (Fr) – horse-drawn carriages
begijn/béguine (Nl/Fr) – inhabitant of a begijnhof (see p137)
begijnhof/béguinage (Nl/Fr) – community of *begijnen/béguines*; cluster of cottages, often around a central garden (p137)
beiaard (Nl) – carillon
Belasting Toegevoegde Waarde (BTW) (Nl) – value-added tax, VAT
Belgische Spoorwegen (Nl) – Belgian Railways
Benelux – Belgium, the Netherlands and Luxembourg
benzine (Nl) – petrol
betalend parkeren (Nl) – paid street parking
biljart/billard (Nl/Fr) – billiards
billet (Fr) – ticket
boulangerie (Fr) – bakery
BP (boîte postale) (Fr) – post office box
branché (Fr) – trendy, hip
brasserie (Fr) – brewery; café/restaurant often serving food all day
brocante (Fr) – bric-a-brac
brouwerij (Nl) – brewery
brown café – small, old-fashioned pub with wooden-panelled interior
bruine kroeg (Nl) – *brown café*
Brusselaar (Nl) – inhabitant of Brussels
Bruxellois (Fr) – inhabitant of Brussels; name of the city's old dialect (p84)
bureau d'échange (Fr) – foreign-exchange bureau

café – pub, bar
carte (Fr) – menu
centrum (Nl) – centre
chambre (Fr) – room
chambre d'hôte (Fr) – B&B guesthouse
Charles Quint – Holy Roman Emperor Charles V (p27)
château (Fr) – castle, country mansion
chocolatier (Fr) – chocolate-maker
commune (Fr) – municipality
confiserie (Fr) – chocolate and sweet shop
couvent (Fr) – convent
cuistax – see kwistax
curiosa (Nl) – bric-a-brac

dagmenu (Nl) – fixed-price, multicourse meal of the day
dagschotel (Nl) – dish of the day
demi-pension (Fr) – half board (ie accommodation, breakfast and dinner)
dentelle (Fr) – lace
dienst voor toerisme (Nl) – tourist office

eetcafé/eetkroeg (Nl) – *café* serving food
église (Fr) – church
entrée (Fr) – entry
essence – petrol
estaminet (Fr) – tavern
étang (Fr) – pond
EU – European Union
Eurocrat – EU administrative official
Europese Instellingen (Nl) – EU Institutions

fiets (Nl) – bicycle
fietspad (Nl) – bicycle lane
frieten/frites (Nl/Fr) – chips or fries
frituur/friture/friterie (Nl/Fr/Fr) – chip shop

galerij/galerie (Nl/Fr) – covered shopping centre/arcade
gare (Fr) – train station
gastenkamer (Nl) – B&B/guesthouse
gaufres (Fr) – waffles
gebak (Nl) – cakes and pastries
gemeente (Nl) – municipality
gemeentehuis (Nl) – town hall
gezellig (Nl) – cosy, convivial atmosphere
Gille (Fr) – folkloric character typical of the Binche carnival (p216)
gîtes d'étapes (Fr) – rural group accommodation, sometimes also a hostel (p286)
gîtes ruraux (Fr) – countryside guesthouses
glacier (Fr) – ice-cream shop; glacier
godshuis (Nl) – almshouse (p137)
GR (Fr) – long-distance footpaths
grand café (Fr) – opulent historic *café*
gratis/gratuit (Nl/Fr) – free
grotte (Fr) – cave, grotto

hallen/halles (Nl/Fr) – covered market
herberg (Nl) – old-style Flemish pub
hof (Nl) – garden
holebi – LGBT (*ho*mosexual-*les*bian-*bi*sexual)
Holy Roman Empire – Germanic empire (962-1806) that was confusingly neither theocratic nor predominantly Italian/Roman for most of its history
hôpital (Fr) – hospital
horeca (Fr/Nl) – the hospitality (*ho*tel-*re*staurant-*ca*fé) industry

hôtel (Fr) – hotel, historic townhouse
hôtel de ville (Fr) – town hall

ingang (Nl) – entry
Institutions Européennes (Fr) – EU Institutions
ISIC – International Student Identity Card

jardin (Fr) – garden
jenever – (Nl) Flemish/Dutch gin
jeu-de-balle (F) – see *balle-pelotte*
jeugdherberg (Nl) – youth hostel

kaartje (Nl) – ticket
kamer (Nl) – room
kant (Nl) – lace
kasteel (Nl) – castle
kerk (Nl) – church
kwistax – pedal-carts popular on Belgian beaches

laverie (Fr) – laundrette
landelijke verblijven (Nl) – countryside guesthouses
loodvrije benzine (Nl) – unleaded petrol

magasin de nuit (Fr) – 24-hour shop
marché aux puces (Fr) – flea market
markt/marché (Nl/Fr) – market
menu (Nl & Fr) – fixed-price meal with two or more courses (what is called the menu in English is the *kaart/la carte*)
menu du jour (Fr) – fixed-price, multicourse meal of the day
molen/moulin (Nl/Fr) – windmill
Mosan – from the Meuse River valley
moules-frites (Fr) – mussels and chips
musée (Fr) – museum

nachtwinkel (Nl) – 24-hour shop
NATO – North Atlantic Treaty Organisation military alliance headquartered in Brussels (NAVO/OTAN in Dutch/French)
niet rokers/non fumeurs (Nl/Fr) – nonsmoking
NMBS (Nl) – Belgian National Railways

office de tourisme (Fr) – tourist office
ondertitels (Nl) – subtitles
oude (Nl) – old
OV (originele versie) (Nl) – nondubbed (ie movie shown in its original language)

patinage à glace (Fr) – ice skating
pâtisserie (Fr) – cakes and pastries; shop selling them
pékèt – Walloon for *jenever*
pension complète (Fr) – full board
pharmacie (Fr) – pharmacy
piste cyclable (Fr) – bicycle lane
pitas (Fr) – stuffed pitta bread
place (Fr) – square

plat du jour (Fr) – dish of the day
plein (Nl) – square
poort/porte (Nl/Fr) – gate in city wall
potale (Walloon term) – niche for the Virgin Mary
premetro – trams that go underground for part of their journey (found in Brussels and Antwerp)
prior[itaire] (Fr) – priority mail
priorité à droite (Fr) – priority-to-the-right traffic rule

RACB (Fr) – Royal Automobile Club de Belgique
rommelmarkt (Nl) – flea market
rond punt/rond point (Nl/Fr) – roundabout
routier (Fr) – trucker (also truckers' restaurant)

SHAPE – NATO's 'Supreme HQ Allied Powers Europe' near Mons
slijterij (Nl) – shop selling strong alcohol
SNCB (Fr) – Belgian National Railways
sortie (Fr) – exit
sous-titres (Fr) – subtitles
spijskaart (Nl) – menu
stad (Nl) – town
stadhuis (Nl) – town hall
stadsbelasting (Nl) – city tax
stationnement payant (Fr) – paid parking
STIB (Fr) – Société des Transports Intercommunaux de Bruxelles (Brussels Public Transport Company)
syndicat d'initiative (Fr) – tourist office

taxe de séjour (Fr) – visitors tax
téléférique (Fr) – cable car
terreinfiets (Nl) – mountain bike
toeristische dienst (Nl) – tourist office
toneel/théâtre (Nl/Fr) – theatre
toren/tour (Nl/Fr) – tower
trekkershut (Nl) – hikers' hut (see p285)
tuin (Nl) – garden
TVA (Fr) – value-added tax, VAT

uitgang (Nl) – exit
ULB (Fr) – Université Libre de Bruxelles

vélo (Fr) – bicycle
vieille ville (Fr) – old town or city
vijver (Nl) – pond
VO (version originale) (Fr) – nondubbed film
voorrang van rechts (Nl) – priority-to-the-right traffic rule
VTT (vélo tout-terrain) (Fr) – mountain bike

wassalon (Nl) – laundrette
weekend gastronomique (Fr) – accommodation plus breakfast and some meals
wisselkantoor (Nl) – foreign-exchange bureau

ziekenhuis (Nl) – hospital

Behind the Scenes

THIS BOOK

This 4th edition of Belgium & Luxembourg was researched and written by Mark Elliott. The three previous editions were written by Leanne Logan and Geert Cole. This guidebook was commissioned in Lonely Planet's London office, and produced by the following:

Commissioning Editor Lucy Monie, Caroline Sieg
Coordinating Editors Elisa Arduca, Nigel Chin
Coordinating Cartographer Jolyon Philcox
Coordinating Layout Designer Margaret Jung
Managing Editors Melanie Dankel, Bruce Evans
Managing Cartographer Herman So
Managing Layout Designer Sally Darmody
Assisting Editors Carolyn Boicos, David Carroll, Laura Crawford, Martine Power, Kirsten Rawlings, Angela Tinson, Jeanette Wall
Assisting Cartographers Andras Bogdanovits, Alex Leung, Peter Shields
Cover Research Naomi Parker, lonelyplanetimages.com
Internal Image Research Aude Vauconsant, lonelyplanetimages.com
Project Manager Eoin Dunlevy
Language Content Branislava Vladisavljevic

Thanks to Lucy Birchley, Paul Iacono, Annelies Mertens, Trent Paton

THANKS
MARK ELLIOTT

In a sense I've been researching this book for over a decade. Indeed during the last 15 years I've fallen more and more in love with Belgium and with one special Belgian in particular. Both are inspiringly surreal and adorable. So a million thanks to my wife, Danielle Systermans and to all her/our Benelux friends, who have taught me so much over the years. Not quite all of it was washed away with all the beer and bubbles. Endless thanks also to my unbeatable family back in England who first took me up the Atomium nearly 40 years ago. Their love and inspiration has long given me the joy and freedom to live and learn. I can never thank them enough.

For this particular edition, I'm extremely grateful for the patient help and suggestions of Jan van Akker, David de Graef, Valerie De Kerpel, Guy Jacobs, Rémi Durand, Wieland de Hoon, Hans Rossel, Vince in Tournai, Matthieu Segard & Brandon Nobel, and of dozens and dozens of others who have been so kind as to help me understand the mysterious complexities of everything from flax-scutching to BHV to 18th-century porcelain to Antwerp gay raves.

At Lonely Planet thank you Caroline Sieg for (finally!) trusting me with this project and to Lucy

---

THE LONELY PLANET STORY

Fresh from an epic journey across Europe, Asia and Australia in 1972, Tony and Maureen Wheeler sat at their kitchen table stapling together notes. The first Lonely Planet guidebook, *Across Asia on the Cheap*, was born.

Travellers snapped up the guides. Inspired by their success, the Wheelers began publishing books to Southeast Asia, India and beyond. Demand was prodigious, and the Wheelers expanded the business rapidly to keep up. Over the years, Lonely Planet extended its coverage to every country and into the virtual world via lonelyplanet.com and the Thorn Tree message board.

As Lonely Planet became a globally loved brand, Tony and Maureen received several offers for the company. But it wasn't until 2007 that they found a partner whom they trusted to remain true to the company's principles of travelling widely, treading lightly and giving sustainably. In October of that year, BBC Worldwide acquired a 75% share in the company, pledging to uphold Lonely Planet's commitment to independent travel, trustworthy advice and editorial independence.

Today, Lonely Planet has offices in Melbourne, London and Oakland, with over 500 staff members and 300 authors. Tony and Maureen are still actively involved with Lonely Planet. They're travelling more often than ever, and they're devoting their spare time to charitable projects. And the company is still driven by the philosophy of *Across Asia on the Cheap*: 'All you've got to do is decide to go and the hardest part is over. So go!'

SEND US YOUR FEEDBACK

We love to hear from travellers – your comments keep us on our toes and help make our books better. Our well-travelled team reads every word on what you loved or loathed about this book. Although we cannot reply individually to postal submissions, we always guarantee that your feedback goes straight to the appropriate authors, in time for the next edition. Each person who sends us information is thanked in the next edition and the most useful submissions are rewarded with a free book.

To send us your updates – and find out about Lonely Planet events, newsletters and travel news – visit our award-winning website: **lonelyplanet.com/contact**.

Note: we may edit, reproduce and incorporate your comments in Lonely Planet products such as guidebooks, websites and digital products, so let us know if you don't want your comments reproduced or your name acknowledged. For a copy of our privacy policy visit lonelyplanet.com/privacy.

Monie for making things run so smoothly once I'd started. And many thanks to Herman So and his team of cartographers for doing the best that time allows with my zealous map corrections.

OUR READERS
Many thanks to the travellers who used the last edition and wrote to us with helpful hints, useful advice and interesting anecdotes:

Terrie Anderson, Florence Best, Graeme Brock, Wouter De Sutter, Joe Dervan, Eva Digneffe, Nick Dillen, Dj Lady Sunshine Dixon, Mark Foisy, Annette Freymueller, Matthias Gehling, Mary Hom, Baudouin Hubert, Rosie Jaffer, Fiona Mcallister, Paul Nordhaus, Tatiana Praxis, Hajime Sasaki, Margaret Saunders, Bradley Smith, Juergen Stierhof, Emanuela Tasinato, Olivier Van Den Borre, Olga Van Maele, Melina Van Scharrenburg, Geert Vanhecke, Conor Waring

ACKNOWLEDGMENTS
Many thanks to the following for the use of their content:

Globe on title page ©Mountain High Maps 1993 Digital Wisdom, Inc.

Index

000 Map pages
000 Photograph pages

000 Map pages
000 Photograph pages

INDEX

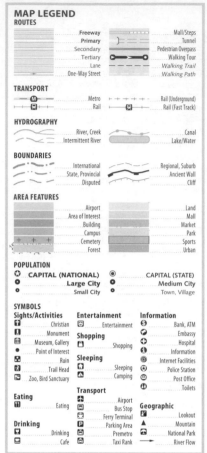

MAP LEGEND

ROUTES

Freeway
Primary
Secondary
Tertiary
Lane
One-Way Street

Mall/Steps
Tunnel
Pedestrian Overpass
Walking Tour
Walking Trail
Walking Path

TRANSPORT

Metro
Rail

Rail (Underground)
Rail (Fast Track)

HYDROGRAPHY

River, Creek
Intermittent River

Canal
Lake/Water

BOUNDARIES

International
State, Provincial
Disputed

Regional, Suburb
Ancient Wall
Cliff

AREA FEATURES

Airport
Area of Interest
Building
Campus
Cemetery
Forest

Land
Mall
Market
Park
Sports
Urban

POPULATION

○ CAPITAL (NATIONAL)
● Large City
○ Small City

◉ CAPITAL (STATE)
● Medium City
○ Town, Village

SYMBOLS

Sights/Activities
Christian
Monument
Museum, Gallery
Point of Interest
Ruin
Trail Head
Zoo, Bird Sanctuary

Eating
Eating

Drinking
Drinking
Cafe

Entertainment
Entertainment

Shopping
Shopping

Sleeping
Sleeping
Camping

Transport
Airport
Bus Stop
Ferry Terminal
Parking Area
Premetro
Taxi Rank

Information
Bank, ATM
Embassy
Hospital
Information
Internet Facilities
Police Station
Post Office
Toilets

Geographic
Lookout
Mountain
National Park
River Flow

LONELY PLANET OFFICES

Australia (Head Office)
Locked Bag 1, Footscray, Victoria 3011
☎ 03 8379 8000, fax 03 8379 8111
talk2us@lonelyplanet.com.au

USA
150 Linden St, Oakland, CA 94607
☎ 510 250 6400, toll free 800 275 8555
fax 510 893 8572
info@lonelyplanet.com

UK
2nd fl, 186 City Rd,
London EC1V 2NT
☎ 020 7106 2100, fax 020 7106 2101
go@lonelyplanet.co.uk

Published by Lonely Planet
ABN 36 005 607 983

Printed by China Translation and Printing Services Ltd
Printed in China

Mixed Sources
Product group from well-managed forests and other controlled sources
www.fsc.org Cert no. SGS-COC-005002
© 1996 Forest Stewardship Council